THE ENTERPRISE OF LAW

THE ENTERPRISE OF LAW

QUESTIONS IN LEGAL EXPERIENCE AND PHILOSOPHY

MALCOLM CLARK
Loyola College in Maryland

WEST PUBLISHING COMPANY
St. Paul • New York • Los Angeles • San Francisco

Copyediting by Faren Bachelis
Interior design by Adrianne Onderdonk Dudden
Cover by Adrianne Onderdonk Dudden

COPYRIGHT © 1987 By WEST PUBLISHING COMPANY
50 W. Kellogg Boulevard
P.O. Box 64526
St. Paul, MN 55164–1003

All rights reserved

Printed in the United States of America

Library of Congress Cataloging-in-Publication Data

Clark, Malcolm.
   Philosophy of law.

   Includes indexes.
   1. Law—Philosophy.   I. Title.
K230.C59E58 1987   340'.1   86-24582
ISBN 0–314–93531–2

Other Books by the Author

    Logic and System, A Study of Hegel
    Perplexity and Knowledge
    The Need to Question
    Invitations to Thinking

CONTENTS

Preface xi

Note to the Student xvii

CHAPTER 1 WHY WORRY ABOUT LAW? 1

    1   Woe to You Lawyers! 2

    2   The Integrity of an Advocate 7
          Rites of Initiation 9
          Legality and Humanity 11

    3   Dilemmas of a Judge 16
          Trouble at the Chess Tournament 17

    4   The Accelerated Inheritance 22
          Riggs v. Palmer 23

    5   Life through Homicide 29
          The Case of the Speluncean Explorers 31

    6   Thinking Like a Lawyer 40
          Doing Things with Words 42
          Formalism and Compassion 45

    7   What Is Legalism? 52
          The Primacy of Rules 53
          The Legal Iceberg 56

    8   The Ambiguity of Justice 60
          Why the Blindfold? 60
          Aristotle on Justice 63

CHAPTER 2 THE RANGE OF LAW 71

9 Primitive Law 72
  Law without Central Authority 75
  Who Makes the Rules? 80

10 Customary Law 86
  Pre-Legal Societies? 87
  On Not Laying Down the Law 89
  The Example of China 94

11 The Development of Legality 99
  The Stages of Law 100
  Anarchy and Despotism 102

12 The Project of Living Legally 107
  Basic Agreements 109
  The Need to Obey Law 112
  The Structures of Legality 113

13 Legal Traditions 117
  Civil and Criminal Law 118
  Common Law and Civil Law 120
  Arbitration and Mediation 124

14 Law Enforcement 129
  Law and Order 129
  Discretion 134

15 The Legal Enforcement of Morals 139
  Where the Law Has No Business 140
  Devlin's Claims 143
  His Critics 147

CHAPTER 3 BASIC THEORIES OF LAW 153

16 The Case of the Nazi Wife 156
  Hart on Law and Morals 156
  Fuller on Fidelity to Law 159

17 Austin's Command Theory 165
  Positivism and Utilitarianism 165
  The Will of the Sovereign 169

18   H.L.A. Hart's Concept of Law   175
         Criticism of Austin   176
         Primary and Secondary Rules   179

19   Dworkin on Principles and Rights   188
         Criticism of the Model of Rules   189
         Invitation to a Thesis about Rights   194

20   Legal Realism   202
         The Living Law   206
         The Mores of the Times   211

21   Natural Law: Aquinas   218
         The Ambiguity of Nature   220
         The Reason behind Law   225
         The Content of Natural Law   229

22   Fuller's Legal Naturalism   236
         The Structures of Law   238
         The Internal Morality of Law   242

CHAPTER 4   LEGAL EPISTEMOLOGY AND ETHICS   247

23   Questions of Fact and Questions of Law   249
         Fact Skepticism   251
         Questioning and Objectivity   253

24   The Adversary System   258
         Trials as Contests   259
         Procedural Justice   261

25   Alternatives in the Civil Law Tradition   267
         A German Example   268
         Trials as Conferences   272

26   Truth in Legal Procedure   275
         Telling the Whole Truth   276
         Truth and Other Obligations   281

27   The Conscience of a Lawyer   287
         The Play at the Old Bailey   287
         Counseling a Client   292

28 Rational Conclusions   296
   Objectivity and Prediction   298
   Intuition and Justification   307

CHAPTER 5   LEGAL REASONING   315

29 The Trail of Precedents   318
   History and Criticism   319
   How the Trail Starts   322
   Strict and Loose Applications   324

30 Analogical Reasoning   329
   Deduction, Induction, and Analogy   331
   Defining the Question   337

31 Manufacturers' Liability   342
   Search for a Concept   343
   Classification under the Concept   345
   A Landmark Case   347

32 Enacted Law   354
   Problems of Codification   356
   Drafting a Statute   358

33 Theories of Interpretation   363
   Legislative Intention   366
   Teleological Interpretation   370
   Dworkin on Interpretation   378

34 Just Decisions   385
   Morality and Equity   387
   Utility and Principles   389
   The Fusion of Approaches   395

Index of Cases   401

Index of Names   403

Subject Index   409

PREFACE

A few pages may help to indicate what sort of book this is: for whom it is intended and what it does, and does not, propose to do. The most likely reader of the preface to a textbook is a teacher considering classroom needs. So some comments about undergraduate courses on law will be followed with a survey of the five chapters. After the preface I have added a brief note to the student, where I suggest how the book is to be read.

"Undergraduate legal education" is still a largely undefined term, yet the rubric has given scope for much experimentation over the past fifteen years. College offerings in the substance of law (notably constitutional and business law) have increasingly been supplemented with courses on "the nature and functions of law," to quote the title of one of the original ventures in this direction. Free from the craft demands of a professional school, instructors and students have been able to explore questions about law as a basic aspect of our experience. The legal mentality has for better or worse, and especially in the West, been a dominant factor in the way we see people and things. If we boast of living according to a government of laws, then we may investigate the legal imagination as seriously as we discuss the creative contributions of poetry to our culture. The liberal atmosphere of a college, where many disciplines come together, is well suited to asking what law in general is, rather than what the law in particular happens to be.

The available teaching materials for such courses on law cover a broad range. We may, however, see a spectrum that runs from the abstract questions of a philosopher to the empirical inquiries of a political scientist. At one extreme there are textbooks (largely anthologies) for the philosophy of law. The authors suppose a reader who has some familiarity with the language and methods of contemporary philosophy. At the other extreme there are books on "the legal process" that supply an account of how the law works in this country. The authors either come from the legal profession or belong to departments of the social sciences; rarely is more than passing reference made to theoretical questions about law, and neglect of other systems and traditions of law results in a limited view of an enterprise as varied as man himself.

The course I began teaching ten years ago, and out of which this book grew, was offered within the philosophy department of a liberal arts college. The staple, therefore, was an exploration of traditional and contemporary philosophies of law. However, I tried to give as much space as possible to discussion of both important and little-known fields of legal experience. An account of diverse ways in which people live legally may not only add substance to abstract questions but also help to suggest why these questions have received such different replies. Even a philosopher starts with facts, and his voice often betrays the vision that comes from the particularity of his experience and interests.

The enrollment in this course was as varied as the project; less than a third of the students were philosophy majors. There was an even division between those who seriously thought of a legal career and those who had no such commitment but appreciated the opportunity, once in a lifetime, to ask seriously what law is about in its many forms. Lacking a specialized audience and a corresponding textbook, I began to collect materials and develop comments on them in response to student interests. This book marks the present stage of the endeavor.

It has been my experience that the structure of an undergraduate course on law need not be much affected by the distinction between students who do and do not intend to go to law school. Those who have such an ambition know that they will there receive professional training in the content and procedures of the law they are to apply. However, it does seem odd (at least by European standards) that high school graduates in this country, preparing for a legal career, spend four years at college studying anything but law and then three years at law school in concentrated learning of a trade. Such students look, in their stay at college, for courses that clearly pertain to their future work and yet go beyond the precise tasks of a professional school, concerned as it is to ensure the competence of a practitioner. Interest is shown, for example, in the legal experience of other times and places. What are the roots of law in custom? What has anthropology to tell us about the basic structures of law? How are our assumptions challenged by legal procedures today outside the common law? Why do so many of us turn away from lawyers and courts to other methods of dispute settlement? What, indeed, is a legal system? Why should we have one and what are our obligations toward it?

Moral questions have taken on a new life in law schools, though mainly in the form of problems about detailed professional responsibilities. Yet such discussion tends to be superficial unless grounded in a comprehensive philosophy. It is all too easy to voice one's opinions on the issues. A more solid response calls for roots that penetrate to undergraduate years. There, basic ideas still have a freshness that may be lost once the technical requirements of legal training take over. In my own course, it is the contribution of nonprofessional students that has often proved most fruitful. These show a healthy disrespect for the official thinking of lawyers and judges. Complaints that advocates are interested only in victory, and that courts do little more than repeat "the law is the law," are misinformed; but the grain of truth can grow into questions that lead to the heart of jurisprudence.

Of more concern is the distinction between students with some training in philosophical thought and those who have none. Students who come from academic fields where information and techniques are at a premium often show resentment when asked to challenge the security of facts and to put their own questions into question. As children they faced life with wonder; they were natural philosophers, creating worlds. Yet the discipline of education set them on the paths of a ready-made land, and their progress to college was along the road of fact gathering and reporting. The practical mind dismisses reflective questions as "up in the clouds." This metaphor, however, is seldom analyzed. The juxtaposition of the words *experience* and *philosophy* in the subtitle of this book is intended as a parallel rather than as a contrast.

How then may such a course be organized? I have, until now, left the more explicitly theoretical questions of law to the end. It seems good pedagogy to proceed from that which is more easily understood to that which presents greater difficulty. Theory is a reflection on practice; I have tried to draw the former out of what a lawyer does in his or her office and in court. However, this leads to problems of orderly development. Should we, for instance, make many passing references to legal positivism before explaining the legal philosophies of Austin and of Hart? Is it wise to illustrate the departure of legal reasoning from usual models of logic, and to show the dependence of judicial decisions on extracurial factors, before discussing legal realism as a movement? Some preliminary reviewers of the manuscript agreed that this is permissible. Most said no. I have accepted the latter advice as sound and have advanced what used to be the final chapter, Basic Theories of Law, to the position of chapter 3. Whether I shall follow this suggestion in my own teaching is for the future to tell. I have, at least, tried to give a sufficient independence to the five chapters that they can be used in varying order to suit the nature of the audience and the purposes of the instructor.

Chapter 1 is introductory and could scarcely come elsewhere than at the beginning. No two teachers will agree on the best way to evoke foundational questions about the law. How should we invite a critical exploration of the moral, social, and epistemological bases of law and show that reflective questions do matter? Without trying to play "law school," the student must be encouraged to read a variety of legal materials, to gain some familiarity with the terminology, and to develop his or her spontaneous questions. I have chosen to begin with some remarks on problems of advocacy and on initiation to the legal mentality that law schools propose. Then a variety of cases turn to the dilemmas of a judge. Fuller's dramatic "Case of the Speluncean

Explorers" is reproduced almost in full, since it is still—in my opinion—the best introduction to the basic theories of law; the cave has its lessons today as it did for Plato. *Riggs v. Palmer* (recently revived by Dworkin as a specimen of the move from rules to principles) is offered as an actual case. Thoughts are then directed to the vital but ambiguous question what we mean when we accuse lawyers or judges of legalism. After a glance at cases that furnish striking illustrations of the legal mind at work, an extract is presented from Judith Shklar's critical study, along with a reply from a law professor. Finally, hesitations about justice in the law are discussed in an extract from Jerome Frank and a summary is given of how Aristotle has formed our thinking on this topic.

Chapter 2 provides an excursion into comparative law that is lacking in most introductory books. The enterprise of law is not limited to one country or to modern times. Though I know of a teacher who puts this chapter at the end of his course, some such tour through the broad field of what people have (rightly or wrongly) set under the name of law seems to me of importance before raising theoretical questions. If we are to ask what X is, should we not first inquire into the scope of instances to which we apply the term X? A philosophy of science that is drawn primarily from astronomy and physics will presumably differ from one that is more generous in regard to sociology and psychiatry. Austin's theory of law makes most sense if we look to legislation as the paradigm. But why should we? Is there no law in the family or in societies that have no legislature? I begin, therefore, with sections on primitive and customary law. What about the Eskimos, or the Cheyenne Indians, or the traditional emphasis of China on the *li* over the *fa* (on implicit assumptions rather than explicit rules)? Do our own judges depend on unwritten custom as well as on published law? Some account is given of the likely stages of legal development, and gradually the question is introduced about the boundaries to what we may reasonably call law. What is this enterprise and what are its inescapable structures? Since the book employs many examples from civil law countries, a section is added to explain the basic legal traditions in the world today. The concluding topics have to do with law enforcement (police and prosecutors, facing subtle problems of discretion, have a share in lawmaking) and with the legal enforcement of morals, where the Hart-Devlin debate continues to raise fundamental questions about the limits of law.

Chapter 3 turns explicitly to the underlying philosophies of law. The Hart-Fuller exchange of 1958 supplies an introductory case. Then I examine the history of legal positivism from Austin to Hart. Students respect the logic of this theory but have some questions, especially about the claimed lack of intersection between law and morality. A summary of the position of Ronald Dworkin follows, starting within this tradition yet deeply critical of it. His defense of individual rights, embedded in the institutional history of a legal system, leads us to an examination of other theories that allow, in various ways, for the entry of moral considerations into the law that *is*. Legal realism is a doctrine that never fails to evoke a positive response; judges are human and they reflect, in their decisions, whatever passes as the mores of the times. Finally, I look at the ancient claim that judges are constrained by less ephemeral principles drawn from the nature of society or of law. This proposal, so often disparaged in the past, may deserve some reconsideration today. Aquinas (clearly dependent on the Greeks) is taken as a benchmark, and Fuller is presented as offering a contemporary, though modest, version. This chapter is the longest, and most abstract, in the book. How it is used, where it is placed, and how its sections are ordered will depend much on the instructor's own philosophy and on the concerns of students. It is my hope that the chapter supplies a firm enough backbone to satisfy a course in the philosophy of law, yet that the instructor in a legal studies course may be highly selective in use of these pages; there is no lack of theoretical questions in the rest of the book, and a teacher can either stress or de-emphasize the bearing these topics have on the basic schools of legal philosophy.

Chapter 4 carries the forbidding title of "Legal Epistemology and Ethics." The latter, of such renewed importance in the post-Watergate era, is—I submit—thoroughly dependent on the former. Before I ask what I should do on the basis of the facts, I must first inquire what counts as facts within a certain enterprise. Discussion that tends to diminish the seemingly obvious distinction between legal facts and legal rules is therefore offered. Moral questions have affected every page so far, but now they become explicit. There follows a section on the status of the adversary system: how does this satisfy or frustrate our demand for justice? A critic looks for viable alternatives, and some from the civil law tradition, illustrated by trials in Germany and France, introduce the question what we mean by *truth*. The seemingly abstruse question whether truth is a matter of correspondence or of coherence may vitally affect the practice of a legal advocate, whose role can ask him or her to do what would otherwise be immoral. A famous trial from Victorian England serves as an example, and the topic of legal counseling takes us to the law office. The chapter ends with an extended look at judicial behavioralism. I have found that political science students appreciate this and are open to questions about the viewpoint from which they devise their own approach.

Chapter 5 passes to the staple diet of law schools, but in a way that recognizes critical questions raised throughout the book. What limitations are put on judges by their duty of fidelity to past decisions? How, in recognizing the individuality of the case at bar, can legal officials move between strict and loose application of the precedents? Is the reasoning that judges give, to justify their decision, controlled by the models of induction and deduction with which logic supplies us? If not, by what else? A traditional series of cases on manufacturers' liability, culminating with Cardozo's opinion in *MacPherson v. Buick*, is offered as an illustration. And questions of enacted law (codes and statutes) lead to a discussion of theories of interpretation in general. The book closes with a section on judicial decision making that, taking Wasserstrom's work as a foundation, poses questions about how a judge should act if a verdict is to be respected by those for whom the law exists—that is, by you and me. Are we merely consumers of law, or also producers?

Those who read this book, or use it for teaching, will interpret and organize it in various ways. The question of interpretation is basic to all I have written, and I follow Dworkin's view that no privileged account comes from whatever the author had in mind. There is considerable flexibility in finding "what is so." No field offers such ripe examples as the law.

Textbooks invite a supplement from other readings. To each of the thirty-four sections I have added a short reading list and a variety of questions for discussion; there should be ample material for student research, for brief essays or term papers, and for the give-and-take of an intelligently conducted classroom. The detailed index could also help.

The style I have tried to adopt throughout is one that achieves clarity and maintains interest, in order to make dry legal and philosophical questions live. The risk of oversimplification and of levity is present. I have written for the audience I know, and the acknowledgment I wish to make is—above all—to those students whose questioning minds have directed this limited enterprise.

NOTE TO THE STUDENT

Many a bookstore will offer you various paperbacks that carry some such title as *Law for the Layperson.* Though these handbooks leave some place for help from a lawyer, they dispense a black-and-white account of what the law is when we marry or divorce, make a contract or a will, damage a car or a reputation.

This is not such a book. You will learn little of what to expect from the courts if so unfortunate as to land there. Indeed, some of what you read could give poor advice, for the cases are often antiquated, and many are drawn from other lands and even from primitive law. This book is not intended as a course *in* law. It is proposed as a work *on* law, raising basic questions about why we live according to rules and what this means. Even children reveal a surprisingly legalistic mentality; how do we thus make sense of the world in which we live, and how do we distort it?

Though it could sound perverse to say so, my plan is to challenge what you already know of law rather than to extend your information. One theme of the book is our inability to supply a clear and distinct report of what the law is. The color is gray, not black and white. This is not merely because lawyers, threatening one rule through some other, can attack the claims of a book on law-made-easy. There are deeper problems. The very enterprise of "rule following" is open to questions not easy to state and more difficult to answer. What are legal rules and why are we obliged by them? Though they may be found in books and carry a definite pedigree, do they draw their life and authority from principles that enjoy no such precise statement or origin?

One of the classics in philosophy is entitled *On Learned Ignorance,* by Nicholas of Cusa. Questioning what we hold as obvious leads to an ignorance that is very different from simply forgetting or never learning. An ancient claim is that wisdom arises in wonder.

There is a frustration in being told repeatedly that we do not really know what we thought we did; the fate of Socrates stands as a warning. However, the beginner can find some consolation where this is the strategy. Whatever answers may come are to be drawn from an experience common to us all and not from the expertise of detailed information. You must endure law school to learn the particular rules; but you have engaged since childhood in the project of following rules. Legislators and judges produce the law in the books, yet we are the ones who supply the mentality that renders lawmaking possible. It is your mind that is finally in question.*

These remarks have a purpose. Some of the readings in this book are thorny. The language of the law is not simple, and theories about law may tax our understanding. Nevertheless, the book will have failed if it does not conduct its reader back into his or her own experience. That must be the touchstone for all you receive and contribute. It is hoped, for instance, that the questions at the end of each chapter will serve as more than an academic exercise. They are not intended to send you off to the library in a search for what someone else said. The proposal is that, with little reading but much thinking, you will find your own words for what is as open to you as to any of the authors.

Three comments with which to close; the first two are practical. Law schools have a tradition of group study; likewise, it may prove fruitful if your circumstances enable you to meet with others for discussion of the questions raised here. Secondly, do not think of the law as one sphere of life, isolated from others, in the way that chemistry is from accounting. Law is literature—it is an exercise in thinking and in writing. The judge or advocate is one of the few remaining generalists in an age of specialization. If you reflect on law, you treat of life, and please do not say that your reading of poetry or your study of history belongs elsewhere. Nothing is irrelevant to the law, and the law is not foreign to any human experience.

The third comment is more theoretical. Running through this book is a distinction between an *external* and an *internal* viewpoint for talking about law. An example may help. Suppose an extraterrestrial visitor arrives on our planet and sends home an account of what we do. He reports, among other details, on the manner in which we suffer poverty, sickness, and mortality. Suppose further that (as is most unlikely) he suffers none of these. However brilliant his intelligence and power of observation, his account will be seriously flawed. No proliferation of statistics about causes, symptoms, and effects will supply for a failure to appreciate (from within) what it means to suffer.

The analogy, and the challenge, may be apparent. When we discuss law, it is easy to adopt the situation of an external observer, listing the prescriptions of a legislator and the penalties that follow noncompliance. Legal behavior then falls into the pattern of descriptions in physics and physiology.

---

* I should like to support this blunt assertion by quoting from an excellent book on law, one that I frequently recommend to my students: *The Legal Imagination*, by James B. White (1973). "Another way to explain what this course is about is to say that its ultimate question is how an intelligent and educated person can possibly spend his life working with the law, when life is short and there is so much else to do" (Introduction to the Student, p. xxxii). The author is there writing for students already committed to a legal career. My concern is rather with the great majority who live legally without even knowing the name of the local law school. The question remains. How should they, intelligent as they are, continue to "work with the law," when they have reached the age of asking why and recognize the brevity of life and their responsibility for what they make of it?

What is lacking? It is for you to say as you make your way through the book. But the appeal is to what we actually experience. In regard to law, this means our experience of what it *means to be* a person who accepts the obligation of following rules and their underlying principles. Our ordinary language is ill adapted. We talk readily about how one thing relates to another. We stammer when asked what it means to be a subject who does the relating, under rules he or she imposes. Language is largely expressed in the "third person." However, we live in the "first person." Failure to find adequate words is inevitable, yet it may be relative. It is possible that a raw beginner can prove more faithful to our most personal enterprise than many respected writers on the philosophy of law have been.

THE ENTERPRISE OF LAW

1

WHY WORRY ABOUT LAW?

Law, says the judge as he looks down his nose,
Speaking clearly and most severely,
Law is as I've told you before,
Law is but let me explain it once more,
Law is The Law.

(W. H. Auden)[1]

I must say that, as a litigant, I should dread a lawsuit beyond almost anything else short of sickness and of death.

(Judge Learned Hand)

All of us, whether we realize it or not, are surrounded by the law as by the air which we breathe.

(Judge Joseph N. Ulman)

Auden's judge, though doubtless learned in the law, has little to tell us on the law. It is an unwelcome fact. Judge Hand, in a much-quoted statement, captures our fear of legal involvement. Some would go further: better even the hospital than the courthouse. However, there is a difference. Medicine is invoked to cure or to forestall sickness. But law, as Judge Ulman suggests, belongs to physiology as well as to pathology.[2] Remove it, and we collapse. For our life as persons, we depend on the law as we do on the air we breathe. Our alarm at each arises

---

1. From "Law Like Love," in *The Collected Poems of W. H. Auden*, © 1945 W. H. Auden, Edward Mendelson ed., Random House, 75. Printed with permission.
2. In an all too rare book of reflections by a judge on his trade: Joseph N. Ulman, *A Judge Takes the Stand* (New York: Alfred A. Knopf, 1933).

when a storm breaks out; what is life supporting becomes obtrusive, and we take cover to protect ourselves.

This image may serve to introduce all that follows. We shall try to explore the airlike quality of law. It is not just a foreign force that threatens to strike when we deviate; it is constitutive, structural. Rules make games and traffic possible before they intervene through the shout of the umpire or the whistle of the policeman. Purchasing an article, crossing a street, or dwelling in a house are all legal acts. Law appears in the intimacy of the family, and even morality is expressed as a set of rules.

Nevertheless, the claim that almost everything we do falls under the rubric of law offers a poor starting point. Talk about everything is suspiciously like talk of nothing. So this first chapter is an effort to begin by clarifying some of the questions that lead us to ask about law rather than simply taking it for granted. This, at least, is the approach to be expected from a philosopher. Every statement we make is an answer to a question we have posed. It helps little to learn what Copernicus or Calvin or Kant said unless first we appreciate what worried him. Hence this book will start by examining some of the stormy aspects of law that lead us to dread the courthouse and adopt a more suspicious attitude toward legal professionals than toward any other.

1. WOE TO YOU LAWYERS!

If we are to talk with clarity about law, surely we should begin with a definition. Many can be quoted, but this book will supply none.[3] The reader may, by the end, have fashioned some basis for a definition of the law, or at least for a rejection of other accounts. At the beginning, however, we have no more than our common talk, which will need to be refined and expanded as we proceed. But we do know that legislators make laws, police officers enforce them, and we obey or circumvent them. If we run afoul of the system, we approach a lawyer to guide us through the statutes and cases and to present our own position in court. Though lawyers may do their best to resolve the dispute before it reaches the courthouse, we realize what sort of drama would face us there, at the hands of judge and jury. If the verdict is unfavorable, we are aware that appeals can reach the highest court of the land. And, should the results still be disappointing, we may be prepared to invoke—through our language of rights and of fairness—some "law beyond the law."

Whether the policeman is seen as friend or foe depends much on the country (and perhaps the social stratum) in which we live. Our view of the judge varies with the verdict. Our attitude toward the legislator is a matter of politics.

---

3. Roscoe Pound, whose approach to law is solidly empirical, warns his readers to beware of definitions, and of the ideologies they suppose; he gives twelve examples. See *An Introduction to the Philosophy of Law*, 2d ed. (New Haven: Yale Univ. Press, 1954), 25–30.

Yet what is most surprising is that criticism of the law has so often focused on the lawyer, who supposedly is dedicated to help us find our way through the forest and protect us from its dangers.

> Woe to you lawyers! For you load men with burdens hard to bear, and you yourselves do not touch the burdens.... Woe to you lawyers! For you have taken away the key of knowledge; you did not enter yourselves, and you hindered those who were entering.
>
> (Luke 11:46, 52)

Jibes that lawyers belong to one of the world's oldest professions are inaccurate; what we know today as a legal profession is a precarious development of history, largely Western in its origin and often threatened. However, the implied reference to prostitution is biting. The Gospels are not even-handed in their tolerance. The woman taken in adultery is presented with sympathy, but the sustained attack on the legalistic mentality of the Pharisees has led some to interpret the Gospels as antinomian (against all law).

> The first thing we do, let's kill all the lawyers.
> (*Henry VI, Part II*, act 4, scene 2)

Shakespeare is not indulging in caustic exaggeration. He is repeating a slogan from peasant revolts and other popular uprisings. It is not only today that lawyers have been seen as representing the powerful and denying their services to the oppressed.

If witticisms count as evidence, the legal profession has proved an enduring target.[4] "Lawyers use the law as shoemakers use leather; they rub it, press it, and stretch it with their teeth, all to the end of making it fit their purposes" (Louis XII). "A lawyer is a learned gentleman who rescues your estate from your enemies and keeps it himself" (Lord Henry Brougham). "I used to be a lawyer, but now I am a reformed character" (Woodrow Wilson).

Such remarks carry the hidden compliment that lawyers form an essential part of the social fabric, and dependence breeds dislike. However, this reliance upon legal professionals is distinctly Western. We have recently been reminded of alternatives, and of a deeper criticism of institutional law, through the revival of trade with China. Western businessmen have found great difficulty in locating Chinese laws, courts, and advocates for handling questions that arise about commercial contracts.[5] This is no recent development to meet the Marxist ideal

---

4. See, for example, "An Insulting Look at Lawyers through the Ages," *Juris Doctor* 8 (Oct./Nov. 1978): 62.

5. This account needs some, but not much, qualification in view of the stream of legislation that has issued in China since 1981. A sudden manufacture of "propositional law" may have little effect on underlying attitudes. Western legal critics have complained about the "special-case mentality" whereby a narrow rule is enacted to meet some particular need, with little concern for how this fits into the overall structure of law. No system of law is seamless, yet the generality of law should be respected and its degeneration into mere

that law should wither away when a truly Communist society is formed. Such a demand has built upon the Confucian tradition that regards law as external and impersonal. Western societies have been despised for their legalism and their reliance on litigation. The dynastic codes of China were almost entirely criminal, and recourse to law was looked upon as a last resort, when all natural means had failed. The right relations between people were to be learned in the family and extended outward to form the basis for friendship and business. The individual, unguided by any published directives, was to harmonize his or her behavior with an order perceived within.

We are suspicious of such talk, yet it finds echoes in the West. And it may be possible to reject legalism without deriding law. Even so, it is difficult to avoid the suspicion that what we in the West reverence as the rule of law has led us to overreliance upon courts and lawyers for arranging what we could well do ourselves. There are more lawyers in Washington, D.C., than in all of Japan; two-thirds of all the lawyers on earth today are in the United States.[6]

It would seem a relatively simple matter to say in a will who is to get your money when you die, and then for the executor to meet the requirements for showing the will to be valid and for paying taxes, satisfying debts, and distributing what remains. In England this is usually done without a lawyer. The result is that the process takes one-seventeenth as long as here and costs one-hundredth as much. In the United States, where it is the rare exception to go through complex probate procedures without a lawyer, the typical legal fee amounts to about 5 percent of the estate (apparently the abolition in 1975 of legal price-fixing has not much changed this). Since the work involved on a large estate may not be proportionately more than on a small one, some lawyers have admitted to probate fees of more than $1,000 per hour.

The leaving of possessions at death occurs no more than once to each of us. Buying a house may be repeated, as is likely to be the payment of fees for title examination to a lawyer, though the routine work of searching records is often done by someone without legal qualifications. Again, other countries find simpler procedures and make no call upon the lawyer.

Behind such complaints is not merely the accusation of excessive fees for little work. There are parallels in medicine and elsewhere. However, physicians do not cause sickness in order to cure it. What most troubles the layperson about the legal profession is that it seems to create requirements in order to lead us through them. And it is here that we pass from a mundane shock at high prices to questions that may eventually prove philosophical. I know when I have a cold in the head or a pain in the back. I know when they disappear, with or without the expertise of an M.D. But the existence of law raises more theoretical problems than the existence of pain. Is law simply man-made, or does the

---

commands is to be avoided. We shall ask, in following chapters, what is meant by the "structures" of law and by the distinction between rules and commands.

6. I have taken these figures, and those of the following paragraph, from Philip Stern, *Lawyers on Trial* (New York: Times Books, 1980). The book is sharply critical but well documented.

individual legislator fill in details on an outline from some higher source? Most of us are rightly wary of higher sources, though there are dangers also in the earthbound claim that laws are merely the product of those who happen to have the power to impose them. If so, there is power enough in the bar associations of this country at present. It can be a criminal offense to engage in the unauthorized practice of law; this may be so small an infraction as filling out a form without employing a lawyer. Yet it is the local, state, or national bar association that defines what is the legal or illegal practice of law.

However, those who attack the "lawyer's monopoly" should perhaps first look to themselves. We may be making a request rather than receiving an imposition. Legalism (whatever this ambiguous term means) lies close to our heart and pervades our culture. Those who think in legal terms must expect appropriate institutions. For Jew, Christian, and Mohammedan, God is a legislator and judge. Correctly or incorrectly, we have deified the law:

> Of Law there can be no less acknowledged, than that her seat is the bosom of God, her voice the harmony of the world: all things in heaven and earth do her homage, the very least as feeling her care, and the greatest as not exempted from her power, both Angels and men and creatures of what condition soever, though each in different sort and manner, yet all with uniform consent, admiring her as the mother of their peace and joy.
> (Richard Hooker, 1593)

When John Dean was appearing before the Senate Watergate Committee (Feb. 3, 1974), he exclaimed: "My God, how could so many lawyers get involved in something like this?" There is a certain pathos in the remark. We should not utter it of plumbers who allow their own basement to flood. However, if we create a secular priesthood, we invite the anguish and shame of defrocking. Much of the fascination and danger of law may come from the way it gets involved in metaphysics.

FURTHER READING

A short list of books has been added to each section. With a few exceptions, these books are readily available in college or law-school libraries. Students considering a legal career may find the following two bibliographies helpful:

Marke, Julius J., and Edward J. Bender. *Deans' List of Recommended Reading for Prelaw and Law Students.* 2d ed. Dobbs Ferry, N.Y.: Oceana Publications, 1984.

Mersky, Roy M. *Law Books for Non-Law Libraries and Laymen.* Dobbs Ferry, N.Y.: Oceana Publications, 1969.

The former includes a brief statement about each of the 2,330 books recommended by law school deans, and an asterisk identifies those entries most useful to a prelaw student. The latter bibliography (unfortunately out of print at present) lists about twelve hundred books and puts them under such headings as "professional non-law reading for the lawyer" and "books to help the lawyer's writing style."

6 Why Worry About Law?

The following books supply a range of common complaints about the legal profession and the litigious society that we have helped to form:

Auerbach, Jerold S. *Unequal Justice.* New York: Oxford Univ. Press, 1976.
Bartlett, Joseph W. *The Law Business: A Tired Monopoly.* Littleton, Colo.: F. B. Rothman & Co., 1982.
Carlin, Jerome E. *Lawyers on Their Own.* New Brunswick, N.J.: Rutgers Univ. Press, 1962.
Goulden, Joseph C. *The Million Dollar Lawyers.* New York: G. P. Putnam & Sons, 1977.
Lieberman, Jethro K. *Crisis at the Bar.* New York: W. W. Norton & Co., 1978.
———. *The Litigious Society.* New York: Basic Books, 1981.
Nader, Ralph, and Mark Green. *Verdicts on Lawyers.* New York: Crowell, 1976.
Rodell, Fred. *Woe Unto You, Lawyers!* New York: Reynal & Hitchcock, 1939.
Stern, Philip M. *Lawyers on Trial.* New York: Times Books, 1980.

QUESTIONS FOR DISCUSSION

1.   The Gospel verses quoted above appear in the context of a general condemnation of the scribes and Pharisees but are addressed specifically to the lawyers among them. Two charges are made: (a) lawyers add needlessly to the burden of life and (b) they render ineffective our normal know-how for confronting our difficulties. Do you find any basis for such complaints today?

2.   Antinomianism, though officially declared heretical, has formed a recurring theme among Christian writers. The claim is that right action comes from an inner spirit and requires no obedience to external laws. Put such a doctrine into words of your own and give your assessment of it. Are there laws in a family? How are laws and lawyers treated in the views of Utopia that literature presents? If you believe in heaven, do you expect it to involve laws?

3.   The concentration of legal services on the side of the powerful and wealthy may be more dramatic today than it was in Shakespeare's time. Legal studies are strongly directed toward corporate law, and three Wall Street law firms employ more lawyers than all this country's public-interest law firms. Recognizing the vast disparity in salaries, do you blame law students for sacrificing their idealism and heading where the money is? Is the uneven access to justice inevitable?

4.   Comment on the claim that whereas physicians heal ills that come to us from nature, lawyers play a part in the creation of problems that demand legal expertise for solution. See, for example, "How to Avoid Lawyers," by Jethro Lieberman, in Nader and Green (1976), pp. 105–17. What about recourse to small claims courts, the use of paralegals rather than lawyers, and the simplification of legal language?

5.   The term *metaphysics* carries many meanings. Used loosely and pejoratively, it suggests what is mystical and unsupported by evidence. More precisely, and neutrally, it involves a claim to reveal some necessity going beyond the empirical facts that come through our senses. The remark that "ice must be slippery" is empirical and is short of absolute necessity (try very low temperatures?). The claim that "every event must have a cause," or that "God does/does not exist," asserts a necessity that no factual reports could justify.

What do you make of the closing comment of this section, that law is involved with metaphysics? The particular tax laws depend on who is in power at the time. They are conventional, changeable. But what about the more basic law that we should support the society to which we belong? That recompense should be made for injuries we inflict? That people should not be treated simply as things? Are such laws simply man-made, a fact of the current legislator's will?

2. THE INTEGRITY OF AN ADVOCATE

> *In the law courts nobody cares a rap for the truth about what is just or good, but only about what is plausible.*
>
> (Plato *Phaedrus* 272d)

Some adjustments would be needed to apply Plato's criticism to the modern legal scene.[7] However, his dialogues form an extended attack on the Sophists, and there are interesting parallels between these ancient Greek teachers and the lawyers of modern times. The early experiment in democracy, where political and judicial decisions were made in open assemblies, set a premium on the techniques of argumentation. It was the Sophists who, for fees that were not always modest, displayed and taught such skills.

The fact that this name (which literally means "wise people") has acquired the dubious connotations of "sophistry" is much to the point. The Sophists were not charlatans. They contributed to the development of Greek prose and to the analysis of language. But their approach was that of competitors rather than scholars. The role of the advocate became more absorbing than that of the adherent, conquest more important than truth. A discussion was a battle in which one must be victor and the other must be vanquished.

They formed no philosophical school to which a system of doctrines can be assigned. However, certain slogans suggest the direction of their work. "Man is the measure of all things." "Nothing is of nature, all is of convention."[8] Their skill was in spotting the issue, finding exactly how the position that one disputant was taking differed from that of another. Thus the pressure of argument could be applied where most effective. They were practical, pragmatic. They refused to enter into abstract questions of truth or justice: "good" means always "good for" some particular purpose, and it is up to the client to specify that purpose.

If Plato's opposition is to be put into contemporary terms, we may say that the Sophists had little sense of professional responsibility. The Middle English word *profess* means living under a vow. Though reasonable fees might be accepted, the goal of one's work was to be a total submission to some absolute demands. The three faculties in a medieval university that prepared for such a life were divinity, medicine, and law. If we dismiss Plato as an idealist, the term is accurate. He held that only ideas are fully real; we judge wheels by circles, not vice-versa. The Sophists were hired technicians who failed to respect the reality of the ideal.

---

7. See also his comments on the legal advocate in *Theaetetus* 172d–175d.

8. These claims were interpreted variously; see, for example, W. K. C. Guthrie, *The Sophists* (Cambridge: Cambridge Univ. Press, 1971), 55–134. We have come to view such assertions as statements of a relativism that leaves the individual or the community as final arbiter of what is so or ought to be. For instance, slavery would be right in ancient Athens, wrong today; there is no "nature" of man, or norm beyond the current measures we happen to apply, that crosses over the ages and must judge the conventions of time and place.

It is said that a student at law school, asking his professor in class if a certain legal decision was just, found himself politely directed to the divinity school for such questions. Whether he would have been satisfied there is far from evident, but the story is suggestive. The popular conception is of a lawyer as one who simply serves the interests of his client. He is paid to rehearse one side of any question. He aims at neither truth nor justice but at victory.

There is possibly no occupation, outside of managing an athletic team, where the competitive element of winning is so much to the foreground as it is in law. And of all legal traditions, none dramatizes this more than the common law of England and America, based as it is so thoroughly on the adversary system. All is in view of an actual or potential trial, and when judgment is delivered the score is made public. From the first class at law school, life is formulated in terms of adversaries.

The realization that a lawyer is trained to see and argue either side of any question does not of course justify the conclusion that he or she is simply a "hired gun." Admittedly, the layperson may wonder at the status of lawyers who are employed solely by a particular corporation or who devote their talents exclusively to plaintiff or defendant (for example, in medical malpractice suits). Yet the ethical problems are complex, and we shall return to them (in chapter 4) when more is at hand for stating the question.

Nevertheless, our preliminary inquiries into the legal mentality should not ignore the sort of hesitations that Plato might have voiced if he were around to view our courts and law offices. His idealism has been supplanted by a form of positivism. Facts are more highly respected today. And a law is seen as a fact generated by some particular legislator's will, rather than as a norm proceeding from a reason common to all. Actions are illegal because the legislature happens to ban them, rather than because we understand why they are wrong. Moral relativism is often assumed; even those who appeal to justice are reluctant to suggest that there are any universal principles. The lawyer's task is to know and to use the law that *is*. If he has strong feelings that this fails to be what it *ought to be*, then let him use his strength (though not precisely as a lawyer) to introduce legislation and bring new laws to power.

Chapter 2 of this book will explore the wide range of a lawyer's tasks and will suggest that these play an important part in the way we formulate the social order required for living humanly: the lawyer is a creative artist before he or she engages in the tactics of advocacy. Chapter 3 will investigate some of the many ways in which a deep concern for moral principles is allowed by contemporary theorists to enter into a lawyer's or a judge's reading of what the law really says. And the two final chapters will try to arrive at a balanced account of the adversary system and hence of the often agonizing demands we place on legal professionals who are committed to truth and justice. But the present chapter is merely introductory. Its concern is to raise questions rather than to solve them.

Rites of Initiation

Should we doubt the correctness of calling law a discipline, we may glance at what goes on in the three years of law school in this country. There the student is trained to think like a lawyer. He or she learns to see any human situation as never before, with a clarity and rigor that make previous perceptions appear sloppy and uncoordinated. What passed all too easily for thinking acquires the sharp edge of precise concepts and rigorous arguments.

However, it is a sad truth that every discipline serves to limit inquiry as well as to extend it. Thinking like a scientist is an achievement that has made the modern world. Yet the very success of science has come from the resolute project of excluding all qualities that cannot be transformed into numbers. We convert warmth to temperature because we can apply numbers to the length of a column of mercury. We then learn to disregard our feelings as "subjective" and to concentrate on those few characteristics that are quantifiable. Molecules are not warm and have no color, but they do have mass, size, and motion.

There are parallels in every other discipline. The merchant sees a painting for its price, the historian for its date. The philosopher, lost in thoughts of aesthetics, may miss much of the feeling that produced the painting. No harm comes from this so long as a person does not identify himself with the abstractions of his discipline. The dentist can still regard his dinner guests as more than people who chew. However, it is not always easy to maintain one's integrity, where this word be taken literally as *wholeness*. The more demanding a career is, the more it threatens the viewpoints and languages and sense of reality that we had before entering it. The specialist can glide easily from saying "talk of X does not work in my job" to saying "X is not real."

It is hoped that these introductory remarks are general enough to set in context the following comments on initiation to a legal career. Few who pass through law school, for all the tears, regret the habits of mind it produces in them. Their worries are that the sharpness of vision has come at the expense of breadth and variety. Complacency in the power of the law often yields to a painful sense of its weakness. Confronted with profound and delicate human problems, the lawyer can do no more than apply impersonal categories; he is not helped to understand the roots of the conflict. He can predict an outcome in court; he cannot heal the trouble that leads there. Laypeople often classify lawyers as hardened cynics. The causes of cynicism, however, may be more subtle than we suspect.

Perhaps the most frightening experience of students at law school is the discovery that previous strategies for success no longer work. Your manner of studying, your way of reading, your language, your very distinction between what is important and irrelevant—all these are challenged to the extent that no foothold seems to remain. And the competitive requirements are increased as your means for meeting them are threatened.

One writer on legal studies goes so far as to apply to law school the analysis that Erving Goffman makes of "total institutions" in his work *Asylum* (Chicago:

Aldine Publ. Co., 1961).[9] Goffman studies asylums, prisons, and monasteries for the way in which they eliminate the home world of the entrant and replace it with their own perceptions and evaluations. The physical techniques of removing personal possessions, restricting privacy, and imposing uniform dress clearly do not apply to law schools. But these may employ psychological strategies that penetrate even deeper. Terms such as *mortification* and *self-abasement* are not far-fetched if the convictions of more than twenty years are systematically assaulted and can be reinstated only when a new self, speaking an unfamiliar language, acquires some facility at the strange game of balancing citations from documents and forming a consistency where "even the devil could make no sense."

One institution of American law schools seems to stand out for the intensity of praise and blame it has received; this is the so-called "Socratic method." Though more than a hundred, or even two hundred, students may be present, the professor does not lecture. He or she tries to develop a systematic understanding of the law by questioning students on cases they have read. You are called at random from the mass and are told to state the case. What you say is then subjected to intensive interrogation. For every reply there is a further question. What might be inspiring in the privacy of a tutorial can become a grievous humiliation in such a forum, where students are pitted so dramatically against each other.

Arguments for this method range from the claim that it is the most effective way of teaching large numbers to the conclusion that a student who survives the process will never be daunted by any courtroom appearance. At least, the emphasis on learning through questioning cannot be faulted. Critics of the method, though admitting that its use is highly variable and can in worthy hands be beneficial, have seen it employed as a primary weapon in fashioning the less admirable aspects of the legal mind. Everything becomes a defense of one position against another, rather than a communal search for truth. And though the appearances may be of an equal battle, the raw fact is that the professor is the interrogator and has the armaments on his side. Nowhere is the dogmatism of the law, and its identification with the status quo, more evident. One law professor characterized the method as "placing a premium on being able to outdraw a student at twenty feet." Ralph Nader, no friend of the current legal balance of power, spoke of the Socratic method as "the game that only one can play."

There has been some move away from such a procedure in American law schools today. And if we return to the beginning of this section, one conclusion is likely: the Socratic method has little to do with Socrates. It is to be granted that Socrates always met a reply with a further question and seemed set to destroy all that was taken for evident and was not justified in an appropriate way. It is granted, too, that Plato did not always succeed in making Socrates a

---

9. John J. Bonsignore, *Before the Law*, 3d ed. (Boston: Houghton Mifflin Co., 1984), 258–61.

humble inquirer who recognized his own ignorance more painfully than his interlocutors did theirs. But the Socrates of tradition has become the model for reflective thinking that puts one's own questions into question. His Delphic vocation was to poverty, to a renunciation of any sure possession of knowledge. He would not have rejected Descartes' argument that "I think therefore I am," but he would at once have been troubled at any assurance of comprehending who is the "I," what is the "thinking," and what is the "being." If Socrates' method involved troubling others, it was because he himself did not know. "As for myself, if the sting ray paralyzes others only through being paralyzed itself, then the comparison is just.... I infect others with the perplexity I feel myself.... I am ready to carry out a joint investigation and inquiry." (Plato *Meno* 80)

The average law student is unlikely to recognize the picture. When his name is called, he does not feel invited to a joint search for ignorance. The law is there to be known, and the professor knows it; he may not even have had to glance through his notes. A comment that raises doubts on details may be applauded. But far-reaching questions about the topic are likely to be dismissed—or referred to the divinity school.[10]

Legality and Humanity

For the conclusion to this section I refer to a recent account of how one of this country's most prestigious law schools appeared to a first-year student, Scott Turow. The author, who seems to have survived his honest and often critical account of his initiation at Harvard Law School, describes his passage from early enthusiasm to the depths of disillusionment and then to a more balanced perspective. Through the narrative, readers follow the effects of legal training on a variety of the most highly qualified students. We witness the growth of an unscrupulously competitive atmosphere that no medical training can match. We observe how the early devotion of students to public service through the law gives way to the demands of a system where nine-tenths of the lawyers serve one-tenth of the people.[11]

Of special interest are comments on the professors and their various uses of the Socratic method. The one whom Turow ranked in September as the best teacher was the one he was most bitter in rejecting, by May, as reprehensible in the use of his own position and the power of legal knowledge. More significant, perhaps, is the fact that the professor who seemed most like Socrates, in

---

10. "For the lawyer, jurisprudence is that part of the law which he never gets time to read—the part adorned with learned names ... and separate from the legal arguments he uses in court" (from Thurman Arnold, *The Symbols of Government*, New Haven: Yale Univ. Press, 1935, 57).

11. Two years before Turow wrote, a poll of law students in California showed that whereas 37 percent of first-year law students intended public-interest work, the figure had fallen in the third year to 22 percent. Those who listed their primary motivation in legal studies as alleviating social or individual problems had dropped from two-thirds to one-third.

repeatedly questioning standard legal answers and categories, was at first unanimously dismissed by the students as incompetent: "The guy can't teach; no wonder they laid him off for twelve years." To the credit of Harvard students, appreciation of him slowly grew: "I sat still, then suddenly I realized his point: there are no answers. This is what he has been inviting us all semester to realize. Rules are declared, but the theoretical dispute is never settled."

The book, in its entirety, should be of interest to any prospective law student. The following three extracts may suggest some questions and invite reflection on what has been said in this section.

ONE L
by Scott Turow

Excerpts: pp. 89–93, 221–22, 296–97.
Reprinted by permission of the Putnam Publishing Group from One L by Scott Turow.
Copyright © 1977 by Scott Turow.

When we started jurisdiction in Procedure, Nicky Morris made what seemed an important comment.

"About now," he said, "law school begins to become more than just learning a language. You also have to start learning rules and you'll find pretty quickly that there's quite a premium placed on mastering the rules and knowing how to apply them.

"But in learning rules, don't feel as if you've got to forsake a sense of moral scrutiny. The law in almost all its phases is a reflection of competing value systems. Don't get your heads turned around to the point that you feel because you're learning a rule, you've necessarily taken on the values that produced the rule in the first place."

The remark struck a number of people, and as we left class for lunch, I talked about what Nicky had said with Gina Spitz. Gina came on as the last of the tough cookies. She'd just graduated from Barnard and she was full of the bristle of New York City. She was big, feisty, outspoken, and glitteringly bright. But what Nicky had said had touched her in a way that left her sounding plaintive.

"They're turning me into someone else," she said, referring to our professors. "They're making me different."

I told her that was called education and she told me, quite rightly, that I was being flip.

"It's someone I don't *want* to be," she said. "Don't you get the feeling all the time that you're being indoctrinated?"

I was not sure that I did, but as Gina and I sat at lunch, I began to realize that for her and many of the other people in the section, there was a crisis going on, one which had not yet affected me as acutely....

In the fourth week of school, Professor Mann promoted a class debate on various schemes for regulating prostitution, and I noticed the differences in style of argument from similar sessions we'd had earlier in the year. Students now spoke about crime statistics and patterns of violence in areas where prostitution occurred. They pointed to evidence, and avoided emotional appeals and arguments based on the depth and duration of their feelings.

But to Gina, the process which had brought that kind of change about was frightening and objectionable.

"I don't care if Bertram Mann doesn't want to know how I *feel* about prostitution," she said that day at lunch. "I *feel* a lot of things about prostitution and they have everything to do with the way I *think* about prostitution. I don't want to become the kind of person who tries to pretend that my feelings have nothing to do with my opinions. It's not *bad* to feel things."

Gina was not the only classmate making remarks like that. About the same time, from three or four others, people I respected, I heard similar comments, all to the effect that they were being limited, harmed, by the education, forced to substitute dry reason for emotion, to cultivate opinions which were "rational" but which had no roots in the experience, the life they'd had before. They were being cut away from themselves.

Many of the people with such complaints were straight out of college. Thinking about it, I concluded that having survived the '60s, held a job, gotten married—having already lived on a number of principles—made me less vulnerable to a sense that what we learned in class would somehow corrupt some safer, central self. But there was no question that my friends' concern was genuine; listening to them made me more self-conscious about the possible effects our education in the law was having on me.

At home, Annette told me that I had started to "lawyer" her when we quarreled, badgering and cross-examining her much as the professors did students in class. And it seemed to me there were other habits to be cautious of. It was a grimly literal, linear, step-by-step process of thought that we were learning. The kind of highly structured problem-solving method taught in each of Perini's classes, for instance—that business of sorting through details, then moving outward toward the broadest implications—was an immensely useful technical skill, but I feared it would calcify my approach to other subjects. Besides rigidity, there was a mood to legal thinking which I found plainly unattractive.

"Legal thinking is nasty," I said to Gina at one point in our conversation, and I began to think later I'd hit on a substantial truth. Thinking like a lawyer involved being suspicious and distrustful. You reevaluated statements, inferred from silences, looked for loopholes and ambiguities. You did everything but take a statement at face value.

So on one hand you believed nothing. And on the other, for the sake of logical consistency, and to preserve long-established rules, you would accept the most ridiculous fictions—that a corporation was a person, that an apartment tenant was renting land and not a dwelling.

What all of that showed me was that the law as a way of looking at the world and my own more personal way of seeing things could not be thoroughly meshed; that at some point, somehow, I would have to *learn* those habits of mind without making them my own in the deepest sense. I had no idea quite how I'd go about that, but I knew that it was necessary.

"Every time we have one of these discussions in Criminal," Gina said, "I want to raise my hand and say, The most important thing is to be *compassionate*. But I know what kind of reaction I'd get from Mann—he'd tell me, That's nice, or just stare at the ceiling. I mean, am I wrong?"

I agreed that she was not, either in predicting Professor Mann's answer or in the opinion she'd expressed.

* * *

Some members of the section were infuriated by Morris's approach. They found it abstruse, confusing, and—worst—impractical.

"He's in outer space," Ned Cauley told me one day. "We're not learning Civil Procedure; we're learning Nicky Morris's theory of rules. What's going to happen to all of us when we go into a courtroom and make a motion under Rule Twelve E? Do you think the judge is going to give a damn whether it's a model of legal informalism?"

But the majority of the section were enthusiasts and I was among them. Like Ned, I had come to law school for professional training, but I was lost when teachers concentrated more directly on the kind of professionalizing Ned desired. In those classes, law study was treated primarily as the means for learning the circumscribed skills and customs of a sort of elevated priesthood. The uniqueness of legal thought was emphasized. In consequence, I and many other classmates were often left with the sense of a gap between legal ideas and those we had known in other areas of study. Nicky was out to efface that boundary.

"The law," Nicky said at one point in the second term, "is a humanistic discipline. It is so broad a reflection of the society, the culture, that it is ripe for the questions posed by any field of inquiry: linguistics, philosophy, history, literary studies, sociology, economics, mathematics."

Nicky did not touch on all those subjects, but his teaching was always animated by a sense of the law's search as unlimited and profound. In Morris's class I found myself launched once again on that kind of scrutiny of the most fundamental assumptions regarding the way we lived each day—the manner in which we treated each other—which had seemed so important when I had come to school. Each time I walked into Morris's classroom all that rapturous discovery of the first six weeks returned. And I knew I would leave after each meeting with that same crazy feeling, half heat, half thirst—the sensation of being nearly sucked dry by excitement.

* * *

The ultimate risk of allowing students to make their first acquaintance with the law in such an atmosphere, in that state of hopeless fright, is that they will come away with a tacit but ineradicable impression that it is somehow characteristically "legal" to be heartless, to be brutal, and will carry that attitude with them into the execution of their professional tasks.

Those objections to heavy-handed Socraticism are, in a fashion, only a part of a larger concern with legal education of which I began to become conscious after my conversations with Gina last fall. The law is at war with ambiguity, with uncertainty. In the courtroom, the adversary system, plaintiff against defendant, guarantees that someone will always win, someone lose. No matter if justice is evenly with each side, no matter if the issues are dark and obscure, the rule of law will be declared. The law and the arbitrary certainty of some of its results are no doubt indispensable to the secure operation of a society where there is ceaseless conflict requiring resolution.

But a lot of those attitudes toward certainty seem to rub off on the law world at large. Many of the institutions of legal education show a similar seeking after sureness and definition, a desire to subdue the random element, to leave nothing to chance: the admissions process, where statistical formulas serve as the basis for decision; the law school classroom, where all power and discretion are concentrated in the professor; the stratifications so clearly marked in the law school population, with the best students segregated on the law review, and the faculty remote from all; and the notion of the meritocracy, the attempt to rank and to accord privilege by some absolute standard. All of these things amount in my mind to a fighting of the war against ambiguity and uncertainness in quarters where it is not called for, where the need which supports the custom of the courtroom is not present. Not even the law can abolish the fundamental unclearness of many human situations, but in the law schools there is precious little effort made to address the degree to which human choice is arbitrary. We are taught that there is always a reason, always a rationale, always an argument. Too much of what goes on around the law school and in the legal classroom seeks to tutor students in strategies for avoiding, for ignoring, for somehow subverting the unquantifiable, the inexact, the emotionally charged, those things which still pass in my mind under the label "human."

FURTHER READING

Some Studies of the Legal Profession:

Countryman, Vern, et al. *The Lawyer in Modern Society*. 2d ed. Boston: Little, Brown & Co., 1976.

Harnett, Bertram. *Law, Lawyers, and Laymen.* New York: Harcourt Brace Jovanovich, 1984.
Mellinkoff, David. *Lawyers and the System of Justice.* St. Paul: West, 1976.
Patterson, L. R., and E. E. Cheatham. *The Profession of Law.* Mineola, N.Y.: Foundation Press, 1971.
Pound, Roscoe. *The Lawyer from Antiquity to Modern Times.* St. Paul: West, 1953.
Schwartz, Murray. *Lawyers and the Legal Profession.* Indianapolis: Bobbs-Merrill, 1979.

Some Books on Life at Law School in the United States:

Dobbyn, John F. *So you want to go to Law School.* St. Paul: West, 1976.
Ehrlich, Thomas, and G. Hazard. *Going to Law School?* Boston: Little, Brown & Co., 1975.
Kinyon, Stanley. *Introduction to Law Study and Law Examinations.* St. Paul: West, 1971.
Osborn, John J. *The Paper Chase.* Boston: Houghton Mifflin, 1971.
Seligman, Joel. *The High Citadel.* Boston: Houghton Mifflin, 1978.
Stevens, Robert. *Law School: Legal Education in America from the 1850's to the 1980's.* Chapel Hill: Univ. of North Carolina Press, 1983.

There is a wide range of novels that give an insight into the daily life of a lawyer. See, for example:

J. J. Marke, *Deans' List of Recommended Reading* (2d ed. Dobbs Ferry, N.Y.: Oceana Publications, 1984), 144–65.

R. M. Mersky, *Law Books for Non-Law Libraries and Laymen* (Dobbs Ferry, N.Y.: Oceana Publications, 1969), 41–42.

QUESTIONS FOR DISCUSSION

1. Were not the Sophists correct in insisting that *good* is always a relative term, meaning good *for* some purpose you choose to assign? Think of examples (a horse, a car, a college, tax laws, a person). Does the same apply to *just* and *true*? Apply your conclusions to the obligations you would face as a lawyer (when your client specifies his or her purposes).

2. To describe someone as an idealist is often to dismiss that person as an impractical visionary. Could you, however, be thoroughly practical and businesslike in the way you try to bring justice (an ideal or model) into a world where it exists so far only in faint copies? The language of model and copy is Plato's. The question What is real? may seem the height of abstraction, but could your answer to this decide how you spend your life as a lawyer?

3. The concept of positivism involves the claim that any statement should be put in a form where its truth or falsity can be found through observable facts. What facts would verify or falsify the following statements:

    The college is dissatisfied with your performance.
    Religion is the opium of the people.
    All people are created equal.

How might a positivist interpret the "reality" of a law? For example:

    No eating in the classroom.
    A will is invalid unless there are two witnesses.
    You have a right to read but not to publish pornographic literature.

4. Mention examples from your experience of how disciplines and occupations limit perception as well as extending it. Think of friends (or teachers), each engaged in a different field of study. How would you characterize a prelaw student?

5. How can the pressure to learn legal rules lead to an imperceptible assumption of the values that produced the rules? Should a lawyer have a definite answer for his client's question, What is the rule?, and yet realize that there are, behind each rule, theoretical disputes that yield no clear answer?

6. Clarity, consistency, and certainty seem to be virtues in all disciplines. Would you employ a lawyer who confronts problems emotionally? Does Gina (in the extract from Turow's book) set up a misleading opposition between reason and feeling? Or is she protesting against limitations in the form of reasoning that lawyers have adopted? What is dry reason? Linearity? Argument? Reread the extract carefully and try to come up with a more satisfactory version of the two sides.

3. DILEMMAS OF A JUDGE

So far we have spoken of lawyers rather than of the law. The target is more concrete. Yet our ambiguous attitudes toward the former have much to do with the intangibility of the latter. We usually have to consult a lawyer to know whether and how a law exists. And though we may hesitate to say that the average lawyer makes laws, we know that he or she stands at the door. Those who have read Kafka's *The Trial* will appreciate that control of the door is close to command of whatever lies within.

This, and the following two sections, will look for questions that arise in the work of judges. These are, of course, also lawyers. But their right to the title of a "profession" seems secure. Their public office usually carries a sacrifice of salary from the possibilities of private practice (though it is of interest that in countries outside the common law tradition, judges are not drawn from private practice but go their particular way after law school). The title, Your Honor, seems well deserved.

If the legal profession does require a patient discovery of truth and submit to the demands of justice, then we should look above all to the work of the bench. Is not good judgment one of the highest qualities we can ascribe to a person? Ironically, however, it is precisely here that we detect the ambiguity of the law. To commend someone for good judgment is to praise him for what he has contributed rather than for a routine following of instructions. But if a judge is creative in his decision making, how can he be following the law?

We think of the law as a collection of rules that prescribe what we ought or ought not to do. In the prosaic workings of a court, the judge is evidently following rules in applying the rules. Yet if he adds *more* than this, how does this "more" derive? From some other rules within the law? From rules outside the law? Would these be personal convictions of the judge? Would he then please those who share his beliefs but expose himself to the charge, from others, of acting beyond or against his office?

Such questions go much closer to the heart of our concern with the law than do complaints about legal fees. The topics will be with us throughout the book, but these sections offer three suggestive examples. The first is an analogy drawn from games. The second is an actual, though ancient, law case arising out of an attempt to hasten the effect of a will through a touch of poison. The third is an imaginary case written by a master of "jurisprudence through fiction."

Trouble at the Chess Tournament

In this book I shall from time to time, to illustrate the law at work, draw examples from the games we play. There we are on familiar ground, and our activity is structured by rules that are often codified in books, enforced and adjudicated by referees. All we lack is a lawyer (unless the manager of the team takes on the role of advocate).

The following example is drawn from chess.[12] I chose this game because few pursuits offer less of a penumbra for judicial dilemmas. In soccer, the referee has considerable discretion whether to call a penalty or wave play on when the offending team may profit from such an interruption. But in chess the rules have the exactitude of mathematics. Surely even an inexperienced judge can oversee all moves and declare the winner when checkmate occurs.

Suppose, then, that you are asked to serve as referee in a local chess tournament. You have all you need in case of doubt. At your side is the official book of rules. So is a set of more particular rules adopted by the committee to govern this tournament. Nothing can go wrong.

JONES v. SMITH

Jones is an elderly man who may have been sharper in his youth but now makes some fatal moves. The game is over in fifteen minutes. However, to the surprise of all, Jones asks that he be declared the winner, on grounds of justice: he can scarcely make ends meet on his pension and badly needs the prize money, whereas Smith is wealthy by any standards.

As referee, you are likely to deny this appeal. But how, precisely, would you justify your rejection of it (write your judicial opinion)? Did you not sympathize with Gina's protest that the law should be compassionate? Are you talking like Auden's judge, "The law is the law"?

An adequate answer to such an apparently simple question would introduce many problems about the nature of law. Is law composed simply of rules that we can readily locate, or are these backed by unwritten principles? Chapter 3 will take us further into such topics. For the present, we may notice an apparent distinction between the rules in a game and those we find in our law books. A game, it seems, is entirely specified by its rules. The moment Jones sat at the chess board, he agreed to exclude all considerations beyond those of this particular game. His limited purpose became that of achieving checkmate by moving the pieces in prescribed ways. He may have had further goals, like pleasure and the sharpening of his mental powers; but such aims are not listed in the book of rules, which simply define the moves that lead to winning or losing. No umpire in baseball can allow a batter a fourth strike because this will

---

12. I have developed this example from suggestions in Ronald Dworkin's book, *Taking Rights Seriously* (Cambridge: Harvard Univ. Press, 1977), 101–5.

add to the player's pleasure or even contribute to the interest of an otherwise one-sided game.

In this sense, games may be called "closed practices."[13] They are such that a player cannot raise the question whether a rule applies to his case, in view of purposes that are not explicitly set forth in the rules. Some "sovereign" (the commissioner of baseball?) or some "master rule for the making and changing of rules," may eventually allow us four strikes in baseball or eliminate the possibility of queening a pawn or of castling in chess. But a game allows no appeal beyond the rules presently in the book.

There are philosophers (we shall later examine the views of John Austin and of H. L. A. Hart) who see a close parallel in the law of the land.[14] They admit that laws can be changed, yet their concern is more with the *how* than the *why* of change. They are understandably suspicious of talk about any universal purpose in all legal systems or in the game of living legally. Other philosophers (Ronald Dworkin and Lon Fuller may serve as contemporary examples) are less sure that law forms a closed system of rules. They see law as an "open practice," in the sense that some unwritten principles enter into our statement of what the law really is and into a judge's decision of a particular case. Such theorists would doubtless send Jones on his way from the tournament. However, they might be less ready to dismiss his argument, in a court of law, that he has a right to win a taxation case for moral considerations that are not explicitly stated in the law books. We may say that, in an open practice, moves are "underdetermined" by rules. If we respect a judge for his judgment, it is because he is asked to look repeatedly beyond the rules he learned. The question is, of course, to what?

WHYTE v. GREENE

This game is closely contested. After several hours neither is clearly ahead and the tension has grown. At this point, Greene begins tapping his fingers on the table and whistling softly. Whyte asks for silence. Greene deliberately continues. Whyte appeals to you. What do you do?

One of the spectators draws your attention to a tournament rule that holds a game forfeit if one player unreasonably annoys the other. Can you apply this rule to declare Whyte the winner?

The term *unreasonable* is one of many that have been called "weasel words." Other examples would include *proper, appropriate, substantial, due care, fair dealing,* and *in the public interest.* Such phrases, like the animal, are flexible and evasive. They allow for considerable initiative on the referee's part rather than specifying exactly how the rules apply.

---

13. I take the distinction between closed and open practices from Thomas Morawetz, *The Philosophy of Law* (New York: Macmillan, 1980), 46–52.

14. The theories of these philosophers, along with the ideas of Dworkin and Fuller, will be explained in the appropriate sections of chapter 3. Austin sees law as stemming from the explicit or tacit command of a sovereign. Hart substitutes rules for commands and replaces the sovereign with some master rule in relation to which all particular rules are valid.

What, then, limits your discretion in ruling against Greene? If he had started kicking Whyte under the table, you would intervene. If he sneezed loudly, you would not. The rules of a game call for acceptance when people agree to play. You can safely suppose that those who entered this tournament excluded physical interference when making their implicit agreement; the project of chess is known by all to differ in this respect from wrestling.

Perhaps you would be advised to explore other contrasts. Shooting craps is also not a body-contact sport, but it is a game of chance (or so I innocently suppose) rather than one of strategy. A closer example would be poker, but the intellectuality of this game invites psychological maneuvering whereas the understanding by which we become chess players seems to remove such an approach to victory as far as possible.

If the case of *Jones v. Smith* tended to suggest some differences between games and law, that of *Whyte v. Greene* diminishes the difference and prompts us to ask whether a game is quite as closed by its written rules as it seems. Should not even an umpire be open to the precarious venture of giving good judgment by reference to purposes that go beyond the book? Chess offers few such examples. We find more evident instances in our popular spectator sports. The rules of basketball tell when the whistle should be blown (e.g., for traveling). But I suspect that most referees would admit to some choice in repeatedly stopping the game or in allowing its flow as a game. How do we judge the judge? Can we eliminate all references to some purposes that make the game, even though not listed in the book of rules? What about the football referee who must decide what is or is not dangerous play? Boxing, in view of serious current criticisms that threaten its existence as a sport, offers evident examples.

Those who, like the author, speak at some distance from organized sports may consider a final example from which none of us can escape. We have to talk, and we encounter the rules of grammar and syntax. Should we, for instance, ever split an infinitive ("My aim is to further clarify . . ." rather than "My aim is further to clarify . . .")? Childhood training makes me shudder at the prospect. Yet I read from an authority that "A real split infinitive, though not desirable in itself, is preferable to either of two things, to real ambiguity, and to patent artificiality".[15]

Many illustrations are needed, but the proposal seems eminently sensible. The rules for writing are precise, and we are advised to follow them closely. Yet our very obedience is in view of basic goals or principles. We want to avoid misunderstanding (Did I mean above a "further clarification" or a "further aim"?). We want also to achieve ease and simplicity of expression. Such purposes, being behind the rules in general, can serve to moderate the rules on particular occasions.

---

15. H. W. Fowler, *A Dictionary of Modern English Usage*, 2d ed. (New York: Oxford Univ. Press, 1965), 581.

FINCH v. SLYE

Shaken by your difficult decision and by the public controversy it has aroused, you turn to your third game late in the day. The opponents are both good players but are of markedly different temperaments. Finch is timid, hesitant, tortured. Slye sits like a Buddha, fixing an enigmatic smile on his adversary. After only a few moves, Finch (aware of the precedent set by your previous ruling) whispers to you asking if you can prevent Slye from intimidating him. Your request is met with an enigmatic smile.

I leave you with the case, and with the anguish of a judge. In most undertakings we remain free to say the evidence is inconclusive. But the judge is bound to give a decision on each case before him and to be able to justify that decision, distinguishing his reasons clearly from those that he (or others) gave in whatever seems to be a contrary judgment.

The key, abstract as it is, to such dilemmas is offered by Dworkin:

> A player consents not simply to a set of rules, but to an enterprise that may be said to have a character of its own; so that when the question is put—To what did he consent in consenting to that?—the answer may study the enterprise as a whole and not just the rules.
>
> (*Taking Rights Seriously*, 1977, 105)

Those who know chess well can tell us about the enterprise as a whole and about the forms of intimidation that do or do not fit. Similarly, we all develop skill in interpreting the many projects of our life. A teacher of some experience understands the complex enterprise of education and follows particular rules in the light of this understanding. A family member is constrained by few formal rules but he or she has an intimate knowledge of the enterprise; the mistake is unlikely of thinking that what is not explicitly forbidden is therefore allowed.

It is, however, much more of a problem when we come to a judge or to anyone planning activities with an eye to what might end up in court. There is wide disagreement where to set the law of the land on a spectrum that runs from the highly open practices of family life to the almost entirely closed practice of chess. Much of what follows in this book will be concerned with the question whether we can sensibly talk about common purposes in a legal system or about "the legal enterprise as a whole."

FURTHER READING

Books on the decision-making process of judges, and on the question whether and how they make law, will be suggested in the final three chapters, notably in sections 19, 28, and 34.

For a study of the main fields of human activity as games, see: Huizinga, Johan. *Homo Ludens*. Boston: Beacon Press, 1950 (especially chapter 4, "Play and Law").

For an account of how children develop intellectually through various understandings of the meaning of rules, see: Jean Piaget, *The Moral Judgment of the Child* (1932; reprint, New York: Free Press, 1965), 13–108.

QUESTIONS FOR DISCUSSION

1. In his comment on the analogy of games, Dworkin points out that chess is "an autonomous institution," where the right to be declared the winner comes entirely from the rules of the game (*Taking Rights Seriously*, 1977, 101). His thesis, to be described in section 19, is that the legal rights a judge should consider are not thus independent of the moral and political rights we have: "legislation is only partly autonomous." This important claim is much disputed in contemporary discussions on the philosophy of law. At least, we notice an obvious distinction between chess and the law of the land—we do not have to play the former but we cannot escape membership in a political society. Would Jones have been more sensible to meet his financial problems in some undertaking better fitted to his abilities than chess? But if we think of Jones as the dissatisfied citizen of a nation, such options are restricted. Is "love it or leave it" practical advice in regard to the land of your birth? How can we explain that the law of the land makes players out of those who have not chosen to join the game and would prefer not to be in it?

2. You organize games, with prizes, for a children's party. One little boy has so far won nothing. Might you arrange things so as to increase his chances of winning (e.g., by stopping the music in his favor at musical chairs)? Would this be just? Would it be legal? Compare your decision with the one you gave in *Jones v. Smith*.

3. The novelist, C. P. Snow, bases one of his stories on a lengthy legal dispute over a contested will (*In Their Wisdom*, New York: Scribner's, 1974). A rich octogenarian changed his will shortly before his death; his needy and worthy daughter was disinherited and the estate was willed to a social drone, the utterly selfish son of a woman who had insinuated herself into the testator's life as nurse in his final years. On purely legal terms, the case was borderline. The daughter won in the trial court but lost the appeal by a two-to-one vote of the judges. Exclusive concern was given in both proceedings to legal technicalities about "undue influence." In your opinion, should the judges have looked beyond the rules they found in the books of law? Do you think that some considerations of justice should have tipped the decision the other way? Or might such treatment of the rules of law have been unjust, and have worked social harm, by making the law less certain (for the rest of us)?

4. Do rule books ever suggest the purpose of a game? If they are silent on this, does it make sense to talk about common purposes and (if so) how would you find them? What unwritten principles might help you to rule on unsportsmanlike behavior?

5. An interesting challenge to the view that games are entirely closed practices occurred during a 1983 baseball game. In the ninth inning, George Brett hit a home run to win the game for Kansas City against the New York Yankees. However, the Yankee manager (Billy Martin) had been waiting for his opportunity. He had noticed that Brett put more pine tar on his bat than allowed by the rules. Martin chose this moment to draw the violation to the attention of the umpires, who followed the book in disallowing the home run and declaring the Yankees the winner. Kansas City finally won, on appeal to the president of the American League. But how would you have decided the case? Would you have found it relevant to ask *why* pine tar is limited to eighteen inches on a bat? Is this to deprive the batter of some advantages over the pitcher and thus keep the score from mounting? Or is it simply to keep dirt off the baseball? Do the principles and purposes behind a game enter into our interpretation of the rules?

6. What reply might you expect from an experienced judge if you naively asked him what is the purpose of the law he has spent much of his life applying? If you asked him what is the purpose of some particular law? Suppose it is a statute passed by a legislature of several hundred members?

4. THE ACCELERATED INHERITANCE

Legal language strikes us as designed to exclude the layperson. Since this section contains the first extended example in the book, a few words of introduction may help. What are the cases you find in a law library or in the casebook of a law student? If you are taken to court, do not expect such publicity. All that is openly said will be recorded, but publication in law books can (with some exceptions) be achieved only if you or your opponent appeals the decision. The cases that a lawyer reads, and on which he bases his understanding of the law, are—in this country—the published arguments of appeals court judges. It is from such judicial writing that the venerable *common law* has been derived.[16]

How then are you to read a case such as the one below? Put yourself squarely in the adversarial situation. Who are the opponents? Who won? Here the initiative came from Mrs. Riggs and Mrs. Preston. These were daughters of the late Francis Palmer, whose will had left the family farm to his grandson, Elmer Palmer. Since the demise of Francis had been hastened by poison from the hands of Elmer, the two sisters saw not only injustice but illegality in Elmer's ownership of the farm. When they approached the courts for redress, they thus became the *plaintiffs* and Elmer the *defendant*. They lost but then appealed the decision. It is here that we find their suit, in the highest court of New York State, where they are referred to as the *appellants*. Elmer became the *appellee*, or *respondent*. You may, if you value morality more than cunning, be pleased to find that the court decided in favor of the sisters: the estate was taken from Elmer and they were declared its owners.[17]

What such an appeals court publishes is one or more *opinions*, composed by the judges involved. The majority opinion (appearing first) justifies the court's decision; what Judge Earl writes here is an argument for reversal of the previous judgment. Judge Gray, who opposed Earl's conclusion, then writes a minority opinion to explain his objections. Sometimes other judges who sat on the appeal case add their own opinion on one side or the other.

In learning who won, you will have discovered something of what originally happened to create a legal controversy. Now study, in as much detail as possible, the facts of the case. This is not easy, for we are reading at several removes. Appeals courts do not call witnesses; factual knowledge is limited to the record of the trial court. Your grasp of the facts must come from whatever the upper court judges have repeated, usually at the beginning of their opinion. Here it

---

16. The distinction between the "common law" and the "civil law" will be explained in section 13. The former is the law of England and the United States (and related countries, such as Australia); it is mainly *case law*, drawn from earlier judicial decisions that are respected as precedents. The civil law, by contrast (though beware of a separate use of this term in opposition to criminal law), is found in countries whose legal system is derived from continental Europe and ultimately from Roman law; it is largely *enacted* in the guise of comprehensive *codes*. The following case indicates something of the difference: the civil law had more to say in propositional form, as articles in the books, on the interesting question at stake.

17. Many names are applied to these "upper courts." They are known generically as "appellate courts"; I shall refer to them by the less daunting title of "appeals courts."

may help to draw a family tree and ask pertinent questions. How does Susan Palmer fit in, and was she simply ignored in Francis's will? What threat did Elmer see in the marriage to Mrs. Bresee? How did the will respect the interests of Mrs. Riggs and Mrs. Preston? Why, if the estate is taken from Elmer, should it go to them? Your report on the facts will include what happened in the trial court, the decision that is to be confirmed or denied in the appeal.

Now you come to the essentials, the legal arguments on each side. Notice what the disputants agree upon and what they contest. Remember that the criminal trial is over. We no longer ask whodunit? Elmer had, in a separate court, been found guilty of poisoning his grandfather and is satisfying the sentence of that court by serving a term for second-degree murder in the state reformatory (remember his age). We are not told how long he will remain a guest of the governor. However, ownership of a prosperous farm must give him some solace; he can follow its fortunes while in prison and enjoy it when released. So this is a civil trial, where all dispute is about who legally possesses the estate.[18]

Notice also that the opposing judges seem interestingly to agree on what is morally better. They combine in thinking it somehow unjust that Elmer should so profit from the fruits of his iniquity. Where, then, is the exact point of the dispute? Why does Judge Gray set his moral opinions aside and conclude that Elmer should retain the estate? How does Judge Earl transform his moral convictions into legal conclusions at variance with those of Gray? This case is not a masterpiece of law but should draw upon the imagination of the beginner. Try to appreciate both sides and to pass from feelings to arguments. Recognize also that what was on trial here may have been the status of law itself, as it comes to us through our lawyers and judges. Comments on the case will be added in an extended set of questions for discussion at the end of this section.

RIGGS v. PALMER[19]
Court of Appeals of New York, 1889

115 N.Y. 506, 22 N.E. 188.

EARL, J. [Judge] On the 13th day of August, 1880, Francis B. Palmer made his last will and testament, in which he gave small legacies to his two daughters, Mrs. Riggs and Mrs.

---

18. Here we have the other meaning of "civil law." It deals with the suit of one individual against another (*Riggs v. Palmer*), rather than with the action of the community against an individual for what have been defined as crimes (*State of New York v. Palmer*, or *People v. Palmer*).

19. There is, in this country, a standard way of listing cases. The title is that of the adversaries, with plaintiff's name first in civil suits (though the order is sometimes reversed if the defendant loses and appeals). Next comes the name of the court and the year of the hearing. Then (in this example) 115 N.Y. 506 means that the report will be found, in a law library, starting on page 506 of volume 115 in the *New York Reports (Court of Appeals)*. A further identification, 22 N.E. 188, means that the case can also be found starting on page 188 of volume 22 of the *North Eastern Reporter*, in the West Publishing Company's system; these reports began only a few years before the *Riggs* case.

Preston, the plaintiffs in this action, and the remainder of his estate to his grandson, the defendant Elmer E. Palmer, subject to the support of Susan Palmer, his mother, with a gift over to the two daughters, subject to the support of Mrs. Palmer in case Elmer should survive him and die under age, unmarried, and without any issue. The testator [one who makes a will], at the date of his will, owned a farm, and considerable personal property. He was a widower, and thereafter, in March, 1882, he was married to Mrs. Bresee, with whom, before his marriage, he entered into an antenuptial contract, in which it was agreed that in lieu of dower [a wife's right to all or part of her dead husband's property] and all other claims upon his estate in case she survived him she should have her support upon his farm during her life, and such support was expressly charged upon the farm. At the date of the will, and subsequently to the death of the testator, Elmer lived with him as a member of his family, and at his death was 16 years old. He knew of the provisions made in his favor in the will, and, that he might prevent his grandfather from revoking such provisions, which he had manifested some intention to do, and to obtain the speedy enjoyment and immediate possession of his property, he willfully murdered him by poisoning him. He now claims the property, and the sole question for our determination is, can he have it? The defendants [Elmer and the administrator of the estate] say that the testator is dead; that his will was made in due form, and has been admitted to probate [the process of proving that a will is valid and of giving effect to it]; and that therefore it must have effect according to the letter of the law.

It is quite true that statutes regulating the making, proof, and effect of wills and the devolution of property, if literally construed, and if their force and effect can in no way and under no circumstances be controlled or modified, give this property to the murderer.

The purpose of those statutes was to enable testators to dispose of their estates to the objects of their bounty at death, and to carry into effect their final wishes legally expressed; and in considering and giving effect to them this purpose must be kept in view. It was the intention of the law-makers that the donees in a will should have the property given to them. But it never could have been their intention that a donee who murdered the testator to make the will operative should have any benefit under it. If such a case had been present to their minds, and it had been supposed necessary to make some provision of law to meet it, it cannot be doubted that they would have provided for it. It is a familiar canon of construction [principle of interpretation] that a thing which is within the intention of the makers of a statute is as much within the statute as if it were within the letter; and a thing which is within the letter of the statute is not within the statute unless it be within the intention of the makers. The writers of laws do not always express their intention perfectly, but either exceed it or fall short of it, so that judges are to collect it from probable or rational conjectures only, and this is called "rational interpretation"....

Many cases are mentioned where it was held that matters embraced in the general words of statutes nevertheless were not within the statutes, because it could not have been the intention of the law-makers that they should be included. They were taken out of the statutes by an equitable construction [*equity* means fairness in a particular situation]; it is said in [Matthew] Bacon: "By an equitable construction a case not within the letter of a statute is sometimes holden to be within the meaning, because it is within the mischief for which a remedy is provided. The reason for such construction is that the law-makers could not set down every case in express terms. In order to form a right judgment whether a case be within the equity of a statute, it is a good way to suppose the law-maker present, and that you have asked him this question: Did you intend to comprehend this case? Then you must give yourself such answer as you imagine he, being an upright and reasonable man, would have given." (9 Bacon's Abridgment 248).

... What could be more unreasonable than to suppose that it was the legislative intention in the general laws passed for the orderly, peaceable, and just devolution of property that they should have operation in favor of one who murdered his ancestor that he might speedily come into the possession of his estate? Such an intention is inconceivable. We need not, therefore, be much troubled by the general language contained in the laws.

Besides, all laws, as well as all contracts, may be controlled in their operation and effect by general, fundamental maxims of the common law. No one shall be permitted to profit by his own fraud, or to take advantage of his own wrong, or to found any claim upon his own iniquity, or to acquire property by his own crime. These maxims are dictated by public policy, have their foundation in universal law administered in all civilized countries, and have nowhere been superseded by statutes....

Here there was no certainty that this murderer would survive the testator, or that the testator would not change his will, and there was no certainty that he would get this property if nature was allowed to take its course. He therefore murdered the testator expressly to vest himself with an estate. Under such circumstances, what law, human or divine, will allow him to take the estate and enjoy the fruits of his crime? The will spoke and became operative at the death of the testator. He caused that death, and thus by his crime made it speak and have operation. Shall it speak and operate in his favor? If he had met the testator, and taken his property by force, he would have had no title [legal ownership] to it. Shall he acquire title by murdering him? If he had gone to the testator's house, and by force compelled him, or by fraud and undue influence had induced him, to will him his property, the law would not allow him to hold it. But can he give effect and operation to a will by murder, and yet take the property? To answer these questions in the affirmative it seems to me would be a reproach to the jurisprudence of our state, and an offense against public policy.

Under the civil law, evolved from the general principles of natural law [see question 10 at the end of this section] and justice by many generations of jurisconsults, philosophers, and statesmen, one cannot take property by inheritance or will from an ancestor or benefactor whom he has murdered.... But, so far as I can find, in no country where the common law prevails has it been deemed important to enact a law to provide for such a case. Our revisers and law-makers were familiar with the civil law, and they did not deem it important to incorporate into our statutes its provisions upon this subject. This is not a *casus omissus* [a case for which no legal provision has been made]. It was evidently supposed that the maxims of the common law were sufficient to regulate such a case, and that a specific enactment for that purpose was not needed....

My view of this case does not inflict upon Elmer any greater or other punishment for his crime than the law specifies. It takes from him no property, but simply holds that he shall not acquire property by his crime, and thus be rewarded for its commission....

The facts found entitled the plaintiffs to the relief they seek. The error of the referee [who decided at the lower court level] was in his conclusion of law. Instead of granting a new trial, therefore, I think the proper judgment upon the facts found should be ordered here. The facts have been passed upon twice with the same result,—first upon the trial of Palmer for murder, and then by the referee in this action. We are therefore of opinion that the ends of justice do not require that they should again come in question. The judgment of the general term and that entered upon the report of the referee should therefore be reversed, and judgment should be entered as follows: That Elmer E. Palmer and the administrator be enjoined from using any of the personalty or real estate left by the testator for Elmer's benefit; that the devise [gift] and bequest in the will to Elmer be declared ineffective to pass the title to him; that by reason of the crime of murder committed upon the grandfather he is deprived of any interest in the estate left by him; that the plaintiffs are the true owners of the real and personal estate left by the testator, subject to the charge in favor of Elmer's mother and the widow of the testator, under the antenuptial agreement, and that the plaintiffs have costs in all the courts against Elmer. All concur, except GRAY, J., who reads dissenting opinion, and DANFORTH, J., concurs.

GRAY, J. (dissenting) This appeal presents an extraordinary state of facts, and the case in respect of them, I believe, is without precedent in this state. The respondent, a lad of 16 years of age, being aware of the provisions in his grandfather's will, which constituted him the residuary legatee of the testator's estate, caused his death by poison, in 1882. For this crime he was tried, and was convicted of murder in the second degree, and at the time of the commencement of this action he was serving out his sentence in the state reformatory. This action was brought by two of the children of the testator for the purpose of having those provisions of the will in the respondent's favor canceled and annulled.

The appellants' argument for a reversal of the judgment, which dismissed their complaint, is that the respondent unlawfully prevented a revocation of the existing will, or a new will from being made, by his crime; and that he terminated the enjoyment by the testator of his property, and effected his own succession to it, by the same crime. They say that to permit the respondent to take the property willed to him would be to permit him to take advantage of his own wrong.

To sustain their position the appellants' counsel has submitted an able and elaborate brief, and, if I believed that the decision of the question could be effected by considerations of an equitable nature, I should not hesitate to assent to views which commend themselves to the conscience. But the matter does not lie within the domain of conscience. We are bound by the rigid rules of law, which have been established by the legislature, and within the limits of which the determination of this question is confined. The question we are dealing with is whether a testamentary disposition can be altered, or a will revoked, after the testator's death, through an appeal to the courts, when the legislature has by its enactments prescribed exactly when and how wills may be made, altered, and revoked, and apparently, as it seems to me, when they have been fully complied with, has left no room for the exercise of an equitable jurisdiction by courts over such matters.... The reason for the establishment of such rules, we may naturally assume, consists in the purpose to create those safeguards about these grave and important acts which experience has demonstrated to be the wisest and surest. That freedom which is permitted to be exercised in the testamentary disposition of one's estate by the laws of the state is subject to its being exercised in conformity with the regulations of the statutes. The capacity and the power of the individual to dispose of his property after death, and the mode by which that power can be exercised, are matters of which the legislature has assumed the entire control, and has undertaken to regulate with comprehensive particularity.

The appellants' argument is not helped by reference to those rules of the civil law, or to those laws of other governments, by which the heir, or legatee, is excluded from benefit under the testament if he has been convicted of killing, or attempting to kill, the testator. In the absence of such legislation here, the courts are not empowered to institute such a system of remedial justice....

The statutes of this state have prescribed various ways in which a will may be altered or revoked; but the very provision defining the modes of alteration and revocation implies a prohibition of alteration or revocation in any other way. The words of the section of the statute are: "No will in writing, except in the cases hereinafter mentioned, nor any part thereof, shall be revoked or altered otherwise," etc. Where, therefore, none of the cases mentioned are met by the facts, and the revocation is not in the way described in the section, the will of the testator is unalterable. I think that a valid will must continue as a will always, unless revoked in the manner provided by the statutes....

The appellants' argument practically amounts to this: that, as the legatee has been guilty of a crime, by the commission of which he is placed in a position to sooner receive the benefits of the testamentary provision, his rights to the property should be forfeited, and he should be divested of his estate. To allow their argument to prevail would involve the diversion by the court of the testator's estate into the hands of persons whom, possibly enough, for all we know, the testator might not have chosen or desired as its recipients.

Practically the court is asked to make another will for the testator. The laws do not warrant this judicial action, and mere presumption would not be strong enough to sustain it.

But, more than this, to concede the appellants' views would involve the imposition of an additional punishment or penalty upon the respondent. What power or warrant have the courts to add to the respondent's penalties by depriving him of property? The law has punished him for his crime, and we may not say that it was an insufficient punishment. In the trial and punishment of the respondent the law has vindicated itself for the outrage which he committed, and further judicial utterance upon the subject of punishment or deprivation of rights is barred.... The judgment should be affirmed, with costs.

FURTHER READING

There are many textbooks for undergraduate legal studies courses, and most of these books are well stocked with cases that are of interest to the nonprofessional reader. For an evaluation of eighteen such textbooks, see *Journal of Legal Education* 28 (1976): 112–19. However, not one of these books was put in the top three out of five possible ratings for its treatment of theories of law or law as a generic concept. It is not so easy to find books that concentrate on cases that bring to light the way in which law is an open practice, dependent on unwritten purposes and principles rather than on explicit rules. One anthology, not listed in the above article, presents thirty-six cases that were chosen for their relevance to philosophical questions in the law: Philip E. Davis, *Moral Duty and Legal Responsibility* (1966; reprint, New York: Irvington Publishers, 1980).

For a case that occurred almost seventy years after *Riggs* and offers analogies to it, see Neiman v. Hurff (1952), 11 N.J. 55, 93 A.2d 345. See also Oleff v. Hodapp (1935), 129 Ohio St. 432, 195 N.E. 838.

QUESTIONS FOR DISCUSSION

1. Judge Gray's opinion may first be examined, since he shocks the layperson who hastily assumes that a judge should support the position that leads in the morally superior direction. If you think this, reflect on the diversity of what we find under the ambiguous rubric of "morality." Suppose you apply for a divorce, following the laws of your state, and then discover that the judge denies it because of his moral convictions about the sanctity of marriage? Or suppose, as a businessman, you engage in a promising contract only to find it struck down by a liberal judge who thinks it unfair? Returning to the case we have read, what if Francis Palmer had left his money to an armaments firm? To a gambling establishment?

2. Is Gray concerned to defend the relative certainty of law against the uncertainty of morality? And is not his insistence on the certainty of law more applicable to wills than (say) to contracts between people still living? Does not the very rigidity of testamentary laws come from the fact that you are no longer there to defend your intentions? Again, see the danger in Earl's principles.

3. Gray suggests some possibly immoral consequences of Earl's moral way. Did not Earl unjustly add to the punishment that the criminal court held sufficient for Elmer's contribution to his grandfather's death? And here is a perhaps more serious complaint: is Earl not guilty of one of the most grievous charges made against Hitler, of indulging in *retroactive* legislation? Suppose that, toward the end of the semester, I change (for the whole semester) the way of calculating grades that I announced in September. Would you protest, in the name of both law and morality? Does Earl make a ruling in 1889 and antedate it in order to catch what was done in 1882?

4. There may be deeper fears to which Gray gives expression. Should law be sought in unwritten and unpublished sources? Did the Emperor Caligula make valid laws by inscribing them so high on the walls of Rome that no one could read them? Were Hitler's laws valid if announced only through secret directives to his officials? Can a secret law be a law at all? What, then, of Earl's appeal to unwritten principles in the law? Where do we find the "general, fundamental maxims of the law"? Are these secret if not published in writing?

5. Shortly after *Riggs*, an Ohio appeals court criticized Earl's decision. In the 1892 case of Deem v. Millikan (6 Ohio Circuit Courts 357, 3 Ohio Circuit Decisions 491), it was decided that a son who murdered his mother did not forfeit his inheritance. Bacon's principle was said by Judge Shauck to "afford no warrant for adding an important exception to a statute which, in clear language, defines a rule of public policy. . . . When the legislature speaks in clear language upon a question of policy, it becomes the judicial tribunals to remain silent." Is this a restatement of Gray's dissent? Would you agree that legislators make law and that judges are limited by their office to applying the law that *is*? If we think that the law *ought to be* otherwise (or ought to be more specific on what we regard as hard cases), should not the change in law come from the legislature rather than from judicial decisions?

6. Judge Earl's decision usually wins the spontaneous support of undergraduate students. Some, however, are wary of what they regard as appeals to emotion rather than to the law. Do you find examples of this in the language he uses? The question of a judge's dependence on precedents (earlier legal decisions in analogous cases) will be discussed in a later chapter, and all reference to precedents has been removed from the opinions quoted above. However, the cases cited seem, by about three to one, to support Gray rather than Earl; previous courts enforced the terms of a will even where the beneficiary forcibly prevented the testator from changing it. Again, does Earl rely on moral considerations outside the law?

7. If we want to know the meaning of a statement, we inquire into the intention of the author. Both Gray and Earl speculate on this. However, whose intentions are they investigating? Is Gray concerned with those of Francis Palmer, when the question is raised what the testator would have wanted, if he had known? Is Earl more concerned with the intentions of the legislators, if they had anticipated such an event?

8. Both Francis and the legislators were dead and could not support such claims about hypothetical intentions. Is it plausible that Francis might still (if he had known) have preferred that his farm go to Elmer than to Riggs and Preston? In discussing hypothetical intentions, are we asked to play the psychologist? Though this may be what Gray indicates, is it all that Earl is demanding? He quotes an ancient *Abridgment of the Law*, by Matthew Bacon, as telling us to suppose the lawmaker present and to ask him: "Did you intend to comprehend this case?" The dead do not reply. Yet notice Bacon's further requirement: "You must give yourself such answer as you imagine [reason?] he, being an upright and reasonable man, would have given." What is Bacon suggesting? An imaginative fantasy? Or a philosophical and moral inquiry into the reasons behind what particular legislators happen to say? Here we touch upon questions that require many pages to expose. Theorists such as Dworkin claim that the law depends, to some extent, upon an inquiry into "the best philosophical theory" behind what the rules state. Intentions are particular, but reasons are universal.

9. How does Earl apply these very general principles to the case at issue? The legislators in Albany made no explicit provision for what happened. But, says Earl, we must not merely look for words; we should use our intelligence to discover the reason or purpose that regulates laws of inheritance. This, he claims, must be the "orderly, peaceable, and just devolution of property." Many questions of detail are left open, yet this much at least is said to be clear: anyone who commits murder in order to inherit property is contradicting the purpose of the laws of inheritance. Failure to write an explicit provision comes, not from oversight, but from simple presupposition of what is basic and essential. Your comments? Even if you agree that all laws have a reason or purpose, is this so easy for us to find? Could it be other than what Earl discovers in the laws of inheritance?

10. Earl is appealing beyond the written rules to what some call "natural law." He uses the term himself and refers to the "universal law" of all countries; this seems to go back to disputes between Plato and the Sophists on the question of nature vs. convention. It is claimed that such

law is not made by human legislators and cannot be changed by them; indeed, any statutes they pass in violation of it would be disqualified. Earl speaks of fundamental principles that control all acts of legislators and rulings of judges. What examples does he give of such principles? Are they principles of morality external to the law, or are they principles of the law itself? How might Earl defend them if challenged?

5. LIFE THROUGH HOMICIDE

Writers on the theory of law seldom contrive to entertain their readers. An exception is the late Prof. Lon L. Fuller, of Harvard. One of his devices for explaining and illustrating the philosophies at work in law was to construct a supreme court in the fictional Commonwealth of Newgarth. Each member of the court represents a different philosophy of law in writing his opinions, and Fuller thus brings to abstract controversies the wit and richness of all too human personalities.

Some of the cases are designedly trivial (such as a dispute over a purchase of pickled squids). Most of his cases, however, portray an extreme situation where the familiar signposts of law are missing and the actors are forced to engage afresh in the very enterprise of living legally. It is such a "boundary situation" that forms the facts of the case we are to read in this section.

Fuller mentions that he had two actual cases in mind. The earlier one (*United States v. Holmes*) came from an incident in 1841. An American ship sank and the longboat was seriously overladen with nine seamen and thirty-two passengers. When it seemed certain that this boat would go under unless lightened, the officer in charge exclaimed "Help me, God; men, go to work." Holmes was a seaman who had shown notable courage throughout. Hearing these words, he proceeded to force several of the passengers overboard. Though the fate of the other survivors is not recorded by the court, Holmes was taken into custody and tried for unlawful homicide. His defense attorneys argued that, in the longboat, Holmes found himself facing death and was thus in a "state of nature" where the laws of human society had no application. The judge rejected this notion, holding that "the law of nature" can be suspended by no human law and in no situation. An ambiguity in the term *nature* is evident (and this will be discussed in section 21). Holmes was found guilty but given a light sentence of six months and twenty dollars.

The other case (*Queen v. Dudley and Stephens*) also arose from a lifeboat situation. After a British yacht sank in 1884, three seamen and the cabin boy spent three weeks without food in an open boat. The condition of the boy deteriorated most rapidly. Two of the seamen (Dudley and Stephens) decided, after prayer, that they should kill the boy for food. The third seaman (Brooks) dissented, though he did not refuse to join the others in the sustenance obtained after the act was committed. Four days later, rescue arrived. Dudley and

Stephens were convicted of murder, but the sentence of death was commuted by the Crown to six months imprisonment.

Fuller moves the setting for his own case from the open sea to the depths of the ground. Five members of the Speluncean Society were exploring a limestone cavern when their only escape route was thoroughly sealed by a series of landslides. The cave lacked any edible materials, and after three weeks they were informed by radio that the rescue operation would take at least ten more days, by which time they would have died of starvation. They then proposed the remedy in the *Dudley* case and asked for legal or moral advice. None was offered. Radio silence followed. When the rescuers finally got through, they found that the Speluncean Society was short a member.

It was this one, Whetmore, who had first proposed the grim expedient and had suggested that dice be cast. Then he withdrew from the agreement, though he allowed the dice to be thrown for him. The outcome indicated him as the victim.

Juries are known for their way of rendering a humane verdict despite the rigor of the law. To guard against such a solution, and to set the dilemma squarely on the judiciary, Fuller invokes what actually occurred in the *Dudley* trial. The foreman of the jury asked permission to return a *special verdict*. This means that the jury had simply to assess whether the facts were as reported, leaving the judge to decide, on applying the rules of law, whether the defendants were guilty. The judge did so find them and imposed the statutory penalty of death. However, both the trial judge and the jury at once petitioned the chief executive of Newgarth to commute this sentence to six months (as in *Dudley*).

The appeal then went to the supreme court, and it is the five opinions of this august but eccentric body that Fuller presents. Those of Justices Foster, Keen, and Handy are reprinted below with minor omissions. They form the heart of the dispute. You may recognize some version of Earl and Gray (section 4) in the first two. Handy stands for a distinctly American contribution to theories of law and may be described as a legal realist—one who asks us to look at the full way in which legal decisions are made.

In the interests of brevity I have chosen to omit one opinion entirely, that of Justice Tatting. Though he offers valuable criticisms of Foster, he represents more a legal style than a philosophical school. In another of Fuller's parables, Tatting is described by a colleague as "weaving about every case an encircling filigree of irrelevant distinctions." And here he is so perplexed that he declares his withdrawal and casts no vote.

We begin with Chief Justice Truepenny. After stating the facts of the case (summarized above), he then does no more than to propose a convenient division of labor. Let the judges maintain the law by upholding the trial court's decision. And let the chief executive defend morality by showing mercy.

THE CASE OF THE SPELUNCEAN EXPLORERS
"In the Supreme Court of Newgarth," *by* Lon L. Fuller

Harvard Law Review 62 (1949): 616–45.
© *1949 by the Harvard Law Review Association. Printed with permission.*

TRUEPENNY, C. J.: . . . It seems to me that in dealing with this extraordinary case the jury and the trial judge followed a course that was not only fair and wise, but the only course that was open to them under the law. The language of our statute is well known: "Whoever shall wilfully take the life of another shall be punished by death." N.C.S.A. (n.s.) 12–A. This statute permits of no exception applicable to this case, however our sympathies may incline us to make allowances for the tragic situation in which these men found themselves.

In a case like this the principle of executive clemency seems admirably suited to mitigate the rigors of the law, and I propose to my colleagues that we follow the example of the jury and the trial judge by joining in the communications they have addressed to the Chief Executive. There is every reason to believe that these requests for clemency will be heeded, coming as they do from those who have studied the case and had an opportunity to become thoroughly acquainted with all its circumstances. It is highly improbable that the Chief Executive would deny these requests. . . . We may therefore assume that some form of clemency will be extended to these defendants. If this is done, then justice will be accomplished without impairing either the letter or spirit of our statutes or offering any encouragement for the disregard of law.

FOSTER, J.: I am shocked that the Chief Justice, in an effort to escape the embarrassments of this tragic case, should have adopted, and should have proposed to his colleagues, an expedient at once so sordid and so obvious. I believe that something more is on trial in this case than the fate of these unfortunate explorers, and that is the law of this Commonwealth. If this court declares that under our law these men have committed a crime, then our law is itself convicted in the tribunal of common sense, no matter what happens to the individuals involved in this petition of error [claim that the trial court misread the law]. For us to assert that the law we uphold and expound compels us to a conclusion we are ashamed of, and from which we can only escape by appealing to a dispensation resting within the personal whim of the Executive, seems to me to amount to an admission that the law of this Commonwealth no longer pretends to incorporate justice.

For myself, I do not believe that our law compels the monstrous conclusion that these men are murderers. I believe, on the contrary, that it declares them to be innocent of any crime. I rest this conclusion on two independent grounds, either of which is of itself sufficient to justify the acquittal of these defendants.

The first of these grounds rests on a premise that may arouse opposition until it has been examined candidly. I take the view that the enacted or positive law of this Commonwealth, including all of its statutes and precedents, is inapplicable to this case, and that the case is governed instead by what ancient writers in Europe and America called "the law of nature."

This conclusion rests on the proposition that our positive law is predicated on the possibility of men's co-existence in society [i.e., this is the purpose of *all* law]. When a situation arises in which the co-existence of men becomes impossible, then a condition that underlies all of our precedents and statutes has ceased to exist. When that condition disappears, then it is my opinion that the force of our positive law disappears with it. We are not accustomed to applying the maxim *cessante ratione legis, cessat ipsa lex* [when the reason for a law is extinguished, so is the law itself] to the whole of our enacted law, but I believe that this is a case where it should be so applied.

The proposition that all positive law is based on the possibility of men's co-existence has a strange sound, not because the truth it contains is strange, but simply because it is a truth so obvious and pervasive that we seldom have occasion to give words to it. Like the air we breathe, it so pervades our environment that we forget that it exists until we are suddenly deprived of it. Whatever particular objects may be sought by the various branches of our law, it is apparent on reflection that all of them are directed toward facilitating and improving men's co-existence and regulating with fairness and equity the relations of their life in common. When the assumption that men may live together loses its truth, as it obviously did in this extraordinary situation where life only became possible by the taking of life, then the basic premises underlying our whole legal order have lost their meaning and force.

Had the tragic events of this case taken place a mile beyond the territorial limits of our Commonwealth no one would pretend that our law was applicable to them.... Now I contend that a case may be removed morally from the force of a legal order, as well as geographically. If we look to the purposes of law and government, and to the premises underlying our positive law, these men when they made their fateful decision were as remote from our legal order as if they had been a thousand miles beyond our boundaries. Even in a physical sense, their underground prison was separated from our courts and writ-servers by a solid curtain of rock that could be removed only after the most extraordinary expenditures of time and effort.

I conclude, therefore, that at the time Roger Whetmore's life was ended by these defendants, they were, to use the quaint language of nineteenth century writers, not in "a state of civil society" but in "a state of nature." This has the consequence that the law applicable to them is not the enacted and established law of this Commonwealth, but the law derived from those principles that were appropriate to their condition. I have no hesitancy in saying that under those principles they were guiltless of any crime.

What these men did was done in pursuance of an agreement accepted by all of them and first proposed by Whetmore himself. Since it was apparent that their extraordinary predicament made inapplicable the usual principles that regulate men's relations with one another, it was necessary for them to draw, as it were, a new charter of government appropriate to the situation in which they found themselves.

It has from antiquity been recognized that the most basic principle of law or government is to be found in the notion of contract or agreement.... If the compact was a fiction from an historical point of view, the notion of compact or agreement furnished the only ethical justification on which the powers of government, which include that of taking life, could be rested. The powers of government can only be justified morally on the ground that these are powers that reasonable men would agree upon and accept if they were faced with the necessity of constructing anew some order to make their life in common possible....

This concludes the exposition of the first ground of my decision. My second ground proceeds by rejecting hypothetically all the premises on which I have so far proceeded [here Foster moves from the purpose of *all* law to the purpose of a *particular* statute]. I concede for purposes of argument that I am wrong in saying that the situation of these men removed them from the effect of our positive law, and I assume that the Consolidated Statutes have the power to penetrate five hundred feet of rock and to impose themselves upon these starving men huddled in their underground prison.

Now it is, of course, perfectly clear that these men did an act that violates the literal wording of the statute which declares that he who "shall wilfully take the life of another" is a murderer. But one of the most ancient bits of legal wisdom is the saying that a man may break the letter of the law without breaking the law itself. Every proposition of positive law, whether contained in a statute or a judicial precedent, is to be interpreted reasonably in the light of its evident purpose. This is a truth so elementary that it is hardly necessary to expatiate on it. . . .

The statute before us for interpretation has never been applied literally. Centuries ago it was established that a killing in self-defense is excused. There is nothing in the wording of the statute that suggests this exception. Various attempts have been made to reconcile the legal treatment of self-defense with the words of the statute, but in my opinion these are all merely ingenious sophistries. The truth is that the exception in favor of self-defense cannot be reconciled with the *words* of the statute, but only with its *purpose*.

The true reconciliation of the excuse of self-defense with the statute making it a crime to kill another is to be found in the following line of reasoning. One of the principal objects underlying any criminal legislation is that of deterring men from crime. Now it is apparent that if it were declared to be the law that a killing in self-defense is murder such a rule could not operate in a deterrent manner. A man whose life is threatened will repel his aggressor, whatever the law may say. Looking therefore to the broad purposes of criminal legislation, we may safely declare that this statute was not intended to apply to cases of self-defense [see question 3 below].

When the rationale of the excuse of self-defense is thus explained, it becomes apparent that precisely the same reasoning is applicable to the case at bar. If in the future any group of men ever find themselves in the tragic predicament of these defendants, we may be sure that their decision whether to live or die will not be controlled by the contents of our criminal code. Accordingly, if we read this statute intelligently it is apparent that it does not apply to this case. . . .

The line of reasoning I have applied above raises no question of fidelity to enacted law, though it may possibly raise a question of the distinction between intelligent and unintelligent fidelity. No superior wants a servant who lacks the capacity to read between the lines. The stupidest housemaid knows that when she is told "to peel the soup and skim the potatoes" her mistress does not mean what she says. She also knows that when her master tells her to "drop everything and come running" he has overlooked the possibility that she is at the moment in the act of rescuing the baby from the rain barrel. Surely we have a right to expect the same modicum of intelligence from the judiciary. The correction of obvious legislative errors or oversights is not to supplant the legislative will, but to make that will effective.

I therefore conclude that on any aspect under which this case may be viewed these defendants are innocent of the crime of murdering Roger Whetmore, and that the conviction should be set aside. . . .

KEEN, J.: I should like to begin by setting to one side two questions which are not before this court.

The first of these is whether executive clemency is affirmed. Under our system of government that is a question for the Chief Executive, not for us. I therefore disapprove of that passage in the opinion of the Chief Justice in which he in effect gives instructions to the Chief Executive as to what he should do in this case and suggests that some impropriety will attach if these instructions are not heeded. This is a confusion of governmental functions of which the judiciary should be the last to be guilty. I wish to state that if I were the Chief Executive I would go farther in the direction of clemency than the pleas addressed to him propose. I would pardon these men altogether, since I believe that they have already suffered enough to pay for any offense they may have committed. I want it to be understood that this remark is made in my capacity as a private citizen who by the accident of his office happens to have acquired an intimate acquaintance with the facts of this case. In the discharge of my duties as judge, it is neither my function to address directions to the Chief Executive, nor to take into account what he may or may not do in reaching my own decision, which must be controlled entirely by the law of this Commonwealth.

The second question that I wish to put to one side is that of deciding whether what these men did was "right" or "wrong," "wicked" or "good." That is also a question that is irrelevant to the discharge of my office as a judge sworn to apply, not my conceptions of morality, but the law of the land. In putting this question to one side I think I can also safely dismiss without comment the first and more poetic portion of my brother Foster's opinion....

The sole question before us for decision is whether these defendants did, within the meaning of N.C.S.A. (n.s.) § 12–A, wilfully take the life of Roger Whetmore. The exact language of the statute is as follows: "Whoever shall wilfully take the life of another shall be punished by death." Now I should suppose that any candid observer, content to extract from these words their natural meaning, would concede at once that these defendants wilfully took the life of Roger Whetmore.

Whence arise all the difficulties of the case, then, and the necessity for so many pages of discussion about what ought to be so obvious? The difficulties, in whatever tortured form they may present themselves, all trace back to a single source, and that is a failure to distinguish the legal and moral aspects of this case. To put it bluntly, my brothers do not like the fact that the written law requires the conviction of these defendants. Neither do I, but unlike my brothers I respect the obligations of an office that requires me to put my personal predilections out of my mind when I come to interpret and apply the law of this Commonwealth.

Now, of course, my brother Foster does not admit that he is actuated by a personal dislike of the written law. Instead he develops a familiar line of argument according to which the court may disregard the express language of a statute when something not contained in the statute itself, called its "purpose," can be employed to justify the result the court considers proper....

We are all familiar with the process by which the judicial reform of disfavored legislative enactments is accomplished. Anyone who has followed the written opinions of Mr. Justice Foster will have had an opportunity to see it at work in every branch of the law. I am personally so familiar with it that in the event of my brother's incapacity I am sure I could write a satisfactory opinion for him without any prompting whatever, beyond being informed whether he liked the effect of the terms of the statute as applied to the case before him.

The process of judicial reform requires three steps. The first of these is to divine some single "purpose" which the statute serves. This is done although not one statute in a hundred has any such single purpose, and although the objectives of nearly every statute are differently interpreted by the different classes of its sponsors. The second step is to discover that a mythical being called "the legislator" in the pursuit of this imagined "purpose" overlooked something or left some gap or imperfection in his work. Then comes the final and most refreshing part of the task, which is, of course, to fill in the blank thus created.

My brother Foster's penchant for finding holes in statutes reminds one of the story told by an ancient author about a man who ate a pair of shoes. Asked how he liked them, he replied that the part he liked best was the holes. That is the way my brother feels about statutes; the more holes they have in them the better he likes them. In short, he doesn't like statutes.

One could not wish for a better case to illustrate the specious nature of this gap-filling process than the one before us. My brother thinks he knows exactly what was sought when men made murder a crime and that was something he calls "deterrence." My brother Tatting has already shown how much is passed over in that interpretation. But I think the trouble goes deeper. I doubt very much whether our statute making murder a crime really has a "purpose" in any ordinary sense of the term. Primarily such a statute reflects a deeply-felt human conviction that murder is wrong and that something should be done to the man who commits it. If we were forced to be more articulate about the matter, we would probably take refuge in the more sophisticated theories of the criminologists, which, of course, were certainly not in the minds of those who drafted our statute. We might also observe that men will do their own work more effectively and live happier lives if they are protected against the threat of violent assault. Bearing in mind that the victims of murders are often unpleasant people, we might add some suggestion that the matter of disposing of undesirables is not a function suited to private enterprise, but should be a state monopoly. All of which reminds me of the attorney who once argued before us that a statute licensing physicians was a good thing because it would lead to lower life insurance rates by lifting the level of general health. There is such a thing as over-explaining the obvious.

If we do not know the purpose of § 12–A, how can we possibly say there is a "gap" in it? How can we know what its draftsmen thought about the question of killing men in order to eat them? My brother Tatting has revealed an understandable, though perhaps slightly exaggerated revulsion to cannibalism. How do we know that his remote ancestors did not feel the same revulsion to an even higher degree? . . . All of this is conjecture, of course, but it remains abundantly clear that neither I nor my brother Foster knows what the "purpose" of § 12–A is.

Considerations similar to those I have just outlined are also applicable to the exception in favor of self-defense, which plays so large a role in the reasoning of my brother Foster. . . . As in dealing with the statute, so in dealing with the exception, the question is not the conjectural *purpose* of the rule, but its *scope*. Now the scope of the exception in favor of self-defense as it has been applied by this court is plain: it applies to cases of resisting an aggressive threat to the party's own life. It is therefore too clear for argument that this case does not fall within the scope of the exception, since it is plain that Whetmore made no threat against the lives of these defendants. . . .

Now I know that the line of reasoning I have developed in this opinion will not be acceptable with those who look only to the immediate effects of a decision and ignore the long-run implications of an assumption of a power of dispensation by the judiciary. A hard decision is never a popular decision. Judges have been celebrated in literature for their sly prowess in devising some quibble by which a litigant could be deprived of his rights where the public thought it was wrong for him to assert those rights. But I believe that judicial dispensation does more harm in the long run than hard decisions. Hard cases may even have a certain moral value by bringing home to the people their own responsibilities toward the law that is ultimately their creation, and by reminding them that there is no principle of personal grace that can relieve the mistakes of their representatives.

Indeed I will go farther and say that the principles I have been expounding are not only those which are soundest for our present conditions, but that we would have inherited a better legal system from our forefathers if those principles had been observed from the beginning. For example, with respect to the excuse of self-defense, if our courts had stood steadfast on the language of the statute the result would undoubtedly have been a legislative revision of it. Such a revision would have drawn on the assistance of natural philosophers and psychologists and the resulting regulation of the matter would have had an understandable and rational basis, instead of the hodge-podge of verbalisms and metaphysical distinctions that have emerged from the judicial and professorial treatment of it.

These concluding remarks are, of course, beyond any duties that I have to discharge with relation to this case, but I include them here because I feel deeply that my colleagues are insufficiently aware of the dangers implicit in the conceptions of the judicial office advocated by my brother Foster. I conclude that the conviction should be affirmed.

HANDY, J.: I have listened with amazement to the tortured ratiocinations to which this simple case has given rise. I never cease to wonder at my colleagues' ability to throw about every issue presented to them for decision an obscuring curtain of legalisms. We have heard this afternoon learned disquisitions on the distinction between positive law and the law of nature, the language of the statute and the purpose of the statute, judicial functions and executive functions, judicial legislation and legislative legislation. My only disappointment was that someone did not raise the question of the legal nature of the bargain struck in the cave,—whether it was unilateral or bilateral, and whether Whetmore could not be considered as having revoked an offer prior to action taken thereunder.

What have all these things to do with the case? The problem before us is what we, as officers of the government, ought to do with these defendants. That is a question of practical wisdom, to be exercised in a context, not of abstract theory, but of human realities. When the case is approached in this light, it becomes, I think, one of the easiest to decide that has ever been argued before this court....

I have never been able to make my brothers see that government is a human affair, and that men are ruled, not by words on paper or by abstract theories, but by other men. They are ruled well when their rulers understand the feelings and conceptions of the masses subject to their government. They are ruled badly when the understanding is lacking.

Of all branches of the government, the judiciary is the most likely to lose its contact with the common man. The reasons for this are, of course, fairly obvious. Where the masses react to a situation in terms of a few salient features, we pick into little pieces every situation presented to us. Lawyers are hired by one another to see who can discover the greatest number of difficulties and distinctions in a single set of facts. Each side tries to find cases, real or imagined, that will embarrass the demonstrations of the other side. To escape this embarrassment, still further distinctions are invented and imported into the situation. When a set of facts has been subjected to this kind of treatment for a sufficient time, all the life and juice have gone out of it and we have left a handful of dust.... Once drive a sufficient wedge between the mass of people and those who direct their legal, political and economic life, and our society is ruined. Then neither Foster's law of nature nor Keen's fidelity to written law will avail us anything.

Now when these conceptions are applied to the case before us, its decision becomes, as I have said, perfectly easy. In order to demonstrate this I shall have to introduce certain realities that my brothers in their coy decorum have seen fit to pass over in silence, although they are just as acutely aware of them as I am.

The first of these is that this case has aroused an enormous public interest, both here and abroad. Almost every newspaper and magazine has carried articles about it; columnists have shared with their readers confidential information as to the next governmental move; hundreds of letters-to-the-editor have been printed. One of the great newspaper chains made a poll of public opinion on the question: "What do you think the Supreme Court should do with the Speluncean explorers?" About ninety percent expressed a belief that the defendants should be pardoned or let off with a kind of token punishment. It is perfectly clear, then, how the public feels about the case. We could have known this without the poll, of course, on the basis of common sense, or even by observing that on this court there are apparently four and a half men, or ninety percent, who share the common opinion.

This makes it obvious not only what we should do, but what we must do if we are to preserve between ourselves and public opinion a reasonable and decent accord. Declaring these men innocent need not involve us in any undignified quibble or trick. No principle of statutory construction is required that is not consistent with the past practices of this court. Certainly no layman would think that in letting these men off we had stretched the statute any more than our ancestors did when they created the excuse of self-defense. If a more detailed demonstration of the method of reconciling our decision with the statute is required, I should be content to rest on the arguments developed in the second and less visionary part of my brother Foster's opinion.

Now I know that my brothers will be horrified by my suggestion that this court should take account of public opinion. They will tell you that public opinion is emotional and capricious, that it is based on half-truths and listens to witnesses who are not subject to cross-examination. They will tell you that the law surrounds the trial of a case like this with elaborate safeguards, designed to insure that the truth will be known and that every rational consideration bearing on the issues of the case has been taken into account. They will warn you that all of these safeguards go for naught if a mass opinion formed outside this framework is allowed to have any influence on our decision.

But let us look candidly at some of the realities of the administration of our criminal law. When a man is accused of crime, there are, speaking generally, four ways in which he may escape punishment. One of these is a determination by a judge that under the applicable law he has committed no crime. That is, of course, a determination that takes place in a rather formal and abstract atmosphere. But look at the other three ways in which he may escape punishment. These are: (1) a decision by the Prosecutor not to ask for an indictment; (2) an acquittal by the jury; (3) a pardon or commutation of sentence by the executive. Can anyone pretend that these decisions are held within a rigid and formal framework of rules that prevents factual error, excludes emotional personal factors, and guarantees that all the forms of the law will be observed?

In the case of the jury we do, to be sure, attempt to cabin their deliberations within the area of the legally relevant, but there is no need to deceive ourselves into believing that this attempt is really successful. In the normal course of events the case now before us would have gone on all of its issues directly to the jury. Had this occurred we can be confident that there would have been an acquittal....

I come now to the most crucial fact in this case, a fact known to all of us on this court, though one that my brothers have seen fit to keep under the cover of their judicial robes. This is the frightening likelihood that if the issue is left to him, the Chief Executive will refuse to pardon these men or commute their sentence. As we all know, our Chief Executive is a man now well advanced in years, of very stiff notions. Public clamor usually operates on him with the reverse of the effect intended. As I have told my brothers, it happens that my wife's niece is an intimate friend of his secretary. I have learned in this indirect, but, I think, wholly reliable way, that he is firmly determined not to commute the sentence if these men are found to have violated the law.

No one regrets more than I the necessity for relying in so important a matter on information that could be characterized as gossip. If I had my way this would not happen, for I would adopt the sensible course of sitting down with the Executive, going over the case with him, finding out what his views are, and perhaps working out with him a common program for handling the situation. But of course my brothers would never hear of such a thing [they are less concerned with the facts of the legal process than with the explicit rules (Keen) or the underlying principles (Foster)].

Their scruple about acquiring accurate information directly does not prevent them from being very perturbed about what they have learned indirectly. Their acquaintance with the facts I have just related explains why the Chief Justice, ordinarily a model of decorum, saw fit in his opinion to flap his judicial robes in the face of the Executive and threaten him with excommunication if he failed to commute the sentence. It explains, I suspect, my brother Foster's feat of levitation by which a whole library of law books was lifted from the shoulders of the defendants. It explains also why even my legalistic brother Keen emulated Pooh-Bah in the ancient comedy by stepping to the other side of the stage to address a few remarks to the Executive "in my capacity as a private citizen." (I may remark, incidentally, that the advice of Private Citizen Keen will appear in the reports of this court printed at taxpayers' expense.)

I must confess that as I grow older I become more and more perplexed at men's refusal to apply their common sense to problems of law and government.... I conclude that the defendants are innocent of the crime charged, and that the conviction and sentence should be set aside.

[Since Tatting reiterated his withdrawal, the court was left with a split vote. This cannot reverse the judgment of a lower court. So a date was set for the execution of the explorers, and Fuller tells us no more.]

FURTHER READING

The cases of *U.S. v. Holmes* and of *Queen v. Dudley* are printed in a number of anthologies (e.g.: Ford, Stephen D. *The American Legal System*. St. Paul: West, 1974, 45–63).

Another interesting, but shorter, legal parable from Lon Fuller is "The Problem of the Grudge Informer." See his book, *The Morality of Law* (New Haven: Yale Univ. Press, 1969), 245–53, and many anthologies. Those who wish to follow the squabbles of the Newgarth judges in "The Case of the Interrupted Whambler," or in their conflict over the pickled squids, can consult Fuller's *The Problems of Jurisprudence* (Brooklyn, N.Y.: Foundation Press, temporary edition, 1949).

For a sequel to the case we examined, see "Son of the Speluncean Explorer," by Burton F. Brody, *Iowa Law Review* 55 (1969): 1,233–47.

QUESTIONS FOR DISCUSSION

1. Professor Fuller himself has little sympathy for the expedients of Truepenny and of Keen: to declare the rigor of the law as a judge and then to hope for extralegal remedies (Truepenny) or for a later change in legislation that will little help those caught in the present (Keen). What would you think if you were one of the explorers? Suppose the chief executive did commute your sentence. You would be delighted, but would you be intellectually satisfied? Or would you think that what all took to be the right result had come about in a slipshod fashion, unworthy of a legal system?

2. Foster asks the law to solve its own problems. We should look beyond the words of any statute to find what the law really is. This depends, in his first argument, on the purpose of law as such. If the purpose of games is harmless enjoyment, then rules that encourage serious injury would fail to be rules. How does this argument apply to the explorers facing death by starvation? Would you agree that continuing coexistence in society is the ultimate purpose of all law? Is this the same as individual self-preservation? Suppose that one of the explorers had simply taken it upon himself to kill Whetmore? Would Justice Foster have applied an argument similar to that in the *Holmes* case (remember that Holmes's attorney also appealed to a "state of nature")?

3. Foster's second argument looks, not to "law as such," but to some specific law. What this really is depends, he claims, on the purpose of that particular law. Thus, if the purpose of the law against murder is the deterrence of murder, then this law does not prohibit killing in self-defense. For if I allow myself to be killed by an aggressor, the purpose of deterring me vanishes and so does this law in regard to me. If, however, the law is understood as allowing me to defend my own life, then the purpose of deterrence still applies, raising important questions about whether I may shoot my assailant in the heart rather than in the hand. Do you agree with Foster that "precisely the same reasoning is applicable to the case at bar"? Even if you agree that *one* of the purposes of criminal legislation is deterrence, is this the *only* purpose?

4. Parallels to Judge Earl (in *Riggs v. Palmer*) are evident, though not complete. Earl also argues from the purpose of laws. Those regulating wills are "for the orderly, peaceable, and just devolution of property." And Earl's appeal to unwritten principles of all law seems to suggest some general purpose, though he does not define it. Judge Gray's rejection of such talk, in *Riggs*, is now reinforced by Keen's sarcastic assault on Foster's claim to identify purposes and on his penchant for thus filling the gaps in legislation. What is your attitude toward this controversy? Does a knife have one purpose given by its manufacturer, or do purchasers assign a variety of purposes? Is Keen denying that laws have any purpose, or is he saying there is no privileged purpose? Suppose all textbooks are banned from exam rooms because of the growth of cheating in the college. Would this law apply to a student who brings an accounting textbook into a philosophy exam? Or is Keen's objection based solely on the practical difficulty of *discovering* the purpose of most laws? How can he tell us the scope of a law if he has no idea of its purpose?

5. Keen's position as a *legal positivist* (a term to be explained in chapter 3) is clearly stated at the beginning of his opinion, when he criticizes Foster's "failure to distinguish the legal and moral aspects of this case." Keen makes clear his moral sentiments by suggesting he would, if he were chief executive, pardon the explorers altogether. Yet he is a judge, sworn to apply the law that is. And this he finds to be certain, from the natural meaning of the words in the statute. Indeed he argues, at the end of his opinion, that the sort of "judicial dispensation" that Foster proposes is counterproductive; if judges make hard decisions, in fidelity to the plain meaning of the law though at variance with moral feelings, this will lead eventually to a clear-cut legislative revision of statutes. Such a procedure, Keen holds, is more rational than the "hodge-podge of verbalisms and metaphysical distinctions" that come from Foster's injection of tender-minded moralism into the professional practice of law. What are your comments, on either side of this basic question? Legislators cannot foresee all the cases that will arise. Why should not judges define and adapt the law through the concrete cases that they decide? If this is allowable, what is to guide them in their making of law? Are they submissive to some higher rules or principles? Legal? Moral? Religious? Is morality personal, in the sense of personal predilections, what I do or do not *like*?

6. Handy is a congenial figure, and his name is suggestive. He is a pragmatist who draws upon the sympathies of all who find theory oppressive and want to clear a way for the practical solution; Fuller offers Handy as a perhaps extreme instance of legal realism, which will be discussed in section 20. In regard to this case, 90 percent of the public call for pardon or token punishment. Ironically, four of the justices (plus half of Tatting!) agree on the humane outcome. Why, then, the fuss? All that stands in the way is the dread formality of the law. In another of Fuller's parables, a proposal is made to have Handy impeached; and we may indeed find something unworthy in his appeal to public-opinion polls and his reliance on gossip from his wife's niece. But when you go to a lawyer and ask what is the law, do you want more than his prediction of how the courts would decide in your case? Is such a prediction to be based only on dusty books of law? Surely the decisions of courts do take into account solid movements of public opinion (judges read newspapers also).

7. Handy can be seen merely as an anti-theorist who tries to demythologize the law. Or he can be seen as defending the theory that the law *is* in general, and *ought to be* in particular, an expression of the basic convictions (or mores) of a society. He would thus oppose Keen's rigid distinction of *is* and *ought* in law. Notice, however, the even greater temperamental difference between Handy and Foster. They stand alone, among these justices, in claiming that the spelunceans did not break the law. But Foster, in the spirit of Plato, argues from the rational principles of all law or of life in society, whereas Handy (no less an opponent of metaphysics than Keen) takes the facts as they come. Suppose, for example, that the public-opinion polls had shown 90 percent in favor of execution? What would Foster say? What would Handy? What would you?

6. THINKING LIKE A LAWYER

A hundred and fifty years ago, Alexis de Tocqueville toured this country to learn how the young democracy worked, without the structures of authority to which he had been accustomed in Europe. His comments on the part played by the legal profession are perceptive.[20]

> Men who have made a special study of the laws derive from this occupation certain habits of order, a taste for formalities, and a kind of instinctive regard for the regular connection of ideas, which naturally render them very hostile to the revolutionary spirit and the unreflecting passions of the multitude.... They naturally constitute *a body*; not by any previous understanding, or by an agreement that directs them to a common end; but the analogy of their studies and the uniformity of their methods connect their minds as a common interest might unite their endeavors.... [p. 273]
>
> Lawyers are attached to the public order beyond every other consideration, and the best security of public order is authority. It must not be forgotten, also, that if they prize freedom much, they generally value legality still more: they are less afraid of tyranny than of arbitrary power.... [p. 275]
>
> This aristocratic character, which I hold to be common to the legal profession, is much more distinctly marked in the United States and in England than in any other country. This proceeds not only from the legal studies of the English and American lawyers, but from the nature of the law and the position which these interpreters of it occupy in the two countries. The English and the Americans have retained the law of precedents; that is, they continue to found their legal opinions and the decisions of their courts upon the opinions and decisions of their predecessors. In the mind of an English or American lawyer a taste and a reverence for what is old is almost always united with a love of regular and lawful proceedings.... A French observer is surprised to hear how often an English or an American lawyer quotes the opinions of others and how little he alludes to his own, while the reverse occurs in France....
>
> The French codes are often difficult to comprehend, but they can be read by everyone; nothing, on the other hand, can be more obscure and strange to the uninitiated than a legislation founded upon precedents. The absolute need of legal aid that is felt in England and the United States, and the high opinion that is entertained of the ability of the legal profession, tend to separate it more and more from the people and to erect it into a distinct class. The French lawyer is simply a man extensively acquainted with the statutes of his country; but the English or American lawyer resembles the hierophants of Egypt, for like them he is the sole interpreter of an occult science. [pp. 276–77]

---

20. *Democracy in America*, from the revision by Francis Bowen of the Henry Reeve translation, edited by Phillips Bradley. Copyright © 1945 by Alfred A. Knopf. Printed with permission.

De Tocqueville assigns to the legal profession a vital part in maintaining the stability of a democracy against the "passions of the multitude." He sees a parallel between lawyers and the aristocracies that he knew in Europe. However, the cohesion of an aristocracy comes from its inherited privileges and interests. Lawyers form a body, and play their part, through the peculiar stamp of their training and their method. The lawyer is separated from others by his mind and his language.

Little comment is needed on the claim that lawyers speak a mysterious language, and that their "occult science" is rendered even less accessible to the layperson by the precedent system of the common law countries. The uninitiated runs a risk by walking into a law library to look up the law on any but a very simple matter. Nevertheless, every profession develops its technical language to secure precision and historical continuity. Apparently, an effort was made in the early years of the Communist regime in Poland to express the law in terms open to the worker and peasant, but this resulted in uncertain and capricious court decisions; the law was less knowable than before. There is, however, a movement at present in this country to require legal documents to be expressed in plain English, and so far the flood of litigation, predicted by some opponents within the profession, has not been realized.

It is more interesting to explore the quality of legal language than to protest at its mystery. Creation myths attribute the formation of worlds to the uttering of words. When Adam named the animals, he was not compiling a dictionary but deciding how to see things. So it is that each occupation develops its own perception, its precise but limited way of talking about people. Banks speak to their customers in a special manner, corporations to their stockholders, advertisers to buyers. The restricted view, with the distance involved, is expected; if a salesman addresses me by my first name he has lost a sale.

Legal language works with its own professional abstraction. But there are problems here that we face with few other institutions. The lawyer holds a person's life in his or her hand. If I am summoned to court, my future welfare and my self-respect depend on how my advocate puts me into words. This can be no less true when the courtroom remains a distant possibility and the words are on paper. Language is incidental to the surgeon but it is the whole life of the lawyer. Words that capture only a superficial view of complex human situations are like a knife that will not cut.

Here it is easy to exaggerate. The wording of a contract may rightly be as impersonal as the trade it enables. A will should ensure the desired devolution of property but need not capture the testator's feelings in the face of death (though there is no reason why the style of the document could not also convey something of the awe that this theme inspires). However, anyone considering a career in law might be advised to examine a fair sample of what lawyers and judges write. That is their literary world, and hence their professional world. What sort of people do they present in this world? Do you find real persons or caricatures, abstractions fit only to carry legal labels?

Doing Things with Words

Personal questions are involved, and the best that can be done here is to offer a few introductory illustrations. Some guidelines may be taken from de Tocqueville's account of the legal mind. What is the "legality" that is prized even more than freedom and that protects us from the threat of arbitrary power? How are lawyers distinguished by their "habits of order," their "taste for formalities," their "regard for the regular connection of ideas"?

We may start with an example of an oversimple approach to the problems of legal language. The case of Temple v. City of Petersburg reached the Supreme Court of Appeals of Virginia in 1944 (182 Va. 418, 29 S.E.2d 357). In order to enlarge a cemetery, the city had acquired an acre of land adjacent to it; this would allow for the reinterment of bodies that would be exhumed when a road was widened along the other side of the cemetery. Those who lived nearby protested on the basis of section 56 of the Virginia Code:

> No cemetery shall be hereafter established within the corporate limits of any city or town; nor shall any cemetery be established within 250 yards of any residence without the consent of the owner.

The residents lost their case and then appealed. But the appeals court also ruled in favor of the city's proposed extension. The judge defended his decision in this rather delicate matter as follows:

> The word "established" is defined in Webster's New International Dictionary, second edition, 1936, thus: "To originate and secure the permanent existence of; to found; to institute; to create...." Just why the legislature, in its wisdom, saw fit to prohibit the establishment of cemeteries in cities and towns, and did not see fit to prohibit enlargements or additions, is no concern of ours. Certain it is that language could not be plainer than that employed to express the legislative will.

The interpretation of statutes is a complex matter, to be discussed in section 33. An inquiry into the intention of a legislature is often made by a court, and the statement above, that this "is no concern of ours," is untypical. Nevertheless, the layperson may be forgiven for suspecting some difference between the approach of a lawyer and of (say) a sociologist to a dispute of this kind. The latter would focus on such topics as the changing attitudes toward death and their effect on land values around cemeteries; how exactly is it relevant that the area in question was a peaceful burial ground rather than a noisy athletic field? Yet the judge in *Temple* appears intent to see complex human relationships as determined by the rules he finds in a book.

The notion of legalism, of drawing decisions from published rules rather than from a weighing of social interests, will be examined in the following section, where an attack on the legal mind by a political scientist is answered by a lawyer. For the present, we may look simply at the theory of language that seems to underlie the *Temple* decision. The judgment in favor of the city rests largely on questions about the meaning of a word, *establish*, and the solution is found by recourse to a dictionary as the repository of meanings.[21]

Such a search for meaning may be adequate when we are learning a foreign language. Encountering the word *Tisch* in a German text, I turn to my dictionary and discover the word means *table*. The thing, I happily suppose, first exists and then English-speakers and German-speakers apply words to it as labels. However, would more of a problem be involved if the word in question were *Geist*? Or suppose a foreign-language dictionary allows one word to be translated as *house, home, dwelling*, and *residence*. In translating, am I simply shuffling labels, or might I be advised to ask how speakers in different languages make themselves at home?

Meaning may not be so much *what words have* as *how we do things with words*. The dictionary reports on the most common ways we use words, but it is purely descriptive. The object before me is an ashtray because most people would use it in the context of smoking. Yet so long as my resolutions stand, I use it as a paperweight, and hence it is one. Though the example is trite, it may suggest the inadequacy of a dictionary as a source for solving *Temple*. To find the meaning of "establishing a cemetery," we must inquire into what people (legislators? city officials? residents?) are doing and wanting and feeling.

The proposal that we should look beyond the definition of words to their use in various human projects has been formulated notably in the work of a recent philosopher, Ludwig Wittgenstein. He emphasized that language is an activity, that words are what we do in giving expression to a variety of intentions. He spoke of the multiplicity of "language-games" that we play:

> How many kinds of sentence are there? Say assertion, question, and command?—There are *countless* kinds: countless different kinds of use of what we call "symbols," "words," "sentences." And this multiplicity is not something fixed, given once for all; but new types of language, new language-games, as we may say, come into existence, and others become obsolete and get forgotten.... The term "language-*game*" is meant to bring into prominence the fact that the *speaking* of language is part of an activity, or of a form of life.
>
> Review the multiplicity of language-games in the following examples, and in others: giving orders, and obeying them—describing the appearance

---

21. Much contemporary philosophy, in England and America, shows a praiseworthy concern to tie words down to ordinary usage, for which the dictionary is the arbiter. It may not follow, however, that those who compile dictionaries are thereby solving philosophical questions. One writer on law has expressed the following hesitation: "The meaning of 'justice,' linguistic philosophers would insist, is to be found in ordinary usage, and ordinary usage is to be found in the *Oxford English Dictionary*. The O.E.D., it seems, is the *Q.E.D.* I have some misgivings about the uses and usages of dictionaries ever since an illustrious professor of English, taxed with violating a dictionary pronunciation, replied serenely: That's wrong—I must change it in the next edition" (Paul A. Freund, *On Law and Justice*, [Cambridge: Harvard Univ. Press, 1968], 82).

of an object, or giving its measurements—constructing an object from a description (a drawing)—reporting an event—speculating about an event—forming and testing a hypothesis—presenting the results of an experiment in tables and diagrams—making up a story—... asking, thanking, cursing, greeting, praying. (*Philosophical Investigations*, 3d ed., New York: Macmillan, 1968, section 23)

The reader can extend the list and test some examples. Suppose a person enters the room and says "Peace." If I say "The policemen signaled me to proceed," am I reporting or speculating? What about the very word *meaning*?

Perhaps it is a too general question to ask whether legal talk represents one language-game among the many we play. But some suggestions may be permitted. Any law student will tell you of his painful initiation to the requirements of speaking like a lawyer. A word such as *malice* must be stripped of its rich layers of common meaning and assigned the precision it is accorded in a court of law.[22] Here the lawyer is following the path of any other professional, such as a scientist. Terms like *force* and *energy*, or the cardinal numbers themselves, have a wide variety of uses in primitive languages and in the talk of a young child. The scientist restricts this abundance to one precise employment on which all can agree. *Two* applies in the same way to people and coconuts and ideas (though notice some differences!). The lawyer likewise defines a univocal (one meaning for each word) language in his search for order and regularity.

However, there is a counter-direction that language has followed. The model of the technical dictionary is not the only one. Words show also a tendency to break out of their precise, constant meanings and reveal the broader possibilities of the user. More is intended in the context of any act of speaking than the words themselves can make explicit. The word for the potter's activity became the word for turning and shaping, then for imitating and creating, and for purely intellectual forming. A study of the history of the word *form* could supply an interesting introduction to the history of philosophy.

Few legal cases have so caught popular feeling as that of Karen Ann Quinlan.[23] At the age of twenty-two, Karen became unconscious and was kept alive on a respirator. Doctors gave no hope of recovery and allowed for an indefinite continuation in a comatose state. Her parents, deeply religious people, went through agonies of decision and eventually asked that the respirator be removed. The doctor responsible for her at first agreed but then told the Quinlans that legal advice had been taken: the painful request must be refused because the parents no longer had the rights of a legal guardian. In the television dramatization (NBC, Sept. 26, 1977), Mrs. Quinlan asks who could

22. For example: "The mental state constituting malice aforethought does not presuppose or require any ill will or hatred of the particular victim.... An intentional act that is highly dangerous to human life, done in disregard of the actor's awareness that society requires him to conform his conduct to the law, is done with malice regardless of the fact that the actor acts without ill will toward his victim or believes that his conduct is justified." (People v. Conley, 1966, 64 Cal.2d 310, 411 P.2d 911)

23. In the Matter of Karen Quinlan, Supreme Court of New Jersey (1976), 70 N.J. 10, 355 A.2d 647.

possibly be more of a guardian than those who had watched over Karen with ceaseless concern since babyhood, had nursed her through her illnesses, had rejoiced with her in her triumphs, had shown the unhesitating love that only a parent can have. The reply of the hospital lawyer: "I'm afraid our problem has to do with law and not with love." To which Mrs. Quinlan answers: "Then I want no part of such law."

To the credit of the New Jersey Supreme Court, great sensitivity is revealed in a lengthy opinion. But our question stands. Does the very precision of legal language militate against what laypeople (perhaps naively) regard as real?

Formalism and Compassion

A more pointed attack upon lawyers, dating back to Plato, is that they degrade language to the status of an instrument. It is the end result that counts. If your words secure the desired result from the court, they were well chosen. The lawyer is at the service of his client, but the weapons of a primitive society are replaced by language in an advanced one. This charge may seem crude, yet it is reinforced by the way law is so often seen as a tool of social control or as a means for social engineering. Anyone who is on the mailing list for legal publishers can attest to the amount of material for sale that teaches the techniques of pleading effectively for greater damages or lower responsibility.

In regarding language as a way of doing things with words, we should certainly not gloss over its function as a means toward desired ends (its effective or performative purpose). However, we may be reluctant to view this as the sole end of talking. The youthful Descartes expressed his disillusionment with philosophy as a way of "speaking plausibly on all subjects and winning admiration," even though he knew little at first hand of what was involved. Later writers have admitted that philosophical or legal argumentation became for them a purely intellectual exercise, a verbal punning, a type of mental gymnastics in which know-how took the place of the passion for truth. After reading many judicial opinions, one may well ask whether the learned judge is led to his conclusion by his legal training or whether he falls back on unsophisticated convictions he has held since youth and then uses his legal technique to give these professional respectability.[24]

If de Tocqueville's account of the legal mind is to be assessed, various terms become problematic. We must ask what is meant by *legality*, by *order*, by *regularity* (and hence by *rules*). One of the most elusive terms is *formalism*. Interestingly, *form* was the word taken above as an example of the way in which terms expand their meaning. There is nothing superficial about forming clay or associations or hypotheses. If we face a final judgment, it is about how we have formed or formulated our life. Yet formalism often suggests some remove from

---

24. The charge will be examined in section 28, that judges first come to their decision in an intuitive way and then proceed to support this extralegal decision by putting it in the form of a legal argument.

reality, and this is a common complaint against the legal mind; as the real person goes through the legal process, he becomes increasingly shadowy, until he appears in the decision of an appeals court as a caricature of a caricature.

The very ambiguity of the term *form* suggests the dilemma of a student confronting the possibility of a legal career. The danger is evident: to view life from the distance of the law library and to use words as weapons. Yet the challenge is no less clear. Dentists and industrialists, even politicians, are expected to see life from a narrow perspective. But not lawyers. They are among the few surviving generalists in a specialized world. The client who approaches a lawyer has more at stake than health or financial gain; words must be precise and effective but also adequate to the respect we owe a person.

Consider the advocate who has half an hour for his say in court. What choices shall he make? What arguments shall he produce? How can he cover so much in so little time? How can he do justice to the fellow being he is appointed to represent? Think of the demands in a simple case of personal injury. How can he compass, in his writing and pleading, the sudden terror, the physical pain, the tedium of hospital, the worries about money, the anxieties of going to law, the emotions of asserting a claim? Think of the many viewpoints (and languages) the lawyer must adopt with compassion if he is even to understand what is involved. He must be one person with his client in the hospital, another with the opposing lawyer in his office, another in addressing the judge before the trial, or in the courtroom, another person with each witness. I exaggerate, perhaps, but this comes from regard for the ideal.

Though law may be described as a science, its practice is certainly an art. As a conclusion to this section, extracts from two cases are offered by way of illustration. The first suggests formalism in its bad sense; the second gives an example of legal talk that reveals sympathy for a personal situation. But read with caution. Could the former judge be both legally and morally correct? Could the latter judge be indulging in a sentimentality that detracts from the law and confuses the question?

The first case touches upon the serious question of "informed consent" to medical treatment. Should I be allowed to offer my consent before doctors go to work on me? The general reply of the law is yes. Notice, however, two important qualifications here. First, there is the involvement of an infant, who would be left without a mother if her say were simply accepted. And second, the judicial opinion that is quoted abstracts altogether from these substantive questions; the argument is based exclusively on the procedures or formalities of law.

On September 17, 1963, the mother of a seven-month-old child was brought to the Georgetown University Hospital for emergency treatment. She had lost two-thirds of her body's blood supply from a ruptured ulcer. An immediate blood transfusion was required to save her life. Yet the woman and her husband were Jehovah's Witnesses, and the husband refused to allow the transfusion as against their religious beliefs.

Hospital authorities sent their lawyers at once to the District Court of the District of Columbia, asking the judge to sign a hastily prepared approval for a transfusion. The judge, Edward Tamm, refused to sign the order. Instead, he wrote the word *denied* on the paper. In his view, no formal written application had been filed.

At 4:00 P.M. the hospital lawyers located one of the judges of the circuit court, the appeals court that has power to overrule the district court. No further document was produced, and there was no time for the full circuit court to discuss the case in the normal way, but an immediate reversal of the lower court's decision was requested. Judge Wright acted quickly. He telephoned the responsible physician, Dr. Westura, and then the husband, Mr. Jessie Jones, who repeated his refusal. The judge went to the hospital and saw Mrs. Jones; her only audible statement was "against my will." At 5:20 P.M. Judge Wright signed the order that Judge Tamm had refused to approve. The transfusion was given immediately and the patient lived.

On October 14, 1963, Mr. Jones, having presumably obtained the services of a lawyer, filed a petition with the circuit court for an order to review the events of September 17 and declare the order of that date to be a *nullity* (having no legal effect). The outsider, while fully respecting the sincerity of the religious convictions involved, may be excused for wondering at the legal mentality that now appears. The wife was alive. The infant child still had a mother. And most would think that a sufficient defense had already been made of religious beliefs.

Our question, however, is what the legal professionals should do. Irregularities had taken place, in the name of life. Should the matter be laid to rest? Or would this admit an unwelcome precedent in the law? Here are some extracts from the written opinion of one of the colleagues of Judge Wright on the circuit court, dissenting to the court's decision that Mr. Jones's petition of October 14 be denied.

APPLICATION OF THE PRESIDENT AND DIRECTORS OF GEORGETOWN COLLEGE, INC.

United States Court of Appeals, District of Columbia Circuit, 1964

331 Federal Reporter, 2d Series, 1010.

MILLER, J. (dissenting) ... Although the proposed order was styled "Application of the President and Directors of Georgetown College, Inc., a Body Corporate," there was no such proceeding pending in the District Court; there had been no complaint, petition or formal written application filed. The only "application" was the oral request of the attorneys that the tendered order be signed and entered.... It is plain, I think, that at the very least Judge Tamm's denial was based on the fact that there was nothing before him upon which he could act, that the jurisdiction of the District Court had not been properly invoked, and that there was no pending controversy....

I am not now concerned with the substantive questions presented by the petition for rehearing; I am disturbed by the procedural aspects of the situation.... It seems clear to me that the matter did not properly come before this court and that, had it been duly presented on appeal, one judge of this court was not authorized to make a summary disposition of the matter on the merits. These procedural defects are, therefore, fatal to the validity of the purported orders entered September 17 by a single judge when no appeal had actually been filed. Argument that a court is justified, in physical circumstances such as were present here, in ordering blood transfusions against the will of an adult patient necessarily presupposes a properly constituted court and an action actually filed and pending before it. Such an argument, no matter how extensive and persuasive, cannot validate the action which was taken here because it cannot destroy the basic facts which make the purported orders mere nullities: that no action was filed in the District Court and that no appeal was filed in this court; and that, had there been an actual appeal, a single appellate judge was not authorized to act....

I think that, instead of merely denying the petition for rehearing, we should dismiss it on the ground that there was no case or controversy presented or determined and that consequently there is nothing to rehear. But, whether the petition for rehearing be denied or dismissed, the purported orders of September 17 should be expunged so there would be nothing in our records which could be cited as a precedent for future similar action by a single appellate judge. We have inherent power to take that action sua sponte [on our decision].

I do not mean to impugn the motives of our colleague who signed these orders. He was impelled, I am sure, by humanitarian impulses and doubtless was himself under considerable strain because of the critical situation in which he had become involved. In the interval of about an hour and twenty minutes between the appearance of the attorneys at his chambers and the signing of the order at the hospital, the judge had no opportunity for research as to the substantive legal problems and procedural questions involved. He should not have been asked to act in these circumstances.

For the second case we have the majority opinion of an appeals court, ordering a retrial in a murder case. The layperson may approve of this decision, but it is worth mentioning that two of the judges dissented.

To understand the case, we need to know that New York Penal Law 1120 excused from criminal liability anyone who, at the time he acted, satisfied *either* of two conditions:

1. He did not know the nature and quality of his act (he simply did not realize what he was doing), or

2. He did not know the act was wrong (he knew what he was doing but sincerely thought it right).

The defendant, Mrs. Sherwood, drowned her two-year-old son and was found guilty of murder in the first degree. An appeal was sent to the New York Court of Appeals on the ground that the trial court judge had not adequately informed the jury that either of the above two conditions could relieve Mrs. Sherwood of the charge. In justifying the call for a retrial, it might have been enough to dwell upon the formal distinction between *either/or* and *both/and* and show from the record that this distinction had not been clearly put to the jurors. But the judge who wrote the majority opinion saw fit to explain himself at length. The following extract may relate to a discussion of what the legal mind should include and exclude as relevant.

PEOPLE v. SHERWOOD
Court of Appeals of New York, 1936

271 N.Y. 427, 3 N.E.2d 581.

CROUCH, J. . . . The claim of the defense was that the mother killed the child because she had become obsessed with a delusion that in death alone could there be safety and freedom from pain, suffering and misery for her son. The time has gone by when such a claim could seem fantastic, either to judge or juror. While we still—and rightly—accept the validity of such claims with the utmost caution, we nevertheless know now that they may be valid. The claim here rests upon evidence which, on the one hand, neither discloses nor even suggests any rational motive for the tragic act; and, on the other hand, does build up a personality which might well crack and crumble under the hard blows which fate, within a brief period, dealt it. Born of indifferent stock in a small western town, the defendant at nine years of age had lost her mother. For a time she was in an orphanage, and then for a period served her itinerant father and his successive wives as a household drudge. There followed a period of a few years when she lived at various places in the middle west with a succession of Salvation Army families, doing household and other work, and getting some scattered and interrupted schooling. Following that insecure and sorry young girlhood, she commenced when about sixteen years old to earn her own independent way. Shortly she went on the stage as a chorus girl with traveling companies. When she was nineteen years old she met and married her husband, a stage electrician, whose job, like her own, kept him moving from place to place. Within a year a baby girl was born. The couple finally came to rest in Newburgh on the Hudson, where the man secured a job with a moving picture house. After a period of comparative peace and security, what small prosperity had come to them was ended by the illness of the husband. Early in 1933 the boy baby was born. The evidence of the doctor who attended the defendant and of the nurse at a prenatal clinic, shows clearly that the child was not an unwanted one. On the contrary it was desired, welcomed, and after birth was lovingly and carefully attended to and looked after. The husband's illness developed into tuberculosis. The home, the only one the defendant had ever known, was broken up. He went to a sanitarium, the little daughter was taken by the mother-in-law, and the defendant with the infant son went to a lodging house, the landlady of which looked after the child while the defendant, as her sole means of support, worked as a waitress in a restaurant. In April, 1935, her husband died. Several months later the defendant met a man who, after a time, offered to provide a home for her and her son, to marry her and to educate the boy. On a day fixed they were to leave Newburgh for a new home in the west. She gave up her job. She made ready to go. The day came but not the man. She waited until she realized she had been deceived. She tried to get work and failed. Without a job, without means, she and her little son were evicted by the landlady—though the latter denied that—and thereupon was committed the act for which her life is forfeit. A laconic statement made to the police the same day tells the story: "My husband, Fred Sherwood, died about four months ago, and since that time I have found it very difficult to make a living for myself and my two children, Dorothy, aged seven, and James, aged two. This afternoon, August 20th, 1935, shortly before twelve o'clock noon I took my younger child, James Sherwood, in a stroller down to Caesar's Lane at New Windsor, New York. There is a very shallow brook there and I let him wade in the brook until he seemed to get tired of it, and then I picked him up in my arms and held him under water for about half an hour. During this period of time his head was completely covered with water. I picked him up then, put a clean suit on him and held him in my arms for some time. . . . Later I walked up to the state road and was given a ride to the City of Newburgh. After I got into the City I walked into Police headquarters and told the lieutenant at the desk what I had done." . . .

In the main charge it was not made clear that a defect of reason which inhibited a knowledge *either* of the nature and quality of the act *or* that the act was wrong, excused a person from criminal liability. At various points the two matters were referred to in the conjunctive, with the word "and" instead of the word "or." The error was called to the attention of the court at the close of the main charge, and the court said merely: "If I made that error, I so charge." Left in that way, the distinction might doubtfully be considered as having been made clear. But thereafter—and it was the court's last word before the jury retired—the court upon request charged that a mere false belief would not be sufficient to excuse her, "unless it was the result of some mental *disease* which prevented her from knowing the nature and quality of the act *and* that it was wrongful." Here was a repetition of the same error, complicated with a reference to "some mental disease," i.e., some pathological condition, instead of a "defect of reason," as the statute reads. No disease, no pathological condition, existed or was claimed to exist. It may be doubted whether the jury had a clear conception of when a person is or is not criminally liable under section 1120....

The judgment of conviction should be reversed and a new trial ordered.

FURTHER READING

Those interested in a thorough and creative textbook of legal writing can be referred to James B. White, *The Legal Imagination* (Boston: Little, Brown & Co., 1973; abridged edition, Univ. of Chicago Press, 1985). A few other books:

Austin, J. L. *How to Do Things with Words.* 2d ed. Cambridge: Harvard Univ. Press, 1975.

Brand, Norman, and John O. White. *Legal Writing: The Strategy of Persuasion.* New York: St. Martin's Press, 1976.

Cardozo, Benjamin. *Law and Literature.* 1931. Reprint. Littleton, Colo.: F.B. Rothman & Co., 1986.

Cooper, Frank E. *Writing in Law Practice.* Indianapolis: Bobbs-Merrill, 1963.

Gopen, George D. *Writing from a Legal Perspective.* St. Paul: West, 1981.

London, Ephraim (ed.). *The Law as Literature.* New York: Simon & Schuster, 1960.

Mellinkoff, David. *The Language of the Law.* Boston: Little, Brown & Co., 1963.

———. *Legal Writing: Sense and Nonsense.* New York: Scribner's, 1982.

Probert, Walter. *Law, Language and Communication.* Springfield, Ill.: C. C. Thomas, 1972.

Rossman, George. *Advocacy and the King's English.* Indianapolis: Bobbs-Merrill, 1960.

Stryker, Lloyd P. *The Art of Advocacy.* 1954. Reprint. Washington, D.C.: Zenger Publ. Co., 1979.

QUESTIONS FOR DISCUSSION

1. De Tocqueville's conclusions about the political dependence of this country on the legal profession are well supported today by the fact that more than half the members of Congress are lawyers, as have been a majority of the presidents. But the conclusions are not dependent on finding lawyers in high places. We boast that our government is "one of laws and not of men." May we not all value legality more than freedom? How is power transferred after an election? Where does authority finally lie?

2. It is through your own experience of writing that you become most aware of the limitations and merits in the writing of others. Find a legal document that covers a somewhat personal situation and try to put it into more fitting language. Or write a will, in the customary legal style, for an imaginary testator; then compose a letter in which he/she explains to one of the beneficiaries the provisions you have made.

3. Do you think that the language of section 56 of the Virginia Code clearly expresses the legislative will? What more would you need to know if you are to discover the mind of the lawmakers? Lon Fuller offers an interesting example (*Harvard Law Review* 71 [1958]: 664). A city ordinance reads: "It shall be a misdemeanor, punishable by a fine of five dollars, to sleep in any railway station." A passenger for a delayed train is found sitting upright but plainly asleep. A tramp has brought a blanket and is discovered sprawled on a bench but not yet asleep. Which of the two would you fine under this ordinance?

4. (a) What language-games might Wittgenstein find in the following: "There are seven dilapidated houses on that side of the street, and it was the one in the middle that burned. Faulty wiring was the cause. The owner had too little insurance." (b) Classify the act of yelling "fire!" in two ways. (c) What is the difference between giving an order and stating a rule? (d) If there are many oceans, are there also many skies? (e) How many chairs are there in this room? (f) How does acquiring a second language differ from learning your mother tongue?

5. How do you distinguish between the "literal" and the "metaphorical" meaning of a word? Consider, for example, the phrase "the winter of our discontent." Is *winter* defined literally by the astronomer and then extended metaphorically by the poet, or does the latter perhaps come closer to our initial or original experience here? Did you observe strong forces in nature before you experienced strong feelings (or uttered strong words)? Do negative particles attract positive particles? Should a lawyer, though conforming to the legal dictionary, be sensitive to the origin and development of words outside the law?

6. How would you, as a lawyer, plead damages for the parents of a young child killed by a negligent driver? If the only question is about money, remember that it can cost over a hundred thousand dollars for a parent to bring up a child.

7. A lawyer may well regard his courtroom appearance as an act put on to secure the results desired by his client. He speaks other languages in other settings. Do you think it pertinent to ask in which language he thinks to himself? Could there eventually be a danger of merely talking for effect and never truly "saying" anything?

8. Does the Georgetown Hospital case show a choice between legality and humanity? Or a choice between different interpretations of legality? Did Miller and Tamm speak as judges rather than as men, and did Wright act as a man but not as a judge? Or do Miller and Wright represent different philosophies of law?

9. Comment on Miller's claim that "there was nothing before Tamm on which he could act." Notice the words *properly* and *duly*. Why was Miller so concerned that the order of September 17 should be removed from the court records? Notice his final paragraph; when he says that Wright "should not have been asked to act in these circumstances," what sort of obligation is meant here?

10. If you were Judge Wright, and acted as he did, how would you defend yourself in a written opinion? Include a reply to the following objection. A judge has no legal power as an individual; he cannot order a fight to stop in the saloon he attends when off duty. His sole authority comes from his place on the bench, as defined by the formalities of the law. Since Wright was clearly violating these formalities, he was—for all his noble sentiments—pretending to be a judge when not a judge.

11. The two paragraphs printed from Judge Crouch's opinion in *Sherwood* speak two languages (we might even say, those of Wright and of Miller). Would not the shorter paragraph have sufficed? Perhaps the basic question for any lawyer is What is *legally relevant*? And this depends on the prior question, What is *law*? Was Crouch indulging in sentimentality and usurping the function of a defense attorney? Or does the point of the second paragraph depend upon the biographical details and sympathetic presentation that transform Mrs. Sherwood from the defendant to a plausible person?

7. WHAT IS LEGALISM?

There is ambivalence in the attitude of many people toward the law. They recognize the law as life-sustaining, as a condition for holding a job, making a marriage, planning for retirement; they commend legality and take it as their guide. Nevertheless, the respect of even worthy citizens for the law is often challenged. It seems not merely to fall short of ideals but often to oppose them by blocking the path that is humane and compassionate; the courts, we are sometimes told, exist to apply the law and not to work out the intricate ways of justice.

Many ambiguities lurk in the notions of both law and justice, and hence in any claim that identifies or opposes them. The question whether legal rules and decisions depend on moral principles takes us to the heart of disputes about the nature of law and hence to the topics of chapter 3. The final two sections of this introductory chapter will look for examples of how we use some key terms in such discussions. Section 8 will see how an ancient and a contemporary author talk of *justice*. The present section examines opposing views on the merit of formulating our questions in terms of *law*.

Our language may be suggestive. I am happy to be told that I acted *lawfully* or *legally*. But I am offended to be accused of *legalism*. This word seems to indicate the dark side of law or to imply that a legal mentality distorts rather than discloses the true situation.

What exactly is meant by legalism, and how far does it extend? Are all people who view an issue in terms of laws thereby legalistic? Or is there both a good and a bad way of abiding by the laws? Is rule-following a matter of degree, where legality is good in moderation but bad in excess, becoming legalism?

The first reading comes from a book that bears the title *Legalism*. The author, who approaches law from outside the profession, identifies legalism as the attitude of seeing human relationships primarily in the form of rules. This attitude, she holds, shows a narrow viewpoint that culminates in the legal systems of the West. She sustains a lengthy attack on legalism, so understood, and argues for approaches that lessen our dependence on rules. Think, for example, of the way a psychiatrist understands clients and of the problems that he and a lawyer have in communicating when brought together in a case.

The second reading is a reply from a professor of law. He would not himself have given so broad a scope to the term legalism. But he argues that if the word be allowed to cover all thinking governed by rules, then we should be prepared to distinguish many forms. The legal mind can be faulted in particular ways, yet such a general condemnation of rule-following is unhelpful and is lacking in perception for the merits of law.

The Primacy of Rules

Dr. Judith Shklar is a professor of government at Harvard. Her purpose and position are made clear in the preface:

> This is a book about legal theory by someone who is not a lawyer.... Many historians and political scientists, who have a real interest in law, in the legal profession, and in legal theory, find the lawyer's approach to these subjects irrelevant to and remote from their concerns. This book tries to show why one historian of ideas has come to share this view.

You will have no difficulty in following her attack on the dominance of attitudes that are clearly congenial to lawyers and judges. But it may help to bear two questions in mind as you read:

1. What precisely are these attitudes? Shklar traces them to the way we structure our experience and see people in terms of established rules that yield claims and counterclaims. If this suggestive proposal is to be understood, it needs considerable illustration from the reader's own experience. Do you see people this way?

2. A just appreciation of her attack on legalism demands some survey of the alternatives. Notice what she lists and commends as opposing positions. Do these survive without rules?

LEGALISM
by Judith N. Shklar

Cambridge, Mass.: Harvard University Press.
Copyright © 1964 by the President and Fellows of Harvard College.
Excerpted by permission of the publishers.

> What is legalism? It is the ethical attitude that holds moral conduct to be a matter of rule following, and moral relationships to consist of duties and rights determined by rules. Like all moral attitudes that are both strongly felt and widely shared it expresses itself not only in personal behavior but also in philosophical thought, in political ideologies, and in social institutions.... Legalism, so understood, is often an inarticulate, but nonetheless consistently followed, individual code of conduct. It is also a very common social ethos, though by no means the only one, in Western countries. To a great extent it has provided the standards of organization and the operative ideals for a vast number of social groups, from governmental institutions to private clubs. Its most nearly complete expression is in the great legal systems of the European world. Lastly, it has also served as the political ideology of those who cherish these systems of law and, above all, those who are directly involved in their maintenance—the legal profession, both bench and bar. The court of law and the trial according to law are the social paradigms, the perfection, the very epitome, of legalistic morality....
>
> Even though it is no sign of disaffection for legalism to treat it as but one morality among others, such a view has not been congenial to any of the traditional theories of law. These have been devised almost exclusively by lawyers and philosophers who agree in nothing

but in taking the prevalence of legalism and of law for granted, as something to be simply defined and analyzed.... The habits of mind appropriate, within narrow limits, to the procedures of law courts in the most stable legal systems have been expanded to provide legal theory and ideology with an entire system of thought and values. This procedure has served its own ends very well: it aims at preserving law from irrelevant considerations, but it has ended by fencing legal thinking off from all contact with the rest of historical thought and experience.... [pp. 1–3]

As one English lawyer [J. A. G. Griffith] has put it, "A lawyer is *bound* by certain habits of belief ... by which lawyers, however dissimilar otherwise, are more closely linked than they are separated ... A man who has had legal training is never quite the same again ... is never able to look at institutions or administrative practices or even social or political policies, free from his legal habits or beliefs. It is not easy for a lawyer to become a political scientist. It is very difficult for him to become a sociologist or a historian... He is interested in relationships, in rights in something and against somebody, in relation to others... This is what is meant by the legalistic approach... [A lawyer] will fight to the death to defend legal rights against persuasive arguments based on expediency or the public interest or the social good... He distrusts them ... He believes, as part of his mental habits, that they are dangerous and too easily used as cloaks for arbitrary action."

... The dislike of vague generalities, the preference for case-by-case treatment of all social issues, the structuring of all possible human relations into the form of claims and counterclaims under established rules, and the belief that the rules are "there"—these combine to make up legalism as a social outlook.... As law serves ideally to promote the security of established expectations, so legalism with its concentration on specific cases and rules is, essentially, conservative. It is not, however, a matter of "masking" a specific class and economic interest. Not only do lawyerly interests often differ from those of other conservative social groups, businessmen's, for example, but legalism is no mask for anything. It is an openly, intrinsically, and quite specifically conservative view, because law is itself a conservatizing ideal and institution. In its epitome, the judicial ethos, it becomes clear that this is the conservatism of consensus. It relies on what appears already to have been established and accepted. When constitutional and social changes have become inevitable and settled, the judiciary adapts itself to the new order. The "switch in time" from 1937 onward, after all, involved the whole federal bench eventually, not just one Supreme Court justice....

The ease with which the English judiciary not only accommodated itself to socialist legislation, but even bent backward to facilitate its enforcement, shows how the belief in statute law as "there" can help an immensely conservative set of lawyers to adapt itself to political *force majeur*. Yet in 1911 Winston Churchill had said in Parliament that it was impossible for trade unionists to expect fairness or understanding of the nature of social conflicts from the judiciary. Even before turning to Marxism, Harold Laski assumed that no amount of personal impartiality could save the English judiciary from its upper-class outlook. That English barristers have not as a group been drawn to the cause of socialism remains true. It is not likely that the judiciary is now composed of ardent Labour sympathizers. Far from it. However, men live up to the expectations that their own ideology imposes upon them and to the demands of public office. Faced with the consensus that supported the reforming legislation of the first years after the war, the judiciary demonstrated its neutrality by adapting to the new order as it had supported the old.... To seek rules, or at least a public consensus that can serve in place of a rule, must be the judge's constant preoccupation, and it affects his choices in ways that are unknown to less constrained political agents. To avoid the appearance of arbitrariness is a deep inner necessity for him.... [pp. 9–12]

The antiquity of legalism as an ideology is, in fact, one of the wonders of history. It is itself the expression of the continuity of the legal profession and its basic tasks. Whereas science has rendered the practice of modern medicine quite unlike the pre-nineteenth-century profession of the same name, the heirs of Coke resemble him closely in vocabulary, outlook, and concerns. De Tocqueville's description of the legalistic ethos is as accurate today as it was when it was written. Order and formality being the marks of the legal mind, he wrote, it is natural for lawyers to support the established social order.... "They are less afraid of tyranny than of arbitrary power." One might add that, if they fear tyranny, it is because it tends to be arbitrary, not because it is repressive....

Almost a hundred years after de Tocqueville wrote, Max Weber could still present a picture of the ideology of the legal profession that was virtually unaltered. Lawyers remained as wedded to formal justice as ever and so to all the interests that relied on permanence and predictability in social procedures.... What he and de Tocqueville saw was that a legal caste, once it had established the "rule of law" securely against threats from absolutist arbitrariness, was bound to prefer order to liberty. What de Tocqueville called aristocratic habits of thought, Weber believed (rightly) to be more a matter of "internal professional ideology." The importance of the inner dynamic of legal reasoning and the professional preferences of lawyers tend to separate them from other social groups. Capitalist entrepreneurs have their own interest in stability and calculability, but the excessive formalities of lawyers' law are uncongenial to them. The conflict between jurists and psychiatrists is another example of tension engendered by incompatible professional views.... [pp. 14–16]

Adolf Hitler's pretensions to legitimacy, the support they gave Nazism until its radical anti-legalistic tendencies revealed themselves (and even after), more than justify de Tocqueville's and Weber's suspicions. It cannot be repeated often enough that procedurally "correct" repression is perfectly compatible with legalism.... What Hans Frank, the governor general of Poland, objected to was not Nazi policy, of which he fully approved, but its being carried out in a formally nonlegal manner. He wanted rules for extermination, stable procedures for condemning.... [pp. 17, 208]

The differences in the respective attitudes of American lawyers, psychiatrists, and businessmen are still much as [Weber] described them.... The resort to arbitration under chamber of commerce auspices, from which lawyers were at first explicitly excluded, represented a significant preference for direct negotiations over formalism and, worse, litigation. On another level, businessmen do not want regulatory governmental agencies to become too courtlike, but prefer to maintain direct access to them in order to bargain with officials. The official program of the A.B.A., on the other hand, calls for judicialization. In this the lawyers, true to their ideology and habits, express their traditional distaste for the politics of negotiation, expediency, and arbitrariness. It is the popular acceptance of this legalism in America that surely contributes its share to the general cynicism toward politics as inevitably "dirty." The belief that negotiations aiming at peaceful settlements represent defeats for justice, for the politics of legalism, has led the official American bar to take at least one stand that separates it noticeably from most other conservative groups. From the first it has lent its support to international law, and especially to the International Court of Justice, on the ground that adjudication alone can prevent war and establish the reign of justice. Here, as in domestic politics, disputes between states are treated in isolation, apart from world politics in general.... [pp. 17–18]

The conspicuous concentration on "*the* West" today is clearly a response to the Cold War and to the political organization of ex-colonial societies which now challenge the European world. These events have made us all culturally self-conscious. The result is a search for an identity, for a positive and uniquely Western tradition.... The most elaborate, erudite, and influential of modern efforts to expose the contrast between "the Occident" and the rest of the world has been that of Max Weber.... To him it seemed that it was a matter of "rationality," by which he meant exactly what has here been called legalism. The predisposition to discover, construct, and follow rules was, in his view, the distinguishing mark of European culture. This alone accounted for those phenomena which appear "only in the Occident": Roman law, the legal profession, judicial institutions, capitalist economics, rational social ethics, and Puritanism in religion. In glaring contrast to these stand the patrimonial and kadi justice of China and Islam and the inner-worldly ethic of the Orient. [pp. 20–21]

The Legal Iceberg

The following reply originally formed part of a panel discussion of Shklar's book. The tone is light but the questions are serious. Professor Coons would not himself have applied the word legalism to all rule-governed action (he prefers the term *conceptualism*). His contention, however, is that so broad a meaning for the word does not then leave Shklar free to present legalism as but one possibility open to us among many. He claims that rule-following is, for better or worse, our fate. The question of options is transferred to the way we live with rules. We have no one big problem (law or not?) but many specific problems (Is this particular rule or procedure the best? Is our solution too conceptual or not sufficiently?).

It is for the reader not merely to side with one author or the other, but to say how vital is the disagreement. On many points, both Shklar and Coons would settle for the same "bottom line." Coons goes out of his way to introduce criticisms of current legal procedure that Shklar neglected. The reader may have other accusations. Should these be addressed to law from outside law? Or should they be seen as rule-criticisms made from within the inescapable project of living according to rules and principles? Coons's image of a "legal iceberg" is suggestive. Perhaps, as with an iceberg, the visible part of law is supported by vast regions of legality that escape our notice? There may be some analogy in the position of those legal philosophers who hold that the explicit rules of law are dependent for their interpretation on unwritten principles below the surface.

"LEGALISM"
by John E. Coons (professor of law, Univ. of California, Berkeley)

Paper presented at the 1965 meeting of the Association of American Law Schools.
Printed with permission of the author.

Our subject—despite its name—is not simply a book on legalism.... The book she has so beautifully written is a comment, rather, on the general problem of conceptualism in ethics, even though her examples have been largely limited to public law. She has adopted a meaning for legalism so broad that it could include questions ranging all the way from the destructibility of contingent remainders to the problem of the appropriate number of cocktails at the publishers' party. "What is legalism?" she asks. "It is the ethical attitude that holds moral conduct to be a matter of rule-following." This, then, is a book about an ethical attitude—an attitude holding that only specific verbal propositions have functional significance in moral and legal discourse; about an attitude that it can be a meaningful and sometimes necessary thing to construct and promulgate such formulas as "all dogs must be leashed" or "six martinis is too much." Dr. Shklar is a student of that insidious habit of human intelligence—generalization. Though her book is aimed at lawyers and speaks mostly of law, it is less a critique of lawyers and law than of all philosophies that strive to organize reality into verbal categories—in short, of practically all philosophies. Perhaps the book is not an outright rejection of conceptualism in ethics, but its author rather clearly wishes that it could be. She may suffer rules gladly for society's sake, but she does suffer. For her the center of ethical experience is not to be found in the hoary dicta of judges and moralists. It lies rather in a hope for something she describes as:

> ... social diversity, inspired by that barebones liberalism which, having abandoned the theory of progress and every specific scheme of economics, is committed only to the belief that tolerance is a primary virtue and that a diversity of opinions and habits is not only to be endured but to be cherished and encouraged.

This—to me—sentimental attachment to diversity for its own sake informs the entire work. It may help to explain Dr. Shklar's ambivalent attitude of hostility coupled with occasional grudging admiration for what she supposes to be the mind of the American lawyer—he of the constipated psyche, hugging his comfort blanket of true rules, suspicious of diversity, yet oddly fastidious in supplying procedural equality for dissenters. So, at least, she seems to view him. This is not merely a book about an attitude. It is an attitude about an attitude.

Few of us would deny that conceptualism can be harmful in law as elsewhere. There is nothing like an overdose of hair splitting to render a legal or ethical system dysfunctional.... We can agree that the compartitioned mind is badly equipped for Law and Politics without concluding much at all about the bulk of the legal iceberg below the water line chosen by Dr. Shklar. I'd like to know what's going on in the murkier depths below the level of high policy....

To suppose that lawyers think of rules in ontological terms as "there" is to mistake the shorthand of professional discourse for the deposit of truth. We do not believe in the contingent remainder because it is there. It is there because we believe in it; or, perhaps more accurately, it works, therefore it is.

I believe the lawyer's attitude to be as skeptical as Dr. Shklar could possibly wish. We swim in a sea of indeterminacy, and, if we don't love it, we at least are aware of it. Our problem is not that of being fooled by concepts but of dominating them with practical reason. Where simplistic absurdities exist—and they do—we must slay them, and we do so with regularity. Yesterday we killed the fellow servant doctrine; today we have mortally wounded *Shelley's* case.... In race relations, anti-trust policy, civil liberties, and criminal law, the courts have been anything but conceptualistic....

All I have said amounts to this: there is no general problem of legalism but only problems of legalism. There are merely solutions that are dysfunctional, some because they are too conceptual, others because they are not sufficiently conceptual. It is our business and Dr. Shklar's to expose and correct them. She has ably identified several problems of excessive conceptualism at high levels. I would suggest another example that has previously occupied me—indeed, a pet of mine—one of a humbler character than war crimes but nonetheless important and pervasive. For lack of a better description, I would call it the cult of winner-take-all. It is imbedded in the unspoken premise that for any given dispute submitted to adjudication, only two solutions exist: for plaintiff or for defendant; it makes litigation what the game theorists describe as a zero sum game. A judge may strive for compromise in pre-trial, but his own decision from the bench must be polarized, however neatly the issues of fact and law may be balanced....

Are rules of conduct inevitably prisons? Dr. Shklar is properly schizophrenic on this issue, but there is little doubt that rule-oriented systems cause her a good deal of uneasiness. I may be merely proving Dr. Shklar's fundamental point about lawyer's attitudes in what I'm about to say, but it is hard for me to think of rules as the enemy of freedom and diversity. It may be true, as Dr. Shklar suggests, that mystical moralists like Nietzsche and Sartre think of rules as confining and cold—as confining and cold as the asylum that was eventually reserved for the original superman. Freedom is not the absence of form. Indeed, the history of human liberty is in large measure the history of form manifested in the organization and complication of matter and psyche. In the human species the development of structure is the beginning of choice; and the essence of structure is the development of rules....

But I would go even further in praise of rules: they are not merely a precondition of freedom. They are the guardians of the enthusiastic society, for they provide the limiting conditions under which romance is possible. Romance is not the offspring of formlessness; rather, it is the child of order. It depends in a fundamental way upon letting man know the risks he runs and then leaving him free to run them.... What was it about Beauty and the Beast, or even Cinderella, that made our childish hearts leap? Precisely this: we had confidence that the plan would be observed, the promise kept, the rule enforced. We were excited by the knowledge that what the girl did or failed to do really mattered. It was of no great importance that the rule itself be sensible but only that it be enforcible....

The application of this same line of thought to the institution of marriage is obvious.... The romance of marriage is in the commitment, in a man's willingness to cast his lot for life on a judgment that is both difficult and dangerous. Like accepting the challenge to a duel, it may be unwise, it may be regretted, it may be a disaster. But all this is simply to say that there is risk, and without risk there is no romance.

This line of thought can be carried too far, as perhaps I have unwittingly demonstrated. The content of the rules does make a difference. And, as Dr. Shklar demonstrates, a limited tyranny is conceivable, even under the rule of law. But at least insofar as legalism, like Mother Goose, preserves fidelity to human principle and institutions, it protects the essence of a zestful life. In preserving the rule of the game, the law keeps the game worth playing....

FURTHER READING

For some of Shklar's references to Max Weber, see M. Rheinstein (ed.): *Max Weber on Law and Economy in Society* (Cambridge: Harvard Univ. Press, 1954), 301–21.

A celebrated brief attack on the mentality of finding and following rules comes in Sartre's essay, "Existentialism and Humanism." What he calls "essentialism" is parallel to Shklar's "legalism" and Coons's "conceptualism."

The Rule of Law, edited by Robert P. Wolff (New York: Simon and Schuster, 1971), contains an interesting collection of partisan attacks on legal institutions and of investigations into contemporary hesitations about law.

For an example of how a judge may view his task in political rather than legalistic terms, see Walter F. Murphy: *Elements of Judicial Strategy* (Chicago: Univ. of Chicago Press, 1964).

QUESTIONS FOR DISCUSSION

1.   Suppose a student is dissatisfied with the score he or she got on a test and hopes to have the grade changed to a higher one. Suggest how the student can proceed in the manner of (a) a lawyer, (b) a political scientist, (c) a businessman.

2.   Shklar refers to legalism as an ethical attitude, a habit of mind, a social outlook, an ideology. It is found in individuals, in professions, and even as the basic predisposition of European culture. It is opposed to the attitudes of a historian, a sociologist, a political scientist, a

psychiatrist, and a businessman. Many distinguishing marks are listed, but the fundamental one seems to be that the legalist interprets any human situation in terms of rules that specify the rights of one person against another. The alternative attitudes are concerned with the facts of expediency or with whatever currently appears to be the public good. Suggest how the legalistic outlook may differ from the others in such examples as these: (a) a business dispute, (b) an international conflict, (c) the desegregation of schools, (d) assessment of "mental disease or defect."

3. Max Weber lists "Puritanism in religion" as a typically Western example of legalism. Explain what you understand by the term. Comment again on the Gospels as a protest against legalism (see section 1). From what you know of moral philosophy, would you regard Aristotle or Kant as more legalistic? Which of the justices on Lon Fuller's supreme court of Newgarth (section 5) offers the strongest criticism of legalism?

4. The meaning of "kadi justice" will be explained in section 11. The image is of an Oriental ruler deciding on the pleas of his subjects, with no rules or precedents to guide him but with an intuitive sense of what is best. That is, the forms of law are lacking but the individual situation is respected. Think of the very different approach offered by Judge Miller in the Georgetown Hospital case (section 6); did he defend "formal justice" at the expense of the "substance"? Might he stand, in Shklar's view, as the epitome of legalism? Why does bargaining (perhaps the symbol of Oriental business) strike many of us as unworthy? Do you think politics is dirty? That plea bargaining is wrong?

5. Judge Gray (in *Riggs v. Palmer*, section 4) argues from the need for certainty and predictability in the law. Shklar says much on the conservatism of the legal mind, the desire to avoid arbitrariness and "promote the security of established expectations." How do you reconcile this with the interesting illustrations of how the judiciary changed rules (after 1937 in the U.S. and after 1945 in Britain)? The example of the legal profession under Hitler is more dramatic. What has this to do with the mentality of viewing rules as simply "there"? Could German judges have opposed the rules they received from Hitler by appealing to rules that go beyond the immediate legislator?

6. Coons argues that Shklar's definition of legalism is so broad that it fails to exclude what she offers as alternatives. Can you escape from all rules? What about the liberalism and pluralism that Shklar advocates? Does not the tolerance essential to support these require rule-guidance?

7. Though the businessman prefers arbitration and bargaining to adjudication in the courts, has he thereby escaped from rules or merely changed their form? Political science, sociology, and psychiatry are products of the Western mind and are dedicated to viewing human behavior in terms of descriptive laws; are such sciences not themselves the result of rules for a "right" way of seeing and reporting?

8. Do you agree with Coons that rules are the structure for freedom rather than its enemy? Shklar protests against the formalism of law, but Coons claims that "freedom is not the absence of form." Does freedom grow in proportion to the number of choices you have, or could you possibly become more free as the range is limited to that which is evidently right for you? Who is more free, the student with little idea of what to do on graduation or the one who knowingly channels his efforts toward one appropriate career?

9. Coons suggests that, rather than vainly trying to drop rules, we cultivate a sensitivity to their wide variety and an appreciation of the flexibility that the legal profession shows in their regard. Consider the examples he gives of notable adaptations that the law has made. Did the initiative come from within the judiciary? Even if not, did the judges simply submit to extralegal influences (as perhaps under Hitler)? Or did they find grounds within the law for a change in rules? It is here that Coons's image of the iceberg may be helpful. Above the waterline is the law as "seen" (the rules that we find by inspecting written statutes and judicial opinions). But Coons expresses interest in the "murkier depths below." What may lie there, assuming it is also part of the law? More rules? Or could we speak of principles of law, unwritten perhaps, but both limiting and enabling changes in the rules above?

8. THE AMBIGUITY OF JUSTICE

What is justice? In some sense, we all know. One of the first phrases we learned in childhood was That's no fair! Of all the virtues, it may be justice that most appeals to the child's sense of a world untroubled by "interiority." He is twice as naughty if he breaks two cups accidentally as if he breaks one cup intentionally.[25] For us, justice is "the precise virtue." If I borrow $10 and return $9, I have failed in justice. If I return $10 without a word of thanks and later refuse a small loan to you, then I have satisfied justice though I may have failed in other virtues.

Perhaps our difficulties in understanding, and even appreciating, justice come from its competitive status. Politeness and kindness do not involve violation of other virtues; if a polite person is lazy, this is not because he is polite. But justice seems often to be at the expense of other virtues. Portia, in *The Merchant of Venice*, protests against the enforcement of justice unless mercy is introduced to season it (that is, to diminish it as justice, to lessen its precision).

Hence our problem. Justice is the specifically legal virtue. It is to the courts of justice that we go for whatever the law supplies. Yet we may leave them with the paradoxical complaint that we failed to get justice because the unsympathetic judge did not sit lightly to the harsh demands of justice!

Terminology evidently needs some attention. Two approaches will be considered in this section. The first is from a recent judge, the second from Aristotle.

Why the Blindfold?

Jerome Frank gave up his ambitions for a career as a novelist and entered the law. The sacrifice was not total. He wrote on the law and, after becoming a federal judge at the appeals court level, brought to his opinions the style and sensitivity he would have applied to his novels. He maintained a firm grasp of the concrete situation and repeatedly criticized his colleagues for their insufficient awareness of the difficulty of finding the facts; he proposed that law students study less law and more sociology, and that their encounter with law should be in trial courts as well as through upper court writings.

In the extract below, he asks us to consider the traditional figure of justice that adorns our courthouses. We remember the scales and the sword. But it is to other features that Judge Frank draws attention. The figure is of a woman (the Greek divinities who represent justice are goddesses). And her eyes are covered. He is strongly in favor of the symbol of femininity: even the precise virtue should reveal a heart and show flexibility. He is opposed to the image of a blindfold: rules should be adapted in full view of the many subtle facts that alter cases.

---

25. Piaget discusses the development of the child's sense of justice in *The Moral Judgment of the Child* (1932; reprint, New York: Free Press, 1965), 197–325.

THE UNBLINDFOLDING OF JUSTICE
by Jerome Frank

From Courts on Trial: Myth and Reality in American Justice.
Copyright 1949 by Jerome Frank; © renewed 1976 by Princeton Univ. Press.
Excerpts (pp. 378–80, 383–89, 391) reprinted with permission of Princeton Univ. Press.

In the Athens of Aristotle's day, most non-criminal suits began as arbitrations, and became contentious litigation only if the parties refused to accept the decisions of the arbitrators. In the light of this practice, Aristotle significantly discusses the differences between "legal" and "equitable" justice. (1) "Legal justice," he said, rests on "arithmetical" equality. According to such justice, "it makes no difference whether it is a good or bad man" who has violated a legal rule; "the law looks only to the distinctive character of the injury, and treats the parties as equal...." (2) But the "equitable," although also justice, is a "correction of legal justice," a "better" kind. "The equitable man ... is no stickler for his rights in a strict sense, but takes less than his share though he has the law on his side.... Equity bids us to be merciful to the weakness of human nature ...; not to consider this or that detail so much as the whole story. It bids us to settle by negotiation and not by force; to prefer arbitration to litigation—for an arbitrator goes by the equity of a case, a judge by the strict law, and arbitration was invented with the express purpose of securing full power for equity." Here was a defense not only of negotiation and arbitration but of individualization of cases, of a relaxation of legal rules to meet the unique circumstances of each particular case.

In actual practice in ancient Athens, even if arbitration failed, and a case went (as most cases, if litigated, finally did) to a "popular" court consisting of a large multitude of judges (whom moderns sometimes call "jurors"), nevertheless "equity" played a large role. For the Greeks openly recognized (as Aristotle's writings show) that these judges had no obligation strictly to apply the legal rules, that they could and frequently did use the rules only as general guides, with full allowance for the unique facts. "In the Greek administration of law," wrote Wigmore, "the emphasis was less on the strict law than on the general justice of the case."

No doubt this system had some of the disadvantages of our own jury system, since the Greek judges in the popular courts returned something like our general verdicts. However, most Greek "jurors," unlike ours, were constantly in court and were fairly well acquainted with the legal rules. The indications are that their avowed method of individualizing cases, and the absence of any rigid doctrine of following the precedents, produced excellent results.

Many modern students, however, have denigrated the Greek legal system, comparing it unfavorably with that of Rome which they picture as having desirably evolved an elaborate network of legal rules and principles. Typical is the comment by Sir Henry Maine: "... The Greek intellect, with all its nobility and elasticity, was quite unable to confine itself within the strait waistcoat of a legal formula; and, if we may judge them by the popular courts of Athens, of whose working we possess accurate knowledge, the Greek tribunals exhibited the strongest tendency to confound law and fact. The remains of the Orators and the forensic commonplaces preserved by Aristotle in his Treatise on Rhetoric, show that questions of pure law were constantly argued on every consideration which could possibly influence the mind of the judges. No durable system of jurisprudence could be produced in this way. A community which never hesitated to relax rules of written law whenever they stood in the way of an ideally perfect decision on the facts of particular cases, would only, if it bequeathed any body of judicial principles to posterity, bequeath one consisting of the ideas of right and wrong which happened to be prevalent at the time. Such jurisprudence [unlike the Roman] would contain no framework to which the more advanced conceptions of subsequent ages could be fitted...."

What a remarkable attitude Maine voices! He grants that the Greeks "never hesitated to relax" legal rules "whenever they stood in the way" of just decisions "on the facts of particular cases." He grants, too, that "the immediate benefit [conferred] on their citizens may have been considerable." But he criticizes the Greeks because, bent on justice in particular cases, they bequeathed no "body of judicial principles to posterity." Surely it is strange that those Greeks, from whom we have acquired many of our most precious political and philosophic ideas, and the foundations of our natural sciences, should be regarded as backward legally. I suggest that in concerning themselves with the considerable benefit to their citizens rather than in contriving rules to benefit posterity, they showed that they were enlightened in the legal realm as elsewhere. I suggest that we have much to learn from the Greek view of the judicial process....

Years ago, I suggested (à la Aristotle) that legal rules which, because of their generality, necessarily omit much, should, in their application to particular states of fact, be taken with a keen perception of their unexpressed qualifications. I went on to say that, in this sense, the rules might be considered "fictions," and that consequently, they should be dealt with as the courts deal with legal fictions when aware they are employing them. I noted that the courts have often said that legal fictions are "intended for the sake of justice" and should "not be permitted to work any wrong." The rules, I said, if applied without awareness that (in the sense above noted) they are "fictional," do work harm. "They can," I continued, "be immensely useful and entirely harmless if used with complete recognition that they are but convenient hypostatizations, provisional formulations, signposts, guides." (*Law and the Modern Mind*, 1930, p. 167)

I now turn to a somewhat fanciful idea I offered in the same book. I suggested that the quest for a practically unrealizable legal certainty might *partially* be explained by the carry-over into adult life of a hankering for the strict rules of the father which, in our kind of society, the young child cherishes as a means of procuring emotional stability. Now it is notable that the Roman legal system—admired for its elaboration of rules and principles, and far less given to acknowledged, flexible, individualizing than the Greek system—arose in a society in which the power of the father (the patria potestas) was a dominant characteristic. In the maturity of Greek civilization, this power of the father had much diminished. I suggest that it is barely possible that, as a result, the role of the mother emerged as an influence on Greek legal attitudes, so that equity, greater lenience, more attention to the "circumstances that alter cases" in the application of rules, became an accepted legal ideal....

Think, for instance, of the role of Mary, the mother, in the 12th and 13th centuries, as pictured by Henry Adams: "She alone represented Love.... The Trinity ... must admit only one law. In that law, no human weakness or error could exist.... There was no crack and no cranny in the system, through which human frailty could hope for escape. One was forced from corner to corner by a remorseless logic until one fell helpless at Mary's feet.... Mary [was] the only court of equity capable of overruling strict law." Abelard wrote that "all of us who fear the wrath of the Judge, fly to the Judge's mother."

... In 1884, Theodore Roosevelt, then 26 years of age, sneered at the legal profession as "especially fitted for the weaker sex." I think that the young Roosevelt was right in his conclusion, wrong in his attitude. For I believe that the judicial process is one of the best means worked out by human society for the adjustment of many of its difficulties. I believe also that flexibility, tact, and the understanding of people, are more important in the practice of the "law" than what has usually (but erroneously) been considered legal logic—the rigorous application of fixed legal principles. To what do these beliefs add up? To the conclusion that it is the so-called "feminine" attributes, rather than the so-called "masculine," that are essential in the task of administering justice....

You will perhaps recall the famous English judge who gave this advice to a newly-appointed member of the bench: "State your conclusions, but never your reasons. Your conclusions will probably be right; your reasons will usually be wrong." How often, to my youthful awe, had not my mother and sisters successfully used this device: "Let the reasons go hang." Women usually have a way of piercing to the core of the matter....

"The heart has reasons, which reason does not know," wrote Pascal.... Mercy, charity, compassionateness, respect for the unique attributes of the men and women who come before our trial courts—these would seem to be needed components of a civilized judicial process. I find some solace in the fact that, in spite of contrary pretensions, those are actual components of many decisions. But I ask myself why our judges must continue to do merciful justice by stealth.... In the Juvenile Court we have rejected such stealth. "The ingredients of this court's approach," says Lucas, "are understanding, sympathy, and unvarying resolve to unravel the relentless web of conditions which determine human behavior...." Is it not possible that the techniques of the Juvenile Court could desirably, in some measure, be taken over by all our trial courts?

Our traditional image of Justice is a blindfolded goddess, who treats all persons alike, disregarding extenuating circumstances. "Lately," says George Boas, "Justice has been peeking from under her blindfold to distinguish between children and adults.... She is of course blamed occasionally for this, since she is no longer impartial; but in time, it will probably be the proud boast of her worshippers that she treats no two individuals alike" (i.e., that she mercifully individualizes in the spirit of the Aristotelian arbitrator's "equity"). Otherwise, Justice may provide an artificial or fictitious "equality before the law," an "arithmetical" equality which is cruel.

Aristotle on Justice

Aristotle had few answers to our questions. But his comprehensive treatment of justice, in book 5 of the *Nicomachean Ethics*, along with the great authority he acquired, led subsequent writers to adopt his terms and divisions. It is unfortunate, then, that the work does not make for easy reading. It was probably taken from rough lecture notes and certainly involves gaps and transpositions. So a summary will be given here of some of the main classifications of justice that he handed down to us.

His analysis is based, not on speculation, but on a study of plain language. Aristotle first excludes the way we sometimes speak of a "just person" as one who does whatever is good. Such a term is coextensive with all the virtues. It includes, for example, mercy and generosity. If you send me a gift, I may feel moved to make you a gift on some appropriate occasion. But am I obliged to this *out of justice*? If you reply yes, then I suggest that the situation has become one of *quid pro quo*. It may be well to send Christmas cards to those who send one to you, but the notion of a gift (gratuity) is somehow lost. Giving a gift in order to receive a gift sounds rather like a contradiction in terms.

Hence Aristotle is quick to isolate justice as a *specific* virtue. Let us call it *particular* justice and avoid confusion by not allowing the term *justice* any wider range (as Plato, for example, does in *The Republic*). The key note of justice, so restricted, is *reciprocity*: there is a definite proportion between what I did to you and what I can justly expect from you. Indeed, the notion of *proportions* runs through Aristotle's whole treatment of justice. The Greeks were a people with a deep sense of harmony, whether it be in mathematics, music, or architecture.

DISTRIBUTIVE AND CORRECTIVE JUSTICE

Who is involved in such reciprocal relations? If it is the whole society on one hand and individuals on the other, then we have *distributive* justice. Examples would be the assignment of taxes and of police protection. Little need be said here, for we see this as the province of the legislature rather than of the courts. Yet it may be worth mentioning that Aristotle, like Plato, held that just distribution should be according to *merit*. He was no egalitarian. The better, and more highly qualified, workers should—like victors in the games—get the larger prizes. He did admit, though, that many legitimate disagreements come from questions about the *standards* of merit.

If, however, the reciprocity is between individuals (as with a contract or injury) then we have what Aristotle called *corrective* justice. The term is unfortunate, because it suggests subordination to distributive justice; I merit only a third of the pie but seize a half, so I am hauled into court to correct my wrong. This is the approach of Communist systems of law. If you take an extra room in the apartment block, this is unjust, not because the room belonged to another individual, but because the state distributed living space at a rate of fifty cubic meters per person. In Communist law, contracts are with the state.

However, Aristotle does not explicitly make this subordination. Indeed, one could argue for the reverse priority. If we see the state as an abstraction apart from the people who constitute it, then we may find a presupposition for distributive justice in the basic respect that one person shows for any other. Though we think of the courts following the legislature, it may be that the latter depends on the spirit of the former. Whatever rules govern income tax have little bite apart from my project of living with you and with others according to rules.

VOLUNTARY AND INVOLUNTARY TRANSACTIONS

This is Aristotle's subdivision of corrective justice. At first glance it is obvious, but some important questions remain. If I make a bargain with you, the transaction is voluntary, and my failure to satisfy it comes under what we should call the law of contracts. But if I injure you, the "transaction" is involuntary and my obligation to make good your loss comes under what we call the law of torts.

Aristotle's treatment of voluntary transactions is interesting. He insists that the proportions involved, though precise, are not *natural* but *conventional*. He takes as an example the exchange made between a farmer (grain) and a doctor (healing). In our day the doctor would get much more grain for his remedies than in ancient Greece. Aristotle makes no protest in the name of justice. The value we set on health is conventional and is subject to fluctuations in the market.

What about the proportions we are bound to restore after violations that Aristotle sees as involuntary transactions? He holds that such proportions are *arithmetical* and explains himself in this way:

> It makes no difference whether a good man injures a bad one or a bad man a good one. Nor does it matter if it is a good or a bad person who has committed adultery. The law looks only to the specific character of the injury and treats the parties as equal.
> (Aristotle *Nicomachean Ethics* 1132a)

Here we seem to have a basis for the many criticisms of justice as a harsh virtue. If I take your book and lose it, am I bound only to pay you the market value? Is it irrelevant that the book bore a handwritten message from a parent now dead? That I destroyed the book so that you would suffer? The blindfold of justice seems firmly in place.

Is it not strange that Aristotle should respect the inequality of people in distributive justice but not here? A possible explanation is that he is turning from inequalities in what we *have* to the basic equality in what we *are*. My judgment of unreasonable behavior in chess (see section 3) is based, not on inequalities in performance, but on the basic fact that both players have accepted the project and the spirit of chess. Arithmetical proportion does at least apply to the way in which we all accept the very rule of law that makes violation possible and restoration obligatory. Such a transaction is involuntary in the sense that, far from being an elective (as is chess), we are all bound to enter into it, and we do so on a one-to-one basis. You are involuntary when your pocket is picked; but you are also involuntary (though in a different sense) when you find that you must act for a reason, that you must take some political stand (even by not voting), and that your choices are limited by death. We are equal in our mortality.

It is sometimes said that the basic demand of justice in law is for like cases to be treated in a like manner (this has been called the *formal* principle of justice). If a line of precedents shows that people who did X are found liable for Y, then it would be unjust for me to be exempted from Y if I am proved to have done X. However, this abstract statement raises more problems than it solves. Jerome Frank's stress on "particular states of fact," and his appeal for the "individualization of cases," remind us of the differences between each instance of what appears as X. Some differences are clearly irrelevant (for example, the name of the defendant). Other differences may lead us to ask whether X was really committed (the case of the speluncean explorers, in section 5, offers an example from criminal law; section 31 will look for relevant differences in a series of cases in tort law).

In other words, a principle of equality needs to be supported by some principles of relevance (or *material* principles of justice), which specify how discrimination between cases is just rather than arbitrary. If I understand the run of Aristotle's analysis, he is making two claims in this regard. One is that, though we must solve complex questions about relevant distinctions before we can satisfy the demands of justice for equality of *treatment*, these very questions presuppose that we grant each person a more basic equality of *respect*: we must allow each participant an adequate hearing. Justice Keen may finally have concluded that no legally relevant distinction removed the four explorers from the class of murderers and from the statutory penalty of death; yet by giving full consideration to the questions of fact and of law involved, by trying to see a complex situation from each point of view, Keen accorded the explorers equality before the law and thus satisfied some fundamental requirement of justice.

Aristotle's second claim has to do, at least by implication, with the development of law. The class of X (murderers) was ill defined when the spelunceans came to trial. Was it more clearly expressed as a result of the appeal? Perhaps the division of the court forces us to reply no. But the opinions of Keen and of Foster, though opposed, were at least efforts to pass from a sheer individualization of cases toward a more precise statement of the nature or scope of murder. Aristotle would probably have little sympathy for Jerome Frank's talk of intuitive decisions that cannot be supported by reasons (or are buttressed with reasons that "will usually be wrong"). If the blindfold of justice is lifted, this is surely not for us to indulge in inarticulate mercy or compassion; it is for us to see and explain why what appeared to be X was or was not really so. Aristotle did not regard arithmetical equality as cruel. He saw it as belonging to a requirement that the law, if it is to be just, must ever seek a conceptualization that does distinguish like from unlike cases.

There is much interpretation in this account of Aristotle. And a reader who finds more inspiration in the extract from Jerome Frank may also look for support in Aristotle's comments on the concept of equity. These were passing remarks but they have had an immense influence, and even Judge Frank solicits Aristotle to the cause of individualization through the distinction between legal justice and equitable justice. The chapter will close on this theme, and the topic will recur, notably in discussions of judicial decision making.

EQUITY

Before introducing this final division of justice that Aristotle discusses, a word of summary may help. Justice is based on *proportions*, and at least four stages can be distinguished:

1. virtue without proportion (e.g., mercy, generosity);
2. justice with conventional proportions (voluntary transactions);
3. justice with variable but natural proportions (distribution on merit); and

4. justice with invariable proportions (the basis for corrective justice).

An example is needed. What models of justice can we find in the case of the speluncean explorers?

1. Stage 4 is neglected at the risk of losing the story's point; if Whetmore's life were in no sense equal to that of the others, the drama fails.

2. Stage 2 enters when lots are drawn; what proportions could be more conventional than those determined by the fall of dice?

3. Stage 3 would have been involved if, instead, the explorers had decided who should die on the basis of merit; suppose, as in the *Holmes* case, death had been assigned to the one least able to contribute to the survival of those in peril (or to the future benefit of society).

4. Stage 1 the only basis offered by Truepenny; he appealed beyond law and justice to the sheer generosity of the chief executive.

Such comments are a prelude to the question of *equity*. Aristotle discusses this only toward the end but may not have intended it as a postscript. Unfortunately, it has been so treated in the history of the common law, where the courts of equity were established in England to supply the justice that the regular courts no longer offered. Jerome Frank likewise seems to appeal to equity as a remedy introduced to meet a failure. What about Aristotle?

> Equity is not identical with justice, but neither are they simply different.... It would seem strange to praise an equitable decision if it were not also a just one, and the goodness of equity comes from its justice.... Our problem arises with the realization that the equitable decision is just because it involves some correction of legal justice. The reason is that all law must be universal, and about some things it is not possible to make universal statements.... Hence equity is a correction of law where this fails owing to its universality.
>
> (Aristotle *Nicomachean Ethics* 1137a–b)

A weak interpretation of Aristotle is possible: he is merely pointing to the obvious fact that a legislator does not envisage all possible cases and that judges are expected somehow to supply for this lack of provision and precision. But a stronger interpretation is often made. Aristotle is said to be claiming that some situations would escape from general rules of any kind, even if we allow Herculean foresight to the legislators and supreme precision to the judges when they discriminate cases and write their opinions. One author offers an account of this interpretation as holding that "for any given general rule which prescribes how any member of a class of cases is to be treated, there will always be some particular fact situation which is indisputably a member of that class of situations, but which nevertheless ought not to be treated in accordance with that law."[26]

Aristotle supplies no examples. And the question of a commentator is whether examples can be given to support this latter interpretation. We are all able to think of cases where we complain that a judge's decision was unjust because he did not sufficiently investigate the situation set before him or the applicable law. Yet can you envisage a case so removed from linguistic expression that you could not suggest some formulation of a rule to cover it and any other case *of the same kind*? Wittgenstein's dictum, that we should keep silent about that of which we cannot speak, may apply here. Life consists in making exceptions to rules, but these exceptions come as further rules, based on underlying principles. If I hold that I should not tell lies, I may still lie to save your life, and this challenges me to enunciate a qualification of the given rule; I do not retreat into the ineffable. Judge Earl, in *Riggs* (section 4), may possibly have seen himself as exercising equity, but he knew his ruling would be cited in future cases and would, it is hoped, deter any subsequent Elmer Palmer who could read or who would employ a lawyer to do this for him.

These remarks offer little guidance to legislators when they face the question how general their language should be. They may well be advised to leave "open texture" in their words and rely upon the courts to decide how broad or narrow are the classes captured by the law. It may be prudent to speak vaguely of unfair competition in commercial laws but much more precisely of dangerous play in the rules for ice hockey. However, this is not to concede that a judge, in applying antitrust laws to a particular corporation, will enter further into the realm of the unutterable than a referee who is called to explain why he put one combatant rather than another into the penalty box. If I hold that corporation A was acting unfairly and corporation B was not, I am obliged to say why, and in so doing I face the recurring problem of avoiding a too-general or a too-precise ruling; yet ruling there is, in concepts expressed through words.

> Given an indefinitely large number of rules there is no reason why all cases could not be decided justly by means of an appeal to rules. But as a practical matter, rules cannot become too specific and still fulfill their most important function as rules.[27]

Aristotle was no anti-conceptualist, and I suspect he was not proposing the strong interpretation outlined above. Even if he was, we must still ask whether he makes sense. The problem of equity affects us all, as Aristotle saw, even in our ordinary talk. How can we put what we think or wonder into words? We try, we fail, we try again. But the question is *how* we try again. Do we somehow go

---

26. Richard A. Wasserstrom, *The Judicial Decision* (Stanford, Calif.: Stanford Univ. Press, 1961), 107–8. This book, which will be discussed more fully in section 34, offers a clear analysis of various claims that a judge's decision is based on some intuition of particular factors that escape from exact legal expression (84–117).

27. Wasserstrom, *The Judicial Decision*, 112.

outside all language? The tone of an expression counts, the smile or shrug that accompanies our words. Yet even there, the person who is sensitive to the demands of language will repeatedly try to rectify inadequate words with more words. Aristotle's own encyclopedic writings may suggest his answer.

A final comment. Put yourself in the position of a person who appeals a judicial decision as falling short of justice. If you invoke *equity*, are you asking the judge to intervene through his generosity, his love, his mercy? Or do you appeal to him for imagination and sensitivity and (above all) for *serious thought* in finding justice *within* the law? Equity, some would say, is not a foreign element to be summoned from beyond the enterprise of living legally; equity enlivens the law and prevents it from being purveyed as rules without policy or as policy without principle.

FURTHER READING

There are many books that discuss the nature of justice. Extensive bibliographies are to be found, for example, in:

Bedau, Hugo A., ed. *Justice and Equality.* Englewood Cliffs, N.J.: Prentice-Hall, 1971.
Bird, Otto A. *The Idea of Justice.* New York: Praeger, 1967.
   Some books with particular reference to law include:
Cahn, Edmond. *The Sense of Injustice.* Bloomington, Ind.: Indiana Univ. Press, 1964.
Feibleman, James K. *Justice, Law and Culture.* The Hague: Martinus Nijhoff, 1985.
Freund, Paul. *On Law and Justice.* Cambridge: Harvard Univ. Press, 1968.
Kelsen, Hans. *What is Justice?* Berkeley: Univ. of California Press, 1957.
Morris, Clarence. *The Justification of the Law.* Philadelphia: Univ. of Pennsylvania Press, 1971.
Pound, Roscoe. *Justice According to Law.* New Haven: Yale Univ. Press, 1951.
Stone, Julius. *Human Law and Human Justice.* Stanford, Calif.: Stanford Univ. Press, 1965.
Strick, Anne. *Injustice for All.* New York: G. P. Putnam & Sons, 1977.
Wasserstein, Bruce, and Mark Green. *With Justice for Some.* Boston: Beacon Press, 1970.

QUESTIONS FOR DISCUSSION

1. Comment on the ambiguity in the notion of justice contained in two quotations that Jerome Frank juxtaposes on page 267 of *Courts on Trial*:
   "A rule which is certain and fixed promotes justice more than do good laws which are liable to change or modification."
   "It is essential for the law to be certain, and to attain that certainty it is worthwhile to sacrifice justice in occasional cases."
2. What did Sir Henry Maine mean in saying that "the Greek tribunals exhibited the strongest tendency to confound law and fact"? If the train on which you commute is always ten minutes late, does this important fact change the "rule," or does the timetable continue to state the law? If prosecutors have simply ignored violations of a certain law for many years, has this fact changed the law? As a parent, might you think that justice is served by some confusion of fact and law when you referee games played by your children of various ages and abilities?
3. Why, in our courts, is the criminal record of a defendant inadmissible in the trial but pertinent in the sentencing? Would the removal of this "blindfold" increase or decrease justice? Our juvenile courts, though concerned to give an accurate verdict on legal guilt, also view their

task very much in terms of therapy. Do you approve of this, in the name of justice, or see it as a confusion of the roles of judge and social worker?

4.   Jerome Frank suggests that legal rules should be treated as "signposts or guides." How do proverbs, the slogans of practical wisdom, differ from legal rules? Notice how proverbs often seem to contradict each other. Do they invite, not literal following, but what Frank calls the "perception of unexpressed qualifications"? Does a rule rely upon unwritten principles that help us to decide how narrowly the rule should be taken?

5.   Pascal's claim, that the heart has reasons to which we are blind in our normal thinking, is often quoted. Is this a form of irrationalism? Or is it a plea for an extension of the legitimate boundaries of reason? Are you impressed by the advice quoted as being given by one judge to another, that his conclusions will probably be right but his reasons wrong? Apply such advice to mathematics. To business decisions.

6.   Is there something odd in the suggestion that God's justice is defective through want of love and mercy? Or does Henry Adams view medieval religious devotion as recognizing the complexity of justice and thus spreading it over various actors?

7.   Forty years have passed since Jerome Frank wrote, and these have seen a notable integration of women into the legal profession. Do you agree with, or find offensive, his claim that women lawyers and judges contribute to the realization of the ideals of law and justice through the attributes that Frank praises? For a recent account of the psychiatric distinction between a "patriarchal and matriarchal superego," with applications to the conscience that is institutionalized in law schools, see Ann Belford and Barry Ulanov: *Religion and the Unconscious* (1975).

8.   Much of our success in any pursuit depends on our sensitive grasp of what is relevant and irrelevant. Think of a historian, a sociologist, a military commander, a mortgage official, or a policeman. Aristotle, unaware of our own legal system, certainly does not tell the judge what should be noticed and what should be disregarded. But by mapping out the swampy field of justice, Aristotle at least supplies us with some of the markers. However, be open to the possibility that he has misled us:

   a. Is he correct in seeing reciprocity as the key to justice? Do we not acquire our deepest intuitions of justice from within the family, and is not reciprocity strangely lacking here? Do not the members of a close family act toward each other with a love that calculates no return and to which the notion of proportions is foreign? Is sacrifice based on thought of return?

   b. Though much is made in contemporary religion of the need for social justice, is justice (as seen by Aristotle) really a vital part of religious doctrine? How do you interpret the parable of the laborers in the vineyard (Matthew 20:1–16)? What is meant by *grace*?

   c. Comment on the suggestion that our courts are concerned with *corrective* rather than *distributive* justice. Has the U.S. Supreme Court become increasingly concerned with the latter? What can be said in favor of the Communist notion that contracts are basically with the state?

   d. Aristotle inherited the "conventional/natural" distinction from the Sophists, and his illustrations of "natural proportions" are rather unsatisfactory. Can we do better, given our emphasis on the market? Distinguish, for example, between your judgment of whether a doctor or a manual worker should get a higher salary and your answer to the question whether the former should get preferential treatment in the traffic courts.

   e. Comment on the claim that all people are created equal. Where, in Aristotle's terms, should we apply "arithmetical proportions"? What is meant by "equality before the law"?

9.   Do you think that Aristotle's convoluted discussion of equity is largely a matter of semantics? Does it make any difference whether a correction to justice is itself within or outside the basic project of justice? Refer again to the case of the speluncean explorers and to Truepenny's solution, or to the difference between Gray and Earl in *Riggs v. Palmer*. Why might you be dissatisfied to receive mercy *rather than* justice?

2

THE RANGE OF LAW

> *Your first duty is obedience to all the rules and regulations, and to the orders of the officers of this institution.*
>
> *Loud and boisterous talking or shouting is strictly forbidden in any building of the institution. Whistling anywhere, at any time, is forbidden....*
>
> *Keep in mind that these rules do not cover every contingency. Any deviation from good behavior or common decency will be considered as a rule violation even though it may not be specifically stated in the rules....*
>
> (from the Rules of the Colorado State Penitentiary, 1967)

> *Should this be found I want these facts recorded. Oates' last thoughts were of his Mother but, immediately before, he took pride in thinking that his regiment would be pleased with the bold way in which he met his death.... He went out into the blizzard and we have not seen him since.... We knew [he] was walking to his death, but though we tried to dissuade him, we knew it was the act of a brave man and an English gentleman.... I can write only at lunch.... The cold is intense, minus 40° at midday.*
>
> (from the Journals of Capt. Robert Falcon Scott)

Those with a clearly formed philosophy of law may be quick to draw a line between what is and what is not law. We have certainly not come so far, and there are dangers in premature definition. Living as we do in a society with well-established legal institutions, we may be inclined to exclude from our consideration the less-articulate forms of law that have occupied most of human history. Whatever theory of law we produce can be prejudiced by the narrow range of examples from which it is drawn; our position would be like that of a person whose philosophy of science is based on a prior elimination of sociology or psychiatry or even biology.

The first quotation above clearly falls within the range of law. It has to do with rules formulated in great detail to cover all behavior of prisoners. These rules are published in writing and are made known to each inmate in a variety of ways. There are agencies for deciding, in particular cases, whether the law has or has not been broken. And the prison authorities have at their disposal the means to enforce each prescription, down to the length of hair and the tone of voice. Notice also the catchall provision at the end—even what escaped the lawgiver's meticulous mind can, at the discretion of enforcement officials, be treated as though covered by the specific words of a rule.

You will not limit your view of law to the regulations of such an institution. Yet most of us, when asked about law, tend to draw our examples from written regulations made by an authority that is backed by the power of sanctions (Do this, or else . . .).

The second quotation is taken from Captain Scott's ill-fated expedition to the South Pole in 1911–12. Although recent studies have demythologized this exploit, the reader of Scott's journals is still invited to wonder how he or she would have behaved on the return journey, facing almost certain death from cold and starvation. The personnel were military, yet it is of interest to inquire how much of what they did in such extreme conditions came from the following of explicit rules. Titus Oates was suffering from severe frostbite in his feet, and his plight seemed to remove the last hope his companions had of survival. He received no order (only persuasion) to stay in the tent. Nor was he told to face the blizzard. In the absence of commands and of rules, did he act capriciously? As the story is narrated, he was guided by "roles" that came to him from the spirit of a society rather than from its written ordinances. The ideal of the "gentleman," though influential since the Renaissance, may no longer speak to us, and our last thoughts are unlikely to be of a regiment. Have no other standards of this sort arisen? If you were in the situation of Captain Scott, would you have continued your journal to the end and have died with pen in hand? If so, why? Suppose no naval requirement made this a matter of written law. Might your conduct still have been, in some sense, law-inspired?

9. PRIMITIVE LAW

I experience a sort of terror when, at the moment of setting to work and finding myself before the infinitude of possibilities that present themselves, I have the feeling that everything is permissible to me. If everything is permissible to me, the best and the worst, . . . every undertaking becomes futile.

(Igor Stravinsky)[1]

1. *Poetics of Music* (Cambridge: Harvard Univ. Press, 1947), 63; quoted in *The Principles of Social Order*, K. I. Winston, ed. (Durham, N.C.: Duke Univ. Press, 1981), 51.

It may be strange to compare a lawyer to an artist. There are evident contrasts in temperament and training. Yet think for a moment of the analogy. Both bring order out of chaos. The artist begins with an infinite range of possible sounds or shapes and colors. Better, perhaps, he starts with incoherent feelings and his vocation is to bring these, through his creation, to the light of intelligence and to the reach of communication. Similarly, a person whose work is in the law tries to construct from the confusion of human relationships some pattern of intelligibility and communication. His task is also to make order. The materials may be different but certainly no less worthy. The call upon imagination and sensitivity is as demanding.

Our dominant myth of creation speaks of what was "without form and void" gradually gaining the articulation of a world in which human beings can live and sin and be redeemed. Such a story is not put before law students at their first class. Instead, they are set in a ready-made world of statutes and cases. The students are told to use their ingenuity to find a way through what is given. They learn to predict how the courts will decide, and hence to advise a client whether to settle out of court or to follow trained leadership through the pitfalls of the courthouse and the casebook. Lawyers work within a framework. They can easily forget that we have ourselves developed this framework and that they, as professionals, share some responsibility for what it is. If they are asked to draw up a contract, they may recover some sense of their creative power. They know that a carefully negotiated contract can be filed away and forgotten, for understanding has been achieved through their preliminary work in exploring possibilities. But, for the most part, they see themselves as applying rules or procedures that are already in existence.

If these remarks suggest criticism, this extends far beyond the law. It is, unfortunately, a mark of maturity that we have acquired the know-how to accept and manage whatever is prescribed in our field. The investment analyst shows his or her ability in moving money from one place to another, with no distracting thoughts on the nature of investment or the quality of life that such manipulations render possible.

We have lost the thrill and anxiety of childhood. Nothing in our adult life comes as close to the myth of creation as did our own infancy. The newborn child has no guidelines, no orderly world to which he or she can adapt, no signposts that lead along well-beaten paths. There is only a buzzing confusion in which the basic distinction of self and world seems lacking. An infinitude of possibilities lies open. The fact that we grow into a society in which we live together and talk to each other is a remarkable feat.

Others tell, in detail, the story of these dramatic journeys that most of us have now forgotten.[2] We passed through a succession of worlds, but we created each. Is it surprising that the young child is first a convinced *animist*? He

---

2. In what follows I draw upon the work of Piaget. Perhaps the best introduction is through his *The Child's Conception of the World* (1929; reprint, Totowa, N.J.: Littlefield, Adams & Co., 1969).

struggles to find himself by discovering other selves. The sun and moon are spirits that follow him with curiosity; when he turns they turn also. Rivers flow in order to get to the sea. Stones sink because they are less intelligent than wood. Only much later does the child formulate a world in which *artificialism* is the guiding theme; clouds are understood as made from smoke that is produced by subjects like us. Then the child comes to experiment with *naturalism*, a world view in which rivers and clouds and floating are interpreted through such impersonal factors as gravity and pressure and density. We are happy today with a scientific explanation of magnetism or electricity in terms of "attraction," though we politely forget the animistic origins of this term.

Piaget's best-known experiments have to do with "conservation." Pour liquid from a tall narrow container (A) into one that is short and wide (B). Self-respecting children under seven (unless indoctrinated by parents or teachers) will tell you that there is less in container B than there was in A. How will you show the mistake? Pour the liquid back, and there is the same amount in A as before? Children will justly claim that as the volume decreased before, so now it increases! Can you *prove* them wrong? Or does your *a priori* "law of conservation" simply come into conflict with their poetic world in which things (or volumes) are created and destroyed?

What has this to do with law? Children and adults make their laws for seeing the world, for drawing order out of the sheer confusion of raw experience; the world we find depends somehow on an implicit agreement about a way of seeing it. Galileo is one of our heroes. But was he a world-finder or a world-creator? Did he discover how things really are (in themselves)? Or did he offer an imaginative proposal for a new way of legislating to experience? If Galileo simply reported what is really there (in itself), apart from his creative schemes, then his quarrels with the Inquisition form a sordid story. But suppose that Galileo's place in history comes from a daring legislative idea, that one model of explanation should replace another? There we have the seeds of a profound dispute, a drama that might even justify the blood it shed. Our deepest conflicts are about the models or paradigms we bring to experience.[3]

These lengthy comments are intended to offer grounds for a study of the varieties of legal experience before we turn to any of the details of law. In particular, some excuse is sought for an inquiry into examples of primitive law. This is no topic for the average law school. Primitive law seems infantile, an early venture into what we know so well today. However, the project or enterprise of law may be better revealed in its early forms than in its developed systems. Can the lawyer ask what he or she is doing by investigating an age when there were no lawyers but only people on their way toward the creation of what we should call legal procedures and institutions?

---

3. The clearest expression of such suggestions, in the field of science, is to be found in the writings of Thomas Kuhn and Michael Polanyi.

Law without Central Authority

The case of the speluncean explorers put us in a situation where (according to one of its characters and probably also to its author) the enacted law of a modern state failed to penetrate and where the actors faced afresh the enterprise of making law in a void. This was no more than a story. But, even today, when we reach the limits of inhabitable temperatures on our earth, we discover people who approximate to such survival conditions. An extract follows on one of the most primitive of legal systems, that of the Eskimo.

Most Eskimos have of course been affected by our own culture and ways of thinking legally. Yet we can still find, along the northern fringes of land from Siberia to East Greenland, scattered settlements living much as they were when first investigated by anthropologists. Rarely are there more than a hundred in a single community, and no organization exists to bind these small groups into a tribe or other social whole. Within the community there may be a shaman, endowed with religious powers, and a headman whose position depends on his demonstrated ability as a hunter. But the landmarks we associate with law seem lacking. There are no written rules. There is no legislator to make or change laws, no regular police to enforce them, no permanent judge or court to apply them to cases.

Some will say that it is then foolish to investigate Eskimo law. Perhaps. Yet there is a surprising uniformity in Eskimo culture. One language could enable the traveler to communicate across the six thousand miles of settlements. And he would find much the same way of organizing experience, of evaluating actions, of distinguishing "mine" and "thine," of defining relationships and deviant conduct. In the absence of any codified law or clearly legal institutions, we may possibly speak of a "living law" that is operative, of some set of presuppositions and norms that give guidance to what is done.

The extract below is from *The Law of Primitive Man*, by E. Adamson Hoebel, one of the most widely used introductions to an anthropology of law. Hoebel there studies seven primitive cultures. Each account begins with a description of what the author calls the "jural postulates" of that culture. He describes these as "the broadly generalized propositions held by the members of a society as to the nature of things and as to what is qualitatively desirable and undesirable" (p. 13). Such postulates are "felt by those who live by them but so much taken for granted that they are but rarely expressed or exposed for examination" (p. 333). They are, as it were, the basic ways of formulating experience that distinguish (for example) the world of the Eskimo and provide a framework for whatever law exists there or might supposedly be codified.[4] They are the principles behind the rules or below the surface.

The religious postulates of the Eskimo are plainly animistic. Nature is a community of spirits, so that prudent action consists in placating these and not

---

4. In another work, to be discussed below, Hoebel did experiment with a codification of the unwritten law of the Cheyenne on homicide.

giving offense. It is, for instance, vital that at certain times caribou meat should not be eaten and walrus tusks should not be carved. We find it difficult to take such tabus seriously but should not forget that our removal of personality from nature is as much an option for "seeing things" as is theirs. Facts are theory-laden. Our own law reveals some conflicts in the way we perceive "insanity."

The closest the Eskimo comes to a courtroom scene is the public confession of tabu-violations.[5] The shaman plays the part of prosecutor and judge, but the villagers rally to the defense. Justice wears no blindfold, and the goal seems therapeutic, a healing of guilt rather than the imposition of a verdict.

Hoebel evidently regards the economic postulate as basic, that "life is hard." This leads to interesting conclusions about the nature of property, in line with the needs of a nomadic hunter, and to some fine distinctions that are respected without benefit of codes or cases. The narrow margin of survival also challenges our own postulates about the sanctity of life, and the story of the speluncean explorers would have called for some different incident to arouse the Eskimo legal mind.

In regard to the taking of life, two opposing tendencies may be noticed. On the one hand, social disorder seems encouraged by the lack of formal law. Most murders come from strife over the possession of women, and such conflicts are promoted by the lack of rituals that clearly announce a state of marriage. The defining of relationships may be one of the primary functions of law. On the other hand, the basic instinct to engage in blood feuds, avenging death with death, seems to have been channeled into legal forms. Though single murders may be private wrongs to be met with private remedies, an extension of the killing becomes a public crime to be punished by agents of the community. Execution now takes place in the name of the people and we come close to the adjudication and law enforcement of a more formal system.

In the following extract, Hoebel describes what he calls "the bare-bones of the legal." He speaks with hesitation of "law" in such Eskimo communities, but largely because he regards the presence of "official force" as essential to any legal system. Indeed, his definition of law is classical: "A social norm is legal if its neglect or infraction is regularly met, in threat or in fact, by the application of physical force by an individual or group possessing the socially recognized privilege of so acting" (p. 28). The requirement that a legal system should contain an agent who is accepted as having the power to make and enforce laws is central to the legal philosophy of John Austin, which will be discussed in section 17 below. Other writers place less emphasis on the presence of sanctions.[6] Indeed, Hoebel stresses also the way in which laws create social order by formulating "interactional expectancies": each member of a society "must be

---

5. The extract reprinted below closes with a further parallel: the Eskimo way of resolving conflicts in a forum where the improvisation of songs is judged by the applause given to the most insulting.

6. For a criticism of Hoebel and Austin on this point, see: Lon Fuller, *The Morality of Law* (New Haven: Yale Univ. Press, 1969), 106–18. See also the writings of Malinowski for an anthropologist's criticism of such views.

able to predict what the others will do when confronted with certain situations.... He is ordering his own conduct in relation to the expected conduct of others" (p. 12). Even in the absence of a policeman carrying a weapon and a rule book, unwritten customs and religious assumptions lay some claim to stand at the informal end of a legal spectrum.

THE LAW OF PRIMITIVE MAN: A STUDY IN COMPARATIVE LEGAL DYNAMICS
by E. Adamson Hoebel

Chapter 5: "The Eskimo: Rudimentary Law in a Primitive Anarchy," pp. 68–99, Cambridge: Harvard University Press. Copyright © 1954 by the President and Fellows of Harvard College, © 1982 by E. Adamson Hoebel. Excerpted by permission of the publishers.

So simple is the social life of the Eskimo, and so rudimentary his legal institutions, that the basic premises of his culture translatable into jural postulates are few.... Although the Eskimo does not subject himself to self-analysis, nor consciously try to formulate a logically consistent system of social behavior, his system does make sense in terms of its own premises—premises that may be extracted from what has been reported of his beliefs and practices by numerous observers and formulated as they are here. The underlying postulates of jural significance in Eskimo culture are the following:

Postulate I. Spirit beings, and all animals by virtue of possessing souls, have emotional intelligence similar to that of man.
 Corollary 1. Certain acts are pleasing to them; others arouse their ire.
Postulate II. Man in important aspects of life is subordinate to the wills of animal souls and spirit beings.
 Corollary 1. When displeased or angered by human acts they withhold desired things or set loose evil forces.
Postulate III. Life is hard and the margin of safety small.
 Corollary 1. Unproductive members of society cannot be supported.
Postulate IV. All natural resources are free or common goods.
Postulate V. It is necessary to keep all instruments of production (hunting equipment, etc.) in effective use as much of the time as is possible.
 Corollary 1. Private property is subject to use claims by others than its owners.
 Corollary 2. No man may own more capital goods than he can himself utilize.
Postulate VI. The self must find its realization through action.
 Corollary 1. The individual must be left free to act with a minimum of formal direction from others.
 Corollary 2. The measure of the self for males is success as a food getter and in competition for women.
 Corollary 3. Those who are no longer capable of action are not worthy of living.
 Corollary 4. Creation or personal use of a material object results in a special status with respect to "ownership" of the object.
Postulate VII. Women are socially inferior to men but essential in economic production and childbearing.
Postulate VIII. The bilateral small family is the basic social and economic unit and is autonomous in the direction of its activities.
Postulate IX. For the safety of the person and the local group, individual behavior must be predictable.

Corollary 1. Aggressive behavior must be kept within defined channels and limited within certain bounds.

... From the fearful state of mind emerge the thousand and one tabus that hedge every moment of the Eskimos' waking day. A people more tabu-ridden would be difficult to find. The multitude of tabus are mostly directed to spirits of animals or their controlling deities in order to guard against conduct offensive or disrespectful to them. So comprehensive is the tabu system that the paucity of legal rules in Eskimo culture is in large part caused by the encompassing supernatural sanctions which dominate Eskimo social and economic life. Magic and religion rather than law direct most of their actions. Violation is sin. And the Eskimos in their own terms are most sinful.

The immediate personal consequence of sin is illness. Each sin contributes to the formation of a dark, noxious vapor that envelops the vital soul of the offender.

Among the Central Eskimos of Canada and those of West Greenland, confession in a public gathering purges the soul. With dramatic intensity the shaman (*angakok*) draws forth confessed tabu violation after tabu violation from the patient. Co-villagers form a background chorus to his chanting—washing the polluted soul clean with their cries for forgiveness. The Eskimo public, although the sins of one may endanger all, is gently tolerant and compassionate of the sinner in most cases.... The powers of the shaman as revealed in his direction of the public confessional are not to be taken as immediately legal. The action on the part of the sinner is "voluntary" and no compulsive legal sanctions are indicated when complete and abject confession is forthcoming....

The third basic postulate and its corollary are expressed not in the form of legal injunctions but, on the contrary, in privilege-rights. Infanticide, invalidicide, senilicide, and suicide are privileged acts: socially approved homicide.

Infanticide may be considered first. Infants are only potentially productive. If conditions permit, the Eskimos will always endeavor to raise their babies to adulthood. Too often, however, harsh circumstance does not permit. It is then up to each family to decide for itself: are its present resources (both human and material) sufficient to maintain the baby through its nonproductive years? There will be no social blame or legal sanction if a negative decision is reached and acted upon....

Senilicide, invalidicide, and suicide are expressions of the same postulate that underlies infanticide—life is hard and the margin of safety small. Those who cannot carry their full share of the productive load forfeit the right to live.... Yet another privilege-right resting upon the third postulate is that of cannibalism under famine conditions....

From the fourth postulate it follows that land is not property in any form: communal, joint, nor private. It is not even to be thought of as public domain, for it is and ever remains no-man's-land in an absolute and unconditional sense. Although each local group is traditionally associated with a particular district, it makes not the least pretension to territorial sovereignty. Anyone, whatever his local group, may hunt where he pleases.... Eskimo interest is in game per se; land is ignored and therefore not conceptualized as property.

Game and most articles of personal use, on the other hand, are objects of property notions. Deep-rooted Eskimo individualism, expressed in the postulate that the self finds realization through action, breeds law-ways in support of private property by way of the corollary idea that the creation of an object makes it the private property of the creator, as it also does, up to a point, in hunting. Game that can be taken by individual effort belongs to the person who makes possible the kill. Consequently, among the Ammassalik of East Greenland the hunter who chops a seal hole "has a potential right to seal caught in it." More definitely, a seal which escapes with a harpoon head in it belongs to the hunter who actually succeeds in capturing and killing the creature, although the harpoon, identifiable with ownership marks, should be returned to its owner. But—any seal harpooned with a bladder float attached to its line goes to the owner of the float no matter who captures it, since it is reasoned that the capture is made possible by the drag and visibility of the float....

Against this postulated extension of individualism, however, the fifth postulate, that no man can have more than he can effectively use, comes into play.... Nelson reported that the entrepreneur who accumulated too much property, i.e., kept it for himself, was looked upon as not working for the common end, so that he became hated and envied among the people. Ultimately he would be forced to give a feast upon pain of death, distributing all his goods with unrestrained largess. Nor might he ever again undertake to accumulate goods. Should he postpone the distribution too long, he was lynched, and his goods distributed among the people by his executioners....

The Eskimo is what some would call an anarchist. He has no government in the formal sense, either over a territory or at all. There is no pre-eminent center of authority. In this, Eskimo society is notably democratic. Yet, as is the case with every human group, skills are unequal.... The secular leader, or headman, of which there is one in each local group, is he who is tacitly, half-unconsciously recognized as first among equals. He is almost invariably the best hunter, always up first in the morning and the first man out on the ice, the one who makes all the plans for hunting trips—and the lesser men respect his wisdom and intuition.... He possesses no fixed authority; neither does he enter into formal office. He is not elected, nor is he chosen by any formal process. When other men accept his judgment and opinions, he is a headman. When they ignore them, he is not.

... Although direct personal power of man over man finds no place in the Eskimo scheme of things, competitiveness and rivalries are strong.... Outright appropriation of another man's wife is a gratuitous challenge to his status, and one of the recurrent consequences is homicide.... In part, the Eskimo difficulties are enhanced by the lack of marriage and divorce rituals which might demarcate the beginning and the end of a marital relationship. Marriage is entered into merely by bedding down with the intention of living together; divorce is effected simply by not living together any more.... Things and wives are both easily borrowed and lent....

The single murder is a private wrong redressed by the kinsman of the victim. Repeated murder becomes a public crime punishable by death at the hands of an agent of the community.... The important element is that the executioner, who undertakes the slaying, seeks and obtains, in advance, community approval for his act of riddance. When such approval is obtained no blood revenge may be taken on the executioner, for his act is not murder. It is the execution of a public sentence in the name of the people....

Homicidal dispute, though prevalent, is made less frequent in many Eskimo groups by recourse to regulated combat—wrestling, buffeting, and butting. Buffeting is found among the central tribes along the Arctic Circle from Hudson Bay to Bering Straits. Wrestling occurs in Siberia, Alaska, Baffinland, and Northwest Greenland. All three forms are a type of wager by battle without the element of divine judgment....

Deserving of fame are the *nith* songs of the eastern and western Eskimos. Elevating the duel to a higher plane, the weapons used are words—"little, sharp words, like the wooden splinters which I hack off with my ax."

Song duels are used to work off grudges and disputes of all orders, save murder. An East Greenlander, however, may seek his satisfaction for the murder of a relative through a song contest if he is physically too weak to gain his end, or if he is so skilled in singing as to feel certain of victory. Inasmuch as East Greenlanders get so engrossed in the mere artistry of the singing as to forget the cause of the grudge, this is understandable. Singing skill among these Eskimos equals or outranks gross physical prowess.

The singing style is highly conventionalized. The successful singer uses the traditional patterns of composition which he attempts to deliver with such finesse as to delight the audience to enthusiastic applause. He who is most heartily applauded is "winner." To win a song contest brings no restitution in its train. The sole advantage is in prestige....

In these ways, Eskimo society, without government, courts, constables, or written law, maintains its social equilibrium.... Here we have come the nearest we can, in observation, to the bare-bones of the legal.

Who Makes the Rules?

Anthropologists and lawyers speak a different language.[7] Hoebel's interest in the law of primitive people came through his friendship with Karl Llewellyn, a professor of law at Columbia University. In 1935 they spent a summer together among the Cheyenne Indians in Montana. The result was one of the classics of legal studies, *The Cheyenne Way* (1941). From patient listening to stories told by aged members of the tribe, they compiled what may be called a book of Cheyenne "case law." The skills of anthropologist and lawyer combined to portray a living law that had been effective for centuries but had never before been committed to writing. Six chapters elucidate the law in such fields as homicide, marriage, and property. Another five discuss methodology and conclusions.

Here we find ourselves still in the law of a primitive culture, far from the materials that our law schools take for granted. Yet our own legal institutions can be seen in embryo. We discover a central authority; though scattered for most of the year, the whole tribe assembles in the summer and the tribal chiefs and soldier chiefs meet to pass judgment on prevailing disputes. Their rulings are publicized by word of mouth and are enforced by various equivalents of our police. There is no legal profession, but the requirement that all sides to a dispute be heard seems to be well recognized.

The jural postulates show similarities to those of the Eskimo. All land is public property, and the religious view is animistic (though the spirits are more benevolent than hostile). The individual realizes himself by action, but this is shown primarily in warfare. That is, aggression is directed outwards, and murder within the tribe (or abuse of marital rights) is a serious crime.

Hoebel and Llewellyn devote their first chapter to five introductory cases. The third is reprinted below. However, before we discuss this, some remarks may be made on the first case. A modern lawyer could well ask what this case has to do with law, for the story is of heroic exploits. A father (Red Robe) mourns the loss of his two sons, killed by a neighboring tribe, and voluntarily abandons his possessions in spite of all entreaties. A chief (Two Twists) then offers vengeance by exposing his own life in a war exploit of daring beyond the call of duty.

There are many parallels to such a story, which we can imagine to have been repeated around campfires for generations. If this is "law," then it is certainly public. But can we speak of rules that form a system and apply generally?

---

7. "Lawyers ... proceed within the view permitted by the blinkers of their own society. Indeed, they help to make them.... The province of the lawyer and that of the social anthropologist are once and for all different." (Paul Bohannan, *Justice and Judgment Among the Tiv* [Oxford Univ. Press, 1968], xi.)

Perhaps we find a parallel in many of the sayings of the Sermon on the Mount (e.g., "If anyone strikes you on the right cheek, turn to him the other also."). Are such exhortations to be understood as rules that are to be taken literally? Could a society so survive? Is this the basis of our courthouse?

There are books in the Bible that plainly consist of laws (e.g., Leviticus and Deuteronomy). However, the Bible as a whole achieves its place in literature for its proposal of ideals that cannot be regarded as literal rules for all. So if law be limited to rules, then most of the Bible and much of Cheyenne tradition must be excluded. Yet do literal rules, deprived of guiding ideals, lose their spirit? The Cheyenne, in the informal state of their law, would probably see no problem here. I suggest that we should. Law schools teach the rules, and rightly so. But our law may be broader, or deeper.

Now to the case that is printed below. A contemporary lawyer will probably feel more at home, for the discussion is about explicit rules. Perhaps, though, he will notice two types (and sources) of rules and hence suggest that we distinguish two parts to the case. The first fits surprisingly well into a lawyer's categories and may be termed a "case of first impression" (one without clear precedents). Sticks-Everything-Under-His-Belt shows initiative by simply removing himself from the jurisdiction of the courts. He declares himself out of the tribe. So the court meets. They come to a decision and promulgate a clear ruling. What he did is illegal, being against the spirit of the tribe, and the penalty is ostracism, which is duly enforced. Sticks-Everything follows the camp, at a discreet distance, happy with his horse but suffering from lack of tobacco. Years pass. Then one of the chiefs, his brother-in-law, takes pity and draws attention to a clause in the ruling. Ostracism can be abolished if someone will give a Sun Dance. He will do so. And this story has a happy ending (if we ignore the unfortunate effects of tobacco after such long denial).

Then we come to the second part of the case, more challenging to us than the first. Black Horse, summoned to the Sun Dance but reluctant to expose an ugly growth on his body, appeals to the court for exemption. The court denies that it has jurisdiction in this matter and directs him to the brother-in-law. The latter at first rejects the request on the grounds of *his own* ruling, that all must attend. Black Horse counters by making *his* rule. Negotiation takes place, and eventually a settlement is achieved.

The first part of the case is not foreign to our experience, but it does raise the question how a court is to decide, when it has no precedents. No appeal can be made to the will of a legislator or to the way that previous courts tipped the balance. Can we say that the court asked, in traditional terms, what the "reasonable man" would do? Much fun has been made of this mythical figure. He does not pass easily from culture to culture. Yet, in any society, he seems to be a person well aware of the general purposes at work and of his place within them. You know, in some detail, the rules of the road. But will you drive through a red light when the road is thick with snow over ice, you are climbing a hill, and no danger is in view? If this is against the law, the author must admit his violation, though he tried to be reasonable in precarious conditions. More serious problems (not clearly answered by the written law) come with the delicate question how much force you may direct against an intruder who threatens you with something less than the loss of your own life.

We have already seen something of the dilemmas of a judge or referee. Perhaps the basic question is what exactly is being judged. It may be the best cow at an agricultural fair. Or a play in a game. Or style in figure skating. Judgment has most commonly to do with the quality of performance in meeting a complex set of anticipations. The chiefs, knowing well from detailed experience what it means to be a Cheyenne, were probably right in their estimate of illegality in the behavior of Sticks-Everything.

Yet what about Black Horse? How could he, no member of the court, dare to make a rule? The question takes us far in our assessment of law. Surely he was engaged in private negotiation rather than public legislation? Would not Judith Shklar, though approving of what he did, classify his procedures as "extralegal"?

These are questions that suppose a clear view of the limits of law. But think for a moment of what Black Horse and the brother-in-law achieved. Though they met outside the jurisdiction of the courts, they established a relationship that had nothing to do with the balance of power. We do not know who was the stronger. They accepted a relationship that was juridical without benefit of judge or jury.

Apart from the formalities of law, a settlement was attained that had the effect of law. "Interactional expectancies" were clarified; each person knew well what he could or could not do in view of the other. And it is not ridiculous to suggest that their agreement, though directed toward that particular Sun Dance, could serve as a precedent for future negotiation in analogous cases. However private our agreements, we live under pain of generalization, of anticipating "the like" in the future.

THE CHEYENNE WAY: CONFLICT AND CASE LAW IN PRIMITIVE JURISPRUDENCE
by K. N. Llewellyn and E. Adamson Hoebel

Case 3: Tribal Ostracism and Reinstatement (pp. 9–12).
Copyright © 1941 by the University of Oklahoma Press. Printed with permission.

Once, at a time when all the Cheyenne tribe was gathered together, Sticks-Everything-Under-His-Belt went out hunting buffalo alone. "I am hunting for myself," he told the people. He was implying that the rules against individual hunting did not apply to him because he was declaring himself out of the tribe—a man on his own.

All the soldier chiefs and all the tribal chiefs met in a big lodge to decide what to do in this case, since such a thing had never happened before. This was the ruling they made: no one could help Sticks-Everything-Under-His-Belt in any way, no one could give him smoke, no one could talk to him. They were cutting him off from the tribe. The chiefs declared that if anyone helped him in any way that person would have to give a Sun Dance.

When the camp moved, Sticks-Everything-Under-His-Belt moved with it, but the people would not recognize him. He was left alone and it went to his heart, so he took one of his horses (he had many) and rode out to the hilltops to mourn.

His sister's husband was a chief in the camp. This brother-in-law felt sorry for him out there mourning, with no more friends. At last he took pity on his poor brother-in-law; at last he spoke to his wife, "I feel sorry for your poor brother out there and now I am going to do something for him. Cook up all those tongues we have! Prepare a good feast!"

Then he invited the chiefs to his lodge and sent for his brother-in-law to come in. This was after several years had passed, not months.

When the chiefs had assembled, the brother-in-law spoke. "Several years ago you passed a ruling that no one could help this man. Whoever should do so you said would have to give a Sun Dance. Now is the time to take pity on him. I am going to give a Sun Dance, to bring him back in. I beg you to let him come back to the tribe, for he has suffered long enough. This Sun Dance will be a great one. I declare that every chief and all the soldiers must join in. Now I put it up to you. Shall we let my brother-in-law smoke before we eat, or after?

The chiefs all answered in accord, "*Ha-ho, ha-ho* [thank you, thank you]. We are very glad you are going to bring back this man. However, let him remember that he will be bound by whatever rules the soldiers lay down for the tribe. He may not say he is outside of them. He has been out of the tribe for a long time. If he remembers these things, he may come back."

Then they asked Sticks-Everything-Under-His-Belt whether he wanted to smoke before or after they had eaten. Without hesitation he replied, "Before," because he had craved tobacco so badly that he had split his pipe stem to suck the brown gum inside of it.

The lodge was not big enough to hold all the chiefs who had come to decide this thing, so they threw open the door, and those who could not get in sat in a circle outside. Then they filled a big pipe and when it was lighted they gave it to Sticks-Everything-Under-His-Belt. It was so long since he had had tobacco that he gulped in the smoke and fell over in a faint. As he lay there the smoke came out of his anus, he was so empty. The chiefs waited silently for him to come to again and then the pipe was passed around the circle.

When all had smoked, Sticks-Everything-Under-His-Belt talked. "From now on I am going to run with the tribe. Everything the people say, I shall stay right by it. My brother-in-law has done a great thing. He is going to punish himself in the Sun Dance to bring me back. He won't do it alone, for I am going in, too."

After a while the people were getting ready for the Sun Dance. One of the soldiers began to get worried because he had an ugly growth on his body which he did not want to reveal to the people. He was a good-looking young man named Black Horse. Black Horse went to the head chiefs asking them to let him sacrifice himself alone on the hilltops as long as the Sun Dance was in progress.

"We have nothing to say to that," they told him. "Go to the pledger. This is his Sun Dance."

Black Horse went to the brother-in-law of Sticks-Everything-Under-His-Belt, who was a brother-in-law to him as well. "Brother-in-law," he begged, "I want to be excused from going into the lodge. Can't you let me go into the hills to sacrifice myself as long as you are in there, to make my own bed?"

"No," he was rebuffed, "you know my rule is that all must be there."

"Well, brother-in-law, won't it be all right if I set up a pole on the hill and hang myself to it through my breasts? I shall hang there for the duration of the dance."

This brother-in-law of his answered him in these words, "Why didn't you take that up when all the chiefs were in the lodge? I have agreed with them that everyone must be in the lodge. I don't want to change the rule. I won't give you permission to go outside."

Then Black Horse replied, "You will not make the rules my way. Now I am going to put in a rule for everybody. Everyone in there has to swing from the pole as I do."

"No," countered the brother-in-law. "That was not mentioned in the meeting. If you want to swing from the pole, that is all right, but no one else has to unless he wishes to."

When they had the Sun Dance everyone had a good time. Black Horse was the only one on the pole, and there were so many in the lodge that there was not enough room for all to dance. Some just had to sit around inside the lodge. Though they did not dance, they starved themselves for four days. This dance took place near Sheridan, Wyoming, seven years before Custer. I was only a year old at the time, but what I have said here I was told by Elk River and others. We call this place "Where the Chiefs Starved Themselves."

FURTHER READING

Apart from the two books from which extracts were given above, varied approaches to primitive law may be found in the following:

Barton, John H., et al. *Law in Radically Different Cultures.* St. Paul: West, 1983.

Bohannan, Paul. *Justice and Judgment among the Tiv.* New York: Oxford Univ. Press, 1968.

———, ed. *African Homicide and Suicide.* Princeton, N.J.: Princeton Univ. Press, 1960.

———, ed. *Law and Warfare: Studies in the Anthropology of Conflict.* Austin, Tex.: Univ. of Texas Press, 1976.

Diamond, A. S. *The Evolution of Law and Order.* 1951. Reprint. Westport, Conn.: Greenwood Press, 1973.

———. *Primitive Law.* 2d ed. London: Watts, 1950.

Gluckman, Max. *The Judicial Process Among the Barotse.* Glencoe, Ill.: Free Press, 1955.

———. *Politics, Law, and Ritual in Tribal Society.* Oxford: Blackwell, 1965.

Krader, Lawrence, ed. *Anthropology and Early Law.* New York: Basic Books, 1966.

Maine, Henry. *Dissertations on Early Law and Custom.* 1883. Reprint. Salem, N.H.: Ayer Co., 1975.

Malinowski, B. *Crime and Custom in Savage Society.* 1926. Reprint. Westport, Conn.: Greenwood Press, 1984.

Nader, Laura, ed. *Law in Culture and Society.* Chicago: Aldine Publishing Co., 1969.

Nader, Laura, and Harry F. Todd, eds. *The Disputing Process: Law in Ten Societies.* New York: Columbia Univ. Press, 1978.

Newman, Katherine S. *Law and Economic Organization.* New York: Cambridge Univ. Press, 1983.

Pospisil, Leonard. *Anthropology of Law.* New York: Harper & Row, 1971.

———. *The Ethnology of Law.* Menlo Park, Calif.: Cummings Publishing Co., 1978.

Roberts, Simon. *Order and Dispute: An Introduction to Legal Anthropology.* New York: St. Martin's Press, 1979.

Shuchman, Philip, ed. *Cohen and Cohen's Readings in Jurisprudence and Legal Philosophy.* Boston: Little, Brown & Co., 1979, 755–833.

Wigmore, John H. *A Kaleidoscope of Justice.* Washington, D.C.: Washington Law Book Co., 1941. Reprint. Littleton, Colo.: F. B. Rothman & Co., 1983.

This is an extensive anthology of legal settlements around the world, described by the compiler as "informational entertainment."

QUESTIONS FOR DISCUSSION

1. One of Piaget's claims is that a child derives a notion of moral laws long before he can see nature in terms of purely descriptive laws. Clouds are "naughty" in obscuring the sun. Does this suggest that the legal world, far from being a late and sophisticated development, finds its roots in our earliest efforts to make sense of things? Can you contribute to this theme from your own observation of young children? Though they show a strange understanding of rules, are they at times remarkably legalistic?

2. The Eskimo postulate (or corollary) that "unproductive members of society cannot be supported" conflicts with our own postulate about the sanctity of each human life. Is this difference simply one of convention, or could some universal standards be involved? Animal herds leave injured and aged members to die. Is it a mark of humanity that we protect those who cannot help themselves? Have we passed from a purely biological world, based on relations of strength, to a legal world where rights exist apart from strength? Think, however, of the Titus Oates incident (quoted on the introductory page of this chapter). Many see his action as noble. If so, was it "legal"?

3. Do we accept the postulate that property is based finally on making or on some equivalent, such as productive use? If you think so, would you expect a judge ever to quote such a notion as a principle of law? Can you give a generalized statement of the Eskimo rule from which they derive the conclusion that, whereas you possess an escaping seal that I had harpooned, I possess the seal if a bladder float had been employed? It is interesting to find that such subtleties antedate the development of courts and of written law.

4. Would you want a situation where, as with the Eskimo headman, status depends entirely on demonstrated ability and strength? It is an ancient claim that law was manufactured by the weak to preserve an unwarranted position they had attained. Consider the related problems that come from the Eskimo failure to give clear legal status to marriage. Does one's security as a person come from self-acceptance, and this from a social acceptance that depends on the definition of legal relationships?

5. Homicide among the Eskimo takes a variety of legal forms, including the exposure of an unwanted female child to the Arctic cold, private revenge on a rival who has taken one's wife, and the community-sanctioned killing of a repeated murderer. We regard (with many protests) only the last as legal. Why? Does this suggest that a legal system is a form of contract, an agreement of the whole society to practices that would otherwise be sheer expressions of private motives? Could the Eskimo reply to our criticisms by claiming that infanticide and blood revenge also draw their legality from group approval that is given through immemorial custom?

6. The story of Red Robe and Two Twists was mentioned because Hoebel and Llewellyn saw fit to include it in a book of law. If they are correct, then would the *Iliad* and the *Odyssey* form part of Greek law? The Greeks read these as a poetic statement of ideals that bound them together as a society. Though the battlefield of Troy and the perils of Odysseus were remote, certain norms of conduct and views of what really matters were absorbed. Does this apply in any way to us? Few go to law school. Few would know where to find the statutes of our state or the ordinances of our city. Yet, to a surprising extent, we know the law. Have we taken in its "spirit" from extralegal sources? Do we correspondingly, without any reading in the books of case law, recognize the right solution to concrete cases?

7. Do the Cheyenne chiefs form a court or a legislature or both? However you reply, you will probably recognize their authority to make rules. Though their ruling in the case we read mentions a specific person, is it a general law for the tribe? Did this ruling simply impose a penalty for anyone who helped an ostracized member, or did it allow ostracism to be lifted if anyone accepted the penalty? If doubt remained on the meaning of the original rule, did the brother-in-law then seek a clarification of legislative intention or did he approach the chiefs for a further ruling? Or are such formal questions irrelevant here?

8. The chiefs deny that they have jurisdiction over Black Horse's request. There are parallels in the refusal of our own courts to rule on some disputes within a family. Then the brother-in-law and Black Horse each makes a rule and specifies it as applying to everybody. On what legal authority? Or are we too restrictive in seeking a chain of command for rules that apply to all? Suppose a business dispute. Do you simply say "I want this"? Or do you present arguments that "this" is reasonable? The courts have, by and large, followed commercial practice, the well-tried results of claim adapting to counterclaim.

9. Suppose we say that this was an instance of negotiation rather than of legal procedure. We are free to make the boundaries of law as narrow as we wish—no court, no law. But are some vital attitudes and postulates to be found on both sides of such a boundary? Black Horse and the brother-in-law did not fight it out. Each exercised forbearance, recognizing the other as a partner in a contract. Do we come close here to the basic requirement for legality, the recognition of a person as having rights that are independent of his current power? Do animals make contracts? Do they engage in a "market"?

10. Suppose that, years later, another Sun Dance is given. You refuse to take part because of a dispute over the possession of horses. Might you cite the Black Horse settlement as a precedent for whatever alternative you propose?

10. CUSTOMARY LAW

> *The dominant schools of jurisprudence examine the law they find in books to the exclusion of all other legal phenomena, because it is tacitly assumed that law must be expressed in propositions.... Customary law is held to be so unimportant that no effort is made to investigate it or to devise methods for its study.... As to the law of the family, I doubt whether there is a country in Europe where the relation between husband and wife, parents and children, or between the family and the world outside, shows much resemblance to what is written in the law books.... The only branch of law which does accurately portray life is commercial law, because this is based closely on the customary law of business transactions.... In other realms, we must distinguish the living law of what people actually do from the propositional law that is enforced in the courts.*
>
> (from Eugen Ehrlich, *Fundamental Principles of the Sociology of Law*, Munich, 1913; chapter 21)

Few forms of training involve such extensive reading as does the law. And in few is the student exposed to so great a variety of human problems. Yet he or she works at a certain remove from life. What comes through law books is a pale reflection, and often a distortion, of what actually happened before it became "a case." Ehrlich's claim, in the quotation above, is that if we are to find the law that directs what people really do, then we must look beyond the propositions of statutes and cases. The living law of the family is known to all who have grown up in a viable one. But books of family law have to do only with what is no longer a functioning family; and even in break-up situations, the participants are disturbed by the lack of perception they meet when they stand before the law.

However, this contrast between propositional law and living law, between explicit rules and tacit understandings, can be overdrawn. Every word in a ruling depends on a network of shared assumptions. And even in a well-ordered family, there are times when someone cries Let's have some rules around here!

Pre-Legal Societies?

We noticed Hoebel's hesitation in speaking of law among the Eskimos. They certainly have a system of social behavior and recognize a variety of rules that guide their conduct. But such rules were said to come from "magic and religion rather than law." Nevertheless, Hoebel studies a set of "underlying postulates of jural significance." Though these underlie what may currently be no more than the "bare-bones of the legal," they could be seen as supplying the basis for development of a clearly legal system.

Hoebel's definition of law (see p. 76 above) involves the existence of some agency that is privileged to apply physical force when rules are broken. Hence his first requirement for the growth of a more definite legal system in Eskimo societies would presumably be some extension to other realms of what he found only in the handling of repeated murderers; there alone, punishment is regularly inflicted in the name of the community. Most of us tend to think of laws in terms of official enforcement. We know our rules for driving to be *legal* when a policeman can have us fined for breaking them; we should, however, be less ready to regard the rules of etiquette as *laws* (suppose, for example, you are waiting at a side road to enter a line of crawling cars on the main road).

What other agencies might we expect if a contemporary lawyer were to be less reluctant to speak of Eskimo law? One would be some analogue to our own system of courts. This would have as its task to make the decision when rules have or have not been broken. We saw an approach to this in the procedure for eliciting confessions of tabu violations. Such "trials," however, seem to start with a presumption of guilt. We should expect a procedure better fitted to express and weigh both sides and to locate the many lines that separate legal from illegal behavior. It might, for instance, be a delicate question to decide when the killing that is allowed to redress private wrongs becomes "repeated" and hence a public crime.

A further agency would have as its task the settling of disputes between individuals (rather than adjudication on crimes). The song duels offer an interesting move in that direction, though we may wonder at Hoebel's insistence that such types of "wager" heal disputes without any claim to invoke divine judgment (or to achieve strict justice?). The Cheyenne case seems also to distinguish between the clearly legal procedure that led to ostracism and the perhaps extralegal negotiation by which Black Horse and the brother-in-law resolved their dispute. Though our own legal system recommends that disputes be settled as far as possible out of court, it is the possibility or threat of "going to law" that may have the greatest effect in bringing serious disagreements to conclusion.

The above account lists three agencies that we expect but that we find present only in germ among the Eskimo. However, discussion about what is to count as law is less concerned with the agencies involved than with the distinction between rules that are legal and those that are not. Etiquette was mentioned as an example of the latter. Most people would similarly list a range of social conventions, models of conduct, religious standards, and moral precepts as not properly belonging to the law. Why? Is it simply because such legal agents as policemen and judges happen to show no official concern in these areas? Or should we ask the further question why concern is not shown? Is this explained by the rules themselves and by their origin?

One philosopher who has given an influential answer to such questions is H. L. A. Hart.[8] He pictures a "pre-legal" society, without any legislature or courts. It is held together by what most people refer to as "custom," but which Hart prefers to call "primary rules." These are recognized by the members as obliging them to abstain from specific antisocial activities and to perform services or make contributions to the general welfare. So long as the community is small, stable, and united by common sentiment, these rules will suffice and Hart sees no reason for calling them legal rather than moral or religious.

However, development toward a more complex society will produce uncertainty about what the rules are and how they apply. Procedures are needed for identifying *valid* rules, for adapting them to changing circumstances, and for settling disputes about whether an individual has actually broken a rule. At some point, according to Hart, the society will move from the pre-legal to the legal world by supplementing the primary rules with "secondary rules." The latter are rules *about* the former. We shall expect to find a "rule of recognition" that specifies which primary rules are valid, some "rules for change" that create an agency to make new rules or adapt old ones, and some "rules of adjudication" that empower agents to sit in judgment on cases and that define procedures to be followed.[9]

This account will be expanded, and some critics will be heard, in chapter 3. But Hart does supply us with a simple way to distinguish legal rules from others. Why does a police officer stop me for traveling at 65 m.p.h. on a clear road but not for making angry gestures at a fellow driver? Not because one

---

8. What follows is drawn from H. L. A. Hart, *The Concept of Law* (New York: Oxford Univ. Press, 1960), 89–96.

9. Can an analogy be supplied from games? The origins of lacrosse were certainly customary. If we had witnessed the ways in which this was played by the Iroquois as far back as the fifteenth century, we might have spoken of primary without secondary rules. The sport is recorded in multiple varieties, allowing as many as a thousand players on each side, with goals that might be miles apart and a game lasting for several days. Europeans began to adopt lacrosse in Canada around 1840, and their legal mentality, with its notions of hierarchical order, rapidly led to some equivalent (within games) of a "rule of recognition." Rule books were written to define which of the many variants were valid, and associations were created with authority to approve changes and to oversee what could then be called an organized sport.

action is necessarily more dangerous than the other, but because one rule has a "legal pedigree" and the other has not. Speed limits are rules that were made by legislators who are empowered to do this by other rules that derive finally from some master rule. The rules of politeness are simply "in the air": though of considerable importance for the functioning of a community, their authority cannot be traced to any constitution or other rule of recognition.

Hart allows for an immense variety in the ways a society may establish its secondary rules. A primitive version of a rule of recognition could state that only whatever is inscribed on this tablet or written in that book is law. Or we may find a complex system such as that of England, where laws issue from "the queen in Parliament" according to an unwritten constitution. But Hart's claim is that we can, by tracing primary rules to secondary rules, always distinguish the legal from the extralegal.

It is evident that this account would meet with some opposition from Eugen Ehrlich. He would not brand a primitive society, having only customary practices, as pre-legal. And he directs us, even in our own highly developed society, to look beyond statutes and judicial decisions to a living law that lacks the clear pedigree demanded by Hart.

Perhaps the most interesting example is commercial law. Much of this, when first appearing in legal opinions, was regarded as *already* being part of the law because it belonged to customary practice. Hart concedes, in view of this, that some customs might count as law even before officially recognized by the courts.[10] However, the question is *why* these particular customs do so count and others do not. If the reply is that the community already regards a custom as *legally* binding, then the point of tracing pedigree to a rule of recognition seems threatened or lost.[11]

On Not Laying Down the Law

> Deepy embedded traditional ways of carrying out state policy—or not carrying it out—are often tougher and truer law than the dead words of the written text.
>
> (Justice Frankfurter, in Poe v. Ullman, 1961, 367 U.S. 497, 81 S.Ct. 1752)

It may be helpful to replace sharp distinctions with a more relaxed view of law as a spectrum that runs from the highly informal to the very formal. At the left side we should place institutions such as the family and spontaneous associations, where rules are kept to a minimum and members know what to expect of each other through the ideals they share but never put into words. At the right extreme we should set "total" institutions (those that legislate for all

---

10. Hart, *The Concept of Law*, 45–46.
11. For a more detailed statement of this criticism, see: Ronald Dworkin, *Taking Rights Seriously* (Cambridge: Harvard Univ. Press, 1977), 41–43.

aspects of a person's life), such as prisons, where scarcely any assumptions are made about a shared spirit, and law is spelled out in explicit rules that apply even to the most trivial behavior. Locating other groups of people and branches of law between the extremes would raise many questions. If Ehrlich is correct in seeing commercial law as an accurate reflection of the bargaining that constitutes the market, then we should be approaching the left side of the spectrum; but what can be more formal than a commercial contract? Criminal statutes would be well to the right of the cases of civil law; we require that there be a written law before a crime can be charged, and the police are now directed by explicit rules as they proceed to an arrest. Constitutional law is an interesting mixture of highly formal provisions and deliberate "open-texture."

Evidently the lawyer, the judge, and the lawgiver face a task that demands considerable sensitivity. No one way of seeing law is enough, even if attention is confined to one field of law. There are situations where written rules are demanded, as detailed and unambiguous as possible. In others, Ehrlich's warnings about propositional law pertain, and awareness is needed of understandings that challenge precise statement.

Ehrlich justly claims that writings about law concentrate on the formal side of the spectrum. If "customary law" is his term for the informal side, then this gets little serious examination. The reason is obvious. Writing builds most easily on other writing. Custom may guide much of what we do, but it comes to the attention of the lawyer only when claimed or challenged in a court, by which time we are firmly engaged in propositional law. Indeed, the title "customary law" is sometimes rejected as a contradiction in terms.

If one author chooses to limit law to what involves a clearly developed court system, so be it. Then the Eskimos have no law, and the Cheyenne may also be excluded. But it is still important to ask what common elements belong on both sides of the fence; if Eskimos are without law, they nevertheless accept norms of conduct and interact with each other in ways that are strangely similar to those of legal societies. Though the dividing line is drawn by some to the right of center on our spectrum, it may be of interest to look leftward and ask what is there that still affects the world of legal propositions where we are at home.

When you are in a position of authority, you are likely to find yourself at times saying that you refuse to lay down the law on some point at issue. Possibly what you fear is that your ruling will be generalized in a way that you are at present unprepared to allow. You know that your proposition or permission is correct in the circumstances. However, you do not want it to be put into writing and quoted as a precedent for future cases. Though timeless truth may be an ideal, you have not achieved it here.

Do judges show a similar reluctance? They suffer the burden of being obliged to give a ruling on each case put before them. Yet they often show care in selecting language that will move their decision to the right or to the left on the spectrum. An example is supplied in this country by two cases that reached the Supreme Court and dealt with negligence claimed of a driver whose vehicle was struck by a train at a grade crossing. In one, Justice Holmes gave this ruling:

> If a driver cannot be sure otherwise whether a train is dangerously near he must stop and get out of his vehicle, although obviously he will not often be required to do more than to stop and look.[12]

Seven years later, Justice Cardozo commented in his opinion:

> Standards of prudent conduct are declared at times by courts, but they are taken over from the facts of life. To get out of a vehicle and reconnoitre is an uncommon precaution, as everyday experience informs us. Besides being uncommon, it is very likely to be futile, and sometimes even dangerous.... [Caution is needed] in framing standards of behavior that amount to rules of law. The need is the more urgent when there is no background of experience out of which the standards have emerged. They are then, not the natural flowerings of behavior in its customary forms, but rules artificially developed, and imposed from without.[13]

Here Cardozo refuses to lay down the law, in the form of a precise rule, on what a driver should do in such conditions. He appeals rather to the nebulous but genuine "background of experience" we have as drivers, to "behavior in its customary forms." At the wheel, you probably show great skill and obey norms of safety in turning left against oncoming traffic. Could you legislate for all drivers in this? Doubtless you could join the driving instructor in giving some advice to the beginner. But in time he will cease to be a beginner. As a passenger, I should feel safer with a driver who relies on the inarticulate norms of experience than with one who still follows rules of thumb literally.

The example is taken from traffic law, an area where we may think rules should be precise and unambiguous. Yet even in judicial opinions on traffic accidents, we find frequent recourse to such weasel words as "due care" and "reasonable conduct." I should protest if a policeman hauled me into court for nothing more specific than violating customary standards of prudence. Yet what about the very basic rule of keeping to whichever side of the road your country has prescribed? Suppose a statute has ordained that pedestrians walk on the left side of a road, thereby facing oncoming traffic. You know from experience, however, that almost all Sunday evening traffic on a certain road is in a direction opposite to the one in which you are walking. Might it be reasonable for you to walk on the right side rather than the left? In a case from the New York Court of Appeals, it was held that a pedestrian was not negligent in so acting when struck by one of the few cars coming from behind.[14] The statute, it

---

12. Baltimore & Ohio R.R. Co. v. Goodman (1927): 275 U.S. 66, 48 Sup.Ct. 24.
13. Pokora v. Wabash Ry. Co. (1934): 292 U.S. 98, 54 Sup.Ct. 580.
14. Tedla v. Ellman (1939): 280 N.Y. 124, 19 N.E.2d 987.

was maintained, merely codifies custom and does not remove the exceptions that custom and good sense have supported.

A similar turn from propositional law to common understandings is shown in an earlier New York case.[15] Inadequate maintenance by the New York Central Railroad caused overhead electric wires to fall at a point where the local youths had set up a diving board over the Harlem River. Harvey Hynes, standing on this board, was killed. But the railroad was held free of liability on the grounds that the diving board was technically an extension of their property and Hynes was thus a trespasser, though over public waters. The majority opinion of the court of appeals, reversing this decision, was written by Cardozo. "This case" he said, "is a striking instance of the dangers of a jurisprudence of conceptions, the extension of a maxim or a definition with relentless disregard of consequences to a dryly logical extreme.... Rights and duties in systems of living law are not built upon such quicksands." The diving board had been so used for more than five years without protest. The question what Hynes was doing is not to be answered from the law books but rather from an investigation of customary perceptions. How do people see and classify other people? Here he was no trespasser but a lad engaged in the enjoyment of the public waters. "The use of the springboard was not an abandonment of his rights as a bather. It was a mere by-play, an incident, subordinate and ancillary to the execution of his primary purpose."

Cardozo's book entitled *The Nature of the Judicial Process* (New Haven: Yale Univ. Press, 1921) is a helpful antidote to the view that judges draw their conclusions by deduction from the propositions of law. We should not forget that much of what a judge does proceeds from the unformulated customs of his own profession:

> He must learn for himself as he gains the sense of fitness and proportion that comes with years of habitude in the practice of an art. Even within the gaps, restrictions not easy to define, but felt, however impalpable they may be, by every judge and lawyer, hedge and circumscribe his action. They are established by the traditions of the centuries, by the example of other judges, his predecessors and his colleagues, by the collective judgment of the profession, and by the duty of adherence to the pervading spirit of the law (p. 114).

In the examples above, we have looked for custom as it appears in the words of case law, correcting abstract propositions but being raised thereby to the level of propositions itself. Harvey Hynes is now a case. What can be said of custom altogether *outside* adjudication? Here we face the problem of putting into words what seems to defy words. Perhaps a negative strategy is best. How does propositional law make a fool of itself when it strays too far into the realms of living law?

---

15. Hynes v. New York Central R. Co. (1921): 231 N.Y. 229, 131 N.E. 898.

One example will have to do. The paradigm we have taken for customary law is the family. The courts have shown a reluctance to apply their formalities to rule on the obligations of husband to wife or parents to children: "Judicial inquiry into matters of that character would be fraught with irreparable mischief."[16] However, in recent generations the tacit assumptions behind earlier marriages have been threatened, and some partners have turned to the courts in an effort to draw support from more formal arrangements. Brief reference may be made to one such "reconciliation agreement."[17] A six-page document is incorporated in a court order that renders either party, in violating the terms, liable to be found in contempt of court. With embarrassing detail, the document lists what the husband and wife stipulate in regard to their interests and social activities, tolerance of friends and relatives, nagging and sarcastic remarks, grievances and the silent treatment, affection and lovemaking. The tone of voice is regulated, a time limit is set for grudges, and excuses from sexual intercourse are duly classified as reasonable or not.

Fun should not be made of such a document where the intent is sincere and, it is hoped, the outcome was successful. Yet the temptation to do so is significant. Most jokes are based on some confusion in language-games. And the formality of this document seems more appropriate to institutions at the right extreme of the legal spectrum than to the intimacy and indefinability of the left.

Each of us started as an infant, and our initial awareness of social practices came within the family. Though we may now decline to call these "law," our understanding of enacted law and case law draws upon such sources. Mother and infant develop a complex set of "interactional expectancies" without written words. The roles of mother and father are distinguished for the child, and siblings are incorporated into the society. The complex rules of language are mastered without benefit of formal lessons in grammar. Household duties are allocated without statutes, and adaptability is all the greater to meet unforeseen contingencies. Life is organized by the interplay of affections and through rituals of celebration rather than by any calculation of conformity and violation.

Each group on the spectrum of law is held together by some principles of association. These are many, and it is sensitivity to their variety that makes for skill in the art of law. At one extreme the principles have to do directly with the purposes of the group. Whether this be a family or a small club or possibly an Indian tribe, all members are aware "in their bones" of what favors or threatens their shared ideals. The written expression of norms is not merely unnecessary but destructive. However, the complexity and impersonality of a group leads toward different principles. Purposes are still there (else why the group?), but these are no longer evident and a need arises for formal structures of association. Since we do not know intuitively what is mine and thine, we have to define this, as we do our rights and responsibilities. Families do not expel members,

---

16. Miller v. Miller (1889): 78 Iowa 177, 42 N.W. 641.
17. Reprinted in James B. White, *The Legal Imagination* (Boston: Little, Brown & Co., 1973), 558–64.

but a club that grows in size will have to put on paper its criteria for membership. And a state will develop its criminal law, with statutes and courts and prisons.

These are generalities, and they are rather obvious. But neglect of them can lead to both confusion and clumsiness. As we pass in life from the informal sources of law to its formal expressions, we forget our origins at risk of pain and disharmony. Instead of developing legality, we produce a creeping legalism.[18]

The Example of China

It is in small groups that custom seems at home; our examples so far have had to do with assumptions about the correct way to walk on a local road, the privileges of neighborhood youths at play, the ownership of animals and weapons on a hunting exploit. Can we speak about the customary law of a large group? Or does it follow that, as central authority appears, law must assume the formality of explicit statement and definite institutions? We saw some beginnings of this change as we turned from the unorganized Eskimo village to the council of Cheyenne chiefs.

If terminology helps, we are asking about the differences and oppositions between *customary* law and *bureaucratic* law.[19] The former consists of tacit standards that people find spontaneously in their social roles and rituals; they know without reflection what is the right way of doing things and what simply is not done. Bureaucratic law, however, is consciously made, systematized, and enforced by officials who are in a position to achieve this. If we are to illustrate the contrast, and ask about the possible existence of both forms together, we need distance to gain perspective. So the following remarks are about some manifestations of these two forms of law in ancient China.

The earliest political organization in China has been called feudal, since it bears interesting resemblances to our own Middle Ages. From the twelfth to the third century B.C., the country was divided into hundreds of local fiefdoms, united by no effective authority. Social structure revealed a class of hereditary nobles at one extreme and landless serfs at the other. In between were the *shih* (gentlemen) who served the lords as stewards, sheriffs, and warriors. There was no written law, but each rank understood its standards of proper behavior, regulating what was to be done in various circumstances. The individual recognized his position in society and what was expected of him. He knew this without published rules, and the only official sources to which he could point were collections of moral anecdotes. Evidently such norms met with violations. But these were not made in the light of claims to alternative systems or of

---

18. See Lon Fuller's contribution to *Voluntary Associations* (Nomos XI), eds. Pennock, J. Roland, and John W. Chapman, New York: Lieber-Atherton, 1969.

19. For a discussion of these terms, and a general account of the two approaches to law, see: Roberto Mangabeira Unger, *Law in Modern Society* (New York: Free Press, 1976), 48–52, 58–66, 127–33.

higher principles applying to all people. In brief, feudal China shows an almost pure form of customary law.

By 221 B.C., however, China had become a unified imperial state. The process took about three centuries of warfare in which feudal units gradually absorbed each other. They fell in number to seven and grew correspondingly in size and in difficulty of administration. The shared values and assumptions of the feudal period were largely destroyed, and a replacement was sought for custom. It is here that the intermediary class of the *shih* came into prominence. They offered themselves to the ruling princes as advisers, as experts in ways to govern where the old foundations had gone. Such officials assumed control through their ability to locate and manage the centers of power. There are parallels with the Sophists in ancient Greece.

At this time an important terminological distinction appeared. The old norms that organized the society of feudal China were called *li* (which some today translate as "natural law"). The new controlling rules were called *fa* (translated by some as "positive law"). These were directives that imposed policies with no evident regard for traditional norms. Bureaucratic law took over from customary law, and there was a dramatic movement rightward on the legal spectrum. What served the current needs of the prince was formulated publicly and enforced by the measures he controlled.

Law passed from a complex network of assumed values to a codified rulebook. We find similarities with the rise of nations in the West. But our own experience was less dramatic. The Sophists had been met by Plato. Expediency was subordinated to the limitations set by universal norms of reason. In China, however, written law was seen as a product of the will of those who happened to have the power to enforce it. There were no courts, no legal profession, no form of legal reasoning that could challenge managerial direction.

We shall later find grounds to ask whether government by directive does not exceed the natural (rather than conventional) bounds of law. If I show my greater strength and command you to hand over what I want, then you may say you were obliged to do so. But did you have a legal obligation?[20] Are we held to some distinction between law and the sheer administration of policy decisions? Is the government a "gunman writ large"?

Such questions come from a later age and a different culture. Terminology, or prudence, served to hide them in ancient China. The *fa* were often promulgated in the language of the *li*. However, we should not ignore the giant step that had been taken, from a view of law as *found* to one in which individuals *make* it. Law does create social order, but this insight appeared in China in its most threatening form, where power used law without the restraints of generality.

The question whether law is the product of individual will or of universal reason remains with us today. It is rash to impose our own statements on a

---

20. This distinction, to be discussed in section 18 below, forms an important part of H.L.A. Hart's book, *The Concept of Law*.

distant time and society. Yet we may end with some remarks on a dispute that dominated the early years of imperial China. Though the first emperor relied on the *fa*, there was soon a strong and lasting reaction in favor of the *li*. Those who supported social control through positive law were called *legalists (fa chia)*. Their opponents drew support from the teachings of Confucius (551–479 B.C.). The doctrines of this obscure keeper of the granary and supervisor of flocks were brought to prominence and became the basis of one of the world religions. Confucianism guided China to the present century and formed the mainstay of a legal tradition that is the longest of any enduring political community in the world.

In its simplest terms, the debate was whether bureaucratic law should be expanded with the centralization of power in an emperor, or whether there should be a return to customary law and to its informal basis for social order. The legalists saw man as an insatiable individual, enslaved by passions of pride, envy, and greed; order can be secured only by the clear but external directives of a powerful ruler.[21] The Confucianists claimed that order is internal and rules are a form of self-legislation. Admittedly, we do respond to the *fa* of superior power. But these touch only the symptoms of our discontent. External conformity to rules is no more than a palliative for social problems. The state is distant, the family is immediate. If we pay our taxes for proper reasons, it is not because the tax collector is knocking at the door but because we have learned from our primary relationships a true sense of the laws by which one person is harmonized with others.

There is much in Confucianism that means little to us in the West. We are unlikely to be inspired by the claim that the harmony of passions in our own person, or of people in society, should reflect the order of heaven and earth. Astronomy, for us, is a descriptive rather than a normative science. Yet our distinctions may be contrived and we may do violence to our earliest perceptions. The basic question, once again, is how we create order out of chaos. There is no simple answer. But the Confucianist is clear in his reply that order is self-imposed, that it comes from our primary encounter with other people and things rather than from the will of an external legislator or manager.

These, again, are generalities and we should ask for their historical result. The Confucianists won their debate with the legalists and supplied a basis for the Chinese attitude toward law that has lasted for at least two thousand years. Whether the advent of Communist China has contradicted or reinforced this long tradition is a fascinating question that goes far beyond our present one.

Following the Revolution of 1911, the Chinese adopted a series of legal codes based on Western models and on the Western tradition. To the outsider, Chinese law became almost European. But not to the men and women who lived under it. They sought their notion of social order and justice from more traditional springs. Courts were established, yet the legal profession never

---

21. Those familiar with the theories of the philosopher, Thomas Hobbes, may see a parallel.

flourished. Lawyers were regarded as the imposition of an alien spirit. Chinese jurisprudence is almost nonexistent. A popular maxim states that "of ten reasons by which a judge may decide a case in court, nine are unknown to the person submitted to the court." We read with no little sympathy. And perhaps we see a common problem in the way that propositional law has taken over from living law.

Some Western writers have turned to the Chinese legal experience for suggestions of how justice can be fulfilled in equity.[22] Litigation, as the claim to a day in court and the hope for a legal victory, is despised in China. There, the hope is that disputes be dissolved through conciliation rather than resolved by one party winning over the other. Neither side should lose face. Mediation takes a little from each rather than satisfying some logical but impersonal notions of right.

> If, in some exceptional cases, one did go before the courts, the Chinese judges still decided according to the standards set by Confucius rather than by an application of the rules of written law. They would, for example, refuse to evict a poor tenant who had committed no fault if the landlord were well-off and not in need of the premises; they granted delays to borrowers in embarrassed circumstances if their creditors were rich. And, as feared, the enactment of new codes resulted in an increased number of trials and this, to the Chinese, was a sign of decadence. Even the most advanced thinkers considered a return to the principles of Confucius to be desirable.[23]

FURTHER READING

For the nature and origin of custom, see Sir Carleton Kemp Allen: *Law in the Making* (7th ed., New York: Oxford Univ. Press, 1964), 67–111.

Some legal anthologies give a variety of extracts on customary law; for example, John H. Barton, *Law in Radically Different Cultures* (St. Paul: West, 1983); Stephen D. Ford, *The American Legal System* (St. Paul: West, 1974), 1–27; Jerome Hall, *Readings in Jurisprudence* (Indianapolis: Bobbs-Merrill, 1938), 875–948.

For Chinese law, see the following:

Bodde, Derk, and Clarence Morris. *Law in Imperial China.* Philadelphia: Univ. of Pennsylvania Press, 1973.
Chen, Philip M. *Law and Justice: The Legal System in China.* Port Washington, N.Y.: Dunellen Press, 1973.
Cohen, Jerome A., ed. *Essays on China's Legal Tradition.* Princeton, N.J.: Princeton Univ. Press, 1980.
David, René. *Major Legal Systems in the World Today.* New York: Free Press, 1978, 477–91.
Kim, Hyung I. *Fundamental Legal Concepts of China and the West.* Port Washington, N.Y.: Kennikat Press, 1981.
Li, Victor H. *Law Without Lawyers.* Stanford, Calif.: Stanford Univ. Press, 1977.

---

22. See, for example: Jerome Frank, *Courts on Trial* (Princeton, N.J.: Princeton Univ. Press, 1949), 381–83.
23. René David, *Major Legal Systems in the World Today* (New York: Free Press, 1978), 483–84.

Terrill, Ross, ed. *The China Difference.* New York: Harper & Row, 1979.
Unger, R. M. *Law in Modern Society.* New York: Free Press, 1976, 86–109.

QUESTIONS FOR DISCUSSION

1. A school or college illustrates a broad legal spectrum. There are formal rules for academic and personal conduct, but customary law is also at work in interesting ways. Think of examples and ask how Eugen Ehrlich would find the "living law." For instance, you notice cheating during a test. What do you do about it, if anything? From what sources do you draw guidance?

2. Suppose you are appointed dean of students. All students receive a handbook that contains rules of conduct. Are there some areas of your concern where you might want to make the published rules more detailed? Others where you would decide to put the rules in less precise form?

3. Cardozo held that explicit rules, rather than being "imposed on us from outside," should be "the natural flowerings of behavior in its customary forms." Take as an example the often delicate problem of driving in a parking lot without marked lanes. All goes well for many years in the lot of a shopping plaza. Then a series of accidents occur and you are asked to mark lanes and post signs. How, following Cardozo's suggestion, could you do this either well or badly?

4. If you have ever driven through various countries abroad, you will be aware that a reading of the laws is not enough. Also important is an understanding of various driving temperaments and of diverse attitudes toward the enacted law. Comment on this in terms of the claim that law is "a series of interactional expectancies." Or, if you have no such experience of driving, think of similar examples. A simple one has to do with the etiquette of talking to another person. What is the right distance? Could the "hands on" attitude of some nations verge upon "assault" in the law books of our own?

5. "In the absence of official law and its agencies, the early gold miners abided by unwritten understandings of considerable complexity. If you claimed a ravine as your site of operation, you had only to leave a pick or shovel to secure immunity from theft and trespass." The picture may be rather idealistic, but was the frontier lawless before the sheriff appeared?

6. Can the complaints of Judith Shklar against legalism (section 7) be reinterpreted if a broader spectrum of law than the one she allows be accepted? Suppose legal training were less exclusively occupied with propositional law? Suppose the courts, in resolving disputes, were less concerned to quote rules and more open to the possibility that legal relationships precede what legislators and judges write? One lawyer remarked that his greatest successes in settling business conflicts came when he was able to persuade the parties to ignore the written rules and recover some sense of mutual trust.

7. What happened in ancient China is remote from our experience, but the dispute between *fa* and *li*, between legalist and Confucianist, may still be with us. Do you, for example, find it suggestive that a labor union can express its discontent by ordering its members to "work to rule" (cause a slowdown through punctilious observance of even the slightest regulation)? Is this fidelity to law? Or is it promoting the *fa* to an extent that ridicules the law?

8. What is your opinion of a court-backed reconciliation agreement as a remedy for marital problems? Some relief may be found, as for example in clarifying financial procedures and responsibilities. But do you suspect that the general direction, from *li* to *fa*, is wrong? Why are explicit rules so foreign in defining the relationship between husband and wife? Try writing some. Law may be involved in establishing even such intimate roles. Yet is this the law of formal rules? Or should you, as counselor, try to liberate the parties from such dependence, to break up formalized conceptions, and to cultivate an open relationship of mutual respect in face of the unknown and indefinable?

9. Do you see parallels to the Chinese experience in our own disenchantment with political solutions (resolving deep-seated questions through legislation)? When we find a wrong, we turn to

Congress to heal it. What can this strangely assorted body do? Something. Yet does a new law get to the heart of the problem or merely play with the symptoms? Consider legislation on taxes, on drugs, on abortion.

10. Can you interpret Professor Coons's comments on legalism (section 7) as advocating an extension of law from *fa* to *li*? Does his opposition to the "winner takes all" notion of court proceedings parallel the Chinese rejection of adjudication in favor of conciliation and mediation? When is a dispute "settled"?

11. THE DEVELOPMENT OF LEGALITY

> *There, under the Tree of Justice, was the Image of Perfection, seated on a stool, with one indigo soldier to his right bearing high the sword of State and another to his left holding over his head one of the Imamic umbrellas. Before him sat cross-legged on the ground a scribe, and around him was a crowd of people of every rank and class, in turbans and shawls of all colors as well as in rags, waiting to be heard. And everyone was heard. Quietly, the pristine scene rolled before my eye and to the satisfaction, evidently, of the Imam and the people.... More than once I have seen the Imam sitting for one or two hours at a stretch, without once raising his voice. Attentively, patiently, cheerfully, compassionately, he heard and judged.*[24]

Arabian judges were called *kadis*, and their procedure gave birth to a popular mythology of the ideal judge who discriminates intuitively between innocent and guilty and shows great subtlety to solve the case and edify the multitude. The *Book of the Thousand Nights* contains such tales. In the Bible, Solomon's wisdom in revealing the true mother of a child is well known (1 Kings 3). There is a close parallel in Chinese literature, which also abounds in stories of the shrewd judge who reads hearts and gives justice without a formal system of proof. In medieval Europe, Louis IX of France was admired for his dispensing of kadi justice under an oak tree at Vincennes.

Rudyard Kipling was familiar with this version of law but brought to it the Westerner's evident hesitation: "The king may be pleased and raise the speaker to honour for that very bluntness of speech which three minutes later brings a too imitative petitioner to the edge of the ever-ready blade."[25] History shows some development of the legal process. All may not be gain, but if we are to estimate profit and loss or even to understand what is sought under the name of legality, we need some rough notion of the stages through which we have come.

---

24. From Ameen Rihani, *Arabian Peak and Desert* (Boston: Houghton Mifflin Co., 1930), 89; quoted by J. H. Wigmore in *A Kaleidoscope of Justice* (Washington, D.C.: Washington Law Book Co., 1941), 239–40.
25. From *The Ameer's Homily*, quoted by Roscoe Pound in *Jurisprudence* (St. Paul: West, 1959), 2: 355n.

The Stages of Law

Charles Darwin, perhaps more than any other, impressed upon English speakers the task of explaining in terms of development. An animal or plant sums up the stages through which its ancestors have passed. As humans, we know through biography.

Sir Henry Maine was a professor of law at Cambridge and at Oxford. He was born only a dozen years after Darwin and brought to legal studies the same imperative to understand the present through an investigation of the long journey that led there. His book entitled *Ancient Law* (1861) had an influence in legal scholarship comparable to that of Darwin's *Origin of Species* (1859) in science. Maine's factual basis was limited, but legal anthropology is to this day far short of the agreement shown in biology. There is no consensus on how it was that early law developed, if indeed any uniform pattern is to be found. Maine had at least the benefit of a simple vision, and this may be worth recounting if warnings are given of the need for qualification.

One parallel with biology can be mentioned at the beginning. The notion of individuality grows as the story proceeds; our topic in the early stages of animal species may be the colony rather than the particular. So, with law, it is only in the developed forms that the conflicts and crimes and rights and duties are normally taken to be of one individual in regard to another.

> Society in primitive times was not what it is assumed to be at present, a collection of individuals, [but rather] an aggregation of families.... [Such] corporations never die, and accordingly primitive law considers the ... patriarchal or family groups as perpetual and indistinguishable.... If the community sins, its guilt is much more than the sum of the offences committed by its members; the crime is a corporate act.[26]

The development of the subject in law from a family or tribe to an individual parallels another key theme in Maine's analysis, the passage from law as *found* to law as *made*. Customs come to us from the social air we breathe. We discover them, and no one could say I hereby create a new custom. The notion that rules are made by an individual, whether he be an Indian warrior or a monarch, is an innovation that supposes a long history.

The first two of Maine's ten chapters outline the principal stages that he found in the development of law. We need not worry whether he claimed that each culture passed through them in strict sequence. They may perhaps be interpreted as logical stages, vaguely historical components in the complex notion we have today of law.

Accounts of the beginning are especially precarious, and Maine says little here. Do animals have law? At least they have a complex instinctual life that leads to regular behavior. So, we may suppose, at our own origins we followed

---

26. *Ancient Law* (London: Oxford Univ. Press, World's Classics Edition, 1931), 104–5.

regular procedures; this is the way we hunt game, make fire, propitiate the spirits. Individuality, and hence deviance, had not entered. There was as yet no distinction between *is* and *ought*. If we want a term, we may speak of **habit**. Here we have a "stage" only in the sense of a basis for the development of law.

With the stage of **custom** Maine is within what we have described as the spectrum of legality. Alternative ways of acting have appeared, at least as possibilities. The sheer habit of taking a regular day of rest from work in the fields has become a tribal practice with the force of an *ought*. The question of violating it (in obedience to some other imperative?) has at least occurred.

The third stage is a critical step. It comes with the introduction of writing, and Maine arrived at his own field of expertise, Greece and Rome. This is the move to **codification**. Our prejudice for written law should not blind us. An oral tradition can be more public than a written one, and no less permanent; what is promulgated around the campfire can be hidden in the library. But the discipline of writing gave to legality the requirement of commentary and the ideal of a system. Granted that work is forbidden on certain days, what exactly is work and what exceptions may be legitimate? Does a journey count as work? If so, how far is a journey?

The fourth stage is that of **legal fictions**. This is less easy to identify in time, but for Maine the change is vital. He begins his second chapter by remarking that even codification was seen merely as a dutiful recording of what already existed. However, from that point, the notion of *making* law appears, surreptitiously and then with increasing openness. A legal fiction is a device for making a new law under cover of retaining an old one. Maine lists the adoption of a child as his prime example: what is not biologically a family becomes one legally. Here, the expansion of law is certainly salutary; an adopted child can be as "really" a family member as any other, thanks to the lawyer rather than the doctor. We may or may not be so happy about modern corporations having residence in Delaware though their factories are elsewhere. And if we continue our prosaic example, I can now make a lengthy journey on a holy day by repeatedly pausing to establish a temporary residence.

The next stage is more radical. We appeal beyond all the laws we find in our experience to some **transcendent law**. Maine had in mind especially the derivation of a *ius gentium* (law of all peoples) by the Romans in order to supply grounds for settling disputes that crossed the boundaries of the many nations in their empire. The motive may have been largely commercial, but under the influence of Greek thought this notion became a basis for altering our law by adapting it to the "real" law (that may never have existed adequately in any legal system). Is this a blatantly idealistic changing of the law? Or is this still a discovery of law, invoking the philosopher as well as the legal practitioner? The question remains with us.

Of the final stage, that of **legislation**, little need be said. We are all too familiar with it, to the extent that some will regard as law only that which has been enacted by a legislature. Law this certainly is, but law with a history. What

Maine asks us to remember is that legislation appeared only at the end of a long development. We know today that we make law. But we do not do so in the sense that I make some resolution for my personal behavior. The making of a particular law cannot, without violence, be divorced from the finding of legal guidelines that stretch back to the discovery of norms in custom.

This needs illustration. Suppose we take the simplest case of legislation, where rules are made by a chief or monarch who holds power in his hands. He may order the death of a rival. This, however, can be called legislation only if he promulgates rules that define treason and make it a capital offense. We may think this just as much a sheer exercise of power as giving the command to kill. Yet there are vital differences. The existence of a rule depends on its acceptance as *legally* made. The criterion is complex but it takes us beyond the words of the king and back to earlier stages of law. The notion of treason has deep roots in customary law. The king can no more conjure it out of his own will than he can thus construct the idea of marriage or of property.

So what? The rival is as dead at the hands of law as he would have been through a sheer command. However, we noticed that even the Eskimos make a sharp distinction here. And we must recognize at least one thing that the king cannot enforce as a command, namely what happens in the realm after his death. The events may of course be lawless, a sheer struggle for power. But if we speak of succession, we talk of a complex notion that draws from all stages of law. And there are fascinating questions that test the legal mind, primitive as well as advanced. Suppose a lawless takeover is achieved, and a few years later the legal succession is reestablished. What now is the legal status of arrangements created during the interregnum? The example is not entirely fanciful, as the German courts can tell us from many delicate cases with which they were presented after the death of Hitler.

Anarchy and Despotism

> First came the Golden Age, when uncorrupted reason was the guide. Freely man lived, unforced by law or fear of trial. No harsh decrees were written on tablets of bronze. No suppliant throng scanned in awe the face of a judge. No courts there were, and harmony prevailed.
>
> (Ovid *Metamorphoses*, I, lines 89–93)

The Roman poet repeats an ancient theme: human origins lie in an age free from the sin and suffering that followed some fall from grace. What is of significance for us is that he identifies law with the fall and holds it was absent in the paradise before.

Here we confront again the question of defining law. A definition, as the etymology of the word indicates, sets a limit. This limit may be purely conventional, a matter of the speaker's choice in the way he uses words. If my definition of science excludes psychiatry, I am giving expression to my preference for the highly mathematical form of objectivity that is found in physics. However, it may also be claimed that the limit set by a definition follows from the topic itself rather than from my own decision about a helpful use of words. Those who speak of the nature of law are likely to be making such a claim for the definition they propose.

Discussion of human life before law, or without law, evidently raises the question how law is defined and which of the above two types of definition is maintained. Is the dispute similar to an argument whether a bicycle is a vehicle? This is far from irrelevant if I have been fined by a policeman for riding one in a park where vehicles are banned. Must vehicles be self-propelled? My wallet may suffer from the decision, but no one will detect a metaphysical problem here—vehicles are conventionally defined.

Or is the dispute over the limits of law similar to current controversies whether a human fetus is a person? Some say that this delicate question is also a matter of semantics and that legal arguments over abortion are asking little more than how those who wrote a constitution were using words. Others hold that much more is involved, having to do with the nature of a person. Could talk of "a fetus that is not a person" be a contradiction in terms, stemming from what really exists, in itself?

Notice that the first dispute is about things, the second about persons. Things are evidently what we make of them through the purposes we happen to impose. An object (ashtray, car, mountain) is what it is for a subject. But what about a subject? There is something odd in talk of a "thing in itself." Things have no self to be in. Yet we certainly talk about a person in himself or herself.

Law may seem to fall in the latter category: it concerns persons, and things only through such personal relations as possession. I can make a bicycle that is not a bicycle; if I adapt one for exercising while stationary, I thereby remove it from the definition I have assigned of a "two-wheeled machine that is pedaled to move from one place to another." But suppose I accuse a legislator of making a law that is not really a law? Some commentators will see no difference from the first example. Others hold that more could be involved here than my tastes in language. Despots have created statutes and secured court decisions that violated the nature of law and hence imposed no legal obligation, whatever the police did to enforce the despot's will.

What about Ovid? He joins a lengthy tradition by conceiving a golden age without law. We are familiar with this idea from Jewish and Christian sources: "Sin was not counted where there was no law" (Romans 5:13). In our age, it is the future that dominates our myths. The nineteenth century produced accounts of law as belonging to an ugly past and present; its abolition is our goal for the future. Godwin taught this in England, Bakunin and Kropotkin in Russia. Tolstoy inherited their anarchist ideals and tried, with little success, to establish communities that would live by the gospel of love rather than by the dictates of law. This was the setting in which Karl Marx developed his own intense thoughts on the eventual abolition of a coercive state and on the inevitable "withering away of law."

If such views be seen as a form of anarchism, then we must say that there is something of the anarchist in all of us. We hope to exclude the dark side of law, all that we have described as legalism. But does this mean excluding law as such? Again, the question is one of definitions. And again, we must ask whether these are purely conventional. Ovid identifies law with force, fear, and adjudication; it must also be written on tablets of bronze or in statutes and casebooks. He clearly excludes custom from law; the golden age without law was one of "uncorrupted reason," not merely the animal-like "habit" that Maine sets prior to custom.

Maine's version of the many stages of law involves oversimplification, but he does at least suggest the complexity of the developed product. The temptation of all who define law is to concentrate on one stage at the expense of others. The legalist identifies law with legislation, the Confucianist with custom. Maine would hold that all belong to a balanced definition, layers of legality coexisting with creative tensions. Those who try to solve their problems through more legislation may be threatening the very source that law has in customary assurances. And those who idealize custom may be denying law the precision it can achieve through positive enactment.

The most notable anarchist writings are visionary and draw little support from experience. Attempts to abolish institutional law have ended either in chaos or in more exorbitant forms of repression. However, should anarchism be taken to mean the abolition of customary understandings as well as positive rules, then we seem to have a more than conventional limit to law at one extreme of our spectrum. If no common assumption defines what I am and you are, and no norms are supplied for each to expect how the other will face him in various circumstances, then it may be no mere matter of language to say we are outside law. No one has seriously advocated such a situation, but we can take the notion as a limiting case toward which customary law inclines if it simply renounces its development toward formality.

Can we move outside law at the other extreme of the spectrum? Some writers refer to law as an instrument of power. There is no problem if they simply mean that we can achieve policies by working through the courts as well as by paying money or making threats. Yet a vital distinction is missed that was suggested above in our discussion of the stages of law. Making rules is not the same as issuing commands. Having a legal obligation to obey is very different from being forced. Does this distinction come from some "nature" that belongs to the very enterprise of living in community, or does nothing more than the conventions of language lead us to draw this line? The question will reappear in the theories of law discussed in chapter 3, but here we may describe the difference provisionally.

If we are examining distinctions between the rule of law and the existence of despotism, it is no credit to our century that we need look no further. Hitler received only 44 percent of the votes in the 1933 elections, and he prudently declared that the Weimar Constitution would continue as the basis of government. But under appearance of legality, far-reaching changes were soon introduced. Those who see legitimacy (a rise to power within the laws) as the only criterion of legality will have to conclude that Hitler proceeded to do what a legislator does: he made laws. Most of the German judges held these to be valid and applied them in the courts. Some judges, however, had hesitations leading to resignation.

A writer at the time put it this way: "The will of the Führer is expressed by commands. He decides at his own absolute discretion and vouchsafes no glimpse into the workings of his mind. The Führer is not himself bound by the law. Today he may permit what he forbade yesterday."

Scandals in our own legislature may lead cynics to view politics as no more than the interplay of forces competing for power. Yet the claim to a rule of law needs to be taken seriously. Perhaps the basic element is that a legislator proposes to decide, not as an expression of his own will, but under guidance from reasons that are in principle public. Will is private, reason universal. Of course we dispute which are "good" reasons, and a legislator is not required to write his justification in the manner of an appellate judge. However, there is no necessary link between winning an election and making laws: power is not equated with reason. A legal society does not abandon itself to its officials but keeps them under supervision through complex institutions of sustained criticism. Congressmen may indeed have failed to pay their taxes, but they cannot simply exempt themselves from the generality of the laws they make.

By contrast, the command of a despot draws upon the power he possesses rather than upon the validity of his reasoning, as exposed to community acceptance and ratification. When Hitler decided, in 1934, that it was expedient to eliminate Ernst Röhm and check the power of the S.A. ("Brownshirts"), no law was there to legitimize this on the grounds of treason. The murders were accomplished swiftly. It is true that a law was then created to "justify" the deed after it had been perpetrated. But the question whether such retroactive legislation can make valid laws, or whether it contradicts the very nature of law, may well suggest the point of our inquiries into the limits of legality.

For the average German of those times it was the secrecy of legislation that most threatened him and best challenged the notion of law. Few of us read the statutes of our country or city. Yet this is a far cry from a situation where the published laws are changed by secret directives to the courts. What is left of the notion of "interactional expectations" if I can find no structures by which to guide my actions? Alice discovered, in Lewis Carroll's fantasies, a strange parody of courts but no law.

The legalists of ancient China proposed to extend the power of the ruler by systematically weakening the family, the village, the guild, and other institutions of customary law. The eventual failure of this policy illustrates the tension existing between different stages of law or areas of the legal spectrum. Custom can be inarticulate and ineffective without legislation; we may even, without such development, be led beyond the pale to a situation that is truly lawless. But legislation that loses its sources in custom can pass from authority to naked power and likewise become lawless. If a ruler succeeds too well in stifling the unwritten laws, he pollutes the air he breathes.

A detailed account of the boundary between legislation and a potentially extralegal use of power, in our own culture, goes beyond present purposes. Such a study would call for an analysis of the distinction between the rule of law and the policies of the ruler. It would call for an examination of our doctrine of the separation of the courts from the administration and the legislature. An investigation would have to be made of the distinction between legal reasoning and the way that administrators issue and defend their commands. Above all, perhaps, the question would have to be raised of the existence and independence of a legal profession. This book began with cheap complaints against lawyers. Yet if Germany under Hitler was lawless, this was possibly best shown by the degradation of the legal profession to the status where it was a mere extension of administrative policies.

FURTHER READING

Eugen Ehrlich's *Fundamental Principles of the Sociology of Law* (Buffalo, N.Y.: W. S. Hein & Co., 1979) is not for light reading, but a helpful selection of extracts, entitled "Law and the Inner Order of Associations," is presented in M. P. Golding, ed., *The Nature of Law* (New York: Random House, 1966), 200–213.

The same anthology (98–103) contains an extract from Sir Henry Maine in which he attacks the views of those who (notably the legal positivists) draw their theory of law from the final stage, legislation, to the neglect of prior ones.

On the distinction between law as found and as made, see Lon Fuller, *Anatomy of the Law* (1968; reprint, Westport, Conn.: Greenwood Press, 1976).

For an approach to the boundaries of a "rule of law," see the writings of Philip Selznick (e.g., his article on "Sociology of Law" in the *International Encyclopedia of the Social Sciences* 9 (1968): 50–59; his views are summarized in Edwin M. Schur, *Law and Society* (New York: Random House, 1968), 54–59.

QUESTIONS FOR DISCUSSION

1. We have all at times received, and possibly dispensed, some form of kadi justice. Think of examples from a parent, a teacher, even a traffic court. Where would you situate such examples on the legal spectrum? Did the lack of formal elements, such as explicit rules and precedents, leave you dissatisfied? If laws were involved, did they tend to be secret? Or public but customary?
2. Can you think of any examples where we still think of corporate responsibility? Are you shocked by the religious doctrine of original sin (that all share in the sin of Adam)?
3. Today we see a clear distinction between finding and making. Yet our language is more subtle. James Watt invented the steam engine. But Edmund Spenser's heroine would not return "till him alive or dead she did invent." The Latin word *invenire* means "to find." Do you simply find facts in science or contribute toward their making? Is inertia found or made? Notice that the term *fact* comes from the Latin "that which has been made." Suppose you and a few friends

meet regularly with a common interest; later, a club is formed and needs rules. Are these made or found?

4. Philosophers of law tend to favor one of the stages of law and either to exclude or minimize others. Which of Maine's stages seems to have dominated the reasoning of Justices Keen, Foster, and Handy of Newgarth (section 5)?

5. The notion of war crimes rose to prominence in the international trials after World War II. What offense had been committed by Germans who followed orders of their legitimate ruler, Hitler? Three main categories were used. War crimes, in the strict sense, were "violations of the laws or customs of war." Then there were "crimes against peace" that were violations of international agreements about the legitimacy of warfare. And finally there was the catchall provision of "crimes against humanity." How might your use of a developmental approach to law differ if you were a prosecutor or defense attorney at such trials?

6. Questions about the conventionality of definitions have been illustrated above. Here are a few more examples. What is the difference between a college and a university? Is East Germany a democracy? Does light travel in straight lines? Can a person found guilty by all the courts really be innocent? Suppose that an extraterrestrial has no freedom (is completely determined); can he be human? Do you have a soul?

7. One dictionary defines *anarchy* as "disorder and confusion, lawlessness." This is certainly not what Godwin, Proudhon, and the Russian anarchists advocated. They spoke rather of a return to "laws that stem from the nature of society itself." Does your own experience offer any support to the dictionary? Do we make a mistake in viewing the state on the model of small groups such as the family? A parent or teacher may well say, "I leave it to your discretion. . . ." But could the Internal Revenue Service so speak?

8. Have you encountered despotism? When you approach the dean's office with a reasonable request, do you find yourself in a legal situation or in one of sheer power? Clarify the distinction, with examples. Students were politically more active in the seventies. Were they then simply opposing administrative policies or protesting against an insufficiently legal situation for voicing opposition?

9. Hitler did not operate in a vacuum. There is a strain in German jurisprudence that goes beyond legislation to the "community spirit" (*Volksgeist*) of a nation. Could Hitler reply, to the criticism in these pages, that he was thus acting legally, drawing on a law beyond the laws? Again, see the dangers of reliance upon unwritten law. Who knows what precisely custom is until it has been written and so accepted?

10. Perhaps the clearest opposition of law to despotism, of rules to commands, has to do with our distinction between the publicity of the former (reason) and the privacy of the latter (will). How would you express this distinction, with examples? Within the family, the college, the state, how are disagreements settled? In spite of any complaints you may have against lawyers, do you see their profession as dedicated to a more general settlement of conflicts, to a social order based on reason rather than on will and on power?

12. THE PROJECT OF LIVING LEGALLY

> *Do you wish to understand the true history of a neolithic Ligurian or Sicilian? Try, if you can, to become a neolithic Ligurian or Sicilian in your mind. If you cannot do that, or do not care to, content yourself with describing and arranging in series the skulls, implements, and drawings which have been found belonging to these neolithic peoples.*
>
> (Benedetto Croce, *Theory and History of Historiography* [London, 1921], 134)

Croce, writing as a philosopher, puts to the archaeologist a basic question that extends to all of us. We understand our field of study or of work by discovering its laws. But we must distinguish between laws that are descriptive and those that are normative, and we need to establish an appropriate priority. If the physicist reports that water seeks its own level, or that water obeys the law of gravity, his anthropomorphic language will not conceal the fact that these laws are purely *descriptive*, accounts of what he observes repeatedly. The archaeologist, however, aspires to more than a correlation between the capacity of skulls that he unearths and the physical features of adjacent arrowheads and pottery. His task is to get within the experience of people who fought with those weapons and expressed themselves in the ornamentation on their implements. The laws he tries to bring to light are *normative*: they are "obeyed" in terms of what ought to be done.[27]

An example of the distinction may come from your own visits to foreign lands. You observe, and describe in letters home, how the locals behave—what they wear and eat, how they go about their work and relax when it is over. Your account may be as "external" as the one you give of the flora and fauna. However, it is likely that you will at times try to identify with the inhabitants and see their actions from their point of view. Your report of what they do as a rule will then be supplemented by some account of what they make it a rule to do. There is a difference between observing typical menus or garments and understanding why eating practices are changed during Lent or why traditional costumes are worn on days of celebration.

The distinction is not always easy to make. A visitor to our own shores who sets out to describe the clothing worn at various levels of employment in the business or industrial world can scarcely avoid some references to roles which people think they ought to satisfy; the terms *white-collar* and *blue-collar* are more than purely descriptive. And even in what I do myself, I move repeatedly between the external viewpoint of descriptive laws and the internal viewpoint of normative laws. If I reach first base in a baseball game, my decision whether to steal second depends on a close scrutiny of the behavior of others, an estimate of my own behavior in running, and an assessment of my obligations in making a gamble or playing it safe.

In commenting on the range of law, we have shown respect for anthropology and sociology and other sciences that aim to describe the variety of what is done under the name of law. Yet at times, especially in the distinction between commands and rules, a reminder has been given of the internal viewpoint that formulates law as an *ought* rather than an *is*.

This section will ask about the *ought* of normative laws. The question goes far into moral philosophy, and our treatment will be superficial. However, an account of human laws that simply ignores this will miss the drama of the topic.

---

27. This distinction will be examined again in section 18 when we discuss H. L. A. Hart's account of external and internal points of view in regard to rules.

One way of dodging the question of *ought* is to reduce all such statements to a combination of desires and sanctions. I ought to go to Germany if I want to learn the language well (but why should I want this?). I ought to be honest in trade if the penalty of failure at the hands of irate customers is not eventually to fall on me (but suppose I am wealthy and do not care about the loss?).

Some definitions of human law are along such lines. For example, as we have seen (p. 76 above), Hoebel found laws to be present only where their violation "is regularly met, in threat or in fact, by the application of physical force by an individual or group possessing the socially recognized privilege of so acting." He had no hesitation in identifying a law when he discovered that agents of the Eskimo village regularly executed those who engage in repeated murders. A visitor to our own country could similarly learn that we have income-tax laws by observing public agents at work on those who choose to avoid making contributions to the government each April 15. The fact that most citizens do comply would be explained as a choice to part with money rather than face the consequences of noncompliance. Again, a series of *is* statements about sanction and choice removes the mystery from talk of what we *ought* legally to do or avoid.

This account of law is likely to appeal to an anthropologist who is aware of his distance from the people he studies and of the scientific standard that he should report only what can be observed. Similar difficulties and ideals apply to the archaeologist, yet Croce's warning is appropriate. If a purely external viewpoint can lose the "true history" of an ancient civilization, such an attitude toward law may likewise miss the essential. To understand the law of a primitive tribesman, or of a feudal lord in China, or of a contemporary Frenchman, we certainly start with detailed observations; but our full task could call also for us to "try to become one in our mind."

If I say there is a law about this or that, how does it come to me as an *ought*? Am I simply noticing the power of the police or the strength of peer-group pressures? Do I merely weigh the discomfort of compliance and the pain of likely sanctions? Or do I recognize some interior obligation that external factors may support but cannot replace? Such questions take us back to the basic way we encounter other people and live as members of a community rather than as animals in a herd.

Basic Agreements

When Martin Luther was asked where, if the ban were put upon him, he would go, he replied: "Under the sky." In the moral ambiguity of the twentieth century we shall do well to imitate his example. Consider simply a community under the sky, the community constituted by two parties who have, out of the wilderness of the world, entered into a relation of exchange....

Tom Sawyer trades with Huck Finn an apple core for a bent nail. Tom and Huck are persons, the subjects of exchange.... Tom examines the apple core, Huck the nail. Visibly, the objects have changed hands. An exchange has therefore occurred? No, the exchange waits upon an agreement, which is not yet. The transfer essential to exchange is a transfer not of things, but of rights. The objects may or may not pass between hands. But unless ownership passes, there has been no exchange. This consists in a transfer of titles which are held, and are commonly admitted to be held, by the two parties....

Tom and Huck stand related as persons for the one sufficient reason that each admits the other to be the bearer of a right. For that, and never anything short of it, is what we mean by being a person....

There lies the paradox of all property: my property in anything depends not on my interests or my claims but on the acknowledgments and forbearances of others. We here confront the fundamental condition of all peaceable intercourse among men. It is the radical sense in which all property is public. Private property is a public fact, or it is no fact at all.... We have property only because first we consent to have community, and there is no greater mystification of human understanding than the belief that men establish community in order to preserve rights of property which they had apart from it: "The great and chief end of men's uniting into commonwealths, and putting themselves under government, is the preservation of their property." (John Locke)

... It is the habit of social theory in our day to suppose that Tom and Huck behave in so civilized a fashion each out of fear of a black eye. But that at least is not as Tom and Huck see their relationship. A black eye in a community is a punishment; beyond community it is as morally inconsequent as a thunder shower. Property is an institution of the market, not of the state....

Tom's and Huck's community is grounded neither on force nor on fear. It is grounded on a simple respect for each other's claims, on what (if I dared to say it in the presence of constables, priests, and doctors of political economy) is simple good will. Each respects in the other a simple dignity, confers upon the other the status of being party to the community which they have realized as their proper new creation out of nature's ignorant solitudes.... Their community is in nature but not of it. For under their covenant they stand related to each other, not as apple core to nail, nor as man to thing, but as person to person. That is the irreducible significance of such community as they have, that in it they stand related as I and thou....

Competition is so characteristic a feature of capitalist economy that one is apt to see in the economic community a simple extension of that struggle for survival which occurs in nature. Power and collisions of power are as real in society as they are real in nature. The demand for adjustment is inexorably the same in both. There is nevertheless the most radical distinction. Men compete in the market; yet, in spite of competition, they deny themselves the unquestionable advantages of theft. For they hold no act permissible which shall suspend the conditions of their permanent intercourse with each other.... Power is exercised according to rule.... The behavior of marketers is not, in short, mere behavior; it is normative behavior, behavior in obedience to a rule.[28]

---

28. John F. A. Taylor, *The Masks of Society* (New York: Appleton-Century-Crofts, 1966), 106–9, 113–17. Printed with permission of the author.

These extracts are taken from a book that the author presents as a study of *juristic philosophy*, "an inquiry into the phenomenon of obligation in each of the several domains of civilized society" (p. 10). Only one of these domains is "the law," in the narrow sense of what is formally adjudicated in courts. His concern is with the basic but implicit agreements by which we make possible such enterprises as the market, science, and art. We have suggested before that science becomes a body of information only if we have entered into an agreement on what shall count as a fact, as evidence, as explanation, as verification. The drama precedes the details of the play; before the curtain can rise we must first form, or simply have, an agreement on what *is* a play.

It is clearly not suggested that a constitution was established for science before we began to make observations, or for trade before we engaged in the first barter. Rules implicit from the beginning were only later expressed formally and have been repeatedly challenged and amended. It may take a crisis for us to ask what we are doing.

Professor Taylor comments (pp. 41–48) on Sir Henry Maine's account of civilization as an advance "from status to contract." No denial is made of the claim that we have moved from the informal arrangements of custom to the explicit statement of our relationships that we find in business contracts and in enacted law. However, Taylor stresses that the basic question has to do with the acquisition of status in any form. And he offers, by way of introduction, a description of the covenant by which the Hebrews became a people and recorded their self-awareness in the books of the Old Testament. This is a clear example of the way in which a society is constituted, not by the facts of geography, but by acceptance of a law that defines shared aspirations. The oppressor may drive a people into exile, or disperse them, or render their enacted law ineffective, but he does not thereby destroy what unites them: "Now therefore, if you will obey my voice and keep my covenant, you shall be my own possession among all peoples" (Exodus 19:5). Though the Bible tends to speak, vertically, of a covenant with God, it can also be read horizontally as the report of fundamental agreements on how to see and evaluate the world. Genesis talks of God's creation of the world, but we should not forget that man is appointed lord of creation and is assigned the vocation of "naming the animals," of agreeing on the particular worlds in which he is to live.

In our age of business, it is the commercial world that draws most clearly on our thoughts of community. The disparity between jungle and market calls for reflection. Animals recognize only the fact of power, and the laws of the jungle are purely descriptive. But the market is a juristic creation. Adam named a world of property and of exchange, of rights and titles. Relations of strength are involved, yet these are subordinated to the forbearance by which one person recognizes another as a fellow subject rather than as an object of desire and manipulation. Science tells us of the relation of object to object (without probing into the question how we made or defined what we accept as an object). In my present use of pen and paper, I am engaged in a subject-object relationship, imposing my will on things. However, when you claim that the pen is one I borrowed from you and forgot to return, or that I am wasting limited resources in a vain project, then we face the basic question how you and I encounter each other as subjects. We have done so, from the day we met. But what is the "covenant" that defines our status as *I* and *thou*?

Taylor is evidently arguing for an investigation of the normative laws that make a human community possible. We find these in the hunting customs of the Eskimos and on the floor of the New York Stock Exchange. We find these laws in the assumptions that Ptolemy took for granted and in the radical proposals of Galileo. Detailed descriptions must be left to the economist and the scientist. Our own question turns from particular laws to law in general, from the covenants we may accept or decline to the covenant where obligation comes out of our inescapable status as subjects.

The Need to Obey Law

The question Why obey this particular law? is one we face almost every time we park our car. The question Why obey law? may seem too philosophical for serious consideration. Yet it lies at the heart of all we do. A closer examination of this serious topic is in order.

I assume some agreement on the theme that each of us inhabits various worlds that are the the product of human creativity. You belong to a nation, a social class, a family, to various groupings of your peers. Movement is possible. You can reject your origins in the suburbs and identify with a ghetto (or vice-versa). You can deny your pledge to the flag and defect to another state and economic life. You can withdraw from a court-dominated legal system and enter a customary community (as so many tried in the seventies). No problem. But can you defect from law? Or are you so tied into the project of living legally that your attempted escape will turn out to be merely a passage from one legal system to another?

These are not questions that first appeared in our disturbed century. They are perennial. At least, they go back to ancient Greece (and perhaps no less to ancient China). The claim to unlimited defection was made by the Sophists: "All is of convention, nothing of nature." If you dislike the ways of Athens, move to Sparta or to Egypt, or establish your own life style. We may be reminded of the delightful myth of Robinson Crusoe. Yet we should be warned by the fact that Crusoe, in his solitary paradise, and seemingly with all possibilities open, remained depressingly English!

Plato, as we have seen, offered a reply to the Sophists. What he said was put more clearly by his rebellious disciple, Aristotle.[29] Here we come to the good common sense of a biologist who had observed a wide variety of people as well as animals. No argument against the Sophists can prevail if it is *positive*, if it

---

29. The reply of Plato and of Aristotle to the Sophists will be discussed in more detail in section 21.

rely upon some premise that will at once be questioned. But a *negative* proof may be possible and no less valid. Let us not forget the obvious. The Sophist is not alone and unknown on a distant island (and even if he were?). He talks within a community. He uses words with a claim to meaning and to truth. Let us start, not with the *content* of what he says, but with his *activity* of talking. What is he presupposing even when he explicitly denies it? If he says there are no standards of truth, is he not affirming these in his very activity of denying them? To take a more recent example, if someone (like Professor B. F. Skinner) claims that we are all completely determined by forces in our environment, does he not (in asserting this theory to be the valid result of his long and responsible inquiries) affirm his own freedom in his very denial of it?

You see, perhaps, what is suggested in regard to our need to obey some laws, our obligation to legality. The contradictions above are not "logical" (like talk of a square circle); they are "juristic," having to do with the relation of subject to subject in community. The details of language are conventional, but formulating a statement as meaningful and true is not. When they meet, speaker and listener form a community that legislates norms for judging meaning and disclosing truth. Else nothing is said. Disagreement is possible only on the platform of a more basic, and normative, agreement. Nor can we escape from this in the privacy of our own mind. Even private thoughts submit to public norms for our rational assessment. Hence, if I assert that law is a sheer fact of power to which I conform or not as I choose, then I am recognizing normative laws in my very denial. Under penalty of reducing my claim to a meaningless exclamation, I am acknowledging a juristic community of inquirers; I stand, with forbearance, as a subject before other subjects. Though I may with reason despise the judge on the bench, I do so legally, protesting some details of law from within the context of law.

The Structures of Legality

Such generalities are unlikely to impress those who are eager to pass on to what happens in court. However, what does happen there is theory-laden. The common view that law is an instrument of power, an order backed by sanctions, deserves some questioning. Even such abstract discussions may affect what you do as judge or lawyer; certainly they should color the way you see a career in the law. There is a significant difference between devoting your life to the power of rules and to power exercised according to rule.

A gradual return will now be made to the variety of legal experience that is the topic of this chapter. If the enterprise of legality is inescapable, in the bare sense of accepting some normative laws of community, do we then plunge unaided into the ocean of legal possibilities? Or do we have some guidelines as we confront again the passage from the shared ideals of customary law to the well-defined institutions of a modern legal culture?

There are many steps in this journey from the informal to the formal and from finding law to making it. Put yourself at any stage where there is a call to pass from implicit to explicit, from assumption to codification, from a feeling for what is traditional and right to the legislation of definite statutes. The task is to make or clarify a *rule*, in some meaning of this broad term. Certain authors limit rules to what legislatures and judges write. Others are prepared to speak of unwritten customary rules. However you use the term, the question will arise whether there are limits to ruling. In view of what has been said about the inescapable project of living legally, are there some rules you could propose that would, from the nature of this enterprise, fail to be law? The question applies to a tribal chief, to an absolute monarch, to a modern legislator. Can a rule-giver so violate the *structures of legality* that he fails to make valid laws, even though his power is such that he can force his will upon others? The question is still abstract but far from irrelevant. If the Gestapo or the KGB (or even the officials of a federal administrative agency) knock at your door, you will likely be obliged to let them have their way. But the fate you receive (what you *do*, viewed from within) depends much upon your estimate of whether you have a legal obligation to comply.

For an initial statement of this question we may turn again to the mythical illustrations that Lon Fuller has supplied for legal discussion. He presents the allegory of a hapless king whose ambition was to join Solon and Lycurgus in the ranks of the great lawgivers.[30] The reader is led to understand that the predecessors of Rex on the throne had supplied a well-codified law that had become antiquated and cumbersome. With minor adaptations, however, the story could be set within the deliberations of the Cheyenne chiefs, who made rules without writing them.

Rex's first act as king was to repeal all previous law and draft a new code. The project was audacious to the point of folly. And failure was assured by Rex's highly concrete mind. He had some sense for a wise decision in particular cases but could not articulate the reasons that placed like cases under uniform rules. So his code proved unworkable—neither his subjects nor the courts could make anything of it. Justice, however, did not cease in the kingdom. Rex drew upon his native abilities and dispensed a form of "kadi justice" without benefit of code or precedent. We may allow him some success, yet his subjects proved strangely ungrateful. Their respect for legality demanded more than isolated decisions. Rex, and his law, failed sadly in *generality*. A basic structure of all law, drawn from our very enterprise of living legally, was being seriously violated.

So Rex tried again and revised his code. His concomitant studies in logic were not altogether fruitless. But he was unable to convey to his subjects the principles that guided his own decisions. Fuller tells us that Rex declared the new code a state secret, known only to himself and his scribe. We are sadly

---

30. Fuller, *The Morality of Law*, 33–38.

familiar with codes that remain secret for less obvious reasons, such as the technicality of their language. In any event, the subjects rejected the new law as failing in *publicity*.

Rex then decided to make public the reasons that informed the law. On the first day of each year he reflected on and publicized the reasons behind his decisions of the previous year. Here we take a giant step toward valid law. However, Rex insisted that past decisions would in no way control future ones. Fuller's parable is weak on this point, since reasons that governed the past must somehow extend to the future—reason is universal. However, we see his point and sympathize with the rebellion of Rex's subjects. If we are to live according to law, then its rules must be forward looking, or have *prospectivity*.

We can pass rapidly over subsequent stages in the fable. Rex retired to his study and, without help from critics, produced a new code that was a masterpiece of obscurity and was honeycombed with contradictions. His pained but patient subjects suggested that the structures, and rationality, of the legal enterprise require both *clarity* and *consistency*.

Rex then abandoned his own claims to authorship and transferred the task to a miscellaneous group of experts. These were isolated from judicial functions, and they absorbed many years in their task. Changes took place meanwhile in the economic and social conditions of the realm. The eventual result was a prize of legal draftsmanship. The only trouble was that, in the altered circumstances, compliance with many of the provisions was impossible. So there followed a daily stream of amendments, and people wondered if rules that changed so radically could really be law. The protests implied that *possibility* and *constancy* belong somehow to the structures of law.

Rex decided that he must intervene again. He reassumed charge of law in the kingdom and began judging cases with a belated experience that restored generality and publicity to his decisions. His prowess as a judge had blossomed. There was only one problem. The official code, according to which he should judge, was no longer of his authorship. His subjects were unable to see much correspondence between enunciated law and its administration. They complained that *conformity* between the two, or uniform application of the law, is a further requirement if we are to live legally.

The end of the story is significant. Rex died, aware of his failure to make law, and his successor to the throne turned from lawyers to psychiatrists for help. People, he said, can be happy without rules. In other words, repeated violation of the structures of legality implicit in our existence as a community led to a change in viewpoint from law as normative to law as purely descriptive.

The details of Fuller's argument remain to be clarified. He does not hold that his eight structures of legality are exhaustive. And it is interesting to see how aware he is of the subtlety of each in practice, and of the problems in coordinating one with the other (pp. 39–94).

Fuller's philosophy of law, and criticisms of it, will be presented in section 22; his concern is to argue that there is some nature to law, as an enterprise. In terms of this chapter, his suggestion is that the boundaries of law are more than a matter of convention. Even if a rule is backed by sanctions, and even if it has a pedigree tracing it to a rule of recognition that empowers the legislator, the rule he makes may nevertheless fail to be valid law. The project of living legally, to which we are committed as members of any society, is not open to infinite variety. In our enterprise there are structures that, when violated, make what otherwise seems a law to be not "really" a law.

FURTHER READING

The distinction between "internal" and "external" viewpoints in the study of history is developed at length by R. G. Collingwood in *The Idea of History* (New York: Oxford Univ. Press, 1946).

The notion that some basic agreement underlies all forms of culture is presented in many different forms of the theory that human society rests upon a social contract. Thomas Hobbes (*The Leviathan*, 1651) proposed that we first existed as individuals, under no law but self-interest, and that we then formulated society and laws for protection against the excesses of this power struggle. Kant developed an alternative account of the social contract theory, that mutual agreement and the respect of person for person are the basis for any human existence and are presupposed even by competition. For a contemporary version, see: John Rawls, *A Theory of Justice* (Cambridge: Harvard Univ. Press, 1971).

The argument that legality is an enterprise with natural structures, and that the self-contradiction involved in breaking these can declare some laws to be invalid, is found in chapter 2 of Lon Fuller's *The Morality of Law* (New Haven: Yale Univ. Press, 1969).

A more empirical study of the purposes and structures of a legal system is offered by Iredell Jenkins, *Social Order and the Limits of Law* (Princeton, N.J.: Princeton Univ. Press, 1980). Though the perspective is different from Fuller's, there are interesting parallels between the account each author gives of the requirements and problems of the legal enterprise.

For a recent anthology that presents much material on "mythic, dramatic, rhetorical, and philosophical" versions of the origin of law and on the ways in which law has organized experience, see: J. C. Smith and D. N. Weisstub, eds., *The Western Idea of Law* (London: Butterworths, 1983).

QUESTIONS FOR DISCUSSION

1. Do you understand other people by observing and learning to predict their behavior? Think of a teacher, a political candidate, a close friend. What about yourself? What distinction do you see between saying that you *cannot* run a mile in four minutes and that you *cannot* stand your job or family any longer? Is it possible to intend doing your best in a contest and still predict that you will lose? What is odd about predicting your own intentions? Apply such examples to the distinction between descriptive and normative laws.
2. The parallel between laws and games is precarious, but could you describe a game in terms of penalties for breaking the rules? If there is no referee and you repeatedly gain advantages by breaking the rules, does your purpose stray from winning the game?
3. Is obeying a custom more than following a habit? Think of examples that may distinguish between habits and customs in eating, in responding to sickness. Can you understand guilt through its symptoms, or do you need to have some experience of what it means to be guilty?

4. Distinguish between a lion's possession of a deer it has caught and your ownership of a deer you have shot; between a bird's territory and your real estate. Distinguish between succeeding in the struggle for survival and winning in the market.

5. What problems do you see in John Locke's theory that people first acquired property and then, under threat from others who wanted it, contracted into a community for defense of property? Does property depend on your strength to keep it or on acknowledgment by others who respect your title to that property?

6. Contrast the frustrations that come from things and from persons. What do we learn from each form of opposition? Distinguish between the use of things and respect for persons.

7. Much discussion has taken place over the days of creation in the Genesis account. How does the creation of worlds (scientific, economic, legal) depend on human intentions? Could God create valuable properties, or harmonious colors, or even time (let alone days), without man?

8. What is odd about these statements, and how do they illustrate Aristotle's notion of "negative proof"? There is no truth. All is a mistake. Life is utterly absurd. Everything I say is false. Life is just a dream. The only advice I give you is to do the opposite of what you are advised.

9. One of the films that claimed most attention in 1983 was *E.T.*, the story of an extraterrestrial who found himself within an American family. Physically, this lizard-like creature was rather repulsive. Why did viewers recognize him as "one of us"? Did he take his place in our system of rules and accept our underlying agreements? Suppose you encountered such a being; how would you distinguish between "who?" and "what?"

10. Perhaps the basic structure of law that Fuller suggests is "generality." This means more than that a rule should mention a class of people rather than simply an individual. The suggestion is that a valid law expresses a general reason rather than simply stating an act of will. Rex, let us suppose, issues two proclamations. All able-bodied males shall enter the king's service in time of war. All red-headed females shall enter the king's service at his pleasure. Is one a law, the other merely a command?

13. LEGAL TRADITIONS

A student of science may attend to its history and find important differences before and after Darwin or Einstein; yet contemporary science pays little respect to geographical frontiers. In law it is otherwise. A case from a hundred years ago can retain its authority, but a law degree earned in one country will have little value for practice in another.[31] The layperson today reads popular science journals that tell each month of developments around the world. There is no equivalent in law; indeed, "comparative law" is an arcane subject even for the professional.

The variety of legal systems, however, is not without order, and this section will mention some family resemblances. Though a lawyer in this country may show extreme modesty if your legal problem stretches to Italy, he will feel much more at home with any reference to the law of Australia, as will an Italian lawyer in regard to that of Argentina. Something can at least be said on the two most influential legal traditions, that of the "common law" and that of the "civil law."

---

31. One American law professor states that when European-trained lawyers come to him for graduate studies, his first word of advice is: "Try to forget that you have ever studied law."

The term *civil law* is unfortunately ambiguous, and this section will start by examining a very different meaning, in which the term is used in opposition to *criminal law*, a division that seems to belong in all traditions. The section will close by discussing a further distinction that affects all legal families, between adjudication and other forms of settlement.

Civil and Criminal Law

Anyone who finds himself before the law today will need to learn whether he is involved in a criminal or a civil trial. If it is the former, he is open to severe disgrace. If it is the latter, his job is secure and his neighbors will not shun him. The distinction is often made concrete by assigning different floors of the courthouse, or different buildings, to the two proceedings.

The rules of criminal law specify certain acts as wrong, not merely in regard to the individuals directly harmed, but to the community as such. Public officials (policemen, prosecutors) take the initiative in bringing the wrongdoer to justice. He must, at least in theory and with minor qualifications, be charged with violation of codified statutes, and in court his case will be entitled *State* (or *People*, or *U.S.*, or *Queen*) *v. Smith*.

Civil law, when opposed to criminal law, has to do with disputes between individuals such that the stigma of harm to the community is lacking. The injured person (plaintiff) must himself take the initiative in bringing his opponent (defendant) to the courts, where the case is entitled *Jones v. Smith*. In our regions, reference is more likely to be made to previous court decisions than to statutes, and the outcome is normally a money settlement, never a verdict of guilt followed by imprisonment.

Such is the shame of being convicted of a crime (and hence becoming a "criminal" or a "convict") that most legal systems employ terminology to salvage the self-respect of their generally law-abiding citizens. A minor infraction of traffic laws, though the charge is initiated by public officials, is called an *offense* or (in France) *contravention*. In Germany such "violations of order" have been removed from the jurisdiction of courts. Crimes in the narrow sense are usually distinguished as *felonies* and *misdemeanors*, the former being more serious in public esteem and open to longer prison sentences.

However, this sensitivity to labels does not hide the apparently sharp distinction between criminal and civil law. We are reminded of Aristotle's division between distributive and corrective justice. Those who violate law or justice may be disrupting a relationship between themselves and their society as a whole. Or they may be breaking some agreement, explicit or implicit (Aristotle would say "voluntary" or "involuntary"), between one individual and another. Surely there is a difference between the grave view we adopt toward a pickpocket with long experience but petty takings and our attitude to a businessman who, by failing in some contract, has deprived his associate of more than the total lost by others to a hand on their wallet?

Or are we so confident of the distinction and of the philosophy behind it? What the statutes list as a crime differs notably from one legal system to another and varies with time in each. Witchcraft is no longer on our own list, but we have added air pollution and embezzlement. And what about the very notion that some wrongs are public and others only private? If breach of contract is a private matter, why have we put our legal institutions at the disposal of aggrieved parties? Surely we are defending a public assumption that promises should be honored? Similarly, our public interest in the good name we have makes libel cases more than private vendettas. Much as private property is a public fact, so civil law draws upon concerns that are vital to the entire society. It is not only in criminal courts that a relationship is involved between the part and the whole.

The other side of this assertion is evident. No one who has been robbed or raped sees this as a purely public affair. A personal grievance comes to the fore. The part-whole relationship makes little sense without the conflict between part and part.

One conclusion from this weakening of the distinction is that our assignment of some cases to criminal courts and others to civil has much to do with factors outside the formal rules of law. If contract violations go to our civil courts, this is largely because those who can suffer from such infractions have managed fairly well to secure fidelity to contracts without help of the police. The civil courts are here an appendage to a business community that operates smoothly from its own bases in customary law.

Consider negligence on the roads and in the home. If I drive negligently but injure no one, I may still be stopped by the police and brought into a lowly branch of the criminal courts. However, say you visit me and suffer injury from my negligence in maintaining my house. All I have committed is a tort (civil wrong) and my venue is the civil court. The reasons have little to do with logic but come from such mundane factors as the number of accidents, the supply and disposition of policemen, and our reluctance to have them checking private homes as they do private cars.

A further conclusion is that an oversimplification is involved in the traditional account of the origins of criminal law. It is said that murders and thefts were originally dealt with by the aggrieved individual or group; the blood feud dominated primitive society. Eventually, central government appeared, a police force was established, and the state took over such order maintenance by defining crimes and prosecuting those who thus became criminals. Only within the last century or two is the process said to have been completed, and this is hailed as a triumph of civilization.

There is much truth in the account, but we should be wary. The distinction between private and public injuries is not easy to draw in primitive societies. And the notion seems deep-seated that some wrongs have an importance beyond the individual or family immediately affected, even where much of the machinery of criminal law is lacking. Psychologists, and perhaps theologians, may have much to tell us here. Why, for example, was witchcraft raised to its peak of evil from the many offenses of a bygone day? Some peculiar threat to the community's self-concept was recognized. There may well be religious origins to the notion of "crime" that have to do with our basic covenants rather than our particular contracts. Some things we do are an affront to the gods and not merely a violation of secular order. Even if we allow a symbolic value to the payment of money, some offenses so threaten our status as a community that no such transfer can achieve a settlement. A radical cleansing is required.

The killing of one Cheyenne by another was certainly a crime. It bloodied the Sacred Arrows and no personal revenge would rectify this. The whole tribe had been assaulted. There would be no success in war, and game would shun the territory. A general purification was required, so the tribe would attend the solemn rituals by which the Arrows were renewed (see Llewellyn and Hoebel, *The Cheyenne Way*, chap. 6). If a society is the hard-won result of basic agreements, and of the normative laws that express these, then its very existence may involve some form of criminal law.

Common Law and Civil Law

Comparative law, as a developed discipline, is but half a century old. World trade has lifted it from the scholarly journal to make it a speciality that pays. But it is not altogether foolish to ask what exactly is compared to what when we study comparative law. The reply, at a superficial level, is clear. We examine the rules and institutions of law in different parts of the world. A firm that proposes to set up a branch in Brazil or Saudi Arabia will want to know how contracts are interpreted in courts there.

The formal rules are quite easy to find. Yet enough has been said to suggest that these are only the tip of the iceberg. They come from a complex basis in customary understandings, and propositional law may not well reflect the depths of the living law:

> Large numbers of Guatemalans, Brazilians, Ethiopians, and Congolese live much of their lives relatively free of any substantial contact with the official legal system.... The paper legal system will look much like that of France or Spain or Italy, or of England or the United States. But if one looks at the actual role of law in the lives of important elements of the population the resemblance is only superficial.[32]

In this book we are concerned with questions about law in general rather than with any particular topic in law, and examples will come mainly from home shores. Nevertheless, an effort is being made to look backward to primitive law and to supplement local cases with some awareness of foreign alternatives. This section needs only to give the beginner an idea of how the many different legal

---

32. J. H. Merryman and D. S. Clark, *Comparative Law* (Indianapolis: Bobbs-Merrill, 1978), 28.

systems of today are classified. The following brief reply comes from Max Rheinstein, a contemporary expert:

> Among all the legal systems of the world we distinguish between the two great families of the common law and the civil law, and within the latter the two groups of the French and the German patterns.[33]

In the United States we may speak of a federal legal system and of another system belonging to each of the states. The lawyer you hire is familiar with the legal rules and procedures of his state but is likely to seek outside help if your case goes further. Legal systems are defined by geographical boundaries; however, on the basis of resemblances in structure, procedure, and history, these systems are grouped into legal families or traditions. We belong to that of the "common law," which derives from England and is found where British or American influence was strong at the time when legal institutions were formed: for example, Australia and Ireland. Other countries can be so associated if the admixture of different cultures is recognized: for example, India and the Philippines. The other dominant legal tradition has its home on the continent of Europe and is referred to as the "civil law" or (by some) the "Romano-Germanic" family.[34] It is found today in countries that came under colonial influence from this source, such as Latin America and parts of Africa. It is also a feature of varying significance in some pockets of the common law, such as Scotland, Quebec, Puerto Rico, and Louisiana. A third important legal tradition is comprised today by the countries that have turned Communist. However, as we noticed in China, law cannot be changed overnight; before these developments, most of the nations concerned either were solidly within the civil law tradition or accepted codes based on it. Finally, what remains can be put under the heading of religious law (Islamic, Hindu, Confucian) or tribal law (in Africa), with many supplements from the first three traditions.

It is civil law that claims to be the most ancient legal family. Its origins are to be found in Roman law and its spirit is still much that of the systematic Roman mind, developed by the rationalistic tendencies of the French and Germans. Perhaps the most abiding influence of the Roman Empire came from the codification of law that was achieved under the Emperor Justinian in the sixth century A.D. The cultural unification of Europe in the Middle Ages depended on the Latin language and on Roman law, as interpreted and adapted in the medieval universities. Indeed, to this day the atmosphere of civil law is more suggestive of the lecture hall than the courthouse. The law professor, deriving conclusions from principles, has had a greater influence on legal style than the judge who settles disputes that may ill fit the principles.

---

33. Merryman and Clark, *Comparative Law*, 13.
34. It is the dependence of this tradition on Roman law that accounts for this use of the term *civil law*. The Romans, in speaking of *ius civile*, were not excluding criminal law but were distinguishing the ancient law of the *city* of Rome from the law thought to be common to other peoples in the Empire (*ius gentium*).

The power of Roman law on the European continent was fostered by the late development of centralized national authority. Law was viewed, by its teachers, as crossing local boundaries, and the substance on which commentaries were made was drawn from the codes of the Roman Empire rather than the customary law of particular regions. This ideal of a highly systematic codification of law persisted when national unities formed. Each nation wrote its law in a comprehensive code. The French civil code appeared in 1804, followed shortly by commercial, criminal, and procedural codes. The later unification of Germany delayed the German civil code till 1896, but its careful construction has given it an influence in civil law countries parallel to the Napoleonic codes of France.

Many qualifications are needed. For example, the Scandinavian countries have largely resisted the call for codification. But in general, the European mind to the east and south of the English Channel has wanted to see the law stated concisely in a system of statutes. The contrast with our own approach comes forcefully if we notice how one studies law at a French or German university.[35] There is no discussion in the lecture hall, where the professor makes his way through the articles of the codes, thus supplying a panoramic view of the law rather than introducing it piecemeal through cases. In his interpretation of the articles, the professor will of course refer to cases, yet the attitude is theoretical and only vague guidelines are offered for the solution of practical problems. The student does reading in commentaries on the law and in "doctrine," scholarly discussion of academic points of law. He also engages in practical exercises, but his familiarity with what goes on in law offices and courts is expected to come almost entirely in the apprenticeship years that follow his university studies.

The history of the development of law is far different when we cross the Channel and notice how the common law tradition arose. There are interesting parallels between English and Roman law.[36] However, dependence on the latter is far less marked in England than on the Continent. The basic difference is that a powerful monarchy dated from the time of the Norman kings (interestingly, French remained the language of the royal court until the end of the fifteenth century and the spoken language of the law until the seventeenth). Disputes were at first settled, according to customary law, in a variety of local courts. But the king also dispensed justice from his own court (notice the reference this term has outside a purely legal setting). Since he represented the final authority, appeals from local decisions began to be made to him. The story of the gradual extension of royal "jurisdiction" (authority to state and apply the law) is a complex one. Yet the result was an effective by-passing of local law and the establishment, under the king, of a "common law" for the realm.

It was the piecemeal character of this process that was vital for the form taken by the law. At no time did the king propose to found a system of law. His

---

35. See: H. J. Liebesny, *Foreign Legal Systems* (Washington, D.C.: George Washington Univ. Press, 1981), 167–73; and Merryman, *Comparative Law*, 397–401.

36. Liebesny, *Foreign Legal Systems*, 19–21.

representatives decided particular cases and slowly discovered a logic in what they were doing by conforming later decisions to a line of earlier ones. The basic approach of the common law had more to do with procedures than with substance.[37] There was no set of statutes to which a plaintiff could relate his own request for justice. His concern was to find some way of getting the royal judges to hear his case. He had to present a detailed statement of the facts and then hope that the court would find some basis for coming to a judgment in analogy to other cases. There was no need to quote principles of (say) negligence from Roman law or from university speculations; all that existed legally was a range of "negligence cases."

Understandably, those educated in the Continental legal tradition find the common law opaque and irrational. Where are the general principles from which we derive particular conclusions? They *are* there—law, as King Rex discovered, must be general and systematic or fail in its project, and the common law has proved most effective. But the principles are not published in a code, nor are they even precisely formulated. Some commentators have said that the rationality of the common law is drawn from the "general immemorial custom of the realm." This may itself be a legal fiction, yet in terms of the stages or spectrum of law it seems fair to suggest that common law is closer to custom, civil law to legislation. Legal training and the legal profession have been less obviously concerned with theory than in the civil law. What counts is the mastery of techniques that secure a hearing and win a trial.

The fruit, for good or evil, of this preference for case law over enacted law is shown in our modern law libraries. These vast structures give but a small space to books that codify the law (notably criminal) and devote the rest to a maze of appellate decisions in particular cases. The work of discovery is immense, and the layperson is incompetent. However, what he or she reads in these cases is likely to seem closer to reality than what appears in the writing of a civil law judge. It is not merely that one cites previous cases and the other balances the meaning of articles in a code. The civil law writer seems almost embarrassed to admit that the pure system of law refers to the messy details of actual disputes.[38] The facts of the case are often limited to cryptic hints, whereas even the most technical discussion in a common law decision starts with a lively account of the human conflict that was brought to the court for judgment. Indeed, as we shall notice in chapter 5, the judge severely limits his claim to speak for cases beyond the concrete one before him.

We thus have two interpretations of the project of living reasonably. One sees reason as primarily deductive (moving from general principles to particular conclusions). The other challenges us to ask how we move from instance to instance without a plain view of the principles that are involved; again, there are depths to the legal iceberg that we may not clearly understand, but they are far from irrelevant to what happens above the surface.

---

37. Sir Henry Maine writes that the common law was "secreted in the interstices of procedure."
38. See Liebesny, *Foreign Legal Systems*, 94–100, for comments and for the example of a German case.

The two traditions present us with notable variations in the legal enterprise. Some of these, such as the contrast between the strongly adversarial procedure of common law courts and the more inquisitorial process under the civil law, will be discussed later (section 25). For the present, some overlapping comments may suggest important differences between the two legal approaches.

The mentality of the civil law is often classified as rationalist and that of the common law as empirical. How are plaintiff and defendant helped to see the reason at work in the judgment they receive? In the civil law, they are directed to the abstract assertions of statutes; if these are taken individually (as the layperson does), a rule is stated but the reasons for it are not discussed. In the common law, we feel lost when referred to a mass of cases, but we do get the impression of various minds trying scrupulously to discover and express the subtlety of rules that have no life apart from their applications. One significant mark of common law decisions is that these allow for a plurality of judicial opinions, some openly dissenting and others concurring for different reasons.

Both traditions threaten to violate some of the structures of law. The common law is likely to fail in systematic unity. A judge can rule on cases only as they are presented; the position is analogous to that of a builder who has to construct a house without control over the order in which materials are delivered (suppose the roofing arrives before the joists?). In the civil law, codes may form a coherent whole, but the virtue of generality is likely to come at a cost (the builder's instructions tell about setting joists but make no provision for the peculiarities of this particular custom-built house). For example, article 1382 of the French civil code states: "Every human act which causes harm to another obliges the one through whose fault it has occurred to pay damages." We nod in approval, yet we recognize the need for guidance from case after case before we can bridge the gap between such a principle and the concrete situations we confront. We may also remember the troubles in Rex's kingdom when a lack of conformity appeared between a self-consistent code and the ways in which it was applied.

Finally, one of the problems of case law is that rulings seem to be retroactive. Statutes and codes are certainly prospective—they govern what is to come and supply us with a guide for the future. But recall the fate of Elmer Palmer in the *Riggs* decision (section 4). Could he have protested that Judge Earl's ruling in 1889 was made to cover what Elmer did in view of what most took the written law to be in 1882? Is not the common law, by its dependence on such judicial decisions, infected with retroactivity?

Arbitration and Mediation

Tiv litigants [of northern Nigeria] would seem to believe that the proper and correct solution of a dispute 'exists'. It 'is'. The task of the judges is to find it. In the old days the principal litigants would go from one elder of the community to another until they discovered one who could penetrate the details of the case and emerge with this 'correct' solution. To a lesser extent, they still do so today. It is obvious to Tiv that when a right decision has been reached, both litigants will concur in it, even though the particular judgment may not be wholly in favor of either.

The importance of such concurrence by the litigants cannot be overemphasized. It is to misunderstand the Tiv view to say that Tiv courts have or have not the 'authority' to 'enforce' a 'decision'. 'Authority', 'enforcement', and 'decision' are all Western legal concepts which spring from our notions and ideas of authority hierarchies. They are part of the Western folk system concerning our jural and governmental institutions. If Tiv judges make a settlement in which both parties can concur, there is no problem of 'enforcing a decision'. . . .

Concurrence of the litigants never occurs without concurrence of the entire community: no one is ready to make concessions while any portion of public opinion still supports him. It is the opinion of the community which forces concurrence. Judging, like all other activities of Tiv leaders, consists largely in the timely suggestion of what the majority thinks is right or desirable.

The 'correct solution' changes as the situation of both litigants changes. Tiv, therefore, tend to deplore 'final decisions', which their European administrators, of course, prefer. Tiv feel that making a final decision, in the English sense, often perpetuates conditions which will eventually become unjust. It sometimes appears to foreigners that Tiv do not want their courts to make decisions at all, but it seems more accurate to say that they want the judges to point out a *modus vivendi*, which will endure while the situation endures.[39]

The extract above may suggest some caution in our use of such terms as *judge* and *court* when we encounter dispute settlement in this semi-Bantu tribe. Perhaps we should prefer to talk of negotiations where the elders serve as counselors and facilitators rather than as legal officials. What can we make of a judge who is at the mercy of shifting opinions and lacks the authority to impose a decision of his own, indeed refrains from making a final decision?

It is healthy to be reminded that our concern to find a hierarchy of authority in legal institutions, and a pedigree in laws, is distinctly Western. Agencies and rules that do not fit this scheme can easily be classified as extralegal. However, the image of a spectrum of law, suggested in this chapter, may invite us to look further at what unites and distinguishes procedures that we readily see as legal and those that we regard as dubiously so.

We remember the opposition traditionally shown by the Chinese to litigation in courts and the preference for help from people who are neither judges nor lawyers. We have heard, in our society, the complaint about legalism that turns many away from the courthouse toward forms of settlement outside. We have

---

39. Paul Bohannan, *Justice and Judgment Among the Tiv* (New York: Oxford Univ. Press, 1968), 64–65. Published for the International African Institute and reprinted with permission.

seen that the common law arose through requests to a respected person for help in settling disputes where no fixed rules were at hand. And it is likely that today's lawyer, for all his training in the formalities of rule-directed procedures, finds that much of his work is of a more informal nature, involving him in bargaining rather than in rule-citing.

Terminology is not very precise, but the following suggested distinctions may prove helpful.

Adjudication requires submission to a formally constituted court that works under the provisions of a legal system equipped with definite rules. The parties know in advance the rules (substance of the law) that are to be applied, whether these be expressed in statutes or in previous judicial verdicts. They know also the rules of procedure according to which the trial will be conducted (e.g., evidence, burden of proof, examination of witnesses).

Arbitration takes place when those in conflict agree to accept some neutral third party and to abide by his or her verdict when they have fully presented their arguments. The disputants may follow the procedural laws that apply in a formal court of law but not depend on the substantive law of the court. Or they may allow the arbitrator to work outside even the procedural laws of adjudication.

Mediation covers any form of negotiation where the "good offices" of a third party are accepted, even though the opponents make no prior commitment to abide by the decision. For example, international conflicts are often resolved in this way. So are many disputes where the lawyer manages to steer away from the courts.

The boundary lines are not impenetrable and this could be of importance to lawyers as they inquire repeatedly what they are doing. If their task is to help in the creation of social order, they may have to ask which of various tools they should apply in any situation. Their assistance in a marital or commercial or criminal case can run the whole range.

Perhaps the basic question, crossing all differences, is why we allow anyone to help in the resolution of our problem. Even the qualified acceptance of a mediator is a giant step from the power struggle of the jungle to the province of law. Indeed, the distinction between force and legality may be more evident in the work of mediation. A judicial order is backed by power and seems to some like a command. But the mediator must convince diverse parties, who have come together in a compact of reason, that the proposed solution is a work of reason.

Acting according to rational principles carries restraint; the judge is bound by statute and by precedent. The most relaxed mediator must respect some consistency in a line of decisions and allow some guidance from the living law. We find the obligation to follow precedent appearing even in the informal conditions of primitive law: "The chiefs of the later tribal societies, by pronouncing the same judgments in similar situations, were unwittingly creating a set of abstract principles."[40]

The judge, who seems assigned to adjudication by our very terminology, plays many roles within and outside the courtroom. He may have been appointed rather than chosen, and he is sworn to uphold a system of formal rules, but he is committed to a highly particular settlement in each case he faces. At least, our expectation today is that he should not merely render a verdict that defines wrongs but should also make some move toward healing them. In the trial itself, the judge's liberty of maneuver is limited. Yet, as we shall see later, the civil law judge can spread the trial over a series of conferences, and his role comes close to that of an arbitrator. Even in our own tradition there is a growing emphasis on keeping the case from court through pre-trial conferences.[41]

In adjudication, arbitration, and mediation, the goal is *settlement* of a dispute. This term is ambiguous. For some, a conflict is settled when it is ended by an authoritative decision. For others, the term has connotations of therapy. A true settlement involves a change of perception in both parties. What before seemed to deny any solution, since the claims were logically opposed, now is resolved because each side has been helped to see its own position and interests differently. As has often been said of a commercial exchange, each is the gainer.

FURTHER READING

Perhaps the best introduction to the various legal traditions is René David, *Major Legal Systems in the World Today*, translated and revised by J. E. C. Brierley (New York: Free Press, 1978). For the historical development of the civil law and common law, see pp. 33–69, 286–308.

A shorter account of the civil law, common law, and Communist traditions is supplied by Mary Ann Glendon, et al., in *Comparative Legal Traditions in a Nutshell* (St. Paul: West, 1982).

Henry W. Ehrmann's *Comparative Legal Cultures* (Englewood Cliffs, N.J.: Prentice-Hall, 1976) arranges material by topic rather than by legal tradition.

John H. Merryman's *The Civil Law Tradition*, 2d ed. (Stanford, Calif.: Stanford Univ. Press, 1985), is a brief description from a recognized expert.

A recent history of the civil law tradition is Alan Watson's *The Making of the Civil Law* (Cambridge: Harvard Univ. Press, 1981).

Other available, though weighty, books on comparative law include:

Glendon, Mary Ann, et al. *Comparative Legal Traditions: Text, Materials and Cases*. St. Paul: West, 1985.

Liebesny, Herbert J. *Foreign Legal Systems*. Washington, D.C.: George Washington Univ. Press, 1981.

Merryman, J. H., and D. S. Clark. *Comparative Law: Western European and Latin American Legal Systems*. Indianapolis: Bobbs-Merrill, 1978.

---

40. L. Pospisil, *Anthropology of Law* (New York: Harper & Row, 1971), 145–46.
41. For example, see H. J. Berman and W. R. Greiner, *The Nature and Functions of Law* (Mineola, N.Y.: Foundation Press, 1972), 181–94.

Schlesinger, Rudolf B. *Comparative Law.* Mineola, N.Y.: Foundation Press, 1980.

von Mehren, Arthur T., and J. R. Gordley. *The Civil Law System: An Introduction to the Comparative Study of Law.* 2d ed. Boston: Little, Brown & Co., 1977.

For a discussion of techniques in arbitration and mediation, see: Harry T. Edwards and James J. White (*The Lawyer as Negotiator*) St. Paul: West, 1977.

Lon Fuller has written helpful articles on the part that mediation plays in law; these are collected in *The Principles of Social Order*, edited by Kenneth I. Winston (Durham, N.C.: Duke Univ. Press, 1981).

QUESTIONS FOR DISCUSSION

1. In an age when spy stories are so popular, we all know about "moles" and others who betray the intelligence service and the nation. Treason is the clearest example of a crime. Can you apply, in other realms, this notion of people turning against the very community that produced them? Why is the killing of elderly people a crime among the Cheyenne but not for the Eskimo? Why might robbery and fraud be crimes? Is any suggestion offered for understanding the rather paradoxical notion, in some jurisdictions, that suicide is a crime?

2. In the common law tradition, rulings are given by judges without codes to guide them. An exception, however, is made today for criminal law. Apart from the precariously surviving notion of common law crimes, no judge can find you guilty unless he can show you to have violated a statute passed by the legislature. Why this exception?

3. The above exception was not always so. English criminal law was once drawn from the decisions of courts. If codification is possible, and apparently desirable, in criminal law, why not for the whole law? Do you see any reasons for not writing comprehensive rules?

4. Comment on Max Weber's claim that "the degree of legal rationality is essentially lower in the common law nations than in continental Europe." Do historians show an essentially lower degree of rationality than mathematicians? And what about scientists? The philosopher, A. N. Whitehead, wrote that science was "an anti-rationalist" revolt against the "rationalistic orgy of the Middle Ages." Is "rationalism" a particular form of "rationality" and not necessarily superior to forms that rely more on the varieties of experience?

5. At the beginning of his book, *The Civil Law Tradition*, J. H. Merryman points out that a lawyer in the undeveloped nations of Central America "thinks of our legal system as undeveloped and of common lawyers as relatively uncultured people" (p. 3). If law has grown (and progressed?) from custom to legislation, must this charge not hold? Would Eugen Ehrlich, himself from a civil law nation, agree?

6. Legal training and judicial opinions in the civil law tradition do not ignore the facts of a case, but a more restrictive view is taken of what facts are legally relevant. Is the fact that I was speeding to an important meeting relevant to my violation of traffic laws? Does the principle that all people are created equal depend on the facts we find of unequal need, work, and merit? Does the meaning of such a principle shift as we apply it in a range of factual situations (the family, the workplace, the law court)? In various applications of a principle, can you separate how it is the same from how it is different?

7. You are appointed to defend a person charged with a crime. Does the fact that only a small percentage of such cases go before the courts suggest that the procedure has as much to do with negotiation as with adjudication? What is "plea-bargaining"? Do prosecutors always prosecute, even when the evidence seems in their favor?

8. The U.S. Supreme Court has recognized the lawful status of negotiations between prosecutor and accused where these are conducted even on the grounds of expediency, expense, and court congestion (North Carolina v. Alford, 1970, 400 U.S. 25, 91 Sup.Ct. 160). Does this go beyond a concern for the individualization of justice, into the realm of a purely business deal? I get a bargain because my business competitor is occupied with grander schemes; I get a bargain

because the courts are busy or the prosecutor has bigger fish in mind. Is this justified through our acceptance of "the luck of the game" when we somehow or other contract into the game?

14. LAW ENFORCEMENT

If we are told that the law is at hand, it is probably a policeman we expect to appear. This tendency to identify law with enforcement officials goes beyond our evident interest in the pain of sanctions. We have come to place an extraordinary burden on the police, adding to their tasks much that we supposedly assign to legislators and judges. The problems of law enforcement run beyond practical difficulties into theoretical questions of what law is and how it is interpreted.

Statutes and ordinances in this country generally require the police to enforce all laws, regardless of any judgment about the justice or cost involved. It is well known, however, that the police exercise broad discretion in deciding whether to arrest. They often do not enforce gambling laws against social gamblers or in taverns where local sentiment on law and order allows for the practice. The police do not enforce laws they think obsolete or trivial, especially when this would place a strain on resources. Crimes are classified as worthy of attention, or not, depending on the cultural subgroups in which they occur. And the police may show considerable judgment in their approach to an informant (e.g., in narcotics cases) who could help them to more serious arrests.

We are neither surprised nor shocked. But the problems of a police officer serve to focus some questions about our generally unthinking use of such terms as *law and order* and *discretion*.

Law and Order

The task of enforcement agents is usually pictured in terms of preventing or handling crimes, from felonies to traffic violations. Policemen compare behavior with the norms that are precisely defined in statutes, and the available weapon is arrest for subsequent adjudication. However, police officers soon learn that most of their time is spent playing a variety of other social roles, for which training has offered little preparation. They find themselves responding to family quarrels and mediating disputes about offensive sounds or sights or remarks. The work is commonly at the outer limits of criminal law, and often beyond in the realm of tort. Even where support comes from statutes, these can be so vague that the police must take over as rule makers. They may discover that they are strangers in a community with standards foreign to them. Or, if they are blessed with tact and sympathy, they may appropriate the mantle of a counselor. There are, even today, societies where people turn to a policeman for personal help before they think of a priest or social worker.

When we speak of law and order, we are either using the same term twice or are implying the above difference of functions. If we suggest a distinction, it is between the application of enacted law and the maintenance of customary order. Murder, theft, and speeding fall under the former category. The keeping of public peace is a fair account of the latter. What we are here discussing as law enforcement is restricted by some to the former. But the plight of a police officer, or of equivalent enforcement agents in earlier times, invites the broader meaning. The two roles may show the complex interplay of legislation and custom, of law that is made and found.

An illustration of one approach to this question is offered in an article by a former Yale law professor, Charles A. Reich.[42] His problem has to do with the right of police to stop and question us. It was the pleasure and relaxation he found in walking, at night as well as during the day, that brought him into confrontation with the police on nine or ten occasions. In at least five states, he was halted by a patrol car, told to identify himself and even threatened with arrest for "vagrancy" (which, as those who know Latin will confirm, means "wandering"). To such incidents he adds many in which he was stopped without cause while driving. Professor Reich then clarifies his problem:

> These circumstances define the problem that I wish to discuss. In this article, I am not concerned with police investigations after a crime has been reported, or with circumstances which suggest that the individual who has been stopped may be doing something illegal. My problem is this: no crime has been reported, no suspect has been described, there is no visible sign of an offense, there is nothing whatever to direct police attention to this particular individual. I am concerned with what is called *preventive* police work.
>
> Although the experiences I have had are in themselves trivial, the increasing preventive activities of the police present an issue of first importance. What happens when the person stopped is a Negro, or poor, or frightened? What intrusions upon privacy, what affronts to dignity, occur? How much discretion do the police have to invent an offense for anyone who objects to being questioned? May the police establish a regular routine of requiring pedestrians to carry identification and explain their presence, or of requiring motorists to stop and tell where they are going? I do not have answers, but I have some questions. Let us focus on the moment of contact between the citizen and the police.
>
> The first issue that troubles me is whether the police have any power at all to stop a law abiding person on a public street. Of course any individual has a right to approach any other individual—to ask him the time, to ask him how to find the Yale Divinity School, or to ask his opinion about foreign policy. But it is not quite the same when the police stop someone.

---

42. Charles A. Reich, "Police Questioning of Law Abiding Citizens," *Yale Law Journal* 75 (1966): 1,161–72. The extracts that follow are printed with permission of the Yale Law Journal Company and Fred B. Rothman & Company.

There is authority in the approach of the police, and command in their tone. I can ignore the ordinary person, but can I ignore the police? Police officers tell me that they have a *right* to stop anyone in a public place, without having a reason. I think I have a *right* not to be stopped. So far as I know, reported court decisions do not supply us with an answer.

The next issue is what questions the police may ask. Name? Address? Occupation? Age? Marital status? Explanation of presence and destination? Documentary proof of identity? Many people might have no objection to giving out any or all of these facts about themselves. But I have a strong sense that however innocuous the facts may be, some things are nobody's business. I do not particularly like to be probed, and I like it much less when the probing is official. I certainly do not think that every police officer has a roving commission to satisfy his curiosity about anyone he sees on the street.

Closely related to questioning is the issue of the individual's replies. May he refuse to answer? May he demand to know the identity of the officer? May he demand to know why he is being stopped? May he lie to the officer about his age, or why he is out on the street? May he turn and go on his way? I submit that very few people know what their rights are under such circumstances. I do not even know how to find out.

The next issue is what *actions* the officer may take if the individual attempts to claim some rights. May the officer detain him? Frisk him? Search him? Take him to the police station? Hold him there for questioning? Here the law does supply an answer in general terms, for we know that arrests and searches can be made only upon probable cause. But concrete answers really depend upon what we conclude about the right to stop and to ask questions.

The last issue is what remedies are available to the citizen to test out the law in the circumstances I have described. There is always a tort action for false arrest. Perhaps in some extreme circumstances there might be grounds for an action under one of the civil rights statutes, or for an injunction against a continuing police practice. But these remedies are often costly, time-consuming, and ultimately unsuccessful. No one effectively "polices the police." [pp. 1,162–63]

Evidently, a professor of law is well equipped to defend himself, but Reich worries about those who are not. He sees such action of the police as a particular threat to minorities, to the poor, and to teenagers. This, he says, is the raw material of alienation and rebellion. Abusive language and calculated humiliation can be as grave as physical violence. He adds: "What is at stake is the respect and dignity due to each individual from his government."

The problems raised lie at or beyond the borders of enacted criminal law. If police officers wish to appeal to this, they have at their disposal a variety of charges so indefinite as to give them almost unlimited discretion. They can threaten arrest for disorderly conduct, for loitering, or even for the catchall concept of "suspicion." And the motorist can be charged with having faulty equipment or an obstructed window, or for careless driving. Reich describes a case where a driver in Colorado was stopped by the police and used language that was not sufficiently deferential. He was then followed for six miles and arrested for failing to dim his lights correctly. After a night in jail he secured his release by pleading guilty to a charge of drunken driving, was fined $355 and lost his driver's license for a year. The case is known to us because it finally reached the federal appeals courts and the driver was held entitled to damages for "arbitrary misuse of official power."

The happy ending, if such it be, does not answer any of our questions about law enforcement where clear statutes fail to guide it and the tenuous notion of public peace is involved. The reply given by many, Professor Reich among them, is that the province of written rules should be extended. Order maintenance should also be governed by enacted law. Reich continues as follows:

> The broad outline of a set of rules for the police can be suggested briefly.
> 1. The police should not be allowed to stop anyone unless something particular about him, as distinguished from the mass of people, gives cause to believe that he has committed a crime.
> 2. When a person is stopped, the officer should identify himself, and explain, with particularity, his reasons for stopping the person.
> 3. The person may be questioned, but he cannot be required to answer. He may be asked, but not required, to produce identification.
> 4. The officer must conduct himself in a manner that would be proper in ordinary business relationships between equals.
> 5. The officer may search a person only if he reasonably believes that he (the officer) is in danger, or if he has probable cause in the constitutional sense.
> 6. If the person stopped desires to continue on his way, the officer may not detain him unless he has probable cause to arrest him for a crime.
>
> These guidelines are a beginning: there is much room for working out details, but almost any rules will have the virtue of some certainty in an area where unlimited uncertainty now exists. Perhaps such instructions might be effectively enforced by a civilian police review board which could provide the sort of sanctions and remedies that the courts are unable to provide.
>
> Perhaps this article sounds as if I have something against police officers—as if I do not appreciate the difficulties and dangers they face, the impossible demands upon them, and how well most of them perform their duty. But this is not my meaning. My meaning is that everyone, including the police, must live under rules. All organizations, and all officials, get out of hand if they do not have rules to guide them, if they do not do their work within limits. [pp. 1,170–71]

This suggested extension of rules is unlikely to meet with the approval of police officers who find that recent court decisions on the procedure for arrest (e.g., Miranda v. Arizona, 1966, 384 U.S. 436, 86 Sup.Ct. 1602) supply obstacles to police efficiency and even endanger the officer's life. One wrote that "the toughest adversary a cop confronts is the law he must enforce." However, our concern is more theoretical. Are there contemporary parallels to the ancient Chinese experience of the extension of *fa* into realms previously organized by the *li* (section 10)? Does the growth of enacted rules touch only the symptoms of discontent and even stifle the air that legislation draws from customary law?

Think, for example, of law and order in the flow of traffic. Here, rules are defined as precisely as possible and the discretion of police is kept to a minimum. However, two questions are pertinent. Can a police officer enforce all the rules? And, even if this is possible in theory, should it be tried in practice?

The answer to the first question is clear. A study of traffic violations at one intersection in Berkeley, California, showed that (if we assume similar conditions at other intersections) around three million violations of traffic laws take place each day in that city. Evidently the rules cannot be enforced in their entirety. But suppose the budget were sufficient to increase the police force a thousand times? The answer to our second question seems to be that total enforcement would be intolerable. Traffic does move through our busy streets with sufficient order for most of us. And this is not achieved by rules alone. Behind the rules lie common understandings that both support rule following in general and allow for a multitude of violations without loss.

The theme has been discussed earlier in this chapter. There are times when it is either ridiculous or self-defeating to lay down the law. Indeed, most of the examples we took of cases where the courts have allowed customary views of reasonable conduct to stand against competing statutes were from the realm of traffic. It would be excessive to insert the word *reasonably* into each law we write, but it is commonly assumed to be there. Propositional law cannot spell out all we understand.

This is not to say that Professor Reich is wrong in his particular suggestions. The problem he discusses may be one that calls for a move "rightward," toward a formulation of rules. The six he suggests are modest and might well be effective. However, our own question is more general and is not necessarily satisfied by the statement that everyone must live under rules. If we grant that the police need to be policed by other officials, the logician may ask who is then to police these. There can be no infinite regress of rules. Somewhere we must stop and rely on what lies beyond or under the rules.

Perhaps it is healthy, then, to stress the distinction in our term *law and order*, and to phrase our detailed problems in terms of a boundary line and a relative priority. The vague assumption of customary order may need to be given form through enacted laws. But we should realize that the latter feed upon some deeper level of customary assumptions. The civilian police review board that Reich advocates would soon have to ask how, within the many communities of a policeman's work, conduct and talk "between equals" is understood. The very uniform of a police officer precludes the equality of businessmen making a contract, or of husband and wife, or of teacher and student. Policemen face a delicate task in adapting to the complexity of roles they play, but no mere multiplication of rules can suffice to lead them in this project.

Discretion

In his full article, Reich refers several times to the discretion that policemen exercise. He objects to unlimited discretion. Yet surely we also praise a person for acting with discretion? There are ambiguities in our talk, and they will surface again in the following chapters when we ask about the decisions that judges make.

Some preliminary clarifications of a vital term are needed. We shall look first at an analysis of the term *discretion* that has been made by Professor Ronald Dworkin.[43] Then, with some analogies drawn from games, we shall return to the problems facing a police officer.

Dworkin looks for various meanings of discretion in our ordinary language. Common to all is a context in which someone is charged with making decisions in the light of standards set by an authority. Discretion implies some area left open by a belt of restriction—it is like the hole in a doughnut. The question is about the surrounding standards and the resulting scope for decision. In such terms, Dworkin distinguishes between two "weak" senses and one "strong" sense of discretion.

One of the weak senses needs only to be mentioned, for it has figured little in subsequent discussion. An official in a hierarchy of authority is said to have discretion if his decision is taken to be final, not to be set aside by a higher official. Thus, a linesman in soccer may have discretion in holding a player to be offside if the referee on the field will not overrule such a decision.

It is the other weak sense of discretion that has drawn comment, and when I refer in what follows to "weak discretion," this is what will be meant. Dworkin defines it as saying no more than that an official must use sound judgment in applying standards that have been given him from above. Dworkin's example is of a lieutenant's instruction that a sergeant should take his five most experienced men on patrol. The sergeant will fail if he simply picks the first five men he encounters or if he includes the raw recruit who has just arrived. However, we can still say that the sergeant is left a great deal of discretion in using his judgment to decide which five men are truly the most experienced (much as the manager of a soccer team must use discretion in picking the best players to encounter an opponent that relies on sudden breakout from a packed defense).

In contrast to this Dworkin sets the strong sense of discretion in which "an official is simply not bound by standards set him by the authority in question." The example given is of a sergeant being told to pick any five men for patrol.

---

43. Ronald Dworkin, *Taking Rights Seriously*, 31–39. For a detailed criticism of these pages, and one on which I have drawn in what follows, see Kent Greenawalt, "Discretion and Judicial Decision," *Columbia Law Review* 75 (1975): 359–99.

Where then are the "surrounding standards" that allow us still to picture "a hole in the doughnut"? Dworkin is quick to add that strong discretion is not license and does not exclude criticism. There are standards of rationality, fairness, and effectiveness that allow us to say the sergeant made a mistake. Suppose, for example, he picked his patrol stupidly (if he includes a man with a leg injury) or unjustly (if he exposes only his personal enemies to danger or selects the five men who refused to bribe him). Even strong discretion does not leave us free to indulge our private prejudices.

Dworkin's purpose in making this distinction between weak and strong discretion is to argue that judges have the former but not the latter when they decide issues of law. Hence, even in hard cases, plaintiff and defendant are entitled to a legally correct decision and are not at the mercy of whatever may take place in some gap in the law. Dworkin is here attacking what he understands to follow from the approach of legal positivists such as Hart. Discussion of such claims will be left to section 19.

How clear, in our ordinary language and in contexts outside the courtroom, is this distinction between weak and strong discretion? Is the good judgment required in the former altogether covered by authoritative standards, or does it allow for some of the freedom of choice that Dworkin tries to restrict to strong discretion? How do you, as a sergeant, decide which are your five most experienced men? By length of service in the army? By length of service in this particular campaign? By length of service and by some measure of ability that makes for a truer form of "experience"? By demonstrated ability on patrols? You may well assume that the standards set you by the lieutenant are governed by the purpose that the patrol should be as successful as possible. But, even so, you may realize that officers in your battalion would be split on which of the above criteria should be the guiding one. It could well be that your judgment is scarcely covered by authoritative standards and that little more is left than general norms of rationality.

The problems of a basketball referee have already been mentioned (see section 3). The rule book tells you fairly precisely what actions do or do not count as fouls. And, when you often have to decide on hard cases, you may find some authoritative standards such as that you should prevent a game from becoming too rough and that you should maintain the flow of the game. Yet such standards can conflict. Perhaps you will talk of some superior standard, such as "the good of the game," but this is so vague that it allows for the fact that different referees would blow the whistle more or less frequently in the same contest. Do we criticize some of them for a violation of weak discretion or do we cover the difference by allowing for strong discretion?

One other example is taken from Kent Greenawalt.[44] As a teacher you are instructed to select the ten pupils "who would get the most out of it" to have seats at a Shakespeare play. Fidelity to this standard allows for choices that

---

44. Greenawalt, "Judicial Decision," 366. The two previous examples are discussed on pp. 370–71.

might extend to all students in your class. Should it be those who have read the most Shakespeare? Those who are best at acting? Those who might be most inspired to improve their reading of plays? Those who might least profit from an alternative activity planned for the ones not seeing the play?

A possible conclusion is that "we might more accurately think of a spectrum of ranges from simple factual judgment to wide freedom of choice than to think of a dichotomy of two senses [of discretion]."[45] At least, we may now return to the predicament of a police officer.

You are sent to arrest a suspect who has clearly offered probable cause. If you are told to use your discretion in making the arrest, this presumably comes close in meaning to what Dworkin describes as weak discretion. You are working under well-defined standards for what counts as a legal and efficient arrest. You will have to use judgment in deciding how best to execute these standards in the concrete situation. But you will fail in more than general rationality if you forget to warn the suspect of his rights or if you otherwise create unnecessary problems for the prosecutor. The discretion you use is akin to that of a baseball manager who is instructed by the owner to pick the strongest starting line-up to face a left-handed pitcher.

When, however, we turn from the usually precise rules of law enforcement to the more nebulous area of order maintenance, we move toward discretion of greater strength. As a police officer, you are sent to settle a neighborhood dispute and are told to act with discretion. Here, the goal is less simple. What constitutes settlement? The mere fact that bloodshed is avoided, for the time? Or some degree of therapy by which the disputants come to recognize the need to coexist? Nor are you equipped with clear rules. The laws you may employ are called discretionary, meaning that they rely upon such ill-defined terms as disturbing the peace, offensive behavior, indecent language. And the rules you can draw from experience run the gamut of threat, persuasion, and a casual defusing of the drama. Humor may prove more effective than handcuffs. Much depends on the way you present yourself, on your level of language and tone of voice.

Does this mean that you enjoy unlimited discretion, in the sense that Professor Reich seems to accuse some police officers as claiming? We have seen that Dworkin refuses to identify strong discretion with license. Policemen, in deciding whether and how to stop and question a citizen, are certainly bound by norms of rationality and fairness. Many of the instances that Reich cites can be criticized on this score. And the vagueness of such terms is surely lessened by some standards that come from the very understandings that give authority to the police and make possible its abuse. A police uniform may be seen as a symbol for the social order by which we regulate our interaction even where no definite rules penetrate. Arbitrary power contradicts the grant of authority that

---

45. Ibid., 366.

we make to protect a community of people who come together in ways other than those of power.

Let us imagine that the baseball manager telephones the club's owner to report a problem: his star player has achieved local publicity by provoking a drunken brawl at the hotel on the night before a championship game. The owner grants full discretion to the manager in handling the situation. Here, there is no one goal involved, and rules are lacking. If you were manager, would you still field your strongest team? Or would you exclude the player to maintain discipline and protect the team's good name? The strong degree of discretion you have does not mean that anything goes. At stake is the very respect on which your position and effectiveness as manager depends. Even in the absence of definite rules, you can make serious mistakes; you may find that, in spite of the discretion granted to you, your contract is not renewed for the following season.

Suppose the various forms of discretion are seen on the model of a spectrum rather than in the manner of a dichotomy. Some commentators (like Greenawalt) will then emphasize the way in which freedom of choice extends into regions we thought to be governed by authoritative standards. Other commentators (like Dworkin) will argue for the extension, in the opposite direction, of standards such as unwritten principles of law. Whether Dworkin is right to put judges at a point on the spectrum where they must look for the one correct decision to which a plaintiff or defendant is entitled can remain an open question. However, there is a sense in which the growth of the common law has itself shown this repeated search for underlying principles. A further baseball analogy may help.

You agree to act as umpire in a neighborhood game where the players range in age from six to sixteen and abilities reveal an even greater span. At first you conduct the contest (game A) entirely according to the official rules, calling a strike whenever the pitch passes over the plate and between the knees and armpits of the batter, large or small. The score proves very unequal, so you switch to a procedure (game B) in which you call strikes and balls according to no principle that the players can detect. You show unlimited discretion. Protests mount, for this fails as a game. Eventually you change to a procedure (game C) in which you call strikes and balls according to principles not clearly enunciated at first but gradually becoming more evident as time passes. For example, what would be a strike against an older player is not so called when the player is younger. A similar difference applies where there are variations in ability at the same age. And when one team is several runs behind, you avoid calling strikeouts on them until the scores are more even.

Game A allowed discretion only in regard to your judgment of how the ball crossed the plate. Game B permitted unlimited discretion, which is really only license; it was not a game because it was lawless and tyrannical. Game C, however, changed to what may be called *principled discretion*. Order came from undefined principles (fairness, sportsmanship, the interest of a close contest). Rules were not simply rejected but were left fluid because they repeatedly adapted to principles in the process of discovery. When challenged, the umpire was not able always to explain his decision adequately but was not immune from the obligation to attempt some justification. Nor was the challenging player deprived of his rights for reconsideration. Beyond all law is anarchy (in the pejorative sense). Yet behind the explicit rules of law are some implicit principles that allow the rules to change and to be bent legally.

FURTHER READING

Bard, Morton, and Robert Shellow. *Issues in Law Enforcement.* Reston, Va.: Reston Publishing Co., 1976.
Davis, Karl. *Discretionary Justice.* Baton Rouge, La.: Louisiana State Univ. Press, 1969.
Davis, Kenneth Culp. *Police Discretion.* St. Paul: West, 1975.
Kadish, Mortimer R., and Sanford H. Kadish. *Discretion to Disobey.* Stanford, Calif.: Stanford Univ. Press, 1973, 1–94.
McDonald, Lynn. *The Sociology of Law and Order.* Boulder, Colo.: Westview Press, 1976.
Wilson, James Q. *Thinking about Crime.* 2d ed. New York: Basic Books, 1983.
―――. *Varieties of Police Behavior.* Cambridge: Harvard Univ. Press, 1968.
Wright, Jack, and Peter Lewis. *Modern Criminal Justice.* New York: McGraw-Hill, 1978.

QUESTIONS FOR DISCUSSION

1.   The *Encyclopaedia Britannica* defines a policeman as one whose function is "to maintain civil order and to investigate breaches of the law." Can you have the former without the latter? The latter without the former? Do literary utopias include a police force? Would law enforcement belong to the utopia you envisage?
2.   If a plainclothes detective of thirty-five years' experience notices two men walking furtively to and from a certain store window, does his police function demand that he interrogate and frisk them (see Terry v. Ohio, 1968, 392 U.S. 1, 88 Sup.Ct. 1868)? Suppose Professor Reich were so interrogated, and his repeated visits to the store window were prompted by hesitation about buying jewelry for a lady? Do you object to passing through a metal detector, or even to being frisked, before you board a plane?
3.   Are you ever guilty of careless driving? Does this charge apply if you remove one hand from the steering wheel? If you take your eyes off the road to look behind (mirrors leave blind spots)? If you restrain a boisterous child? If you attend to a more attractive passenger? Can you define what level of noise in a house constitutes a nuisance to neighbors?
4.   One police expert lists twenty grounds for stopping and interrogating a person. These include "exaggerated unconcern over contact with the police officer" and "visible concern when he approaches." What problem do you see in a complete codification of police conduct?
5.   Policemen have, in recent years, been driven to the conclusion that law enforcement is impeded by the proliferation of law, in the form of rules for police action. Can this complaint be generalized? "Faced with a climbing rate of crime, America is often said to be a lawless nation. Yet we probably have more law per square inch than any other nation in the world. It is an overgrowth of law and regulation that prevents us from carrying out our most needed and basic functions" (Alvin Toffler). Is this an overgrowth of law or of formal regulations?
6.   Statistics suggest that police officers deliberately fail to make arrests in more than half the felonies and misdemeanors where they could show probable cause. Such selective enforcement becomes more dramatic when we consider the next decision, whether to prosecute or not. Must we conclude that the trial begins long before the judge enters the court? Most trials have already

been concluded by the policemen and prosecutor. Can this be justified in terms of what has been discussed in this chapter? A customary society passes judgment without benefit of the distinctions we make between legal personnel.

7. What specific proposals can you draw from the suggestion that much of law enforcement has to do with the maintenance of customary order rather than the application of formal rules? Instead of insisting on one (propositional) law for all, should we promote self-policing of subcultural groups? Should we expand petty claims courts (adjudication and arbitration) and citizen dispute centers (mediation)?

8. "Engraved on the Department of Justice building are these five words: *Where law ends tyranny begins.* I think that in our system of government, where law ends tyranny need not begin. Where law ends, discretion begins, and the exercise of discretion may mean either beneficence or tyranny, either justice or injustice, either reasonableness or arbitrariness" (Karl Davis). Comment on this in light of the distinction between rules and a form of discretion that goes beyond rules, between the license of unlimited discretion and the gradual development of principled discretion.

15. THE LEGAL ENFORCEMENT OF MORALS

> *The only purpose for which power can be rightfully exercised over any member of a civilized community, against his will, is to prevent harm to others. His own good, either physical or moral, is not a sufficient warrant.*
>
> (John Stuart Mill, *On Liberty*, chapter 1)

The present chapter, on the range of law, has been more concerned to indicate the wide variety of what may count as legal experience than to draw lines that distinguish law from other social rules and standards. However, we have noticed at least three possible ways of marking limits to law.

1. Hoebel, in the spirit of John Austin, confines law to those norms that are regularly backed by physical force on the part of an individual or group that enjoys social recognition for so acting.[46] A legal system is defined in terms of a pedigree that identifies laws as stemming from a sovereign. Custom, for example, belongs to law only through the tacit command of such an authority. In such terms, the Eskimo and others without any central government can at best claim "the bare-bones of the legal."

2. H. L. A. Hart has adapted the pedigree of a legal system to put its apex in a "rule of recognition."[47] What gives validity to a law is not the command of a leader, backed by force, but the derivation of that law from a "rule for identifying laws." When one king dies, and his commands cease, the law persists and another king ascends the throne "by law." The limits of law are thus those set by the rule of recognition; for example, what has been enacted by the Congress in accord with the Constitution is within the law. Moral convictions, however important, are outside the law unless they are given the force of law by enactment in accord with the master rule. What the

---

46. See p. 76.
47. P. 88.

Cheyenne chiefs decide in their lodge is law but what Black Horse rules is probably not.

3. Lon Fuller, in his parable of King Rex, places further constraints on law.[48] Though Rex may have announced his many rulings from the the throne, and have otherwise satisfied the kingdom's master rule for making laws, he is said by Fuller to have failed to make valid law. Pedigree is not enough. The boundary of law excludes any rules that violate certain requirements in the very project of living according to rules. Yet it may be noticed that Fuller, with a great respect for the place of custom and mediation in law, would include within the range of law much that Austin and Hart exclude.

These questions will be set in a broader context in the next chapter. However, it is likely that many readers feel some impatience for such academic arguments about the nature of law and the compass of a legal system. If we are interested in the limits of law, this is surely for the practical purpose of keeping the legislator and the policeman out of our private affairs. Popular discussion today is more concerned with the normative question where law *ought* to extend than with the descriptive question where law *does* extend. As we all know, laws have been passed and enforced that tell us what we may or may not do in our private sexual lives, in our use of alcohol or drugs, and in matters such as suicide, which some would say are questions for the individual but no business of law officials. Although societies have legislated in such personal areas, ought they do so?

The topic that has been put under the heading of "the enforcement of morals" is loaded with ambiguities and has provoked a great deal of philosophical discussion. This section will offer little more than introductory comments. It may serve as a transition to chapter 3, for the difference between theories of law has much to do with disagreements on the relation of law and morality.

Where the Law Has No Business

> ... There must remain a realm of private morality and immorality which is, in brief and crude terms, not the law's business.
> (The *Wolfenden Report*, 1957, paragraph 61)

This quotation comes from the report of a committee charged to discuss whether changes should be made in the British law that treated homosexuality and prostitution as criminal offenses. The report, which recommended the decriminalization of such activities, was strongly defended by H. L. A. Hart. He admitted that the laws in question, coming from the monarch in Parliament, were valid. But he argued that they were bad laws and should be changed by the legislature (as they were shortly afterwards).

Before we turn to the specific debate that the Wolfenden Report brought about, it may be helpful to ask the very general question whether there are any

---

48. Pp. 114–15.

realms of our life that invite some moral assessment but should be beyond the competence of law, criminal or civil. We start in relatively neutral regions rather than in the much discussed area of sexual behavior.

Earlier, we saw that Aristotle prefaced his discussion of justice by distinguishing between this as a general virtue and as one that is specific or precise.[49] I may possibly speak of someone who shows generosity and mercy, or who exhibits heroism and extraordinary courage or self-sacrifice, as a just person. However, it would seem odd to say that I am obliged by justice to be generous or heroic. We know that current practices in this country require a 15 percent tip at a restaurant; such a sum has become part of the waiter's pay rather than a recognition for exceptional service. The money thus ceases to be a "gratuity," given in a spirit of pure generosity (though a voluntary 25 percent might recover the origins of the practice). What law or custom demands is destructive of the form of "private morality" that is called "supererogation" (doing over and above what is usually asked). Thus there are some moral virtues that seem to require a limit to legal obligations. A person who heroically plunges into the icy Potomac to rescue survivors from a crashed airliner deserves our moral esteem and perhaps even calls upon our imitation in some less dramatic circumstances. But if the law, backed by a policeman on the bridge, had required him to do this, his very possibility of exhibiting an important range of moral action would have been destroyed.

Legislatures do not, in fact, try to enforce heroism or generosity as a matter of law. Indeed, civil cases indicate a reluctance to demand even minimal standards of help toward a person in distress. One example, from a bitter January in Minnesota, may suggest the question whether our legal obligation not to harm another involves a duty (as morality certainly does) to avoid exposing him to inevitable harm from other sources.[50] Depue was a cattle buyer who went to Flatau's house on business. Becoming ill, he asked if he could stay the night. Flatau refused, putting the visitor on his sleigh and setting the reins of the horse around his shoulders. About a mile away, Depue fell off, nearly froze to death, and suffered amputation of several fingers. The trial court ruled that he had no legal claim to sue; the decision relied on a precedent of several years earlier, in which it was stated that "those duties which are dictated merely by good morals or by humane considerations are not within the domain of the law.... Suffering humanity has no legal complaint against those who pass by on the other side."[51]

However, the appellate court reversed the order. It was agreed that the precedent correctly reported the failure of the law to impose on us the obligation or heroic ideal of imitating the good samaritan. Yet it was held that in this case a jury should be allowed to decide from the facts whether Flatau was legally

49. See section 8.
50. Depue v. Flatau (1907): 100 Minn. 299, 111 N.W. 1.
51. Union Pacific Ry. Co. v. Cappier (1903): 66 Kan. 649, 72 Pac. 281.

liable for the consequences of "negligent failure" in regard to Depue. No contract obligation was present, and Depue may not have had a legal right to stay as a guest, but expedients could well have been available less drastic than "exposing him in his helpless condition to the merciless elements." This reversal gives us no clear guide where the line is to be drawn between law and morality, but it does not question the existence of such a line.

The reader may remember the case of Red Robe and Two Twists.[52] It was an example, common to much of the literature in primitive societies, of a heroic exploit proposed to all for serious consideration and possible imitation. The question was asked whether this is part of the law, and ideals of the Sermon on the Mount were suggested as parallels. The question, perhaps, was rhetorical. The law does not oblige us to expose our life in so valiant a way, or even to turn the other cheek. Such moralilty belongs to a realm beyond the explicit business of civil or criminal law. Yet we should not simply dismiss the presentation of moral ideals from all talk of living legally. Even if a legal rule (in the strict sense) limits our duties to those of contract obligations, the very notion of a contract or promise involves moral principles that go beyond what the law books specify.

A possible complaint is that when we talk of heroism or generosity, the difficulties about applying a legal obligation to these extend also to talk of a moral duty. Am I even morally obliged to plunge into an icy river to attempt a rescue? Perhaps it would be wiser to look at some everyday moral virtue that seems to escape from the reach of law. What about friendship? Aristotle defines this loosely as the virtue by which "people are mutually recognized as bearing goodwill and wishing well to each other."[53] I can scarcely see an obligation to enter into a relation of friendship with those who sell me groceries or cash my checks; mutual respect as persons, with genuine politeness, may be enough. However, there are particular relationships, and some legalized ones, where one may plausibly speak of a duty to offer and receive friendship. The most obvious examples are within a family, nuclear or extended. There the law defines the minimum, and moral requirements go far beyond. The reluctance of the law to step "behind the curtain" has been discussed before.[54] In such relationships, at least, Aristotle seems correct in saying that "those who are friends have no need of justice," though he proceeds to complicate the distinction by adding that "the truest form of justice is friendship."[55]

The role of a medical doctor offers some interesting problems in defining a moral area beyond a strictly legal connection. Changes have taken place over the years. A century ago, the local doctor may have been largely a friend with

---

52. See section 9.
53. Aristotle *Nicomachean Ethics* 1156a.
54. See section 10 for a discussion of the family as a paradigm for customary law. It was with hesitation that the law agreed to allow suits for wife-beating. A more pertinent question today is whether a husband can be legally accused of raping his own wife.
55. Aristotle *Nicomachean Ethics* 1155a.

specialized knowledge; he was the neighbor who could express his goodwill with the aid of prescriptions for the pharmacy, though the friendly manner was often as important in effecting cures. Yet we know that today's physician can be as much concerned with legal as with medical questions; the threat of a malpractice suit shackles the good samaritan, and detailed professional codes define practices and even attitudes. Those of us who remember the old-style family doctor may wonder if there is still a sufficient "realm of private morality which is not the law's business."

The reader can offer comments on the intricate expectations of the teacher-student relationship. Here, our law makes few obvious inroads, showing unwillingness even to support a suit that poor teaching is a failure to meet contractual requirements. However, the trial of Socrates may remind us that it is not impossible for a manner of teaching to produce criminal charges.

Examples have run their course. They should suffice to indicate that law and morality are not coterminous and yet that the problem where we ought to draw lines is not easily solved.

Devlin's Claims

Two years after the *Wolfenden Report*, Sir Patrick (later Lord) Devlin, a prominent judge, was invited to give the prestigious Maccabaean Lecture in Jurisprudence to the British Academy. He initially approved of the report and of its recourse to the moral philosophy of John Stuart Mill. This is perhaps best known today through Mill's so-called "harm principle" (quoted at the beginning of this section). Put bluntly, the claim was that, at least as far as the law of the land is concerned, what we do is our own business unless our actions harm other people. Under such a norm, homosexuality between consenting adults seems an evident candidate for immunity from legal interference. So Devlin, agreeing at first with Mill, decided to devote his lecture to the recommendation of further changes in the criminal law, as this applied to "private immorality." However, he tells us that his studies then led to an important change in his convictions. When he delivered his lecture, it turned out to be a criticism of "errors of jurisprudence" in the *Wolfenden Report*.

The lecture provoked a storm of protest. Devlin responded by moderating some of his views and adding six chapters in which he applied his position to various realms of law.[56] What follows is a series of extracts from the basic lecture.

---

56. Patrick Devlin, *The Enforcement of Morals* (New York, Oxford Univ. Press, 1965).

THE ENFORCEMENT OF MORALS
by Patrick Devlin

© *Oxford University Press 1965 (pp. 6–17, 22, 24).*
Reprinted with permission of the Oxford University Press.

There is only one explanation of what has hitherto been accepted as the basis of the criminal law and that is that there are certain standards of behaviour or moral principles which society requires to be observed; and the breach of them is an offence not merely against the person who is injured but against society as a whole.

Thus, if the criminal law were to be reformed so as to eliminate from it everything that was not designed to preserve order and decency or to protect citizens (including the protection of youth from corruption), it would overturn a fundamental principle. It would also end a number of specific crimes. Euthanasia or the killing of another at his own request, suicide, attempted suicide and suicide pacts, duelling, abortion, incest between brother and sister, are all acts which can be done in private and without offence to others and need not involve the corruption or exploitation of others. Many people think that the law on some of these subjects is in need of reform, but no one hitherto has gone so far as to suggest that they should all be left outside the criminal law as matters of private morality. They can be brought within it only as a matter of moral principle. It must be remembered also that although there is much immorality that is not punished by the law, there is none that is condoned by the law. The law will not allow its processes to be used by those engaged in immorality of any sort. For example, a house may not be let for immoral purposes; the lease is invalid and would not be enforced. But if what goes on inside there is a matter of private morality and not the law's business, why does the law inquire into it at all?

I think it is clear that the criminal law as we know it is based upon moral principle. In a number of crimes its function is simply to enforce a moral principle and nothing else. The law, both criminal and civil, claims to be able to speak about morality and immorality generally. Where does it get its authority to do this and how does it settle the moral principles which it enforces? Undoubtedly, as a matter of history, it derived both from Christian teaching. But I think that the strict logician is right when he says that the law can no longer rely on doctrines in which citizens are entitled to disbelieve. It is necessary therefore to look for some other source.

In jurisprudence, as I have said, everything is thrown open to discussion and, in the belief that they cover the whole field, I have framed three interrogatories addressed to myself to answer:

1. Has society the right to pass judgement at all on matters of morals? Ought there, in other words, to be a public morality, or are morals always a matter for private judgement?

2. If society has the right to pass judgement, has it also the right to use the weapon of the law to enforce it?

3. If so, ought it to use that weapon in all cases or only in some; and if only in some, on what principles should it distinguish?

I shall begin with the first interrogatory and consider what is meant by the right of society to pass a moral judgement, that is, a judgement about what is good and what is evil....

What makes a society of any sort is community of ideas, not only political ideas but also ideas about the way its members should behave and govern their lives; these latter ideas are its morals. Every society has a moral structure as well as a political one: or rather, since that might suggest two independent systems, I should say that the structure of every society is made up both of politics and morals. Take, for example, the institution of marriage. Whether a man should be allowed to take more than one wife is something about which every society has to make up its mind one way or the other. In England we believe in the Christian idea of marriage and therefore adopt monogamy as a moral principle. Consequently the Christian institution of marriage has become the basis of family life and so part of the structure of our society. It is there not because it is Christian. It has got there because it is Christian, but it remains there because it is built into the house in which we live and could not be removed without bringing it down. The great majority of those who live in this country accept it because it is the Christian idea of marriage and for them the only true one. But a non-Christian is bound by it, not because it is part of Christianity but because, rightly or wrongly, it has been adopted by the society in which he lives. It would be useless for him to stage a debate designed to prove that polygamy was theologically more correct and socially preferable; if he wants to live in the house, he must accept it as built the way it is.

We see this more clearly if we think of ideas or institutions that are purely political. Society cannot tolerate rebellion; it will not allow argument about the rightness of the cause. Historians a century later may say that the rebels were right and the government was wrong and a percipient and conscientious subject of the State may think so at the time. But it is not a matter which can be left to individual judgement....

I return to the statement that I have already made, that society means a community of ideas; without shared ideas on politics, morals, and ethics no society can exist. Each one of us has ideas about what is good and what is evil; they cannot be kept private from the society in which we live. If men and women try to create a society in which there is no fundamental agreement about good and evil they will fail; if, having based it on common agreement, the agreement goes, the society will disintegrate. For society is not something that is kept together physically; it is held by the invisible bonds of common thought. If the bonds were too far relaxed the members would drift apart. A common morality is part of the bondage. The bondage is part of the price of society; and mankind, which needs society, must pay its price....

You may think that I have taken far too long in contending that there is such a thing as public morality, a proposition which most people would readily accept, and may have left myself too little time to discuss the next question which to many minds may cause greater difficulty: to what extent should society use the law to enforce its moral judgements? But I believe that the answer to the first question determines the way in which the second should be approached and may indeed very nearly dictate the answer to the second question. If society has no right to make judgements on morals, the law must find some special justification for entering the field of morality: if homosexuality and prostitution are not in themselves wrong, then the onus is very clearly on the lawgiver who wants to frame a law against certain aspects of them to justify the exceptional treatment. But if society has the right to make a judgement and has it on the basis that a recognized morality is as necessary to society as, say, a recognized government, then society may use the law to preserve morality in the same way as it uses it to safeguard anything else that is essential to its existence. If therefore the first proposition is securely established with all its implications, society has a prima facie right to legislate against immorality as such.

The Wolfenden Report, notwithstanding that it seems to admit the right of society to condemn homosexuality and prostitution as immoral, requires special circumstances to be shown to justify the intervention of the law. I think that this is wrong in principle and that any attempt to approach my second interrogatory on these lines is bound to break down. I think that the attempt by the Committee does break down and that this is shown by the fact that it has to define or describe its special circumstances so widely that they can be supported only if it is accepted that the law *is* concerned with immorality as such.

The widest of the special circumstances are described as the provision of 'sufficient safeguards against exploitation and corruption of others, particularly those who are specially vulnerable because they are young, weak in body or mind, inexperienced, or in a state of special physical, official or economic dependence'. The corruption of youth is a well-recognized ground for intervention by the State and for the purpose of any legislation the young can easily be defined. But if similar protection were to be extended to every other citizen, there would be no limit to the reach of the law. The 'corruption and exploitation of others' is so wide that it could be used to cover any sort of immorality which involves, as most do, the co-operation of another person....

I think, therefore, that it is not possible to set theoretical limits to the power of the State to legislate against immorality. It is not possible to settle in advance exceptions to the general rule or to define inflexibly areas of morality into which the law is in no circumstances to be allowed to enter. Society is entitled by means of its laws to protect itself from dangers, whether from within or without. Here again I think that the political parallel is legitimate. The law of treason is directed against aiding the king's enemies and against sedition from within. The justification for this is that established government is necessary for the existence of society and therefore its safety against violent overthrow must be secured. But an established morality is as necessary as good government to the welfare of society. Societies disintegrate from within more frequently than they are broken up by external pressures. There is disintegration when no common morality is observed and history shows that the loosening of moral bonds is often the first stage of disintegration, so that society is justified in taking the same steps to preserve its moral code as it does to preserve its government and other essential institutions. The suppression of vice is as much the law's business as the suppression of subversive activities; it is no more possible to define a sphere of private morality than it is to define one of private subversive activity. It is wrong to talk of private morality or of the law not being concerned with immorality as such or to try to set rigid bounds to the part which the law may play in the suppression of vice. There are no theoretical limits to the power of the State to legislate against treason and sedition, and likewise I think there can be no theoretical limits to legislation against immorality. You may argue that if a man's sins affect only himself it cannot be the concern of society. If he chooses to get drunk every night in the privacy of his own home, is any one except himself the worse for it? But suppose a quarter or a half of the population got drunk every night, what sort of a society would it be? You cannot set a theoretical limit to the number of people who can get drunk before society is entitled to legislate against drunkenness....

In what circumstances the State should exercise its power is the third of the interrogatories I have framed. But before I get to it I must raise a point which might have been brought up in any one of the three. How are the moral judgements of society to be ascertained? By leaving it until now, I can ask it in the more limited form that is now sufficient for my purpose. How is the law-maker to ascertain the moral judgements of society? It is surely not enough that they should be reached by the opinion of the majority; it would be too much to require the individual assent of every citizen. English law has evolved and regularly uses a standard which does not depend on the counting of heads. It is that of the reasonable man. He is not to be confused with the rational man. He is not expected to reason about anything and his judgement may be largely a matter of feeling. It is the viewpoint of the man in the street—or to use an archaism familiar to all lawyers—the man in the Clapham omnibus. He might also be called the right-minded man. For my purpose I should like to call him the man in the jury box, for the moral judgement of society must be something about which any twelve men or women drawn at random might after discussion be expected to be unanimous....

I do not think that one can talk sensibly of a public and private morality any more than one can of a public or private highway. Morality is a sphere in which there is a public interest and a private interest, often in conflict, and the problem is to reconcile the two....

Nothing should be punished by the law that does not lie beyond the limits of tolerance. It is not nearly enough to say that a majority dislike a practice; there must be a real feeling of reprobation. Those who are dissatisfied with the present law on homosexuality often say that the opponents of reform are swayed simply by disgust. If that were so it would be wrong, but I do not think one can ignore disgust if it is deeply felt and not manufactured. Its presence is a good indication that the bounds of toleration are being reached. Not everything is to be tolerated. No society can do without intolerance, indignation, and disgust; they are the forces behind the moral law, and indeed it can be argued that if they or something like them are not present, the feelings of society cannot be weighty enough to deprive the individual of freedom of choice. . . .

There is a general abhorrence of homosexuality. We should ask ourselves in the first instance whether, looking at it calmly and dispassionately, we regard it as a vice so abominable that its mere presence is an *offence*. If that is the genuine feeling of the society in which we live, I do not see how society can be denied the right to eradicate it. . . .

The error of jurisprudence in the Wolfenden Report is caused by the search for some single principle to explain the division between crime and sin. The report finds it in the principle that the criminal law exists for the protection of individuals; on this principle fornication in private between consenting adults is outside the law and thus it becomes logically indefensible to bring homosexuality between consenting adults in private within it. But the true principle is that the law exists for the protection of society. It does not discharge its function by protecting the individual from injury, annoyance, corruption, and exploitation; the law must protect also the institutions and the community of ideas, political and moral, without which people cannot live together. . . .

I return now to the main thread of my argument and summarize it. Society cannot live without morals. Its morals are those standards of conduct which the reasonable man approves. A rational man, who is also a good man, may have other standards. If he has no standards at all he is not a good man and need not be further considered. If he has standards, they may be very different; he may, for example, not disapprove of homosexuality or abortion. In that case he will not share in the common morality; but that should not make him deny that it is a social necessity. A rebel may be rational in thinking that he is right but he is irrational if he thinks that society can leave him free to rebel.

His Critics

The argument that comes across most clearly in this lecture is that a society, being a community of ideas, has a right to protect its existence against ideas that seriously threaten it, whether these be in the realm of treason or of sexual behavior. Devlin distinguishes between principles that individuals may choose to adopt or not, for their own guidance, and principles, such as monogamy, that go to the heart of what a society is. Those of the latter sort are, he holds, rightly within the competence of the criminal law. How does he say we are to identify practices that thus fall under the law? Individual freedom is an important value, but we can restrain it by law when public feeling against some practice rises to "intolerance, indignation, and disgust."

Professor Hart was among the first of many distinguished commentators to put his criticisms in print.[57] He surveys the field of arguments from Mill to Devlin but brings the discussion to earth with an appeal to facts:

57. H. L. A. Hart, *Law, Liberty, and Morality* (Stanford, Calif.: Stanford Univ. Press, 1963).

... Though [Lord Devlin] says that society has the right to enforce a morality as such on the ground that a shared morality is essential to society's existence, it is not at all clear that for him the statement that immorality jeopardizes or weakens society is a statement of empirical fact. It seems sometimes to be an *a priori* assumption, and sometimes a necessary truth and a very odd one. The most important indication that this is so is that, apart from one vague reference to "history" showing that "the loosening of moral bonds is often the first stage of disintegration," no evidence is produced to show that deviation from accepted sexual morality, even by adults in private, is something which, like treason, threatens the existence of society. No reputable historian has maintained this thesis, and there is indeed much evidence against it. As a proposition of fact it is entitled to no more respect than the Emperor Justinian's statement that homosexuality was the cause of earthquakes.[58]

Hart admits that some shared morality may indeed be essential to the survival of a society. There are formal values that establish relationships where "the individual sees questions of conduct from an impersonal point of view and applies general rules impartially to himself and to others; he is made aware of and takes account of the wants, expectations, and reactions of others; he exerts self-discipline and control in adapting his conduct to a system of reciprocal claims."[59] Anthropologists would agree that some such norms of morality have to do with what it means to say that a society exists. But the focus of Devlin's argument is not here.

Devlin replied to Hart by adding a lengthy footnote to his lecture.[60] He points out that deviations from a society's shared morality *need not* threaten its existence any more than all subversive activities do; his contention is only that such deviations *may* constitute a threat and hence cannot "be put beyond the law." This clarification, however, serves only to shift the burden of Devlin's argument from the first two to the third of his "interrogatories."[61] If we grant that challenges to our common morality may pass the threshold of the law's concern, how are we to know when this danger is *sufficient* to constitute a serious threat to society's existence? Devlin replies in terms of the intensity of public indignation and disgust. The expression of feeling that warned us the law could intervene now becomes itself a reason for intervention.

Another critic of Devlin, Ronald Dworkin, interprets this shift in the discussion as helping to expose the underlying question.[62] He gives little space to Devlin's argument about a society's right to protect its own existence and he concentrates on what he considers to be a disjointed but more important argument running through Devlin's essays, that a political majority "has a right to

---

58. Ibid., 50.
59. Ibid., 71.
60. Devlin, *The Enforcement of Morals*, 13.
61. See p. 144 above.
62. Dworkin, *Taking Rights Seriously*, chapter 10.

follow its own moral convictions in defending its social environment from change it opposes."

That is, the question is no longer seen as one regarding the very survival of a society. It is a question about the rights involved in legislating to prevent changes of which a majority disapproves on moral principle. Devlin's proposal is that the majority does have a right to protect, against change, those institutions that it regards as central, where the majority claims to find a threat to common morality and where the existence of this threat is established through appeal to the moral indignation that is aroused. Dworkin's reply is that, even if we go as far as possible in accepting Devlin's assumptions, the proposal must fail because it rests on a fundamental misunderstanding of what it means to approve or disapprove *on moral principle*: "What is shocking and wrong is not his idea that the community's morality counts, but his idea of what counts as the community's morality."[63]

Dworkin offers a valuable examination of what it means to base any claim on a moral position.[64] I must, basically, be able to produce *reasons* for my claim. This does not mean that I should offer a developed moral theory. But it does mean (a) that I do not speak from sheer prejudice (e.g., asserting that racial or ethnic distinctions render some classes of people less worthy of respect, without regard to what such people have done); (b) that my moral position justifies my emotional reactions, rather than vice-versa ("such people make me sick"); (c) that facts to which I appeal do not fail to meet clear standards of evidence (as in saying that "homosexual acts are physically debilitating"); (d) that I have made the reasons my own and am not simply parroting what I have heard; and (e) that I am open to exploring and defending the consistency of my position (e.g., if my appeal is to texts in the Bible, I must be prepared to face the challenge of other biblical texts).

Hence the question whether the opposition of most citizens to homosexuality amounts to a moral position requires, according to Dworkin, more than a report of majority feelings, however much these meet the heading of indignation and disgust. Devlin's argument may not be mistaken in advising a legislator to act with reference to moral consensus, but little guidance is given for testing the credentials of a consensus that is moral. "The argument would have some plausibility if Lord Devlin meant, in speaking of the moral consensus of a community, those positions which are moral positions in the discriminatory sense we have been exploring. But he means nothing of the sort."[65]

Admittedly, the legislator cannot hold hearings on the Clapham omnibus. However, he should go behind a poll of what people feel; he should examine the rational grounds on which such feelings may be justified. He must, for instance, distinguish plausible arguments from prejudices based on principles

63. Ibid., 255.
64. Ibid., 249–53.
65. Ibid., 253.

that we could not seriously be expected to hold. Devlin was quick to discount the correlation of homosexuality with earthquakes as "irrational." Yet he fails to help us to exclude sheer aversion and arbitrariness from our appeal to morality.

If I understand Dworkin's reply correctly, he is turning our attention from a superficial to a profound level in our reliance upon a "common morality." Questions about where we should draw the line between the criminal law and what we loosely call private morality will always be with us. No one can say that the last word has been uttered on homosexuality or pornography or any similar dispute over the boundary between public and private. Yet the deeper moral questions involved are about the way we (as citizens, legislators, or judges) conduct the discussion and arrive at specific laws. Our basic problem is not about conflict between moral rules and legal rules. It is about the principles that underlie both. More will be said in chapter 3 on Dworkin's contested claim that some moral principles lie at the heart of law and need to be considered when legal decisions are made. However, he does raise the essential question what we are doing when we make law or adjudicate it or merely find ourselves constrained by it. Whether the rules of criminal law violate the rights of a homosexual becomes subordinate to the question whether his right to respect as member of a law-abiding community is violated by procedures that rely upon the weight of feelings rather than inviting a thorough examination of reasons.[66]

FURTHER READING

Devlin, Patrick. *The Enforcement of Morals.* New York: Oxford Univ. Press, 1965.
Dworkin, Ronald. *Taking Rights Seriously.* Cambridge: Harvard Univ. Press, 1977, chapter 10.
Feinberg, Joel. *Harm to Others.* New York: Oxford Univ. Press, 1984.
Golding, Martin P. *Philosophy of Law.* Englewood Cliffs, N.J.: Prentice-Hall, 1975, chapter 3.
Grey, Thomas. *The Legal Enforcement of Morality.* New York: Alfred A. Knopf, 1983.
Hart, H. L. A. *Law, Liberty, and Morality.* Stanford, Calif.: Stanford Univ. Press, 1963.
Morawetz, Thomas. *The Philosophy of Law.* New York: Macmillan, 1980, chapter 3.
Pennock, J. Roland, and John W. Chapman, eds. *The Limits of Law* (Nomos XV). New York: Lieber-Atherton, 1974.

66. Dworkin will figure in various discussions still to come in this book, and these may help to remove the abstractions of this paragraph. One comment could help, for the present, to lessen the academic tone. Dworkin outlines a precarious but important distinction between *personal* preferences (for our enjoyment of goods) and *external* preferences (that such goods should not be assigned to others). So far as we accept the way in which democracies allow majority decisions on policies and laws, it is important—he holds—to make this distinction. If most of us are heterosexual, it is to be expected that the laws will favor this "personal preference" in the designing of our institutions. The "standard form" of marriage will be based on the union of male and female. But laws should not be made through "external preferences" that homosexuals be prevented from developing their own conceptions of an appropriate life style. The very respect for a person as one who assumes responsibility for his own life is at stake. See, for example, chapter 9 of *Taking Rights Seriously*, where Dworkin argues that "reverse discrimination" does not violate the rights of an individual to admission as a student at law school.

Ratcliffe, James M. *The Good Samaritan and the Law.* 1966. Reprint. Gloucester, Mass.: Peter Smith, 1981.

Wasserstrom, Richard A., ed. *Morality and the Law.* Belmont, Calif.: Wadsworth, 1970.

QUESTIONS FOR DISCUSSION

1. In these days of tolerance, there is widespread respect for the principle that we may interfere with the free decisions of people only when this is necessary to prevent them from harming others. The police should devote their resources to stopping assault or theft but not to "victimless" crimes. If you agree in general with this principle, how would you make it more precise? Does the sale of pornographic magazines in bookstores harm people? Suppose similar material appeared on the regular TV channels? During times when a good proportion of the viewers are children? Are we right to require a doctor's prescription for the purchase of antibiotics, tranquilizers, and other medicines? Suppose a person comments that he recognizes the harm likely to be produced but that he elects it just the same (a short and pleasurable life rather than a long one of abstention)?

2. Much has been written on the moral education of children. If you were a parent, would you respect the right of your child, from an early age, to make up his or her mind on moral matters? Or would you think (with Aristotle and Piaget) that some training in habits is required if the child is eventually to appreciate and "ratify" moral standards? Think of examples (e.g., orderliness, politeness, respect for alternative viewpoints). Are you extending parental law into the realm of private morality?

3. In the light of your replies, comment on the question whether "rational virtues" are innate or are learned. Do you interfere with a child's privacy if you employ punishment to help him or her recognize that other people see things differently and have interests that conflict with the child's?

4. Every family establishes some rules for conduct. Is there a danger that these will achieve conformity but hinder development of an appreciation of the reasons behind them? How would you help a child to realize that morality involves doing more than the rules require?

5. In 1925 Joe Webb acted heroically by diverting the fall of a pine block in a mill, in such a way that McGowin's life was saved but Webb was badly crippled for life. McGowin, in gratitude, maintained Webb by regular payments; but these ceased when McGowin died, and Webb went to law to secure continuation of the payments by the estate. The trial court decided that Webb had no legal claim, since the law stops short of enforcing any moral virtue of generosity. How would you have decided if you were on the appeals court? (Webb v. McGowin, 1935, 27 Ala. App. 82, 168 So. 196)

6. The legality of euthanasia, or "death with dignity," is much debated today. Is this a matter of private morality, of an individual's decision about the manner in which he or she will meet death? Or is it also a matter of public morality, involving all of us in our respect for the sanctity of life?

7. The basis of Devlin's lecture lies in his claim that the criminal law exists, not simply for the protection of individuals, but for the protection of society, which is a community of moral and political ideas. Devlin uses treason as an example. A rebel may think he is right but should not expect society to leave him free to effect his rebellion. How do different political societies draw the line between the legitimate expression of opinion and rebellion? Do they all agree that there is such a line?

8. What do you make of the claim that a society is essentially a "community of ideas"? What constitutes a nation today? Is it geography (people living within boundaries)? Common language, laws, traditions? Do we come closer to the heart of the question as we approach some notion of shared ideals and ideas? Apply your answer to specific ideas. Monogamy and the family?

Heterosexuality? Standards of self-discipline? Recognition that disputes be resolved through some system of reciprocal claims?

9.   When Sticks-Everything-Under-His-Belt went hunting on his own (see pp. 82–84 above), was he threatening to destroy the community of ideas that constituted the Cheyenne society? Should the chiefs have engaged in a dispassionate weighing of the benefits (to be found in an expression of idiosyncratic ideas) and the clear and present threat of social harm (such as disruption of social control over various forms of deviancy)? If you suspect that we may miss something of the symbolic importance of hunting together, could it be that Devlin's critics show a similar blindness to the complexity of our own social cohesion?

10.   There is a difference between advancing a claim on the ground of sheer self-interest and basing it on some moral position. Do you agree with Dworkin that we can adopt a moral position only when we can support it with reasons? Is not Devlin more realistic in recognizing that most people can be "reasonable" without being "rational" (think of his own example of the jury that gives a sound verdict without being required to justify it)? Or do you support Dworkin in trying to specify some minimal standards for any "moral" claim (e.g., some understanding of arguments, satisfaction of norms for evidence, consistency of the position with other "logical" conclusions)? If you do agree with Dworkin, how would you act as a legislator in face of strong indignation about homosexuality or any other challenge to "common morality"?

3

BASIC THEORIES OF LAW

> HILLARY, J.: *Plaintiff, have you anything more to say?*
>
> R. THORPE (counsel for plaintiff): *I think you will do as other judges have done in the same kind of case, else we shall not know what the law is.*
>
> HILLARY, J.: *Law is the will of the Justices.*
>
> STONORE, C.J.: *No, law is reason, that which is right.*
>
> <div align="right">(<i>De Flaundres v. Rycheman</i>, 1346, Y.B. 19 Edw. III 375)</div>

> To be sure, there are lawyers, judges, and even law professors who tell us they have no legal philosophy. In law, as in other things, we shall find that the only difference between a person "without a philosophy" and someone with a philosophy is that the latter knows what his philosophy is....
>
> <div align="right">(F. C. S. Northrop, <i>The Complexity of Legal and Ethical Experience</i>
[Boston: Little, Brown & Co., 1959], 6)</div>

The first quotation comes from the earliest reports we have of courtroom arguments in the common law. Though more than six centuries have passed, we see the same philosophies of law at work that are with us today. One justice states plainly that law is a command or rule generated by the lawmaker or law-interpreter, by king or judge. Counsel for the plaintiff insists that identifying the law is a matter of predicting decisions; law is a guide for our dealings with others, and we depend upon some constancy in it, whether this be revealed by our reading of the precedents or by the calculations of computers. The chief justice, however, maintains that *ley est resoun*. The law French of the time allows for various translations, but his position seems clear. Our answer to the question What is the law? demands more than submission to what a judge happens to rule, and more than an estimate based on previous exercises of judicial will. We must ask if the decisions of a judge are against reason and if they are in violation of justice. Such questions are not satisfied by a study of the law books.

Those of us who have stood before the law may recognize the scene, however remote the time. Are we at the mercy of whatever verdict we receive? Or do we find ourselves protesting beyond this to some "higher" rule or principle? If so, is this norm a policy that reflects the thinking of our age, the commercial or sexual mores that evolve with history and are often at variance with the written law? Or, when we complain that the decision was "unreasonable" and "unfair," are we invoking criteria that transcend time and would apply as well to an ancient Greek or a medieval Englishman?

We are unlikely to put our disappointment in theoretical terms. We grumble that the law is out of touch, or that the judge lives with his books and has little sensitivity to real situations, or that the law on this point is grossly wrong and irrational. But, as the second quotation above suggests, even those who make no claim to follow a "philosophy" do act from speculative positions that give a consistent course to their decisions. We are condemned to be theoreticians, and our very denial of this involves some theory.

The first two chapters, in discussing specific legal problems and in describing different forms of legal experience, mentioned some of the basic theories of law. This chapter will offer a more systematic treatment. Perhaps we can begin with a reminder of the way in which the parable of the speluncean explorers in section 5 embodied three philosophies of law in the fictional characters of Justices Keen, Handy, and Foster. Then the rest of the chapter will turn from fiction to history, will fill in details and add variations to each position.

Justice Keen based his opinion on a clear distinction between legality and morality. He was sympathetic toward the explorers and suggested that the relevant statute ought, for moral reasons, to be amended by the legislature. But a judge is committed to apply the law that *is*, without so interpreting it that it becomes a different law under the guidance of the judge's moral ideals. Any confusion of the law that *is* with the law that *ought to be* exposes us to opposite dangers. One is indicated by the anarchist who claims that, because he morally disagrees with a law, it is no law at all. The other danger is illustrated by the legalist who says that, simply because it is a law, he is morally obliged to keep it.

Keen's position is that of legal positivism, which has been the dominant philosophy for over a century. There are many variations under this title, but the distinction between legality and morality has proved a common and enduring theme (though, as we shall see, one that has been seriously challenged by Ronald Dworkin in recent years). It is important, from the outset, not to conclude that those who defend this position are amoral. Indeed, legal positivism is largely a product of utilitarianism, which is a moral theory. It was much the concern of thinkers such as Jeremy Bentham and John Austin to reform the law in order to achieve "the greatest good of the greatest number." Nevertheless, this is a task for the legislature, or for the judge acting as a delegated legislator when rules have been left open in "hard cases"; it is not part of the judge's work when, in the great majority of cases for adjudication, he finds and applies the existing law (there, bad law is still valid law).

In the explorers' case, Justice Handy presented an opinion that is congenial to the layman but is unlikely to be heard from the bench in quite such raw terms. However, his scorn for the theoretical contortions of his brethren does reflect a program, if not a school, that flourished in this country and is called legal realism. Law is not so much a formal discipline, where conclusions are derived by logic, as it is a practical art. Handy claimed in his judicial opinion that "the problem before us is what we, as officers of the government, ought to do with these defendants.... When the case is approached in this light, it becomes one of the easiest to decide." Almost everyone in Newgarth, and even on the bench, thought the defendants should be pardoned or let off with a token punishment. The facts of public opinion, the mores of the time, were evident.

There is a solidly empirical mentality that unites the realist with the positivist. Yet whereas the latter tends to see law as a set of rules produced and changed by the legislator, the former looks more to the judge, the prosecutor, the policeman, and other officials who (it is said) make and alter law in the very performance of their function. The "book of rules" is but one element in a complex process that needs to be studied thoroughly and honestly. The realist looks beyond the law library and toward the findings of the human sciences; what is called "sociological jurisprudence" offers a similar approach. Since legal realism is a program suspicious of theoretical formulations, any commentator has to be cautious in his account. The layman, though, will understand the claims that are made. He looks, above all, for common sense in a judge. And morality is, in popular discussion, identified with what most serious people at the time think right or obvious. The judge, it is felt, should spend more of his hours in the workplace and the market, fewer with his books.

Justice Foster was the only one to join Handy in voting for the explorers. Here again, the law that *is* depends on the law that *ought to be*. However, there are important differences between Handy and Foster, and the language shifts from the empirical to the metaphysical. Suppose Handy's poll had revealed that 90 percent of the people were *against* the explorers. He would presumably have submerged his own convictions and followed the facts of public opinion—the mores were other than he thought. Not so for Foster. As a representative of what have been called natural law theories, he insisted that morality is a matter of reason and not of polled opinions. Euclid did not look for a show of hands on the validity of his theorems. Similarly, from Plato to the present, this school of moral theory has maintained that reasoning can prove some moral conclusions to stand independently of whatever shifts a historian or sociologist may record. Law, then, is not simply given to us either in the rules of the legislator or in the spirit of the times. The details of law will certainly change, but there are underlying purposes or structures that make law possible and support the obligation it imposes on us. The judge should take these into account in finding what the law really is, even in opposition to what the rules clearly state. It was along such lines that Foster argued in defense of his conclusion that the

Newgarth statute did not apply to the explorers. This article, as taken in its plain meaning by Keen, failed to be law where it turned, in these unusual circumstances, to contradict the basic agreements or purposes or nature of law.

A concrete illustration would be of some help before we look at the range of legal philosophies. We have at our disposal a published debate between Lon Fuller, author of the speluncean story and a prominent advocate of a modified natural law position, and H. L. A. Hart, the leading theorist of legal positivism in recent years. The extracts below are taken from a part of the discussion where a dramatic German case is examined by the two proponents. Unfortunately, the contribution of a legal realist is lacking, though the reader can imagine the comments of a "Justice Handy."

16. THE CASE OF THE NAZI WIFE

The following extracts come from a debate that runs for eighty pages of the *Harvard Law Review* and has been called by one commentator "perhaps the most interesting and illuminating exchange of views on basic issues of legal theory to appear in English in this century."[1] Hart begins by trying to clarify the meaning of legal positivism. He distinguishes five theses commonly ascribed to the positivists.[2] Hart claims one of these (that law forms a "closed logical system") to be so ascribed "without good reason." He applies another ("non-cognitivism in ethics") to some positivists, but not to others. Of the remaining theses, he disagrees with John Austin on the identification of law with the commands of a sovereign (see sections 17 and 18 below). But Hart agrees on the other two. One is that the analysis of legal concepts is the main task of a legal philosophy and is to be distinguished from the historical and sociological studies advocated by the realist. The other is the basic thesis that there is no necessary connection between law and morals. We may now proceed to the section of Hart's article where he applies a positivist account to the German case, and then to Fuller's reply, where Hart's interpretation is attacked.

POSITIVISM AND THE SEPARATION OF LAW AND MORALS
by H. L. A. Hart

Harvard Law Review 71 (1958): 615–20.
Copyright © 1958 by the Harvard Law Review Association.
Printed with permission.

... The third criticism of the separation of law and morals is of a very different character; it certainly is less an intellectual argument against the Utilitarian distinction than a passionate

---

1. Robert S. Summers, *Lon L. Fuller* (Stanford, Calif.: Stanford Univ. Press, 1984), 10.
2. Hart repeats this distinction in *The Concept of Law* (New York: Oxford Univ. Press, 1961), 253n.

appeal supported not by detailed reasoning but by reminders of a terrible experience. For it consists of the testimony of those who have descended into Hell, and, like Ulysses or Dante, brought back a message for human beings. Only in this case the Hell was not beneath or beyond earth, but on it; it was a Hell created on earth by men for other men.

This appeal comes from those German thinkers who lived through the Nazi regime and reflected upon its evil manifestations in the legal system. One of these thinkers, Gustav Radbruch, had himself shared the "positivist" doctrine until the Nazi tyranny, but he was converted by this experience and so his appeal to other men to discard the doctrine of the separation of law and morals has the special poignancy of a recantation. What is important about this criticism is that it really does confront the particular point which Bentham and Austin had in mind in urging the separation of law as it is and as it ought to be. These German thinkers put their insistence on the need to join together what the Utilitarians separated just where this separation was of most importance in the eyes of the Utilitarians; for they were concerned with the problem posed by the existence of morally evil laws.

Before his conversion Radbruch held that resistance to law was a matter for the personal conscience, to be thought out by the individual as a moral problem, and the validity of a law could not be disproved by showing that its requirements were morally evil or even by showing that the effect of compliance with the law would be more evil than the effect of disobedience. Austin, it may be recalled, was emphatic in condemning those who said that if human laws conflicted with the fundamental principles of morality then they cease to be laws, as talking "stark nonsense."

> The most pernicious laws, and therefore those which are most opposed to the will of God, have been and are continually enforced as laws by judicial tribunals. Suppose an act innocuous, or positively beneficial, be prohibited by the sovereign under the penalty of death; if I commit this act, I shall be tried and condemned, and if I object to the sentence, that it is contrary to the law of God ... the court of justice will demonstrate the inconclusiveness of my reasoning by hanging me up, in pursuance of the law of which I have impugned the validity. An exception, demurrer, or plea, founded on the law of God was never heard in a Court of Justice, from the creation of the world down to the present moment.

These are strong, indeed brutal words, but we must remember that they went along—in the case of Austin and, of course, Bentham—with the conviction that if laws reached a certain degree of iniquity then there would be a plain moral obligation to resist them and to withhold obedience. We shall see, when we consider the alternatives, that this simple presentation of the human dilemma which may arise has much to be said for it.

Radbruch, however, had concluded from the ease with which the Nazi regime had exploited subservience to mere law—or expressed, as he thought, in the "positivist" slogan "law as law"—and from the failure of the German legal profession to protest against the enormities which they were required to perpetrate in the name of law, that "positivism" (meaning here the insistence on the separation of law as it is from law as it ought to be) had powerfully contributed to the horrors. His considered reflections led him to the doctrine that the fundamental principles of humanitarian morality were part of the very concept of *Recht* or Legality and that no positive enactment or statute, however clearly it was expressed and however clearly it conformed with the formal criteria of validity of a given legal system, could be valid if it contravened basic principles of morality. This doctrine can be appreciated fully only if the nuances imported by the German word *Recht* are grasped. But it is clear that the doctrine meant that every lawyer and judge should denounce statutes that transgressed the fundamental principles not as merely immoral or wrong but as having no legal character, and enactments which on this ground lack the quality of law should not be taken into account in working out the legal position of any given individual in particular circumstances. . . .

After the war Radbruch's conception of law as containing in itself the essential moral principle of humanitarianism was applied in practice by German courts in certain cases in which local war criminals, spies, and informers under the Nazi regime were punished. The special importance of these cases is that the persons accused of these crimes claimed that what they had done was not illegal under the laws of the regime in force at the time these actions were performed. This plea was met with the reply that the laws upon which they relied were invalid as contravening the fundamental principles of morality. Let me cite briefly one of these cases.[3]

In 1944 a woman, wishing to be rid of her husband, denounced him to the authorities for insulting remarks he had made about Hitler while home on leave from the German army. The wife was under no legal duty to report his acts, though what he had said was apparently in violation of statutes making it illegal to make statements detrimental to the government of the Third Reich or to impair by any means the military defense of the German people. The husband was arrested and sentenced to death, apparently pursuant to these statutes, though he was not executed but was sent to the front. In 1949 the wife was prosecuted in a West German court for an offense which we would describe as illegally depriving a person of his freedom. This was punishable as a crime under the German Criminal Code of 1871 which had remained in force continuously since its enactment. The wife pleaded that her husband's imprisonment was pursuant to the Nazi statutes and hence that she had committed no crime. The court of appeal to which the case ultimately came held that the wife was guilty of procuring the deprivation of her husband's liberty by denouncing him to the German courts, even though he had been sentenced by a court for having violated a statute, since, to quote the words of the court, the statute "was contrary to the sound conscience and sense of justice of all decent human beings." This reasoning was followed in many cases which have been hailed as a triumph for the doctrines of natural law and as signaling the overthrow of positivism. The unqualified satisfaction with this result seems to me to be hysteria. Many of us might applaud the objective—that of punishing a woman for an outrageously immoral act—but this was secured only by declaring a statute established since 1934 not to have the force of law, and at least the wisdom of this course must be doubted. There were, of course, two other choices. One was to let the woman go unpunished; one can sympathize with and endorse the view that this might have been a bad thing to do. The other was to face the fact that if the woman were to be punished it must be pursuant to the introduction of a frankly retrospective law and with a full consciousness of what was sacrificed in securing her punishment in this way. Odious as retrospective criminal legislation and punishment may be, to have pursued it openly in this case would at least have had the merits of candour. It would have made plain that in punishing the woman a choice had to be made between two evils, that of leaving her unpunished and that of sacrificing a very precious principle of morality endorsed by most legal systems. Surely if we have learned anything from the history of morals it is that the thing to do with a moral quandary is not to hide it. Like nettles, the occasions when life forces us to choose between the lesser of two evils must be grasped with the consciousness that they are what they are. The vice of this use of the principle that, at certain limiting points, what is utterly immoral cannot be law or lawful is that it will serve to cloak the true nature of the problems with which we are faced and will encourage the romantic optimism that all the values we cherish ultimately will fit into a single system, that no one of them has to be sacrificed or compromised to accommodate another.

> All Discord Harmony not understood
> All Partial Evil Universal Good"

---

3. Hart here adds a lengthy footnote, the gist of which I have repeated at the end of this section, under "Further Reading."

This is surely untrue and there is an insincerity in any formulation of our problem which allows us to describe the treatment of the dilemma as if it were the disposition of the ordinary case....

POSITIVISM AND FIDELITY TO LAW
by Lon L. Fuller

Harvard Law Review 71 (1958): 649–57.
Copyright © 1958 by the Harvard Law Review Association.
Printed with permission.

... I should like to undertake a defense of the German courts, and to advance reasons why, in my opinion, their decisions do not represent the abandonment of legal principle that Professor Hart sees in them. In order to understand the background of these decisions we shall have to move a little closer within smelling distance of the witches' caldron than we have been brought so far by Professor Hart. We shall have also to consider an aspect of the problem ignored in his essay, namely, the degree to which the Nazis observed what I have called the inner morality of law itself.

Throughout his discussion Professor Hart seems to assume that the only difference between Nazi law and, say, English law is that the Nazis used their laws to achieve ends that are odious to an Englishman. This assumption is, I think, seriously mistaken, and Professor Hart's acceptance of it seems to me to render his discussion unresponsive to the problems it purports to address.

Throughout their period of control the Nazis took generous advantage of a device not wholly unknown to American legislatures, the retroactive statute curing past legal irregularities. The most dramatic use of the curative powers of such a statute occurred on July 3, 1934, after the "Roehm purge." When this intraparty shooting affair was over and more than seventy Nazis had been—one can hardly avoid saying—"rubbed out," Hitler returned to Berlin and procured from his cabinet a law ratifying and confirming the measures taken between June 30 and July 1, 1934, without mentioning the names of those who were now considered to have been lawfully executed. Some time later Hitler declared that during the Roehm purge "the supreme court of the German people ... consisted of myself," surely not an overstatement of the capacity in which he acted if one takes seriously the enactment conferring retroactive legality on "the measures taken."

Now in England and America it would never occur to anyone to say that "it is in the nature of law that it cannot be retroactive," although, of course, constitutional inhibitions may prohibit certain kinds of retroactivity. We would say it is normal for a law to operate prospectively, and that it may be arguable that it ought never operate otherwise, but there would be a certain occult unpersuasiveness in any assertion that retroactivity violates the very nature of law itself. Yet we have only to imagine a country in which *all* laws are retroactive in order to see that retroactivity presents a real problem for the internal morality of law. If we suppose an absolute monarch who allows his realm to exist in a constant state of anarchy, we would hardly say that he could create a regime of law simply by enacting a curative statute conferring legality on everything that had happened up to its date and by announcing an intention to enact similar statutes every six months in the future.

A general increase in the resort to statutes curative of past legal irregularities represents a deterioration in that form of legal morality without which law itself cannot exist. The threat of such statutes hangs over the whole legal system, and robs every law on the books of some of its significance. And surely a general threat of this sort is implied when a government is willing to use such a statute to transform into lawful execution what was simple murder when it happened.

During the Nazi regime there were repeated rumors of "secret laws." In the article criticized by Professor Hart, Radbruch mentions a report that the wholesale killings in concentration camps were made "lawful" by a secret enactment. Now surely there can be no greater legal monstrosity than a secret statute. Would anyone seriously recommend that following the war the German courts should have searched for unpublished laws among the files left by Hitler's government so that citizens' rights could be determined by a reference to these laws?

The extent of the legislator's obligation to make his laws known to his subject is, of course, a problem of legal morality that has been under active discussion at least since the Secession of the Plebs. There is probably no modern state that has not been plagued by this problem in one form or another. It is most likely to arise in modern societies with respect to unpublished administrative directions. Often these are regarded in quite good faith by those who issue them as affecting only matters of internal organization. But since the procedures followed by an administrative agency, even in its "internal" actions, may seriously affect the rights and interests of the citizen, these unpublished or "secret" regulations are often a subject for complaint.

But as with retroactivity, what in most societies is kept under control by the tacit restraints of legal decency broke out in monstrous form under Hitler. Indeed, so loose was the whole Nazi morality of law that it is not easy to know just what should be regarded as an unpublished or secret law. Since unpublished instructions to those administering the law could destroy the letter of any published law by imposing on it an outrageous interpretation, there was a sense in which the meaning of every law was "secret." Even a verbal order from Hitler that a thousand prisoners in concentration camps be put to death was at once an administrative direction and a validation of everything done under it as being "lawful."

But the most important affronts to the morality of law by Hitler's government took no such subtle forms as those exemplified in the bizarre outcroppings I have just discussed. In the first place, when legal forms became inconvenient, it was always possible for the Nazis to bypass them entirely and "to act through the party in the streets." There was no one who dared bring them to account for whatever outrages might thus be committed. In the second place, the Nazi-dominated courts were always ready to disregard any statute, even those enacted by the Nazis themselves, if this suited their convenience or if they feared that a lawyer-like interpretation might incur displeasure "above."

This complete willingness of the Nazis to disregard even their own enactments was an important factor leading Radbruch to take the position he did in the articles so severely criticized by Professor Hart. I do not believe that any fair appraisal of the action of the postwar German courts is possible unless we take this factor into account, as Professor Hart fails completely to do. These remarks may seem inconclusive in their generality and to rest more on assertion than evidentiary fact. Let us turn at once, then, to the actual case discussed by Professor Hart....

The defense [of the wife] rested on two statutes, one passed in 1934, the other in 1938. Let us first consider the second of these enactments, which was part of a more comprehensive legislation creating a whole series of special wartime criminal offenses. I reproduce below a translation of the only pertinent section:

> The following persons are guilty of destroying the national power of resistance and shall be punished by death: Whoever publicly solicits or incites a refusal to fulfill the obligations of service in the armed forces of Germany, or in armed forces allied with Germany, or who otherwise publicly seeks to injure or destroy the will of the German people or an allied people to assert themselves against their enemies.

It is almost inconceivable that a court of present-day Germany would hold the husband's remarks to his wife, who was barred from military duty by her sex, to be a violation of the final catch-all provision of this statute, particularly when it is recalled that the text reproduced above was part of a more comprehensive enactment dealing with such things as harboring deserters, escaping military duty by self-inflicted injuries, and the like. The question arises, then, as to the extent to which the interpretive principles applied by the courts of Hitler's government should be accepted in determining whether the husband's remarks were indeed unlawful.

This question becomes acute when we note that the act applies only to *public* acts or utterances, whereas the husband's remarks were in the privacy of his own home. Now it appears that the Nazi courts (and it should be noted we are dealing with a special military court) quite generally disregarded this limitation and extended the act to all utterances, private or public. Is Professor Hart prepared to say that the legal meaning of this statute is to be determined in the light of this apparently uniform principle of judicial interpretation?

Let us turn now to the other statute upon which Professor Hart relies in assuming that the husband's utterance was unlawful. This is the act of 1934, the relevant portions of which are translated below:

1. Whoever publicly makes spiteful or provocative statements directed against, or statements which disclose a base disposition toward, the leading personalities of the nation or of the National Socialist German Workers' Party, or toward measures taken or institutions established by them, and of such a nature as to undermine the people's confidence in their political leadership, shall be punished by imprisonment.

2. Malicious utterances not made in public shall be treated in the same manner as public utterances when the person making them realized or should have realized they would reach the public.

3. Prosecution for such utterances shall be only on the order of the National Minister of Justice; in case the utterance was directed against a leading personality of the National Socialist German Workers' Party, the Minister of Justice shall order prosecution only with the advice and consent of the Representative of the Leader.

4. The National Minister of Justice shall, with the advice and consent of the Representative of the Leader, determine who shall belong to the class of leading personalities for purposes of Section 1 above.

Extended comment on this legislative monstrosity is scarcely called for, overlarded and undermined as it is by uncontrolled administrative discretion. We may note only: first, that it offers no justification whatever for the death penalty actually imposed on the husband, though never carried out; second, that if the wife's act in informing on her husband made his remarks "public," there is no such thing as a private utterance under this statute. I should like to ask the reader whether he can actually share Professor Hart's indignation that, in the perplexities of the postwar reconstruction, the German courts saw fit to declare this thing not a law....

The real issue dividing Professors Hart and Radbruch is: How shall we state the problem? What is the nature of the dilemma in which we are caught?

I hope I am not being unjust to Professor Hart when I say that I can find no way of describing the dilemma as he sees it but to use some such words as the following: On the one hand, we have an amoral datum called law, which has the peculiar quality of creating a moral duty to obey it. On the other hand, we have a moral duty to do what we think is right and decent. When we are confronted by a statute we believe to be thoroughly evil, we have to choose between those two duties.

If this is the positivist position, then I have no hesitancy in rejecting it. The "dilemma" it states has the verbal formulation of a problem, but the problem it states makes no sense. It is like saying I have to choose between giving food to a starving man and being mimsy with the borogoves. I do not think it is unfair to the positivistic philosophy to say that it never gives any coherent meaning to the moral obligation of fidelity to law. This obligation seems to be conceived as sui generis, wholly unrelated to any of the ordinary, extra-legal ends of human life. The fundamental postulate of positivism—that law must be strictly severed from morality—seems to deny the possibility of any bridge between the obligation to obey law and other moral obligations. No mediating principle can measure their respective demands on conscience, for they exist in wholly separate worlds. . . .

If a summary is needed of the German dilemma and of the solutions offered by Hart and Fuller, it may be well to notice that five dates are involved. Three were of laws: the 1871 German Criminal Code and the Nazi statutes of 1934 and 1938. The incident took place in the second half of 1944, when less than a year remained of Hitler's rule. The trial of the wife took place in 1949, four years after Hitler's death. The prosecution appealed to the code of 1871, the wife to the statutes of 1934 and 1938.

The position taken by Radbruch, and followed in various ways by the post-Nazi courts, was based on natural law theories. A statute in conflict with fundamental principles of justice would fail to be law. Hence it would be possible for the courts to deny any claim that rested on what the court could find never to have achieved the standing of a valid law. This would not be a retroactive decision, because such a law never really existed to be changed.

Hart condemned the satisfaction with such thinking as "hysteria." Assuming that the statutes of 1934 and 1938 met the legal requirements for becoming law, he held that they were indeed valid, and no moral considerations could change the fact. Hence the court in 1949 should, for Hart, have chosen between two possibilities. One was simply to admit that the woman had acted legally but immorally—we should "leave her to heaven." The other was to engage in frankly retroactive legislation to punish her: laws valid in 1934 and 1938 would be declared, in 1949, to form an invalid defense for what happened in 1944. Hart is certainly not happy about such "odious" criminal legislation. However, he well characterizes his positivism in the final remarks that were quoted from his essay. The facts of life do not come together to form a coherent system. The glib metaphysician hides our quandaries through his romantic optimism, but an honest confrontation with the facts (Hart's view of the merits of positivism) forces us repeatedly to choose between evils.

Fuller writes in qualified defense of Radbruch and of the German courts. He does so by arguing that the immorality of some Nazi practices did indeed "intersect" with the legality of their legislation, so that some rules never attained the status of valid law. Fuller's position on this general question will be discussed later, but we should notice briefly here an important distinction between his version of "natural law" and Radbruch's. The latter held that morality presents us with a variety of principles that can serve as a measuring stick to evaluate statutes and other legal decisions (much as the laws of a state can show certain rules of a private association to be illegal). Fuller makes no appeal to morality as an external measure of law and looks for it instead at the heart of law, in the requirements that follow from our basic obligation to live according to rules rather than by force.

His concern, then, is with the form or structure of the legal enterprise at the hands of the Nazis. And what he finds is a multiple violation of the "inner morality of law." It is not, for example, that occasional resort was made, for good reasons, to retroactive legislation. Retroactivity permeated the whole conduct of law and defeated the project of legality. A similar threat was made against the publicity and other essential structures of law. It is in this sense that Fuller asks us to look closely at the 1934 and 1938 statutes, not for specific ways in which they break the Ten Commandments, but for the retroactivity and secrecy that infect these laws. The husband could have been sentenced to death, for remarks made in private, only through a series of secret interpretations communicated to the courts but never publicized. Such are the traditional ways of a regime that itself violates the purposes of legality. Hence Fuller finds it no surprise that the post-Nazi courts saw fit to declare such statutes not to have been valid law.

In the closing remarks that were quoted, Fuller asks the reader not merely to talk about the dilemma facing the postwar German courts, but to ask exactly what it was. Did they perhaps see it more acutely than the positivists? That is, Fuller here takes up Hart's challenge that natural law theorists conceal the harsh dilemmas of our moral life. There are doubtless some moralists who contrive a facile way of making all principles fit into a neat system. Most, however, are well aware of the remaining problems and offer no swift solution to the conflict of principles. The question of civil disobedience, for example, is an agonizing one, but it is a genuine dilemma only if we allow for a moral obligation to keep the law and for a competing obligation to break it in some instance. At least, Fuller's own philosophy of law shows a sensitivity to persisting conflicts, even between basic structures of law. The clarity and publicity of law may be at the expense of its certainty. And, though prospectivity belongs to the normal requirements for law, there are many situations in which retroactive legislation is advisable.[4]

Fuller returns the challenge by asking what dilemma Hart allows us when we find bad law. There is evidently a moral obligation to change it. But what exactly is the competing legal obligation if it is entirely divorced from morality? When the Gestapo hammer at my door, they impose on me a command that is well backed by force. Yet do they exact a legal obligation? Even if they cite a clear statute, legally made by a valid legislator, what obligation do these facts create if law itself remains an "amoral datum" rather than being grounded in a moral enterprise? As we shall see later, in Hart's criticism of Austin, these questions were recognized. However, Fuller continued to be unsatisfied with the

---

4. Ironically, even in the case of the Nazi wife, Fuller expresses limited approval of Hart's suggestion for retroactive legislation: this would serve "as a way of symbolizing a sharp break with the past, as a means of isolating a kind of cleanup operation from the normal functioning of the judicial process." (See end of section 6 in his essay.)

answers given. The title he chose for his article, "Positivism and Fidelity to Law," suggests what he sees as the basic problem: Why do we have laws at all and why do we owe them our fidelity?

FURTHER READING

For a version, in parable form, of the dilemma facing the postwar German courts, see: Lon Fuller, "The Problem of the Grudge Informer," *The Morality of Law* (New Haven: Yale Univ. Press, 1969), 245–53.

An account of the German case, discussed by Hart and Fuller, is given in *Harvard Law Review* 64 (1951): 1,005–7. It should be noticed, however, as Hart points out in a footnote to his own article, that the 1951 report is not altogether accurate. The German court did accept the theoretical possibility that statutes may be invalid if in conflict with the natural law. However, the decision against the accused woman was not based on such a judgment of invalidity but simply on her violation of the German Criminal Code of 1871. She was held to have informed against her husband for purely personal reasons that were "contrary to the sound conscience and sense of justice of all decent human beings."

QUESTIONS FOR DISCUSSION

1. Hitler came to power just thirty-three years after effect was given to the German Civil Code, a model work of lawmaking. Presumably there were some judges whose careers spanned both events. If you were a German judge, how would you describe the dilemma you faced as you became aware of the laws that Hitler was making and as you received secret directives for interpreting these and older statutes? Judges who were put on trial after the war were asked why they had not resigned under Hitler. If you chose to resign, why precisely? Was your choice between a legal obligation to apply valid but bad laws and a moral obligation not to do so? If Fuller were in such a position, how would he have stated the dilemma?

2. The charge has often been made, and as often rejected, that the almost wholesale adoption of positivism by the German legal profession in the early decades of this century helped toward the acceptance of Hitler and his legal techniques. Certainly a positivist should be as strongly opposed, on moral grounds, to unjust laws as is any other person. Fuller discusses this dispute in section 6 of his essay. He adds an interesting suggestion to distinguish between Radbruch's view of natural law and his own notion of the "inner morality" of law. How do you understand the following claim by Fuller that Radbruch failed to free himself from the underlying assumptions of positivism? Does this charge apply also to some religious accounts that identify natural law with the will of God?

> If you were raised with a generation that said "law is law" and meant it, you may feel that the only way you can escape one law is to set another off against it, and this perforce must be a "higher law." Hence these notions of a "higher law," which are a justifiable cause for alarm, may themselves be a belated fruit of German legal positivism.

3. In time of war, most countries are led to expedients that are on the borderline of legality (witness the treatment in this country of citizens of Japanese extraction after the attack on Pearl Harbor). Translate the Nazi statutes of 1934 and 1938 into U.S. laws of 1942 and 1943, and imagine the husband-wife incident took place here. Suppose you were the prosecutor of the husband in 1944. Would you have expected to gain a conviction? If not, why not?

17. AUSTIN'S COMMAND THEORY

> *Laws properly so called are a species of commands. But, being a command, every law properly so called flows from a determinate source, or emanates from a determinate author. . . . For whenever a command is expressed or intimated, one party signifies a wish that another shall do or forbear: and the latter is obnoxious to an evil which the former intends to inflict in case the wish be disregarded.*
>
> (John Austin, Lecture 5)

If the average person is asked to define law, he or she will probably speak in terms of that which a legislature enacts and a policeman enforces. The approach, if unsubtle, has the merit of being thoroughly factual. The question whether a law exists is answered by looking in the books to see if it was passed and by looking at incidents to see if it is carried out.

The term *positivism* was coined early in the nineteenth century to designate the method that had proved so successful in the natural sciences. *Factualism* would be one possible translation of a word that remains highly ambiguous; all knowledge starts with, and is limited by, facts that can be observed. Austin's position as the father of legal positivism comes from no extensive writings but from the clear conception of a policy: law should be demystified and should be described by means of what we see as commands being issued and obeyed, and sanctions being imposed if the orders are disregarded. The program would then extend to a similarly objective account of the "cash value" in legal talk about such terms as rights and duties, fault and liability, contracts and property.

This section will give a brief historical account of the tradition on which Austin drew and then will outline some of his basic conclusions. Criticism, at the hand of one of his most eminent disciples, will be left to the following section.

Positivism and Utilitarianism

> The world required centuries of contemplation of irreducible and stubborn facts. It is difficult for men to do more than one thing at a time, and that was the sort of thing they had to do after the rationalistic orgy of the Middle Ages. It was a very sensible reaction; but it was not a protest on behalf of reason.
>
> (A. N. Whitehead, *Science and the Modern World* [1925; reprint, New York: Free Press, 1967], 16)

The Middle Ages are sometimes dismissed as a period of dark superstition. It would be more just to see the fault of the medievals in a complacent confidence that the light of reason can answer all questions. God rules the world, and God is the epitome of reason. Creation is a rational activity and if we want to know why the planets move as they do, or what is the right structure of society, we have only to use our own reason to penetrate the reasons that God has embodied in the world. Thinking, rather than observation, is the correct way to solve our problems.

Science is often hailed as a rational approach to knowledge about the world and man and society. But science was able to develop only with the collapse of such medieval rationalism. The scientific method flourished when men turned from the effort to think out reasons and began to observe sheer facts. The law of gravity is not deduced, *a priori*, from any self-evident general principles, and it does not explain why objects fall; it simply supplies a unified mathematical description of the facts of falling bodies and moving planets.

Galileo ran into many difficulties with the Inquisition. But the source of his problems may have been, in part, that he substituted an "irrationalism" for the Greek and medieval rationalism that the Inquisitors strangely took to be a requirement of religion. He was content to organize sheer facts. In medieval terms, Galileo represented a "voluntarism" that saw creation as a product of God's will, not a rational expression of God's intellect.

Of course, Galileo won. He and his scientific followers enjoyed far greater success in predicting what would happen in nature than did the disciples of Aristotle and Aquinas. Even if the world does run on "ultimate reasons," they are hidden from us; so we make our way to more impressive results if we treat the world as though it were the product of some impenetrable will, "commanding" facts without any final reasons. The laws of nature are defined from the position of a "superior" issuing orders: let it be so. We, as "inferiors," simply observe and obey.

David Hume (1711–1776) provided the scientific method with a clear philosophical expression. His conclusion was put dramatically in the advice to inspect the books in any library. Preserve those, such as books of science and history, that record the *matters of fact* in any field but without trying to deduce that the world must be this way. Save also those books, such as works of mathematics and logic, that do indeed reason to the necessary conclusions of principles but without claiming that such *relations of ideas* tell us anything about facts in the world. However, Hume insisted, we should burn all books of metaphysics, for they attempt the impossible, to prove by reason that facts must be as they are.

Hume did not develop a philosophy of law. His concern was to justify the method of the natural sciences as the way to truth and to extend that method in the direction of the human sciences. He saw metaphysical thinking as the main obstacle to success. Thus Hume finds a place in the parentage of both legal realism and legal positivism; these two philosophies unite in their rejection of the metaphysics of natural law theories. The contrast between the two empirical approaches to law is basically one of viewpoint, the position from which facts are recorded. The legal realist adopts the situation of an observer of judicial decisions—the facts of law are the behavior of courts and of other legal agents (such as prosecutors). The legal positivist, however, tends to identify law with the commands or rules of those whose express function is to make laws: just as there is no ultimate reason behind what we discover in nature, so our laws are simply what a human legislator happens to have willed.

John Austin (1790–1859) is commonly regarded as the father of legal positivism, for he was the first in the positivist tradition to develop a comprehensive theory of law. However, two of his predecessors, Thomas Hobbes and Jeremy Bentham, may be mentioned briefly. Hobbes (1588–1679) was perhaps the first major thinker who offered a systematic application to human affairs of the ideas of the natural sciences. Impressed by Galileo's mechanics, he saw society as a complex of individuals motivated by no higher force than the desire for self-preservation. Mutual destruction is avoided, and order established, by the expedient of submitting to the power of a "sovereign," one who has the strength to act as ruler and to command obedience from others. An account of Hobbes's political philosophy would require much detail, but his approach to law comes across clearly. Law is "the word of him that by right hath command over others." The "right" is an expression of social mechanics and allows no concession to theologians or metaphysicians or even to those who look for authority in long-standing customs. The basis of law is set unambiguously by Hobbes in the legislator. Laws are not found but made, and the question What is the law? must be purified from any thought we have about whether a rule is reasonable or just.

Jeremy Bentham (1748–1832) was the immediate source of Austin's ideas. Bentham deserves his place in the history of philosophy but can better be approached as a social reformer than as a theorist. It was, he thought, the influence of metaphysical thinking that most seriously blocked the introduction of needed improvement in the social and political institutions of his day. For instance, prisons were in an appalling condition because punishment was seen as a retribution required by justice, even if the process added greatly to the sum of suffering without lessening crime or healing the criminal. Bentham held that, by removing metaphysics from our inquiry, we should be in a position to assess each institution and each law calmly and empirically, calculating the balance of good and evil that it produces. We should look to the consequences of our acts and policies. If we simply abolish prisons we shall increase the pain in the world. But we can work for an improvement of prison conditions that will notably lessen the pain of those inside without producing more harm outside. Deterrence and rehabilitation, both matters of factual calculation, take over from the absolutes of retribution.

In this example we can detect the apparently clear doctrine of legal positivism, that "the law that is" should be logically separated from considerations of "the law that ought to be." First find what various punitive laws *are* and *do*, and then use calculations of social benefit and cost to decide how we *ought* to legislate. Just as our concern for which fertilizers ought to be banned requires that a value-neutral study be made by chemists of what fertilizers are and do, so our moral obligation (as citizens) to ensure enactment of the laws we ought to have is best secured if the "science of law" first makes a value-free analysis of what the law is and what its concepts mean. To be respectable and useful, the study of law must initially be descriptive and analytical.

The example of prison reform also suggests the moral theory that Bentham proposed for then moving on to normative questions about which laws we ought, as legislators, to enact. Bentham attacked those philosophers who would legislate for prisons by applying some "principle of retribution" that they claimed to draw from their own thinking or to find as a self-evident norm. He similarly opposed the solution of moral problems by appeal to a variety of principles such as those affirming the sanctity of life or the indissolubility of marriage. For this multiplicity of principles he substituted *one* that he held to be obvious and to save us from the dangers of moral dogmatism by turning our attention to the objective calculations in our genuine disputes.

A simple example. Two doctors disagree whether they should amputate a leg at once or try to save it. They agree about the end they accept, the health and mobility of the patient; they disagree on their technical estimate of the best means to achieve this. Gangrene and death would clearly show the policy of saving the leg to have been the wrong one. Suppose we now complicate the example by imagining the casualty room to be crowded with victims from a serious accident and the medical resources to be inadequate. Who should be assisted first, and how? Those whose lives are most likely to be saved? The elderly or the young? Those whose contributions seem most important to society? There is no easy answer, and serious conflicts are possible. But, Bentham would hold, disagreement is as much about the means to an accepted end as in the case of the single patient. All would agree that they should maximize the benefits they are able to confer. Similarly, disputes about national defense policy and social legislation are based on the assumption that all parties want peace rather than war, health rather than sickness, wealth rather than poverty. As abstract as it may be, one principle underlies all such discussion, that we should adopt whatever policy achieves the greatest good of the greatest number.

A legislator who accepts Bentham's "principle of utility" as the sole moral guide is thus relieved from an inquiry into various norms and finds his attention turned to a calculation of consequences. What will result if the proposed law is enacted or if it is not? The course should be adopted that will produce the greater balance of benefits over harms. Evidently, the notion of benefit and of harm calls for thorough analysis. For instance, is the greatest good achieved if as many people as possible get their preferences satisfied, or is it for the legislator to estimate what is good for them even if they might vote otherwise? However, the most serious objections to utilitarianism have come from those who claim that this seemingly innocuous principle can lead to patently immoral conclusions. Suppose that the majority benefit greatly at the expense of a minority? Slavery is a traditional example. A more contemporary one might involve the conduct of fatal medical experiments to discover a cure for widespread diseases. The victimization of some people could be an effective means to majority benefits. If such procedures are morally wrong, must this not be on the basis of some principle other than that of utility? Bentham dismissed talk of natural rights as "nonsense on stilts," but the defense of utilitarianism has been concerned largely with efforts to preserve justice against possible excesses of utility.

Adequate explanations and discussions of utilitarianism belong to other books. One reply of its proponents is that the measure of utility should be applied, not to individual acts, but to general rules. Thus, I should not ask whether performing dangerous medical experiments on a particular patient might contribute to the greatest benefit of the greatest number. I should ask whether having or not having a rule forbidding such experiments would produce a happier society. In these terms, a "rule utilitarian" can plausibly talk of "rights," such as the right not to be experimented upon without informed consent. However, it remains true that only utility is ultimately binding; rights are justified instrumentally, because they are calculated to produce the greatest benefit for most people in the long run. Since rights are not based on any absolute obligation to respect the autonomy of the individual, they remain at the mercy of empirical calculations, and the possibility is not excluded of some conflict between utility and what we may otherwise regard as justice.

Such discussions take us far beyond the intellectual climate in which Bentham and Austin developed their theories. However, questions of this sort have influenced the growth of legal positivism from Austin to Hart and to such contemporaries as Ronald Dworkin. Indeed, the term *positivist*, once relatively definite as a mark of praise or blame, is no longer secure. There is still a firm opposition to the approach of a traditional natural law theorist who might claim, in reasoning from the nature and purpose of society, to derive conclusions about human law that would reject some legislative acts as invalid (in the manner of Radbruch: see section 16). But utilitarianism is no longer the faithful companion of positivism in normative jurisprudence.[5] And some philosophers who grew up in the tradition of legal positivism now find a place for moral principles at the heart of their investigation of what the current law really is.

The Will of the Sovereign

What pleases the Prince has the force of law.

(Justinian's *Digest*)

John Austin occupied a house overlooking Bentham's garden in London. In spite of the difference of forty-two years in age, the two shared their intellectual

---

5. Nor was it ever a logically necessary one. It would, I suppose, be theoretically possible for a person to adopt positivism as his or her legal theory and to maintain some natural law position in moral philosophy. Or it is certainly possible to be a legal positivist and to support a "deontological or intuitionist school of moral philosophy," such as that of Sir David Ross, who holds that there are many moral obligations "not reducible to one single principle, as utilitarians argue" (Neil MacCormick, *Legal Reasoning and Legal Theory* [New York: Oxford Univ. Press, 1978], 257).

concerns, and Austin's home became a meeting place for the utilitarians. Austin took up the practice of law but soon realized that his interests were too scholarly for success as an advocate. When the University of London was established, he was appointed to the chair of jurisprudence. By way of preparation, he spent two years in Germany. On returning to London, he started a course of lectures and attracted some notable students, including John Stuart Mill. But attendance declined and, when it fell to five, he resigned his chair. His published lectures form almost the sole written work he left. Few scholars received, after death, so much fame from so few pages.

In his opening lecture, Austin proceeds rapidly to his basic position, that laws are commands. To be more precise, laws are general commands, addressed to a class of people for a class of acts, rather than the specific orders one might give to a servant to go on a particular errand. A command, in turn, is an expression of desire. Yet clearly more is involved than wanting something. The desire must be communicated to people in such a way that they will suffer a penalty if they do not comply; for Austin, there is no law without sanctions. Likewise, there must be some definite author of a command. Reasons can perhaps be "in the air," or at least in the general assumptions of a society. However, the will that issues a command must be the will of a determinate person or group.

The individual or body that thus issues laws was called by Austin the "sovereign." We need not think of a king or dictator. The sovereign can, for example, be an elected parliament or a state in a federal union. There are grave problems of identification today. But, in most general terms, Austin found in any legal society a factual distinction between superiors, who make laws, and inferiors, who obey them or suffer penalties for not doing so.[6] And such superiority is no mysterious notion: "Superiority is the power of enforcing compliance with a wish." (Lecture 1) "The bulk of the given society are in a habit of obedience or submission to a determinate and common superior ... and that individual or body of individuals is not in a habit of obedience to a determinate human superior." (Lecture 6)

Since the identification of law with commands is the part of Austin's legal philosophy that has been most open to attack, even by his disciples, it may seem surprising that he offers little justification for this position and shows scant awareness of the objections to be posed. He slips easily, for instance, from the psychological talk of "a habit of obedience," and the mechanistic talk of "power" relations, to the normative language of "obligations": "Being liable to evil from you if I comply not with a wish which you signify, I am bound or obliged by your command, or I lie under a duty to obey it." (Lecture 1)

However, Austin's great merit is consistency. His starting point is faithful to the positivist tradition, and his analyses follow step by step from his beginning.

---

6. Austin himself held that in any democracy we find the sovereign not in the elected representatives but in the electors themselves. This seems to involve a complex conclusion in which the electors habitually obey themselves, though in different capacities (see Hart, *Concept of Law*, 72–74).

Disciples who qualified his position may have come closer to our experience of "following laws," but the consistency that Austin had shown was threatened.

The notion of a "fact" invites many questions. Yet if our approach to law is to be factual, in the sense that we are guided by models that the natural sciences offer, then there is much to be said for identifying human laws with commands. Laws are not found through telescope or microscope. They come in words. And our concern to view them as facts, rather than as the conclusions of reason, may direct us to the products of will rather than the expressions of intellect. If a sign merely formulates an imperative (Don't Spit), I submit to the sheer fact of the author's will, assuming that he can impose a sanction for noncompliance and that my inclination is for temporary discomfort rather than for this penalty. But if the sign states a rule that is backed, at least implicitly, by reasons (Expectoration Spreads Disease), then my attention is taken to arguments and values that may lead beyond the realm of clearly observable facts.

The followers of Austin have tended to abandon his command theory; however, with recent qualifications, they have remained loyal to his doctrine of the distinction between the law that is and the law that ought to be. Whether they have thereby abandoned consistency is a question to be discussed; that they did so is perhaps the burden of the criticism that Fuller levels at Hart. Yet Fuller applauds the logic of Austin's analysis, though rejecting his groundwork. If laws are commands, they take their place among the sheer data of our experience; it is when I give my reasons that I expose myself to public assessment and may find that I am wrong morally as well as technically. If I simply claim that "It is my will," then indeed it is my will. The question whether what I want is reasonable or not, moral or not, is valid and important; but it is a distinct and subsequent question. There is a raw analogy between will and sensation. If I go to the doctor and say I have a pain, he cannot deny this brute fact. But when I embody the fact in reasons, using language that seems to diagnose the pain, the doctor will warn me of my incompetence for such ventures that stray beyond simple observation.

It may be well to quote Austin's unambiguous conclusions on the separation of law and morality:

> The existence of law is one thing; its merit or demerit is another. Whether it be or be not is one enquiry; whether it be or be not conformable to an assumed standard, is a different enquiry. A law, which actually exists, is a law, though we happen to dislike it, or though it vary from the text [e.g., the Bible] by which we regulate our approbation and disapprobation. This truth, when formally announced as an abstract proposition, is so simple and glaring that it seems idle to insist upon it. But simple and glaring as it is, when enunciated in abstract expressions, the enumeration of the instances in which it has been forgotten would fill a volume.
>
> Sir William Blackstone, for example, says in his *Commentaries* that the laws of God are superior in obligation to all other laws; that no human laws should be suffered to contradict them; that human laws are of no validity if

> contrary to them; and that all valid laws derive their force from that Divine original.
> Now he may mean that all human laws ought to conform to the Divine laws. If this be his meaning, I assent to it without hesitation.... But the meaning of this passage of Blackstone, if it has a meaning, seems rather to be this: that no human law which conflicts with the Divine law is obligatory or binding; in other words, that no human law which conflicts with the Divine law is a law.... (Lecture 5)

Austin's aim, in so separating law from morality, was not only to facilitate reform of the law by the objective approach of utilitarianism. He also wanted to make possible the dispassionate study of basic legal concepts that has become known as "analytical jurisprudence." Austin wrote that we should "strip legal terms of a certain mystery." The mystification comes from legal professionals as well as from metaphysicians. The lawyer learns the meaning of his terms in regard to what the courts demand; he knows what he has to prove in order to establish "negligence" or "voluntary conduct" or "diminished responsibility." He can classify "intentions," speak justly of "motives" and "causes," distinguish the many types of "ownership." But use of a term, for practical purposes, does not always involve a satisfactory understanding of it or of its relation to other such terms. The lawyer knows what he does, yet his knowing may be fragile. There remains room for a thorough conceptual analysis that reduces this complexity and confusion to the simplest notions involved, studies them, and reveals their logical relations. It is in such tasks that the mind of a philosopher, particularly with training in the analytic school, can prove helpful.[7]

Austin did not himself go far in this direction, but he did serve as an initiator. His proposal was to ground a "general jurisprudence" that would analyze the essential features of any legal system. Having given a precise idea of law in terms of commands, he devoted much of his effort to showing that he could thereby comprise many apparently different aspects of law. What, for example, is to be said of case law, that which seems to be made by a variety of courts? How can this stem from the will of the sovereign? Or what about customary law, which so much occupied the Germans with whom Austin studied on his travels? The following quotation indicates how Austin tried to absorb such forms of law into his general theory.

> At its origin, a custom is a rule of conduct which the governed observe spontaneously, or not in pursuance of a law set by the political superior. The custom is transmuted into positive law when it is adopted as such by the courts of justice, and when the judicial decisions fashioned upon it are enforced by the power of the state.... For, since the state may reverse the

---

7. Wesley Hohfeld, a leading exponent of analytical jurisprudence, claimed that such classification of basic concepts can lead not only to an improvement of legal language and reasoning, but to what he called "tacit codification" of the law. The study of the most general legal ideas and relations is termed "pure law" in France and "general legal theory" in Germany.

rules which a judge makes, and yet permits him to enforce them by the power of the political community, its sovereign will "that his rules shall obtain as law" is clearly evinced by its conduct, though not by its express declaration.... When customs are turned into legal rules by decisions of subject judges, the legal rules which emerge from the customs are *tacit* commands of the sovereign legislature. (Lecture 1)

We have already (in section 10) seen something of the formative and continuing influence of custom on law, and we have (in section 11) noticed the criticism that scholars such as Sir Henry Maine directed at Austin for subordinating all prior stages of law to that of legislation. Again, Austin cannot be faulted for inconsistency. He set legal positivism on a course that may be characterized as seeing law in terms of the legislator. From this perspective, it is logical to submit all customary practices and judicial decisions to the supervision of a sovereign who could say no but decides to let them be, as an extension of his will. The following section examines the important qualifications introduced by later legal positivists. However, the reader can perhaps anticipate the more radical criticisms made by a legal realist and by a natural law theorist. Is the viewpoint of the legislator the correct one to adopt? Should we not think rather of the judge who has to decide which rules to invoke and how to apply them to the messy circumstances of a particular case? From such a perspective, does not "custom" or "positive morality" (in the vague sense of current estimates of rightness) often prevail over legislated rules? Can we perhaps even give some credence to the ancient claim that such rules are to be submitted to what we know, through reason, about principles underlying all law and measuring whatever the legislator happens to have prescribed?

FURTHER READING

Austin, John. *Lectures on Jurisprudence.* St. Clair Shores, Mich.: Scholarly Press, 1976 reprint. The first six of these lectures were published in 1832 under the title of *The Province of Jurisprudence Determined*; they have been reprinted under the same title and with an introduction by H. L. A. Hart (New York: Humanities Press, 1965), and extracts are to be found in many anthologies (for example, see G. C. Christie, *Jurisprudence*, St. Paul: West, 459–601). After Austin's death, his wife published her reconstruction, from his notes, of an additional forty-five shorter lectures.
Benditt, Theodore M. *Rights.* Totowa, N.J.: Rowman & Littlefield, 1982.
Bentham, Jeremy. *An Introduction to the Principles of Morals and Legislation.* 1789. Reprint. New York: Free Press, 1970.
Hart, H. L. A. *Essays on Bentham.* New York: Oxford Univ. Press, 1982.
Mill, John Stuart. *Utilitarianism.* 1863. Reprint. Indianapolis: Hackett, 1979.
Morison, W. L. *John Austin.* Stanford, Calif.: Stanford Univ. Press, 1982.
Smart, J. J. C., and Bernard Williams. *Utilitarianism: For and Against.* Cambridge: Cambridge Univ. Press, 1973.

QUESTIONS FOR DISCUSSION

1. The distinction between facts and reasons is not easy to make precise. Facts are theory-laden. And our talk of "reasons" covers a range that runs from preferences (He has his odd reasons) to deductive proofs. Yet there is a profound contrast between the respect we show for facts and the priority given by Greeks and medievals to reasons. It was the neglect of obvious facts that postponed for so long our realization that the blood circulates. Can you support the primacy of reasons? Are there facts in mathematics? When you say that he is only a technician, what do you mean? *Techné* was the Greek term for grasping "the fact that," without knowing "the reason why."

2. No one will deny the success of science in finding new facts. But does it truly explain anything? I should laugh at a doctor who diagnosed my pain as the effect of a "vital humor" and then answered my obvious question by saying that "a vital humor is what causes your pain." Is it better to be told that things fall because of gravity, which is what makes things fall?

3. A scientist may reply by asking what you expect as an explanation. Surely not the sort of reasons that Aristotle gave in his account of the heavens? Hume held that science provides "matters of fact" but no reasons; reasoning, though valid in a noninformative field such as mathematics, is ridiculous when applied to prove any truth about the world in which we live. Comment on this example (which may remind some of Voltaire's remarks on the disaster at Lisbon). An earthquake kills thousands of innocent persons. The agnostic says humbly, "I don't know the reason." The theologian says, "There is one and God knows it—but what God knows God only knows."

4. We talk of the reasons for a law. Should we not instead talk of facts about preferences? Long-standing proposals that all cars be equipped with air bags (passive restraints) have not as yet been made into law. Suppose such legislation is finally passed. Are there not reasons for the law? Yes, but these are not drawn (except perhaps by Justice Foster of Newgarth) from thoughts about the nature of automotive man. What we should find is the fact that more people prefer safety to economy than prefer economy to safety (or that the consumer lobby has more power than Detroit can muster).

5. Most people today probably subscribe to utilitarianism as their moral theory. Our basic obligation is to increase the happiness and decrease the misery in the world. Most may also see it as a problem of making objective calculations. Do the likely economic advantages of nuclear power stations outweigh their potential for disaster? Call in the experts and not the philosophers. In view of this, why did Bentham and Austin distinguish law from morality? Suppose I base my argument against nuclear power on the metaphysical claim that life is sacred, so that a law promoting so grave a risk to life is no law at all? Or suppose I ban euthanasia on such a claim rather than on a dispassionate balancing of the good and harm to be expected from the many possible forms of legislation?

6. A traditional argument against utilitarianism is that it allows the condemnation of an innocent person in order to achieve the greatest good of the society (e.g., national security; think of the Dreyfus Affair in France, 1894–1906). How might a rule utilitarian reply? Could an act utilitarian argue that the French Army, in accusing Dreyfus, made a serious miscalculation of the full consequences of this act of victimization?

7. Criticisms of Austin's reduction of laws to commands will be left to the following section. But apply this doctrine, and the related one of the need for sanctions, to various parts of the spectrum of law. In total institutions, Austin seems correct. A prison warden legislates that hair shall not be over three inches in length, and this order is backed by strong penalties. At the other extreme, however, the element of will is less prominent, and sanctions (if any) exist only in the background. Austin would reply, of course, by relegating families and private associations to the realm of custom and limiting law "properly so called" to the state. Yet is he correct, even there? As crowds move through a busy city, is the good order of this complex process really achieved by

commands and sanctions or by shared assumptions that never reach the attention of the sovereign?

8. Austin would meet this argument by insisting that such customary procedures are the result of *tacit* legislation by the sovereign; he could interfere but chooses not to. This reply is not without value. Every teacher turns a blind eye to some practices and thereby assumes responsibility for them. However, is this an adequate account of what goes on at the level of the state? Legislatures and judges exclude vast areas of life from their concern, not to show tacit approval, but rather to express their incompetence and to register respect for privacy. Does this raise the question whether Austin's model of a superior/inferior relation is inappropriate for "the living law"?

9. More specific questions arise when we ask Austin to identify the sovereign. In an absolute monarchy there may be no difficulty. But what about in the United States? Is it the Congress? Or the people who elect the Congress? Or the Supreme Court that can negate the laws that are passed? Or the body that can change the Constitution? Again, the basic question is one of model rather than of detail. Does law emanate from any "determinate source" as an act of will, or does it belong rather to the reasons that form people into a society structured by common purposes?

10. "Bentham was an empiricist, but he had little experience" (John Stuart Mill). Does this criticism, from a refined and subtle utilitarian, apply also to Austin? Is there an important distinction between the (objective) experience of a law as a show of strength and the (subjective) experience of being legally obliged?

11. "Manslaughter can be committed by inadvertent negligence if this is sufficiently gross." What questions do you have about this claim? Are there degrees in negligence? Degrees of what? What is "inadvertence," such that you are "responsible" for it? What is the "fault" or "guilt" (*mens rea*) required for a crime? Can you be blamed if you do not foresee the consequences of your act? No easy answer is expected for such questions. Do they call first for a thorough analysis of the basic words involved? Should a law school include a course in what Austin termed "general jurisprudence"?

18. H. L. A. HART'S CONCEPT OF LAW

> *If the observer really keeps austerely to this extreme external point of view and does not give any account of the manner in which members of the group who accept the rules view their own regular behaviour, ... his view will be like the view of one who, having observed the working of a traffic signal in a busy street for some time, limits himself to saying that when the light turns red there is a high probability that the traffic will stop. He treats the light merely as a natural sign that people will behave in certain ways, as clouds are a sign that rain will come. In so doing he will miss out a whole dimension of the social life of those whom he is watching, since for them the red light is not merely a sign that others will stop: they look upon it as a signal for them to stop, and so a reason for stopping in conformity to rules which make stopping when the light is red a standard of behaviour and an obligation. To mention this is ... to refer to the internal aspect of rules seen from their internal point of view.*
>
> (H. L. A. Hart, *The Concept of Law*, 87–88)[8]

---

8. This and other extracts from *The Concept of Law* by H. L. A. Hart, ©Oxford University Press 1961, along with the summary comments in this section, are printed with permission of the Oxford University Press.

In the 150 years since Austin published his lectures on general jurisprudence, there have been many who have adapted his legal positivism to meet the criticisms it provoked. A notable example is Hans Kelsen (1881–1973), a scholar who started his career in Vienna and emigrated to the United States in the Hitler years. His "pure theory of law" is perhaps the most radical effort to free law from metaphysics, morality, and any admixture of psychology, sociology, and politics. However, for those in the common law tradition, the figure of greatest influence in refining and applying Austin's position has been H. L. A. Hart (1907–   ). After eight years in the practice of law he returned to Oxford and became Professor of Jurisprudence in 1952. His *Concept of Law* (1961) is a landmark in legal philosophy. The account that follows, as a criticism and development of Austin, is based on this work, to which the page references refer.

Criticism of Austin

In 1861, two years after Austin's death, Sir Henry Maine published his *Ancient Law* (see section 11 above). Maine refers explicitly to Austin's reduction of law to the commands issued by a sovereign and admits that the theory applies, with qualifications, to "mature jurisprudence." However, it was the purpose of Maine's studies in the evolution of law to reveal the many stages in the way that led to the modern dominance of legislation. Before that, law was "in the air": no distinct author was even contemplated, and Austin's theories would be irrelevant.

In his brief discussion of the origins of law (pp. 43–48), Hart tends to agree with Maine. Even if we do in fact look to the courts to give legal recognition to customs, there is no absurdity in the suggestion that courts could apply customs as something that is already law, in the same way that they apply statutes. But customs do not proceed from a sovereign, and Hart argues that "no comment" from the legislator need not involve the tacit approval that Austin postulated.[9]

However, the bulk of Hart's criticism is directed at the command theory even where it seems most plausible, in modern municipal law. Chapters 2–4 of *The Concept of Law* develop such criticisms, four of which may be summarized as follows.

1. Though many laws, and particularly those listed as criminal statutes, could seem to be commands backed by sanctions, a large body of law has to do with the conferring of powers on individuals and groups. Such laws enable us to will our estate to descendants, or to enter into a marriage, or to make commercial contracts. They also authorize assemblies to legislate and courts

---

9. Nevertheless, Hart refers to a purely customary society as "pre-legal." And the coherence of his position in allowing that customs can be received by the courts as "already legal" has been questioned (see p. 89 above).

to give judgment. It would, says Hart, be absurd and grotesque to construe such laws as orders backed by threats (pp. 27–41).

2. If I issue a coercive order, I am not commanding myself; the sergeant who orders the platoon to scrub the barracks floor does not get down on his own knees. However, legislation is not essentially other-regarding. When the members of Congress pass a new tax law, they do not exempt themselves from its provisions. Both examples could require qualification: sergeants may make laws, and Congress may also issue orders. But Austin's model of "superior" and "inferior" seems inadequate to meet the self-inclusion that laws allow. The generality of a law, as a work of reason, involves more than an act of will, even when this is directed to a class of people for a class of acts (pp. 41–43).

3. An absolute monarch, Rex, may issue commands to his subjects, who gradually develop what Austin calls a "habit of obedience." Yet critical questions appear when Rex dies. Who takes over as sovereign? If there are laws of succession, do these come from habits inculcated by Rex? Or do we have a gap in the law until Rex II manages to build up further habits of obedience? In fact, we find people talking of the *title* of the eldest son to succeed, of his *right* or *authority* to make laws. And when Rex IV has ascended the throne, we notice that the courts still refer to enactments of Rex I as law. The continuity and persistence of law requires some account that liberates rules from present personalities; at least, Austin's simple idea of orders, habits, and obedience under threat proves inadequate (pp. 49–64).

4. Though an absolute monarch can issue commands that satisfy Austin's narrow definition of law, almost all that we find today as legislation escapes this definition because we recognize legal limitations on legislative authority. Rex I may have encountered *practical* limits to the issuance of commands (e.g., fear of an uprising); but if law is no more than coercive orders, there can be no *legal* limits. These are disabilities contained in special rules that qualify a legislator to make laws. Members of Congress have an authority that is legally restricted. If we accept what they say as law, this is not because we have developed a habitual obedience to their commands, but because we find that their rules are free of conflict with the rules that authorize them to make rules (pp. 64–76).

With chapter 5, Hart begins his own account of law. This relies on a move from commands to *rules* as the basic element in a legal system. First, however, he goes to the root of his criticism of Austin by investigating the concept of *obligation* (pp. 79–88). He presents the command theory as viewing law in terms of a "gunman writ large." Austin's sovereign is, in effect, a gunman who orders us to hand over our money and threatens to shoot us if we do not comply. We do obey, and we remark that we *were obliged* to do so. What do we mean? Simply that (a) his will was backed by superior power and (b) our will was to prefer the loss of money to the loss of life. We might have reacted differently if we knew the gun was not loaded or if his threat was only to pinch us. However, being *obliged* (in this sense) is very different from *having an obligation* (or being *obligated*) to hand over our money. I could, for example, say that I had a legal obligation to report for military service, though I escaped to a country where my government could never reach me; but such an expression would have no meaning in terms of Austin's reduction of obligation to an encounter with coercive orders. In short, Hart begins his theory by trying to draw a clear distinction between coercion and obligation, where Austin moved without scruple from one notion to the other.

Having thus distinguished between commands (which coerce) and rules (which obligate), Hart proceeds to an important analysis of a further confusion in our talk of rules. The quotation at the beginning of this section can help to convey his meaning. In giving an account of what people do, we should clarify whether we adopt the viewpoint of an observer (external point of view) or that of the agent himself (internal point of view).

1. The observer will report that people do, as a rule, stop at red traffic lights. The law is purely descriptive. It is not different from the statement that dark clouds generally lead to rain or that Americans watch five hours of television per day. The observer, perhaps from Mars, makes no distinction between the obligation we have toward traffic regulations and our habits of entertainment. Hart is not unsympathetic toward those who keep an observer's viewpoint. Positivism has much to do with this, in its varied history. And the objectivity of such an account has contributed toward the elimination of metaphysics from both science and law. However, Hart insists that the appeal to experience and to clear analysis, in law, badly distorts the topic if it is equated with the adoption of an external point of view. Here he is attacking not only positivists in the strict tradition of Austin, but also those (legal realists) who identify law with a prediction of judicial behavior (pp. 81–82, 101–102).

2. The agent, the person who himself lives under the law, is little concerned with what people do as a rule; this is a theme for the sociologist. It is the normative status of rules that is important. Even if most people race the traffic lights as these turn to red, or cheat at exams, we have an obligation to stop and not to cheat. Violation does not (at least within limits) affect the standing of a normative rule, whereas it would lead to reformulation of a descriptive one. Rules, in their internal aspect, embody a reason to which we subscribe; and they supply a standard by which we measure conduct as right or wrong. Such notions go back to the beginnings of human thought, but it is Hart's merit to have given them renewed respectability within the requirements set by positivism. Experience is not merely "objective" (the data we see, from outside) but also "subjective" (what we do and intend, the quality we give to our acts). However, discussion of Hart's distinction

between external and internal viewpoints has suggested that some ambiguities remain. Those who are not positivists may accuse him of retaining a certain externality in his account of the internal viewpoint. In terms to which we shall return soon, his language may be "heteronomous" rather than "autonomous."

Primary and Secondary Rules

Hart substitutes rules for the coercive orders of Austin's sovereign. Yet this raises the vital question what rules are and where they come from. If the umpire at baseball declares me to be out, and I see his will as ultimate, then I am out even though I touched the base before the ball arrived.[10] More likely, however, I shall appeal beyond the umpire's will in this matter and I shall cite rules in the book. Should I be so rash as to appeal beyond these, it is to someone at the top, perhaps the commissioner of baseball. Beyond that? To the spirit of the game? Few will go so far to avoid a return to the dugout, but the question is relevant to any system of law. Rules depend upon rules, and these upon more rules. Where do we stop? The Supreme Court? The Constitution? The rights of man?

Before we embark on an account of Hart's version of this hierarchy or "pedigree" of rules, we may pause to think of his likely strategy. It will be that of a sound middle course. On the one side we have Austin reducing law to the sheer facts of a sovereign's will; this forces compliance but creates no genuine obligation. On the other side, however, we have the natural law theorists who will pounce on any concession in order to equate legality with a moral obligation that derives from some metaphysical talk of human nature and inalienable rights. From what we know of Hart, we cannot expect him to go so far, and the rest of his book is as much a defense against the claims of natural law as the opening chapters were an attack on Austin. The range of rules will be subtle but will rest finally upon some sheer facts rather than upon conclusions drawn from reasoning about what we really are.

Hart's proposal was mentioned in section 10 above. He makes a distinction between primary and secondary rules. *Primary* rules are to be found, in an unsupported manner, only in a primitive society that Hart calls "pre-legal." Such rules formulate the varied obligations we have to engage in some acts and abstain from others. We know that violence toward members of the in-group should be avoided, that we should not marry outside the tribe, that certain foods are tabu at prescribed times of the year, that promises in trade should be honored, and so forth. Other primary rules provide for sanctions if violation of the above rules occurs. However, as any primitive society grows, certain problems appear. There is uncertainty about what precisely the rules are or which ones prevail when they seem to conflict. There is need to change the rules to

---

10. One famous umpire is said to have formulated a version of the command theory of law as follows: "They ain't strikes, they ain't balls, they ain't nothin' till I call 'em!"

meet new situations. And confusion arises about whether a rule has been violated in particular circumstances.

According to Hart, a legal society in the strict sense develops only as such problems are met and the primary rules are supplemented by the introduction of *secondary* rules, or rules about rules. He mentions three examples (pp. 92–95):

1. A *rule of recognition* is introduced to specify which primary rules have authority as such. This may simply identify what is carved on a public monument. Or the secondary rule may classify as law whatever Rex decrees, in ritual terms, when on his throne (rather than in his bedroom). Or we may have the complex secondary rules that enable us to recognize a valid act of Congress or of Parliament, or the much more ambiguous rules that abstract a *ratio decidendi* (see section 29) from a judicial opinion. In a sense, much of what we shall discuss in chapter 5 raises questions about our own sophisticated rule of recognition. In both case law and enacted law we spend our time asking what exactly is the rule.

2. *Rules of change* allow for deliberate alterations in primary rules. Moses showed little interest here, yet subsequent religious history—from glosses on the Torah to papal encyclicals and ecumenical councils—reveals the need. The simplest answer is legislative enactment, but most rules of change have lived in the murky regions of judicial interpretation. The art of changing without seeming to change, of making under the guise of finding, belongs to all legal systems.

3. *Rules of adjudication* establish agencies (such as courts) and procedures (such as trials and appeals) to determine when a primary rule has been violated in a particular case. Chapter 4 is directed largely to questions about rules of adjudication: what is a trial, and how do adversarial or inquisitorial systems of law apply rules to facts in order to arrive at judgment?

Hart allows for many possible historical developments from a pre-legal to a legal society. It is likely, for example, that the third of the above secondary rules usually appeared before the first two. However, there is little doubt, for Hart or his reader, that the critical secondary rule is that of "recognition." A legal society is characterized by its ability to offer an account of what does or does not pass as law. A rule exists as a rule in a certain legal system if its pedigree can be traced to the rule of recognition that defines legality within that system. Questions about Hart's philosophy have been concerned largely with the status of his rule of recognition.[11]

---

11. Much of what follows has to do with the way in which the concept of a "rule" changes as we pass from primary to secondary rules, and notably to the rule of recognition. See Lloyd L. Weinreb, "Law as Order," *Harvard Law Review* 91 (1978): 924–30.

Before we suggest such questions, it may be well to indicate how he draws from his theory the traditional positivist conclusion of the independence of law from morality. Suppose we know, without hesitation, the rule of recognition that is pertinent. The only thing that counts as law (primary rules) is that which is inscribed on the tablets that Moses brought down from Sinai; or that which is solemnly declared to be law by Rex from the throne; or that which is passed by Congress and found by the Supreme Court, if challenged, to be in accord with the Constitution. We must adopt an internal viewpoint and ask whether the primary rule in question (e.g., allowing divorce or capital punishment) satisfies the secondary rule of recognition. If it does, it is valid law; if not, it is invalid.

Moral questions will also arise. We may think a valid law to be wicked or unfair. We are then morally obliged to work for its repeal through the secondary rules of change. We may even find ourselves morally required to question the rule of recognition. The Mosaic tablets could be resulting in more harm than good for most people. Rex may have divided us into freemen and slaves. The Constitution may have defended property at the expense of justice. But, Hart concludes, the question of a moral obligation to change the law, and even the norms of law, is logically distinct from the question whether a primary rule is currently valid as law by derivation from the secondary rules.

In chapter 9, Hart presents a persuasive argument in defense of the separation of legal validity from moral obligation. He notes that the passage from a pre-legal to a legal society exposes us to moral abuses. The very institutions that derive from our secondary rules may lead to tyranny against minorities, even to a slave state. But, he asks, so what? Is it better to say, of a morally wrong law, that this is no law at all, or to say that it is indeed law but too iniquitous to obey or apply? He argues in various ways for the latter, though admitting that his preference is less convincing in some situations than in others.

Many readers will be tempted to view the whole learned discussion as a game with words. When the Gestapo knock at the door, it does seem rather academic whether we say they are backed by no law at all or by valid laws that are immoral and ought not to be applied or obeyed. Hart considers this objection but joins the natural law theorist in holding that an important difference is at stake. For what is in question is the status of legal obligation. Those who will not follow Austin in reducing our *ought* statements to an admission of superior force need to know what they mean when they so venture beyond fact to duty.

A brief word on the "pure theory of law," defended by Hans Kelsen, may be relevant. The purity of law represents, for him, its independence from both moral reasoning and sociological facts. Laws are amoral *ought* statements; neither a moralist nor a sociologist can justify them. Each law has its validity from its place in a hierarchy of norms. A particular law is valid because it is made through procedures authorized by a superior law. But what happens when we come to the top? Here Kelsen affirms the conceptual necessity of a supreme norm (*Grundnorm*). It cannot, he says, be pointed out in any written constitution or other enactment but is the logical requirement of a legal system and can be stated only with complete generality as: One ought to behave as the first constitution prescribes. For Kelsen, it is this abstract norm, rather than the will of God or of any sovereign, that stands behind the tablets of Moses or the written constitution of a state.

Lon Fuller, in criticism, remarks that Kelsen has substituted his own "fiction" for Austin's picture of a sovereign.[12] But the average person may be more sympathetic. Surely we have to stop somewhere? The appeal of positivism comes with its claim that life rests on no ultimate reason. All Kelsen is doing is to state that, in law, we must find a resting place in some very general norm and not in any observation about the commands of sovereigns or the behavior of courts.

Does Hart's rule of recognition serve a similar function? He is more empirical, inviting us to look specifically for whatever a definite legal system accepts as its ultimate rule, and he discusses some very practical legal questions (such as what happens when a colony gains its independence and sets up its own law). His opposition to natural law theories is shown most clearly when he discusses the status of the rule of recognition (pp. 97–114). This is *ultimate* in the sense that an official within the system will eventually answer all questions of validity in terms of it: "When the validity of an English statute has been queried and assessed by reference to the rule that what the Queen in Parliament enacts is law, we are brought to a stop in inquiries regarding validity" (p. 104). If we then ask about the morality of the statute, we have passed to an external point of view. But equally we desert our internal questions of validity when we ask whether the enactments of the queen in Parliament are law:

> The assertion that a rule of recognition exists can only be an external statement of fact. For whereas a subordinate rule of a system may be valid and in that sense 'exist' even if it is generally disregarded, the rule of recognition exists only as a complex, but normally concordant, practice of the courts, officials, and private persons in identifying the law by reference to certain criteria. Its existence is a matter of fact (p. 107).

Hart illustrates this with a simple analogy. The accuracy of my measuring rod derives from its correspondence with a standard meter bar in Paris. The wooden ruler on my desk is valid or not from the internal viewpoint of this system. But the meter bar in Paris is neither valid nor invalid. Its existence as a criterion depends upon the matter of fact (and the external viewpoint) that the practice of engineers and surveyors happens to accept this as a norm of length.

In the light of this, to reread Hart's account of the internal point of view is to notice important ways in which his departure from Austin is less dramatic than it seems. For example, Hart explains the connection between rules and obligation as follows: "Rules are conceived and spoken of as imposing obliga-

---

12. See Fuller, "Positivism and Fidelity to Law," *Harvard Law Review* 71 (1958), 641.

tions when the general demand for conformity is insistent and the social pressure brought to bear upon those who deviate or threaten to deviate is great" (p. 84). One commentator asks whether such talk of pressure for conformity really distinguishes Hart from Austin, and adds: "If the acceptance of a rule is based on fear, aren't we at the level of 'being obliged' rather than at that of obligation? Shouldn't there be some moral ground for the acceptance?"[13]

Questions of this sort can be made more concrete by brief reference to a book that was written while civil disobedience stirred this nation's conscience and while protests against the war in Vietnam were at their height. Sanford Kadish and Mortimer Kadish, a lawyer and a philosopher respectively, combined to prepare a scholarly study of how the American system of law legitimizes departures from clear legal rules by citizens and by officials (juries, prosecutors, judges).[14] The authors claim that a legal system, and notably the American one, embodies not only rules but also "principles of acceptance." The former tell us what our specific obligations are, but the latter give guidance on the more delicate topic of "how those obligations are to be taken."[15] No simple talk of discretion will help. Even if the law explicitly grants us discretion in hard cases, this statement formulates our problem rather than solving it: "Discretion is one thing; discretion to determine competence to exercise discretion is quite another."[16] We see the acute question of when we are justified to go against the apparently clear provisions of a legal rule, and we ask what help the law itself may give us; how can we legally contravene what the law seems to say?

It is beyond our purposes here to explain the complex and detailed theory developed by the authors. But perhaps the reader will see the difficulty presented by any philosophy of law that derives legal validity exclusively from a rule of recognition. This advises us against any departure from legal rules (valid in terms of their pedigree), and it has to classify any such deviation as extralegal: "A departure from a mandatory rule may be justifiable on moral or social grounds, but not on legal grounds."[17] The target that the authors have in mind

---

13. Martin P. Golding, *Philosophy of Law* (Englewood Cliffs, N.J.: Prentice-Hall, 1975), 44n. Another writer also queries whether Hart "preserves the distinction between legal and coercive systems—the basis, after all, for his criticism of Austin." If the distinction between "obligation" and "being obliged" is to be maintained, then the validity of law must depend, not only on the fact that the officials of a legal system happen to accept certain norms, "but also on a good-faith claim that the system and standards thus described are 'acceptable' to those governed by the system" (E. Philip Soper, "Legal Theory and the Obligation of a Judge," *Michigan Law Review* 75 [1977]: 518–19). Ronald Dworkin likewise questions whether Hart's account of the "acceptance" of a rule of recognition manages to preserve the distinction between commands and rules. Dworkin points out, for example, that many officials of Nazi Germany obeyed Hitler's commands out of fear. "Does that mean they accepted a rule of recognition entitling him to make law? If so, then the difference between Hart's theory and Austin's becomes elusive...." See Ronald Dworkin, *Law's Empire* (Cambridge: Harvard Univ. Press, Belknap Press, 1986), 35.

14. Mortimer R. Kadish and Sanford H. Kadish, *Discretion to Disobey* (Stanford, Calif.: Stanford Univ. Press, 1973).

15. Ibid., 185.

16. Ibid., 44.

17. Ibid., 195.

is very general, including most of the traditional philosophies of law, which are classified as presenting "the producer's view of legal obligation" and as implying what Max Weber called "the rational-bureaucratic model of a legal system." Our concern here is solely with the attack on Hart's effort to ground legal systems in a rule of recognition and on his claim that such a master rule is accepted only from the *external* point of view which is adopted likewise in recording the social fact that surveyors accept the meter bar in Paris as their standard of measurement.

> Prof. H. L. A. Hart's views, as they bear on principles of acceptance, are of particular interest. One might think that Hart, who has cogently argued against the adequacy of the "external point of view" that underlies a predictive theory of law and in favor of an "internal point of view" that emphasizes the binding force of an obligation, would have been sensitive to the problems to which principles of acceptance respond....
>
> Yet in truth Hart's rule of recognition serves to obscure the need for principles of acceptance, not to satisfy it. In "disposing of doubts as to the existence" of a rule, the rule of recognition establishes legal standards for determining a rule's validity; but it does not resolve the doubt of the receiver of the rule about whether he is free to act on his own judgment of how those standards apply to a rule confronting him. If the receiver of the rule must act before an authorized official or body has pronounced on the issue, how will he know whether to act on his own judgment or not? Rules of recognition do not provide the answer, but principles of acceptance do."[18]

The vital question of a distinction between legal rules and legal principles will be posed in the following section, for it is essential to Dworkin's criticism of Hart. But for the present our interest is limited to the way in which Hart's rule of recognition, as the basis for deciding on the pedigree (and hence validity) of any primary rule, leads us to abandon the internal point of view that he has stipulated for understanding our obligation toward ordinary rules. There is no great problem for surveyors; if the meter bar in Paris were destroyed, they could perhaps easily substitute agreement on some replica in Brisbane or Buenos Aires. However, our agreement on the U.S. Constitution and on two hundred years of interpretation may be a bit more subtle. A cataclysm that silenced the Supreme Court and even obliterated much of the record of past decisions would pose major problems in constitutional law; yet the reconstructive process in a happier time could possibly draw upon some principles of acceptance, both moral and political, that involve more than the social fact of how officials happen to behave.

Hart has offered an eminently plausible account of legal obligation from within the perspective of a positivist philosophy. Those who reject or question this philosophy are less sure that he satisfactorily describes how we and judges submit to the law. In the following section, a dissenting vote will be considered

---

18. Ibid., 191–92.

from a source that developed within the positivist tradition. But first we may look at questions raised from a philosophical school that arose largely in opposition to that of Hume. Kant is seen today as offering a serious alternative to positivism and utilitarianism. He would be sympathetic to Hart's call for an internal point of view on the law but would hesitate to allow that Hart succeeds in explaining a genuine sense of fidelity toward law. Some important distinctions may help to clarify a difficult question.

Suppose I tell you that you ought to work harder and that you ought not to make promises without any intention to keep them. The first "ought" is *hypothetical* and *heteronomous*. You ought to work harder *if* you want appropriate rewards and a better job. This is a matter of choice rather than of obligation. And the law that I suggest is imposed on you by another (from the Greek, *hetero-*, other and *nomos*, law). But the second "ought," in regard to promises, is at least potentially different. There may be no concealed "if-clause," no hypothesis or reliance on your own choice. The law may be self-legislated—you recognize it, not simply because of the fact that others tell you and the situation is such, but because you understand and ratify the reasons for the rule. Here, for Kant, the law would be *categorical* (absolute) and *autonomous*. It is here alone that he would be prepared to speak of having an obligation.[19]

Kant certainly regards the gunman situation as heteronomous, involving a purely hypothetical imperative (your money, if you want your life). The author, who was assaulted at gunpoint while correcting the galley proofs, can speak from limited experience—the question What would Kant have said? did surprisingly occur to him in the chaos of the moment. Yet how would Kant interpret Hart's account of legal obligation? Kant would respect the adoption of an inner point of view as an effort to move from heteronomy to autonomy, but he is unlikely to see Hart's version as adequate. This would be because the internal viewpoint reverts to the external as we pass from the validity of a particular rule to the existence of the rule of recognition. The rule that what the queen in Parliament enacts is law is itself a matter of fact, consisting of a complex practice of the courts and legal officials. This authority remains heteronomous. I am still in the realm where I wash my hands before meals because custom demands it and I also happen to like cleanliness (or I hand over the $20 in my pocket because I happen to like life).

Evidently, Kant is much restricting the area for talk of obligation. Most of our "ought" statements are heteronomous. My honesty in business may come largely from fear of consequences if I get a reputation for shady dealings. My religious observance may have much to do with rewards and penalties after death or with sheer submission to authority.[20] And the obedience I give to

---

19. For Kant's own account of the distinction between hypothetical and categorical imperatives, see his *Foundations of the Metaphysics of Morals*, Library of Liberal Arts edition (Indianapolis: Bobbs-Merrill, 1959), 31–34.

20. Kant, no friend of institutional religion, held that obedience to the will of God is heteronomous. The biblical story of Abraham's compliance with God's command that Isaac be sacrificed, though possibly some

traffic and tax laws may be covered completely by Hart's account. But Kant argues that true obligation belongs to our status as rational beings: "It has its origin in the pure, but practical, reason." If, then, there is obligation anywhere in regard to positive laws, it must at least be in our basic obligation of fidelity toward the laws of the land in general. This, we have seen (pp. 161–62 above), is what Fuller claimed that Hart failed to justify.

Hart's likely reply to such objections can be supposed. If any rules, in morality or law, are to be autonomous, this must be because I can derive them by reason. Then I should be self-legislating, submitting to a conclusion as both universal and mine. Yet the possibility of drawing such conclusions is exactly what the whole tradition of positivism has denied. We cannot go beyond positive law or positive morality. If we do argue that a certain law is morally wrong, this is because we measure it in terms of values we now happen to regard as more important than the legislators did. Or it is because we have made a more thorough calculation than they did of the balance between helpful and harmful consequences. Even the principle of utility cannot be proved by reason from the nature of man.

The rationalist philosopher is, for Hart, a romantic who vainly claims to derive both legal and moral rules from a common origin in reason. Hart prefers the honesty of admitting a variety of factual sources for our many "oughts." We must expect to face dilemmas. But we should grasp the nettle and not hope to think it away (see pp. 158–59 for Hart's closing remarks in the extract printed in section 16). Above all, we should not try to achieve this bogus solution by failing to distinguish the validity of a law from its morality. Hart does, however, attempt to locate "a minimum content of Natural Law, in contrast with its more grandiose constructions." He finds this in the mundane fact that almost all of us happen to choose survival in a world that at present threatens this in various ways. Though he will not thereby satisfy either Aquinas or Kant, we shall mention his proposals toward the end of this chapter (p. 233).

FURTHER READING

Hart, H. L. A. *The Concept of Law.* New York: Oxford Univ. Press, 1961.
_____. *Causation in the Law.* 2d ed. New York: Oxford Univ. Press, 1985.
_____. *Essays in Jurisprudence and Philosophy.* New York: Oxford Univ. Press, 1984.
_____. *Law, Liberty, and Morality.* Stanford, Calif.: Stanford Univ. Press, 1963.
_____. *Punishment and Responsibility.* New York: Oxford Univ. Press, 1968.
_____. "Problems of Philosophy of Law." In *The Encyclopedia of Philosophy*, vol. 6, edited by Paul Edwards. New York: Macmillan, 1967, 264–76.
MacCormick, Neil. *H. L. A. Hart.* Stanford, Calif.: Stanford Univ. Press, 1981.

Discussions and criticisms of Hart's theory of law can be classified according to the philosophical school of the author. Increasing "distance" is shown in these three examples:

> model for religious virtues, has been seen by many philosophical commentators as raising questions about a true "fidelity to law."

Raz, Joseph. *The Concept of a Legal System.* 2d ed. New York: Oxford Univ. Press, 1980. This is the work of a legal positivist who asks how adequately Hart answers his own questions.

Dworkin, Ronald. *Taking Rights Seriously.* Cambridge: Harvard Univ. Press, 1977. Dworkin argues that a legal system is based not only on primary and secondary rules, but also on principles of law that bind judges to respect certain basic rights apart from any rule of recognition. His views will be described in the following section.

Fuller, Lon. *The Morality of Law.* New Haven: Yale Univ. Press, 1969. A critic of all legal positivism, Fuller offers alternatives that will be discussed in section 22 below.

QUESTIONS FOR DISCUSSION

1. Talk of commands is seldom heard outside the army, and that is a highly legal society. When a company "commander" orders an attack on a village, is this a command or a rule (think of incidents in Vietnam)? Was Eichmann simply "following orders" in his mass extermination of Jews?

2. Do members of Congress break the law when failing to stamp a letter sent to constituents? If generality belongs to the essence of law, does this mean that all laws oblige the legislators? Are there any circumstances in which a gunman could invoke laws rather than imposing commands? Write a statute to which he might appeal.

3. When a dictator dies, is there a gap in the law? If a different regime follows a revolution? What happens to law when a colony becomes independent?

4. Distinguish between internal and external viewpoints in the following:
   a. I was speeding because I was late for an important appointment
   b. The divorce rate has increased because marriage is outmoded
   c. Both birds and tourists seek warmer regions when winter comes
   d. Gentlemen prefer blondes
   e. He has an I.Q. of 130
   f. The shades of dusk are falling

5. A city ordinance makes it illegal to park your car in front of a driveway, even if it is your own (the author speaks from his criminal record!). You are visiting a friend, and he suggests you leave your car in front of his driveway, since no other space is available for several blocks. Analyze your obligation to the ordinance, in terms supplied by Austin, Hart, and Kant. Does Hart's distinction between "being obliged" (coercion) and "having an obligation" apply here? If you see no reason for the rule in this case, would the law be heteronomous (in Kant's sense)? If so, how would your obedience to it differ from your compliance with a gunman's order? Does your obligation of fidelity to laws in general extend to laws that seem unreasonable?

6. Such questions are imprecise, because the term *unreasonable* runs from mere inconvenience (in the above example) to evident immorality. Few would hesitate to violate parking laws in order to get prompt medical assistance for an injured person. Would you say that the law remained valid but that you were morally obliged to break it?

7. Hart argues against Austin's command theory by saying that it neglects "some of the most characteristic elements of law," the "fundamental accepted rules" that "lie at the root of a legal system" (Hart, "Positivism and Separation," 603). He then insists, however, that such rules need have no connection with morality. Do you agree that your acceptance of the rules that lie at the root of your legal system is altogether distinct from moral questions? Fuller, in reply (Fuller, "Positivism and Fidelity," 642–43), asks you to suppose you are drafting a constitution for a country emerging from a period of violence. Austin might consistently speak of the force of such a document, meaning the power of the new sovereign. But, if Hart suggests more, how can the acceptance of this constitution avoid relying on general assumptions of what is reasonable and just? In the light of such an example, would you regard the existence of the rule of recognition as a sheer matter of fact or as an embodiment of moral principles?

8. Are moral obligations imposed on you by your society, your upbringing, your superego? If so, why should you respect and follow such commands? If you conclude that all morals are relative, what about your own obligation toward the truth of this conclusion? Can respect for truth be explained in terms of heteronomous forces? Is there some self-contradiction in Hume's basic position that there can be no necessary facts but only sheer matters of fact (what about this fact?)?

19. DWORKIN ON PRINCIPLES AND RIGHTS

> *I do not think that anyone familiar with what has been published in the last ten years, in England and the United States, on the philosophy of government can doubt that this subject, which is the meeting point of moral, political and legal philosophy, is undergoing a great change. We are currently witnessing, I think, the progress of a transition from a once widely accepted old faith that some form of utilitarianism, if only we could discover the right form, must capture the essence of political morality. The new faith is that the truth must lie not with a doctrine that takes the maximisation of average or aggregate general welfare for its goal, but with a doctrine of basic human rights....*
> (H. L. A. Hart, "Between Utility and Rights," *Columbia Law Review* 79 [1979]: 828)

In 1969, Hart was succeeded in the chair of jurisprudence at Oxford by Ronald Dworkin, an American who had been a professor at Yale. The change is perhaps symbolic of a relaxation in legal positivism toward theses that had previously been associated with rival philosophies. The legal realists have seen law in terms of the judicial rather than the legislative process, and Dworkin has developed his legal philosophy largely from an examination of the problems in judicial decision making. His theory of law is also open to the traditional claim of natural law philosophers that the judge must take moral principles into account when finding what the law really is. Yet Dworkin seems to remain faithful, with many qualifications, to the positivist notion that the validity of a law depends on its pedigree; for the moral considerations he envisages are largely those found to be "embedded" in the positive rules of a particular legal system.

Articles published by Dworkin up to 1976 have been collected in a book entitled *Taking Rights Seriously*, to which page references in this section will refer unless otherwise indicated.[21] Since the articles (or chapters, arranged logically rather than chronologically) cover about ten years of developing thought, interpretation of his complex and subtle theory is precarious. In 1986

---

21. Ronald Dworkin, *Taking Rights Seriously* (Cambridge: Harvard Univ. Press, 1977). The paperback edition (1978) reprints pages 1–290 and adds a lengthy appendix (pp. 291–368) in which Dworkin replies to seven of his critics. Further articles by Dworkin, published between 1977 and 1983, have been collected under the title *A Matter of Principle* (Cambridge: Harvard Univ. Press, 1985); in this work Dworkin applies his legal philosophy to a wide range of contemporary issues, such as the theoretical and practical status of liberalism, the claim that judges should decide cases by aiming to maximize social wealth, and problems of reverse discrimination and freedom of the press.

Dworkin published *Law's Empire*, a further account of his legal philosophy.[22] The book appeared only as these pages reached the typesetter. Time, and the process of criticism and rejoinder, will tell whether the task of a commentator has been made less or more precarious by Dworkin's restatement of his position. It is likely that the questions so keenly debated over the past ten years remain open. *Taking Rights Seriously* marked Dworkin's appearance as a legal philosopher, and this may still be an appropriate text to use as an introduction to his thought.

Criticism of the Model of Rules

> The rule of law is a nobler ideal than the rule of legal texts.
> (Dworkin, *Taking Rights Seriously*, 338)

> Interpretations struggle side by side with litigants before the bar. Each judge's interpretive theories are grounded in his own convictions about the "point"—the justifying purpose or goal or principle—of legal practice as a whole....
> (Dworkin, *Law's Empire*, 87–88)

We have seen, through the cases in our opening chapter, something of the problems that face a judge, whether he or she acts as referee in a chess tournament or as a Supreme Court justice who must decide on matters of life and death. Law comes to us most evidently in the form of rules. These govern the majority of cases in a way that leaves little room for initiative. The judge enjoys what Dworkin calls "discretion in the weak sense" (see section 14 above). Judgment is required only in applying standards clearly expressed by the law, as in the example of a sergeant told to pick his five most experienced men for a patrol. However, many cases come before a judge where the rules do not guide the decision so clearly, and it is in terms of such hard cases that we can best approach the opposition of Dworkin's legal theory to that of Hart.

When legislators make a rule, they may unintentionally leave gaps in the law (by failing to think of a case that is likely to arise), or they may intentionally use "open-textured" words that invite judges to render the rule more precise as cases call for decision. By way of a simple example we can refer again to *Temple v. City of Petersburg* (section 6 above). The Virginia legislators made a rule forbidding that any cemetery should "hereafter be established" within a city or town. The court decided that this statute did not prevent the enlargement of an existing cemetery; the word *establish* was taken as limited to the creation of a new cemetery, and no investigation was conducted into the history of the statute. It would, however, be plausible to hold that the wording was sufficiently

---

22. Cambridge: Harvard Univ. Press, Belknap Press, 1986. For a collection of interpretations and criticisms of Dworkin's thought, along with a further reply that he has made to each critic, see *Ronald Dworkin and Contemporary Jurisprudence*, edited by Marshall Cohen (Totowa, N.J.: Rowman & Allanheld, 1984).

open that it either might or might not cover the purchase of new land for an extension, or to say that there was here a gap in the law; the legislators simply had not anticipated this delicate problem. How then would the court decide?

Hart's reply is that the court's "specification of a variable standard is very like the exercise of delegated rule-making power by an administrative body."[23] Where rules do not give adequate guidance for a decision, the judge has discretion in the sense of becoming a legislator to fill the gap or make a more definite ruling. "The open texture of law means that there are, indeed, areas of conduct where much must be left to be developed by courts and officials striking a balance, in the light of circumstances, between competing interests which vary in weight from case to case."[24] As a deputy legislator, the judge is of course not acting arbitrarily or following his personal preferences. He will, like any legislator, be open to moral considerations. If he is a utilitarian, he will presumably be under a moral obligation to find that decision which maximizes social benefits. In the *Temple* case, the court should have so decided between the competing interests of cemetery officials and of nearby property owners. However, according to Hart, such considerations are moral ones about the question which law ought to be made by a legislator; they are not principles within the law that already *is* and that gives one party to the dispute a legal right to a favorable decision.

Dworkin's reply is that an examination of how judicial decisions are reported when judges write their opinions shows Hart's analysis to be incomplete and flawed. A court does not simply act under legal rules and, when these are inadequate, move into an area where the judge exercises "strong discretion" by making new rules without guidance from legal standards. In addition to primary rules, deriving from a rule of recognition, the law contains a variety of *principles* that prescribe a correct legal decision even in hard cases. The court may have great difficulty, and reveal disagreement, in finding the relevant principles and arriving at the legally correct decision, but we do not thereby pass from adjudication to legislation.

Two cases are offered by Dworkin as an example, though he claims that "almost any case in a law school casebook would provide examples that would serve as well" (p. 23). The first case is that of *Riggs v. Palmer*, which we discussed at length in section 4. There the majority opinion was based on "general, fundamental maxims of the common law"; these were accepted as unwritten principles of the law rather than as rules specified in statutes or in case law. Dworkin's second example is Henningsen v. Bloomfield Motors, Inc. (1960, 32 N.J. 358, 161 A.2d 69). This is a landmark decision on the obligation of a manufacturer or retailer for defective products. Henningsen bought a Plymouth (Chrysler) car from Bloomfield Motors. He signed a contract on the

---

23. Hart, *The Concept of Law*, 129.
24. Ibid., 132. For Dworkin's most recent criticism of such views, see his account of "conventionalism" in *Law's Empire*, chapter 4.

reverse of which were eight inches of fine print that limited the warranty to defective parts sent back to the manufacturer. After 468 miles, the steering mechanism seems to have cracked and the car veered off the road. Damage was so extensive that no defective parts could be recovered. Henningsen could point to no established rule of law that prevented the manufacturer from standing on the narrow contract. The jury nevertheless found for Henningsen, and the defendants (Chrysler and Bloomfield) appealed. The Supreme Court of New Jersey, with no dissenting votes, affirmed the earlier verdict.

Though there is a complex history of decisions on manufacturers' liability (as we shall see in section 31), the interest of this case comes partly from the extent to which the court opinion turned from citing precedents to a discussion of principles that can be less readily identified in specific statements. On Bloomfield's side was the freedom to make contracts and the principle that a person is held to what he signs even if he has not read it. On the other side, it was pointed out that freedom of contract is not an immutable doctrine and that car manufacturers have special obligations in view of the needs and dangers of an automotive culture. Finally, appeal was made to principles of justice supposedly underpinning the law: "Is there any principle which is more familiar or more firmly embedded in the history of Anglo-American law than the basic doctrine that the courts will not permit themselves to be used as instruments of inequity and injustice? . . . More specifically the courts generally refuse to lend themselves to the enforcement of a 'bargain' in which one party has unjustly taken advantage of the necessities of the other" (Henningsen, 32 N.J. 389, quoting Justice Frankfurter).

Accustomed as we are to the notion that laws should be written somewhere, for our inspection, and to the perhaps Western conviction that there should be a hierarchy of authority in the making of rules, we may have some sympathy with the defendants in this case. Where are the "principles" that led to the judgment against Bloomfield? What authority made them part of the law? Can judges summon the law out of thin air?

Dworkin's claim is that *Henningsen* is far from untypical. A study of judicial decision making is said by him to reveal that judges appeal beyond rules to principles that, even if clearly moral ones, are assumed to be part of the law and a basis for adjudication rather than an extralegal ground for legislation. Many of the laypeople who applauded the *Henningsen* decision may have been socialists who saw this as a political move against a large corporation. Were they legislators, there would have been nothing inappropriate in their vote for policies that curb big business. But Dworkin's thesis is that judges enjoy no such freedom to decide in court on the basis of their own convictions either for or against large corporations. The New Jersey judges, for all their reliance on moral principles, were claiming to find the law as it really is rather than to make laws as they think these ought to be. Dworkin clearly does not deny the fact that some judges are politically motivated; that is a sociological fact, as is the observation that some judges yield to bribery. His claim has to do with the logic of the law:

judicial decisions rightly and legally involve reference beyond rules to principles that inhere in the legal system of which judges are officials. Though boundaries may be hazy, this is different from citing Karl Marx or the Sermon on the Mount (unless some view of alienation or of turning the other cheek has indeed become part of the very fabric of the society and legal system that the judge is called to represent).

How do principles differ in form from rules? Dworkin's account of principles varies, and he may (as we shall see) restrict these to moral standards of justice involving rights. However, his initial version is broad and is stated in contrast to the clearly defined rules of law. Legal rules apply in an "all-or-nothing" fashion, as do the rules of a game. Three strikes and you are out (if not, there is another rule to cover the situation, as when the catcher drops the ball). The umpire does not have to weigh the relative merits of protecting a player's self-esteem and of keeping a close score in the game (unless, perhaps, in a neighborhood or family contest: see section 14, p. 137 above). Similarly, the rules in *Riggs* (taken without regard to principles) told the court that Francis Palmer's will was valid and that Elmer should enjoy the estate.

However, principles are in unsettled conflict, and the judge or referee must assign them relative weight. That was the point of our simple example from the chess tournament (section 3). Did Greene unreasonably annoy his opponent by whistling, or Slye by smiling? No rules specified the decision, yet it was not a matter of mere choice by a referee who acted as legislator. Recourse was had to the undefined purposes that bring people together as chess players and make this a game with a particular quality. Principles of sportsmanship might weigh against Greene. Yet principles inherent in the very project of competitive play, of winning by one's wits, might weigh in his favor. Field games offer more obvious illustrations of how a referee is invited to turn from the rule book to underlying principles that promote fairness, safety, and even the interest of spectators in a fluid contest.

Does the analogy of games extend to law? What about the requirement that each side in a dispute must be heard? That no one shall judge in his own case? That a wrongful act does not improve one's legal situation? That liability is a corollary of fault? That an act is not culpable unless accompanied by a guilty mind? That no one can complain of a harm to which he consents? That one who acts by another acts himself? What about the fundamental requirement that precedents should be followed, that like cases should receive a like decision? Such basic notions are somewhat different from the rules of a strikeout or for making a valid will. Where two rules conflict, one must be dropped or suitably extended by a rule-like qualification. However, Dworkin sees principles as being in *competition* rather than in *contradiction*, so that when they intersect, "one who must resolve the conflict has to take into account the relative weight of each" (p. 26). He gives the example of adverse possession, that a person who trespasses long enough on another's land eventually gains a right of way. The principle that no man may profit from his own wrong is here outweighed but not superseded; it lives to fight another day, as in *Riggs*.

Principles are evidently the home ground for words like *reasonable*, *unjust*, and *significant*. Indeed, it is often an important question before a court whether a legal provision should be treated as a rule or as a principle. The example is cited of the Sherman Act, which stated that every contract in restraint of trade shall be void (p. 27). It makes a vital difference whether this provision play the part of a rule or be interpreted as a principle forbidding unreasonable restraint of trade.

The distinction between rules and principles has been challenged,[25] and Dworkin admits that it is not always easy to apply in specific instances. However, there are considerable differences between viewing the legal enterprise on "the model of rules" and seeing it as comprising an indefinite range of principles. If law is composed only of rules, the task of advocates is to find and urge the rules most favorable to their client. And the client is at the mercy not only of the many rules located by the opposition, but also of the judge who is free to contribute a ruling of his own. Dworkin, however, directs us to look below the waterline and to discover the underlying principles that give the law its life and meaning. The task imposed upon judges is, in this account, demanding. They are denied the liberties of strong discretion and must go beyond the rule of texts to recognize and assess the principles at work. For the litigant is entitled to the legally correct decision in any case, rather than appearing as a suppliant for favorable legislation where the rules run out. There is an important difference between saying that a litigant has a right to win and deciding that it is good for that person to win. We may even be reminded of the case of the speluncean explorers, where each judge thought that these men should be saved from the executioner, yet there was disagreement whether this was a matter of legal right or of extralegal benevolence.

Some commentators have tried to minimize the distinction between Hart and Dworkin by allowing for the addition of principles to rules within the law but by claiming that legal principles can also be drawn from the rule of recognition, provided that this be interpreted in a sufficiently broad fashion. Dworkin has rejected this conciliatory move (see, for example, pp. 64–68). However, it would be wrong to view him as altogether abandoning the tradition of legal positivism and as proposing a natural law theory such as that of Justice Foster in the speluncean story. It will be necessary now to ask more precisely what Dworkin means by legal principles, how he suggests we should find them, and what this has to do with the rights we can thus expect to be defended by a court.

---

25. Dworkin, *Taking Rights Seriously*, 46 n. 2. Chapter 3 consists largely of Dworkin's reply to such critics. In *Law's Empire* he adds a distinction between *borderline* and *pivotal* cases: the former have to do with more or less arbitrary decisions about rules, whereas the latter test the underlying principles of law (pp. 41–43).

Invitation to a Thesis about Rights

> In place of the misleading question, whether judges find rules in the 'existing law' or make up rules not to be found there, we must ask whether judges try to determine what the parties have a right to have, or whether they create what they take to be new rights to serve social goals (p. 293).

The influence that Dworkin's complex theories have had in this country may be related to the fact that the courts became effective champions of civil rights at a period when the legislatures failed to supply remedies. Dworkin's attention to the judiciary as the defender of individual rights, and his argument that utilitarianism is an inadequate basis for them, may have appeared as a timely suggestion that some values need institutional support against much that passes as the will of the majority or even as a calculation of policies serving the greatest good of the greatest number. Utilitarians can of course be expected to indicate failure in such calculations rather than to admit it in their moral theory. But citizens who look to the courts for defense against the tides of policy are likely to view Dworkin's account more favorably than one that allows the judge discretion to act as a deputy legislator.

Though Dworkin initially defined principles, broadly taken, by their contrast to rules, his discussion of rights calls for a distinction, within this broad sense, between principles and policies. A policy "sets out a goal to be reached, generally an improvement in some economic, political, or social feature of the community" (p. 22). Thus, it is a policy to devote a certain percentage of the budget to national defense, to restrict immigration, or to lessen fatalities on the roads. A principle, however, is observed "because it is a requirement of justice or fairness or some other dimension of morality." Thus, it was to a principle in the strict sense that the courts appealed in holding that no man shall profit by his own wrong (*Riggs*) and that one party not be allowed to take unjust advantage of another (*Henningsen*). Dworkin shows the direction of his inquiry by giving as examples the principles on which the rights of minorities and the right to free speech are based. He admits to the difficulty of applying this distinction: principles become policies (e.g., in deciding how much education to make available to all), and policies are based on principles (e.g., in social security legislation). But Dworkin insists on the importance of his distinction and criticizes utilitarianism for trying to reduce principles of justice to policies that seek maximization of social benefits.

The application of Dworkin's distinction to judicial decision making may be apparent. Though legislators can act on the basis of policy, he holds that judges are constrained to give their decisions on the ground of principles. In reply to one of his critics, Dworkin distinguishes between two questions that occur to a judge in an ordinary civil action. "Does the plaintiff, all things considered, have a right to what he asks? That is the question of principle. Will it make the community better off as a whole if I decide for the plaintiff? That is the question of policy."[26] Suppose, for example, a property owner is threatened with loss through the contruction of a new road. The city or county administrator is likely to see the dispute as a question of policy. But a judge, even if likely to vote as a citizen for policies that weaken the position of property owners, is bound to give the decision of the court on the basis of a thorough investigation of the principles embedded in the law.

The rights with which Dworkin is concerned are individual ones, and he defines them as "trumps" we hold against the pursuit of policies. "Individuals have rights when, for some reason, a collective goal is not a sufficient justification for denying them what they wish, as individuals, to have or to do, or not a sufficient justification for imposing some loss or injury upon them" (p. xi). Specifically, our rights are "trumps over some background justification like utility, and I argue that judges in ordinary common law cases try to decide which party has a right to win rather than which decision would be best for the community on the whole."[27] One example may be mentioned. In discussing the complex question of civil disobedience (chapter 7), Dworkin claims that even if rejection of this practice adds to the sum of social benefits, "the prospect of utilitarian gains cannot justify preventing a man from doing what he has a right to do" (p. 193).

If we expect judges to give their verdicts on the basis of legal principles rather than of current policies, the critical question is how Dworkin helps us to find such principles within the law. Two introductory comments may be relevant.

1. Dworkin expressly rejects Hart's theory that adjudication (rather than quasi-legislation by a judge) depends exclusively on legal rules whose validity stems from a rule of recognition. Dworkin sets a further source of adjudication in legal principles that do not derive from such a master rule. Has he thereby abandoned the notion of a legal "pedigree" that is one of the distinctive marks of legal positivism? There is no easy answer to this question, and Dworkin's thought may have shifted, at least in emphasis. Chapter 2 ("The Model of Rules") was originally published in 1967, and there he seems to look for legal principles through a historical investigation into the traditions at the heart of a particular legal system. Such principles have their origin "in a sense of appropriateness developed in the profession and the public over time. Their continued power depends upon this sense of appropriateness being sustained" (p. 40). Indeed, such principles can lose their legal effect, not from repeal but from erosion. This continuing inquiry into legal history is certainly an extension, but not an abandonment, of the

---

26. Cohen, *Contemporary Jurisprudence*, 263. For an interesting application of this distinction, see chapter 4 of Dworkin's *A Matter of Principle*; with a view to nuclear protest movements, Dworkin studies how the case for civil disobedience changes when the official decisions under challenge are seen as mistakes in policy or as errors of principle. Chapter 3 discusses some of the theoretical problems in distinguishing between principle, policy, and procedure.

27. Cohen, *Contemporary Jurisprudence*, 268.

notion of pedigree. However, it was eight years later that the vital fourth chapter ("Hard Cases") was originally published, and here Dworkin gives a detailed account of how legal principles are discovered. Concern for institutional history still plays an important part, but emphasis is now placed on the importance to judges of a "comprehensive theory of general principles," the disclosure of which is philosophical rather than empirical. The distance from Hart seems to have increased, and the task of a judge approaches that of a moral philosopher.

2. Dworkin's theory evidently serves to lessen the distinction that Austin made between analytical (descriptive) and normative jurisprudence. For we are now told that an objective examination into ways in which judges decide what the law really is may involve recognition of how they take into account moral principles about what ought to be. Moral norms can apparently tell what our rights are under the law that really prevails. Nevertheless, the critic of Dworkin may be confounded all too easily. For Dworkin claims to rest his theory of law on a study of how judges *do* decide. Yet any fact that seems to oppose his conclusions is met by the reply that the judge *ought* to have proceeded otherwise. Natural law theorists, from Plato to Fuller, hold that they are talking about an ideal law that we realize only in "copies." Dworkin's philosophy of law is not easy to situate on a spectrum that runs from this extreme to that of a purely empirical inquiry.[28]

To expound his theory of judicial decision making, Dworkin develops a parable. He portrays an ideal judge, Hercules, who benefits from "superhuman skill, learning, patience and acumen" (p. 105). If his jurisdiction has a written constitution, Hercules will first construct a full constitutional theory that enables him to decide which of the conflicting theories at work in a dispute "provides a smoother fit with the constitutional scheme as a whole" (p. 106). Confronted with statutes of uncertain application, Hercules will not indulge in hypotheses about the mental state of particular legislators but will interpret enacted laws by applying whatever theory best justifies a statute "in the light of the legislator's more general responsibilities." Dworkin cites as an example a judicial opinion that a proposed statutory interpretation "is neither consonant with sound reason, with judicial authorities, with the course of legislation, nor with the principles of our free institutions" (p. 108n).

Hercules' main task, however, is with the discovery of principles at work in the common law. One of the most basic of these is the very principle of justice

---

28. Dworkin might well protest at having his theory so located, for the benefit of beginners, on any "spectrum." His legal philosophy is a complex effort to incorporate both descriptive and normative elements into an account of what the law really is. However, some critics have been puzzled at the way Dworkin moves between "description and recommendation." See, for instance, John Mackie's article, "The Third Theory of Law," in Cohen, *Contemporary Jurisprudence*, 161–70. For an interesting example of Dworkin's criticism of what judges do, see his comment on decisions where the Fugitive Slave Acts were enforced in courts before the American Civil War (Ronald Dworkin, "The Law of the Slave-Catchers," *The Times Literary Supplement* [London], 5 December 1975).

that obliges him to treat like cases alike and hence to recognize "the gravitational force" of precedents (which is largely lacking in the enactments of a legislature on the basis of policies). The complex task of discovering which precedents are relevant and decisive is again a matter that calls for a comprehensive theory. The judge's passage from the general justification for precedents to specific applications involves the question "What set of principles best justifies the precedents? . . . The law may not be a seamless web, but the plaintiff is entitled to ask Hercules to treat it as if it were" (p. 116).

From the picture of Hercules we can see Dworkin's ideal for discovery of the principles in a system of law. "A principle is a principle of law if it figures in the soundest theory of law that can be provided as a justification for the explicit substantive and institutional rules of the jurisdiction in question. . . . This process of justification must carry the lawyer very deep into political and moral theory" (pp. 66–67). "A proposition of law may be asserted as true if it is more consistent with the theory of law that best justifies settled law than the contrary proposition of law" (p. 283). As a literary critic will defend particular claims about a character or incident in a novel by appealing to his interpretation of the work as a whole, so the judge should ground his particular decision on principles that cohere with the best justification of the relevant law.[29] And such coherence involves the making of moral judgments. These are not the private convictions of the judge, nor even the current feelings of the public, but the morality that is "presupposed by the laws and institutions of the community" (pp. 123–28).

Evidently, Dworkin does not think that the ideal he set for Hercules is achieved by any actual judges. These produce "at the best only pockets of a general theory, or, as is no doubt often the case, pockets of different theories" (p. 359). But judges have an intuitive idea of what an ideally comprehensive theory of law would involve. With such a guide, experience can lead in the right direction, much as any official's sense for the spirit of a game will develop over his career and will head toward sound, thoroughly principled judgments.

The difficulty of classifying Dworkin under traditional headings may be apparent. He clearly turns from Hart's version of legal positivism and moves toward natural law positions. Yet he is certainly not asking us to derive general principles of all possible legal systems in abstraction from a thorough investigation of what happens to count as settled law. And Dworkin himself refuses to be placed in customary categories. He rejects the simple alternative proposed by

---

29. The analogy is one that Dworkin has explored; see section 33 below. In *Law's Empire* he prefaces his study of legal theories with a chapter on "Interpretive Concepts." He also makes an investigation of *integrity* central to his theory of law. "We know that people disagree to some extent about the right principles of behavior, so we distinguish that requirement from the different (and weaker) requirement that they act in important matters with integrity, that is, according to convictions that inform and shape their lives as a whole, rather than capriciously or whimsically. The practical importance of this latter requirement among people who know they disagree about justice is evident. Integrity becomes a political ideal when we make the same demand of the state or community taken to be a moral agent. . . . I shall argue that integrity rather than some superstition of elegance is the life of law as we know it" (pp. 166–67).

those who say "We must stand with the positivists, who insist that it is always just a question of fact what the law is. Or we must fly with the most extreme of the natural lawyers, who say that there can be no difference between principles of law and principles of morality. But both of these extreme views are wrong" (p. 342).

One critic of Dworkin, Professor J. H. Ely, takes him to task for suggesting that a study of the law must involve some appreciation of moral philosophy.[30] However, as Ely concedes, the contemporary moral philosophy on which Dworkin most relies is that of John Rawls and is more modest in its pretensions than that which traditional natural law theorists have supposed. Conclusions are no longer drawn from some abstract statement of the nature of man. "The kind of reasoning that is involved in the arguments of contemporary moral philosophers proceeds from ethical principles or conclusions it is felt the reader is likely already to accept to other conclusions or principles he or she might not previously have perceived as related in the way the writer suggests."[31] The description seems to fit Rawls's account of "reflective equilibrium," where we start with an intuitive conviction of what is morally right, develop a theory to justify this, modify our convictions in the light of the theory and then our theory in terms of the intuitions that are thus developed.[32]

We shall shortly (sections 21, 22) inquire into the complex history and contemporary statements of natural law theory. But the common fear is that this proclaims some ideal law as a brooding omnipresence that supplies a ready judgment of whatever legislators enact or judges decide. Dworkin rejects any such proposal, "the assumption that non-positivists must believe in something called natural law, which is taken to be the contents of celestial secret books" (p. 337). He insists that he intends no such metaphysics but means only "to summarize ... many of the practices that are part of our legal process" (p. 216). His concern is not to construct the ideal legal system but to find "the best justification that can be provided for the actual legal system we have."[33] Dwor-

---

30. J. H. Ely, *Democracy and Distrust* (Cambridge: Harvard Univ. Press, 1980), 58. The passage from Dworkin on which Ely comments is reprinted in *Taking Rights Seriously*, 149. Elsewhere, Dworkin remarks that "any judge's opinion is itself a piece of legal philosophy, even when the philosophy is hidden and the visible argument is dominated by citation and lists of facts. Jurisprudence is the general part of adjudication, silent prologue to any decision at law" (*Law's Empire*, 90). And again: "Lawyers are always philosophers, because jurisprudence is part of any lawyer's account of what the law is, even where the jurisprudence is undistinguished and mechanical" (Ibid., 380). Ely's objection may have been anticipated by Learned Hand's remark that we should not be ruled by philosopher-judges even if our judges were better philosophers (Learned Hand, *The Bill of Rights* [Cambridge: Harvard Univ. Press, 1958], 73).
31. Ely, *Democracy*, 54.
32. John Rawls, *A Theory of Justice* (Cambridge: Harvard Univ. Press, 1971), 20–21, 48–50.
33. Cohen, *Contemporary Jurisprudence*, 254. In *A Matter of Principle*, Dworkin gives a simple example of the way in which a judge finds his application of moral principles to be constrained by a coherent general interpretation of the legal tradition in which he works.

Suppose a judge himself approves what might be called a radical Christian principle: that each citizen is morally entitled that those who have more wealth than he does make available to him the surplus. He might wish to apply that principle to hard cases in tort or contract so as to refuse damages against a poor defendant, on the ground that the richer plaintiff's right to damages must be set off against the

kin's links with positivism are maintained by his claim that "the question of what principles are indeed principles of any particular legal system is itself a question of fact" (p. 339).

One of Dworkin's doctrines that has aroused the most protest is the assertion that, even in hard cases, there must be one correct legal answer for the judge if he is to respect the rights of those who await his judgment. Even some who accept the existence of legal principles as well as rules, and who concede that such principles ground our legal rights, see in Dworkin's full theory a rationalism that they cannot allow. Thus, for example:

> Every time I 'correct' a theory as a whole, I am presupposing some further theory. Dworkin postulates a Hercules who can construct a best-possible theory of a given legal system. But Hercules can construct that only at the far end of an infinite regress of theories. Dworkin has landed his Hercules in Augean stables in which the dung cannot run out, because it is in infinite supply.[34]

We see again the question whether reason (in any of its forms) can carry us all the way or must stop with some sheer matter of fact. For Hart this is the social fact that the practice of law officials, seen from an external point of view, takes some master rule as the source of legal validity. Other commentators, closer to Dworkin, admit that principles and rights form a sheer multiplicity, so that the judge who weighs them as they compete is left finally with an act of choice when the decision is made; legislation cannot altogether be excluded from adjudication.

A final comment may be appropriate. Though Dworkin does not, in the manner of a rationalist philosopher, claim to derive any systematic hierarchy of universal legal principles, he does make it clear that one principle, or one right, is of an order distinct from all others:

> The book nevertheless suggests one favored form of argument for political rights, which is the derivation of particular rights from the abstract right to concern and respect taken to be fundamental and axiomatic.... Concern and respect is a right so fundamental that it is not captured by the general characterization of rights as trumps over collective goals, except as a limiting case, because it is the source both of the general authority of collective goals and of the special limitations on their authority that justify more particular rights (pp. xiv–xv).

---

defendant's right to charity. But he cannot do so, because (for better or for worse) that principle is inconsistent with the vast bulk of the rules in the rule book. No adequate justification of what is in the rule book could be given, that is, without presupposing that the radical Christian principle has been rejected (p. 17).

34. Neil MacCormick, *Legal Reasoning and Legal Theory* (1978), 255. This book, both sympathetic to Dworkin and critical of him, is one of the most serious studies that the debate has produced. Dworkin's article, "Is There Really No Right Answer in Hard Cases?" (1978), has been reprinted as chapter 5 of *A Matter of Principle*.

The "fundamental right to equal concern and respect" is defined by Dworkin as the right of all persons to be viewed as human beings "capable of suffering and frustration" and as "capable of forming and acting on intelligent conceptions of how their lives should be lived" (p. 272). This is not to say that all people are to be treated *equally* (e.g., having the same distribution of goods), but it is to hold that each person has a basic right to be treated *as an equal*; that is, his or her claims are to be respectfully considered and are not to be set in lower esteem before the question of distribution is faced.

Dworkin identifies the right to equal concern and respect with the "fundamental equality" that he understands Rawls to take as the basis for developing his whole theory of justice (p. 180). In his lengthy commentary on this theory (chapter 6), Dworkin speaks of this right as an assumption. It is, however, "owed to human beings as moral persons," and we could scarcely reason and argue about morality as we do unless we assumed it (see, for example, pp. 158, 181–82).

Any discussion of such topics would go beyond our purposes here. But we can perhaps see Dworkin as inviting the question why we submit to any legal system at all. Presumably Hercules would come up with a somewhat different set of principles and rights if he were summoned into existence in this country or in China or in an African country where the law is largely tribal. In all human societies there will be collective goals, policies that aim at more than the good of an individual with power; yet the question remains why individuals grant authority to such community purposes. And, if Dworkin is correct, there will always be some rights that can "trump" even these collective goals; but why should the majority allow its aims to be so checked? Those critics who, from their knowledge of history or of anthropology, think Dworkin either too idealistic or too much bound to his own situation, may at least ask if counter-examples do not involve the disappearance of the very notion of a legal system (see the discussion of despotism in section 11 above).

In the article from which he drew the title for his basic book, Dworkin closes by asking Why take rights seriously? He replies that if we want disputes to be settled through law rather than by force, then we need to attend to the ground rules (or principles?) that keep us from being at the mercy of "the conqueror's law." That, of course, is law only in the descriptive sense of how the stronger and weaker behave. The law about which Dworkin has been writing is to be understood "from the internal point of view," and this viewpoint must extend as far as law goes rather than stopping when we come to a rule of recognition. The right to equal concern and respect is more than a topic for a sociologist.

"The Government will not re-establish respect for law without giving the law some claim to respect" (p. 205). The extent to which the law is respected may be a fact on which journalists can comment. Yet all members of a legal system share in the obligation that the law should be worthy of respect.

FURTHER READING

Benditt, Theodore M. *Law as Rule and Principle.* Stanford, Calif.: Stanford Univ. Press, 1978, chapter 4.
Cohen, Marshall, ed. *Ronald Dworkin and Contemporary Jurisprudence.* Totowa, N.J.: Rowman & Allanheld, 1984.
Dworkin, Ronald. *Law's Empire.* Cambridge: Harvard Univ. Press, Belknap Press, 1986.
———. *A Matter of Principle.* Cambridge: Harvard Univ. Press, 1985.
———. *Taking Rights Seriously.* Cambridge: Harvard Univ. Press, 1977.
Greenawalt, Kent. "Discretion and Judicial Decision," *Columbia Law Review* 75 (1975): 359–99.
MacCormick, Neil. *Legal Reasoning and Legal Theory.* Oxford: Oxford Univ. Press, 1978.
Raz, Joseph. "Professor Dworkin's Theory of Rights," *Political Studies* 26 (1978): 123–37.
Ten, C. L. "The Soundest Theory of Law," *Mind* 88 (1979): 522–37.
Weinreb, Lloyd L. "Law as Order," *Harvard Law Review* 91 (1978): 909–59.

QUESTIONS FOR DISCUSSION

1. Think of examples, from your own experience, of how an official may act as what Hart calls a "delegated rule-maker." Suppose the college states that each course shall have an appropriate system of examining and grading. Does this leave the instructor with strong or weak discretion (in Dworkin's sense)? Is the teacher free to balance the competing interests of his or her students? Some will do better at one type of test, others at another. What about a student with dyslexia? Are there underlying principles of justice that entitle each student to be placed in the correct order of merit? Apply the example to a civil suit before a judge.

2. If (as was suggested in section 14 above) we can water down the distinction between strong and weak discretion, do we correspondingly blur Dworkin's distinction between rules and principles? Or could Dworkin reply that, though the instruction to choose any five soldiers for patrol gives less authoritative guidance than does the charge that these be the five most experienced, in both cases we can locate some underlying principles that are distinct from rules or orders? In the former case, Dworkin holds the sergeant to be bound by standards of "rationality, fairness, and effectiveness"; are these principles? Could the latter case be seen as changing one or more of these principles to the status of a rule? Does this seem an appropriate analogy for what happens in the law? Remember the way in which Justice Holmes's rule that a driver, at a grade crossing, must get out of his vehicle was changed by Justice Cardozo to a principle of "prudent conduct" (section 10). Think of other legal examples of the rule/principle distinction.

3. Suppose there is a law on the statutes to the effect that no one shall be denied employment on grounds of race, religion, sex, or place of residence. There is, however, another law requiring that members of the state assembly be residents within the district they represent. If these are rules, and if they apply in an all-or-nothing manner, how would you resolve the conflict? Suppose, however, that the clash was between a general prohibition of discrimination in employment and some legal recognition of the right to stipulate the conditions of a contract that one makes. Think of cases that might go to court and of ways in which the judge might be called to balance competing principles.

4. How secure is Dworkin's distinction between policies (that aim at collective goals) and principles (that ground rights)? Which of the competing standards cited in *Henningsen* fall into each category? Is it a matter of policy or a possible violation of principle if the government decides to tax all social security benefits? If it decides to deny all benefits to those whose income is above a certain level? Think of other examples. Critics of Dworkin hold that his distinction loses its clarity precisely where it becomes relevant in hard cases.

5.   Do referees in games ever make their decisions on grounds of policy? The good of the sport (and the payment of players' salaries) depends on spectator attendance, which is considerably helped by aggressive play and by a close and fast-moving contest. Could this rightly influence your decision in borderline cases of dangerous play? Can you think of analogies in the decision of a judge? Suppose that an anti-pollution statute, passed on a wave of concern for the environment, is leading to widespread unemployment and hardship in your community. Might you (as judge) make your decision, in a case about strict enforcement, on the basis of policy? Could a court refrain from decisions it thought right in principle, on the grounds that such decisions would prove difficult to carry out in general? Suppose that Elmer Palmer's crime, which led to *Riggs*, had consisted of driving his grandfather to a premature death through psychological pressures? Though courts do not simply follow public opinion, might their decisions be influenced by considerations of what people are ready to receive?

6.   Richard Posner is a leading advocate of the application of economic calculations to judicial decisions. In his comment on Dworkin (Cohen, *Contemporary Jurisprudence,* chapter 13) he presents the example of a suit by homeowners against an airline that lowers the value of their property through the noise of its planes. Suppose that noise abatement by the airline would cost much more than the lowered value of the homes. How might your decision, as judge, be formed or influenced by such calculations and by the notion of maximizing utility?

7.   The principles with which Dworkin is concerned are seen by him as supporting individual rights against collective goals. But what about the rights of one individual against another? Criminal law has, in the name of individual rights, offered considerable protection to those suspected or accused of crimes. However, is not a judge who, through his decisions, makes it more difficult to arrest muggers thereby sacrificing the rights of others to be free of such assaults? Should he not base his decisions on the policy, or collective goal, of reducing crime?

8.   If principles have to be weighed against each other, on what principle is this to be done? Does Dworkin's theory present any advantage here over the utilitarian one, which asks us to calculate and weigh the long-term benefits and harms that would come from each possible decision? In wartime it is difficult for a government to balance the competing claims of national security and freedom of speech. Is it more helpful to state the problem in terms of rights than in terms of cost/benefit analysis?

9.   Once moral considerations are introduced into legal judgment, most people begin to fear that decisions will become more subjective. Think of a range of ways in which morality could enter into a judge's verdict. Suppose he or she is highly puritanical? At the extreme left or right politically? Test, in examples, Dworkin's claim that legal principles do not reflect any such personal morality but rather the morality that is embedded in the legal system as a whole. Suppose you were a judge called upon to apply the fugitive slave laws in the years just before the Civil War?

10.   Comment on the following criticism of Dworkin. "This is why I am tempted to speak of Professor Dworkin playing fast and loose with the law. The alleged determinacy of the law in hard cases is a myth, and the practical effect of the acceptance of this myth would be to give, in three ways, a larger scope for what is in reality judicial legislation. First, it would shift the boundary between the settled and the unsettled law, it would make what on another view would be easy cases into hard ones. Secondly, this approach would encourage a holistic treatment of the law, letting very general principles and remote parts of the law bear upon each specific issue. Thirdly, it would encourage judges, in this holistic treatment, to rely upon their necessarily subjective views about a supposedly objective morality" (John Mackie, in Cohen, *op. cit.*, p. 169).

20. LEGAL REALISM

The felt necessities of the time, the prevalent moral and political theories, intuitions of public policy, avowed or unconscious, even the prejudices which

judges share with their fellow-men, have had a good deal more to do than the syllogism in determining the rules by which men should be governed.
(Oliver Wendell Holmes, Jr., *The Common Law* [1881; reprint, Boston: Little, Brown & Co., 1963], 5)

The figure of Justice Handy can be relied upon to present light relief in the fables about the Supreme Court of Newgarth. However, if his attitudes toward law are stripped of caricature, they need to be considered seriously in any account of legal philosophies. The layperson is likely to feel especially at home with such an approach, which has come to be called *legal realism*. This shows the same empirical mentality as does legal positivism but may seem better grounded in the wry ways of courthouse and law office. Empiricists differ among themselves in where they look for their data, the "given" on which they base their account. Positivists have moved, in their search for legal data, from commands to rules and now even to principles underlying the rules. They have asked us to change our viewpoint from the external one, appropriate for commands, to an internal one required for rules and principles. The legal realist is suspicious. His sense of touching ground calls for a report on what people actually do. If he is a commuter, he is more concerned to discover when his train will in fact arrive than to study the systematic, but often misleading, rules in the timetable. Should not a genuinely empirical account of what the law is be drawn from close observation of how courts and other agencies behave, rather than from reading the rules in books and thinking about them at one's desk?

A description of legal realism can be relaxed, because those who are held to belong have denied that they form a school or subscribe to clearly defined theses. Jerome Frank, though happy to be included in such a family, said that it is held together only by collective negations, skepticism, and curiosity. The term *realism* is one of the most ambiguous in philosophy. Here, however, its meaning is that of the ordinary person. A realist is one who is opposed to any form of sham. He is out to detect common illusions and pretenses, to strip away our layers of rationalization and self-deception. He is distrustful of abstraction and generalization. The period in which the movement flourished, the first half of this century, is one when literature, painting, and social criticism looked for the reality behind consecrated formulas.

Some Scandinavian writers on law have also been classified as legal realists, but it is in this country that most of those who accept the title are to be found. This is no mere result of a national coolness toward flights of theory. The United States Constitution converted many a problem that was elsewhere purely political into a topic for courtroom discussion. Hence there has been a focus in American jurisprudence on the question how courts come to a decision. Though Ronald Dworkin, in drawing on this, has turned our attention from policy to principle, the realists stand for what they regard as a more hard-headed approach. They hold that matters of political or social policy, and even the temperament of individual judges, form the basis for an honest report on the way that verdicts are reached.

If a founding figure for this movement is to be identified, it is probably Oliver Wendell Holmes, Jr. His work *The Common Law* (1881) established him as a leading historian of law; but the "manifesto" that was adopted for legal realism is an address, called "The Path of the Law," which he delivered at Boston University in 1897.[35] In it, Holmes suggests that questions about the nature of law should be framed from the viewpoint of the layperson or of the practicing lawyer, whose basic concern is whether he would win or lose a case that goes to the courts. Holmes presents this as the viewpoint of the "bad man," who wants to know what he can do without suffering legal sanctions; but the "good man" may also need to predict the behavior of courts as he plans a life within the law. At any rate, Holmes recommends that we demystify the law by pouring "cynical acid" on legal writings; the conclusion follows, he says, that "the prophecies of what the courts will do in fact, and nothing more pretentious, are what I mean by the law." Karl Llewellyn restated this in his assertion that "what [legal] officials do about disputes is, to my mind, the law itself," though the history of legal realism is suggested by an "error correction" that he added in a later edition.[36]

Whether you should take your grievance to court is a more than theoretical question. You consult a lawyer to find what the relevant law is. The realist will certainly expect him or her to do some research in the law books but will not regard this as adequate; law is more than an impersonal system of rules and principles, bound together by logical consistency. Your decision may, for instance, come to rest largely on a calculation of which judge is likely to hear your case:

> As lawyers we are interested in knowing how certain officials of society—judges, legislators, and others—have behaved in the past, in order that we may make a prediction of their probable behavior in the future.[37]

It has been said that if legal realism receives less publicity today than it did a generation ago, this is because we have all learned to assimilate the truth in the claims that it advanced in an often iconoclastic way. A judicial Hercules might possibly convert into some coherent system the vast maze of constitutional, statutory, and case law. But actual judges fall far short of such a philosophical ideal. They are limited to pockets of different theories, and their intuitions are at the mercy of factors that belong to the domain of sociologists and psychologists. Nor, when we look for the law as it really is, should we confine our attention to judges. We need to know also when prosecutors do or do not

---

35. The address appeared in *Harvard Law Review* (1896/97): 456, and it has been reprinted in various anthologies; for example, see G. C. Christie, *Jurisprudence* (St. Paul: West, 1973), 648–63.

36. Karl Llewellyn, *The Bramble Bush* (Dobbs Ferry, N.Y.: Oceana Publications, 1951), 8–10, 12. The application of modern techniques from the social sciences to the task of predicting legal decisions will be examined below in section 28; the method is known as "judicial behavioralism."

37. Walter Wheeler Cook, "The Logical and Legal Basis of the Conflict of Laws," *Yale Law Journal* 33 (1924): 475.

exercise their office, when police officers turn a blind eye on incidents that clearly involve probable cause, and when jurors openly disobey the instructions of a judge. Jerome Frank appeals to our common sense, and to our experience, in formulating this definition of law:

> We may now venture a rough definition of law from the point of view of the average man. For any particular lay person, the law, with respect to any particular set of facts, is a decision of a court with respect to those facts so far as that decision affects that particular person. Until a court has passed on those facts no law on that subject is yet in existence. Prior to such a decision, the only law available is the opinion of lawyers as to the law relating to that person and to those facts. Such opinion is not actually law but only a guess as to what a court will decide.[38]

Chapters 4 and 5 in this book will examine many of the criticisms that legal realists have made of traditional accounts of adjudication. For example, we shall consider the choice that judges and lawyers seem to have in finding the rules that govern a case. We shall notice the range of strategies open to an advocate in the way he or she treats legal precedents. We shall look at the manner in which legal reasoning departs from familiar models in mathematics and in science. We shall ask whether a court applies legal rules to nonlegal facts, or whether the facts presented to it are already imbued with legal assessments. We shall discover problems in the dedication of even the most sincere judge and lawyer to revealing the truth. And we shall return to questions about how the judge forms and justifies his or her decision.

On all such topics the legal realists have made valuable claims, and the overall position is a skeptical one. Indeed, the basic skepticism may be about the value of any general theory of law. So it could be somewhat unfair to offer criticisms of legal realism as a theory of law. Comments, therefore, will be reserved largely for the particular suggestions of legal realists as relevant topics surface in the following two chapters. Here, all that will be attempted is a rough sketch in the form of a double opposition: How is legal realism to be contrasted with legal positivism and then with natural law theories?

In terms of the question whether law and morality intersect, the realist has little sympathy for the sharp distinctions drawn by Austin and his followers. Realism holds that adjudication, no less than legislation, embodies the variable assumptions a society has about what is right, and that this draws the judge into a perpetual balancing of the divergent interests that lobby for a hearing in that society. Yet the realist is equally opposed to the claim of a natural law theorist that the morality involved is a matter of principles found by reasoning; the living law can be expressed in no more enduring form than a sociological report of what is here and now felt to be fair and appropriate.

38. Jerome Frank, *Law and the Modern Mind* (1930; reprint, Gloucester, Mass.: Peter Smith, 1970), 50.

The Living Law

> Legal realism, with its emphasis on the inevitability of choice and discretion in the life of the law, casts its vote—though for very different reasons—with the tradition of natural law, and against Austin and the positivists, on the old issue of the complete analytic separateness of the law that *is* and the law that *ought to be*.
>
> (Harry W. Jones)[39]

We have seen that Austin's command theory was criticized by Sir Henry Maine on the ground that it draws its model for all law from the final stage in the historical development of law. For Maine, the roots of law are in custom. He might also have been critical of Hart who, though allowing for stages in which there are only primary rules of custom, nevertheless bases his theory of law on the secondary rules that he substitutes for Austin's sovereign; hence societies that live from custom alone are pre-legal.

Emphasis on custom as the basic ingredient of all law may be seen not only as a protest against legal positivism, but as a defense of legal realism. At least, the lineage of this doctrine can be traced to include some important names in legal philosophy. Several will be mentioned in support of the realist's attack on the assumption that we find law by consulting the books.

Perhaps the most famous name is that of Friedrich Karl von Savigny (1779–1861). He devoted his life to scholarly writing on the law and is the founder of what is known as historical jurisprudence. He was a professor at the University of Berlin during the years that Hegel taught there (and also the few that Karl Marx spent as a student). The wave of nationalism that was inspired by the war of liberation against Napoleon led to a demand for a unified German civil code in the manner of the French one.[40] Savigny opposed haste in this direction on the grounds that law springs from deep sources in the spirit of a particular people and cannot easily be put into propositional form. He argued for, and contributed toward, a thorough study of German customary law. Law, he insisted, "takes actual life as its starting point" and proceeds "by internal silently operating powers" in the common consciousness of the people.

Of more influence in English-speaking countries was Eugen Ehrlich (1862–1922), who was briefly discussed in section 10 above. His main work was translated into English as *Fundamental Principles of the Sociology of Law* (Cambridge: Harvard Univ. Press, 1935). It is a lengthy advocacy of the claim that when we ask what the law is, we should look beyond the "propositional law" of statutes and cases in order to examine the living law of custom; there we find the legal relationships that actually guide our life and are poorly reflected in official writings. Ehrlich was certainly not suggesting that judges should ignore

---

39. Harry W. Jones, "Law and Morality in the Perspective of Legal Realism," *Columbia Law Review* 61 (1961): 799, 808.

40. The meaning of "codification," and the formation of the most important contemporary codes in Europe, will be discussed in section 32.

statutes and precedents. His argument was rather that, though the law in general is an expression of the way we actually live, there will always be some gap between the propositional and the living law, and it is the obligation of the judge in a particular case to adapt the former to the latter. This was no novel doctrine, but it deserved and received extensive scholarly treatment.

It is only in this century that sociology became recognized as a science and the title "sociological jurisprudence" gained respectability. The term is associated largely with Roscoe Pound (1870–1964). He abandoned an early career as a botanist in Nebraska (a rare fungus is named after him) to become a professor of law at Harvard for twenty-seven years, twenty of them as dean of the law school. His writings on law are voluminous (according to a friendly critic, Karl Llewellyn, these run without warning from a high level of scholarship to "bedtime stories for the tired bar"). Pound brought to his study of law the meticulous habits of a botanist and found his factual basis in a cataloging of social interests. A scientist observing society will see it as a jungle of wants, ranging from the individual ones on which we disagree to the social postulates that members of a culture assume without stating. There is nothing mysterious about the law. If it is concerned with what we do and want to do, then law is simply a means for holding society together. Just as an engineer adapts stresses and strains to make a bridge stand, so our legal institutions construct a working society out of disparate interests.

Pound introduced, or accepted, the term *social engineering* and viewed law "as a means to an end."[41] Law, for all its complexity, is a tool of social control. We have seen (section 6) the way in which de Tocqueville studied the legal profession as an instrument for the order achieved by the new American democracy. And we notice, as an obvious fact of life, how law is now classified in company with the social sciences, whereas the medieval universities set it alongside the more normative disciplines of philosophy and theology.

Largely under the influence of Pound, the study of law has extended from the trade schools of the profession to other departments of a university. For example, it is assumed by many American prelaw students today that political science offers the best preparation for entry to law schools. In that discipline the courts are viewed as political agencies, on a level with the House Rules Committee, the Bureau of the Budget, the Federal Trade Commission, and the Strategic Air Command. Judges, deprived of their normative mystique, stand side by side with members of Congress, bureaucrats, city councilmembers, and the many technicians who engage in the political process.[42]

A notable example of this move from the rules of formal law to the facts of social science has been the acceptance, by the courts, of what has become known as the "Brandeis Brief." Louis Brandeis came to prominence through his

---

41. *Law as a Means to an End* is the title given to the English translation of a work by Rudolf von Jhering (1818–92), a German legal philosopher whose writings influenced Pound.

42. See, for example, Martin Shapiro, "Political Jurisprudence," *Kentucky Law Journal* 52 (1964): 294.

defense, from 1907 to 1914, of the statutes of various states that prescribed maximum hours of labor and minimum wages. He did so, not by appealing to precedents, but by marshaling masses of economic and sociological data. He then served as a justice on the U.S. Supreme Court for twenty-three years and helped gain respect for the proposal that a thorough factual basis is appropriate in legal decisions. An illustration is the opinion of Chief Justice Warren in the case of Brown v. Board of Education (1954, 347 U.S. 483, 74 Sup.Ct. 686). This defended, by reference to psychological and educational studies, the conclusion that "segregation of white and colored children in public schools has a detrimental effect upon the colored children."

The above comments are offered in support of the claim that much of what the legal realists advocated has by now become common coin. However we formulate the delicate problem of "discretion" (see section 14), there is little complaint at the suggestion that judges do or would give different solutions in many cases, and that such latitude allows, rightly or wrongly, an infusion of changing values into the decisions that are made. It is agreed that judges take an active stance toward the rules they apply; dispute is rather about the room and manner that is allowed for judicial activism and about the place permitted in verdicts for considerations of public policy.[43]

The debate is an ancient one. It found expression, in 1853, in the English case of Egerton v. Brownlow (4 H.L.C. 1; 10 E.R. 359). The House of Lords held that a certain condition in a will was void "as against public policy." In the lower court decision that was thus overruled, Baron Parke strongly urged judicial restraint:

> It is the province of the judge to expound the law only; the written from the statutes: the unwritten or common law from the decisions of our predecessors and of our existing courts, from textwriters of acknowledged authority, and upon the principles to be clearly deduced from them by sound reason and just inference; not to speculate upon what is the best, in his opinion, for the advantage of the community.

The contrary opinion, later supported by the House of Lords, included a compilation of previous decisions, which may be summarized by a quotation from Lord Chief Justice Best:

> If there be any doubt what is the law, judges solve such doubts by considering what will be the good or bad effects of their decision.... That

---

43. For a discussion of this question in the rulings of the U.S. Supreme Court, see John Hart Ely, *Democracy and Distrust* (Cambridge: Harvard Univ. Press, 1980). He presents his own theory in opposition to what he calls the extremes of "interpretivism" (that judges should confine themselves to what is stated or clearly implicit in the Constitution) and of "noninterpretivism" (that they should enforce norms that cannot so be discovered in the document). For Ronald Dworkin's criticism of Ely and of traditional ways in which questions of constitutional interpretation have been framed as an opposition between judicial restraint and activism, see *Law's Empire*, 359-79.

doctrine cannot be law which injures the rights of individuals and will be productive of evil to the Church and to the community.

In this country, a leading advocate of judicial activism in the name of public policy has been Justice Oliver Wendell Holmes. In his work, *The Common Law*, he wrote:

> The very considerations which judges most rarely mention, and always with an apology, are the secret root from which the law draws all the juices of life. I mean, of course, considerations of what is expedient for the community concerned. Every important principle which is developed by litigation is in fact and at bottom the result of more or less definitely understood views of public policy; most generally, to be sure, under our practice and traditions, the unconscious result of instinctive preferences and inarticulate convictions, but none the less traceable to views of public policy in the last analysis (pp. 31–32).

This view guided his own verdicts on the bench: "The true grounds of decisions are considerations of policy and of social advantage."[44] He was largely supported by his successor on the U.S. Supreme Court, Benjamin Cardozo. We have already discussed some of Cardozo's decisions (section 10). For example, in *Hynes v. New York Central R. Co.*, he ruled against the "jurisprudence of conceptions" by appealing to "considerations of policy and of justice." In his work, *The Nature of the Judicial Process* (New Haven: Yale Univ. Press, 1921), he presented a balanced account of the various factors in judicial decision making:

> The directive force of a principle may be exerted along the line of logical progression; this I will call the rule of analogy or the method of philosophy; along the line of historical development; this I will call the method of evolution; along the line of the customs of the community; this I will call the method of tradition; along the lines of justice, morals and social welfare, the *mores* of the day; and this I will call the method of sociology (pp. 30–31).

> Law is, indeed, an historical growth, for it is an expression of customary morality which develops silently and unconsciously from one age to another. This is the great truth in Savigny's theory of its origin (pp. 104–5).

However, we find also a recurring protest in favor of judicial restraint, the most authoritative exponents in this country being Judge Learned Hand and Justice Felix Frankfurter, certainly no enemy of liberal policies. If we want a dramatic version of this opposition, it may come from Justice Blackmun, whose dissenting opinion failed by one vote to change the Supreme Court decision that

---

44. Dissenting opinion in Vegelahn v. Guntner (1896): 167 Mass. 92, 44 N.E. 1077.

capital punishment constitutes "cruel and unusual punishment" (Furman v. Georgia, 1972, 408 U.S. 238, 92 Sup.Ct. 2726). Blackmun wrote:

> Cases such as these provide for me an excruciating agony of the spirit. I yield to no one in the depth of my distaste, antipathy, and, indeed, abhorrence, for the death penalty, with all its aspects of physical distress and fear of mortal judgment exercised by finite minds. That distaste is buttressed by a belief that capital punishment serves no useful purpose that can be demonstrated. For me, it violates childhood's training and life's experiences, and is not compatible with the philosophical convictions I have been able to develop. It is antagonistic to any sense of "reverence for life." Were I a legislator, I would vote against the death penalty for the policy reasons argued by counsel for the respective petitioners and expressed and adopted in the several opinions filed by the Justices who vote to reverse these convictions. . . .
>
> I do not sit on these cases, however, as a legislator, responsive, at least in part, to the will of constituents. Our task here, as must so frequently be emphasized and re-emphasized, is to pass upon the constitutionality of legislation that has been enacted and that is challenged. This is the sole task for judges. We should not allow our personal preferences as to the wisdom of legislative and congressional action, or our distaste for such action, to guide our judicial decision in cases such as these. The temptations to cross that policy line are very great. In fact, as today's decision reveals, they are almost irresistible.

Such judicial decisions are, literally, matters of life and death. What do they have to do with academic questions about the philosophy of law? It would be a gross oversimplification to identify judicial activism with legal realism and to suggest that a legal positivist is committed to judicial restraint. John Austin recognized that judges do in fact make law; and, as a social reformer, he approved of this. However, we should notice two important differences between his approval and that of a legal realist or defender of sociological jurisprudence.

At a theoretical level, legal positivists from Austin to Hart have held that judicial activism is a *moral* question, *outside* the determination of valid law from statutes and precedents. The law, as it stands, derives from the will of the sovereign or from the rule of recognition; where the judge has discretion to act as delegated legislator, he or she operates in a moral realm that is conceptually distinct from the strictly legal one. The legal realist, however, sees no such fine distinctions. A judge's assessment of the law that *is* involves considerations of what it *ought to be.* And these considerations, far from being restricted (as Dworkin holds) to principles that ground rights, involve current social policies, national priorities, changing values, and many other imponderables outside the law books.

At a more practical level, the legal positivist limits such judicial legislation to the "penumbra" of law, the relatively small area where rules are open or underdetermined.[45] For much the greater part of a judge's work, "the law is the law," as adequately expressed in rules. To take a standard example (developed in section 33 below), a rule that bans motor vehicles from a park, or that sets penalties on the transport of stolen cars across state lines, will certainly apply to a Buick or a Cadillac; it is only in the rare case that deals with a moped or a go-kart in the park, or with a stolen airplane, that the judge is called to exercise his or her legislative powers through interpretation. Legal realists, however, seem radically to extend the area of the penumbra or even to eliminate its distinction from the core. Hart is plainly worried by the way in which they have been "preoccupied rather than occupied" with questions of the penumbra: "To assert mysteriously that there is some fused identity between law as it is and as it ought to be, is to suggest that all legal questions are fundamentally like those of the penumbra."[46] And this he holds to threaten "the hard core of settled meaning."

How important are such differences? A possible comment is that the realist and the positivist are in fact answering different questions. The former is concerned only to *describe* what judges actually do, whereas the latter is asking what legal *norms*, deriving from secondary rules, justify or criticize judicial decisions. However, description and justification may not, in this realm, always be easy to separate. The sociologist of law, unlike the meteorologist, is not limited to an observation of sheer behavior. I predict that it will snow tomorrow, and I take what comes as the resultant of impersonal forces. However, my prediction of what the judge will do cannot so readily be divorced from thoughts of how he or she, as a reasonable and just person, ought to decide. In agreeing to submit to the judge, my expectations are for more than a purely personal verdict and for more than the influence of special interests. Legal realists, intent as they are on maintaining the external viewpoint of an observer, have developed no adequate account of this distinction. However, it may not be irrelevant in any theory of adjudication that allows for the entry of morality. Some remarks must now be made on this difficult term.

The Mores of the Times

> It is the customary morality of right-minded men and women which [the judge] is to enforce by his decree. A jurisprudence that is not constantly brought into relation to objective or external standards incurs the risk of degenerating into ... a jurisprudence of mere sentiment or feeling.
> (Cardozo, *Judicial Process*, 106)

Cardozo's sympathy with the legal realists has been suggested, but he is too complex a person to be classified easily, and the above quotation points to an important hesitation. Some comments on it may help to distinguish this legal

---

45. Hart's views on the "core" and "penumbra" of law are presented in section 33.
46. See Hart, "Positivism and Separation", *Harvard Law Review* 71 (1958): 615; cf. 606–7.

philosophy from natural law theories, which also allow for moral considerations to affect our finding of the law.

The distinction has already been suggested by our consideration of the imaginary figures of Foster and Handy in the case of the speluncean explorers. These two justices were the only ones to vote in favor of the trapped explorers, and both judges held that no law had been violated. Morality was the deciding factor in both conclusions, and it was seen as an objective standard rather than as a matter of the judge's private sentiment or feeling. However, Foster claimed the objectivity of principles he could discover by a process of reasoning open to all, in ancient Greece or modern Newgarth. Handy based his claim to objectivity on the facts that a sociologist would discover empirically, at that place and in that time.

The appeal to principles known by reasoning presents many difficulties that we shall examine in the next section. We are more likely to be impressed by the measure of facts. Yet the thought that a judge should base his decision on a poll of current opinions raises questions of its own, reinforced by Cardozo's above restriction of his poll to those who are "right-minded." We may look briefly at a theoretical hesitation about the realist's reliance on customary morality and then examine some of the practical problems.

The theoretical hesitation is twofold. Firstly, we may wonder about our ability to extend the notion of law as "a prophecy of what the courts will do" to cover what we *should* do if we were ourselves *the judge*. As a client or lawyer I may perhaps limit my concern with the law to a prediction of how the judge will decide. But can a judge find the law by predicting his own behavior? The proposal is an odd one, and some shift in language-games may have taken place. I predict that my difficulties in composition are likely to land me with a B in this course, but do I predict my intention to get an A? Or do I simply intend to get an A, as the reasonable and right thing to do? Others may predict the verdict of a judge with a liberal record, but surely the judge comes to a decision for reasons he endorses rather than by simply examining his past behavior? The distinction between predicting and intending calls for a more subtle analysis. Yet we may ask whether the dedication of the legal realist to an external viewpoint does not miss a vital element in an account of judicial decision making.[47]

Secondly, our theoretical question is concerned with what philosophers have called the "naturalistic fallacy." You can get out of an argument only what you put into it. If the conclusion contains an *ought*, a fallacy has been committed

---

47. As the reader may predict, Hart makes much of his distinction between external and internal viewpoints when he criticizes the legal realists. See, for example, *The Concept of Law*, pp. 132–37.

In a community of people who understood the notions of a decision and the prediction of a decision, but not the notion of a rule, the idea of an *authoritative* decision would be lacking and with it the idea of a court.... Laws function in our lives not merely as habits or the basis for predicting the decisions of courts or the actions of other officials, but as accepted legal standards of behaviour.... The rule-skeptic is sometimes a disappointed absolutist (pp. 133, 134, 135).

where the premises involve no more than *is* statements. I may, for example, offer the factual premises that I use my watch for telling the time and that immersing my watch in water damages it. From this I can legitimately draw the conclusion that if I wear the watch while swimming I shall eventually find that it no longer keeps accurate time. I may even translate this conclusion by saying that I *ought* not to wear the watch while swimming. But this remains a purely hypothetical imperative, in Kant's meaning of the phrase.[48] No true obligation, binding me apart from my particular preferences, has been proved. I could, for instance, want to impress others with an elegant gold watch as I take my place at the pool, little caring whether I shall be late for the appointment that follows. At worst, I can be accused of foolishness.

The example is trite, but a logical problem for legal realism may be suggested. So far as this is a doctrine that proposes to tell us what the law "really" is rather than what anyone happens to think it to be, some standards are needed that are objective and external to the capricious preferences of a particular judge. His verdict expresses an *ought*, specifying how the mores of the time are to be followed and how the propositional law is to be adapted to the living law. However, where is the *ought* in the premises? These, it seems, are merely a complex statement of observable facts, of current values and particular situations.[49]

This rather academic objection can be put in terms with which we are more familiar. Though most of us may unthinkingly follow the practices we encounter, at times we wonder if this is right. Failure to report cash payments on income tax returns is increasingly common, but ought I to engage in this form of evasion (even apart from my fear that the IRS will catch me)? If statements of obligation are only accounts of what most people do, then we may wait happily for the fifty-first person out of a hundred to fail to send in his tax returns.

It is clear that neither the legal positivist nor the natural law theorist would support such a transition from the changing facts of behavior to the law of the land. Rules are valid if they derive from other standards, whether these be a human constitution or principles belonging to the nature of a rule-following society. More simply, perhaps, both positions see normative rules as guiding what we do rather than as following from it. An evident danger in the realist position is that the judge, the one who officially declares and applies the law, becomes a slave to current trends and not a source of guidance in finding what we should do in order to live legally.

---

48. See pp. 185–86 above for a brief account of the distinction between hypothetical and categorical imperatives.

49. There are ways out of this logical problem, but at a price that the realist may be unwilling to pay. An absolute *ought* would have to be introduced independently of the mores. For example, a writer such as Savigny, who was influenced by Kant's philosophy, could possibly allow for a "categorical imperative" in the legal process that obliges the judge to adapt his decisions to the evolving *Volksgeist*. The realist, however, is more likely to say simply that our own mores happen at present to favor judicial activism of this sort. At least, there is a certain consistency in seeing legal realism as itself no more than a product of changing times.

The main practical problems in connection with the realist position deal with our knowledge of the mores and our choice between conflicting goals. Though the engineer who is building a bridge can encounter some difficulties of this sort, he seldom has serious doubts that people want his bridge to stand up and that they would regard dangerously inferior materials as a false economy. A glance at any newspaper, however, tells us that the social engineer finds no such unity of purpose.

The term *mores* was coined by W. G. Sumner to describe those largely unconscious conventions of a society that are widely accepted and backed by severe sanctions. The prohibition of incest is an example. So understood, the notion has not much legal relevance. Where we all agree, we have no need to enact statutes or resolve disputes. However, the term has passed into a much looser employment to cover beliefs that are far from unconscious and are open to a significant measure of disagreement. When Cardozo writes that "the judge in shaping the rules of law must heed the *mores* of his day" (Cardozo, *Judicial Process*, 104), he is presumably talking of more problematic questions than incest. If the case before a judge involves euthanasia, or sex discrimination in employment, or the merger of large oil corporations, where does he find the mores in this extended form?

Judges who may heed the prescriptions of a realist in such matters tell us little of the investigations they conduct or the thinking on which they engage. However, there is one class of cases in which the question is made explicit. In the United States, an alien who applies for naturalization must satisfy the requirement that for the previous five years he has been "a person of good moral character." When a decision is appealed, the judicial opinions give us some idea of how difficult it is to identify common estimates of what the mores specify. One such case follows (Repouille v. United States, 1947, 165 F.2d 152).

In 1944, Louis Repouille applied for citizenship. He presented an excellent record, but with one notable blemish. He had been a dutiful parent to four of his children, and, for many heroic years, to the fifth, who was sadly handicapped. At birth the child had suffered a brain injury that left him mentally disabled, blind, mute, and malformed in all limbs, so that he was confined to a crib. The burden on the rest of the family became intense. When the crippled boy was thirteen, Repouille—after agonies of conscience—put him to death with chloroform. The indictment was for manslaughter in the first degree. The jury showed their assessment of the mores by reducing the charge to the second degree (indeliberate) and by recommending the utmost clemency. The sentence was suspended by the judge.

A United States district court ordered the petition for naturalization to be granted. The district attorney, on behalf of the Immigration and Naturalization Service, appealed the decision. The circuit court of appeals reversed the order by a vote of 2–1 and thus turned down Repouille's current request for citizenship. It is of interest that one of the two judges who voted against him was Learned Hand, and the sole supporter was Jerome Frank.

Judge Hand adverted to recent decisions of the courts that had interpreted the phrase "good moral character" as meaning that "the moral feelings, now prevalent generally in this country, would not be outraged." He admitted that the jury and judge in the criminal trial had made their views quite plain. However, "in the absence of some national inquisition, like a Gallup poll, the test is indeed difficult to apply." Lacking any evidence that moral feelings on the topic of private euthanasia had changed, he was obliged to turn down the petition but recommended a new one, now that the act of manslaughter was no longer within the required five-year period.

The opinion of Jerome Frank (*Repouille v. United States*) comes from a legal realist whose dependence on some estimate of the mores goes far beyond naturalization cases:

> The district judge found that Repouille was a person of "good moral character." ... My colleagues, although their sources of information concerning the pertinent mores are not shown to be superior to those of the district judge, reject his finding.... The precedents in this circuit constrain us to be guided by contemporary public opinion about which, cloistered as judges are, we have but vague notions. (One recalls Gibbon's remark that usually a person who talks of "the opinion of the world at large" is really referring to "the few people with whom I happened to converse.") ... But the courts are not utterly helpless; such judicial impotence has its limits. Especially when an issue importantly affecting a man's life is involved, it seems to me that we need not, and ought not, resort to our mere unchecked surmises, remaining wholly (to quote my colleagues' words) "without means of verifying our conclusions." ...
>
> I think, therefore, that in any case such as this, where we lack the means of determining present-day public reactions, we should remand to the district judge with these directions: The judge should give the petitioner and the government the opportunity to bring to the judge's attention reliable information on the subject, which he may supplement in appropriate ways. All the data so obtained should be put on record. On the basis thereof, the judge should reconsider his decision and arrive at a conclusion. Then, if there is another appeal, we can avoid sheer guessing, which alone is now available to us, and can reach something like an informed judgment. Of course, we cannot thus expect to attain certainty, for certainty on such a subject as public opinion is unattainable.

In naturalization disputes, the search for public opinion refers to the facts of the case (did he have a good moral character?). But for a legal realist, the discovery of what people hold belongs to questions of law (e.g., is euthanasia illegal?). What Judge Frank suggested in one case would extend, in some form, to all. There is no need to elaborate the practical problems in getting reliable information. How wide, for example, is the relevant community in which one is to seek data? And is the sample to be limited by some prior standard of what the inquirer regards as right-minded people?

One legal realist who has shown particular awareness of the moral questions in this position is Prof. H. W. Jones of Columbia (see the article cited in footnote 39). He draws an interesting comparison with the existentialist theme that each situation is unique and decisions must be made alone, without the support of guiding principles. Sartre's example is well known, of the student who had to decide between leaving home to join the Free French forces and staying to care for his mother. Neither Christian doctrine nor Kantian ethics could tell him what to do; and if he sought advice, he would already have made his decision by the choice of an adviser. Similarly, it is said, the judge with moral sensitivity stands alone. He cannot, like a scientist, limit his verdict to the evidence at hand; he must decide each case before him, going always beyond what the formal rules prescribe. His discovery and application of the law is a highly personal, and acutely moral, enterprise.

The external observer may well report that judicial decisions are influenced by *morality*, if by this term he means only the mores of the times. Judges are not forbidden to read newspapers or watch the television. However, the question (from an internal viewpoint) whether I should, in judging, follow or oppose current values, is one on which I receive no guidance from the legal realist. He distances himself, on this vital point, from contemporary legal positivists and natural lawyers. For all their disagreement, these hold that the judge should develop some moral philosophy and should rationally submit to its principles, whether acting as a delegated legislator or interpreting moral norms embedded in the law that already exists. However, the realist seems to deprive the judge of any recourse to principled discretion.

Perhaps the lingering question is whether legal realism does, after all, present the judge with a moral situation. Sartre celebrates the lonely responsibility of those who find no guidelines in philosophy or religion or any other normative source. His critics wonder if, where anything goes, the drama is not itself removed. If there are no universals, why the concern about particulars? To repeat Cardozo's remark, a jurisprudence that rejects all objective moral standards, and hence removes all norms for deciding which men and women are "right-minded," will degenerate into mere sentiment or feeling. A purely historical comment may be that the development of the common law, while allowing for the tragic loneliness of a judge who is forced beyond the comfort of secure rules, has not exempted him from all requirements to base his decision on moral principles that he assesses and ratifies.

Any admission that the moral sensitivity of a judge involves his acceptance of underlying principles, as a guideline for his decisions, raises again the question where such principles are to be found. The remaining two sections of this chapter will explore some legal theories that look, in the nature of man or of his legal enterprise, for principles that cut across the institutional history of particular legal systems.

FURTHER READING

Cardozo, Benjamin N. *The Nature of the Judicial Process.* New Haven, Conn.: Yale Univ. Press, 1921.

Christie, George C. *Jurisprudence: Text and Readings on the Philosophy of Law.* St. Paul: West, 1973, 640–787.

Frank, Jerome. *Courts on Trial.* Princeton, N.J.: Princeton Univ. Press, 1949.

———. *Law and the Modern Mind.* 1930. Reprint. Gloucester, Mass.: Peter Smith, 1970.

Friedman, Lawrence M., and Stewart Macaulay, eds. *Law and the Behavioral Sciences.* 2d ed. Indianapolis: Bobbs-Merrill, 1977.

Garlan, Edwin N. *Legal Realism and Justice.* 1941. Reprint. Littleton, Colo.: F. B. Rothman & Co., 1981.

Golding, Martin P., ed. *The Nature of Law.* New York: Random House, 1966, 175–274.

Gray, John Chipman. *The Nature and Sources of the Law.* 2d ed. 1921. Reprint. Buffalo, N.Y.: W. S. Hein & Co., 1983.

Llewellyn, Karl N. *The Bramble Bush.* Dobbs Ferry, N.Y.: Oceana Publications, 1951.

Pohlman, H. L. *Justice Oliver Wendell Holmes and Utilitarian Justice.* Cambridge: Harvard Univ. Press, 1984.

Pound, Roscoe. *An Introduction to the Philosophy of Law.* 2d ed. New Haven: Yale Univ. Press, 1954.

QUESTIONS FOR DISCUSSION

1. Do the claims of legal realism receive support from studies of primitive law? Reread, for example, Paul Bohannan's account of dispute settlement among the Tiv (section 13). Notice how the "pedigree" of law from a sovereign or from a master rule, seemingly so obvious to the Western mind and to the legal positivist, is lacking. Notice further the clear dependence of law on public opinion and the rejection of the idea that there should be a final (or one correct) decision. Has Western theorizing about law tended, in such respects, to hide the realities that are still operative (what Holmes called the "juices" of legal life)?

2. Enrlich took the family as a prime example of living law and of the inadequacy of any propositional law that is formulated. In section 10, reference was made to the amusing appearance of court-backed reconciliation agreements. Think of other instances where "the spirit of a family" escapes expression in the form of rules. Is Savigny mistaken in applying such a model to the state when he speaks of "the spirit of the people" as the basis of law?

3. A textbook of legal studies that adopts the theories of Roscoe Pound is *Introduction to Law: A Functional Approach* (H. R. Hartzler & H. T. Allan, Glenview, Ill: Scott, Foresman, & Co., 1969). The opening chapter is called "Introduction to Social Engineering" and encourages the student to evaluate laws as instruments for achieving social goals. What merits and problems do you see in this approach? Is it not the task of a legislator to bring about social order through the statutes he or she enacts? How would Hart comment on this view of law? How do you find the social goals whose achievement you are to engineer? In the event of conflict, should the current will of the majority always decide?

4. Justice Blackmun's dissenting opinion in *Furman* lists as grounds for his opposition to capital punishment (a) his deepest personal convictions, (b) the failure of such a penalty to achieve any useful social purpose, and (c) philosophical arguments based on the principle of the sanctity of life. Yet he casts his vote for maintaining capital punishment on the sole footing of a judge's obligation of fidelity to the law. Would you agree with the legal realist who sees this as a dramatic consequence of a mistaken answer to the question what law is? Or is Blackmun correct to accuse his brethren of following public opinion and "crossing the policy line"? Should the fate of those on death row be based on the pendulum of public opinion?

5.   Hart accuses the legal realists of ignoring "the hard core of settled meaning" in laws and of rendering all questions "penumbral." He is suggesting that the judge needs to make law only in rare cases, but that the realist would assign him the task of consulting popular opinion in all cases in order to find the law. How important do you think this difference would be in practice? Do we not, in some ways, follow the realist position when we pass responsibility for the verdict to twelve ordinary people on a jury?

6.   Are you obliged to do whatever a parent or teacher or commanding officer tells you to do? Are you obliged to submit to the pressures of your peergroup? Why, then, should a judge be obliged to adapt the law to changes in public opinion?

7.   The case of *Riggs v. Palmer* (section 4) presented a clash between a natural law theorist (Earl) and a legal positivist (Gray). Suppose one of the members of the court had been a legal realist. Would he have decided for or against Elmer Palmer? Write a brief opinion along these lines.

8.   Presidential candidates in this country employ professional pollsters to report, with fair accuracy, the state of public opinion on various issues. Do you think it is right that political candidates and office-holders should follow the results of these polls and vary their pronouncements with each shift that is detected in opinion? Could some such polling service be put at the disposal of judges? Would it be right to do so?

9.   Even if you oppose the suggestion above, would you not agree that judicial decisions have, with some delay, always followed large-scale movements in the public's attitude? Or are there areas where the law has led rather than followed?

10.   Our political tradition has been toward granting each person one vote. However, in other realms, do we not weigh opinions according to the quality of their source (consider how you gather advice)? Do you agree with Cardozo that the judge should base his assessment of the mores on the views of "right-minded" people? What would this mean in practice?

11.   Take any case so far discussed, or one that you otherwise know, and apply to it the various legal philosophies presented up to this point. For instance, how could Judge Wright have written his opinion in the Georgetown University Hospital case (section 6) if he had been a disciple of Jerome Frank? Of Hart? Of Dworkin?

21. NATURAL LAW: AQUINAS

Whereas recognition of the inherent dignity and of the equal and inalienable rights of all members of the human family is the foundation of freedom, justice, and peace in the world...

Now therefore the General Assembly proclaims this Universal Declaration of Human Rights as a common standard of achievement for all peoples and nations....

    Article 1: All human beings are born free and equal in dignity and rights. They are endowed with reason and conscience and should act towards one another in a spirit of brotherhood....

    Article 6: Everyone has the right to recognition everywhere as a person before the law....

(Adopted by the General Assembly of the United Nations, December 10, 1948)

One may well ask: "How can you advocate breaking some laws and obeying others?" The answer lies in the fact that there are two types of laws: just and unjust. I would be the first to advocate obeying just laws. One has not only a legal but a moral responsibility to obey just laws. Conversely, one has a moral responsibility to disobey unjust laws. I would agree with St. Augustine that "an unjust law is no law at all."

Now, what is the difference between the two? How does one determine whether a law is just or unjust? A just law is a man-made code that squares with the moral law or the law of God. An unjust law is a code that is out of harmony with the moral law. To put it in the terms of St. Thomas Aquinas: An unjust law is a human law that is not rooted in eternal law and natural law.
(Martin Luther King, Jr., "Letter from Birmingham Jail,"
April 16, 1963)

Natural law theories trace their lineage to ancient Greece, and their influence on the shape of Western law has been critical. The development of the common law and civil law traditions differed from that of Oriental legal systems notably through the assurance that reasoning can disclose some universal principles, and that these limit government action by defining a legal order.[50] The revolutions and constitutions of modern European and American nations owed much to the language of natural rights and of natural limits to political power.[51] The Declaration of Human Rights of the United Nations (quoted above), though plainly an achievement of compromises in committee rather than of "universal" convictions, employs phrases that suggest a greater authority than that of the current mores or the enactments of a legislature. And the quotation from Martin Luther King, Jr., indicating as it does a philosophical basis for a life of heroic protest, wins popular respect in an age that senses the need both to strengthen the law of the land and to define its limits.

Nevertheless, in contemporary academic discussions, it is talk of natural law that provokes the most suspicion. The term arouses hostility and embarrassment. Those who make statements that might seem to derive from such a theory are often quick to disclaim it.[52] The title "natural law" conjures up a world of absolutes, of metaphysical arguments that ignore history and disregard the variety of human situations; above all, there is misgiving about theological

---

50. See R. M. Unger, *Law in Modern Society* (New York: Free Press, 1976), 76–86, 99–101.

The religious experiences of China in the transformation period and of Europe in the Renaissance diverged radically.... For in Europe science and political philosophy alike started off from the idea of universal principles; government had to contend with the conception of God-given natural laws and with powerful churches; and religious belief emphasized the capacity of individuals to transcend their social circumstances just as their Creator transcends his creation (p. 101).

51. See H. Maine, "The Modern History of the Law of Nature," chapter 4 in *Ancient Law*, (1861; reprint, Gloucester, Mass.: Peter Smith, 1970).

52. For example, in Rochin v. California (1952, 342 U.S. 165, 725 Sup. Ct. 205), Justice Frankfurter speaks of personal immunities that are "fundamental" and "implicit in the concept of ordered liberty," of considerations that are "fused in the whole nature of our judicial process" and "deeply rooted in reason." But he hastens to add that "due process of law thus conceived is not to be derided as resort to a revival of natural law."

questions and ecclesiastical interests that may lurk in the background. Clearly, a story of more than two thousand years has put a complex of theories under one label and has allowed for an assortment of fellow passengers. These few pages cannot pretend to sort out the confusion. They will simply indicate some Greek origins and comment on the medieval version developed by Saint Thomas Aquinas, which has some claim to be a standard for the tradition. The following section will turn to Lon Fuller's more skeletal account as one example of recent progeny; there, the taint of clerical influence has been removed and respectful, though critical, response has been drawn from the legal positivists that he saw as his target.

The Ambiguity of Nature

> MR. ARMSTRONG (for the defense): The crew either were in their ordinary and original state of subordination to their officers, or they were in a state of nature. If in the former state, they are excusable in law for having obeyed the order of the mate.... But if the whole company was reduced to a state of nature, then the sailors were bound to no duty.... All persons on board the vessel became equal. All became their own lawgivers; for official distinctions cease to prevail when men are reduced to the equality of nature. Every man on board had a right to make law with his own hand, and the law which did prevail on that awful night having been the law of necessity, and the law of nature too, it is the law which will be upheld by this court, to the liberation of this prisoner.
>
> THE COURT: It is true that we do find in the text writers, and sometimes in judicial opinions, the phrases "the law of nature," "the principles of natural right," and other expressions of like signification; but, as applied to civilized men, nothing more can be meant by those expressions than that there are certain great and fundamental principles of justice which, in the constitution of nature, lie at the foundation and make part of all civil law, independently of express adoption or enactment.
>
> (U.S. v. Holmes, 1842, 1 Wallace's Circuit Reports 1, 26 Federal Cases 360, No. 15, 383)

What follows is rather abstract and will try the patience of many readers. However, even those with their feet most firmly on the ground do often use the word *nature* in some form (or, notably in this land, the term *absolutely*). Such usage may often carry little more than the emphasis of a clenched fist, but the venture into metaphysics needs to be examined. Is it ever valid? The suggestion that will be proposed, in various ways, is that talk of nature may usually deserve the scorn it receives, but sometimes not. The question is one of viewpoint, whether we speak as observer or as agent. Salvage operations require a conversion from the former to the latter. How relevant this is to talk of law as "natural," rather than merely "positive," remains to be seen; but let us at least begin with the above case, where the defendant's fate, and perhaps his life, depended on such subtleties.

Holmes was a far from ignoble seaman who, when the grossly overladen longboat was sinking, responded to an ambiguous order from the first mate by throwing several passengers into the sea, thus saving the life of the remainder and facing trial for unlawful homicide in a federal court in Pennsylvania. This provoked a courtroom dispute about the meaning of the term nature and about our duties when the limitations of positive law leave us in "a state of nature."

His defense attorney seems to have used such terms in the manner of a scientist. Nature is amoral and outside all normative laws: we adopt the external viewpoint of an observer and give a purely descriptive account of how particles or people behave. In the life-and-death situation of "that awful night," all human laws ceased to apply. The "law of nature" took over. Nature, so viewed, is what we find in the laboratory or in the jungle. Holmes acted appropriately, according to the descriptive laws of survival that were at that very moment being formulated by Charles Darwin.[53]

Unfortunately for Holmes, the judge was less contemporary and relied on an older tradition, according to which "nature" is normative. When the clear rules of positive law fail, as perhaps in the sinking longboat, we are not removed from the reach of law and of human judges but are returned to certain basic norms that are presupposed by any ruling of legislator or judge. The light sentence passed on Holmes revealed the judge's sympathy, but the verdict showed his conclusion that natural law is the basis for all positive law and can decide questions of its extent.[54]

We are probably mistaken if we think that we first understood the term nature in the sense of Darwin and of Mr. Armstrong. The world of Galileo involves a sophisticated human interpretation. Both anthropology and child psychology suggest that our idea of nature is animistic and purposive long

53. Mr. Armstrong had presumably never heard of Darwin and appears to have drawn his notion of a "state of nature" from writers such as Thomas Hobbes. It is fair, however, to equate this with a scientific and descriptive report of human behavior. Hobbes wanted to set his account in the tradition of Galileo, thus liberating morals and politics from metaphysics and theology. Man is to be explained in terms of instinctive drives, the chief of which is the desire for self-preservation. The state of nature is thus that of the jungle. However, man has the intelligence to realize that self-preservation can be achieved most efficiently if he enters into a social contract where individuals submit to the power of a sovereign.

54. Suppose the judge had omitted all reference to nature and had simply remarked that where positive laws fail to apply, people are still bound by moral laws? A traditional legal positivist would have made at least two comments: (1) It is not the office of a judge to convict for breaking moral laws, and (2) The moral laws that applied to Holmes in the longboat extend to legislators and may obligate them to revise the positive laws so that these close such a gap in the law and cover any future immoral acts of this sort. In reply to these comments, the judge would thus have to (1) defend some view of the intersection of legality and morality and (2) explain how his appeal to natural law (and not merely to moral laws) transforms the *ought* questions of legislators into the *is* questions of a judge. The legal realist claims point 1 without the metaphysics of point 2. Natural law theories have tried to ground point 1 in point 2. Hence our basic problem in this section is whether any view of "human nature" can be defended that supplies a common source for morality and legality, and that thus allows for the validity of legal rules to depend on some moral assessment as well as on the pedigree in a legal system. We may find it less easy than a mid-nineteenth century judge to believe that nature (perhaps as the handiwork of God) supplies all human beings with a fixed set of essences or purposes that regulate the private thoughts of an individual and the public enactments of a legislator or a judge.

before it becomes impersonal and factual. When Aristotle wrote that man is by nature social and political, he was not merely recording sociological observations and awaiting exceptions that would refine a descriptive law. He was claiming that all we do involves some submission to norms—to be human is to accept an ordering of our life according to rules.

Such questions about the meaning of nature may focus our attention once again on Hart's distinction between an external and an internal viewpoint for knowing rules. Bees are "social" in the sense that they show to an observer a more orderly pattern of group behavior than does the solitary wasp. But man reveals more than order-for-an-observer. He accepts rules of order and obliges himself to follow them, though he knows he can violate such ideals. We exhort someone to "be a man"; we do not tell an errant insect to "be a bee."

With these introductory remarks in mind, we may return to the way that Greek philosophers spoke of nature. The setting, we have seen, was a running controversy between Plato and the Sophists. The latter plainly adopted the viewpoint of an observer: a look around the world shows the wide variety of moral opinions and suggests that laws depend simply on who happens to have the power to impose them. From that point of view, Plato could only agree: everything we observe through our senses is relative. His reply was based on a conversion to an internal point of view that revealed nature as the absolute norms involved in our very observing and arguing.

This is a sweeping claim but, for our limited purposes, we may merely refer to the way in which Plato's method comes across to the reader who encounters the dialogues. Socrates does not begin his argument by seeking the authority of particular facts or by advocating principles he regards as self-evident. Conclusions appear, as the inquiry proceeds, from what is found to have been presupposed in the very give-and-take of the discussion. As Socrates puts it in one dialogue, "You take me for a sort of bag full of arguments.... You don't see what is happening. The arguments never come out of me; they always come from the person I am talking with" (*Theaetetus* 161). The debate, at this particular point, happens to be about Protagoras's claim that "man is the measure of all things," in the sense that whatever a person thinks to be true is true for him, and whatever any state enacts as law is lawful for it. "Protagoras, admitting as he does that everybody's opinion is true, must acknowledge the truth of his opponents' belief about his own belief, where they think he is wrong" (ibid., 171a). In other words, if Protagoras will but turn from an external to an internal point of view, he must recognize that, in claiming his own theory to be true, he is destroying that very theory, according to which even those theories that contradict his own are true. This may sound like "logic-chopping." But it is a tragic reference to our fate (or nature) as human beings. Man finds himself, in all he says, to be inescapably a truth-affirming being who cannot reduce truth to opinion without destruction of what he is saying. Sad but true, and unavoidably true.

This is likely to be confusing, so a slightly different approach may help. Do not forget the basic fact that Plato is talking to others. So are you, even in the privacy of your "own" thoughts. Now suppose that Plato is confronted, in discussion, with a legal positivist or a legal realist; he thus faces one who grounds his account of law on a rule of recognition or on the mores of the times. Such theories, Plato would admit, are highly plausible from an external point of view. Different states have different constitutions, and anyone who has traveled (as Plato had) will recognize the wide variety of customs. No nature, in the form of a metaphysical absolute, is revealed to the observer. However, let us turn from *what* the opponent says to his very *saying*. He bases his claim on evidence. That is, he freely removes himself from the realm of capricious assertions and offers his adversary the meeting-place of some "objective" ground. He reasonably demands a like return. Plato should accept a like submission to norms that remove what he says from the status of arbitrary or (to use the terms of the positivist) "unverifiable" statements.

Notice the moral tenor of what is happening. Discussion, the mutual search for a truth beyond our particular opinions, is taking place. It does so through forbearance, through the recognition of others as people entitled to proof rather than mere dogmatism. The glory of positivism, whatever it says, is a moral one. There is a "self-legislation" of rules to form a community of inquirers. Behind every appeal to facts lies a norm that specifies our way of revealing and submitting to truth. And this norm is a moral obligation to treat others as persons in a society of rules, rather than to act as our prejudices dictate and as our strength allows. It may not be fanciful to see in this a version of the "fundamental right to equal concern and respect" that Dworkin finds at the basis of all we do as moral persons (see pp. 199–200 above).

Socrates (speaking for Plato) asked simply that the Sophists look to their own presuppositions as honest inquirers. John Austin may have tried to derive legal obligation from the sheer fact of a sovereign's strength, and Hart from the fact that legal officials accept some rule of recognition. But submission to such facts already involves an *ought*, as anyone does who appeals to criteria of truth and engages in discussion with others about particular truths. The nature of man as a questioner in a community of inquirers is not shown by any sociological surveys (which suggest that most of us reveal some disdain for truth). We find the inescapable structures of our nature by trying to reject them and by recognizing the self-contradiction (or self-destruction) disclosed in our very trying or affirming or questioning.

Talk of "natural law" is less commonly associated with Plato than with his disciple, Aristotle. He did not, after some early efforts, write in dialogues; but he had a clear sense for the form of an argument and for the basis that all statements have in dialogue. He recognized, at least, that the Sophists or skeptics could be refuted by no "positive proof," drawn from sheer facts or from evident principles; all of these they would question. Instead, he said, we must adduce "negative proof." We must help the skeptics to turn from their viewpoint as observers to recognize what is involved in our very agency of talking or denying or questioning. We must bring to light the self-contradiction whenever "they make some statement . . . which has meaning both for themselves and for others." (Aristotle *Metaphysics* 1006a; see the whole of book 4, chapter 4.)

Aristotle is a subtle and ambiguous philosopher. He came to philosophy from biology, and this science still exhibits an interesting confusion between the viewpoint of observer and that of agent. The biologist sees living beings as an observer does, and he aspires to the "objectivity" of physics. Yet talk of a "struggle for survival" is teleological and retains something of the viewpoint of the organism itself, trying to achieve its goals. Aristotle is in theory committed to the internal point of view. He makes clear that "the primary and proper meaning of nature is the essence of things which have in themselves, as 'selves,' a principle of development." (Aristotle *Metaphysics* 1015a 13; see also *Physics*, book 2, chapter 1) Though many of his examples would, at least for us, violate this definition, he could not properly speak of the nature of an ashtray or of a car. These are what I choose to make of them. They are not "things-in-themselves." The only material being who certainly has a nature (a "self" to be "in") is man. Animals, and perhaps plants, may fit the definition to a lesser extent, but analogously to what we experience from within.

What Aristotle does offer us is a hierarchical view of reality, based on the ability of anything to be itself. Inorganic things and artifacts are at the lowest level: what they are depends on purposes we assign to them (e.g., a mountain, a hammer). Plants may begin to *be* (in themselves and not just for us), and animals progressively acquire the reality of being-in-and-for-themselves. But it is at the human level that the internal point of view becomes most plausible and Aristotle's talk of nature most relevant. A dissipated person is largely at the mercy of whatever pressures are at work on him from outside. A strong person charts his own course through the contingencies of life. And what lies at the culmination of the hierarchy? Aristotle, who was possibly an atheist in orthodox religious terms, speaks of the ideal of all development as a "self-thinking thought," a self that knows fully what it is and what it intends, without the "self-opposition" that characterizes our own weak efforts "to be."

One conclusion is pertinent to our limited questions. It is well known that Aristotle defined man as a rational being. We tend, erroneously, to interpret him as saying that reason is a property we *have*, much as animals have locomotion and mountains have mass. The viewpoint is that of the observer: people score higher on problem-solving tests than do apes. Aristotle was talking, however, about what we *are*, from an internal point of view. We are beings who know what we are and who set our goals, evaluate our life, and make our way on a course for which we assume responsibility. Here also there is a hierarchy of achievement. We cannot escape from the obligations of *being* reasonable, but we are rational to a greater or lesser extent. Even if I try to act irrationally, I do so for a reason. A life under the influence of drugs, or under the consuming drive for financial success at any cost, is responsibly chosen. I may be less of a "self" as a result, but I have not thereby escaped from the norms of "being reasonable." No animal confronts such demands. Contentedly chewing the cud, it is upset by no failure to "be what it really is." Yet we are condemned, by our "rational nature," to an eternal disquiet that always proposes stages of self-presence beyond any we have so far achieved under the moral imperative of rationality.[55]

The Reason behind Law

> Everything in nature works according to laws. Only a rational being has the capacity of acting according to the conception of laws, i.e., according to principles.
> (Immanuel Kant, *Foundations of the Metaphysics of Morals* [Indianapolis: Bobbs-Merrill, 1959], 29)

The influence of the medieval philosopher-theologians on the formation of Western law was considerable. The law faculties of the universities constructed a system of law from the codes and other records of Roman law, which was no longer in effect; and it should not be forgotten that Roman law was pagan, hence abhorrent to a Christian culture. Some "baptism" of this law was required, and it was radicals such as Saint Thomas Aquinas (1244–74) who dared to perform this. They did so through the accident that the works of Aristotle had recently been rediscovered, after a loss in the West of more than a thousand years. Christian philosophers applied the natural law of a pagan philosopher to the detailed prescriptions of a pagan positive law, in order to form the outlines of our modern law.[56]

Aquinas's so-called "treatise on law" occupies only some fifty pages out of more than four thousand in editions of his *Summa Theologica*, a compendium of the lectures he delivered at the University of Paris. It is well to stress that the ideal of medieval scholarship was a *summa*, an encyclopedia of all knowledge arranged in rational sequence rather than alphabetically, as in our own empirical times. Law was but a small part of a comprehensive inquiry into the reasons that cover all we can know. Our modern attitude, of course, is that this claim is preposterous. Knowledge is too diverse for any one mind, or any one set of principles, to embrace it all. Aquinas was guilty of extreme rationalism. Never-

---

55. Sartre, though no advocate of Aristotelian metaphysics, aptly defines man as a being who "is what he is not and is not what he is" (*Being and Nothingness*, 1957, 70). Critics who have called this slogan an expression of nonsense are evidently adopting an external point of view toward "being."

56. "The work of the universities can really only be understood by reference to a concept of natural law. The law faculties tried to articulate, with the help of Roman law, rules which best expressed a sense of justice and a well ordered society, the existence of which was required by the very nature of things" (René David, *Major Legal Systems in the World Today* [1978], 42). One might add that "the very nature of things" (or better, the very nature of man in society) had become more clearly universal in the transition that "nature" made from ancient Athens to medieval Paris. Aristotle's account of law was largely restricted to the obligations a citizen had toward his *polis*. But for Aquinas, there could be only one source of law, as there is but one God, creator of man and society and of all that is necessarily involved.

theless, the medieval cathedrals were also outrageous structures, yet we may have something to learn from them.

For us, reason tends to be a technique that we exercise upon facts. Astronomers, sociologists, and engineers accept facts as given, and then construct hypotheses that they submit to the control of other observations. However, for the medieval, reason was a life rather than an instrument. We *are* reasonable, to a greater or lesser extent, as we incorporate the diversity of experience into our thinking. In this way, animals are more reasonable than plants, and a highly integrated person is more reasonable than one who suffers, rather than controls, his experience. The nature of a rational being is, in this sense, a matter of degree. The following quotation from Aquinas suggests the manner in which he assimilated Aristotle's rationalism.

> All things exist by expressing themselves, and the higher they are the more intimate is their self-expression. In the inanimate realm this takes the lowest form, that of the action of one body on another [calling for the external viewpoint of science].... At the next level, the plant expresses its inner life in a seed, but this is altogether separated from it.... The level of sensation in animals is higher, involving the interiority of imagination and memory, but lacking self-awareness.... The highest form of life is that of intellect, which reflects on its own operations. Here, however, many different grades are revealed. Our own understanding achieves a self-knowledge that is limited by some degree of self-opposition because of our materiality and reliance on sensation.... Hence the full perfection of rational life belongs only to God, who knows what He is and is what He knows.[57]

An example is needed of what this means in everyday terms, and it may be drawn from the topic of freedom. For an empiricist, such as Hume or Bentham, freedom is a matter of making choices and is opposed by necessity in all its forms. As necessity grows, so freedom declines. But Aquinas would see no such inverse proportion. God is supremely free and supremely necessary. The saints who enjoy the beatific vision are more free than we are, yet they lack choice and cannot sin. In this life our freedom of self-possession grows as does our recognition of what we are, and consequently as our choice to follow different paths decreases. Once I truly understand the reasons for a law, the possibility of breaking it becomes irrelevant, but I am thereby more free rather than less. It is odd that we glory in our situation at the crossroads, not knowing which way to follow. Those who truly understand their goal march straight toward it, and freely so, without much thought for the byways on either side.[58]

---

57. Saint Thomas Aquinas, *Summa Contra Gentiles*, book 2, chapter 98.

58. Spinoza more clearly makes this distinction between freedom of choice ("freedom of the will") and freedom of self-determination (acting "by the necessity of one's own nature, as determined by oneself alone"). It may be of interest to refer also to Dworkin's distinction between "liberty as license" and "liberty as independence, the status of a person as independent and equal rather than subservient": see Dworkin, *Taking Rights Seriously*, 262.

From this we may anticipate that Aquinas, in his account of law, will stand at the opposite extreme to Austin. Austin was a voluntarist who adopted an external viewpoint toward the superior power of a sovereign and the sanctions with which commands are enforced. Aquinas was an intellectualist who saw moral and legal rules as an expression of the ideas by which we become what we truly are.

One result is that, though talk of the obligation (rather than the force) of law is a casual afterthought for Austin, it is central for Aquinas. The question dominating his theory of law is that of the roots of obligation. Granted that the king (or the church, or even God) has the power to impose his will, why *ought* I to offer my obedience? And, in terms of this basic question, what limits are there to the imposition of rules by a superior on an inferior?

Aquinas is often accused of committing the naturalistic fallacy, of passing from *is* to *ought*. As we shall see in a moment, a reading that allows for a maximal account of the content of natural law may invite such criticism. But his proposal was certainly to avoid this modern charge by adopting an internal point of view and investigating those realms where *is* and *ought* have not yet been separated. What I *am* as a rational being involves the *obligation* of overcoming the irrationality at the heart of my nature, and law is a guide rather than a limit.

This may serve as a prelude to a brief account of how Aquinas interprets the various types of law. The source is contained in questions 90–97 of the "First Division of the Second Part" of his *Summa Theologica*.[59] Question 90 is introductory and closes with a provisional definition of law as "an ordinance of reason for the common good, made by him who has care of the community, and promulgated" (pp. 10–11). All would agree that some promulgation belongs to the essence of law, but the critical question is left open whether this needs formal statement in words or comprises also the access we have by use of our reason. The reference to one who "has care of a community" seems to correspond with Austin's demand for a "determinate source" or "sovereign." However, the key note that divides the two theories is the requirement of Aquinas that law should be rational. Austin's legislator says Do this or else. Aquinas's legislator, human or divine, says Do this for these good reasons and with the obligation they supply to a rational being who accepts them through his understanding.

Question 91 distinguishes four types of law. The fourth (divine law) pertains to man's supernatural end. Aquinas discusses it no further at this point, and we can safely leave it to the theologians. Our concern is only with the tripartite distinction into eternal law (question 93), natural law (question 94), and human or positive law (question 95). Question 92, on the effects of law, is relevant only in its stress that law is for the good of its subjects rather than for any benefit to

---

59. References are to these questions, and page numbers apply to the booklet, *St. Thomas Aquinas: Treatise on Law* (Chicago: Regnery-Gateway, 1963).

the legislator. Hence, "tyrannical law is not law at all." But this important doctrine belongs rather to the limits of human law (question 95).

1. *Eternal law* is compared by Aquinas to the "idea in the mind of an artist" and is identified with exemplary ideas in the mind of God, logically prior to creation (p. 38). Whatever your religious convictions, you may express a certain agnosticism about the mind of God. Yet it is possibly here that Aquinas extends a hand to an atheist who accepts a basic rationality in the world. The identification of the Jahweh of the Old Testament with the "supreme form" of Plato and the "self-thinking thought" of Aristotle is an imaginative but precarious leap of history. Underlying this shaky equivalence, however, is Aquinas's claim that there must be some reason behind whatever confronts us; the questioner assumes that an answer is "there," else why should he ask? The objections of positivism to natural law theories are directed fundamentally at the rationalist idea of an "eternal law," whether this be set in the mind of God, or in the absolute spirit of Hegel, or in the dialectical laws of matter and history according to Karl Marx. And the mundane procedures of our courts, asking what a "reasonable man" would do, are solidly in this rationalist tradition. If I dare to tell the judge that I chose to act irrationally, I can certainly predict the verdict!

2. *Natural law* receives surprisingly brief treatment at this point. The bulk of question 94 is concerned with problems about the content and mutability of natural law, and to these we shall return shortly. The opening article, asking what natural law *is*, gets only a short reply, but the basic contention is clear: natural law is an expression of reason, open to our own reasoning. Any particular law that we know "by nature" *is* a reason already contained in the eternal law. An example (given elsewhere by Aquinas) is that the natural law obliges us to temperance because a rational being perceives the contradictions involved when intelligence is clouded through indulgence in material appetites. We are obliged to temperance, not because God commanded it, but because the very exercise of our faculties reveals the subordination of "lower" to "higher" parts of our being. Evidently, a material creation is supposed, making possible both well-ordered passion and inebriation. Natural law is eternal law so far as it is pertinent to creatures and revealed in their exercise of reason.

3. *Positive law* covers, for Aquinas, all human enactments and statements of valid law. These may simply formulate what we already know from natural law, as when a legislature passes a statute forbidding murder. But many questions remain that cannot be solved by merely philosophical thought. Should the statute determine what punishments a judge is to apply (p. 79)? If natural law requires monogamous marriage and some succession to property, what exactly constitutes a marriage and

should property pass by equal shares or by primogeniture? Hence the main task of positive law is to decide on the detailed application of natural law in various social circumstances, without going against such law. Aquinas did not altogether confuse the lawyer with the philosopher.[60]

What we see is a hierarchical view of law, passing from the general affirmation of its grounding in reason (eternal law), through the still-abstract formulation of broad principles (natural law), to the detailed and clearly changeable rules of human origin (positive law). Aquinas indulges in some interesting digressions. For example, he shows a preference for enacted law (and hence codification?) over case law on the ground that the former is more clearly prospective and the latter suffers from the pressure on a court for a verdict (p. 76). We are limited here to a glance at the landscape, but we should at least quote the classical paragraph that is so often cited by friend and foe, as expressing the heart of the natural law position (question 95, article 2, p. 78):

> St. Augustine says that the validity of a law extends only so far as its justice. Now in human affairs justice is a matter of accordance with the principles of reason, which we have seen to form the natural law. Hence any human enactment is a law only to the extent that it is in accord with natural law. If in any point a man-made rule is in conflict with the natural law, to that extent it fails as law and is a perversion of law.

The Content of Natural Law

THOMAS MORE: The law, Roper, the law. I know what's legal, not what's right. And I'll stick to what's legal.

ROPER: Then you set man's law above God's.

MORE: No, far below; but let *me* draw your attention to a fact—I'm *not* God. The currents and eddies of right and wrong, which you find such plain sailing, I can't navigate. I'm no voyager. But in the thickets of the law, oh, there I'm a forester. I doubt if there's a man alive who could follow me there, thank God.

(Robert Bolt, *A Man for All Seasons*)[61]

---

60. Like Dworkin, Aquinas evidently expected the lawyer to be armed with "the soundest philosophical theory," though this would come from Aristotle rather than John Rawls. However, Aquinas distinguished between those enactments of positive law that are "conclusions from principles" and those that are "implementations (*determinationes*) of general directives," arranging the details of life together in very different societies, as an architect may adapt the overall requirements of a home to the plan of a particular house. See *Summa Theologica*, I–II, question 95, and especially article 2: "Whether all law made by man is derived from the natural law." For a commentary, see John Finnis, *Natural Law and Natural Rights* (New York: Oxford Univ. Press, 1980), 281–90.

61. Robert Bolt, *A Man for All Seasons*. Copyright © 1962 by Robert Bolt. Printed with permission of the publisher, Random House, Inc.

> The marriage in question is contrary to the natural law and to the express provisions of New York statute. The court realizes that a discussion of the natural law or a finding under it is not necessary for the determination of this case. However, the point should not be unanswered.
>
> The court assumes that defendants use the term "natural law" in its proper sense. The imperatives of natural law are not the same for the lower animals as they are for man. The moral law as promulgated to man by the light of reason is rightly called the natural law. It was defined by Sophocles and Cicero, Kant, Blackstone and Kent, and mentioned in the Declaration of Independence as "the laws of nature and of Nature's God...."
>
> The natural law was codified in the Ten Commandments. By the natural law, the unity of the matrimonial bond and its indissolubility and permanency are essential properties of conjugal society. Polygamy is opposed to the unity of the bond. When defendant Sodero with one wife in New York married another woman, even in Arkansas, he was then united to more than one person, in violation of the natural law. The natural law is not restricted by state boundaries.
>
> (Sodero v. Sodero, 1945, 56 N.Y.Supp.2d 823)

All was not well between Cesare Sodero and his wife, after thirty-eight years of marriage. When his travels took him to the aptly named town of Hope, in Arkansas, he learned that the state laws for divorce were more lenient than those of New York, where he had been domiciled for all but a year of his married life. So, after he had satisfied the required two months of residence, he applied for and received a divorce and then remarried. The complex question of the recognition accorded to divorces granted in other jurisdictions need not concern us here. What is of interest is the way in which Mr. Sodero found himself to have violated a precept of the natural law that crosses all state lines and defies human enactments to the contrary.

The mores have certainly moved in the direction of facilitating divorce. Legislators and judges have followed, at a discreet distance. Whatever our moral or religious convictions, we perhaps find it strange that an American court, in the mid-twentieth century, should invoke natural law in support of its judgment about divorce. Perhaps we lend an ear to Martin Luther King, Jr., when he calls upon natural law as a justification for denying the validity (or at least the justice) of laws that discriminate between the races. But surely "reason" has little to say on the culturally determined "state of marriage"?

The practical consequences of the dispute between natural law theorists and legal positivists depend largely on our estimate of the detail in the content of natural law. If this is great, descending even to the intimate aspects of married life, then we can understand the protests of positivists against the incursion of metaphysics into the law. But if reasoning about law remains rather general, the conflict may be lessened. We shall, at the end of this section, return to the concessions that Professor Hart makes to some minimal content of natural law. And the figure of Thomas More is pertinent. He sacrificed his life in defense of eternal principles that he regarded as violated by the sovereign. Yet he was no martyr for the exorbitant claims of metaphysics. For most of our life, we take direction from the details of what human law happens to say, in view of the accidents of the times. God knows all the eddies of right and wrong, but "I'm not God."

Some see Aquinas as including in natural law the entirety of his moral philosophy. A good quarter of the *Summa Theologica*, or more than a thousand pages, gives his precise conclusions about our obligations and about the sins by which we fail in that regard. Is a legislator or judge supposed to measure the validity of positive laws by so extensive a chart?

If so, we find much passing as reason that is evidently little more than a reflection of the social and economic conditions of the age. A classic instance is Aquinas's conclusion that usury, the lending of money at interest, is immoral (*Summa Theologica*, II–II, question 78). His homely examples about receiving double payment for wine or corn suppose a society of direct barter. He failed to anticipate the complex commercial life that was to arise before long with the appearance of banks and of exchanges that involved great distance and time (e.g., a voyage of several years). Reasoning from the nature of man offers little basis for an evaluation of modern banking laws.

Another area in which some natural law theorists have shown imprudence through the detail of their conclusions is that of marriage. This venerable institution clearly includes among its purposes the propagation of the race and the rearing of young. But Aquinas deduces that this is the "primary end" of marriage, to which any other purpose, such as the "mutual support of the spouses," is subordinate. Hence contraception must always be wrong. More is involved here than exhortations from the pulpit. In 1948, the case of *Baxter v. Baxter* reached the House of Lords, with a plea for a decree of nullity on the grounds that one spouse had insisted on contraceptive precautions and the other held this to be against "the principal end of marriage." The House of Lords denied both the reasoning and the decree. Some years later, a supporter of natural law argued, in an American law journal, that "this decision was in direct conflict with a primary principle of the natural law.... Persons who have excluded procreation by a positive act of the will have not contracted marriage. This is an absolute and immutable principle which no change of facts will ever vitiate."[62]

Those who see natural law as a comprehensive set of conclusions, enabling us to pass quick judgment in our complex moral and legal problems, are likely to draw normative conclusions about what is natural from observations that justify no more than descriptive generalizations.[63] The following provides a simple example. Aquinas bases his conclusion that telling lies is always sinful on the claim that our words naturally express what is in our mind.[64] That is, it is the nature of our faculty of speech to tell what we take to be the truth and it is

62. Brendan F. Brown, "Natural Law," *Tulane Law Review* 31 (1957): 501.
63. See, for example, the criticism in Golding, *Philosophy of Law*, 32–33.
64. *Summa Theologica*, II–II, question 110, article 3.

wrong for us ever to frustrate this faculty. He concedes that blame is lessened if lies are told as a joke or to help another. But the reader may wonder at the logical passage from an account of how we do use speech to conclusions about how we ought to use it. We bother to condemn lying because we find that people often engage in it; how then can we justify the premise that the nature of speech is only to tell the truth? Such a question becomes most pertinent in exactly those realms where we look for the guidance of a well-founded principle. For example, we need to promote truth in advertising. Yet what norm can we draw from our knowledge of how traders have used their faculty of speech since the days of the first bazaar?

A common accusation against natural law theories is that these make little allowance for the evident changes in social conditions and hence in law. Aquinas may, however, be more cautious than many of his disciples. In question 97, he opposes the claim that human law, because it is based on natural law, is immutable: "Law can rightly be changed in view of the changing conditions of man" (p. 107). In regard to natural law, he acknowledges the conclusion that this, being a participation in eternal law, is immutable. Nevertheless, he is careful to distinguish between degrees of knowledge that we have of the reasons involved. There are indeed certain "first principles" of natural law that are known "in themselves." These include the rather abstract principle that "we are obliged to do what is good" and its immediate conclusions that we should preserve ourselves and the species and that we should, as rational beings, strive to find what is true and "to live accordingly in society" (question 94, pp. 59–61). When, however, we pass from such generalities to more specific conclusions, we find that these "do not apply in the same way to all." As an example, he remarks that the principle obliging us to return goods with which we have been entrusted no longer holds where such return would be "injurious and against reason." Any such principle "fails to the extent that we descend to details" (p. 66).

What summary, in more modern terms, can we give of Aquinas's approach to law? His underlying claim is that law is no mere fact that comes to us from the will of a legislator, human or divine. Law is central to what we are, as rational beings, and we find it at the heart of all we do. Our nature is disclosed not by the reports of an observer, but through the potential self-contradictions we find in acting intentionally. Every failure to act reasonably is a violation of obligations from which we can never escape. Each person thus discovers the general principles of natural law, and of these the most basic ones have to do with our manner of life in a society of rational beings. Our duty to acknowledge each as a reasoner means that we should live according to rules rather than simply drawing advantage from relative positions of strength. This involves settling disputes by discussion, within the framework of accepted standards. It means, in short, the establishment of a system of law, with appropriate institutions. Legislators will be empowered to enact rules of positive law that define the particular ways we conduct our social, political, and economic life. Questions about such rules can for the most part be settled in terms of validity, as we refer to some master rules that we have adopted. Yet this adoption is itself a matter of natural law and involves our basic moral commitments. Hence we do not assess the validity of a particular ruling merely by tracing a pedigree of enactments or cases; what legal officials do can violate the very enterprise that gives them their position. Superior principles can be invoked that are at once moral and legal.

This summary evidently involves a fair amount of interpretation, and the historical Aquinas may well be exposed to many of the common complaints against natural law. He apparently did not limit natural law to inquiry into those principles we can justify from an internal point of view. Perhaps he would have been less dogmatic on usury if he had lived a couple of centuries later, but it is likely that he would still have agreed with the court in the Sodero case that the unity of the matrimonial bond is indissoluble. However, one suggestion at least has helped to restore respectability to his approach, while confining its scope. Suppose that the connection between law and morality applies at the level of an entire legal system rather than at that of particular rules? We may be more ready to condemn despotism, in its many forms, as violating the very nature of legality than to distinguish between valid and invalid rules for marriage on moral grounds. And, if so, are we not more concerned with the *structures* of law that are required by our enterprise of living according to rules than we are with the *content* of particular laws that result? It is along such lines that Fuller has attempted some salvage operations, as we shall see in the following section.

A final comment. Professor Hart has, in a manner notably different from Fuller, attempted to preserve "the core of good sense in the doctrine of Natural Law" (*Hart, Concept of Law*, 189–95). He reduces its principle to the "tacit assumption that the proper end of human society is survival." He suggests that we can "discard, as too metaphysical for modern minds, the notion that this is something antecedently fixed which men necessarily desire because it is their proper goal or end. Instead, we may hold it to be a mere contingent fact which could be otherwise" (ibid., 187–88). Nevertheless, this assumption that all want to survive, when applied to the evident facts of life as we find it (e.g., our vulnerability and limited resources, our approximate equality and limited strength of will), does present us with some guidelines for what Hart calls "natural necessities" in a legal system. We can, for example, argue for laws of property that enable crops to grow and that secure land from indiscriminate entry.

Hart avoids accusations of falling into the naturalistic fallacy; if a superabundance of goods ever becomes possible through science, then the *ought* of property is adjusted accordingly or simply disappears. We may, however, end by suggesting a number of hesitations that even a "modernized" Aquinas would probably express.

1. Hart, in thus limiting the highest necessities in law to whatever stems from our will to survive, is faithful to his own positivist tradition but may not

justify our "duty of fidelity to law" in a way that satisfies critics such as Fuller. Can any such hypothetical imperative (If you want to survive, then you should . . . .) explain obligation, or does Hart effectively rejoin Austin, who viewed obligation in terms of the will of an inferior confronting that of a superior?

2. If we are to base all on "tacit assumptions" about our goals, are these restricted to self-preservation? Aquinas argued that the captain who saw no higher purpose would never sail his ship out of the harbor (*Summa Theologica*, I–II, question 2, article 5). Those aware of the perils of the sea at that time will understand. Hart's "minimal content" seems too restricted for any interpretation of human history. Aquinas did indeed rank self-preservation among the primary principles of natural law, but he subordinated this purpose of all animals to the more demanding imperatives of a rational being. It is not only martyrs, such as Thomas More, who follow him. We all live for ideas that take us far beyond the mere animal state and involve some recognition that "I ought not to place survival before. . . ."

3. What less-restricted content of natural law is then to be envisaged? Its first principle is stated by Aquinas as an obligation "to strive for what is true and to live accordingly in society." Hart sets aside Aristotle's version of natural law as too metaphysical for modern minds. However, the discussion above on the way the Greeks spoke of nature suggested that some self-contradiction may be disclosed in this apparently simple rejection. I affirm rationality in dismissing it for a reason. And I affirm social obligations implicitly in turning my rejection of their metaphysical basis into the form of a reasoned argument, respectful of my obligations as a member of a community of inquirers. Few have argued as well as Hart. But he did argue. He did not just shout and rely upon pressures commanded by his eminent position. Something more is inescapably involved than the triumph of force according to the descriptive laws of the jungle. The categorical imperative in our obligation to reason socially is shown most clearly in the writing of books and articles by a scholar. It is shown also in any legal system. When a judge gives reasons for his verdict, and submits to a process of appeals, he is at least implicitly accepting the natural law by which one person is obliged to acknowledge others as persons, united in the enterprise of living according to rules.

FURTHER READING

Aquinas, Saint Thomas. *Selected Political Writings.* Translated by J. Dawson. Oxford: Blackwell, 1959.
———. *Treatise on Law.* Edited by Stanley Parry. Chicago: Regnery-Gateway, 1963.
Brown, Brendan F., ed. *The Natural Law Reader.* Dobbs Ferry, N.Y.: Oceana, 1960.
Christie, George C., ed. *Jurisprudence.* St. Paul: West, 1973, 1–29.

d'Entrèves, A. P. *Natural Law: An Introduction to Legal Philosophy.* 2d ed. New York, N.Y.: Humanities (Hutchinson Univ. Library), 1964.
Finnis, John. *Natural Law and Natural Rights.* New York: Oxford Univ. Press, 1980.
Golding, Martin P., ed. *The Nature of Law.* New York: Random House, 1966, 9–74.
Hall, Jerome, ed. *Readings in Jurisprudence.* Indianapolis: Bobbs-Merrill, 1938, 3–86.
Luijpen, William A. *Phenomenology of Natural Law.* Pittsburg: Duquesne Univ. Press, 1967.
O'Connor, D. J. *Aquinas and Natural Law.* London: Macmillan, 1967.
Rommen, Heinrich. *The Natural Law.* 1947. Reprint. New York: Arno Press, 1979.
Simon, Yves. *The Tradition of Natural Law.* New York: Fordham Univ. Press, 1965.

QUESTIONS FOR DISCUSSION

1. "It is man's nature to keep his promises." Distinguish between a descriptive (external) and a normative (internal) account of nature in this statement. What happens to each of these laws if 10 percent of all promises are not kept? Apply the same distinction to Aristotle's claim that "man is by nature social and political (lives in a *polis*, or state)." What happens to each of these laws if 10 percent of all people are criminals who seem to recognize no rules of the community?

2. In the light of the above distinctions, explain Mr. Armstrong's argument that, as the longboat began to sink in heavy seas, Holmes reverted from United States law to a "state of nature." Why was he then "bound to no duty" but free to seek his own survival at the expense of others? How would Armstrong have explained the duties that did bind the seaman before the shipwreck? Would Austin agree? Would Hart (notice that the only talk of natural law he allows is based on assumptions of the will to survive)? How did the federal judge differ in his version of the duties that derive from nature, and hence on the obligations faced by Holmes before and after the shipwreck?

3. Contrast these situations. Two children are squabbling and they come to blows after several minutes of counterassertions that "it is, it isn't." Two doctors disagree on the diagnosis of a patient's problem; each carefully presents the evidence for his claim and agrees to submit to the result of further tests that they prescribe. Are normative rules lacking in the former situation that are present in the latter, even though every statement may be purely factual? In such terms, what was Plato's basic argument against the Sophists?

4. What is odd, and self-contradictory, in saying there is no truth but only opinions? In saying that all is utterly meaningless? That I am in no way responsible for my statements? That I am bound by no normal *ought*? In the last example, ought you to accept the conclusions to which your thinking leads you? Ought you to submit your results to criticism by others? Is rationality merely a fact you find by observation, or does it involve some moral norms? Are there "degrees" to rationality? If so, can a legal system reveal a lower or higher degree of rationality? Could some threats to this involve a self-contradiction in our very proposal to live legally?

5. Before you have studied geometry, are you free to think that one angle inscribed in a semicircle is larger than another? Once you have understood the appropriate proof, do you lose your *choice* to think that these angles are not equal? But are you, in some sense, made more *free* through the knowledge you have gained? Was your previous choice better described as capricious than as free? If freedom is a value to be prized, would you have more respect for a motorist who stops at every turning, unsure of which to take, or for one who drives to his goal with little regard for the alternatives? In view of such examples, explain the claim of some philosophers that freedom is a matter of degree, and that it is not simply opposed to necessity.

6. Laws for Austin are in the imperative mood (do this!) or at least in hypothetical form (if you don't, this penalty will follow). Aquinas sees all law, eternal, natural, and even positive, as an expression of reason. Does this distinction correspond to the one between commands and rules? If you want to secure greater obedience to a law, would you appeal to a person's will (exhorting and threatening him) or to his mind (explaining the reasons for the law)? In terms of the therapy that Freud proposed, would you classify him as a voluntarist or as an intellectualist?

7. Both Plato and Aristotle accepted the institution of slavery. So, in the first half of the nineteenth century, did some American political thinkers who appealed to natural law for support. Yet a tradition of opposition to slavery, also in the name of natural law, goes back to the ancient Stoics. Does such a divergence of conclusions seriously threaten the theory? Does slavery belong to the "remote" conclusions that allow for disagreement and for historical change? Or would you hold that treatment of a person as property is a violation of what he is "in himself"?

8. Most uses we make of the word *ought* are certainly "hypothetical imperatives." In the 1970s there was much argument whether supersonic planes ought to be banned at civil airports. Could this *ought* be reduced to a preference for silence in our homes or for speed in transportation? Is it possible, however, to treat every use of the word *ought* as hypothetical? Does the fact that the fight over supersonic planes was conducted in the manner of a public forum, with tacit assumptions about rules of discussion and proof, rest upon no more than hypothetical imperatives?

9. If, in the factual spirit of a positivist, we look at history to find the guiding imperative in human choices, does this turn out to be self-preservation? As Graham Greene pointed out in his screenplay for *The Third Man*, centuries of war in Italy were the setting for the world's greatest art, while a corresponding period of peace in Switzerland gave us chocolate bars and the cuckoo clock!

22. FULLER'S LEGAL NATURALISM

> *After World War II the Manus people [of the Admiralty Islands] learned from their Australian governors that there was a way of dealing with disputes of which they had no previous knowledge. This was the procedure of adjudication. Their own methods of settling disputes had been most unsatisfactory, consisting as they did of "feuds, raids, and subsequent ephemeral peace-making ceremonies often with payments in expiation"* [Margaret Mead, *New Lives for Old*, 1956, p. 306]. *Now they came to see that a dispute could be decided and settled by a submission of it to an impartial arbiter. There followed a veritable fad for adjudication, their own elders being assigned or assuming a quite unfamiliar social role, that of judge. Curiously the justice thus dispensed was a kind of black market commodity since the "judges" who decided their disputes lacked any legal standing with the Australian government; their powers were quite unsupported by any rule of recognition except a very informal and shifting one among the Manus people themselves. The attitude of the indigenous people toward this innovation is thus described by Miss Mead:*

>> To the New Guinea native, newly fired with a desire to keep his society "straight," the whole legal system looks fresh and beautiful. He sees it as a magnificent invention, as wonderful as the airplane, so that far into the interior of New Guinea proper the institution of illegal "courts" is spreading.

If Miss Mead's account is correct, then the rule of recognition among the Manus people ran primarily not toward a human agency empowered by the rule to make law, but toward a procedure. And surely if one is going to speak of an invention comparable to that of the wheel or the airplane, it is appropriate to think of a procedure and not of a mere grant of authority....

I have insisted that law be viewed as a purposeful enterprise, dependent for its success on the energy, insight, intelligence, and conscientiousness of those who conduct it, and fated, because of this dependence, to fall always somewhat short of a full attainment of its goals. In opposition to this view it is insisted that law must be treated as a manifested fact of social authority or power, to be studied for what it is and does, and not for what it is trying to do or become.
(Fuller, *The Morality of Law*, 144–45)[65]

The "opposition" to which Lon Fuller (1902–1978) refers is that of the legal positivists; both he and Hart admit that their lengthy controversy about the nature or concept of law has its root in philosophical differences that run far beyond legal questions. If Hart is the most clearly recognized advocate of modern legal positivism, Fuller has come to stand (though less clearly) for a contemporary version of the more amorphous tradition of natural law. To mark the important differences he saw between his own position and older forms, such as that of Aquinas, the term *legal naturalism* has been applied; the suggestion for this title comes from Philip Selznick (*Harv. L. Rev.*, 83 [1970]: 1,475), a sociologist whom many see to be defending a legal theory close to Fuller's.

Fuller spent most of his academic life as professor of jurisprudence at Harvard. However, it is of some significance that his experience in the practice of law was concerned mainly with the negotiation of labor contracts. This involvement in mediation and arbitration gave him a firm sense of the creative aspect of law. The lawyer, he held, is originally an architect of social order. The courts and the books of law appear on the scene only when institutions have first been designed. Hence Fuller's lasting criticism of legal positivism is that it views the law as a fact already in existence rather than as an enterprise of construction. This has, indeed, been a traditional charge against positivism, at least from the time when Kant accused Hume of taking facts as given rather than investigating the mind's role in making them. In practical terms, Fuller had hesitations about the usual form of legal education, which inculcates analytical skills to be exercised on given cases and statutes, rather than helping toward an awareness of the tacit agreements that make a legal system possible. We may also understand Fuller's leaning toward "boundary situations" in the legal parables he composed: law is best appreciated when we see it arising "from scratch."

---

65. Lon Fuller, *The Morality of Law* (New Haven: Yale Univ. Press, 1964; extended edition, 1969 © 1969 by Yale University. This and the following quotations from the work have been reprinted with permission from the publishers.

It is ironic that Fuller's concern with law as a system we construct was not matched by an adequate formulation of his own system. His writings remain fragmentary, and projects he envisaged were never completed. His best-known work, *The Morality of Law*, is all too polemical. But it is our principal source, and page references in this section will be given to that book in the 1969 edition.[66]

Fuller's ambition was to found a study of "eunomics," which he described as "the theory of good order." Only the first chapter was written, but this is enough to suggest the concerns that led him to legal philosophy. Society is not a value-neutral fact, as may be the "nature" that confronts a modern scientist. The distinction between *is* and *ought*, which is much a product of our scientific culture, has little relevance when we ask how and why people come together in a social order. There are tacit assumptions about the recognition of others as persons, implicit laws of reciprocity, a broad variety of common aims. In new nations or associations, the lawyer is intimately involved in such requisites of order and in the value judgments that infuse them. This creative spirit is bound to fade, and Fuller assigns 1870 as an approximate date in this country. From that time the lawyer has become increasingly remote from the origins of law. His concern has been with pathways already on a map rather than with their creation. Indeed, Fuller sees legal realism as a misguided reaction to this change.

It is not evident that the recognition of values in a project need involve morality. The artist, who also creates order from his materials, may produce good or bad order without thereby submitting to moral criteria. Similarly, we may welcome Fuller's concern with the creation of a legal order, and with the values implicit in this enterprise, without immediately accepting his claim that these are moral values. Hence we face two questions. What are the necessary structures for producing legal order? Is such order moral or purely technical?

The Structures of Law

In nearly all societies men perceive the need for subjecting certain kinds of human conduct to the explicit control of rules. When they embark on the enterprise of accomplishing this subjection, they come to see that this enterprise contains a certain inner logic of its own, that it imposes demands that must be met (sometimes with considerable inconvenience) if its objectives are to be attained. It is because men generally in some measure perceive these demands and respect them, that legal systems display a certain likeness in societies otherwise quite diverse. It is, then, precisely because law is a purposeful enterprise that it displays structural constancies which the legal theorist can discover and treat as uniformities in the factually given (pp. 150–51).

---

66. Fuller's literary executor, Kenneth I. Winston, has tried to make up for these defects by editing *The Principles of Social Order* (Durham, N.C.: Duke Univ. Press, 1981), a collection of published and previously unpublished essays and addresses. The Introduction supplies helpful material and background.

Fuller has consistently distinguished his own account of the "internal morality of law" from any judgment of law through a morality external to it. In this respect he sees himself opposing many Roman Catholic thinkers and also those German philosophers, such as Radbruch, who turned to natural law theories after experience of the Nazi years. Fuller contends that those who limit valid law by morality are in fact usually applying to positive law the external norms that they derive from the will of God, or from papal encyclicals, or from some more secular "higher law." This, he claims, is in effect a reply to one form of positivism through another. Such versions of natural law doctrine, dealing with the full range of substantive obligations that moralists have proposed, are not to be dismissed as worthless but they are not the topic of his inquiry. Instead, what he investigates is the internal or procedural or structural morality of law:

> What I have tried to do is to discern and articulate the natural laws of a particular kind of human undertaking, which I have described as "the enterprise of subjecting human conduct to the governance of rules." These natural laws have nothing to do with any "brooding omnipresence in the skies." Nor have they the slightest affinity with any such proposition as that the practice of contraception is a violation of God's law. They remain entirely terrestrial in their origin and application. They are not "higher" laws; if any metaphor of elevation is appropriate, they should be called "lower" laws (p. 96).

Fuller introduces his account of the structures of legality through the story of Rex's many failures to make law (section 12 above). From this parable Fuller derives eight ways in which Rex, for all his good intentions, simply failed to make law (e.g., failures in generality, publicity, constancy, prospectivity). Our interest here is with what Fuller means by such "structures" of law and, then, with his right to see them as an "inner morality."

One immediate conclusion is that he is working at the level of principles rather than rules. Rules are explicitly stated and discussed (e.g., killing is wrong, except in self-defense; the tax on income is to be proportional). But principles are so basic that they seldom come to the level of statement; legislators are unlikely to pass a statute that all laws (whether enacted or deriving from cases) must be general and public, nor could they easily define what is meant. However, this is the level of the "legal iceberg" in which Fuller is interested. The mediator appeals to no written sources but tries to convince both sides that his solution is a work of reason, an elucidation of what they already implicitly accept in living socially. In one sense he constructs an agreement; in another sense he draws on what is already known but needs to be ratified afresh if his settlement is to be effective and therapeutic. In fact, Fuller suggests that the task of a mediator sometimes consists in liberating the parties from the encumbrance of rules and returning to a more basic level of mutual trust and respect.[67]

---

67. Winston, *Principles of Social Order*, 145.

The creation of rules is not entirely a product of rules. And we can understand, perhaps, Fuller's dissatisfaction with Hart's treatment of customary societies as "pre-legal."

Fuller speaks of the "structural constancies" in the enterprise of legality under a variety of terms. Sometimes they are simply demands or desiderata. At other times they are natural laws. Most commonly they are principles. However, though the term *structure* is the one he uses least frequently, it is this one that may best indicate philosophical connections. The contemporary movement, known as "structuralism" and applied in such fields as linguistics and anthropology, turns from the details of particular languages and cultures to the framework that all these presuppose in order to reveal their individuality.[68]

In an earlier age, it was Kant above all who turned our attention from the particular content of knowledge to the structures that make it possible. He sought the "conditions of possibility" for certain types of experience (e.g., artistic as opposed to scientific) and for any form of experience. To mention the most famous example, he argued at length that causality is not what we find (here and there) but rather a structure, or category, of our finding. Hence the principle of causality, that every event must have a cause, is not a generalization we draw from many observations (as Hume claimed); it belongs to the way we formulate the raw data of experience to make any intelligible world.

Though Fuller never identifies his work with that of either Kant or the structuralists, his proposal is to look for the structures involved in our very project of living legally rather than according to the effect of superior force. The norm by which a law is shown to be invalid is no moral rule introduced from outside. My decision to establish a legal order is vitiated by my making of (for instance) secret or retroactive rules; these fail to be valid law because they contradict the structures that make law possible as such. We see here a firm insistence on the internal point of view and an argument similar to the "negative proof" of Aristotle. Just as I cannot successfully affirm as true that there is no truth but only opinion, so I cannot achieve as law whatever violates the very project of lawmaking and law-abiding.

However, this account of Fuller's position is oversimple. He was no naive rationalist, who would assume that the structures of law fit harmoniously into a system. Following his story of Rex's failures, Fuller engages in a lengthy discussion (pp. 38–94) of "antinomies" in our application of the structures of legality. For example, if the publicity of law is interpreted as meaning its translation into ordinary language, then its use by the courts may become more capricious and less predictable, leading to a loss of clarity and prospectivity. Or a police officer may have to engage in some selective enforcement to ensure that laws can be obeyed by all. Practical questions force us to accept that none of the

---

68. In his book, *Structuralism* (New York: Harper & Row, 1970), Piaget includes under this term a study of legal structures, but he mentions only Hans Kelsen. Piaget adds (p. 106) a criticism of Kelsen that could well have come from Fuller—"What of the 'fundamental norm'? If its legitimacy does not *consist* in its being 'acknowledged' by those subject to the law, on what, then, does it depend?"

structures can be realized fully. The growth of regulatory agencies limits the generality of law, and strict liability narrows the extent to which observance is possible. Clarity does not exclude the "open texture" of legislation. Fuller devotes many pages to a discussion of retroactive laws that are required by the project of sustaining a legal community (pp. 51–62; see also Fuller, *Anatomy of the Law*, 99–105). His conclusion is that making law is a complex and subtle art: "Some degree of 'pathology' attends all legal systems, including the most exemplary" (Fuller, *Morality of Law*, 157).

It remains to be asked whether this investigation of the basic principles of all law is an inquiry into legal morality or only into legal techniques. But first a brief reference may be made to the opening chapter of his main book, in which he examines ambiguities in the term morality. He is certainly correct to locate much of the confusion there, rather than in the notion of *law*.

The common assumption today is that morality is a matter of *duty*. If I make a promise or borrow money, my duty is to fulfil what I said and to return what I took. At a more basic level, I am obliged to recognize people as the subject of rights, and I violate this duty whenever I treat them as things, using them for my private purposes. Kant's moral philosophy is based on such themes, as also is the ethics of Karl Marx (pp. 26–27).

However, the older tradition is a morality of *aspiration*. This has to do with shortcoming rather than with wrongdoing. Implicit in all we do is an ideal of perfection that serves as a measure of our degree of attainment. It is in this way that the Greek philosophers characterized our moral life. Man is a rational and political animal, who achieves to a greater or lesser extent the ideals of a reasonable life in community with others. This is the moral philosophy of Plato, and here the distinction between *is* and *ought* fades into insignificance. Socrates did not first tell us what the good life is and then advance reasons why we ought to lead it. For him, "virtue is knowledge" (pp. 13–15). Aristotle's concept of the "just mean" is no easy way but the hard course that avoids opposing lapses from the ideal of perfection (pp. 18–19).

Fuller suggests three conclusions in regard to the legal enterprise:

1. At a basic level, law involves the morality of duty. We either succeed or fail in the reciprocity by which one person recognizes another to form a community of rational beings. We come together (or fail) as husband and wife, parent and child, citizen and legislator (pp. 19–24).

2. Yet, beyond this fundamental requirement, legality is a matter of degree, guided by the morality of aspiration. Fuller holds, against bitter opposition, that societies are "more or less" legal. The very complexity of the structures of law, and their many antinomies, allow us to "affirm that the government of country A displays a greater respect for the principles of legality than does the government of B" (p. 200). We should never rest complacently in the conclusion that we form a legal

community; the question is How legal? Fuller's estimate of his own country over the past generations is far from optimistic.

3. The dividing line between a morality of duty and one of aspiration is never easy to draw. Overemphasis on the former can lead to a stifling of experimentation and spontaneity, and to all the common accusations of legalism. Yet a single-minded regard for the latter alone can end "with the poet tossing his wife into the river in the belief—perhaps quite justified—that he will be able to write better poetry in her absence" (pp. 27–28).

The Internal Morality of Law

Law is not, like management, a matter of directing other persons how to accomplish tasks set by a superior, but is basically a matter of providing the citizenry with a sound and stable framework for their interactions with one another (p. 210).

Critics of Fuller have generally admitted some validity to his analysis of the structures of law. What the legal positivists have rejected, uniformly and understandably, is his claim that these are moral structures rather than maxims of legal efficiency or craftsmanship.[69] There is a failure in technique, like to that of Rex, when a would-be murderer forgets to load his gun or adds an insufficient dose of poison to the coffee. Failure in mastering the skills of golf does not constitute a violation of any "inner morality" of the game.

A more profound version of this criticism comes from some natural law theorists.[70] Fuller is said by them to conceive of natural law as a "technology," a set of rules for legislating well. This may have been the thinking behind what passed for natural law among the practical-minded Romans. As "legal engineers," they succeeded in constructing a legal system of wide extent and long duration. Fuller, with his project of eunomics and his talk of modest and sober claims that avoid the excesses of metaphysics (p. 146), may seem to present lawmaking as merely an art. If so, then his whole system rests on no more than a hypothetical imperative. If you want good golf, then follow through on your swing. If you want good law, then observe these "desiderata."

Fuller, however, proved unrepentant. He accepted no olive branch to have his thesis endorsed if he would but abandon his talk of morality. Instead, he attacked his critics for betraying "a basic confusion between efficiency and morality." The efficiency of the carpenter in driving a straight nail has no moral overtones, but good law cannot be separated from morality. When Soviet au-

---

69. On pages 243–44, Fuller lists almost fifty reviews of *The Morality of Law* that followed its first edition. For his reply to critics on this point, see pp. 200–224.

70. See, for example, A. P. d'Entrèves, "The Case for Natural Law Reexamined," *Natural Law Forum* 1 (1956): 27–46. This article is abridged and reprinted in Golding, *The Nature of Law*; see particularly pp. 37–42.

thorities countered the illegal exchange of foreign currencies by imposing the death penalty and applying this regulation retroactively, their measures were efficacious; but the questions raised on the score of both legality and morality take us far beyond the world of the carpenter (pp. 202–3).

Austin, according to Fuller, deserves respect for his consistency. The command theory of law was no accident but a necessary support for the separation of morality from law. Faced with the superior strength and sheer will of the sovereign, I prudently decide to submit, yet I have no moral obligation. Contemporary legal positivists abandoned the command theory but, Fuller maintains, their determination still to exclude any moral basis from the law led them to avoid an investigation of why we accept rules; instead, they see law on a managerial model, as a "unidirectional exercise of authority" (pp. 214, 223).

What is Fuller's alternative to a managerial model, and how does he set our fidelity to law on some firm moral grounding? As suggested in section 21, talk of natural law has commonly been based on man's nature as a rational being. I can choose to play golf or not, but I do not choose to make my decisions either for reasons I responsibly accept or for no reason at all. "Reason," so understood, is not a technique I apply (along with investment or murder). It is my inescapable way of being. And this serves as the starting point for both a morality of duty and a morality of aspiration. In the terms of Aquinas, sin is an act "against right reason," and even our acts in accord with reason are but a limited participation in the ideal of rationality.

Reason is often viewed as an individual concern. When I tell someone to be reasonable, I am probably advising him to engage in a calm calculation of his private interest. However, the natural law tradition has seen rationality as inescapably social. The obligation to be reasonable involves the duty to treat others as rational beings, as fellow persons in a community of questioners. This is shown clearly in Kant's various formulations of the one categorical imperative that he derives from pure reason. The initial statement is abstract: I should reject those maxims that cannot be universalized without self-contradiction.[71] However, Kant is quick to move on to more evidently social expressions of this imperative. I should treat persons always as an end in themselves and never as a mere means to my own purposes. I should recognize that I belong to a "realm of ends" by subjecting myself to my own legislation. I should realize that I belong to a "community of free-willing persons."

Such phrases are not found explicitly in Fuller, but he clearly suggests that there are stronger "natural necessities" in the project of living legally than Hart allowed. Fuller was fond of quoting the following passage that dates from 1832:

> Law, in all its divisions, is the strong action of Reason upon wants, necessities, and imperfections. No matter whether its ministration is by a

---

71. For instance, I ought to make promises only with the intention of keeping them. If it were permissible for all to make promises without such an intention, then we should face more than social problems; the very notion of a promise, and hence the possibility of promising, would be destroyed.

legislative or through a judicial faculty, or by the consentaneous acts of individuals under no manifest compulsion; it is still the act of those on whom it has pleased divine Providence to bestow the attribute of reason, as distinguished from those who are guided only by instinct, and can make no rule for themselves.[72]

Fuller's basic complaint against the legal positivists is that they do not fully recognize the place of reason in the grounding of law. The dependence on observed fact is too strong to be countered by changing Austin's "will" into Hart's "rules." Indeed, Hart announced his *Concept of Law* as "an essay in descriptive sociology" (preface, p. vii). The rule of recognition is seen only as a measure of valid law; the critical term *recognition* is scarcely investigated. But why *should* we recognize such a rule? Does it merit to be so accepted? The fact that legal officials go along with it says nothing to the citizen from the internal point of view that introduces talk of obligation. Are there no constraints on the officials themselves that regulate their own acceptance?

The parable of poor Rex and his multiple failures is deceptively simple. Fuller clearly intends more than an amusing story of ineptitude. Rex's failure was an affront to each citizen's dignity as a person who lives socially and hence legally. Fuller quotes Georg Simmel, that "there is a kind of reciprocity between the government and the citizen with respect to the observance of rules ..., a contract between lawgiver and subject" (pp. 39, 216–17). That is, underlying the fact of legislation is a tacit agreement that can scarcely escape formulation in moral terms. And this "vertical" understanding, by which we delegate legislation to authorities, is only part of the "horizontal" understanding by which we come together as persons rather than as animals. According to Fuller, "The law does not tell a man what he should do to accomplish specific ends set by the lawgiver; it furnishes him with baselines against which to organize his life with his fellows" (Winston, *Principles of Social Order*, 234). That is, the structures of legality are more than techniques of legislative craftsmanship: they are conditions for treating others with respect as autonomous subjects, which we are all morally and unconditionally obliged to do.

From the side of those who see an external morality judging the validity of laws, the objections are evident. The charge is that Fuller brings too little morality into the law. He maintains an aloof neutrality in regard to the validity of laws that allow abortion or euthanasia.

Fuller's writings are little concerned with attacks from this quarter. He did, however, apply his theories to produce a condemnation of Nazi laws, of South African racial laws, and of some particular decisions of the U.S. Supreme Court. And his diffidence is not without guidelines. Those who see law as a moral enterprise, based on the respect of one person for another, may be led toward some conclusions of a more substantive nature. The project of living according

---

72. William Rawle, "A Discourse on the Nature and Study of Law," in Winston, *Principles of Social Order*, 86.

to rules in general may well exclude some particular rules that treat our fellow beings as unworthy of this very project and all it implies:

> I have repeatedly observed that legal morality can be said to be neutral over a wide range of ethical issues. It cannot be neutral in regard to man himself. To embark on the enterprise of subjecting human conduct to the governance of rules involves of necessity a commitment to the view that man is, or can become, a responsible agent, capable of understanding and following rules, and answerable for his defaults (p. 162).
>
> Communication is something more than a means of staying alive. It is a way of being alive.... If I were asked, then, to discern one central indisputable principle of what may be called substantive natural law—Natural Law with capital letters—I would find it in this injunction: Open up, maintain, and preserve the integrity of the channels of communication by which men convey to one another what they perceive, feel, and desire (p. 186).

Fuller offers no systematic development of this suggestion. It does, however, bear an interesting similarity to Dworkin's, that the morality embedded in legal systems has to do fundamentally with our right to equal concern and respect. We maintain our channels of communication by adopting those institutional forms that best enable each of us to treat the other as a fellow reasoner. How far this requirement of both morality and legality will take us in assessing the content of rules is a matter for further investigations. At least, we have seen that the basic theories of law are no longer so clearly opposed in the statement of such questions as they once were.

FURTHER READING

Summers, Robert S. *Lon L. Fuller.* Stanford, Calif.: Stanford Univ. Press, 1984.
Winston, Kenneth, I., ed. *The Principles of Social Order.* Durham, N.C.: Duke Univ. Press, 1981.

Apart from *The Morality of Law*, books in which Fuller explains his philosophy of law and confronts his critics include:

Fuller, Lon L. *Anatomy of the Law.* 1968. Reprint. Westport, Conn.: Greenwood Press, 1976.
_____. *The Law in Quest of Itself.* 1940. Reprint. New York: AMS Press, 1978.
_____. *The Problems of Jurisprudence.* Brooklyn, N.Y.: Foundation Press, 1949.

QUESTIONS FOR DISCUSSION

1. Is there an inner logic to enterprises other than law? What about playing games? If there are principles without which you cannot take part in a game (e.g., sportsmanship), are these moral principles?

2. How would you see your task as a mediator in a conflict (experienced or imagined)? Would you appeal to written laws or hope to draw upon the very assumptions that brought the parties to the negotiating table?

3. You are a passenger in my car when it breaks down. I do nothing about it because I say there was no cause for this event. Would you suspect it is more than mechanical knowledge that I lack? Is the principle of causality a structure of all our experience? Or is it based on observations so far? Or on definitions (every effect must have a cause)? What parallel do you see to Fuller's claims about the structures of living legally?

4. Most would say you are morally bound to intend keeping your promises and also to be truthful. Do you see a difference between these two requirements in terms of Fuller's distinction between a morality of duty and of aspiration? Does your obligation to respect people involve both forms of morality? Mention examples of failure.

5. Is your inability to sink a putt at golf purely technical or also moral? What about an artist who produces poor work because he is a shallow person? Can we escape from law as from golf? As from all forms of art?

6. Since World War II, many new nations have come into existence and have founded their legal system on a constitution. Each has a "rule of recognition." If you belonged to such a nation, why would you accept the new constitution? On the basis of a purely hypothetical imperative (if you wish to continue living here....)? Or on the basis of its merits? If the latter, do such reasons have any moral dimension?

7. The figure in the case of the speluncean explorers with whom Fuller, the author, most closely identifies himself is Justice Foster. However, Foster appeals to a "state of nature" as liberating the explorers from the positive law of Newgarth. The language seems to be that of the defense attorney in *U.S. v. Holmes* (see p. 220 above). What differences do you see in the meaning of "nature" suggested by these two? Would Foster have agreed with any contract into which the explorers happened to enter? Or would this have been governed by the "inner morality" of lawmaking?

8. In his alternative argument, Foster relies upon deterrence as one of the principal purposes of criminal legislation. Does this conjunction of deterrence and self-preservation reflect Fuller's view of the purpose of law? How would Fuller have written his own opinion in this case?

4

LEGAL EPISTEMOLOGY AND ETHICS

Reason is the life of the law; nay, the Common Law itself is nothing but reason.

(Sir Edward Coke)

The life of the law has not been logic; it has been experience.

(Oliver Wendell Holmes, Jr.)

On the wall hangs a large photograph, slightly warped, of the President of Austria, and a typed inventory of the furnishings which include a coatrack and a spittoon. On the dais stand a crucifix and a candlestick with one candle. The room remains empty for some ten minutes. Then a judge enters, followed by a kind of beadle... "Where are the files? Get my files." "Which ones?" "How should I know? What are we doing? Who's here?" "Nobody. We should have the mopeds at three o'clock." "It is seventeen minutes past four ..." The judge's eye falls on me. "Do you want anything?" I explain that I have come to study the Austrian legal system. "Jeezus," says the judge.

(Sybille Bedford, The Faces of Justice, 218–20)

We do not have to travel so far as rural Austria for the suspicion to grow that the term *legal system* is a euphemism. The ritual of the courtroom fosters belief in a highly rational process. Facts are scrupulously weighed, rules of law are applied, and a conclusion is derived with clinical severity. But even the uninvolved spectator wonders about each of these stages. Do the real facts gain a hearing? Do the rules that are quoted represent more than a biased selection from a bag of assorted decisions and statutes? And does the outcome depend as

247

much on the psychology of judge and jurors as on the logic of dispassionate argument?

This chapter will dwell mainly on the relation of facts, rules, and decision in a trial. The question of legal ethics will be raised, in very general terms, for some conflict is apparent between the way an advocate employs facts and rules to support his clients and the way he submits to the demands of truth and justice. Yet the main concern of the chapter is with epistemology, a term that calls for a word of explanation.

Epistemology is the branch of philosophy that studies knowledge, and it has become a dominant theme (some say, an obsession) in the last three centuries. The straightforward question What *is* so? has been subordinated to the question How do I *know* what is so? If I have lost my wallet, the question where it is may be of vital interest to me but raises few theoretical worries. If, however, I am told that I lost consciousness for ten minutes after a fall and I ask where my consciousness was for that time, then you may suspect that I do not know what I mean. Similarly, the question whether the Loch Ness Monster exists will turn our attention directly to the depths of the lake—What is there? But the question whether God exists is seen by some as basically epistemological. How could we know if an answer is true or false? Do the facts we observe have any bearing? Is truth here a matter of reasoning, as in mathematics? Are our minds furnished to ask such questions meaningfully and to find an answer? Before undertaking a journey, examine your supplies and equipment.

Traditionally, the two main tendencies in epistemology have been called "empiricism" and "rationalism." The empiricist stresses the part played by experience in knowledge. Every idea originates in what we have observed (grasped through our senses). Our talk does in various ways go beyond this. We generalize, imagine, and speculate. Yet the truth of whatever we say is shown only through further appeal to observation. A statement that could not in principle be verified (or falsified) by reports from our senses, and that does not even contribute toward such tests, is meaningless.

The rationalist, though not denying the importance of sensation, offers a greater role to our thinking and reasoning. Mathematics was a favorite example for Plato: we deduce the theorems of geometry without aid of ruler or protractor. Early astronomy drew its conclusions about the heavens without the support of telescopes. But it is in morality and theology that the influence of rationalism was strongest. Ideas of justice and of God were said to be "innate," present in the mind before we encounter the confusing facts of experience; how else could we know all actual states or rulers to be unjust?

Immanuel Kant is traditionally seen as offering some reconciliation of the two traditions. Ideas without experience are empty, but experience without ideas is blind. An astronomy based on pure thinking is useless, yet each fact of experience is directed by a mental contribution that we make through our *a priori* ideas and our ways of questioning. Though the empiricist can show that oxidation caused the fire, he is powerless to prove that every event must have some cause.

The practicing lawyer is inclined to be an empiricist. He deals with the facts that come to him through witnesses and with rules that are the facts of legislative will or judicial decision. His goal is the further fact of a favorable judgment, secured through the techniques of advocacy. However, many of those who write on the law, or teach it, are somewhat more concerned to work out a system of ideas and principles; they do not aspire to the precision of geometry, but they see their task as one of minimizing the arbitrary and extending the reign of reason.

In one of Arthur Train's many novels about the law, a legal student is warned: "They tell you out at the law school that the law is a wonderful science—the perfection of reason. It is in fact a hodge-podge of Roman law, Bible texts, canon law, superstitions, scraps of feudalism, crazy fictions, and long dead statutes. Your professors try to bring order out of chaos and make sense where the devil himself couldn't find any." Our discussion of the epistemology of law will try to recognize both cynicism and idealism. The raw facts of history account for much that stands as law. Yet reason assumes many forms and, though the devil may work with chaos, no lawyer can avoid the perpetual search for system.

23. QUESTIONS OF FACT AND QUESTIONS OF LAW

On February 24, 1964, in the town of Ralu'a, District of Villa Alta, State of Oaxaca [Mexico], there arrived at nine thirty before this municipal authority a Mr. Ignacio Andres Zoalage, merchant, fifty-five years of age. He explained the following: "I am coming to make a complaint about the chauffeur of the cream-colored truck that is on the platform, in the middle of which is a bruised basket of chiles weighing forty-seven and a half kilograms." The chauffeur of the cream-colored truck was called; he arrived fifteen minutes later and said that his name was Mario Valdez Herrero, chauffeur of the truck. The Court President asked him whether it was true that he had bruised the basket of chiles, and he answered: "Actually, I bruised it, but this happened because I don't have anyone to advise me. It is also the truck owner's fault because he ought to let me have a helper. Also, I could not see because the driver's compartment is high. Besides, it is the señor's fault—they put the things they have for sale on the ground, knowing that there is truck traffic."

The Municipal Court President asked Mr. Ignacio Andres: "Why did you put your merchandise down, knowing that the truck would go by?" Mr. Andres answered that there was room for the truck to pass. The chauffeur then said that this was not true, as the space there was at an angle. Mr. Andres said: "Look, Mr. President, the truck came this way, then this way and that way." The Municipal Court President said it would be most convenient in this case if the chauffeur paid for the damage he had caused, and the basket of chiles should be brought in, so an estimate could be made of how much of it had been spoiled.

The plaintiff left and the Municipal Court President ordered the magistrate to have the merchandise brought in. The magistrate returned with the owner, carrying a basket of chiles. They emptied it on the floor. The court magistrate observed the chiles on the floor and put aside the damaged chiles; he then told the President that the quantity ruined was about one and a half kilograms. The Municipal Court President asked the owner of the basket how much he wanted to be paid for the damage. Mr. Andres answered that it was not much—three pesos. The President told the chauffeur that he had to pay three pesos for the damage. Upon this the chauffeur said: "All right, I will go right now for the three pesos." Meanwhile the Municipal Court President reminded the plaintiff to be more careful on the next occasion and to watch where he put his booth—not to put it just anywhere and especially not in front of a truck. Thus this case was closed and the owner walked out with his load of chiles, leaving the damaged merchandise with the municipal authority.[1]

Few cases brought to the courts of justice are so simple and few reach so happy a settlement. Though the scene is a courtroom, the atmosphere is that of a society with strong roots in custom. We find the living law at work, and no book of law is opened. Suppose, however, agreement had been less easy. What questions of fact would have needed investigation? Was the driver's vision so obstructed that he could not, by taking "reasonable" measures, have seen the chiles? Was there adequate room for legitimate traffic? Did the merchant deliberately place his goods where the chances of such an incident would be increased? Notice that he received a warning from the court president. And what about the unclarified questions of law? There seems to us some difference between being told it is "convenient" to pay for damage and being ordered to do so as a matter of legal obligation. Could the award of three pesos have been lowered through proof of negligence on the part of the merchant? Could it have been increased, by punitive damages, if malice had been shown on the part of the driver? Do you expect that this case, for which no precedent was cited, would serve as a precedent in future decisions?

Consider the shift that takes place from questions of fact to questions of law in a similarly rustic case that reached an appeals court in this country almost a century earlier.[2] Thomas Haslem went to the trouble of gathering into piles the horse manure that had been deposited along some stretch of a public road. Two hours of labor on an April evening collected six dollars' worth, and Haslem intended to cart the fertilizer to his land when he had finished his regular work the next day. In the morning, however, William Lockwood noticed the piles and transported them to his own farm. In the trial that followed, Lockwood claimed that the manure, "being dropped upon and spread out over the surface of the

---

1. Laura Nader, "Styles of Court Procedure," in *Law in Culture and Society* (Chicago: Aldine, 1969), 74. Printed with permission of the author.
2. Haslem v. Lockwood (1871): 37 Conn. 500.

earth, remained part of the real estate of the borough, subject to the public easement," and would have "changed its nature to that of personal estate" only when safely removed to Haslem's farm.

Lockwood won the decision of the lower court, and those who wish to follow the drama further can consult the reports of the appellate court of Connecticut. There they will find half a dozen pages devoted to a profound discussion, not only of real and personal property, but of such concepts as possession, abandonment, and reasonable time. Though six dollars would have bought more in those days, the tone of fantasy is strong. However, the very simplicity of the facts serves to bring home the complex questions of law that pervade our daily life. Whether we are driving a vehicle or making a purchase or earning our daily pay, every fact we encounter is penetrated by rules, and even the most abstruse legal discussion is an effort to convey what actually happens.

Fact Skepticism

> For convenience, let us symbolize a legal rule by the letter R, the facts of a case by the letter F, and the court's decision of that case by the letter D. We can crudely schematize the conventional theory of how courts operate by saying: $R \times F = D$.
>
> (Jerome Frank, *Courts on Trial* [Princeton, N.J.: Princeton Univ. Press, 1949], 14)

Jerome Frank, a legal realist and noted critic of courtroom procedures, distinguishes between "rule skeptics" and "fact skeptics." The former situate the problems and ambiguities of law at the level of rules. That there are grave difficulties in finding what rules apply is evident. This is why a layperson hires a lawyer, one who has passed through a lengthy training in "finding the law." However, Judge Frank's criticism of such training has to do with its excessive concentration on rules and its attention to appeals courts rather than trial courts. He classifies himself as a "fact skeptic" because he holds that our primary difficulty, in the legal process, is at the level of facts. He explains at length the obstacles that our legal procedure contributes to the discovery of "objective facts" and he claims that a court's decision comes from the application of rules to "subjective facts," those that are "processed by the trial court, indeed made by it." Hence, whereas the above formula should read "$R \times OF = D$," it turns out in practice to be "$R \times SF = D$" (Frank, *Courts on Trial*, 24).

He is no less skeptical than others about the "R," and we shall consider the problems of rule-discovery in the following chapter. Also, Frank has severe hesitations about the logical derivation of the decision that is the outcome of the equation. But, for the present, our interest is in questions of fact. Why is it so difficult for a court to disclose what actually happened? And what epistemological problems are raised by the distinction between "objective" and "subjective"?

The practical problems in finding the facts of a case are evident; Frank dwells on them at length. A trial takes place long after the event, and the court works at a double remove—it is a witness to the testimony of witnesses. Little need be said about the fallibility of memory or about the way our mind interprets what our eyes have seen. We have no certainty how many shots were fired in the assassination of President Kennedy or where the sounds originated. Every policeman knows how accounts of a traffic accident are imbued with interpretations; a doctor tries in vain to eliminate amateur diagnosis from his patient's report of an illness. Even the most prosaic description involves fabrication, and memory is highly reconstructive. To this we must add the duress of a courtroom, the concern of witnesses for their stage appearance, and their awareness that each word serves the purpose of one side or the other in a contest.

More interesting is the theoretical question whether interpretation can, or should, be removed from an account of "what actually happened." When I see you reading this page, my report of what you are doing will be rather inadequate if I describe your eye movements and even if I include an account of the physiology of vision. I must be allowed to hazard some interpretation of your "mind," that is, of your intentions and projects and values. Or consider an actual court case about a boy who was struck by a passing car as he and a companion tried to cross the street in front of a stationary bus.[3]

> Plaintiff: The bus driver motioned for us to go on across.
> Defense: Objection.... It's a conclusion on the part of the witness.... He can tell what the operator did but he cannot tell what conclusions he drew from the operator's action.
> The Court: Objection sustained. You can tell us, Arthur, what the operator did.
> Plaintiff: He moved his hand diagonally... for us to go east.
> Defense: We'll object to this as being a conclusion on the part of the witness, what the motion meant. We don't object to his testifying as to what the operator's hands did but we do object to the interpretation of what the operator meant. Object to that and ask the jury be so instructed.
> The Court: Jury is so instructed.

The appeals court upheld the defendant: "Plaintiff was stating, not what he understood the bus driver's hand movements to mean but instead his conclusion as to what the bus driver meant by them."

Far-reaching questions are involved in this brief exchange. In its effort to get at the facts, a court is justified in removing gross interpretations of a state of mind. That you did not visit me in hospital is a fact. That you so avoided me from hatred, or from envy at my getting time from work with pay, is a paranoid

---

3. Smith v. Bocklitz, 344 S.W.2d 97 (Supreme Court of Missouri, 1961).

interpretation of your mind that I have contributed. However, we may ask whether the scrupulous removal of all interpretation from a human action does not demolish the fact itself. A clenched fist is not just a configuration of the hand but is an embodied meaning. Does a child first see the shape of his mother's mouth and then, by lengthy induction, infer anger or approval? Even animals identify moods before they do shapes.

Assault may be defined legally as an act that places a person in actual fear of an unpermitted touching of his or her person. Suppose a woman tells in court of a man's leering looks, threatening gestures, blind passion. Would you, if a judge, dismiss such language as giving conclusions rather than observations? If so, what sort of account would you admit as both objective and relevant to the law of assault?

Perhaps the closest I can come to a pure sensation, or report of the senses, is a pain. Even there, my talk about it must introduce some interpretation. I say where it is, describe it as sharp or throbbing, relate it causally to other facts. An experience devoid of all concepts would be ineffable. So if a court is asking for objective facts, it is specifying some degree of interpretation that is thought appropriate to the case on hand. Take an incident in which A threatens B with a gun and is shot by C. What did C do?[4]

He tensed his forefinger.
He fired a gun.
He shot A.
He shot an assailant.
He saved B's life.

Questioning and Objectivity

Perhaps what has been said can be summarized in the comment that we are fact skeptics, not merely because of poor vision, failing memory, and distorting interests, but because there is no such thing as a fact in itself. Every fact is an answer to questions we ask. The facts of science appear (exist) only when we raise scientific questions. Newton made Newtonian nature. The nature revealed to Wordsworth is no less a fact but results from different intentions.

Hence the topic of legal epistemology has to do with the sort of questions that a court or legal system allows and promotes. The distinction we make between questions of fact and questions of law is important but far from rigid. If you are appointed to a jury, you will be told that you are a "trier of fact." You do not need to know the law. You have simply to decide, on the evidence presented, whether the defendant did in fact do that with which he is charged. However, you are not sitting under a palm tree dispensing kadi justice. Your findings of fact are guided at every stage by complex rules of law.

---

4. This is a shortened version of an example developed by Eric D'Arcy in *Human Acts* (New York: Oxford Univ. Press, 1963), 3.

There are many variations in how this is done, and we shall look at some before long. But in no legal system are the parties simply invited to have their say. The rituals of mediation in some primitive societies can match the formalities of our own courtroom. Some notion of "legal relevance" guides what can or can not be admitted to establish a fact and justify a claim.

A glance at the record of one of our trial courts will show the style in which facts are established. Books are divided into paragraphs (and this is perhaps the way we proceed in the privacy of our mind). Yet the court moves by question and answer, often only a single line to each.

In the common law tradition it is the lawyer, rather than the judge, who occupies center stage. Critics complain about this, but the procedure does well illustrate the dependence of questions of fact on questions of law. What develops in the courtroom started in the lawyer's office. Everything he or she says to the client has one thought behind it: how can this complex human situation be translated into terms that will satisfy a court? A "case" is formulated that fits under established categories. What may seem vital to the client is dismissed, and much that seems trivial is subjected to detailed examination. The degree of importance attached to types of assertions will vary from one area of law to another. For example, more license may be allowed to talk about states of mind in contesting a will than in arguing negligence in a traffic accident.

Lawyers, speaking in court, are trying to win assent to propositions of fact. Those who perform their art well can point to the purpose behind every question they ask, to the subsumption of each fact under a question of law. Those who flounder may show something of the richness of life, but many of the facts they produce are legally irrelevant or turn to the aid of the opposition.

The responsibility an attorney has for the disclosure of what happened goes beyond the choice of questions to the language in which these are framed. To take a trivial but interesting example, a recent study showed that estimates of the speed of a car involved in an accident varied remarkably as the question was put in terms of a "contact," "bump," "collision," or "smash."[5]

Here lies also a basis for the charge of legalism. Legal and human relevance may not coincide. Those called to testify in court are seldom satisfied that they are allowed to tell their full story in the best way. Many a doctor feels frustrated that his effort to report the appropriate medical facts in court is blocked by the alien perspective of the law. Facts that an experienced marriage counselor would regard as critical are ignored and replaced with an effort to prove embarrassing artificialities in order to satisfy legal categories.

Trial by jury arose within the common law. However, the original juries were chosen for their knowledge of the defendant and of the case. This is a far cry from our present system, where the jurors are selected for their lack of knowledge and are condemned to be silent partners while all the questions are

---

5. From Elizabeth F. Loftus, in *Psychology Today* (Dec. 1974): 117–19; quoted by Monroe Freedman in *Lawyers' Ethics in an Adversary System* (Indianapolis: Bobbs-Merrill, 1975), 67.

put by professional advocates. Yet, as we shall see, in criminal trials within the civil law tradition, jurors may sit on the bench with the judge and contribute to the fact-finding process by posing questions themselves.

All that has been said supports Jerome Frank's claim that facts, as well as rules, are highly elusive. However, being a fact skeptic involves some ideal of the sort of facts to which we aspire, even if we fall short. And it is here that epistemological theories have an important bearing. Those of Frank seem to be plainly empiricist. He regrets that the "witness is not a photographic plate," that "the facts as they actually happened are twice refracted, ... shot through with [the] subjectivity" of the witness and of the court interpreting what he says (Frank, *Courts on Trial*, 17, 22). Such language comes straight from John Locke.[6] The mind is, or should be, a mirror that reflects what exists independently. Activity on the part of the mind may be a distortion of what exists apart from it. Frank sees the court laboring under the same disabilities as a historian, who must build his own interpretations upon those of previous ages (ibid., 37).

Nevertheless, doubts have been expressed above about what a fact would be "in itself." What Plato did and wrote is a fact, but certainly not free of interpretation. And it is not ridiculous to suggest that the successive views of historians can contribute to the disclosure of truth; we may be in a better position to know what Plato meant or intended than he did himself.[7]

Law involves a search for objective facts, yet we should not assume the term *objective* to be self-evident. If it means that which is originally given to the senses, then we are in the realm of the incommunicable. A sheer pain is mine and I can say nothing about it. Mirrors may reflect but they do not know what they reflect. Law is concerned with facts only so far as we can talk about them, and this means generalizing them, putting them under categories and rules. Murder, libel, and negligence are made up of facts impregnated with interpretation. Witnesses are fallible, but the complex courtroom procedure may lead us closer to what actually happened, much as the labors of historians try to do.

---

6. John Locke (1632–1704) was a disciple of Newton and proposed to develop an epistemology that would explain why science had succeeded so dramatically in its search for truth. Locke's basic answer was that science, through its stress on observation, respected the passivity of the objective mind. "The understanding is merely passive.... These simple ideas [impressions received from what exists in the world], when offered to the mind, the understanding can no more refuse to have, nor alter when they are imprinted, nor blot them out and make new ones itself, than a mirror can refuse, alter or obliterate the images or ideas, which the objects set before it do therein produce" (*An Essay Concerning Human Understanding*, book II, chapter 2, no. 25). Error enters when the understanding plays an active part and combines such ideas in ways that no longer reflect what exists apart from the mind; this, for Locke, resulted in the "superstition" of pre-scientific thinking (e.g., talk of unverifiable "essences").

7. At least Kant (1720–1804) makes this suggestion in his *Critique of Pure Reason* (B 370). Plato had "not sufficiently determined his concept," those guiding questions that help to disclose all he found to be so. The *Critique* is an investigation of the rightly active part that our mind plays in our very submission to truth. Interestingly, Kant often employs images drawn from legal procedures. He sees his whole work as that of establishing a tribunal or court to assess the claims of reason (A xi–xii). And he comments that, though reason must indeed submit to the facts that are presented, "it must not do so in the character of a pupil who listens to everything that the teacher chooses to say [as Locke held], but rather in the manner of a judge who compels the witnesses to answer questions which he has himself formulated" (B xiii).

Science is the field for which we most readily accept the term objectivity. Yet we should not forget that science is itself the result of social legislation; the enterprise of seeing the world scientifically becomes possible when we apply to experience the laws of conservation and the rule that we shall acknowledge only what is quantifiable. Though every day is unique, we construct a scientific world by designating events as "the same again." What is in no way repeatable escapes from the jurisdiction of science. Facts without rules are empty. The law of the courtroom is different from that of science, but no fact can enter that is not already under some rule or principle.

When, in Brecht's play, *Galileo*, the scientist was opposed by people who asserted the obvious experience that the sun goes round the earth, he replied: "They don't see, they just goggle." Galileo was advocating one rule for interpreting experience over another. And his later recantation was an admission that the rules he adopted as an astronomer might need to be subordinated to the rules that still organized a dominant way of seeing. So it is with all facts—they incorporate laws that express social priorities. Our own conviction that all people are created equal is no report of a raw fact but is a law for encountering others.

Jerome Frank speaks of rules as applied to facts in themselves. Rules certainly are applied, but only to facts already formulated by rules. Stripping away rules from facts is like peeling an onion, finding layer upon layer and no core by itself. Instead of "R × F" we discover:

$$R \{ R [R(RF)] \}$$

The rule of no spitting is not applied in a legal void but is a development of a situation where laws define areas of public and of private acts, and these laws in turn depend on more basic rules for respecting a person as a person.

The distinction we make between questions of fact and questions of law, between the province of the jury and that of the judge, is important but far from clear. Consider, for example, some cases that have so far been mentioned. Was Judge Crouch, in *People v. Sherwood* (section 6 above), invading the province of the jury by writing at length on the facts of Mrs. Sherwood's unhappy life, or was he contributing to a more adequate expression of the question of law? Was Judge Cardozo, in *Hynes v. N.Y.C. R. Co.* (section 10), making a proposition of fact or a ruling of law when he claimed that Harvey Hynes was not trespassing on railroad property but swimming in public waters?

There is an interesting corollary to such questions. Do juries merely pass judgment on facts or do they also criticize and change laws? For generations the law of negligence was that if the plaintiff contributed in any way to an accident, he or she could recover no damages (contributory negligence). But juries, taking this to be unjust, repeatedly failed to follow the rule. As a result, we now have a change in the law to that of proportional negligence, where plaintiff and defendant share the costs. Similarly, however clearly the law is explained to them, some juries are today refusing to return a verdict of murder on a wife who has retaliated for grievous suffering from her husband. Facts and rules are intimately combined in life and are not to be simply distinguished in court. The question raised by this introductory section is whether, in our search for what really happened, we should respect this "confusion" as constructive or should oppose it in the name of a distinction between objective facts and subjective additions.

FURTHER READING

One of the best ways to find how rules and facts come together is to follow a case in detail from the initial incident to the law offices of the attorneys and then through the resulting trial. This whole process has been recorded for a libel suit in Vermont by Marc A. Franklin in *The Biography of a Legal Dispute* (Mineola, N.Y.: Foundation Press, 1968).

For a similar account of a criminal case, see Philip B. Heymann and William H. Kenety, *The Murder Trial of Wilbur Jackson* (St. Paul: West, 1975).

An excellent anthology of what has here been called "legal epistemology" is that of William R. Bishin and Christopher D. Stone, *Law, Language, and Ethics* (Mineola, N.Y.: Foundation Press, 1972).

For a discussion of the relation between questions of fact and questions of law (with some distinctions not mentioned here), see Roy L. Stone, "Metaphysics and Law," *Duke Law Journal* (1969): 897–922.

For an interesting study of how religious and other basic beliefs play a part in what courts have taken to be relevant in cases under tort law, see Guido Calabresi, *Ideals, Beliefs, Attitudes and the Law* (Syracuse, N.Y.: Syracuse Univ. Press, 1985).

QUESTIONS FOR DISCUSSION

1. Suggest various ways in which the dispute over the damaged chiles could have been settled. A fight? A bargain? Mediation? Did the court president act as a judge or as an arbitrator? If he was indeed a court official, should he have revealed more concern for general principles, for a system of law? Did the Connecticut case (*Haslem v. Lockwood*) show inordinate anxiety about building and maintaining a rational system of concepts and rules? If you were the judge, would you have worked within the resources of the law library, or would you have visited the locality to find what people there thought to be right?

2. Suppose you are a judge and the following statements, made by a witness, provoke an objection from the defense attorney on the grounds that they offer conclusions rather than reporting facts. Which objections would you sustain? What purely factual account would you allow?

>He was driving drunkenly (carelessly) down the road.
>There was murder in his eyes.
>He crept furtively around the house.
>He was acting suspiciously.
>He gave me a dirty look and spoke abusively.

3. The libel case that Franklin records originated in a newspaper column that mistakenly reported the plaintiff as convicted of driving while intoxicated, whereas his offense had been to drive when his license was suspended. Suppose you are the lawyer to whom he turns. What legal rules will direct your discovery and presentation of the facts? Does it matter whether the truth of a statement is relevant to libel? Does it matter whether the mistake was made deliberately or not?

Does it matter whether the damage to reputation is specific (e.g., harm to business) or merely general (distress and anxiety)?

4. The complex rules of evidence prevent an attorney, in examining his witness, from asking leading questions. He may not, for instance, say "You did hear the shot before you saw the defendant, didn't you?" An answer is being fed into the mouth of the witness. However, is there not a sense in which all questions are "leading"? They define the issue and leave the respondent with little more to say than yes or no. Would it not be better if the witness were invited to explain at length, and in his own terms, what he knows? The analogy would be a job interview in which you are simply instructed "Tell me about yourself." The civil law tradition is, as we shall see, more open to such narrative accounts from witnesses.

5. Can you give an example of some fact that is not dependent on a rule or convention? What is the real color of the sweater you are wearing? Does this depend on a rule for viewing colors? Electric light or daylight? A north- or south-facing room? What happens as the sun gets older?

6. Is it a question of fact or a question of law whether the defendant exercised reasonable care? Whether A and B are married? Whether A made a promise to B? If I fail to clear my porch steps of ice and you break your leg, did I cause your injury? Does it make any difference whether you are an invited guest, a mailman, or an intruder?

7. A person is killed by a train moving up the trestle to a drawbridge over a river. The plaintiff appeals to a statute limiting the speed of a train crossing a drawbridge. Is the question whether a drawbridge includes the trestle one of fact (for the jury) or one of law (for the judge)? See Savannah, F. & W. Ry. v. Daniels, 1892, 90 Ga. 608, 17 S.E. 647.

8. Are objective facts those that strike our senses, with a minimum of interpretation, or those on which we agree? Suppose you find this room warm and I feel it chilly—how do we arrive at objectivity? Does reference to a thermometer take us closer to sheer facts or transport us into the realm of interpretations? If objectivity means agreement, do we achieve this by imposing rules on experience (such as, let warmth be measured by the length of a column of mercury)? What would you say to a student nurse who, after taking a patient's temperature, held the thermometer and said, "It feels cool"?

9. It is with facts in the past that a court is mainly concerned. Does our distance from the past hinder or help our access to what actually happened? Should memory serve as a mirror or be constructive? Is the true meaning of a text what the author intended at time of writing (see section 33 for a discussion of theories of interpretation)?

24. THE ADVERSARY SYSTEM

The layperson is unlikely to read books on law. More tedious fare is difficult to find. Yet interest is aroused by the crowning stage of a legal case. The trial provides an intense fascination, drawing together the threads of a complex story and giving it a dramatic focus. In sporting terms, we arrive at the final match of the championship.

Truth is revealed through trial. Theories must be put to the test. Opposing hypotheses in science are vindicated or silenced by the trial of an orderly experiment. Competing strategies of generals or economists are revealed as victor or vanquished in the battlefield or marketplace.

In law, divergent claims are made about rules and facts and about the way they come together. The moment of truth arrives in a trial, but this term covers a variety of procedures. At one extreme, these are relatively informal, spread out over time, and the questioning is left much in the hands of the official who gives the final judgment. Admission to a guild through lengthy apprenticeship might serve as a remote example. At the other extreme, the deciding official appears only after the competitors have done all the preliminary work of building their case; in a short encounter they try to prove themselves to him or her through highly formal tests. An analogy is presented in some universities where passing or failing depends exclusively on an examination at the end of the entire three- or four-year course of studies.

It is the latter procedure that is familiar to us in the common law. We refer to it as the "adversary system," and it will be the topic of this section. The former procedure is more characteristic of the civil law tradition, and the following section will indicate examples of what happens there.

Notice that our concern is now with procedural law. If a shipwreck leaves three people on a desert island, it is a question of substantive law or justice whether supplies and tasks should be divided equally among the three or allocated diversely according to need, achievement, merit, and other criteria. But once agreement has been made on the substance of the law, then procedures or rules must be devised for ensuring that resources and duties are so divided. The courtroom trial applies substantive law but is itself governed by procedural law.

Trials as Contests

> That an affinity may exist between law and play becomes obvious to us as soon as we realize how much the actual practice of the law, in other words a lawsuit, properly resembles a contest.... The sporting element and the humor so much in evidence in British legal practice is one of the basic features of law in archaic society.
> (Johan Huizinga, *Homo Ludens* [Boston: Beacon Press, 1955], 76–77)

There are many critics of the adversary system, and a frequent complaint is that the serious search for truth and justice is degraded by a courtroom spectacle that reminds us of a gladiatorial contest or a sporting event. In some societies, even today, it is a common practice for bets to be laid on the outcome of a trial. Our main suspicion about lawyers is that their concern is with gaining a victory rather than with disclosing what is so and following what is right.

It is in primitive societies that the play element in trials is most striking. Among the Eskimo, Hoebel found two remote parallels to our courtroom. One is the public confession for violation of religious tabus. The villagers accompany the penitent's self-accusations with a background chorus of appeals for forgiveness, and Hoebel speaks of the procedure as "theatrics and fun, a welcome diversion in an Arctic world" (E. Adamson Hoebel, *The Law of Primitive Man* [Cambridge: Harvard Univ. Press, 1954], 71). Contest between opponents is lacking there but is found in the settlement of disputes through wrestling, butting, and song duels. The last are a way of exchanging insults by improvising ridicule in highly conventional patterns of composition. The winner is the one who receives the loudest applause, yet no award follows other than the prestige of victory. The opponents are expected to be reconciled and even to exchange presents as a token of settlement.

With our own assumption that a trial must at least claim to be rational, we may suppose the Eskimos to believe that the hand of justice is on the side of the victor. Hoebel denies this. "There is no attempt to mete justice according to rights and privileges defined by substantive law. It is sufficient that the litigants feel relieved.... Supernatural forces do not operate to enhance the prowess of the singer who has right on his side" (Hoebel, *Primitive Man*, 99). If this fails, then, to be a trial by our own standards, perhaps these standards need to be questioned. The transfer of money from one party to another may be less important than a constructive readjustment of the way each party sees the other. And the transformation of a bitter dispute into an amicable contest could have much to do with the way law makes possible a society of people who live with mutual respect and acknowledgment.

It is said that the courtroom is a substitute for private warfare; the blood feud is sublimated into a battle of words.[8] Lawyers are mercenaries hired for their expertise with the appropriate weapons. Even if this is true, reminders of our animal origins should not blind us to the essential difference between a trial of strength and a trial at law. The parallel between a courthouse and a sports arena, though unkind to the legal profession, sets it firmly on the side of those civilizing agencies that replaced force with forbearance.

A history of the development of our modern trial would have to pass through many stages that we regard as strange and barbaric. Guilt or innocence was decided by a variety of ordeals: by the condition of a hand three days after it had been plunged into boiling water or made to carry hot iron, by one's ability to walk blindfold over red-hot ploughshares, by one's sinking or floating when thrown into cold water. Judgment was sought in various forms of competition, in the fall of sticks or the throw of dice. Commenting on such procedures, Huizinga writes: "The original starting point of the ordeal must have been the test as to who will win.... Only in a more advanced phase of religious experience will the formula run: the contest or ordeal is a revelation of truth and justice because some deity is directing the fall of dice or the outcome of the battle" (Huizinga, *Homo Ludens*, 81–82).

In medieval Europe this transition had certainly been made. The mind of God was seen behind all that happened, and an ordeal, when set within the full ritual of the Church, was an appeal to God's judgment as shown through the results. The medieval ordeal was a judicial process in which trust was put in a knowledge far superior to that of any human witness or arbitrator.

In England, under the influence of the Norman kings, the jury was established before the ordeal was abandoned. The earliest juries, however, had to do

---

8. Frank, *Courts on Trial*, chapter 2.

with the prosecution of crimes rather than with the rendering of a verdict. Twelve local knights were appointed to bring accusations, and then the verdict was left to trial by ordeal. An alternative trial was the "wager of law," in which the accused attempted to find twelve people who would, under the most severe religious sanctions, swear an oath to his innocence. In civil cases, a further option was "trial by battle," in which the accused and accuser could employ champions to fight for them, an interesting preview of our modern advocates.

A critical step came when, in 1215, the Fourth Lateran Council included in its thorough reform of the Church an order that the clergy should withdraw from the judicial function of administering trial by ordeal. However, this apparently did not reflect any loss of popular faith in such appeals to the judgment of God, and the resulting growth of the modern trial-jury met with considerable opposition. There was a clear awareness of human bias and of the difficulty of finding the facts through human means.

Yet the scene had been set for the growth of trial procedure as we know it in the common law. The king's justices, traveling on circuit, convened a jury in each village on the basis of the knowledge that the jurors were expected to have of local affairs and persons. This knowledge was thought to be enough for finding the truth in each case. Indeed, it was not until the sixteenth century that witnesses were allowed to present information. The decline of medieval society and the growth of the towns changed the jury's role from contributing information to giving impartial judgment on assertions made by witnesses. And as the common law developed its dependence on precedents, the focus of the trial gradually passed to legal professionals who could find their way through the maze. Each side in the controversy had its hired advocate who planned the strategy, collected evidence, called witnesses, cross-examined those of his opponent, and finally left little more to judge and jury than to give a verdict based strictly on what was presented in the trial through highly formal laws of evidence.

Our own concern is not with the details of this development or with the many variations we find today. But there are a number of philosophical questions we need to ask about the notion of "truth through contest" if we are to pass from legal epistemology to legal ethics.

Procedural Justice

The notion of pure procedural justice is best understood by a comparison with perfect and imperfect procedural justice. To illustrate the former, consider the simplest case of fair division. A number of men are to divide a cake: assuming that the fair division is an equal one, which procedure, if any, will give this outcome? Technicalities aside, the obvious solution is to have one man divide the cake and get the last piece, the others being allowed their pick before him. He will divide the cake equally, since in this way he assures for himself the largest share possible. This example illustrates the two characteristic features of perfect procedural justice. First, there is an independent criterion for what is a fair division, a criterion defined separately from and prior to the procedure which is to be followed. And second, it is possible to devise a procedure that is sure to give the desired outcome....

Imperfect procedural justice is exemplified by a criminal trial. The desired outcome is that the defendant should be declared guilty if and only if he has committed the offense with which he is charged. The trial procedure is framed to search for and to establish the truth in this regard. But it seems impossible to design the legal rules so that they always lead to the correct result.... Even though the law is carefully followed, and the proceedings fairly and properly conducted, [the trial] may reach the wrong outcome. An innocent man may be found guilty, a guilty man may be set free.... The characteristic mark of imperfect procedural justice is that while there is an independent criterion for the correct outcome, there is no feasible procedure which is sure to lead to it.

By contrast, pure procedural justice obtains when there is no independent criterion for the right result: instead there is a correct or fair procedure such that the outcome is likewise correct or fair, whatever it is, provided that the procedure has been properly followed. This situation is illustrated by gambling. If a number of persons engage in a series of fair bets, the distribution of cash after the last bet is fair, or at least not unfair, whatever this distribution is.... There is no independent criterion by reference to which a definite outcome can be known to be just.[9]

The distinctions that Rawls makes can help to clarify discussion about the respective merits of various trial procedures and about the morality of what lawyers do in the name of a certain legal system. The three types of procedural justice are distinguished by the presence or absence of two requirements.

Perfect procedural justice satisfies both requirements: there is an independent criterion of a just result, and there is a procedure that infallibly leads to it. We could independently find whether the slices of cake are equal by (for example) weighing them. And the simple procedure of assigning the last pick to the one who did the cutting ensures that the slices will be equal (if we make the obvious assumptions of self-interest and of accuracy with the knife). Such examples, however, are rare and trivial. Rawls's concern is with the way that one or the other of these requirements fails to be met in the questions of justice that we commonly encounter.

Where there is an independent criterion for the correct outcome but there is no infallible procedure, we have imperfect procedural justice. Rawls takes as his illustration the topic that interests us here, a legal trial. Some hesitations may spring to mind, but the common recognition (or at least fear) that innocent people have been found guilty, and vice-versa, supposes some criterion outside

---

9. Excerpted by permission of the publishers from *A Theory of Justice*, by John Rawls, pp. 85–86, Cambridge: The Belknap Press of Harvard University Press, copyright © 1971 by the President and Fellows of Harvard College.

the workings of the court. I and a few others may know of my innocence, or God does, though the jury found me guilty and all appeals failed. The relative merits of trial by ordeal, by judge, and by jury can be argued. Yet all are imperfect procedures for finding through a court what exists independently.

Pure procedural justice is shown when we overcome the imperfection of our procedures by the simple expedient of abandoning any claim to an independent criterion. Gambling is an evident example. After an hour with dice, a hundred dollars has passed from my pocket to yours. If the dice were not loaded and the rules were followed throughout, the result is perfectly just, and not because of your greater need or of my sin or of any criterion independent of our playing. The following of a fair procedure leads, by definition, to a fair outcome.

Let us now turn to a more pertinent illustration. The analogy of law to games has often been made, and we have noticed the claim that trials originated as sheer contests. The team I support has lost the World Series. Can I still affirm that they were the better team? Such claims are regularly made and may not be utter nonsense. But they can probably be reduced to a number of unverifiable hypotheses. If only our star pitcher had not pulled a muscle, or the ball had not taken a bad bounce, or the series had gone to an extra game! Or, in the realm of the verifiable, I may simply be pointing to a higher percentage of wins during the regular season or making a prediction for "next time." Yet the brute fact remains that justice was done in the actual series because there is no criterion of "better" apart from the result achieved by following the procedures (the example assumes no bribery or other deviation from the rules).

So the question arises whether Rawls is correct in classifying what happens in a trial as an example of imperfect procedural justice. An initial objection is that of the cynic who says, with Robert Frost, that "a jury consists of twelve persons chosen to decide who has the better lawyer." A more serious version of this complaint would put forward the theoretical position that only pure procedural justice is involved; the parallel between trials and games is said to be exact. The legal realist holds that when I ask what the law is, or whether I have a legal right, I am asking for a prediction. How will the courts decide in my case? To say I have a legal right to X is only to predict that I will win my fight for X if I engage in the contest. Talk of any law or rights beyond what the courts decide, or claims that a jury was wrong, are (allowing for full recourse to appeals) as "metaphysical" and as irrelevant as insistence that the losing team was still the better. The bearing of this tough-minded view on legal ethics will be discussed later.

A second, and intermediate, position may be described as "moderate realism": what has just been said is wrong in theory but must unfortunately guide what we do in practice. A vital change in legal theory took place when we passed from the ordeal as sheer contest to the ordeal as a revelation of God's knowledge and justice. The pure procedural justice of the song contest gave way to the imperfect procedural justice of trial by jury. Winning a game belongs to one world, aspiring to truth and justice belongs to another. However, there are grievous problems with such talk of a "second world." What independent criterion do we actually have of innocence in a criminal case or of rights in a civil one? We do not intuit the soul of the defendant. Nor indeed does he intuit his own—the possibilities of self-deception are limitless, and even admission of guilt is but matter for further trial. As for the civil suits, the scales of justice are empty apart from what the court puts in. Hence, though a theory that likens a courtroom to a sports arena is severely lacking, in practice the procedures are very close. Judges and juries, like umpires, must give decisions without delay and under pressure. The law does not make up their mind. All it provides is a process for taking deliberate steps toward a decision. We miss the point of the drama if we exclude all thought of an ulterior norm that could measure the decision as wrong; yet the only norm we can clearly see and apply is that of the formal correctness of the procedures we follow.

Possibly Rawls would not simply disagree, but he does, without such qualifications, offer criminal trials as his chosen example of imperfect, rather than pure, procedural justice. Here his view is the orthodox one and guides most discussions of legal ethics. Winning is not all. In practice as well as in theory there are some independent criteria of a just result. Though we are condemned to imperfect procedures, there are degrees of imperfection; our awareness of this supplies serious questions about the relative merits of different systems and traditions.

Even the firmest proponents of the adversary system admit to defects in it and are open to modifications. The evidence supplied by witnesses is limited and distorted. Should the rules of evidence be less restrictive? Should the witness be better protected against the fears of a stage appearance and the wiles of cross-examination, better helped to speak his own mind in his own words? Should he be so clearly branded as a witness *for* or *against* and be submitted to coaching by a partisan lawyer? And should the client be so much at the mercy of his lawyer for the design and conduct of his case? We expect the richer of two teams to hire the better players, but can we claim that a court discloses justice when we find the unequal competence of lawyers and the correlation this has to the fees they charge? Brains do not always go with money, yet when the investigation of facts and the hiring of expert witnesses is left in private hands, we can look for disparities in the strength of the cases presented.

Those who advocate changes in the adversary system usually suggest a move in the direction of procedures in the civil law tradition. The following section will indicate some of the differences. However, this section may close with a standard defense of the adversary system, consisting of a brief extract from a report of the American Bar Association.[10]

> The lawyer appearing as an advocate before a tribunal presents, as persuasively as he can, the facts and the law of the case as seen from the

---

10. "Professional Responsibility: Report of the Joint Conference," *American Bar Association Journal* 44 (1958); 1,159. Printed with permission from the *ABA Journal: The Lawyer's Magazine*.

standpoint of his client's interest.... In a very real sense it may be said that the integrity of the adjudicative process itself depends upon the participation of the advocate. This becomes apparent when we contemplate the nature of the task assumed by any arbiter who attempts to decide a dispute without the aid of partisan advocacy.

Such an arbiter must undertake, not only the role of judge, but that of representative for both of the litigants. Each of these roles must be played to the full without being muted by qualifications derived from the others. When he is developing for each side the most effective statement of its case, the arbiter must put aside his neutrality and permit himself to be moved by a sympathetic identification sufficiently intense to draw from his mind all that it is capable of giving,—in analysis, patience and creative power. When he resumes his neutral position, he must be able to view with distrust the fruits of this identification and be ready to reject the products of his own best mental efforts. The difficulties of this undertaking are obvious. If it is true that a man in his time must play many parts, it is scarcely given to him to play them all at once.

It is small wonder, then, that failure generally attends the attempt to dispense with the distinct roles traditionally implied in adjudication. What generally occurs in practice is that at some early point a familiar pattern will seem to emerge from the evidence; an accustomed label is waiting for the case and, without awaiting further proofs, this label is promptly assigned to it. It is a mistake to suppose that this premature cataloguing must necessarily result from impatience, prejudice or mental sloth. Often it proceeds from a very understandable desire to bring the hearing into some order and coherence, for without some tentative theory of the case there is no standard of relevance by which testimony may be measured. But what starts as a preliminary diagnosis designed to direct the inquiry tends quickly and imperceptibly to become a fixed conclusion, as all that confirms the diagnosis makes a strong imprint on the mind, while all that runs counter to it is received with diverted attention.

An adversary presentation seems the only effective means for combatting this natural human tendency to judge too swiftly in terms of the familiar that which is not yet fully known. The arguments of counsel hold the case in suspension between two opposing interpretations of it. While the proper classification of the case is thus kept unresolved, there is time to explore all of its peculiarities and nuances.

FURTHER READING

Bloomstein, Morris J. *Verdict: The Jury System.* New York: Dodd Mead & Co., 1972.
Bonsignore, John J., et al. *Before the Law.* 3d ed. Boston: Houghton Mifflin Co., 1984, "The Jury as a Form of Community Participation," 334–98.
DiPerna, Paula. *Juries on Trial.* New York: Dembner Books, 1984.
Forsyth, William. *History of Trial by Jury.* New York: B. Franklin, 1971.
Frank, Jerome. *Courts on Trial.* Princeton, N.J.: Princeton Univ. Press, 1949, 5–13, 80–102.
Frankel, Marvin E. *Partisan Justice.* New York: Hill and Wang, 1980.

Friedland, Martin, ed. *Courts and Trials: A Multidisciplinary Approach.* Toronto: Univ. of Toronto Press, 1975.

Huizinga, Johan. *Homo Ludens: A Study of the Play Element in Culture.* Boston: Beacon Press, 1955.

Kalven, Harry, and Hans Zeisel. *The American Jury.* Boston: Little, Brown & Co., 1966.

Landsman, Stephan. *The Adversary System: A Description and Defense.* Washington, D.C.: American Enterprise Institute, 1984.

Wellman, Francis L. *Day in Court.* 1910. Reprint. Littleton, Colo.: F. B. Rothman & Co., 1986.

QUESTIONS FOR DISCUSSION

1. Think of various ways you use the word *trial* outside the legal context. You proceed by trial and error. You take a new car on a trial run. You attend athletic trials or horse trials. What is common to these uses and to the legal term? Are you testing something to see how it matches expectations or compares with rivals? Distinguish between formal and informal tests. Distinguish between judgments of victory in a race and in figure skating.

2. Would you classify an examination at college as a contest or as a trial? If a student finds that he can score well without a thorough knowledge of the subject, would you accuse him of dishonesty? Would you think the teacher has failed as a judge?

3. Explain Hoebel's remark that the song contests of the Eskimos had nothing to do with substantive law. Explain Huizinga's claim that trial by ordeal passed from a sheer contest to a revelation of truth and justice. If your historical imagination can put you back into the Middle Ages, can you understand the reluctance to accept jury verdicts as a replacement? Knowing as we do how difficult it is for any group of people to agree, do we retain an almost religious acceptance of jury verdicts?

4. In his account of the first year at Harvard Law School (*One L*), Scott Turow describes how students who had shown brilliance in the classroom failed to get high grades when their merit was assessed in a three-hour examination where complete anonymity was maintained for their papers. Does this suggest hesitations about a legal system in which a person's fate is decided in a brief, highly formalized trial, before a judge and jury who know nothing of him or her from outside that event?

5. Think of examples to illustrate Rawls's distinction between imperfect and pure procedural justice. When is it, or is it not, meaningful to say, "I lost but I was right?" At what games might you say, "I lost though I was the better player"? What independent criteria of success or merit can you find in games? In a legal trial? When we speak of a miscarriage of justice, are we appealing to criteria outside the legal process or are we simply proposing an extension of that process from trial to retrial?

6. Can you support the claim that "a legal right is a case you win" by distinguishing between *legal* and *moral* rights? If, for example, the courts of your jurisdiction support racial inequality, a lawyer who tells you that you have no legal right in that regard is simply predicting that you will lose in court; but he may add that your claim is morally justified, or that you are equal before God.

7. Do you agree with the A.B.A. remark above that "a man in his time must play many parts but cannot play them all at once"? Why should you not sympathize fully with two sides and still come to an impartial assessment? Do you not do that much of the time? Plato defined thought as "a dialogue of the soul with itself." Later philosophers have detected (or imposed) a pattern of "thesis, antithesis, and synthesis" in all thinking.

8. If you insist on your ability to play the roles of plaintiff, defendant, and judge at once, are you prepared to admit how this can become very difficult in ill-defined situations? When the question at issue is clear, it may be possible to see all sides. But suppose it is by no means evident

what exactly is the question? Does partisan advocacy help to suggest some statements of the issue that are likely to be missed by one judge, however imaginative his or her thinking? Can a judge be expected to show the practical experience and detailed knowledge that a specialized advocate may bring to the presentation of a client's case?

9. A sustained condemnation of the adversary system is to be found in Anne Strick's book, *Injustice for All* (1977). She sees the main fault of this system as promoting "tunnel vision": "One side gets up and yells white and the other side yells black, but no one is helped to explore shades of gray." Is it significant that an opponent of the adversary system must enter the lists in a partisan way by writing a book that breathes the spirit of combat on every page? Is truth itself the resultant of an adversary procedure?

25. ALTERNATIVES IN THE CIVIL LAW TRADITION

We give high praise to a person when we say that he or she exercises good judgment. What is meant by the compliment will, however, vary with people and situations. The judgment of an engineer about construction materials differs from that of a politician about campaign strategies, and this again from the judgment of a statesman in an international crisis. There are many possibilities for combining rules and facts to yield decisions.

Notable differences appear in the way courts come to their judgment, and a study of this yields insights into national character and into diverse expectations of what legal institutions should accomplish. The traveler abroad observes the architecture and art, the habits of people on their way to work or relaxing in a restaurant, the rituals from passport control to public holidays. However, the visitor is unlikely ever to attend a court of law in session. The reasons are obvious but the loss is great. It is in the daily application of the law that some telling features of a country's life are revealed.

In Communist lands the most striking departure from our own assumptions comes to light. There an individual is on trial, but almost every word suggests a broader design. "The most important function of the Soviet court is the fundamental remaking of the consciousness of the people" (comment of a chief justice of the Soviet Union). The individual stands for those who have not yet fully appreciated their membership in the community and have not yet accepted the total reformation of society that is underway. The goal of the Soviet criminal courts is not to render particular verdicts with a tacit acceptance that the line of defendants will continue indefinitely. The courts take their place in a grand scheme of re-education. The atmosphere is that of a sermon from the bench aimed at confession by the defendant. Proof that he was drunk at work and stole a pair of rubber boots worth five dollars is almost irrelevant compared with the task of helping each person to see that society is *his* and that to rob another is to rob himself. Though there were no previous convictions in this case, the sentence was to one year in a labor colony. This may strike us as harsh, and we wonder about practical results in a land where security measures are so tight and where windshield wipers are locked inside cars to prevent theft. But we should not forget that the courts are doing away, once and for all, with the sad business of courts.[11]

This section, however, is concerned with a less dramatic alternative to the way our common law courts see their function and come to judgment. An example will be given of a criminal trial in Germany, and then some general remarks will be made on the difference, in civil procedure, between our own "concentrated" trials and the "discontinuous" or "episodic" trials of France and Germany.

Though some detail must be supplied, the guiding question is about variations in the way truth is disclosed. Before a trial can resolve an issue, we must arrive at a definition of what the issue is. Here we have a range of options. Perhaps the basic one is whether definition should simply precede resolution or whether the two processes are so related that they should advance together. The logical mind will ask how we can decide a debate without first being able to state the motion with maximum clarity. Yet we may also look favorably on a model where the question comes painfully to light through a number of conferences and a sequence of restatements.

A German Example

Novelists have often set scenes in a courtroom, but Sybille Bedford is possibly the only writer to have devoted a book to reporting actual trials she attended in her travels through five countries.[12] Her visit to Germany started in Karlsruhe, at the highest criminal court of the state of Baden-Würtemberg. Before nine on an October morning in 1959 she found a trial in progress.

> The man who stood talking almost casually without a warder or a guard, punctuated rather than examined by the bench, was the accused telling the story of his life to his judges as the first step of his trial for homicide. He was a [forty-one-year-old] doctor in the German Army and he had shot a man in a public park who had exposed himself indecently to the doctor's small daughter.... The charge was neither manslaughter nor murder but—in the nearest English approximation—wounding with intent to do grievous bodily harm resulting in death.

Near him sat his defense lawyer, and across the room was the prosecutor. There was no witness box. Facing the defendant and spectators was a table with eight men and one woman. Three of these were judges, one presiding and two assisting. The other six were jurors (*Schöffen*). They are taken by lot from a list of substantial citizens and, in this case, included an executive and a factory

---

11. For examples of trial procedure in a variety of Russian courts, see *Justice in Moscow*, by George Feifer (New York: Simon & Schuster, 1964). A graduate of Harvard, Feifer was working for his doctoral dissertation on Soviet law when he recorded this account of a year attending the courts of Moscow.
12. Sybille Bedford, *The Faces of Justice: A Traveller's Report* (New York: Simon & Schuster, 1961). What follows is drawn from pp. 101–51 and is printed with permission of the author.

manager. The number of judges and jurors has been changed since the time of Mrs. Bedford's visit, and it varies with the importance of the case; but such "collegiality" is a principle of trials in the civil law tradition, each member having one vote in the deliberations. It is of interest that the common law system of a jury that sits apart and comes to a verdict on its own was tested in both France and Germany but abandoned.

The most striking departure from common law procedure is that the examination of witnesses is conducted by the judge, not by defense and prosecution, and that the defendant plays a central role throughout rather than sitting still unless his attorney decides to call him as a witness. So, under questioning by the presiding judge, Dr. Brach explained the details of the incident that took place early one Saturday afternoon in February of that year. His daughter had just returned from school and told her father she had been accosted again by the man who had indecently exposed himself to her on various occasions for almost a year. Brach at once took her in his car and retraced the route by which she had come. At the edge of the city park she identified the man. Leaving his daughter in the car, Brach followed him on foot into the park, intending to conduct an arrest and take him to the nearest police station.

The park was almost deserted, but Brach managed to secure the help of a teenage boy. The three of them walked, arguing, across the park and came to the wall. There the fifty-one-year-old man suddenly hauled himself up on a tree and attempted to escape over the wall. The boy caught him by the foot. Brach continues the account:

> "Next thing I knew he was half in the tree and half on the wall and I thought: Oh my God, he's getting away, he's nearly across, and I fired two shots into the air to stop him. To my horror he didn't stop; the only thing left to do was to get him in the leg or foot so that he couldn't go on and escape, and I fired. He came down at once. I thought he must be wounded and went to him to give first aid; he died under my hands...."
> "Dr. Brach, let us be quite clear about this. Did you intend to fire the third shot, or did it go off?"
> "I intended to fire if I had to, it may have gone off before I was ready. I'm not sure...."
> "Dr. Brach, were you accustomed to handling a revolver?"
> "As a medical officer I had nothing to do with such things."
> "You told us earlier today that you were called up and served during the war, before you were even a medical student."
> "Yes, but—"
> "In heaven's name, man, didn't you know that a revolver is about the most uncertain, unsafe weapon there is?"
> ... It was a strange experience to hear this presentation of a case by both sides, as it were, in one; not a prosecution case followed by a defense case, but an attempt to build the whole case, the case as it might be presented in a summing-up, as it went. A strange experience to hear the (attenuated) inquisitorial procedure at work, to hear all questions, probing

questions and soothing questions, accusatory and absolving questions, questions throwing a favourable light and questions having the opposite effect, flow from one and the same source, the bench, and only from the bench, while public prosecutor and counsel for the defense sat mute, taking notes.

When the examination of the accused was over, the witnesses were called. The first, and most important, was Schmitt, the apprentice pastry cook whose help was obtained by Dr. Brach in the pursuit across the park. The judge interrogated Schmitt closely about the vital moment when he had the older man firmly in his grasp and was then made to release his hold by the sudden appearance and firing of a revolver. The judge turned again to Brach to inquire if he agreed with Schmitt's account of what was done and said.

Then the jurors were asked whether they wanted to question the witness, a possibility that some could use with profit in our own courts. After that, the prosecutor asked Schmitt a question and counsel for the defense was heard for the first time (also a single question). Finally—and if anything shows the tenor of such a trial, it is this—Dr. Brach was invited to interrogate Schmitt about his evidence. A similar multiplicity of approaches to the contribution of the other witnesses was allowed. And when it was found that the court had no record of previous complaints to the police from Mrs. Brach, the prosecutor agreed to arrange for an immediate investigation of the files and for the presentation of this evidence on the following morning.

In the afternoon the whole court went to the park to stage a reconstruction of the incident. A law student took the dead man's part and attested to the difficulty of swinging from tree to wall. It was dusk by the time the courthouse was reached again and the testimony of the remaining witnesses could be heard. At 7:30 P.M. the court adjourned.

On the following morning, a professor from Heidelberg University gave a lengthy account of psychiatric explanations of exhibitionism, and Dr. Brach's own character was discussed by those who had interviewed him. The "expert" is, in civil law countries, not classified as a witness; he is summoned by the court, and thus the spectacle is avoided of a clash between highly paid experts who are called to support the position of one side. Whether the resulting testimony is more balanced is an open question.

The evidence was then closed and the prosecutor and defense attorney took the only significant part they played in the trial:

> The prosecutor began straightaway by stating that he was satisfied that there was no evidence of any intent to kill. Then, in a long-winded, lifeless speech, he went through the factual evidence in a review that was more in the nature of a judicial summing-up than a presentation of a prosecution case.... [His duty is] to present the true facts of a case rather than press for a conviction *per se*. Coming to the position in law, he said it was true that under Paragraph 127 of the Code of Criminal Procedure any citizen had the right to arrest an offender caught red-handed. The pursuit of the deceased

might fall within this meaning.... But the law did not admit of any physical violence used or harm inflicted in such an arrest or pursuit. Therefore the third shot fired by Dr. Brach, a shot fired with the intention to wound, was not justified under that law.... He therefore submitted that Dr. Brach be found guilty of intent to do grievous bodily harm resulting in death....

It is the rule for the prosecution, and defense, to end their pleadings with an exact submission as to sentence, and this was now awaited with considerable suspense.... [The prosecutor reminded the court of] the Army regulation under which any member of the armed forces sentenced to one year or more of prison was automatically dismissed from the service. "I therefore submit to the Venerable Court that a sentence of ten months would be the just and sufficient retribution in this case."

... [Counsel for the defense was then called to speak.] The faintly loutish young lawyer, who had sprawled through most of the case, took at once to the wings of rhetoric. Striding the floor and flapping the wings of his gown, he got off on a sustained *vibrato*.... His client had never had the slightest intention of exercising self-justice. His one, his almost obsessive aim throughout had been to deliver up an offender to the lawful representatives of justice. The speech went on for an hour and a half ... and ended on a single sentence: "In the name of the people, I ask you to return a verdict of Not Guilty."

The final word, as always, was offered to Dr. Brach. There was then no judicial summing-up but judges and jurors withdrew at two o'clock to consider their verdict.

The deliberations are in secret. However, there are notable differences from the task of a common law jury, meeting apart from professional judges. Regulations cover the manner in which the discussions are to be held. There is, for example, a precise order of voting, with jurors before judges and the presiding judge last. Voting rules (which have changed slightly since the time of the Brach trial) require two-thirds for conviction and for the sentence, which is then announced along with the verdict. Perhaps most important, the decision must be justified publicly in two ways. An oral statement is made at the end of the trial to indicate general grounds for the disposition of the case. Then, within five weeks, a written judgment must be prepared, following a clearly defined form, and giving an authoritative version of the reasons for the decision. Hence a publicly available "opinion" is required of trial courts. A significant distinction from our own appellate court opinions, however, is that the judgment is impersonal and pretendedly unanimous: no dissenting or doubting opinion is allowed, even if the actual deliberations were sharply divided.

[At 6:00 P.M. the judges and jurors returned.] The presiding judge spoke at once. "In the name of the people—Ulrich Brach has been found Guilty. The sentence of the court is four months prison. This sentence will be deferred for a period of three years.... If within these three years no new

offence has been committed, the prison term will not have to be served....
The defendant will pay the cost of the prosecution."

Trials as Conferences

Had Dr. Brach's fate been decided in a common law land, the process would have reached its climax in a trial that assumed, from beginning to end, the form of a contest between adversaries. The at first amorphous question about what he had done would have been presented as yielding two clearly opposed replies. Initiative in the trial would have passed to the defense and prosecution, each trying to gain the assent of judge and jury to a partisan discovery of the facts and interpretation of the rules. The jury is happily ignorant of both facts and rules before the trial. It is hoped that the judge knows the law, but he or she will allow each lawyer to press a discrepant account of it and of its application to the facts.

The different procedure shown in Dr. Brach's case was described by Sybille Bedford as "inquisitorial," though she added the qualification "attenuated." In a purely non-adversarial inquiry into truth, there would not have been defense or prosecution attorneys to play even the limited role that they did. There would, of course, still have been two sides to the question. It might, however, be more accurate to speak of many sides, many ways of saying what Brach did and how right or wrong it was. The judge, in a pure inquiry, would have gradually explored all possibilities.

What we saw in the Brach case was an attenuated inquisition largely because the trial was separated from the preliminaries that took place between February and October. The leading actor in those was the prosecutor, and his work over the eight months had already reduced the many possible questions to a formulation not so far removed from that of the adversary system when a trial begins. Hence, though the judge dominated the trial and enjoyed a room for maneuver denied to his common law counterpart, his questioning was much restricted to possibilities that had already been defined.

This concentration of the judicial function into what we usually call a trial has much to do historically with the presence of jurors. These make their living in other ways and can spare limited time for participating in the legal process. However, if the term *trial* applies to the way judgment is formed on facts and rules, then a trial is by no means confined to the "day in court" that comes as a public spectacle at the end. In a broad but legitimate sense, Dr. Brach's trial began in February and passed through a complex series of interviews and investigations conducted by many officials.

Though the role of a jury has been much reduced in common law lands, legal procedure is still dominated by the fact or fiction that jurors will eventually appear and give their verdict. Elsewhere, experiments with a jury have been restricted to criminal cases. Hence a rapid look at civil procedure in France and Germany may indicate some possibilities of further departure from an adversary system. Though there is still a progress that leads to culmination in a decision, it is much less easy to separate any trial from what precedes it.

A civil case, in all traditions, differs from a criminal one in that the proceedings must be begun, not by the state, but by an individual with a grievance. Working through a lawyer, he puts this in writing (*assignation* in France, *Klageschrift* in Germany) to report his grounds for appealing to the law, what he intends to prove, and what he demands. He sends one copy to the court and another to his opponent. The latter then also employs a lawyer and submits his reply; this may be brief or detailed or may not even be required in Germany. The court thus takes notice of the case and sets a date, usually within a month, for the two parties and their lawyers to appear. One judge or a panel of judges may be present. In a very simple case, resolution could be possible at this initial appearance. Much more likely, it will turn out to be the first in a series of conferences.

The ideal, at least, is one of informality. In a succession of meetings it will become gradually clear what is at stake, what each side wants to achieve and is prepared to yield, what has to be proved and what documents or oral evidence will secure this. The possibilities of settlement are continually explored. There is no prescribed number of such meetings. Each time the court sets a date for the next one and suggests what part of the case will form the focus and what each party should bring. Proof can be taken in any order as a file is gradually built up on the case.

It is both possible and anticipated that the position of each side will change as the conferences proceed. The pressure of a concentrated trial is taken away, where the attorney must know in advance exactly what he or she is required to prove and must have at hand all the means to do so. Instead, the examination of a witness may open up a new field of inquiry and suggest the possibility of further evidence. The lawyers have time to study such developments, make new investigations, and revise their strategy.

What is sacrificed is the immediacy of the adversary system, where the final judgment is based on what has just been presented, where memories are fresh and the demeanor of all participants enters more directly. The tradition of the civil law still labors under the burden of some medieval procedures; for example, it was once required that all evidence be taken in writing and later be passed, for decision, to a judge who never saw the witnesses. However, there is a move (notably in Germany) to immediacy and "orality" in civil proceedings.

Some commentators protest against the usual description of the civil law tradition as "inquisitorial," insisting that the determination of the issues remains a responsibility of the parties rather than of the judge. The court is in theory bound to decide the case on the basis of what the parties have submitted. Yet there is certainly a difference in degree from the adversary system with which we are familiar. As we saw in Dr. Brach's case, the presiding judge is vocal and dominant and the lawyers relatively silent. In Germany, especially, the judge follows the principle that the court knows the law without depending on the parties to bring it to his attention. He is obliged to discuss the legal possibilities freely with the litigants, to clarify differences, and in a variety of ways to indicate what path is to be followed. The plaintiff and defendant are left to follow suggestions or not, and the responsibility of proof is theirs. But in many respects the manner of the judge may strike us as closer to that of an arbitrator than an adjudicator, and his opportunities for "therapeutic restatement" are greater. In certain details, also, he has considerable powers. He can himself summon experts or ask for documents to be produced or inspect localities that seem relevant to the case.

There are variations in the way that witnesses are examined, but nowhere do we find them exposed to the partisan treatment they receive from counsel for plaintiff or defense in the common law. In both France and Germany it is a breach of professional ethics for an attorney to speak to witnesses before they appear in court. Hence, coaching is eliminated. In court, the witness is first asked by the judge to tell in his own words what he knows about the relevant matter. It is then the judge who interrogates him on what has been said. The lawyer who wishes to question a witness must first submit to the court and to the opposing counsel an account of what is to be asked. These questions are then put by the judge, or if (as in Germany) the lawyer is himself allowed to lead the inquiry, this is brief and lacks the rigors of what we know as cross-examination. An experienced German lawyer mentioned that he is wary of asking more than three questions of a witness, lest he imply incompetence on the part of the court.

This may suggest obstacles to getting at the facts. However, the absence of a jury makes possible a much wider range of questions. The common law rules of evidence were largely developed to protect unskilled jurors from the cunning of a lawyer. One example of the difference is that hearsay evidence is allowed in the civil law tradition, on the assumption that a judge has enough perception to discriminate the many ways in which truth appears.

Truth is a term that belongs both in morality and in our mundane investigations of fact. The range of possibilities in defining questions of fact and applying questions of law may not be irrelevant as we now turn to ask whether legal professionals are acting morally or unscrupulously in doing their job.

FURTHER READING

Descriptions of civil and criminal procedure in countries of the civil law tradition can be found in the following works:

Ehrmann, Henry W. *Comparative Legal Cultures.* Englewood Cliffs, N.J.: Prentice-Hall, 1976, 88–93.

Glendon, Mary A., et al. *Comparative Legal Traditions: Text, Materials and Cases.* St. Paul: West, 1985, 167–91.

Liebesny, Herbert J. *Foreign Legal Systems.* Washington, D.C.: George Washington Univ. Press, 1981, 308–45.

Merryman, J. H. *The Civil Law Tradition.* Stanford, Calif.: Stanford Univ. Press, 1969, revised ed. 1985, chapters 16 & 17.

Merryman, J. H., and D. S. Clark. *Comparative Law.* Indianapolis: Bobbs-Merrill, 1978, 651–740.
Schlesinger, Rudolf B. *Comparative Law.* Mineola, N.Y.: Fundation Press, 1980, 329–435.
von Mehren, A. T., and J. R. Gordley. *The Civil Law System.* Boston: Little, Brown & Co., 1977, 150–208.

QUESTIONS FOR DISCUSSION

1. "Certainly the court will wither away. Why do you think no new courthouses are being built in Moscow? . . . When someone tells me that crime must go on as long as there is human civilization, I feel sorry for him. He's in the dark ages." These words of a Soviet judge (in Feifer, *Justice in Moscow*, 329, 332) strike us as naive. Do our own judges see their task as merely applying the law to particular cases or also as in some way educational?

2. Suppose Dr. Brach was being tried in an American court and you were prosecutor. What particular points would you hope to prove and how would you attempt to do so? How would you expect counsel for the defense to argue against you? Do you think that the two of you could, in this adversarial manner, bring more to light than a single judge could when playing both roles?

3. A lifelong observer of both systems once remarked that if he were innocent, he would prefer to be tried by a civil law court, but that he would choose a common law court if he were guilty. From what you have read, would you agree? If the common law is, as suggested, less likely to give a true verdict, is this because of distortions introduced by the lawyers? Because of the incapacity of a jury to decide objectively? Because of the more restrictive rules of evidence?

4. Our own system of twelve jurors sitting apart, deliberating in secret, and giving the sole verdict of guilt or innocence, was tried for a time in Germany and abolished under the Weimar Republic, partly because the jurors proved more severe and prejudiced than the judges. If you were on trial in a criminal court, would you choose to have the verdict given by a jury? By a single judge? By a panel of judges? By a panel of judges and jurors?

5. A jury in our system makes no public statement of reasons for the verdict it gives. Is this an irrational link in an otherwise rational process? Even if it were feasible, would it be desirable to make the jury prepare a written justification for their verdict?

6. Comment on the claim that every question has two sides. Why only two? Think of some topic of national importance or some decision you faced yourself. Trace the course that was followed from first appearance to the stage when discussion was crystallized into two sides. Do we need at times to recover earlier stages if we are to regain a sense of what the question is really about?

7. "Federal judges are not referees at prize fights but are functionaries of justice" (Justice Felix Frankfurter). It may still be that justice is better served by a neutral referee and two fighters than by a judge who combines all roles. However, does the frustration that a judge feels as a minister of justice come from his confinement to a brief drama in the ring? Does a concentrated legal trial enable justice to function as well as it could through a series of conferences? List the advantages and disadvantages you see in each system and apply this to some example of how truth is disclosed in science or history or in your personal life.

26. TRUTH IN LEGAL PROCEDURE

> *In fulfilling his professional responsibilities, a lawyer necessarily assumes various roles that require the performance of many difficult tasks. Not every situation which he may encounter can be foreseen, but fundamental ethical principles are always present to guide him. Within the framework of these*

principles, a lawyer must with courage and foresight be able and ready to shape the body of the law to the ever-changing relationships of society.
(*A.B.A. Code of Professional Responsibility*, Preamble)

The topic of "legal ethics" covers problems that range from the daily business of a law office to speculative questions about the separation or intersection of law and morality. Details concerning the advertisement a lawyer may make of his services or the fees he may charge his client are matters for professional associations to discuss and regulate. Questions about the relation between legal rules and moral principles, at the level of basic theories of law, were considered in the last chapter.

In this and the following section, however, our concern will be with a middle ground between the very practical and the highly theoretical. The problems of conscience that trouble lawyers are likely to stem from their position as advocates. Each represents a special interest, that of a client. This representation is highly moral, in that it protects the client's basic right to competent defense within the law. But the defense of one may involve an attack on others, even if by no more than conveying a hint of suspicion about the veracity of a witness. The advocacy of any special interest excludes an impartial account of the whole truth and an even hold on the scales of justice.

No one will be surprised at this, and lawyers may have fewer sleepless nights than most of us. Such worries apply also to those who market an appliance, or who support a political party, or who write a book with a certain audience in mind. Yet the questions raised by a life of advocacy within the adversary system of law can be both personal and fundamental. Even those who criticize lawyers for subordinating truth to success may have some thought for the subtlety of truth and some sympathy for the conflicting roles we ask a lawyer to play in helping to disclose it.

This section will offer a theoretical basis by mentioning the two main philosophical theories of truth and will then examine the complexity of an advocate's position. The following section will supply an extended illustration, in an ancient but dramatic case, and will turn from whatever damage a lawyer inflicts on truth in general to the more intimate worry that helping one person means injuring others.

Telling the Whole Truth

The paragraph quoted above from the American lawyer's code of responsibility is suggestive. Though what follows in that document is phrased in the language of rules, these represent the embodiment of more fundamental and largely unwritten principles, which are described as "ethical." No such code imposes on the lawyer a theory of ethics, nor certainly a theory of truth. However, as much as the detective or scientist or historian, the lawyer is dedicated to asking, what is true? He does so from the first appearance of a potential client in his office to the last word in the courtroom. We can, of course, drink water without knowing any chemical theory, just as we talk without a theory of prose. But does our search for truth imply some theory of truth? The following extract may raise a few pertinent questions.

FIELD THEORY AND JUDICIAL LOGIC
by Felix S. Cohen

Yale Law Journal 59 (1950): 238–40.
Printed with permission of the Yale Law Journal Company and Fred B. Rothman & Co.

Are lawyers liars? Anyone who has read the statement of facts in a large number of briefs of appellants and appellees is likely to conclude that any resemblances between opposing accounts of the same facts are purely fortuitous and unintentional. The impression that opposing lawyers seldom agree on the facts is strengthened if one listens to opposing counsel in almost any trial. Now, as a matter of simple logic, two inconsistent statements cannot both be true. At least *one* must be false. And it is always possible that *both* are false, as, for example, when the plaintiff's attorney says the defendant speeded into the zone of the accident at sixty miles an hour and the defendant's counsel insists his client was jogging along at twenty miles an hour, while, in fact, he was moving at forty miles an hour. Thus, a logician may conclude that either (1) at least half of our practicing lawyers utter falsehoods whenever they open their mouths or fountain pens, or (2) that a substantial majority of practicing lawyers utter falsehoods on a substantial number of such occasions. If we define a liar as a person who frequently utters such falsehoods, it would seem to follow logically that most lawyers are liars.

How the edifice of justice can be supported by the efforts of liars at the bar and ex-liars on the bench is one of the paradoxes of legal logic which the man in the street has never solved. The bitter sketch of "Two Lawyers" by Daumier still expresses the accepted public view of the legal profession....

Of course, lawyers know that the popular opinion on these subjects is inaccurate. Lawyers have ample opportunity to know how earnestly two litigants will swear to inconsistent accounts of a single event. Lawyers thus have special opportunities to learn what many logicians have not yet recognized: that truth on earth is a matter of degree, and that, whatever may be the case in Heaven, a terrestrial major league batting average above .300 is nothing to be sneezed at.

The difference between the lawyer's and the logician's view of truth is worth more attention than it has had from either lawyers or logicians....

Take, for instance, a typical humanly constructed sentence, one which has been uttered, down through some 3000 years, by hundreds of millions of human beings of many races, many tongues, and many religions:

"The Lord is my shepherd; I shall not want."

What sense does it make to ask whether this sentence is true or false?

Of course, there may be literal-minded readers of the Bible who will insist that the sentence has only one "correct" meaning, which is true, and that any variant interpretation is simply erroneous.

There are, no doubt, equally dogmatic individuals who will insist that the sentence is simply false. If they are dogmatic atheists, they will tell us: "There is no Lord and therefore He cannot possibly be a shepherd." If they are Montana cattlemen, they may add that nobody in the sheep business could possibly deserve to bear the name of the Lord. Others there are who have outgrown the effort to make God in man's image, but still recite these words with full sincerity. To some such, the words of the Psalmist mean that the forces of evil are somehow self-defeating, that ultimate victory rests with the forces of righteousness, that none of us is self-sufficient, that none of us is capable of protecting himself against all the dangers that surround us from cradle to grave, and that sanity requires a faith in an unseen power that will protect us and guide us as a faithful shepherd guides his sheep, seeing that their wants are fulfilled. But one who thus translates the words of an ancient poet into the context of his own beliefs has no right to assume that this is the only context in which those words have significance. He will be content to say that they have truth for him.

This dependence of meaning upon a personal frame of reference is something that many of us take for granted when we refuse to argue over affirmations of religious faith. May not the same dependence of meaning and truth upon varying contexts be found in non-religious fields as well, even in the mundane fields which concern lawyers and their clients? May we not say, even, that law as, *par excellence*, the field of controversies, is the field in which the imposition of different meanings upon the same verbal formula is most characteristic and most significant?

If anybody asks us whether the first sentence of the Twenty-third Psalm is true or false, we may conclude that the interrogator is lacking in imagination and is guilty of the fallacy of misplaced concreteness. That is because we realize that a sentence of this sort (and perhaps every other humanly constructed sentence, in greater or lesser degree) means many things to many minds. Perhaps, if we look closely enough, a sentence never means exactly the same thing to any two different people. For no two minds bring the same apperceptive mass of understanding and background to bear on the external fact of a sound or a series of marks. Indeed, I doubt whether any sentence means exactly the same thing to me the first time I hear it that it means the tenth or the hundredth time. Of course, for many practical purposes, we are disposed to overlook such variations of meaning. Each of us is likely to try to fix on a particular segment of our thinking, at a particular time, as "the real meaning" of any sentence. We may consider all other interpretations as more or less serious aberrations. Perhaps we are justified in holding that our own specific understanding of the sentence at a particular time is a proposition, and either false or true. But what, then, shall we say of the sentence as a social fact, a source of many interpretations, a matrix of many propositions? Must we not say that the truth of any assertion is a matter of degree, that from certain angles a sentence may give light and that at other angles it may obscure more light than it gives? The angle or perspective and the context are part of the meaning of any proposition, and thus a part of whatever it is that is true or false.

The location of words in a context is essential to their meaning and truth. The fallacy of simple location in physical space-time has finally been superseded in physics. We now realize that the Copernican view that the earth moves around the sun and the older Ptolemaic view that the sun moves around the earth can both be true, and that for practical though not aesthetic or religious purposes the Ptolemaic and Copernican astronomies may be used interchangeably. We realize that Euclidean and non-Euclidean geometries can both be true. What is a straight line in one system may be an ellipse in another system, just as a penny may be round in one perspective, oval in a second, and rectangular in a third.

A prosecuting attorney who assumes that policemen are accurate and impartial observers of traffic speeds will arrive at one estimate of the speed of a defendant charged with reckless driving. The defendant's attorney, if he assumes that his client is an honest man and that policemen on the witness stand generally exaggerate in order to build up an impressive record of convictions, will arrive at another estimate. If each honestly gives his views the court will have the benefit of synoptic vision. Appreciation of the importance of such synoptic vision is a distinguishing mark of liberal civilization....

In a certain sense, it is true that lawyers are liars. In the same sense, poets, historians, and map-makers are also liars. For it is the function of lawyers, poets, historians, and mapmakers not to reproduce reality but to illumine some aspect of reality, and it always makes for deceit to pretend that what is thus illumined is the whole of reality. None of us can ever possibly tell the whole truth, though we may conscientiously will to do so and ask divine help towards that end. The ancient wisdom of our common law recognizes that men are bound to differ in their views of fact and law, not because some are honest and others dishonest, but because each of us operates in a value-charged field which gives shape and color to whatever we see. The proposition that no man should be a judge of his own cause embodies the ancient wisdom that only a many-perspective view of the world can relieve us of the endless anarchy of one-eyed vision.

Cohen opens with the question whether lawyers are liars. He closes with the reply that if they are, it is only in the way we so talk of poets, historians, mapmakers, and other respectable people. In between, he seems to defend what philosophers would call a "coherence theory of truth." This needs explanation and comment. But first we may ask what we mean when, without any complications, we say that someone is lying.

In 1960 the Russians shot down a U2 spy plane, and American authorities initially denied all knowledge of it. In 1983 the Russians shot down a Korean airliner and initially denied that they had done so. Subsequent admissions, in both cases, showed these assertions of "not guilty" to have been lies. The speaker's words contradicted what he knew in his mind to be so. Such a falsehood is to be contrasted with an honest mistake; the speaker says what is false but he sincerely thinks it true, so there is no opposition between mind and words.

Cohen is not claiming that lawyers are liars in this obvious sense. He is less concerned with the correspondence between *mind* and *words* than he is with the more philosophical question whether our *mind* corresponds to *facts that exist apart from dependence on minds*. The poet speaks his mind when he personifies the sun. Our attitude toward the truth or falsity of what he says will come from our reply to the question whether the sun simply exists in itself, and measures our statements about it, or whether what we call the sun is in some way the result of our way of thinking and talking (scientific, poetic, religious, etc.).

The theory of truth that Cohen defends may be illustrated by a prosaic example and then by the two that he draws from science. Suppose I tell those organizing a public lecture that the auditorium will hold three hundred. The audience arrives and thirty are left to sit on steps and window sills or to stand at the back, because there are only 250 chairs. Did I make a mistake? Yes, if "holding" is defined in terms of sitting on chairs. No, if my conventions of posture and language are different. There is no fact in itself apart from the mind of speaker and listener.

What about the victory of Copernicus over Ptolemy? Astronomy would suffer grievously if we went back on this change, yet to say that the sun is the center of the solar system is to stress the dependence of this "fact" on the way we construct a "system" in our minds. That of Ptolemy is much more clumsy, but simplicity and elegance are mental ideals. Our adoption of any system, and our designation of it as true, is much a function of the purposes we bring.

Finally, is straightness a fact? The policeman who stops your car and asks you to walk along a straight line is unlikely to be impressed by your claim that the line marked on the road is not straight. He can prove his point by means of a tape measure. Questions about the tape measure can be met by appeal to the path of a ray of light. However, beyond that we find ourselves in the realm of definitions. We may define "straight" in terms of a ray of light. Or we can find that light does or does not travel in straight lines by electing to use a non-Euclidean or a Euclidean geometry. These are evidently mental conventions, not facts.

The suggestion, then, is that truth is not *the correspondence of what we think to facts that are independent of our thinking* (the so-called "correspondence theory" of truth). This notion works when the definitions are already agreed upon (and forgotten), as by the busy policeman or surveyor or by the manager of a stadium where a ticket is seen by all as giving a right to a seat. Yet as soon as we ask about our agreements, or encounter conflicts between science and religion, or between prose and poetry, we realize that truth is more involved in the *coherence of one idea with another to form a system of ideas* (the "coherence theory" of truth). Rather than turning behind our ideas in search of some independent reality, we examine the different ways in which our thinking can formulate systems to be compared much as we judge works of art or of literature; each is more or less successful at integrating a variety of details in a comprehensive achievement.[13]

Before we ask how Cohen applies this to the law, we may raise an obvious question: If such is truth, then what is falsity? An immediate reaction to the coherence theory is that it misses the sheer dogmatism of claims to truth and leaves us with a relativism where anything we say must be true somehow. Cohen's example from religious language seems to reinforce this doubt. He lists a variety of plausible interpretations of the line from Psalm 23 and suggests that all are true. Each reader brings his own context or frame of reference. Each "will be content to say that the words have truth for him." However, what of Plato's distinction between opinion and truth? Opinions are "mine and thine." Yet surely the questioner must proceed to ask which is true and be prepared to submit his own opinion to some norm that transcends it.

Cohen's reply is interesting and turns us back to the topic of law: "Must we not say that the truth of any assertion is a matter of degree?" A degree of what? His final sentence may supply a clue: "Only a many-perspectived view of the world can relieve us of the endless anarchy of one-eyed vision." Falsity is the

13. Comments made at the beginning of chapter 2 on Piaget's account of mental development may help to illustrate this difference in theories of truth. When we find a young child perceiving the world in animistic terms and failing to accept any law of conservation, we are likely to dismiss his claims as amusing but false; they do not reproduce reality. Our own report of nature in terms of mass, energy, and equilibrium is, we assume, a correspondence to the way things are. We forget the creativity of our own thinking. Scientific paradigms (such as waves, particles, circular motion, positive and negative, fields of force) are as much the contribution of an imaginative mind as are the personal qualities with which a child endows what he experiences. The worlds of animism and of science are each internally consistent; they differ in their suitability for various human projects.

product of a limited viewpoint that fails to incorporate the richness and subtlety of seeing. If we manage to formulate a system, it will be impoverished. But we are more likely to fall short of systematic thinking and remain with the muddle and confusion of the casual viewer. Instead of seeing, we "goggle." From this extreme, the way toward truth passes through many degrees, where each represents a unity that can comprehend a diversity of detail. Great art is simple but tells us more each time we view it. Similarly, science reveals a progressive reduction in the number of explanatory principles and a like extension of their power to comprehend. The criteria are those of economy and fruitfulness. Though we swear to tell the whole truth, all of us are condemned to failure; some, however, come much closer to the proposed ideal than others.

How do these theoretical questions apply to what goes on in the offices and courts of law? Cohen's final examples are not very helpful. They are taken from the narrow world of traffic regulations and have to do with the honesty of the actors (where honesty is the correspondence of words to minds). There facts are closely defined and rules invite little discussion. Cohen's approach could have found more fruitful illustrations, even without deserting the field of criminal law where rules are clearly codified. What, for instance, of *U.S. v. Holmes*, the case that gave some basis for the parable of the speluncean explorers? The rules against taking life were precise, and the facts were clear. It was Holmes who supplied the push that lightened the boat of a number of passengers. Yet what actually happened, and what precisely were the rules? In simple terms, what did Holmes do? Did he drown people? Did he save a much larger number from otherwise certain death? And what was the law? Does the established law of the land apply without qualification in the perils of the sea? Here, questions of truth invite a multiplicity of perspectives. The defense attorneys did what they could to develop the vision of the court and to free it from the limitations of using one eye.

In summary, Cohen is not denying that the legal process aims at truth. He is stressing the social nature of the enterprise. If facts depend on mental contributions, and if the ideal of truth is approached only through the exploration of a variety of perspectives, then the individual advocate plays but one role in a complex and continuing drama. He is a liar only in the way that Ptolemy faces such a charge from Copernicus, or a poet from a scientist. No one person can see all sides or formulate all questions. How, then, do we proceed? Not by canonizing our own limited vision, nor by despairing of the demands of truth and closing our eyes; but by seeing as clearly and systematically as we can from our own chosen or inherited viewpoint, and by allowing others to complement our vision through their own way of seeing.

Truth and Other Obligations

Notice that those who support either a correspondence or a coherence theory of truth are indeed defending truth; neither is reducing the search to that for victory in a game. With regard to a previous discussion (section 24), both theories would support imperfect procedural justice and neither would allow it to lapse into pure procedural justice.

An example is needed to clarify this claim. Take the most pertinent illustration. You are a lawyer and your client insists on pleading "not guilty."

1. If you hold that the legal process offers no more than pure procedural justice, then your position is easy. Not guilty means simply that you challenge the court to prove the charge within the rules. The game is on. Your opponent might have won easily in the jungle, but law has embarrassed him with many restrictions about what moves are acceptable. If you are cunning, you may win. And there is no truth beyond victory.

2. At the other extreme, your task as a lawyer is to discover whether your client's plea does or does not correspond to facts in themselves. If you conclude that it does not, that he is really guilty, then you have a problem; and this is the problem that the layperson sees lawyers facing half of the time (remember Cohen's introduction).

3. Cohen seems to situate himself somewhere in the middle. Your client may turn out to be guilty or innocent (and not simply to have lost or won). Yet the norms are those of coherence. It is your task, as a lawyer, to develop a loyal advocacy of his viewpoint, but to see this as one of many sides of an inquiry that develops in comprehensiveness. You start without adequate knowledge of his guilt or innocence. You are aware, for example, that some confess when innocent and many plead innocent when guilty. You realize that regret can pass for guilt, that moral guilt may not be the same as legal. And, above all, you know of many ways in which the letter of the law falls short of its spirit. The task of disclosing truth is complex, but you do not stand alone—your advocacy is part of a broad social enterprise.

A word needs now to be said for the second position above. It is here, especially, that the layperson finds you, as a lawyer, to be driven into a corner. You may conclude, after due inquiry, that your client's claims are not founded on fact. How can you morally proceed to defend him in a criminal court or to support what he wants in a civil case? If the procedure is no mere game, how can you be morally justified in defending as true what you think to be false?

Perhaps the conflict is overdrawn. Those who, in law school, worry about their later call to advocate causes in which they do not believe will find themselves coming to terms with the problem. They are seldom asked to represent outrageous claims. And initial doubts evaporate after a lawyer has worked on a case for several days. His client's cause soon appears both logical and just. Remaining worries tend to be rather academic. The lawyer knows there is another side, and he wonders if, had he been so employed, the same conversion to logic and justice would have been effected.

Our concern, however, is more with theory than practice. Suppose you do, after all, conclude that your client is guilty or holds the weaker position in a civil case? How can you morally proceed? Do you condemn yourself as a liar? If Cohen's theory is not adopted, then the only answer seems to be that we put truth in its limited place: are there no higher values or duties in question?

A few simple examples. You hated the party, but you tell your hostess at the end that you had a wonderful time. Though you may have offended against some duty to tell the truth, have you not satisfied more important obligations of respect for people? Similarly, you are asked whether you saw Mr. X at a motel with a woman who was not Mrs. X, and you know that a marriage and its children are at stake. Or (a traditional example), a gunman appears and asks if Y is present; you know he is, but you deny it. In all three cases, you seem to have failed toward truth, but so what? You have defended personal feelings, a family, and life itself. If we say that truth should be told, do we not qualify this pale duty in a variety of ways? Is truth the only value, or is it subordinate to many others? What, then, about your vocation as a lawyer? You are called to truth, but not absolutely. Are there higher values or obligations that you support? When we talk of the right that each person has to competent defense in a trial, are we not going beyond the abstract demands of truth to a morality that has more to do with our respect for people?

These comments can serve as an introduction to the following extracts from a much quoted article on the limited obligation of a legal advocate to tell the truth. There are parallels with the Cohen article, but also important differences. Some analysis of these may be instructive. Though the immediate question is ethical, the underlying one is about theories of truth.

THE ETHICS OF ADVOCACY
by Charles P. Curtis

Stanford Law Review 4 (1951): 3–16.
Copyright © 1951 by the Board of the Leland Stanford Junior University.
Printed with permission.

> I want first of all to put advocacy in its proper setting. It is a special case of vicarious conduct. A lawyer devotes his life and career to acting for other people. So too does the priest, and in another way, the banker. The banker handles other people's money. The priest handles other people's spiritual aspirations. A lawyer handles other people's troubles.
>
> But there is a difference. The loyalty of a priest or clergyman runs, not to the particular parishioner whose joys or troubles he is busy with, but to his church; and the banker looks to his bank. It is the church or the bank, not he, but he on its behalf, who serves the communicant or the borrower....
>
> Not so the lawyer in private practice. His loyalty runs to his client. He has no other master. Not the court? you ask. Does not the court take the same position as the church or the bank? Is not the lawyer an officer of the court? Doesn't the court have first claim on his loyalty? No, in a paradoxical way. The lawyer's official duty, required of him indeed by the court, is to devote himself to the client. The court comes second by the court's, that is the law's, own command....
>
> A lawyer, therefore, insensibly finds himself treating his client better than others; and therefore others worse than his client. A lawyer, or a trustee, or anyone acting for another,

has lower standards of conduct toward outsiders than he has toward his clients or his beneficiaries or his patrons against the outsiders. He is required to treat outsiders as if they were barbarians and enemies. The more good faith and devotion the lawyer owes to his client, the less he owes to others when he is acting for his client. It is as if a man had only so much virtue, and the more he gives to one, the less he has available for anyone else. The upshot is that a man whose business it is to act for others finds himself, in his dealings on his client's behalf with outsiders, acting on a lower standard than he would if he were acting for himself, and lower, too, than any standard his client himself would be willing to act on, lower, in fact, than anyone on his own....

A lawyer is called on the telephone by a former client who is unfortunately at the time a fugitive from justice. The police want him and he wants advice. The lawyer goes to where his client is, hears the whole story, and advises him to surrender. Finally he succeeds in persuading him that this is the best thing to do and they make an appointment to go to police headquarters. Meanwhile the client is to have two days to wind up his affairs and make his farewells. When the lawyer gets back to his office, a police inspector is waiting for him, and asks him whether his client is in town and where he is. Here are questions which the police have every right to ask of anybody, and even a little hesitation in this unfortunate lawyer's denials will reveal enough to betray his client. Of course he lies.

And why not? The relation between a lawyer and his client is one of the intimate relations. You would lie for your wife. You would lie for your child. There are others with whom you are intimate enough, close enough, to lie for them when you would not lie for yourself. At what point do you stop lying for them? I don't know and you are not sure.

To every one of us come occasions when we don't want to tell the truth, not all of it, certainly not all of it at once, when we want to be something less than candid, a little disingenuous. Indeed, to be candid with ourselves, there are times when we deliberately and more or less justifiably undertake to tell something else or something different. Complete candor to anyone but ourselves is a virtue that belongs to the saints, to the secure, and to the very courageous. Even when we do want to tell the truth, all of it, ultimately, we see no reason why we should not take our own time, tell it as skillfully and as gracefully as we can, and most of us doubt our own ability to do this as well by ourselves and for ourselves as another could do it for us. So we go to a lawyer. He will make a better fist of it than we can.

I don't see why we should not come out roundly and say that one of the functions of a lawyer is to lie for his client; and on rare occasions, as I think I have shown, I believe it is. Happily they are few and far between, only when his duty gets him into a corner or puts him on the spot. Day in, day out, a lawyer can be as truthful as anyone. But not ingenuous. A lawyer is required to be disingenuous....

"I must be cruel only to be kind," said Hamlet, on his way to his mother. And so likewise a lawyer has to tell himself strange things on his way to court. But they are strange only to those who do not distinguish between truth and justice. Justice is something larger and more intimate than truth. Truth is only one of the ingredients of justice. Its whole is the satisfaction of those concerned. It is to that end that each attorney must say the best, and only the best, of his own case....

The law must give the losing party, and his friends, and his sympathizers, as much satisfaction as any loser can expect. At least the most has been said for him. The whole has been shaken out into the sun, and everyone concerned is given a feeling akin to the feeling of security which you get when you have told yourself the worst before you make a decision. The administration of justice is no more designed to elicit the truth than the scientific approach is designed to extract justice from the atom.

Advocacy requires a lawyer to start with something to be proved, and this is as true of facts as it is of propositions of law. When he goes to the law library, he goes to get something. He will waste a lot of time if he goes with an open mind. He must, of course, first formulate the issue in his mind, but he does this only to make it the easier to find what lies on his side of the issue. He fixes on the conclusion which will best serve his client's interests, and then he sets out to persuade others to agree....

It is profoundly true that the first person a lawyer persuades is himself. A practicing lawyer will soon detect in himself a perfectly astonishing amount of sincerity. By the time he has even sketched out his brief, however skeptically he started, he finds himself believing more and more in what it says, until he has to hark back to his original position in order to orient himself. And later, when he starts arguing the case before the court, his belief is total, and he is quite sincere about it. You cannot very well keep your tongue in your cheek while you are talking. He believes what he is saying in a way that will later astonish himself as much as now it does others....

The classical solution to a lawyer taking a case he knows is bad is Dr. Johnson's. It is perfectly simple and quite specious. Boswell asked Johnson whether as a moralist Johnson did not think that the practice of the law, in some degree, hurt the nice feeling of honesty.

"What do you think," said Boswell, "of supporting a cause which you know to be bad?"

Johnson answered, "Sir, you do not know it to be good or bad till the Judge determines it. I have said that you are to state facts fairly; so that your thinking, or what you call knowing, a cause to be bad, must be from reasoning, must be from your supposing your arguments to be weak and inconclusive. But, Sir, that is not enough. An argument which does not convince yourself may convince the Judge to whom you urge it: and if it does convince him, why, then, Sir, you are wrong and he is right."

Dr. Johnson ignored the fact that it is the lawyer's job to know how good or bad his case is. It is his peculiar function to find out. Dr. Johnson's answer is sound only in cases where the problem does not arise.

A lawyer knows very well whether his client is guilty. It is not the lawyer, but the law, that does not know whether his case is good or bad. The law does not know, because it is trying to find out, and so the law wants everyone defended and every debatable case tried. Therefore the law makes it easy for a lawyer to take a case, whether or not he thinks it bad and whether or not he thinks other people think it bad. It is particularly important that it be made as easy as possible for a lawyer to take a case that other people regard as bad.

We want to make it as easy as we can for a lawyer to take a bad case, and one of the ways the bar helps go about it is the canon of ethics which says, "It is improper for a lawyer to assert in argument his personal belief in his client's innocence or in the justice of his cause." It is called improper just so that the lawyer may feel that he does not have to. This, I think, must be its only purpose, for it is honored in no other way....

No, there is nothing unethical in taking a bad case or defending the guilty or advocating what you don't believe in. It is ethically neutral. It's a free choice. There is a Daumier drawing of a lawyer arguing, a very demure young woman sitting near him, and a small boy beside her sucking a lollypop. The caption says, "He defends the widow and the orphan, unless he is attacking the orphan and the widow." And for every lawyer whose conscience may be pricked, there is another whose virtue is tickled. Every case has two sides, and for every lawyer on the wrong side, there's another on the right side.

I am not being cynical. We are not dealing with the morals which govern a man acting for himself, but with the ethics of advocacy. We are talking about the special moral code which governs a man who is acting for another.

FURTHER READING

Most introductions to philosophy include a discussion of various theories of truth. See also W. R. Bishin and C. D. Stone, *Law, Language, and Ethics* (Mineola, N.Y.: Foundation Press, 1972), 300–345.

For a discussion of how such theories apply in science, see:

Kearney, Hugh. *Science and Change.* New York: McGraw-Hill, World University Library, 1971.

Kuhn, Thomas S. *The Structure of Scientific Revolutions.* 2d ed. Chicago: Univ. of Chicago Press, 1970.

For an extended account of Charles P. Curtis's views on law, see his book, *It's Your Law* (Cambridge: Harvard Univ. Press, 1954).

QUESTIONS FOR DISCUSSION

1.   If what I say is false, does it follow that I have uttered a falsehood? Think of the predictions of an economist, the campaign promises of a politician. If you are a lawyer whose client is found guilty, must you either have lied to the public or been deceived by your client?

2.   Can the statement that "The Lord is my Shepherd" be falsified? If not, can it be true? Is it "more true" that $5 + 7 = 11$ than that $5 + 7 = 10$? Can one witnesses' testimony be more true than another?

3.   Can you show that the principle of inertia is true without somehow presupposing it? If (as has been claimed) medicine men produce a higher rate of cure than psychiatrists in some parts of Africa, how would you show which explanation of a mental disease is the true one? Can a theory be entirely coherent and yet false?

4.   Does a stick bend when partially immersed in water? If you say no, how would you prove this? Suppose I reply that a camera does not lie, and I take a photograph? Does a parent lie to his children when telling them of the existence of Santa Claus?

5.   Can I reasonably say that the typewriter is to the left of the lamp for me but not for you, and that we are both correct? Can I reasonably say that God exists for me but not for you, and that we are both correct?

6.   How does the trial of Dr. Brach (section 25) illustrate Cohen's claim that truth is many-perspectived? Do we know the whole truth about what happened that February in the park? Does Dr. Brach? Do you know what you are thinking or what you want? Can two artists paint the same landscape?

7.   In defending you after a traffic accident, your lawyer makes claims about the speed at which you were driving, the care you were exercising, the reasonableness of what you did, and the reasonableness of the traffic laws that applied. How relevant to each claim is a correspondence theory of truth?

8.   When Boswell voiced the layperson's question about how a lawyer can take a case that he or she knows to be bad, Dr. Johnson replied that it is not the lawyer's but the judge's place to decide whether a case is good and an argument convincing. Curtis disagreed, though notice that he does not follow the exact words of Dr. Johnson. Do you think it is clear, as Curtis holds, that "a lawyer knows very well whether his client is guilty"? How does Cohen differ in regard to this?

9.   Would you expect Dr. Johnson to agree with this statement of a lawyer? "A man who actually committed a murder but whose guilt is not proved beyond reasonable doubt in court is, if nevertheless convicted by judge and jury, himself as much murdered as if he were innocent."

10.   Do you agree with the distinction Curtis sets between the moral standards a person has in acting for himself and in acting for others? Should you tell lies for your wife (or husband) and child, but not for yourself?

11.   Do you agree that, even when you are obliged to tell the truth, you may be allowed to take your time about it? What does Curtis mean by saying that a lawyer is required to be "disingenuous"? Would this suggestion get more support from a coherence than a correspondence theory of truth?

12.   What does Curtis mean in saying that "justice is larger and more intimate than truth"? If, as he evidently holds, the two may come into conflict, why should we subordinate truth to justice?

13. There is no surprise in the comment that every case, having two sides, requires a lawyer on each. But taking Curtis's whole position as presented in these extracts, is he reducing the lawyer's role to that of an instrument? A gun is also ethically neutral. Yet surely a lawyer is more than a hired gun? Is there more to being an officer of the court than being an instrument of the court?

27. THE CONSCIENCE OF A LAWYER

> *It is certain that an advocate commits a serious sin if he knowingly defends an unjust cause.... Nevertheless, if he at the beginning thought the cause to be just, he should not abandon it in such a way as to help the other side or reveal his client's secrets....*
> (St. Thomas Aquinas, *Summa Theologica,* II–II, question 71, article 3)

These words come from the thirteenth century. The opening sentence, if taken by itself, seems to oppose our modern belief in the right of any accused person, however weak his case may be, to have competent defense at the hands of a trained advocate. Yet the qualification that follows does suggest recognition of the conflicting roles of the lawyer in trying to do what is just. Aquinas taught in the theological and not the legal faculty of the University of Paris. He gave no further details. But he was perceptive enough to realize that such general guidelines must raise delicate questions in practice. Once you have undertaken to defend a client, you expose yourself to many possible dilemmas. You cannot simply withdraw without failing in your duty to him. Also, the obligations you have toward your client involve the danger of injuring other people.

This section will supply illustrations of the crisis of conscience that can come to an advocate within our modern adversary system of law. Bar associations have become more definite in the guidelines they supply. Rules, however, are of limited application and often conflict with each other. A conscientious lawyer can find himself standing alone.

The Play at the Old Bailey

One of the most readable and provocative books on legal ethics takes the form of an extended commentary on a famous murder trial in Victorian England. What follows is drawn from the researches of David Mellinkoff into the trial at the Old Bailey, in 1840, of *Queen v. Courvoisier*.[14] The trial itself has drama enough to satisfy those whose expectations come from the sudden moves of television thrillers. But history remembers it for the impassioned discussion of legal ethics that followed. This far outlasted even the life of the famous advocate in that trial who was called, for the rest of his days, to justify an anguished decision he had quickly to make in the courtroom.

14. David Mellinkoff, *The Conscience of a Lawyer* (St. Paul: West, 1973). The summary I have given is printed with permission of the publishers.

Lord William Russell was a widower of seventy-two, who lived modestly in a rented house near Park Lane in London with his three servants: a maid, a cook, and a man who acted as valet and butler. On May 6, 1840, Lord Russell was found dead in his bedroom, with a seven-inch cut across his throat. The incident received great publicity through the newspapers, and suspicion fell at once upon the valet, François Courvoisier. He was Swiss, aged twenty-three, and had been employed for only a few months by Lord Russell. His French name and his previous work in a disreputable French hotel in London told against him—the Battle of Waterloo, at which Lord Russell had fought, was a fresh memory.

The police decided this must have been an inside job. They found that some of the dining room silver was missing, and they discovered small valuables belonging to Lord Russell (such as a medal from Waterloo) hidden under the floorboards in Courvoisier's room. Though an initial search of his possessions revealed nothing suspicious, a later examination produced some bloodstained gloves in his trunk. Courvoisier protested his complete innocence, but on May 27 he was indicted for the murder and put in Newgate Prison to await trial.

No better billing could have been arranged. The prosecutor was to be John Adolphus, now also seventy-two, but for a generation the best-known criminal lawyer in London. Recently, however, his fame had been declining before the rising star of Charles Phillips, an Irishman of great wit and brilliance. Their personal rivalry was notorious. Adolphus publicly accused Phillips of the three B's: blarney, bully, and bluster. Phillips replied that Adolphus never whined about these until they began to suck his honey. And who accepted the defense of Courvoisier? Charles Phillips.

The trial began on June 18. The opening statement of Adolphus was calm and meticulous, attempting to anticipate all the tactics available to Phillips. Witnesses for the prosecution were called, and Phillips was at his best in discrediting their testimony. When the poor confused maid, Sarah Mancer, finally sat down, the packed courtroom felt she was as likely to have committed the crime as Courvoisier. The constable investigating the murder, John Baldwin, returned from the witness stand with the suspicion firmly planted in the jury's mind that police corruption was involved; a reward had been offered of four hundred pounds for information leading to conviction (a considerable sum for those days). When the court recessed, betting was three to one for acquittal of Courvoisier.

However, the second day started badly for Phillips. He already had to counter invidious comparisons with an attack, a week before the trial, on the life of the young Queen Victoria, three years on the throne and only four months a bride. Adolphus had not hesitated to play on the theme of innocent nobility and to remind all that the trial began on the anniversary of the Battle of Waterloo. Then, before the court opened on the second day, a rumor swept London. A key point in Phillips's defense was that the police had neither discovered the stolen silverware nor linked it with Courvoisier. But news was now spread that the silver had been left by him with Madame Piolaine, the proprietor of the French hotel at which he formerly worked. She dramatically came forward as star witness for the prosecution.

Charles Dickens later referred to a trial as "the play at the Old Bailey." Partisan crowds, now feeling that the tide had turned, demanded admission. Even Phillips appeared stunned by the sudden change. He left the courtroom in considerable agitation and returned only as the judges entered to resume the trial.

The proprietor gave her evidence to the delight of the onlookers. Then Phillips rose to cross-examine. His attack on her credibility was vicious. Her establishment and her personal life were impugned. She was in search of a share of the reward. Why had she waited three weeks while all London knew what was at stake? Adolphus, now confident of success, gave his summing-up to the jury. At the end of the second day, the odds had turned to conviction.

On the third and final day of the trial Phillips summarized his weakened case. Seldom has an advocate put on a better show for his client. Phillips spoke for three hours. He was at turns calm and impassioned. He cast renewed suspicion upon Sarah Mancer. He gave a compelling picture of police bungling and villainy: surely the bloody gloves had been planted by them in Courvoisier's trunk? Phillips poured scorn on any argument that depended on the words of Madame Piolaine. And he solemnly warned the jury that they must distinguish clearly between petty thievery and the grievous charge of murder for which no motive had been produced and the evidence remained circumstantial. Courvoisier could later face charges of robbery for the silver and other valuables. But "it is known to the Almighty God alone" who committed the murder. If the jurors pronounced a verdict of guilt on one who is innocent, that would "take the shape of an accusing spirit and confront and condemn you before the judgment seat of God. So beware what you do."

The newspapers reported that tears touched even whiskered cheeks and were observed in the jury box. The opinion was that if the vote had been taken at once, it would have gone for acquittal.

First, however, the presiding judge had to give his charge to the jury. He spoke for three and a half hours, making full use of his right to analyze the evidence, clarify the law, distinguish relevant questions from the many appeals to emotion. It was agreed that all he said was within bounds and in line with his personal reputation for fairness. Nevertheless, the force of Phillips's final appeal had been blunted. The jury returned after an hour and twenty-five minutes with a verdict of guilty.

They were right. Throughout the trial Courvoisier had kept his silence. But from the verdict until he was hanged sixteen days later he scarcely stopped talking. Confession followed confession, each more lurid than the last. He had been influenced by novels he had read. He had resented accusations of inefficiency from his master. He had taken to pilfering articles in retaliation. He had been surprised by Lord Russell when so engaged and had killed him in a frenzy.

He had left the silver with Madame Piolaine. He had compounded his crime with violation of the rest of the Ten Commandments, and so on.

These confessions kept the popular newspapers busy for a couple of weeks. Yet there was one brief statement of Courvoisier, shortly before he died, that occupied the more serious press and the learned journals for several decades and influenced the ethical canons of lawyers wherever the Anglo-American system of law has taken root. Courvoisier mentioned that he had told it all to his defense counsel, Charles Phillips, on the morning of the second day of the trial.

Phillips admitted that this was so. Shortly before the court was to open on that day, Courvoisier privately made a full admission of his guilt. All that the prosecution maintained was true. Phillips was shattered. He urged Courvoisier to change his plea to guilty. "No sir," came the reply, "I expect you to defend me to the utmost."

Phillips went to the courtroom. What to do? The judges would enter in a few minutes. His first inclination was to abandon the case. But this would be to give up his professional responsibility. In desperation, he turned to an odd source of advice. He went to the judge, not the presiding judge but one who sat with him as an assistant. We can imagine the dismay of this official on receiving the information while he was robing. He rebuked Phillips for seriously compromising the duty of the bench to base judgment on public evidence alone. Yet, he insisted, if his client still wanted Phillips to defend him, the brief must be retained. So, a few minutes later, the proceedings of the second day began. Both bench and defense knew the guilt of the prisoner. Only the prosecution and public were in doubt, thinking the drama came from Madame Piolaine.

The popular press now turned its indignation from Courvoisier to Phillips. He knew he was using his eloquence to plead the cause of an assassin and to turn loose on society a villain who would again "imbrue his hands in the blood of the sleeping." Theologians joined the protest, in more measured terms, but crying immorality and extending the charge from the individual to the profession.

However, the attacks that stung Phillips, and marred his reputation, came from within the legal profession itself. Here we must narrow the charge, as serious discussion soon did. It was agreed:

1. that the function of a lawyer is not to make a judgment of guilt but to ensure that the legal procedures of justice are maintained, with an adequate defense of both sides in any question;

2. that, though a lawyer has a right to refuse a case when it is offered to him,[15] his acceptance of that case puts him under obligations toward his client that become more severe as the trial approaches and then starts (withdrawal would be increasingly hazardous to the client); and

---

15. In England, this would need to be put more precisely; the barrister accepts any case that a solicitor refers to him, but the latter has considerable discretion in electing to do so.

3. that Phillips therefore acted correctly in continuing to defend Courvoisier when suddenly led to believe in his guilt early on the second day of the trial.

The question was not *whether* Phillips should continue but *how* he should do so. Specifically, should he have attempted so pointedly to ruin the character of Madame Piolaine on the second day? Should he, in his summary on the third day, have returned to his attacks on the police and, more seriously, to his implications that Sarah Mancer could have committed the crime? If Courvoisier had been acquitted, she might have found herself on trial for the murder.[16] In fact, even with his conviction, she suffered so much anguish from her part in the drama that she eventually died in a madhouse.

More definite guidelines have since been established for the way in which counsel may conduct his argument when he knows his client to be wrong. The lawyer should not be responsible for the presentation of testimony that he knows to be false. And a criminal charge should never be shifted to another identifiable person unless evidence or inferences raise a reasonable suspicion of his guilt. However, boundary lines remain vague. What is or is not the "presentation of testimony?" Is the "suspicion of guilt" to be in the mind of the jury or of counsel? (see Mellinkoff, *Conscience of a Lawyer*, 217)

Madame Piolaine was sprung on Phillips right after his discovery that Courvoisier was guilty. The jury expected a strong attack in the cross-examination. Was it wrong to threaten the reputation of her hotel and to raise suspicions about why she had held back on her vital evidence? And in Phillips's summary on the third day, should he have simply dropped all reference to the attacks he had made in the first day on Mancer and the police? Juries base their verdict partly on the performance of the advocates; so if expectations for a speech in the grand style had been met by a bland address that failed to build on carefully laid foundations, there would have been little doubt of the verdict and of the advocate's failure in defense of his client.

Mellinkoff sees no easy answers. He comments (*Conscience of a Lawyer*, 218): "The specifics of authoritative guidance fall far short of the endless variety the lawyer meets every day in the courtroom. Each time he is on his own.... As in Courvoisier's Case, there are for every lawyer moral crises without precedent; no code section; no case; no rule of thumb."[17]

---

16. More extreme claims have been made than Phillips ever supported. For a discussion of related cases in which advocates, knowing their client's guilt, have not hesitated to expose innocent people to danger of conviction and death, see Mellinkoff, *Conscience of a Lawyer*, 194–203.

17. The ethical questions mentioned in this section are set today under the general heading of "role morality." Some of our social roles seem to allow or require behavior that would be thought immoral outside that role. The parent is expected by society to show particular care for his or her child while other children starve. Is this morally justifiable, and how close is the analogy offered by a lawyer's advocacy of his client? The question of the "morality of role morality" is too complex for serious comments here, but the reader with specifically legal interests can be referred to the collection of relevant articles in *The Good Lawyer*, David Luban, ed. (Totowa, N.J.: Rowman & Allanheld, 1984).

Counseling a Client

> I don't want a lawyer to tell me what I cannot do; I hire him to tell me how to do what I want to do.
>
> (John Pierpont Morgan)

The ethical problems faced by Charles Phillips are suggestive but untypical. This is not merely because few advocates can expect so dramatic a conversion from substantial belief in their client's position to a total loss of faith. It is because much of a lawyer's work has to do, not with defending a client's past actions, but with giving advice for his future ones. The lawyer is above all a counselor, and it is here that he is likely to find many of the problems that can worry a sensitive conscience. A few comments may give an idea of what is involved.

Our concern goes beyond the technical ability of a lawyer. His advice can prove bad if the contract he recommends is challenged or if his prediction of how the courts will decide is wrong. Our question is about counseling that, even if successful, is at or beyond the boundaries of legality. Guidelines are supplied, but little thought is required to suggest how inadequate they will show themselves.

In this country, it is forbidden for a lawyer to "knowingly assist his client in illegal conduct" or to "counsel his client on how to violate the law and avoid punishment therefor." Yet consider a range of problems.[18] One of your clients operates a small store and asks you what penalties he would suffer if he violates "blue laws" that prohibit him from doing business on a Sunday. A second client asks you for a list of countries that have no extradition treaty with the United States, so that a person who has committed a crime here can find refuge there without fear of being sent home for trial. A third client asks you for detailed information on how laws against kidnapping apply if the victim is not transported across state lines. Few lawyers would refuse to give the first client full information about the minor penalties and lack of enforcement in regard to blue laws. Most lawyers would supply the information about extradition treaties, though some would not, on the grounds that it seems a clear offer of advice on how to avoid punishment for crime. However, a serious request for counsel on mitigating the legal sanctions for a possible kidnapping would almost certainly meet with evasive replies from a lawyer of integrity. Do the differences have to do simply with the gravity of the crime? Or with the extent to which the lawyer would pass from bare information to active involvement?

There is one proposal to commit crime that lawyers may frequently encounter. This comes when a client seems clearly to suggest that he will perjure himself in court. The lawyer is explicitly forbidden "knowingly to use perjured

---

18. These examples, and some of the following ones, are taken from Monroe Freedman's *Lawyers' Ethics in an Adversary System* (Indianapolis: Bobbs-Merrill, 1975), one of the few books that well illustrate the problem of legal counseling.

testimony or false evidence." However, it is less clear what is to be done in practice. A client has a right to tell his story when he has his day in court. He can, of course, be advised not to include falsehoods and be warned of the penalties if discovered. But when the story that appears in court turns into what the lawyer knows to be perjury, what course is to be followed? The official advice is that he or she should at that point withdraw from direct examination, allowing the client to continue in narrative fashion, and that the lawyer should then refrain from arguing on the basis of what has been asserted in this way. If we remember the predicament of Charles Phillips, however, we see the problem: both judge and jury will draw obvious conclusions from this tactic at work. The question requires much more discussion, but all solutions seem to opt for one or the other horn of the basic dilemma. If truth is paramount, then lawyer-client confidentiality suffers. Yet if the lawyer is to win the confidence of a client (and to learn the truth from him), then some measure of deception on the court must be tolerated.

The suggestion appears to follow that a lawyer who tries conscientiously to satisfy the various requirements may face a number of trade-offs. A hypothetical case, given in a symposium on legal ethics, can indicate some of these problems of divided loyalty.[19]

You are the court-appointed counsel for defendant in a rape case. He is a drifter who was then working at a filling station. The victim of his alleged attack at the lonely garage is the twenty-two-year-old daughter of a local bank president and is engaged to a minister. Your inquiries produce a jealous suitor who states that he frequently had intercourse with her and describes her behavior toward men as scandalous. He gives information to support this claim, is eager to testify, and says the girl "got what she had been asking for."

The accused at first presents a plausible story of compliance by the girl but later admits, under interrogation in the privacy of your office, that he has been lying to you and is guilty as charged. However, he refuses to plead guilty or to accept any lesser charge. He wants to repeat his initial story in court and insists that he can get away with it as he did once before in California.

Two questions, above all, face you. Should you put your client on the stand, thus exposing the court to what you are sure is a blatantly false story? And should you use the information from the suitor, perhaps calling him as a witness, in order to throw doubt on the testimony of a girl who (whatever her behavior at other times) is telling the truth about this incident?

My suspicion is that many laypeople would reply yes to the first question and no to the second. The prosecution is also vocal and can attack assertions from a dubious source. But there is something offensive about publicly blackening the character of a person who, in this case at least, is on the side of truth.

However, the disagreement about legal ethics is shown by the fact that the symposium produced weighty support for the opposite solution. Perjury was

19. See *American Criminal Law Quarterly* 5 (1966): 8–10.

said to be a fraud on the court and a lawyer who knowingly participates in this to be "perverting an honorable profession." Nevertheless, it was claimed that the requirements of an adversary system involve testing the prosecution case to the full, even where cross-examination severely injures the character of a witness whose statements are known by defense counsel to be true.

The problems that a lawyer faces in counseling a client are perhaps only a particular version of difficulties we all confront in finding truth through talking to others. The statements we normally expect are narrative. I ask you to let me know what happened at the party or at the meeting. I listen while you tell a story that is structured by your own interests and your own assessment of what is important or not. But at some stage in the process, perhaps quite early in it, I am likely to intervene with my own questions. And the resulting account will probably differ in many ways from what an unimpeded narrative would have produced.

As was suggested before (section 23), the guiding hand of judge or attorney may help to disclose truth. At least, some such guide is required if legally relevant facts are to be revealed. However, the possibilities for partisan distortion are great. And these are increased under our blatantly adversary system, where the client and many of the witnesses are extensively interviewed in the lawyer's office before the trial. In the civil law tradition, as we have seen, a witness meets the rival attorneys for the first time in the presence of a judge who does most of the questioning. But one authority in this country recommends as many as fifty full rehearsals of both direct- and cross-examination before the trial. The lawyer can take on the role of director of a play. The boundaries between disclosure and distortion, reporting and fabricating, are not easy to draw.

Two examples may help (Freedman, *Lawyers' Ethics*, 70, 74). Assume that a man and a woman, deciding to get married, contribute five thousand dollars each to start a small business. On one supposition the venture proceeds to wedlock, on another the engagement is broken. What was their intention in pooling the money? Was it to form a partnership? Was the man seen as a trustee? Or did the woman make him a gift of the money? No knowledge of the law is required for us to suspect what scope a lawyer has, be he interested in lowering taxes or in recovering resources where love failed, from the questions he puts in his office to summon distant and inarticulate memories.

Or imagine that a client seeks workers' compensation for a strain incurred while lifting heavy objects. One jurisdiction has, in a long line of cases, made the award only when the worker slipped or tripped in the process. Another jurisdiction requires merely that the incident be work-related. If you, as a lawyer in the former jurisdiction, are trying to crystallize your client's memories, do you think that you could quite easily, with appropriate questioning, discover that he had slipped or tripped?

No more profound conclusion is offered than that a lawyer faces problems of conscience, not only in the way he plays his role on the stage of a courtroom, but in the most mundane questions he formulates when counseling in his office. He is no mere book of law to be opened at will by his client.

FURTHER READING

Questions of legal ethics are discussed mainly in the articles of professional journals. The books by Mellinkoff and by Freedman (nn. 14, 18) offer the best access and have extensive bibliographies.

Other recent books on ethical questions in legal practice include:

Davis, Michael, and Frederick Elliston, eds. *Ethics and the Legal Profession.* Buffalo, N.Y.: Prometheus Books, 1986.
Hazard, Geoffrey C., Jr. *Ethics in the Practice of Law.* New Haven: Yale Univ. Press, 1978.
Luban, David, ed. *The Good Lawyer.* Totowa, N.J.: Rowman & Allanheld, 1984.

QUESTIONS FOR DISCUSSION

1. The previous section considered the positions of Dr. Johnson, of C. P. Curtis, and of F. S. Cohen, as a range of theoretical replies on the way truth is disclosed through the legal process. Suggest how each of the three might have responded to the predicament in which Charles Phillips found himself.

2. One of the most frequently quoted statements of a lawyer's responsibility to his client, even at the expense of injury to others, was made in England twenty years before the Courvoisier case:

> An advocate, in the discharge of his duty, knows but one person in all the world, and that person is his client. To save that client by all means and expedients, and at all hazards and costs to other persons, and, amongst them, to himself, is his first and only duty; and in performing this duty he must not regard the alarm, the torments, the destruction which he may bring upon others.
>
> (Lord Henry Brougham, *Trial of Queen Caroline*, 1821)

Does this language sound excessive when applied to the destruction of a helpless person such as Sarah Mancer? It is well to remember that the opponent Brougham had in mind was none other than King George IV, and that the potential destruction was of the English monarchy. The statement, often taken out of context, has more to do with a courageous defense of the independence of courts than with an attack on innocent witnesses.

3. A game establishes an area that is understood to be separated from ordinary life. The animosity shown, often in ritualistic form, on the playing field is not carried over onto the streets. This notion persists in politics: remarks can freely be made in Congress or in Parliament that would lead to a libel suit outside. Do you think that lawyers tend to think of the courtroom in this light? Does our indignation at their attacks on witnesses come from some failure to appreciate the rules of the game?

4. Hypothetical cases, whether constructed by law professors or by moral philosophers, usually lack the detail required for a sound solution. In practice, the question can often be handled in a way that leads between the horns of the dilemma. What further inquiries might you make in the rape case proposed at the symposium? How would you avoid "fraud on the court"? How might you satisfy both your legal duties toward the defendant and your human duties toward the victim?

5. There seems to be some critical line between the way in which a lawyer simply informs his clients and the way he actively participates in what they do. This needs illustration from outside the law. Suppose a friend comes to you for advice on a matter where legality is not in question (a dispute with teachers or with employers or some marital problem). How can you give "objective" advice without clearly leading the other in a certain direction?

6. There was considerable controversy over a case in Lake Pleasant, New York, where the defendant on a murder charge told his attorneys that he had killed two other people and hidden their bodies. The lawyers located the corpses and took photographs. They did not inform the police, and they denied all knowledge of what had happened when visited by the parent of a girl whose body they had so discovered. Notice that the case for which they had been retained was distinct from the one that resulted in those corpses. Were the lawyers guilty of obstruction of justice? Of hiding a crime? Of becoming an accomplice after the fact?

28. RATIONAL CONCLUSIONS

> *The lawyers have so bemused themselves with words and theories that they have not even yet developed anything like a rational system for performing their principal function of deciding particular controversies. Most decisions are presented behind a verbal facade that is cast in the syllogistic form. But it requires little sophistication to demonstrate that the logical form has little to do with judicial decisions.*
>
> (Lee Loevinger)

Of the three main philosophies of law examined in the previous chapter, it is legal realism that has figured most prominently in this one. The "cynical acid" that Justice Holmes suggested we should throw upon the law has tarnished whatever appearance it had as a perfect work of reason. Any assumption that the rules of law have only to be applied to the facts of a case in order to yield the correct conclusion is now ridiculed under such names as "mechanical" or "slot machine" jurisprudence. If the conclusion that is reached is a rational one, we need considerable flexibility in our understanding of the reason that is at work. Fact skeptics and rule skeptics will also be decision skeptics. So it is to the final term in Jerome Frank's equation that we turn in this section. The topic of judicial decision making will emerge again in section 34, but mainly in light of the question how a judge should arrive at a verdict that is morally correct. Here we are more concerned with the question how his or her decision is said to be rational.

There is a certain paradox in the position of the legal realists. On the one hand, they seem to stress the irrationality of verdicts, the lack of connection between what you put into the slot machine and what comes out of it. On the other hand, they announce that law is a prediction of what the courts will decide. How are we to reconcile irrationality with predictability?

A parallel may exist in the natural sciences. The rationalism that saw the world as controlled by reasons that we could derive by sheer thinking had first to be shattered. Nature then appeared arbitrary before the scientist could begin serious work. He turned from normative laws to a simple observation of the full range of facts involved. Gradually he was able to identify recurrent events and to correlate these, thereby discovering his purely descriptive laws. These are objective, in three senses: (1) they are concerned with objects (the behavior of what he observes); (2) the laws are quantitative (science is interested only in those qualities to which numbers can be applied); and (3) a remarkably high rate of agreement is achieved among all who make such investigations.

The legal realists proposed a similar destruction of the rationalistic mentality that pervaded traditional thinking about the law with which courts are concerned. And the resulting "irrationality" was likewise thought to be therapeutic and constructive, by making possible serious attention to the descriptive laws of the legal process. These would be rational in the sense of enabling us to predict outcomes. If, however, the project is to be feasible, we must take into account all relevant input, as the scientist does whose eyes are no longer blinkered by traditional interests. The judge's conclusion does not follow deductively from the rules in the books and the facts of the case. Nevertheless, a decision can, at least in principle, be predicted if we record and allow for the judge's personal attitudes, social background, political ideology, and all other "extracurial" factors that could bear on the course of a trial.

Such, at least, was the design announced by Holmes and the realists. But though Holmes told us to prophesy the decisions of courts, he gave surprisingly little advice on how we are to do this. His followers wrote at length about the many elements that influence the outcome of a legal case, yet they supplied no basis for measuring and weighing these and hence for making specific predictions.

In this section we shall begin by asking in what direction this call for predicting legal conclusions has led in the past thirty or forty years. Whereas the legal realists made little use of the social sciences, the modern techniques of a political scientist have now been turned to a detailed and quantitative study of many aspects of the law. We shall mention what are known as "jurimetrics" and "judicial behavioralism."

Suppose such a program achieved a high degree of success; objectivity is secured by quantifying all the relevant influences, and experts attain noteworthy agreement on the outcome of cases. Could we thereby say that the law comes to rational conclusions? If a nurse of long experience is able to predict with great accuracy what various doctors will prescribe for a patient, it does not follow that all these doctors are acting rationally. There is an important shift in the term *rational* as we pass from the viewpoint of the observer to that of the agent.

Hence this section will end with some comments on the way a judge can, from his or her own viewpoint, be said to make rational or irrational decisions. The medical analogy may be continued: one doctor arrives at a diagnosis only after conducting thorough tests and following standard procedures, whereas another doctor "divines" the cause of illness and prescribes a remedy on the basis of a "hunch." We should probably say that only the former was acting rationally and (in some further sense of an ambiguous word) "objectively." Yet suppose the patient of the former doctor dies and the patient of the latter is restored to health. The cynic (or the person who sees diagnosis as an art rather than a science) may not think this altogether unlikely. At least, we should remember that we have been adopting the viewpoint of the agent—results are not yet at hand as I choose my procedure and make my decision.

The distinction in viewpoint is more clear when we turn from medicine to law. Doctors may find they were wrong if the patient dies. But a judge is likely to recognize his mistake only if he is reversed, and even then he can still wonder. How does he know which decision is rational? If he departs so far from procedures as to accept bribes or to roll dice, he is acting irresponsibly as a judge (though a knowing observer might have predicted this). Yet what about the claim, often made by legal realists and by laypeople, that a thoroughly honest and conscientious judge may come to his decision intuitively and later compose his opinion as a rationalization or cover-up? The section will include extracts from a celebrated article in which a judge both accepted this as a common procedure and defended it as prevalent even in the evidently rational fields of mathematics and science.

Objectivity and Prediction

> Justice is a personal thing, reflecting the temperament, the personality, the education, environment, and personal traits of the magistrate.
> (Charles Grove Haines)

> Legal method is no more in phase with modern science than it was in the days of Austin.
> (Glendon Schubert)

Let us begin by stating the obvious. Though constancy is claimed for the law, change is also a prominent feature. This is not only because legislatures impose new rules on us by a wave of the hand and a stroke of the pen. Court decisions, at all levels, show a notable movement of their own. Appellate courts bend to the left and back to the right, depending on the judges who constitute them and (less evidently) on social, economic, and political developments. Trial courts fluctuate in more mundane ways; the layperson, who is little concerned with the course of law in its frock-coated form, attends to the psychology of the particular judge on the bench or jury in the box. Montaigne and Dickens warned their readers to recognize the wide range of judicial temperaments and the daily shifts in digestion, gout, and personal humor. Talk of "gastronomical jurisprudence" can be overdone, yet your lawyer will—given any sense of reality—aim to have your case come before the right judge at the right time.[20]

From this important but limited perspective, that of the observer of legal behavior, it is sound to say that a client pays a lawyer for predictive skills. A

---

20. For an extreme account of the psychiatry of judicial verdicts, see Theodore Schroeder, "The Psychologic Study of Judicial Opinions," *California Law Review* 6 (1918): 89–113. For statistics on the remarkable discrepancy in verdicts and sentences given by judges on the same court, see Jerome Frank, *Law and the Modern Mind* (1930; reprint, Gloucester, Mass.: Peter Smith, 1970), 121.

president appoints an economic adviser to make a general prediction of economic trends, to help formulate an appropriate policy, and repeatedly to adapt this in the light of events. A client hires a lawyer to anticipate, in general, how local courts will handle a case, and then (both before and during any trial that develops) to fine-tune these predictions to the mood of a specific judge and to the tactics of opposing counsel.

If your experience is unhappy, your lawyer may (after safely collecting the fee) comment that law is short of being a science, just as the president's adviser remarks on the lack of objectivity in economics. In this context, talk of irrationality or of subjectivity has to do with the reliability of predictive laws. Astronomy is thoroughly objective because we know, to the second, when the next eclipse will occur. Meteorology is more subjective in that it talks only of the probability of precipitation in a particular region. But there is a common goal. The political scientist aims at an objectivity where voting patterns will be more predictable than cloud patterns are at present. Observers of the courtroom scene follow suit. Some may, like the Marxist, hold that the law of a society is in principle determined by the socioeconomic situation, though changes in the former appear with some delay. Yet it is readily admitted by all that we have far to go in our measurement of the full input before we can say with assurance what the outcome of any trial will be.

What is needed on the road to success? When the natural sciences were taken as an example above, three meanings of "objectivity" were distinguished. The third is agreement among experts: all local meteorologists predict rain at rush hour. This supposes the first meaning, the elimination of animistic or metaphysical thoughts that prevent the "field" from being seen as the interplay of pure objects: winds are no longer mindful beings who act with good or bad intentions. But it is the second meaning of objectivity that was basic in the growth of the sciences: the things or events so observed must be open to a method of quantification. It is in this vital respect that the social sciences have lagged behind astronomy and chemistry.

If law is, at some remove, to enter among the sciences, it must be ready for what has been called *jurimetrics*. This term was introduced, at mid-century, by Lee Loevinger in an article appealing for students of the law to adopt measures which would make possible some of the advances that have allowed us to pass from astrology to astronomy and from alchemy to chemistry.[21] He pictured two conventions. The first is composed of the world's greatest legal scholars and takes as its topic the traditional questions of jurisprudence. The second is confined to a dozen competent specialists who limit their concern to specific areas of the law and ask how quantitative measurements can be made of "what goes on."[22] Which convention would produce solid results? Loevinger sees little

---

21. "Jurimetrics—The Next Step Forward," *Minnesota Law Review* 33 (1949): 455.
22. For a recent account of methods used in the operationalization and measurement of judicial behavior, cf. C. Neal Tate, "The Methodology of Judicial Behavior Research," *Political Behavior* 5 (1983): 63–70.

hope of unanimity in the first and asks what would be achieved if the professors did manage to agree on replies to their grand questions. The second, he admits, would produce no sudden or dramatic change in legal procedures. But he sees it leading toward a radical reformulation of legal problems that would "have far-reaching consequences for society and for the individual" and would "establish within the law itself an institutional method for growth and change." Though the quantification of the social factors that legislators regard in making law and of the procedures that judges use in applying this is not in itself oriented to either change or permanence, we should at least "cut windows in the house of law, so that those inside can see out, and we should cut doors, so that those outside can get in."

The article appeared at the start of the electronic revolution that has made computers a fact of life in all fields of knowledge. Perhaps few are so open to such assistance as is the law. A casual visit to a law library can suggest to the layperson what a mass of information a lawyer would need to master if a small area of the law is to be known and used in any particular problem. Even the herculean lawyer or judge who could comprehend the law at present would have difficulty keeping abreast of the spate of new legislation and adjudication. As for law reform, it is scarcely to be expected that an expert committee plowing through the books can devise a product where the left hand realizes what the right hand is doing. It is difficult enough to formulate a complex contract that is consistent with the standing law (or even, through the maze of conditional clauses, with itself).

No one questions the utility of computers in the law as instruments of information storage and retrieval, where they supplement human memory and reason in regard to what is openly discussed in a courtroom. More problematic is the measurement and use of extracurial factors in the prediction of judicial decisions. So we may turn briefly to the movement that has developed over the past generation and is commonly known as "judicial behavioralism."

The suggestion that all we do can be reduced to observable behavior and explained in terms of empirical causes may be as old as Democritus. In the form of a serious program for psychology, the proposal dates from a 1913 paper of J. B. Watson and has been developed most comprehensively in the work of B. F. Skinner. It was Charles Merriam, of the University of Chicago, who stated the case for a similar science of political behavior. What came to be called "political behavioralism" may have remained a minority position in the full range of political scientists. Yet by the 1960s it became increasingly common for graduate students to be trained in statistics and computer technology and to study psychology and sociology as well as (and sometimes instead of) philosophy and history. Articles in professional journals seemed rigorous contributions only when equipped with tables, charts, statistical curves and mathematical functions—to be real is to be quantifiable.

It was not long before judicial behavior was exposed to such research. C. Herman Pritchett brought the quantitative movement to the study of the U.S.

Supreme Court with his 1948 publication, *The Roosevelt Court*. In this research, Pritchett laid the basis for investigations of judicial voting in terms of cumulative scaling and factor analysis. Since that date, many hundreds of articles have been published relating the attitudes and backgrounds of judges to their decisions. Perhaps the most influential and prolific writer in this field has been Glendon Schubert. Reference will be made to some of the qualifications he introduced, but the interested reader may consult *The Judicial Mind Revisited* (1974) for a fair statement of how he built on Pritchett's groundwork for studying causal explanations of why U.S. Supreme Court justices vote as they do.

The field has become highly technical, and the outsider is restricted to a few obvious comments. If the basic model is that of input and output (what leads to a decision, and the vote that results), the question is how we measure each term and how we relate them. The relationship is a mathematical one, and perhaps the only remark an amateur can make is that the certainty of mathematics does not extend to its application. No finding of Euclid can tell us whether the universe we observe is Euclidean. As mentioned above (section 26) we can choose between imposing a Euclidean geometry (to find that light does not travel in straight lines) and assigning a non-Euclidean geometry to allow for light rays to be straight. Similarly, any study of judicial behavior permits some choice in the mathematical method of relating the predispositions of a judge to his disposition of cases. Criticisms, within the field, often center on the selection of the statistical methods employed.

Of particular concern is the question how we measure the influences on a judge and the decisions with which these are to be correlated. Let us turn first to the latter. Our political elections are based on a simple counting of votes, and surely we can categorize judicial decisions in a similar way? Like the voter in the booth, the judge must finally declare himself for or against the claim that reaches him. What difficulty of measurement lies here?

There are a number of vital problems. One is that no appellate judge acts alone. His vote results from interaction with his brethren on the court. Students of judicial behavior have not been blind to this and have used "small group theory" to help explain the process by which votes are formed. But the complications are considerable, and it seems that little has been added to predictive abilities by such studies.

A further problem is that most research has been limited to non-unanimous decisions at the appellate level, and largely to those of the U.S. Supreme Court. Unanimous decisions have been neglected, since these supply no measurable difference in judicial behavior.[23] However, "unanimity" is often a political expedient rather than an expression of genuine agreement. And dissenting

---

23. There is at least one serious study that attempts to use *all* decisions. See Thomas R. Hensley and Karen Dean, "Have We Been Overlooking Something?" Paper delivered at a meeting of the American Political Science Association, Washington, D.C. (1984).

opinions form a literary genre that tends to favor excessive statement rather than balanced views.

Does a judge's vote truly measure his or her attitude? Hundreds of cases may reveal a consistent pattern, but great caution is required in categorizing each decision. A judge voting with the majority to limit the action of a labor union need not be classified as "anti-union." Nor must his vote on a decision for government control over competition classify him as an economic liberal or conservative. The notion of a "vote" translates uneasily from the polling booth to the bench. National elections tell us who won rather than what the public wanted; in judicial votes, which help to formulate our law, the underlying "what" assumes considerably more importance than the question who won a particular case.[24]

Measurement of where an appellate judge stands may turn from his simple vote, for or against, to some analysis of the content of his written opinions. An important example of "content analysis" comes in Schubert's study of the judicial philosophy of Justice Robert Jackson.[25] The popular classification of Supreme Court justices under such categories as judicial activism or restraint had produced ambiguous results here, leading to the conclusion by commentators that Jackson's theories were unsystematic and his votes largely unpredictable. So Schubert, working with two graduate students, read more than three hundred opinions that Jackson wrote as a Supreme Court justice and analyzed them for their content, using correlational, cluster, and factorial methods. An original list of thirty-three "content variables" was reduced to thirteen, and these were related to such other variables as political liberalism or conservatism, economic liberalism or conservatism, and to the chronological variable of three periods in which he sat on the court. The results offered no dramatic reassessment, but they did supply quantitative data for what had previously remained in the realm of loosely supported talk.

Schubert later viewed content analysis of judicial opinions as offering more trouble than it is worth. Others, such as David Danelski, chose to extend the method to a study of judicial speeches. And efforts have been made to clarify judicial verdicts through personal interviews and mail questionnaires.[26] However, the consensus seems to be that such researches are "impressionistic" and that their results belong to the attitudes that influence a decision rather than to judicial behavior itself, which has been increasingly confined to the evidence of a vote in a divided court.

---

24. As an example, consider the 6–3 vote of the U.S. Supreme Court supporting publication of the "Pentagon Papers" (1971: New York Times Co. v. United States, 403 U.S. 713, 91 S.Ct. 2140). It does not follow that six justices were for freedom of the press, in terms of the First Amendment, and three were against. Other questions, such as that of separation of powers, were involved on either side of the vote.

25. Glendon Schubert, *Dispassionate Justice: A Synthesis of the Judicial Opinions of Robert H. Jackson* (Indianapolis, Ind.: Bobbs-Merrill, 1969). See Schubert, *Human Jurisprudence*, chapter 6.

26. Tate, "Judicial Behavior Research," 60–62 (cf. footnote 22 above). Tate looks for some revival of content analysis when computer programs are more readily available for the machine reading and analysis of judicial opinions.

When we turn to the other side of the equation, the influences at work on a judicial decision, we find the morass that has confronted social scientists. Meteorology is still far from popular acceptance as offering reliable predictions, yet those whose vocation it is to tell us from which direction tomorrow's winds will blow have a relatively simple task; the variables, though still not fully explored, are clearly limited. But (to take a simple example) consider the profusion of variables we should have to take into account when predicting disparities between male and female judges in sentencing a woman who has been convicted. We must, for instance, weigh paternalistic attitudes against the claim that female elites are more liberal than male elites.

As an illustration of the complexity of the "input" side of the equation, a few of the many elements involved may be enumerated.

1. There are biological factors. Gender is clearly at stake, as is race and age. So far, however, apparently "obvious" results have not been supported by detailed studies. For example, older judges may become more liberal.

2. "Personality" is an important but ambiguous notion. Is it relevant whether judges like or dislike themselves? Should we take into account such Freudian concepts as projection, rationalization, sublimation, repression, and suppression? Jerome Frank, himself a client of psychoanalysis, said much on the psychological factor in judicial decisions. But more serious studies have proved more humble.

3. "Culture" is a term that covers a multitude of variables. In this context it includes the many affiliations that may have influenced a judge throughout his or her life (religion, politics, education, even language in a multilingual country such as Belgium, Canada, South Africa, or Switzerland). Will a judge educated in private schools and Ivy League colleges be more "establishment" in making decisions than one who was educated in tax-supported schools and state colleges?

4. "Ideology" is one of the terms most generally employed by writers in this field, and it is taken to refer to such headings as "liberal" and "conservative." These terms have to be made operational by recording positions taken on many particular issues, a process that leaves some room for dispute over classification. Gilbert and Sullivan fell slightly short of the rigors of political science in claiming that each of us is born a little liberal or a little conservative.

5. Professional background in the law seems to have been one of the most promising fields of research. Judges with previous experience as prosecutors tend, perhaps surprisingly, to be more conservative on the bench than others. However, in which direction does causality move? Are the more conservative lawyers attracted to prosecutorial positions in the first place?

The simplest model available to a judicial behavioralist is that of a direct, causal analysis in which different attitudes (input) lead to different decisions (output). Attitudes are not directly observable but can be measured in terms of the goals that a person reveals (e.g., support of freedom of speech, of a redistribution of wealth, or of rehabilitation through sentencing). Of importance also is the way that attitudes lead to the perception and weighing of facts in a case.[27] Thus, either a liberal or a conservative judge may be "cued" to give special attention to a case in which the position of the federal government is at stake or in which the issue of free assembly versus social order is involved. Attitudes may assign greater or lesser weight to the fact of physical violence in eliciting a confession. The marital status of a defendant may be seen as important or as irrelevant.

The threat of circularity in such explanations is present. The conclusion that liberal attitudes lead to liberal decisions is unlikely to inspire us. Hence the desire, visible since the early days of legal realism, to explain attitudes in terms of background variables (or attributes). Does the economic standing or political party of the judge account for his liberal or conservative attitudes? Though the distinction is fluid, we may speak of influences present since birth (such as sex and race) and affiliation variables (membership in some social group).

More than twenty years of research on such questions have been primarily "bivariate" (one variable among causes is related to one among effects) and have led to few generally accepted results, even on the seemingly obvious connection between political affiliation and judicial decisions. Stuart Nagel's study of this relationship in 1961 produced only low correlations, and his interpretation of the data has since been challenged. Much the same applies to similar studies of the bearing held by age, religion, region, education, and income. It is difficult to say that any background variable studied so far by judicial behavioralists has a consistent and significant relationship to decisions. Indeed, Schubert's most recent book employs a battery of statistical techniques to suggest that, in South Africa and Switzerland, judicial attitudes may have more influence on political and religious affiliations than vice-versa.[28]

Perhaps we can draw from Schubert's work some indication of current directions. In his 1974 study of non-unanimous cases decided by the U.S. Supreme Court between 1946 and 1969 (*The Judicial Mind Revisited*), he applied cumulative scale analysis to identify certain classes of cases, such as those dealing with civil liberties, on which the justices would divide regularly and consistently. He introduced factor analysis to calculate the degree to which each justice aligns his votes with every other. Cumulative scaling and factor analysis were then combined to use a "scale vector" that would enable the measurement of any justice in terms of such criteria as liberalism and conserva-

---

27. See Fred Kort, "Quantitative Analysis of Fact-Patterns in Cases and Their Impact on Judicial Decisions," *Harvard Law Review* 79 (1966): 1,595–1,603.

28. Glendon Schubert, *Political Culture and Judicial Behavior* (Lanham, Md.: University Press of America, 1985), 224–25.

tism. Schubert thus limited his attention to ideologies (relatively permanent sets of propositions) and made possible a prediction, based on consistent voting behavior, of how any justice would vote on relevant cases.

In this way, votes are used to predict votes, and background variables are ignored. Other scholars have remained more faithful to the original program of the legal realists. For instance, a study by Neal Tate (1981) correlated the decisions of U.S. Supreme Court justices to the variables of party, judicial experience, prosecutorial experience, and appointment by a particular president.

The one background factor to which Schubert has returned is interestingly that of biology, though with considerable refinement on earlier studies. He had, in his 1974 work, suggested that the "change" in Justice Black was due to physiological causes.[29] It is, thus, biological rather than chronological age that needs to be measured, and inquiry has turned to such topics as hormonal balance and the neurological tolerance for ambiguity. Of particular concern to some researchers is the distinction between left hemispheric (logical) thought and right hemispheric (holistic) thought. Attention to the latter, or to its predominance in some people over the former, would allow for the intuitive thinking of judges that runs counter to the paradigm employed by previous behavioralists. Whether this challenge to traditional proposals for prediction will in the end lead to greater predictive ability is for the future to tell.[30]

If the behavioralist is to "cut windows and doors in the house of law," the project is still in its infancy. Though law students are now familiar with the use of computers, the curriculum of law schools remains very much directed toward the old jurisprudence. The dispute is below the surface. No one opposes the advent of predictive methods, so far as these can show themselves reliable and applicable. We know where to look for the proof of the pudding. Critics of judicial behavioralism are largely content to remark that the taste so far is bland. Karl Llewellyn, who made detailed studies of the common law from the perspective of a realist but employed no quantitative methods, claimed that a skilled lawyer, aware of the many subtleties of law in its curial and extracurial forms, should average correct predictions in at least eight out of ten cases that are not pure routine.[31] He left some room for improvement. But there is little evidence that the subsequent twenty-five years have seen this. Indeed, most of the quantitative studies of judicial decisions so far have been in the realm of what is called "postdiction," correlating input with an already present output.[32]

29. "... inexorable physiological changes that accompanied relatively advanced old age" (Schubert, *Judicial Mind Revisited*, 144).
30. For work on "biopolitics," see the journal, *Politics and the Life Sciences*. For instance:
Schubert, Glendon. "The Evolution of Political Science: Paradigms of Physics, Biology, and Politics." *Politics and the Life Sciences* 1 (1983): 97–124.
Masters, Roger. "Human Nature and Political Theory: Can Biology Contribute to the Study of Politics?" *Politics and the Life Sciences* 2 (1984): 120–50.
31. Llewellyn was referring, in such rough figures, to all cases and not just to appellate decisions.
32. There are notable exceptions, as in the article of Reed C. Lawlor, which made a quantitative study of right-to-counsel cases and accurately predicted that *Gideon v. Wainwright* would overrule *Betts v. Brady*. See *American Bar Association Journal* 49 (1963): 337.

In 1966, the *Harvard Law Review* published a symposium on "Social Science Approaches to the Judicial Process."[33] The editors invited Lon Fuller to add an afterword. Fuller gave a sympathetic assessment of the contributions but made a distinction between prediction and understanding. Philosophers of science are divided on the question whether an understanding of nature means more than an ability to predict what will happen; once I predict the full details of the thunderstorm that will arrive in late afternoon, what more can I understand of it (from within the concerns of the scientist rather than those of the poet or the picnicker)? Prediction and understanding may come together in regard to nature, which reveals to us no more than its "face." However, when we turn to human law, there could be room for an important distinction. Suppose I arrive at a probability of 95 percent that I shall lose my lawsuit. Does this mean I have understood the law?

We ask why judges decide as they do, but "why?" questions are ambiguous. You observe me running up a hill on a hot day. Near the top I faint. When I recover, you ask me why I fainted and why I was running on such a day. Grammatical similarity cloaks a vital distinction of viewpoints. The first question invites me to adopt the viewpoint of one who observes physiological input and output. The second question looks for an account of reasons rather than of causes: what my intentions are as one who decides how the facts are to appear and be organized.[34]

Those whose evaluations favor behavioralism in its many forms may reply that we have not yet exorcized the ghost of primitive thinking. What is there in intentions that cannot be recorded by an outsider and quantified? The history of science follows the plan of reducing an agent-viewpoint to that of an observer. Galileo, Marx, and Freud have gradually helped us to restrict the former by transforming it into the latter. However, their very success in following their own project has put before us the fear of a more than theoretical self-contradiction. If Marx is correct in saying that all theories are the necessary effect of socioeconomic forces, then what about the theory of Marxism itself? Freud's theories, in order to be respected and accepted as true, demand something more than a sexual account of their own genesis. Causality and truth dwell in different worlds and demand different viewpoints.

This is certainly not to ask for a reintroduction of the language of intention into physics, or to deny the value of behavioralism in psychology and in law. It is simply to suggest that each of these is a project that, to protect itself, must not exclude some alternative account from the viewpoint of the agent, the one who intends to see the world in certain ways. A legal theorist who reduces all normative laws to descriptive laws will have much to tell us about courts and

---

33. Joel B. Grossman et al., "Social Science Approaches to the Judicial Process," *Harvard Law Review* 79 (1966): 1,551–1,628.

34. For an extended account of such distinctions, see Stuart Hampshire, *Thought and Action* (1959; reprint, South Bend, Ind.: Univ. of Notre Dame Press, 1983).

judges; but if he denies us all access to the viewpoint of those who try to make a reasonable decision, he leaves us wondering about his own judgment.

There is nothing startling in this comment. We have seen it in Hart's distinction between the external and internal view on legal rules. And we have found it also in Dworkin's appeal for a return from rules and policies to questions about the underlying principles of law; this is perhaps largely a recommendation for a clarification of the viewpoint from which legal questions are posed.

Any reader who thinks this too abstract to be pertinent is invited to reflect on his or her personal decision making. Suppose I accidentally drop a wallet before you. From what I have observed of your behavior over the years of our acquaintance, I confidently predict that if you are the finder, the money will be returned to me intact. Does this destroy your freedom in handing me the wallet or the moral praise you deserve for your honesty? The fact that I can predict your behavior does not deny that you act for a reason rather than as a mere resultant of causes. Saint, as well as psychopath, can say, I could do no other. Indeed, it is your very knowledge of reasons and normative laws that distinguishes your "regularity" from that of planets and of plants.[35]

We may assume that some advances have been made in our prediction of judicial behavior, and that more are to be expected. Yet the question remains open about the way in which a judge can rightly classify his own decision-making process as rational or irrational. No legal realist seriously proposed that a judge comes to a verdict simply by extrapolating his own track record. From the viewpoint of the agent, the burden of being a rational animal is confusing and demanding.

Intuition and Justification

> I announced a recess of the court for one week.... I used the greater part of two days reading the briefs and making for myself an outline or analysis of the case. Up to this point I had no clear idea which way I was going to decide.... On the morning of my third day of solitary work, the familiar hunch came to me. Quite suddenly I discovered that I was going to have to decide in favor of the railway company. This discovery came to me with a shock. I was inclined to be what both conservatives and radicals scornfully call a liberal.... Yet now I found myself on the other side; and I did not like it.

---

35. Kant claimed that even if we had so complete a knowledge of a person's character and situation that we could predict his conduct in the way we calculate the next solar eclipse, this person's own viewpoint as a moral agent guarantees his freedom (*Critique of Practical Reason*, Academy Edition, p. 99). Sartre's philosophy is a more eloquent defense of the freedom that belongs inescapably to the viewpoint of a subject: it is we who confer meaning on whatever affects us (tyranny, sickness, even our own birth). We can, of course, elect to question the world in a manner that looks for scientific causes as a reply. But the question of causality is *ours*: if any question we formulate were seen only as part of a causal chain, it would "become unintelligible as a question."

Therefore I determined to test to the utmost the validity of my hunch. The way to do that was to write an opinion. If the half-thoughts and partial conclusions which were forming in my mind would go down on paper and stay there, then they were my deliberate judgment....

I finished writing in about two and one-half days. When I read my opinion again, I had to give up the fight. I was compelled to decide in favor of the railway company.

(Joseph N. Ulman, A Judge Takes the Stand
[New York: Alfred A. Knopf, 1933], 196–200)

The theory of biological evolution has been formulated from the stage of greatest development in what is recorded. Perhaps we are silly to ask how a "lower" stage would regard those above it. From such a position, most novelties may have seemed destined for extinction. Man, at least, would have appeared a biological eccentricity, dedicated to utterly useless pursuits.

With hindsight, we can find utility in our many aberrations. The decline in our ability to roar has led to communication around the world, and the renunciation of wings has sent an average person to thirty thousand feet. Yet each gain was reached through the detour of some loss or degeneration. The rational animal has achieved his or her status by way of what counted locally as remarkable irrationality.

The manner of living together morally through a legal system must rank as a notable example. What could seem more destructive than the question whether we *ought* to hunt and the creation of courts to regulate this basic instinct of a carnivorous animal? Why, for instance, should we protect endangered species? We are less efficient, socially, than a colony of termites. And when we focus on the decisions of particular judges, we may at times be inclined to long for the security of the world of orderly instincts. Perhaps, however, our complaint of irrationality on the bench comes from the application of inappropriate models and from our lack of respect for the incalculable steps that induced us to submit to judges rather than to the proven leader of the herd.

In science we celebrate such figures as Copernicus, Galileo, and Newton. This, however, is not so much for their discovery of further facts as for their imaginative proposal of new ways to see old facts. It is now acceptable to suggest that the dramatic advances of science come from hunches about novel ways of organizing the old, from the intuitive proposal of a revolutionary paradigm.

Our concern here is with the way a judge conceives his or her task of giving a decision. If a verdict in a trial court, or a vote in an appeals court, is to pass muster as an act of reason, does this mean a prosaic submission of facts to established rules? Or could the task of being reasonable in this socially vital area allow for our application of such loose terms as originality and creativity, even of intuition and hunching?

These are introductory comments to an old article that still—in spite of its quaint language—deserves a sympathetic hearing. Good judgment is a high accolade. Can it invite imagination without failing in what we demand under the titles of "objectivity" and "rationality"?

Judges work through highly stylized statements of their decisions. This is expected of them, and there are good grounds for the formality of a judicial opinion. Yet we are naive if we think the account to be a report of how judges actually made up their mind. Few have ventured to tell us about this. The extracts that follow are from one attempt to lift the veil. The article is much quoted, largely because the author seemed out to shock the innocent. The question may remain, however, whether he is telling us of judicial irrationality and subjectivity or whether he is asking us for a more subtle understanding of how we are called to be reasonable and objective in giving judgment.

THE JUDGMENT INTUITIVE
by Joseph C. Hutcheson, Jr.

Cornell Law Quarterly 14 (1928): 274–82, 285, 287.
Copyright © 1929 by Cornell University.
Printed by permission of Cornell Law Review, of Fred B. Rothman & Co., and of the estate of Judge Hutcheson.

Many years ago, at the conclusion of a particularly difficult case both in point of law and of fact, tried by a court without a jury, the judge, a man of great learning and ability, announced from the Bench that since the narrow and prejudiced modern view of the obligations of a judge in the decision of causes prevented his resort to the judgment aleatory by the use of his "little, small dice" he would take the case under advisement, and, brooding over it, wait for his hunch.

To me, a young, indeed a very young lawyer, picked, while yet the dew was on me and I had just begun to sprout, from the classic gardens of a University, where I had been trained to regard the law as a system of rules and precedents, of categories and concepts, and the judge had been spoken of as an administrator, austere, remote, "his intellect a cold logic engine," who, in that rarified atmosphere in which he lived coldly and logically determined the relation of the facts of a particular case to some of these established precedents, it appeared that the judge was making a jest, and a very poor one, at that.

I had been trained to expect inexactitude from juries, but from the judge quite the reverse. I exalted in the law its tendency to formulize. I had a slot-machine mind. I searched out categories and concepts and, having found them, worshiped them. I paid homage to the law's supposed logical rigidity and exactitude....

I knew that judges "are the depositories of the laws like the oracles, who must decide in all cases of doubt and are bound by an oath to decide according to the law of the land," but I believed that creation and evolution were at an end, that in modern law only deduction had place, and that the judges must decide "through being long personally accustomed to and acquainted with the judicial decisions of their predecessors...."

As I grew older, however, and knew and understood better the judge to whom I have in this opening referred; as I associated more with real lawyers, whose intuitive faculties were developed and made acute by the use of a trained and cultivated imagination ... I came to see that instinct in the very nature of law itself is change, adaptation, conformity, and that the instrument for all of this change, this adaptation, this conformity, for the making and the nurturing of the law as a thing of life, is the power of the brooding mind, which in its very brooding makes, creates and changes jural relations....

I loved jury trials, for there, without any body of precedent to guide them, any established judicial recognition of their right so to do, nay, in the face of its denial to them, I could see those twelve men bringing equity, "the correction of that wherein by reason of its universality the law is deficient," into the law. There they would sit, and hearing sometimes the "still, sad music of humanity," sometimes "catching sight through the darkness of the fateful threads of woven fire which connect error with its retribution," wrestling in civil cases with that legal Robot, "the reasonably prudent man," in criminal cases with that legal paradox, "beyond a reasonable doubt," would hunch out, just verdict after verdict by the use of that sixth sense, that feeling, which flooding the mind with light, gives the intuitional flash necessary for the just decision....

And so, after eleven years on the Bench following eighteen at the Bar, I, being well advised by observation and experience, set down ... that, when the case is difficult or involved, and Rabelais' Judge Bridlegoose would have used his "little small dice," I, after canvassing all the available material at my command, and duly cogitating upon it, give my imagination play, and brooding over the cause, wait for the feeling, the hunch—that intuitive flash of understanding which makes the jump-spark connection between question and decision.

And more, "lest I be stoned in the street" for this admission, let me hasten to say to my brothers of the Bench and of the Bar, "my practice is therein the same with that of your other worships...." I speak now of the judgment or decision, the solution itself, as opposed to the apologia for that decision. I speak of the judgment pronounced, as opposed to the rationalization by the judge on that pronouncement....

And I do affirm, and will presently show, that it is that tiptoe faculty of the mind which can feel and follow a hunch which makes not only the best gamblers, the best detectives, the best lawyers, the best judges, but it is that same faculty which has guided and will continue to guide the great scientists of the world, and even those august dealers in certitude, the mathematicians themselves. "For facts are sterile until there are minds capable of choosing between them and discerning those which conceal something, and recognizing that which is concealed. Minds which under the bare fact see the soul of the fact" (Henri Poincaré).

... Now what is this faculty? What are its springs, what its uses? Many men have spoken of it most beautifully. Some call it "intuition"—some "imagination," this sensitiveness to new ideas, this power to range when the track is cold, this power to cast in ever widening circles to find a fresh scent, instead of standing baying where the track was lost.

"Imagination, that wondrous faculty, which properly controlled by experience and reflection, becomes the noblest attribute of man, the source of poetic genius, the instrument of discovery in science" (Benjamin Brodie).

"With accurate experiment and observation to work upon, imagination becomes the architect of physical theory. Newton's passage from a falling apple to a falling moon was an act of the prepared imagination without which the laws of Kepler could never have been traced to their foundations. Out of the facts of chemistry the constructive imagination of Dalton formed the atomic theory. Scientific men fight shy of the word because of its ultra scientific connotations, but the fact is that without the exercise of this power our knowledge of nature would be a mere tabulation of co-existences and sequences.... There is in the human intellect a power of expansion, I might even call it a power of creation, which is brought into play by the simple brooding upon facts. The legend of the spirit brooding over chaos may have originated in experience of this power" (John Tyndall).

"Repeatedly, when one is hard beset, there are principles and precedents and analogies which may be pressed into the service of justice, if one has the perceiving eye to use them. It is not unlike the divinations of the scientist. His experiments must be made significant by the flash of a luminous hypothesis. For the creative process in law, and indeed in science generally, has a kinship to the creative process in art. Imagination, whether you call it scientific or artistic, is for each the faculty that creates" (Benjamin Cardozo).

"When the conclusion is there, we have already forgotten most of the steps preceding its attainment" (William James).

... Max Radin (2 *Am. B.A.J.* 359, 1925) takes the judge's work apart and shows us how his wheels go round. He tells us that the judge ..., having heard the cause and determined that the decision ought to go this way or that way, then takes up his search for some category of the law into which the case will fit. The judge really feels or thinks that a certain result seems desirable, and he then tries to make his decision accomplish that result. "What makes certain results seem desirable to a judge?" he asks, and answers his question that that seems desirable to the judge which, according to his training, his experience, and his general point of view, strikes him as the jural consequence that ought to flow from the facts, and he advises us that what gives the judge the struggle in the case is the effort so to state the reasons for his judgment that they will pass muster.

Now what is he saying except that the judge really decides by feeling, and not by judgment; by "hunching" and not by a ratiocination, and that the ratiocination appears only in the opinion?

Now what is he saying but that the vital, motivating impulse for the decision is an intuitive sense of what is right or wrong for that cause, and that the astute judge, having so decided, enlists his every faculty and belabors his laggard mind, not only to justify that intuition to himself, but to make it pass muster with his critics?

There is nothing unreal or untrue about this picture of the judge, nor is there anything in it from which a just judge should turn away. It is true, and right that it is true, that judges really do try to select categories or concepts into which to place a particular case so as to produce what the judge regards as a righteous result, or, to avoid any confusion in the matter of morals, I will say a "proper result." This is true. I think we should go further and say it ought to be true....

The hunch, sweeping aside hesitancy and doubt, takes the judge vigorously on to his decision; and yet, the cause decided, the way thither, which was for the blinding moment a blazing trail, becomes wholly lost to view. Sometimes again that same intuition or hunch, which warming his brain and lighting his feet produced the decision, abides with the decider "while working his judgment backward" as he blazes his trail "from a desirable conclusion back to one or another of a stock of logical premises."

The term *intuition* literally means "immediate perception or contemplation." An intuitive judgment is one where I see the conclusion without first clearly traveling through all the steps that logically lead to it. Reasoning that does pass systematically through all the stages is described as "discursive." Which, then, is the superior form of judgment? Some say it is intuition, because this goes straight to the point; the intermediate stages are not needed. Others require that judgment be discursive; without all the steps, how is the conclusion known to be valid?

The reply we give may well depend on where we are working. To produce the right answer in mathematics, without showing how it was reached, is unlikely to score high marks. Yet a statesman, a parent, or an artistic director may see a solution and not need (or even be able) to give a step-by-step justification for it. Hutcheson is perhaps not aligning the judge with either extreme. But he is at least asking that we not be too narrow or too unbending in the criteria of rationality that we impose.[36]

Hutcheson seems to set up a dichotomy of hunching and reasoning. It is odd to maintain that "the judge really decides by feeling and not by judgment." If a judge does not judge, then he fails in what he was appointed to do. The question is rather about different types of judgment, and especially about that which appears to be premature. A judge at a beauty contest who gives his verdict before even seeing the competitors is open to serious charges. However, suppose his first glance over the field picks out the winner; need his subsequent statement of the way he justifies the verdict be a "rationalization" in the pejorative sense of this term?

An example is needed from the law.[37] Let us suppose a similar incident of homicide by a drunken driver to occur in two jurisdictions. In one (Iowa), he is charged with reckless driving; the more serious charge of assault with intent to kill cannot be sustained in the courts unless an actual purpose to inflict death is proved. In the other state (Georgia), the driver is indicted for assault with intent to kill, since this requires no more to be proved than reckless disregard for the lives of others. It would seem, under the formula that $R \times F = D$, that a more severe decision results in Georgia because of a difference in the rules as interpreted in the courts. However, the decision that really counts for the driver is the sentence he receives. And the penalty given in Iowa for reckless driving can be far more severe than in Georgia for the same offense. Hence the Georgia courts construe the crime of assault, with intent to kill, in such a way that this crime includes reckless driving while drunk, in order that an appropriately severe sentence may be imposed. That is, the conclusion comes first: an intuition of what the drunken driver ought to get fashions, in different ways, the legal reasoning that supposedly leads to the decision.

There are evidently ways in which "working judgment backwards" can produce gross injustice; the victims of a police state can tell us much of that. Yet Hutcheson claims that the procedure is not foreign to mathematics and science, where the charge of subjectivity is seldom raised. Once the construction line has been drawn in geometry, all fits into its logical place; but knowing where to create such a line is a fruit of intuition that can scarcely be taught. The same applies to the hypothesis a scientist conjures out of his fertile imagination before he proceeds to the more prosaic tasks of experimentation. The apparatus that is built depends on the conclusions it is intended to support. Indeed, as has been suggested before, even vision is highly constructive; the observational scientist would see little if he had not already formed a hunch and knew what would justify his theory.

It does not follow, in mathematics or science or even in art, that anything goes. If a conclusion leads backwards, this must be to steps that will support it.

---

36. We may remember that the suspicion of hypocrisy in the justification of appeals court decisions is fostered by styles of judicial writing. Many judges see their task as similar to that of a debater: it is to support the particular decision reached rather than to weigh both sides and indicate how close the decision was.

37. Frank, *Law and the Modern Mind*, 109–10, quoting Leon Tulin (*Yale L.J.* 37 [1928]: 1,048).

As the chemist Kekulé wrote: "Let us learn to dream, gentlemen. Then perhaps we shall find the truth. But let us beware of publishing our dreams before they have been put to the proof by our waking understanding."[38]

What constitutes "waking understanding" varies from one field to another. The mathematician builds no equipment. And the judge does not deduce conclusions from premises as the mathematician requires. Yet it does not follow that the judicial criteria for objectivity need be less demanding; a sound opinion may even be more difficult to achieve than a reliable experiment or an elegant theorem.

FURTHER READING

Gibson, James L. "From Simplicity to Complexity: The Development of Theory in the Study of Judicial Behavior." *Political Behavior* 5 (1983): 7–49. This article contains a bibliography with more than two hundred entries.

Goldman, Sheldon, and Thomas P. Jahnige. *The Federal Courts as a Political System.* 3d ed. New York: Harper & Row, 1985.

Goldman, Sheldon, and Austin Sarat. *American Court Systems: Readings in Judicial Process and Behavior.* San Francisco: W. H. Freeman & Co., 1978.

Lasswell, Harold. *Power and Personality.* 1948. Reprint. Westport, Conn.: Greenwood Press, 1976.

Nagel, Stuart S. "Political Party Affiliation and Judges' Decisions." *American Political Science Review* 55 (1961): 843–50.

———. "Ethnic Affiliations and Judicial Propensities." *Journal of Politics* 24 (1962): 92–110.

———. *The Legal Process from a Behavioral Perspective.* Homewood, Ill.: Dorsey Press, 1969.

Pritchett, C. Herman. *The Roosevelt Court.* New York: Macmillan, 1948.

Rohde, David, and Harold Spaeth. *Supreme Court Decision Making.* San Francisco: W. H. Freeman & Co., 1976.

Schubert, Glendon. *The Judicial Mind.* Evanston, Ill.: Northwestern Univ. Press, 1965.

———. *The Judicial Mind Revisited.* New York: Oxford Univ. Press, 1974.

———. *Human Jurisprudence: Public Law as Political Science.* Honolulu: Univ. Press of Hawaii, 1975.

———. *Political Culture and Judicial Behavior.* Lanham, Md.: University Press of America, 1985.

Tate, C. Neal. "Personal Attribute Models of the Voting Behavior of U.S. Supreme Court Justices." *American Political Science Review* 75 (1981): 355–67.

———. "The Methodology of Judicial Behavior Research." *Political Behavior* 5 (1983): 51–82.

QUESTIONS FOR DISCUSSION

1. How do the following statements, if judged by contemporary adult standards, fail in objectivity (and in what sort)?

> Nature abhors a vacuum.
> Rivers flow to get to the sea.
> This man was born blind because someone sinned.

---

38. Frank, *Courts on Trial*, 184 n. 27.

2.   Primitive man viewed the winds as capricious spirits. Trace the steps required for a scientific account that allows for prediction of wind direction and velocity. How did empirical psychology arise? Economics?

3.   The verdict of a teacher is given in terms of the grade that he or she assigns. If you wished to make a science of grading, what would you want to measure in the background (attitudes and attributes) of various teachers? Does the grade (vote) adequately represent the decision? Suggest different ways of relating "extracurial" factors to the verdict.

4.   Apply this analogy to the law. Suppose your lawyer can predict how a judge will decide on your case. Does this enable you to understand what the law really is? Explore various realms in which you distinguish between "understanding" and mere "predicting."

5.   If the behavior of a highly moral person is thoroughly predictable, does he or she thereby fail to act freely? Is freedom reducible to choice? Does your freedom decrease or increase as you grow in understanding of the laws of your community?

6.   Distinguish between the rational behavior of chemical compounds and the rationality of doing chemistry. "Without chemicals, life would be impossible" (Monsanto Corp.). Does this mean that the construction of chemical formulas is itself merely the effect of chemical reactions? If this claim were made, would it be self-contradictory (like saying that nothing has any meaning)? Can all normative laws be reduced to descriptive laws?

7.   Why would it be wrong for a judge to decide a case by throwing dice? Is Hutcheson wiping out the lines that separate a modern court from a medieval ordeal? From kadi justice?

8.   We reserve a place of honor for legally uneducated jurors, and Hutcheson seems to suggest that the judge should behave as they do. Yet would this not be legal anarchy? In his novel, *The Just and the Unjust*, James G. Cozzens has a defense attorney address the jury with these words:

> You are free men and women. And if they laugh at you, that's their mistake, because you are the ones and the only ones who can by your verdict deliver over to them victims for the caprices of their law-making. It is your conscience that is decisive.

9.   The term *rationalization*, as it comes to us from Freud, suggests that we make false or superficial statements to justify what we have already elected on non-rational grounds. Yet the word means "making reasonable" or "submitting to standards of reason." The possibility is left open that there are many legitimate ways of achieving this. The astronomer, the historian, and the artist accept different criteria of rationality. Leonardo's personality was expressed one way in his science, another way in his art (though he shows dramatically the place of imagination in the former and of mathematical proportions in the latter). Is the artist, by raising moods from an inarticulate state to one that is public and communicable, less rational than a scientist who talks to us by quantifying and by defining events as regular recurrences? Should a judge settle disputes in his family the same way he does in court?

10.   Hutcheson suggests that, even in mathematics and science, conclusions precede premises in the stage of intuition or invention. However, in those fields, the criteria at work in the following stage of justification are most stringent. The intuitive conclusion may not be supported by the axioms and theorems. The scientific experiment may fail. Even in art, it is a common experience that the brilliant insight will simply not transfer to the canvas or to the orchestra or to the dancers. What analogy applies to the judge? Ulman placed the full burden on a judge's ability to write an opinion: "If the half-thoughts would go down on paper and stay there. . . ." Do you see what he means from your own experience in writing? Is this enough for the law?

5

LEGAL REASONING

> *The law of the Radé [in the highlands of Annam] is not incorporated in a code; it is disseminated in innumerable sayings that have been handed down for ages, and the ancients recite these in guttural tones, while they seem to beat out the measure with lifted hand.... The oldest judge, Magnay, would follow the case in silence and then begin to recite with measured words. All grew quiet. They understood. It was the Bedoué, the ancestral law. The two other judges, nodding their heads, murmured with him. It seemed to all that their ancestors were judging them.*
>
> (Roland Dorgelès) [1]

> *It is a childish fiction employed by our judges that judiciary or common law is not made by them but is a miraculous something made by nobody, existing, I suppose, from eternity and merely declared from time to time by the judges.*
>
> (John Austin)

In the previous chapter we looked at trials in the two main legal traditions of today. We saw the problems facing a court as it attempts to get at the facts and give an objective decision. Little, however, was said of the rules that are applied to the facts and supposedly govern the decision. It is to the rules of substantive law that we turn in this chapter. For ours is no longer the happy assurance of primitive people that the law is to be found, complete and unchanging, in the words of a tradition "whereof the memory of man runneth not to the contrary." We have passed through all the stages of law, in Maine's classification, and are not shocked at the notion that rules are made as well as found. Yet no legisla-

---

1. *On the Mandarin Road*, New York: Century Co., 1926; quoted by J. H. Wigmore in *A Kaleidoscope of Justice* (Washington, D.C.: Washington Law Book Co., 1941), 318–21.

ture starts with a blank legal slate or enjoys unlimited power to rule as it chooses. And even the most creative judge is bound in multiple ways by guidelines from a distant past.

The problems here confronting the civil law and common law traditions may seem to be different. Where the law has been codified, the rules stand before us in the articles of a book; the judge appears to face only the question of interpreting the intention of the legislator or codifier. Where there is no code, the judge has the more complex task of finding the law in a series of previous judicial decisions that form a precedent for his own. However, such differences cut across the boundaries between legal traditions. Our own judges are required to interpret statutes. And it is a truth well known to civil law judges that statutes and codes have to be tested in the courts—the meaning of a rule is shown through a variety of applications in particular cases.

Hence we shall speak of problems about legal rules in case law and in enacted law. The first three sections of this chapter will be devoted to the former, and the fourth will introduce the latter. This is the correct sequence if law has passed historically from finding to making, from settling disputes to formulating rules in a systematic code. A law student in our own country spends most of his or her time on case law, and it is here that much of the fascination and of the intellectual burden of law is to be situated. It is also here that law and life come more closely together; we are not supplied with a book of rules but have to chart the course of reasonable replies through a maze of cases.

The chapter title, "Legal Reasoning," deserves a word of comment. If I protest the judgment of a baseball umpire, it is his eyesight rather than his reasoning that I put in question. He did not see that the pitch dipped below my knees. He failed in answering a question of fact.[2] So too with the traditional view of a jury's task. Was Courvoisier (section 27) the one who did the killing? Did the plaintiff in a libel suit suffer the financial loss he claimed? Reasoning is said to enter only when questions of law are at stake, and these are supposedly left to the judge and to appeals courts. What standard of care must be met if a claim of negligence is to be defeated? Is libel committed if the printed article was erroneous but less damaging than a true report would have been? In answering such questions, the judge needs to do more than polish his glasses. He must be prepared to present a reasoned argument that leads from general statements to a particular application, or from a line of previous decisions to a current one.

Though we separate humans from other beings through our power to reason, it is not easy to say what we mean by this term. Plants and animals adapt well to changes. Leaves diminish loss of moisture in a dry spell. Birds fly to warmer climates when cold days dawn. However, we suspect some difference between responding and meaning. Both we and the animals are mortal. Yet only we, as

---

2. This is not to deny that some "judgment calls" may be required, such as how many bases to award the batter when a spectator touches the ball.

reasoning beings, reckon with the limited possibilities of mortal existence from the day of our birth. Animals are mortal but do not "know" it; the proposition that all creatures are mortal does not give the same tragic quality to a sparrow's daily existence as it does to every painful decision we make.

The example is chosen because the statement that all humans are mortal plays its part in most logic courses and we tend to trivialize it. No proposition is of more importance and few are known with more assurance. But how do we know it? Is this a general principle that we quickly grasp or even have from birth (innate idea?), so that conclusions come through a process of moving from general to particular, from whole to part? In customary terms, is this a major premise to which each of us adds the factual minor premise (I am human) and then deduces the sad conclusion (I am mortal)? Or do we proceed from many encounters with death around us to arrive, by induction, at the conclusion that no one will escape this fate? Do we move from part to whole?

These at least are the models for reasoning that tradition hands us. Do they adequately cover the way in which a legal rule is found and applied? Many commentators have suggested that they do not, and this now forms our theme. Are precedents the inductive basis for general conclusions of law that the trial judge then applies deductively in the case before him? Or do the rules "slide" with the cases? Do we reason from part to part, with only a tenuous grasp of the whole? This chapter will not try to usurp the function of a law school. Years of detailed study are required for a satisfactory answer. Yet some preliminary statement of the options may be helpful.

The final section of the previous chapter raised the question why judges decide as they do. However, the approach was very different from the one to be taken in this chapter. We shall no longer be concerned with the viewpoint of an observer who tries to predict judicial behavior. Nor, in adopting the viewpoint of the judge, shall we be interested in the stage of discovery or in the psychological language of hunches and intuitions. Our attention will be drawn to the justification that is offered in the form of an argument for a decision.

Such justification raises two questions: (1) whether the conclusion follows correctly (validly) from the premises and (2) whether the premises are true. As the chapter proceeds, we shall notice that this distinction is less easy to make in legal arguments than elsewhere. Both questions will appear in each section. However, the emphasis in the first four sections will be on the movement of thought from what is already known (e.g., statutes or previous decisions) to the decision that is to be given. Logicians have until recently paid little attention to the often strange (and some would say, defective) reasoning of courts. The final two sections of the chapter will turn more explicitly to disagreements among judges about the premises. The starting point of a legal argument is not "made up" (as a logic textbook may propose that "all elephants are green" and "all cucumbers are elephants"). However, there is considerably more latitude for interpretation in law than in biology, and topics of moral and political philosophy may take a legitimate role. The conclusion at which a court arrives ought to represent good judgment as well as valid thinking.

29. THE TRAIL OF PRECEDENTS

Justice requires the same ratio between persons and between things. But whereas we agree on the equality of things, we dispute about the equality of persons.

(Aristotle *Politics* 1280a)

One father before going to church says to his son, "Every man and boy must take off his hat on entering a church." Another baring his head as he enters the church says, "Look: this is the right way to behave on such occasions."

(Hart, *The Concept of Law*, 121)

Reasoning has much to do with the passage from a particular situation to a general conclusion, from the immediate "this here and now" to something that can come at another place and time. Sensation tells me that it is warm. By reasoning I dare to affirm that it is always warm in the summer or when the wind comes from the south.

That, of course is a descriptive law, to be revised when the first cold day appears in August. But there is a parallel in the passage from a particular decision to a general (and normative) law. Professor Hart invites us to approach a complex topic through family examples. Suppose a child breaks the living room window with a wild throw of a baseball. The angry father shouts, "You'll pay for that!" Particular command or general law? It all depends. This may have been no more than an outburst of the moment, never to be repeated. Or, at the other extreme, the parent may that evening have gathered all members of the family and announced that any domestic damage will be paid for out of the pocket money of the offender. A legislator has spoken, and a statute exists. Clarification will still be needed; for example, is there a higher tariff for malicious than for negligent damage? But the law is general and public, even if not written.

Suppose, however, the father did not act so formally as a legislator. All he said was, "Jimmy, you'll have to pay for that." The tone was calm, and all realized that life has a future. Might the children reason beyond the present incident to the conclusion that a law is in existence, though never even orally expressed as such? Or put yourself in the position of the father. A week later the window is shattered again. This time the culprit is Jimmy's young sister. You serve as judge rather than as legislator. Are you bound by a precedent? It is a basic principle of justice that like cases should be treated in a like manner. Yet Aristotle hints at the problem. We can readily agree on the sameness of things, because these have no "self" beyond the conventions we establish. It is (for our purposes) the same baseball, though a week older, and the same window, though its glass is only a week old. However, we are less sure of the sameness of incidents (what a person did). Here no legislator explicitly defined the equality of all family members in regard to property damage. If the precedent did establish a law, it is one that allows room for maneuver. Jimmy will argue for a loose construction. His sister will try to confine the case to brothers with ample pocket money.

Before we ask, in the following section, how close legal reasoning is to the forms of induction and deduction that apply elsewhere, it may be wise to say something about the doctrine of precedents. This is basic to case law and, so far as statutes depend on courts for interpretation, to all law. Even if legal arguments do submit to models drawn from science and mathematics, the manner of submission will be vitally affected by the need to move from one human case to another and by the problems of sameness in what people do.

History and Criticism

Since much contemporary criticism of judges has to do with the alleged conservatism of an age-old practice, a few words of history may suggest that the precedent doctrine is less ancient and less rigid than commonly supposed. The earliest records we have of proceedings in English courts belong to the twelfth century. These chronicles are, to some extent, the jottings of a journalist. However, more can be detected. There was a concern to find not only what happened, but what the law is. The court reports show some parallel to a book of case law.[3] Nevertheless, the decisions were not seen as binding; though judges would distinguish their decisions from analogous ones, they did not hesitate to say that contrary judgments were simply wrong. It is only in the sixteenth century that the word *precedent* is found and the practice of citing previous cases became firmly established. An obligation to observe precedents had by then been accepted, but no single case was binding; only a clear line of decisions imposed itself on subsequent cases.

In the seventeenth century a distinction appears that shows an effort to clarify what need and need not be respected in fidelity to the past. A judge was said to be bound by the "holding," or actual decision, in a line of cases, but not by the "dicta," or remarks that judges added. This distinction has remained precarious, and we shall return to it. Yet the previous example may offer an initial explanation.

Imagine that another minor tragedy strikes the family. No window is involved, no game, and no negligence. An older brother is mowing the lawn when the machine breaks down and parts have to be replaced. Surely he will not have to pay for this out of his own money? Not if we attend only to the holding of the

---

3. The earliest treatise on English law, compiled by Bracton in the thirteenth century, refers to about five hundred decided cases; a manuscript of his, discovered in 1884 and called the Note Book, gives digests of two thousand cases.

previous cases. But suppose the father, as judge in the initial case, had added dicta in the form of a lament about the cost of living and an exhortation to keep expenses to a minimum. If the precedent is taken so broadly as to cover all the judge said, the older brother, with money in the bank and the misfortune to have been using the machine at the time, may have to pay. At least, we see the need, in law, for delimiting what carries over from one case to another.

It was in the nineteenth century that the precedent doctrine reached the stage of development that has exposed it to serious criticism. *Stare decisis et non quieta movere*: judges should "adhere to past decisions and avoid challenging what has been settled." The rise of scientific thinking had led to the ideal that case law, though not codified, should form a comprehensive system. Earlier ages had been ones of growth, but the possibility was now present to view the body of law as resting upon well-established precedents.

Even then, there were variations in the reception of the doctrine of *stare decisis*. For example, greater flexibility in regard to precedents was allowed in torts than in property law. After the first quarter of the twentieth century the notion of a well-organized science of law became less persuasive, and judges grew more responsive to changes in social and economic life.[4]

It may be important to distinguish between precedent as a habit and as a legal norm. Every individual and every profession develops habits of working in a regular fashion. The experienced craftsman is one who has reduced much of his task to a routine and can devote his energy to creative touches that add his signature. Officials, in law and outside it, cannot afford to start each problem from scratch. The solution once contrived is repeated, and attention is concentrated on novel features. Such habits are to be expected on the bench, as in the art studio.

Difficulties arise when precedent is canonized as a legal norm. An artist who feels obliged to copy the themes and style of his predecessors condemns himself to mere reproduction. Why should a judge be obliged, in the name of legality, to present each decision as a repetition of past ones? Critics maintain that the norm is merely an extension of the habit, and their explanations remain in the realm of psychology. The motives commonly adduced are sloth and fear. Advocates and judges settle for the law as they learned it; a range of new decisions would mean painful adjustment, a return to school. More damaging is the accusation that legal professionals, as distinguished from those in medicine or business, seek the security of the old and fear exposure to untried ways. Jerome Frank, in particular, has given an unflattering psychiatric account of his brethren on the bench. He even likens judges to the processional caterpillars that can be made to walk happily in a closed ring, head to tail (Frank, *Courts on Trial*, 266).

---

4. For an account of some traditional expositions and justifications of the precedent doctrine, see Richard A. Wasserstrom, *The Judicial Decision* (Stanford, Calif.: Stanford Univ. Press, 1961), 39–83. He then turns to conflicts between precedent and equity, a topic we shall mention again in section 34.

Exaggerations aside, most of us can find some occasion to complain at the precedent-bound administration of justice in our courts. The law is the law, not because reasons are explored and applied afresh but because your case has simply been put under the rubric of a line of "settled decisions." When people speak of "legalism," this is much of what they mean. Bad laws are perpetuated as automatically as good laws, and the individual seems lost in the mill. On a more theoretical level, the Marxist sees the precedent doctrine as an effective instrument by which law is kept in the hands of a ruling class and is insulated from changes in the socioeconomic infrastructure.

No one will deny some value to these criticisms. The question, however, is whether they focus on the precedent doctrine itself or simply on abuses of it. Suppose, for example, it were abandoned and each judge were allowed to give verdicts without regard to those of his predecessors? A reminder of the parable of King Rex (section 12 above) will suggest that some of the structures of law would be in jeopardy. What tries to pass as law would no longer be general or public. If we are to plan our lives rationally according to rules, it may be more important to respect the constancy and stability of law than to accuse judges of laziness. The principle that like cases should be decided in a like manner is a matter of duty rather than of psychology.[5]

The American Bar Association has drawn up canons of judicial ethics, and the twentieth may be worth quoting:

> Ours is a government of laws and not of men, and the judge violates his duty as a minister of justice under such a system if he seeks to do what he may personally consider substantial justice in a particular case and disregards the general law as he knows it to be binding on him....

Kadi justice falls short of a government of laws and perhaps even of the standards of rationality. Whatever "reason" means, it does not cover the possibility that the Imam, seated under the Tree of Justice and presented with two very similar cases, can bestow honors on the first petitioner and say "Off with his head" to the second. The more we stress the particularity of *this* judgment in *this* case, the more we discharge the judge from accountability in what he does. The doctrine of precedent is open to many abuses, but it does require that a judge who seems to depart from a clear line of previous decisions should be able to give public reasons for his apparent departure. He should be able to distinguish the cases and thus preserve general norms rather than destroy them. Age brings some relaxation, but the infant identifies reason with regularity.

---

5. It was suggested above (section 8) that this is the *formal* principle of justice, needing then to be complemented by *material* principles that help us to see which distinctions between cases are just and which are arbitrary. Ronald Dworkin speaks of the "gravitational force" of precedents as going far beyond any social *policy* and involving basic *principles* of justice; we ask, for example, how it could be fair for a negligent car manufacturer to be required to pay damages to an injured purchaser but for a careless building contractor not to face similar damages for resulting injuries (Dworkin, *Taking Rights Seriously*, 113).

How the Trail Starts

> "Take some more tea," the March Hare said. "I've had nothing yet," Alice replied in an offended tone, "so I can't take more."
> (Lewis Carroll, *Alice in Wonderland*)

Those who expect cases to be decided by quotations from earlier verdicts may wonder how the precedent system began before there were precedents. The historical remarks above show this question to be rather artificial. Even if rationality demands some fidelity to the past, this need not always mean research in the books of the past. Bracton's court reports and the case studies of an anthropologist put on paper what is already a going concern.

However, the question what to do when no written precedents are at hand can take an interesting and instructive form in what is called a "case of first impression." The novelty is always limited. Remote similarities must always be available. But consider, for example, a rather sudden technological change, such as the development of the airplane. In the 1920s farmers found that their livestock were disturbed by planes flying over their fields. To what could a plaintiff appeal in case law? Decisions that penalized hunters who fired bullets over private property? Verdicts on the right of a company to string electric wires over someone's land? Or cases in which a property owner on the seashore or by the lakeside sought to prevent boats from sailing past his beach?

Where analogies are as remote as these, their choice and application seems capricious. More likely we suspect that some principle has been at work in the judge's thinking that then seeks illustration in such distant examples. On occasions, we find the judge discussing principles openly and without worrying about the lack of precedents. One such case, trivial but suggestive, may be quoted.[6]

Tuttle was a barber who for ten years owned and operated the only barber shop needed in a small village. Buck was the appropriate name of a rich banker who decided to ruin Tuttle and drive him out of the village. So Buck established a competing barber shop there and paid another barber to occupy it, rent free. Tuttle's modest income was halved. He went to law and won. Buck appealed, and part of the opinion of the Supreme Court of Minnesota follows.

> It has been said that the law deals only with externals, and that a lawful act cannot be made the foundation of an action because it was done with an evil motive.... Such generalizations are of little value in determining concrete cases. They may state the truth, but not the whole truth....
>
> It must be remembered that the common law is the result of growth, and that its development has been determined by the social needs of the community which it governs. It is the resultant of conflicting social forces, and those forces which are for the time dominant leave their impress upon the

---

6. Tuttle v. Buck (1909): 107 Minn. 145, 119 N.W. 946.

law. It is of judicial origin, and seeks to establish doctrines and rules for the determination, protection, and enforcement of legal rights. Manifestly it must change as society changes and new rights are recognized. To be an efficient instrument, and not a mere abstraction, it must gradually adapt itself to changed conditions. Necessarily its form and substance has been greatly affected by prevalent economic theories. For generations there has been a practical agreement upon the proposition that competition in trade and business is desirable, and this idea has found expression in the decisions of the courts as well as in statutes. But it has led to grievous and manifold wrongs to individuals, and many courts have manifested an earnest desire to protect the individuals from the evils which result from unrestrained business competition. The problem has been to so adjust matters as to preserve the principle of competition and yet guard against its abuse to the unnecessary injury to the individual. . . .

Many of the restrictions which should be recognized and enforced result from a tacit recognition of principles which are not often stated in the decisions in express terms. . . . To divert to one's self the customers of a business rival by the offer of goods at lower prices is in general a legitimate mode of serving one's own interest, and justifiable as fair competition. But when a man starts an opposition place of business, but regardless of loss to himself, and for the sole purpose of driving his competitor out of business, and with the intention of himself retiring upon the accomplishment of his malevolent purpose, he is guilty of a wanton wrong and an actionable tort. In such a case he would not be exercising his legal right, or doing an act which can be judged separately from the motive which actuated him. To call such conduct competition is a perversion of terms. It is simply the application of force without legal justification, which in its moral quality may be no better than highway robbery.

The appeals court confirmed the lower court's decision in favor of Tuttle. We may well endorse this. Yet how does the author of the majority opinion (one judge dissented) justify his decision? Against him were two principles. One was an economic policy of our society, that "competition in trade and business is desirable."[7] This is not an eternal truth and is presumably not enforced by Communist courts, but capitalist countries applaud the merits of competition and this approval has been expressed in court decisions. The other principle belongs more closely to the law. It is that a lawful act cannot give grounds for a legal suit simply because the motives were morally bad. If I purchase a rare book merely to prevent you from getting it, you may dislike me and think me wicked, but you cannot sue me with much hope of success. Half a dozen precedents (omitted above) were quoted in the opinion.

---

7. This terminology accords with Dworkin's distinction between principles and *rules*: the desirability of competition is a different sort of standard from the rule that makes a will valid. However, we are dealing with a *policy* and hence not with a principle in Dworkin's narrow sense as a "requirement of justice or some other dimension of morality" (see section 19). The third principle to which the judge appeals in *Tuttle* clearly satisfies this more precise criterion.

How then does the judge avoid reversing the lower court and declaring for Buck? We are first reminded that the common law is open to growth and that judicial decisions establish rules rather than merely repeating what has been said before. Then the judge makes his appeal to a principle that he regards as having greater weight than the two previous ones. It does not simply cancel them but enables us to distinguish between their use and abuse. This principle belongs to those that are "tacitly recognized and not often stated in express terms." Unfortunately, it is not adequately stated in this case either. Yet the key phrase seems to be that Buck's conduct was "the application of force without legal justification." In other words, the principles of economic competition and of the irrelevance of motives would, as interpreted and applied by Buck's lawyer, have resulted in an exercise of force rather than of legality. If I understand correctly, we are invited to go back to those basic agreements by which legal settlements took over from blood feuds and from a trial of strength in the jungle. The two principles in favor of Buck are valid when circumscribed. But, unless controlled by a reminder of what law is all about, they can lead to cutting throats and destroying community. Our attention is drawn from the rules of law, as found in precedents, to the basic principles that oblige us to submit to law and to precedents.

Strict and Loose Applications

> What characterizes the signs of human language is not so much their generality as their mobility.
>
> (Henri Bergson)

No simple statement can be made of the extent to which a judge may exercise initiative in spite of (or even because of) his duty to be faithful to previous decisions. The binding force of precedents is generally stronger in England than in this country. Here, the Supreme Court is less constrained than are lower appellate courts. And commentators certainly disagree on the freedom they see a judge as enjoying.

In the final two sections we shall return to questions about the guidance judges draw from underlying legal principles and from moral considerations about the policies they support in making their decisions. But, for the purposes of this introductory section, it may be useful to adopt the adversarial perspective that gives the courtroom its drama and the legal profession much of its interest. How does the constraint of recognizing precedents appear to the lawyer whose duty it is to act as advocate for a client?

Perhaps the best short answer to this question comes in a series of lectures delivered to beginning students by Karl Llewellyn at the Columbia Law School. These talks were printed as a book entitled *The Bramble Bush*, and a brief extract follows.[8] In it, Llewellyn suggests the range of possibilities open to lawyers who find precedents favorable or detrimental to their clients. He is, however, no supporter of legal anarchy. His scholarly writings are at once a study of the flexibility of the common law and a defense of its rationality.[9]

We turn first to what I may call the orthodox doctrine of precedent, with which, in its essence, you are already familiar. Every case lays down a rule, the rule of the case. The express ratio decidendi is prima facie the rule of the case, since it is the ground upon which the court chose to rest its decision. But a later court can reexamine the case and can invoke the canon that no judge has power to decide what is not before him, can, through examination of the facts or of the procedural issue, narrow the picture of what was actually before the court and can hold that the ruling made requires to be understood as thus restricted. In the extreme form this results in what is known as expressly "confining the case to its particular facts." This rule holds only of redheaded Walpoles in pale magenta Buick cars. And when you find this said of a past case you know that in effect it has been overruled....

Now this orthodox view of the authority of precedent—which I shall call the *strict* view—is but *one of two views* which seem to me wholly contradictory to each other. It is in practice the dogma which is applied to *unwelcome* precedents. It is the recognized, legitimate, honorable technique for whittling precedents away, for making the lawyer, in his argument, and the court, in its decision, free of them. It is a surgeon's knife....

For when you turn to the actual operations of the courts, or, indeed, to the arguments of lawyers, you will find a totally different view of precedent at work beside this first one. That I shall call, to give it a name, the *loose view* of precedent. That is the view that a court has decided, and decided authoritatively, *any* point or all points on which it chose to rest a case, or on which it chose, after due argument, to pass. No matter how broad the statement, no matter how unnecessary on the facts or the procedural issues, if that was the rule the court laid down, then that the court has held. Indeed, this view carries over often into dicta, and even into dicta which are grandly obiter. In its extreme form this results in thinking and arguing exclusively from *language* that is found in past opinions, and in citing and working with that language wholly without reference to the facts of the case which called the language forth.

8. Karl Llewellyn, *The Bramble Bush*, Dobbs Ferry, N.Y.: Oceana Publications, copyright © 1960 by K. N. Llewellyn, pp. 66–68. Printed with permission of the publishers.

9. Karl Llewellyn, whom we encountered as co-author of *The Cheyenne Way*, is classified as one of the most influential legal realists. He was, nevertheless, concerned about a "crisis of confidence within the Bar," stemming from a lack of "reckonability" (stable decision making) in the work of U.S. appellate courts. His book, *The Common Law Tradition* (1960), is a lengthy and weighty answer to such doubts. He argues for a high degree of constancy that comes from the "craft of judging" and from the "period style" that guides all courts at a certain time. The extract from *The Bramble Bush*, and that book as a whole, should be read in light of this broader claim.

Now it is obvious that this is a device not for cutting past opinions away from judges' feet, but for using them as a springboard when they are found convenient. This is a device for *capitalizing welcome precedents*. And both the lawyers and the judges use it so. And judged by the *practice* of the most respected courts, as of the courts of ordinary stature, this doctrine of precedent is like the other, recognized, legitimate, honorable.

What I wish to sink deep into your minds about the doctrine of precedent, therefore, is that it is two-headed. It is Janus-faced. There is not one doctrine, nor one line of doctrine, but two, and two which, *applied at the same time to the same precedent, are contradictory of each other*. That there is one doctrine for getting rid of precedents deemed troublesome and one doctrine for making use of precedents that seem helpful.

We noticed the distinction that appeared in the seventeenth century between the "holding" and the "dicta" of a case. The former was the decision, the latter the verbal embellishment supplied by the judge. Evidently, greater precision is required. The more we stress the particularity of a sheer decision, the less possible it becomes for this to serve as a precedent and carry over to other cases. If the Minnesota decision refers only to barbers (or even to those called Tuttle) then no butcher or baker facing a similar injustice can appeal to the verdict. At the other extreme (generality), it is unlikely that subsequent courts would extend the judge's words to protect any long-established business from facing competition at the hands of newcomers who hoped to take away trade and retire on their profits.

The question Llewellyn raises is where to set a line on either side and how lawyers should plan their strategy in the area between. He talks, not of the holding, but of the "rule of a case" (*ratio decidendi*: reason for deciding). What transfers is not a sheer decision but the thinking that makes the decision rational and hence general. Sometimes the judge tries to put this into explicit words (as an "express *ratio decidendi*"). If so, subsequent judges will certainly attend to what he says, but the words are not authoritative. A later court, while accepting the decision, may reformulate the reasoning that it embodies. The question, then, is how we are to find the *ratio decidendi* in a precedent.

One of the most influential commentaries on this question came from Professor Arthur L. Goodhart, who proposed that the *ratio decidendi* of a case "is found by taking account of the facts treated by the judge as material and his decision as based on them."[10] His defense of this theory, and subsequent attacks on it, go far beyond our limited concerns. But at least we can return to Llewellyn's account in terms of the question which facts are material or immaterial to a judge's decision.

The example given by Llewellyn was of a traffic accident, and already we are in the realm of legal concepts that take us beyond the sheer sight of moving

---

10. See Arthur L. Goodhart, "Determining the Ratio Decidendi of a Case," *Yale Law Journal* 40 (1930): 161.

objects and sound of rending metal.[11] The talk, for example, is of a "defendant." What lies behind this abstraction? His name turns out to be Walpole, and he was driving a pale magenta Buick. He had red hair and a schnauzer dog. An irritable wife sat in the back seat. He also carried life insurance. He turned to his wife just before the accident. The sun was shining. The road was concrete and smooth. And so on. Which facts are material (i.e., relevant to the decision of the court)?

Some we are likely to dismiss at once as immaterial: the defendant's name, the color of his hair, the make of his car. However, there might be situations in which even these could turn out to be relevant to a court. Suppose the event took place in Germany, between 1933 and 1945; the defendant, called Schmidt and driving a German car, had fair hair and Aryan features, whereas the plaintiff, in a foreign car, was called Cohen. But let us return to Llewellyn's example. All he tells us of the plaintiff is that he was named Atkinson. We may fill in the details and imagine that he was alone in his car and well within the speed limit; he was wearing glasses and sounded his horn as he caught sight of Walpole turning in his seat to make a heated remark to his wife. The judge found for Atkinson. When the case went to appeal, the decision was affirmed and the majority opinion included a discourse on the shocking toll of highway accidents.

We must now construct a subsequent case if we are to interpret Llewellyn's account of the strategies opened to lawyers by the precedent doctrine. Atwood was driving on another highway when struck by a car driven by Watson, who was engaged in an argument with his wife. As lawyer for Watson, how will you handle the precedent of *Atkinson v. Walpole*? You will evidently see it as unwelcome and will adopt a strict view to keep this ruling in check. It would be foolish to insist that your opponent is Atwood rather than Atkinson—names are immaterial here. You will, though, confine the precedent to some particular facts that you urge as material to the decision. You will point out (if you are so lucky) that Atwood, in contrast to Atkinson, was exceeding the speed limit, did not sound his horn, and was not wearing glasses while his driving license was so restricted.

Suppose, however, you are hired by Atwood. You base your position on *Atkinson v. Walpole* and adopt a loose view that will use it fully, capitalizing on any welcome features it offers. It is now immaterial that your client did not sound his horn, and the minor infractions of driving regulations pale before the full force of the *Atkinson* decision. Did not the judge then remind us of the grave responsibilities we face whenever we get behind a steering wheel and, in particular, of the lethal dangers imposed on society by those who allow personal matters to detract from the full attention they owe to public safety?

The legal mind exercises itself on strange hypothetical examples, but sometimes these are matched by life itself. A classical case in British law is that of

---

11. Llewellyn, *The Bramble Bush*, 48.

Donoghue v. Stevenson (1932). Miss Donoghue, a shop assistant in Scotland, sued Stevenson for five hundred pounds, claiming to have suffered injury from the discovery of a snail in a bottle of ginger beer that he had manufactured. She won. Subsequent discussion in learned journals asked whether it was material or immaterial that Stevenson was careless in bottling, that ginger beer is not potent enough to dissolve snails, and that the opaque bottle gave no warning of its deadly contents. Can we confine the decision to snails in bottled ginger beer, or should we extend it to all injurious possibilities of manufactured articles?[12]

It is easy to joke about cases that may have been much less humorous at the time. However, the lawyer can face more serious, and moral, problems in this regard. Is it material that your client is rich or poor? A corporation or an individual? Experienced at litigation or faced with the courts for the first time?

Llewellyn offers us no easy answer. His account, however, of the "Janus-faced" quality of the precedent doctrine does suggest the geography of legal strategies. As client or lawyer, you must situate yourself somewhere between the particularity of a decision that cannot be generalized and the generality of words that trespass beyond the limits of a decision.

FURTHER READING

An appreciation of the trail of precedents can be gained only by following it in some detail. Marc A. Franklin does this for the law of libel in *The Dynamics of American Law* (Mineola, N.Y.: Foundation Press, 1968), 192–319. A line of cases on wife-beating is presented by J. J. Bonsignore in *Before the Law*, 3d ed. (Boston: Houghton Mifflin Co., 1984), 15–26.

For an account of *stare decisis* in the civil law tradition, see:
David, René. *Major Legal Systems in the World Today.* New York: Free Press, 1978, 121–34.
Merryman, J. H., and D. S. Clark. *Comparative Law.* Indianapolis: Bobbs-Merrill, 1978, 551–87.

A history of the development of *stare decisis* in England is given by C. K. Allen in *Law in the Making*, 7th ed. (New York: Oxford Univ. Press, 1964), 187–235.

For some criticisms of *stare decisis*, see Jerome Frank, *Courts on Trial* (Princeton, N.J.: Princeton Univ. Press, 1949), 262–89.

A. L. Goodhart's articles are reprinted in G. C. Christie, *Jurisprudence* (St. Paul: West, 1973), along with other provocative accounts: see pp. 921–1,050.

QUESTIONS FOR DISCUSSION

1. Commenting on his example of the boy learning the rule of removing a hat when entering a church, H. L. A. Hart writes: "He is guided by common sense and knowledge of the general kinds of things and purposes which adults think important." In the light of this, how might the boy answer such questions as these? Does it matter whether he uses his right or left hand? Is a toupee

---

12. The writings of Julius Stone contain various studies of this celebrated case. See, for example, *The Province and Function of Law* (1946; reprint, Buffalo, N.Y.: W. S. Hein & Co., 1973), 186–89. There he analyzes the conclusions that could logically be drawn from *Donoghue* as a precedent. He gives eight headings applicable to any conclusion. Since each of these headings contains about four or five possibilities that he lists, the number of combinations is immense.

a hat? Why does the bishop not remove his mitre? Should an aged and bald man with a cold remove his hat in an unheated church?

2.   Distinguish between the material and immaterial facts in the cases of Jimmy, his younger sister, and his older brother. Is negligence a fact? Did it belong to the holding in the initial case? If you were the parent, how might you have then phrased your "express *ratio decidendi*"?

3.   Would you expect a teacher to be guided by precedents in the way he handles requests for exemption from requirements? Would you think it unjust if he denied you a request for delay in taking a test when you know he had allowed this to a fellow student? Alternatively, what would you think if an account of your special circumstances were met with the blunt reply that "you know my fixed procedure on term papers"? Think of your own use of precedents in any position of authority you hold.

4.   Reread the extract from Judith Shklar's *Legalism* (section 7). She defines legalism as "a matter of rule following" and sees the legal mind as insulated "from all contact with the rest of historical thought and experience," so that rule-maintenance becomes more important than support of the public good. Does Professor Coons's reply distinguish between the use and abuse of precedents in law? Does he further suggest that an appropriate adaptation of rules requires some awareness that they are but the tip of the legal iceberg, and that the basis of the law consists of principles below the surface?

5.   In the Minnesota case, Buck broke no rules and faced no clearly opposing precedents. Yet he seems to have been accused of something more serious, of contradicting a basic principle of law itself. Suppose that no statute or precedent tells us that we ought not to make promises without any intention of keeping them. You nevertheless do this. Are you violating the unwritten principle that promises have meaning (and are possible as such) only if the intention of fulfilment is involved? The example (though moral rather than legal) is a classical one, from Kant. Is the judge in *Tuttle* arguing along some such lines?

6.   The English word *law* can be translated by two words in many other languages. *Lex, Gesetz, loi, legge* refer to particular statutes or to the articles of a code. *Ius, Recht, droit, diritto* refer more to the complete legal system and have moral connotations (justice, right). Is this suggestive of the distinction between rules (particular laws) and principles (legality in general)?

7.   Suppose that in a Scottish court in 1933, MacGregor sued MacTavish for cut hands when a bottle of ginger ale exploded. What strategies might the opposing lawyers adopt toward the precedent of *Donoghue v. Stevenson*? If MacGregor won, how would you state the rule of the case? Think of future incidents that might justify an appeal to these precedents (sand in an oyster? an exploding boiler?).

8.   In 1769, Villers was called by Monsley, in a published poem, "a stinking, nasty, itchy old toad." Villers sued and won the appeal. Over the previous 150 years, cases in English courts had decided it was defamatory to call a person a leper or to say he had a venereal disease (the "French pox"), but not to say he was suffering from smallpox. Villers' affliction ("the itch") seems to have been scabies, a serious problem of urban overcrowding. The defense attorney insisted on the difference between smallpox and venereal disease. The judge held to the similarity between Villers' problem and leprosy: "Nobody will eat, drink, or have any intercourse with a person who has the itch." Was *stare decisis* supported or violated?

9.   Make up a novel case that would seriously challenge the precedent set by any decision we have so far encountered (e.g., *Riggs, Hynes, Tuttle*).

30. ANALOGICAL REASONING

> *To argue by example is neither like reasoning from part to whole, nor like reasoning from whole to part, but rather reasoning from part to part.*
>
> (Aristotle *Prior Analytics* 69a)

One interesting aspect of our mythology is that the Devil has been seen as a master logician. He has also been presented as the prince of lawyers. The suggestion, in both pictures, is that argumentation can lead as easily to false results as to true ones. The unscrupulous lawyer, or logician, is thought to employ his dialectical skills to achieve what he wants rather than to disclose what is true.

However, the distinction between truth and validity is one fruit of studies in logic and serves as a defense against such wiles of disputation. At least, we are helped to formulate our reply as either a denial of the truth in our opponent's premises or as an identification of fallacies in his reasoning. Suppose he starts with the claim that anyone who harms another should be punished. He then points out that sneezing, by spreading infectious diseases, is harming others. He concludes that sneezing should be punished. We may reply that the word *harm* is being used in different senses (invalid reasoning). Or we may accept the argument as valid and attack the truth of the major premise, that all harm should be punished.

Truth can be reached without a study of logic, and even without use of logic. I can make a wild guess that happens to be correct. Or knowledge can come in a flash, by some form of intuition. No logician denies the fact, or even the importance, of such processes. What he asks is that the resulting claims should then be submitted to some appropriate form of justification. In this sense, the demand for logic may be our deepest debt to the Greeks.[13] When the Old Testament prophets urged us to be true, they were speaking of commitment, of fidelity to a vocation, of a faith that comes from passionate involvement and is weakened through attempts at reasoning.[14] Many religious people regard the project of proving God's existence to be a sign of loss of faith rather than a means to strengthen it. It was under the influence of Greek thought that simple faith in God passed in the Middle Ages to growth of a theology ("faith seeks understanding"). However we start our journey, the full way to truth requires some detachment from immediate convictions and an exposition of them through an organized process of reasoning. Knowledge became a discipline and we produced biology, geology, anthropology.

Even those of us who are most critical of lawyers do not suggest that logic should be banned from the courtroom in the way that a "fideist" would exclude reasoning from religion. Whatever may have held in primitive dispute-settlement or in trial by ordeal, we demand justice from a court through the rigor of

---

13. See section 21 for comments on Aristotle's account of our status as "rational beings" (those endowed with *logos*). Reason, for him, is not merely a technique for moving from one fact to another, as we commonly suppose today: "Reason, more than anything else, *is* man" (Aristotle *Nicomachean Ethics*, book 10, chapter 7, 1178a). That is, we are involved in some radical self-contradiction if we act without any concern for logical justification. Rationality is not just a classification imposed by an observer to describe behavior: it is a moral *ought* that underlies a legal system as well as our search for truth in general.

14. For an interesting summary of differences in the ideals proposed by the Hebraic and Greek sources of our culture, see chapter 4 of William Barrett, *Irrational Man* (New York: Doubleday, 1958).

proof and the exercise of reason. However, questions can be raised about the *manner* in which lawyers and judges reason, about the sort of logic that is or should be at work if law is to be a discipline. The previous section may have suggested that the claim to reason from particular cases to a general rule, and to apply this logically to a new case, is not well founded. Do judges use a bogus logic where mathematicians and scientists employ a genuine one? Or do different norms of appropriate reasoning apply in the law?

Deduction, Induction, and Analogy

> There are occasions when we must ask which of two rules we should apply, which of two premises we should use, to determine [for example] whether this is negligence.... These questions look deductive because they are reflective. They are unlike deductions because they are resolved not by those adamantine processes of logic and mathematics but by analogy, because the terms of the argument remain riddles. They are resolved as such questions are solved as "Is an infinite number a number?" "Is Einstein's account of relativity a proof?" "Is Freud's account of the unconscious a proof?" "Is time real?"
>
> (Roy L. Stone)[15]

The author of this quotation was an astute analyst of the styles of reasoning employed in various fields of knowledge and at various levels within each field. Mathematics, in the form that most of us have encountered, is a clear instance of deduction. If all rectangles have diagonals that are equal, and all squares are rectangles, then we must conclude that all squares have diagonals that are equal. However, the processes of deductive proof turn out to be inadequate when we come to advanced questions about infinite numbers, for example. There the very terms of the argument remain "riddles": our questions, rather than yielding unambiguous answers, are themselves put in question. And Stone suggests that legal argument, far from being a sloppy form of deduction (or of the induction found in science), is to be likened to the type of reasoning that seems required at the advanced levels of mathematics and science.

This section will try, with the simplest of illustrations, to explore what may be involved in such a claim. We shall start with deduction, that most "adamantine" form of logic. Some writers, at least in the past, have seen this as a sufficient tool for the analysis of legal reasoning:

> Every judicial act resulting in a judgment consists of a pure deduction. The figure of its reasoning is the stating of a rule applicable to certain facts, a finding that the facts of the particular case are those certain facts and the application of the rule is a logical necessity. The old syllogism, "All men are mortal, Socrates is a man, therefore he is mortal," states the exact form of a

---

15. Roy L. Stone, "Ratiocination not Rationalisation," *Mind* 74 (1965): 482.

judicial judgment. The existing rule of law is: Every man who with malice aforethought kills another in the peace of the people is guilty of murder. The defendant with malice aforethought killed A.B. in the peace of the people, therefore the defendant is guilty of murder.[16]

The question immediately arises how we know the major premise or general rule. The classical answer is, through induction: we observe that all men up to now have shown themselves to be mortal and that judges have regularly treated a certain range of crimes as murder. There are, however, difficulties with the claim that reasoning is satisfied through this combination of induction and deduction. Such problems will lead us to an investigation of what Stone may mean by the "analogical" reasoning that he finds in the law as well as in some of the most sophisticated questions of other disciplines.

Deduction is what Aristotle called "reasoning from whole to part." Suppose a judge in a juvenile court sternly tells an offender that he is of an age to know better. If the cryptic reprimand were developed, it might run like this: "All those who are no longer children should obey the law; you are no longer a child; so you should obey the law."

In classical terms, the major premise makes a claim about some "whole" or "class" (all adolescents, all humans, all swans). The minor premise identifies some smaller class, or an individual, as a member of the larger group. And the conclusion applies the claim to this "part." Thus: "All swans are birds, and the animal swimming on the pond is a swan, so it must be a bird." Turning to the law, we may reason: "Anyone defaming a person by false statements in writing has committed libel; but you did this in the article you published about me, so you have libeled me."

We suspect that life is not quite so simple. We can make a closed world of deductive thinking by defining terms as we please. This may work in mathematics: once we have defined the relevant terms according to Euclid, we deduce that the angles of any triangle must add up to 180°. But, if we leave the security of definitions and encounter the world of facts, it does not follow that three rays of light, forming a triangular figure, must create angles that are measured to give a total of 180°. It is easy to win an argument by controlling the definitions. When de Gaulle commented that all true Frenchmen would support his policies, and an opponent protested by arguing against some policy, the general is reported to have replied: "Then, sir, you are no true Frenchman!"

If deduction is to tell us about the world in which we live, the standard criticism is that the premises presuppose the conclusion. How do we know that all men are mortal unless we know that Socrates is mortal? Suppose that Socrates is taken alive to heaven in a chariot of fire?[17] Would you recognize

---

16. John M. Zane, "German Legal Philosophy," *Michigan Law Review* 16 (1918): 337.
17. Those who follow a literal reading of the Bible will face this problem in regard to Elijah (2 Kings 2:11).

that the major premise is false? Or would you, faithful to what turns out to be a definition, hold that Socrates must have been an angel in disguise?

One way to escape from such a problem is to maintain that the major premise involves more than a combination of observations (matters of fact) and definitions (relations of ideas). We might know, from metaphysical reasoning, that mortality must belong to "human nature": the proposition is both necessary and informative. Such claims are precisely what Hume opposed and are unlikely to lead us far in a court of law.

In a case to decide whether the executor of the estate of Mary Baker Eddy could prevent sale of her personal letters by a book auctioneer (Baker v. Libbie, 1912, 210 Mass. 599, 97 N.E. 109), the judge cited authorities and then argued independently "on principle." His reasoning followed this deductive form. All have a right of property to the fruits of their labor. Yet private correspondence is as much a fruit of labor as is "the grain of the husbandman." Hence an author of letters has a right of property to them. The reasoning seems valid, but our problem is again how we find the truth of the major premise. Does everyone have a right to *all* fruits of labor? How do we know, unless we already recognize the estate's right to this correspondence, which was the very question the court had to solve and not to presuppose? Or is the major premise the result of some metaphysical argument from the nature of man and of property?

The answer most would supply is that the court's task was to find the truth or falsity of the major premise by examining a limited number of previous rulings on what people could or could not keep of their productions, then to arrive at some generalization and turn it to the dispute between Baker and Libbie. In other words, deduction can be used only in applying a generalization that comes through the form of reasoning known as induction.

Aristotle was familiar with induction as an alternative or complement to deduction. However, it was with the rise of the natural sciences that induction came into its own as a way of reasoning. Aristotle had tried to deduce truths about the heavens from the general principle that perfect motion must be circular. So, for that matter, did Copernicus. But eventually this "orgy of rationalism" gave way to the realization that we begin with scientific facts as they happen to be observed. Circles yielded to less elegant ellipses. Similarly, we may start by concluding, from our observations, that all living beings must have oxygen to survive; then we find some that can do without, and we humbly revise our conclusion to "most living beings. . . ." Up to now all humans have died before the age of 150 and we conclude inductively from this immense sample that all humans are mortal; but we remain open to the possibility of exceptions or even to some major revision through medical advances.

Induction is a form of reasoning that takes us "from the part to the whole." The classic example in logic textbooks has to do with the color of swans. It does not belong to the definition (or "essence") of a swan that it should be white. However, centuries of observation had found each swan to be white and had justified a sound generalization about the whole class. "A is a swan and is white. B is also a swan ("same as A") and is white. So with C, D, ... Hence all swans are white." This conclusion was certainly informative but lacked the rigor of deduction, as was well illustrated by the eventual discovery of black swans in Australia.

At least we seem to be approaching the way in which the general statements that serve as premises in case law are established. The rule in terms of which you accuse me of libeling you is much more complex than assertions about the color of animals. But your expectation that you will win the suit is based on the observation that for more than three centuries judges have given verdicts against those who engaged in defamation. A line of precedents leads inductively to a general rule, from which you draw, by deduction, your optimistic conclusion about your own case.

Induction, it appears, avoids the dishonesty of winning an argument by smuggling in our own definitions. We simply submit to the facts as they have so far come to us. However, the suggestion was made (in section 23) that the facts we observe embody various rules for observing. No fact reaches us free of a network of concepts and principles that give it meaning as a certain sort of fact. If a sun-like body rose tomorrow morning in the west, we should explore all possibilities of classifying it as a comet or as a mass illusion rather than accept a radical revision of our astronomical theory. A long-standing way of seeing the world is unlikely to be changed through an apparently discordant fact that can be "tamed" as a remaining puzzle in the fit between theory and observations.

One basic problem with induction is that the many instances on which it draws must be classified as instances of "the same." We actually experience no two sunrises as exactly the same, but we define them as such for astronomical or other purposes. Certainly, no student has the same experience of duration in a boring and an interesting lecture; the "hour" is an imposition we have made on life, not one we have drawn from it. Young children show great difficulty, and produce amusing results, in learning to use the words *same* and *different*.[18] However, "normal science" works with such precise definitions of sameness that induction succeeds admirably for practical purposes; biologists face no crisis in seeing all swans as the same and then delighting in their differences.

Piaget held that our earliest form of reasoning is neither induction nor deduction but what he called "transduction."[19] This moves from one particular to another particular without any clear conception of the universal that unites them. Aristotle, though not much interested in children, likewise opposed to induction and deduction a form of "argument by example" or of "analogical

18. While walking with Piaget, a child pointed to a slug on a leaf and said, "There's the slug." A short distance farther, he pointed to a slug on a leaf and said again, "There's the slug." Piaget asked, "Is it the same slug?" The child answered, "Yes." Piaget wisely asked, "Is it a different slug?" The child answered, "Yes." Adults have forgotten the difficulty they had in learning to see the world in terms of different instances of the same.

19. Jean Piaget, *Play, Dreams and Imitation in Childhood* (1951; reprint, New York: W. W. Norton & Co., 1962), 230–37.

reasoning" that goes "from part to part." Roy Stone, in the article cited above and in others he has written on legal argument, coined the term *paraduction* for the case-by-case method of reasoning.

A simple illustration, from outside the law, may help to indicate what is involved. Suppose a student, in his first year at college, did badly in biology and physics but well in history and literature. Among the courses for which he registers in his second year are sociology and philosophy. He predicts he will do badly in the former and well in the latter. Why? Perhaps he proceeded inductively to the conclusion that he gets poor grades in science and good grades in the humanities; then he reasoned deductively on the grounds that sociology is a science and philosophy belongs to the humanities. If he so argued, he should be careful, and not only because his induction was based on so small a sampling. The general terms he used are very shaky. Does "science" cover biology, physics, and sociology in the same way? Can history, literature, and philosophy be grouped together as "humanities," and what does this nebulous term mean? Such reasoning is not invalid, but we have to recognize that the generalities are unclear and the classification systems are allowed to slide as we put new instances under them.

If we want an uncomplicated example from the law of some hypothetical jurisdiction, we may return to Llewellyn's story of Atkinson's suit against Walpole. The facts of the case, material or immaterial (relevant or not to the decision), included such details as the make of car, the speed at which each was traveling, the presence or absence of a distracting passenger, the violation of requirements in a driving license. On the model of pure inductive-deductive reasoning, the judge would have scanned the precedents, discovered the controlling rule in a common *ratio decidendi*, and applied this to the dispute before him. From a range of decisions we arrive inductively at a general rule and then employ this to get our present decision by deduction. There would have been no leeway for the legal maneuvers that Llewellyn describes. And the further case that we invented, of *Atwood v. Watson*, would be unlikely to have reached even a trial court. Watson's lawyer would have told him that he was clearly liable for violating a well-defined rule about distractions while driving. Or, alternatively, Atwood's lawyer might have told him that he had no hope of recovery because the rule excluded this where the plaintiff was exceeding the speed limit or ignoring the requirement for wearing glasses while driving.

People do, however, go to court with hope of winning and fear of losing. The discussion of strict and loose applications of the precedent doctrine was based on the fact that case law does not yield rules of such precision that the business of courts is ended. The field may be narrowed; it is not closed, even when some judge does his best to put into words what he understands as the "express *ratio decidendi*."

How, then, does a judge reason in coming to his decision? The problems of "same and different," so easy to overcome in swans, become obstreperous in case law. The judge has to work by analogy. The case before him is not exactly the same as any other in the precedents (or in the wide variety of cases from which he selects some as precedents). He finds characteristics that are similar, others that are dissimilar. In the cases already decided, he has to estimate how relevant each of the characteristics was to the decision. He has to weigh the present similarities and dissimilarities in regard to such relevance. His task is normative as well as descriptive: he has to inquire, not only at what speed each driver was moving, but how social policies pertain to speed of driving and what principles justify the rights of a driver on a highway. He has to ask, not simply "Is X a Y?", but rather "Should X be treated as a Y for certain legal purposes?"[20]

Much of recent philosophy is an attack on the naive assumption that reasoning requires the abstraction of "essences" in what we are and do. For example, Wittgenstein suggests that we move from one instance to another by seeing what he calls "family resemblances." The illustration he takes is of games, a pertinent one for discussion of laws. We all know whether something is or is not a game, but can we supply a satisfactory definition? Think of board games, card games, ball games, solitary games, games of skill and of pure luck. There is no evident way in which their identity can be separated from their many differences, yet we know they belong together in a far from trivial sense. "I can think of no better expression to characterize these similarities than 'family resemblances'; for the various resemblances between members of a family: build, features, colour of eyes, gait, temperament, etc. overlap and criss-cross in the same way" (Wittgenstein, *Philosophical Investigations*, section 67). We may add that the *purpose* of imposing any such category of "sameness" is relevant. Am I classifying activities or games in order to decide how a special sales tax is to be applied? Or to compose a detailed statute that specifies which types of gambling are illegal? Or to write a book on the history of games or on the philosophy of sport?

Some philosophers, such as Plato, have looked upon our ability to recognize mathematical forms as evidence of "innate ideas"; and it is impressive that a young or uneducated person can immediately classify shapes into triangles and squares and circles. Here at least, it seems, we have a beautifully sharp distinction between what is identical in all triangular shapes (three angles, three sides, etc.) and what is different (size, color, texture). However, primitive languages may not have one set of numbers for all objects: the word for *three* coconuts may be different from the word for *three* people. We should notice what we have lost in abstracting the sameness of the cardinal numbers, and we should remember that counting can serve many purposes.

Though it is not easy to say exactly what form is taken by "analogical," or "paraductive," or "transductive" reasoning, most of us are ready to offer a

---

20. For a detailed analysis of legal argument by analogy, see Martin P. Golding, *Legal Reasoning* (New York: Alfred A. Knopf, 1984), 44–49, 102–11. It should not be forgotten that the use of letters of the alphabet as symbols for the "characteristics" of a legal case is itself an analogy, one that raises some pertinent questions.

quick evaluation of it. Reasoning from case to case without a sure grasp of the unifying rule is primitive. The lawyer (if such be his style) joins the child in his defective reasoning. The assumption, of course, is that the standard for reasoning is to be drawn from mathematics or science. However, we have seen some indications that both of these desert the apparent purity of deductive or inductive reasoning, and perhaps especially in their more "grown-up" questions.

Medieval thinkers would also have been hesitant about this evaluation. They did indulge all too readily in deduction. Yet they insisted that the highest realm of inquiry, talk of God, is concerned entirely with analogous concepts, those that are "partly the same and partly different, such that the sameness cannot clearly be separated from the difference." For example, the medievals held that we cannot say what "knowing" and "being" are in such a way that we can then "add" the distinctions which make this into divine knowledge and that into human, or this into divine being and that into human. They would certainly have denied that theology therefore involves a lower form of reasoning than mathematics.

So we may at least entertain the suggestion that the reasoning of a judge is misunderstood if seen as but an imperfect form of what is done in geometry or geology. And this might involve some criticism of the model that law is merely a set of rules. If analogical reasoning in law has a quality that sets it apart from deduction and induction, this is because the daily task of a judge shows more frequent recourse to unformulated principles than does the normal work of a mathematician or scientist.

Defining the Question

Men do not begin thinking with premises. They begin with some complicated and confused case, apparently admitting of alternative modes of treatment and solution. Premises only gradually emerge from analysis of the total situation.... The problem is to *find* statements, of general principle and of particular fact, which are worthy to serve as premises. As a matter of actual fact, we generally begin with some vague anticipation of a conclusion (or at least of alternative conclusions), and then we look around for principles and data which will substantiate it or which will enable us to choose intelligently between rival conclusions. No lawyer ever thought out the case of a client in terms of the syllogism. He begins with a conclusion which he intends to reach, favorable to his client, of course, and then analyzes the facts of the situation to find material out of which to construct a favorable statement of facts, to *form* a minor premise. At the same time he goes over recorded cases to find rules of law employed in cases which can be presented as similar, rules which will substantiate a certain way of looking at and interpreting the facts. And as his acquaintance with rules of law judged applicable widens, he probably alters perspective and emphasis in selection of the facts which are to form his evidential data. And as he learns more of the facts of the case he may modify his selection of rules of law upon which he bases his case....

> Thinking actually sets out from a more or less confused situation, which is vague and ambiguous with respect to the conclusion it indicates. The formation of both major premise and minor proceed tentatively and correlatively in the course of analysis of this situation and of prior rules.... The conclusion does not follow from premises; conclusions and premises are two ways of stating the same thing...
>
> (John Dewey)[21]

Dewey points out that he is describing what he calls "the logic of search and inquiry," rather than "the logic of exposition." More is involved in the former, however, than a psychological process of intuition or hunching. The manner of searching and inquiring is still given the title of a "logic." What Dewey appears to suggest is that the very questions that lead us to our search are themselves in question. Only in the subsequent stage of exposition can we define such questions sufficiently to present our argument in more traditional forms.

The average student of geometry or physics is seldom drawn to such "foundation questions." The problem is set uncompromisingly by the textbook. Discovery of a fruitful approach may come in a flash, but the burden of all that is to be publicly discussed is in the realm of exposition. Similarly, Galileo may have been more concerned with the observations he made of falling bodies than with the highly imaginative ideas that clarified his questions and cleared the ground for the gathering of information. In such fields it usually takes a crisis before such "stage-setting" questions are themselves put in question. The problem in geometry appears insoluble. Is there a misprint in the book? Or are we led to ask about the foundations of mathematics? Or suppose Galileo could make no sense of his data. Should he explore alternative paradigms that generate different questions and call for other forms of equipment and of observations?

Dewey seems to claim that a lawyer's concern is, from the first, with the question itself. A human incident takes place and a client comes for advice. He tells his story in his own words, but the lawyer, in listening and interrogating, is exploring many different possible versions of the legal question that is involved. Was there a crime and, if so, which of the many classifications of criminal law can be applied to say what happened? Which forms of deliberation and of intention were present in what the client did? How did he understand what he was doing? How would a reasonable person interpret it? In civil law, the choice involved in formulating the question is even wider. Should Henningsen (section 19) claim negligence by the manufacturer or state the case in terms of an implied warranty, or both, or what else? A glance through the headings of codes in the civil law tradition suggests many different ways in which an "ordinary" dispute can be so classified as to become a legal question. And the reliance of

---

21. From John Dewey, "Logical Method and Law," *Cornell Law Quarterly* 10 (1924): 23. Copyright © 1924 by Cornell University. Printed with permission of the *Cornell Law Review*, of Fred B. Rothman & Co., and of the Center for Dewey Studies, Southern Illinois University at Carbondale.

the common law on uncodified rulings may greatly increase the range of possibilities.

Evidently, as Dewey points out, the lawyer's choice of a way to state the question will be guided by considerations of helping his client to win. But, in any adversary system, an opponent will explore a different set of rules and a variant account of the facts. The court is bound to neither side and must eventually come up with its own formulation, which remains open to restatement by successors in the tradition.

A simple example can indicate that no "right" version of a question is given by the gods. Animals carry no label telling how they are to be classified. Biologists find it important to separate those that do and do not have backbones; in the former a fish is denied the title of a mammal and whales are given this dignity. However, the layperson who classifies by habitat and views a whale as a fish is "wrong" only by virtue of his failure to share the odd interests of a biologist. We do not know how Adam named the animals (Genesis 2:19). Perhaps by size or color or shape; he at least saw the snake as importantly different. We can expect a primitive hunter to be more interested in whether animals are dangerous or harmless, edible or not, than in their anatomy and in their manner of feeding young. A final note may suggest the added sensitivity of law to the full range of human concerns: I am told that English law, in deciding cases about liability for acts perpetrated by animals, divides the beasts into wild, domestic, and dogs!

All reasoning is a function of the basic questions we ask. In both deductive and inductive arguments, the stage-setting questions are taken for granted and hidden from view. Whether we are deciding the sum of the angles of a triangle or the rate at which bodies fall, the scene has already been constructed. We still have to follow the theorems or use ruler and clock, and our intuitions may prove wrong. Yet the most important decisions have been made. We know what counts as a premise for the demonstration. Even if we find we are wrong, our way of thinking or looking is not (usually) threatened. It is in this sense that conclusions and premises are two ways of stating the same thing.

In law, however, we are repeatedly thrown back upon the prior questions that crystallize the premise/conclusion relationship. If we regard much legal reasoning as dishonest, this may be because the law confronts us so frequently with foundation questions, with hesitations about what we are really trying to do. Argument "from part to part" makes the guiding question obtrusive and itself questionable.

A further comment may be made and some illustrations added. Legal reasoning can have a therapeutic aspect that neither Euclid nor Galileo would have claimed: we can be healed by changing our basic questions. Our judges certainly propose to apply the law rather than to heal the litigants. However, primitive law may have had more to do with changing the attitude of disputants than with establishing and maintaining a system of rules. And the work of an arbitrator or negotiator today can be more evidently concerned with healing. If the dispute is framed in terms of question 1, then answer A–1 will not satisfy X and answer B–1 will not satisfy Y. The genius of the arbitrator is to restate the dispute in terms of question 2, such that the new answers A–2 and B–2 help X and Y to perceive advantages that had not been there before, because the appropriate question had not yet been brought into existence.

The therapeutic work of a court is much a matter of changing viewpoint and focus. Prof. Herman Oliphant offers a helpful image:

> Each precedent considered by a judge and each case studied by a student rests at the center of a vast and empty stadium. The angle and distance from which that case is to be viewed involves the choice of a seat.[22]

A critic could suggest that a seat in the front row on the fifty-yard line offers a less-biased view than a remote seat behind the goalposts. However, this is to assume that the object in the center is a "thing-in-itself" and that viewing is passive. Height, distance, and angle allow for different interpretations and may contribute to truth. At least, such changes make possible alternative statements of the question that can help toward resolution of a conflict. Oliphant gives an example in the same article:

> A's father induces her not to marry B as she promised to do. On a holding that the father is not liable to B for so doing, a gradation of widening propositions can be built, a very few of which are:
> 1. Fathers are so privileged to induce daughters to break promises to marry.
> 2. Parents are so privileged.
> 3. Parents are so privileged as to both daughters and sons.
> 4. All persons are so privileged as to promises to marry.
> 5. Parents are so privileged as to all promises made by their children.
> 6. All persons are so privileged as to all promises made by anyone.

The example may be rather academic in an age when children suffer little "inducement" from parents. Yet the point can be well illustrated in the settlement of an international dispute, now that the possible results are so grave:

> If a Polish fishing vessel has damaged a transatlantic cable, the party on the "left-hand" side of the dispute might be taken as the helmsman of the ship, the captain of the ship, the department of the Polish government concerned with regulating fishing, the Polish government, Kruschev, or "the Communists." The party on the "right-hand" side might be considered to be the private company owning the cable, the United States, or the West.[23]

---

22. Herman Oliphant, "A Return to Stare Decisis," *American Bar Association Journal* 14 (1928): 72.
23. Roger Fisher: "Fractionating Conflict," *Daedalus* 93 (1964): 920.

The skilled negotiator would probably do his best to defuse this conflict by achieving a narrow focus, perhaps helping all to see only the shipping and telephone companies. In other situations, though, his task might be to open eyes to a broader focus. An incident arising from a plane crash could be insoluble at the level of manufacturer and airline, yet be open to resolution if it is seen to involve the worldwide community of air travelers. Similarly, since the mid-1960s this country has witnessed a range of cases on the arrest of suspects by police; the story is not over, but there is a therapeutic element in a court's decision whether to view the question close up, telling police exactly what to do, or to take a seat high in the stadium and ask about the meaning of law and order or even of human dignity.

FURTHER READING

Cassirer, Ernst. *Substance and Function.* New York: Dover, 1953, chapter 5 (induction).
Golding, Martin P. *Legal Reasoning.* New York: Alfred A. Knopf, 1984.
Hall, Jerome. *Readings in Jurisprudence.* Indianapolis: Bobbs-Merrill, 1938, chapter 3 (logic and law), chapter 13 (analogy).
Morris, Clarence. *How Lawyers Think.* Cambridge: Harvard Univ. Press, 1937.
Perelman, Chaim. *Justice, Law, and Argument.* Dordrecht, Holland: Riedel, 1980.
Radin, Max. *Law as Logic and Experience.* 1940. Reprint. Hamden, Conn.: Shoe String Press, 1971.
Stone, Julius. *Legal System and Lawyers' Reasonings.* Stanford, Calif.: Stanford Univ. Press, 1964.
Zelermyer, William. *Legal Reasoning: The Evolutionary Process of Law.* Englewood Cliffs, N.J.: Prentice-Hall, 1960.

QUESTIONS FOR DISCUSSION

1. We are confident that all humans are mortal. Suppose we eventually receive radio signals from an extraterrestrial civilization. Those who send the information claim to be immortal (i.e., not to die, even bodily). How would you assess this claim? The inhabitants then say that their science denies the principle of causality (that every event must have a cause). Is our own acceptance of this principle based on induction? Or on deduction from definitions we contribute (every effect must have a cause)?

2. You count the posts in a long fence as you walk from north to south and find that you get the same number on returning from south to north. Do you conclude, by induction, that counting is independent of direction? Or, if you got a different result, would you know that you had made a mistake? Why?

3. The Concise Oxford Dictionary takes up Wittgenstein's challenge and defines a game as "a contest played according to rules." Would this make lawsuits a type of game? Would the definition exclude the free play of children? If you cannot arrive at a watertight definition, have you any basis for saying that some activities are games, and others are not?

4. A thunderstorm breaks out while you are walking, so you seek shelter in the porch of my house. You are bitten by my dog. When you sue me, I deny liability on the grounds that you were a trespasser. How would you argue on analogy to Cardozo's ruling in *Hynes* (section 10)?

5. In a primitive agricultural society, A promises to pay ten dollars to B for his cow. B delivers the cow, but A refuses to pay. Decision is made in the courts for B, with the ruling that all promises to purchase cows must be honored when the buyer receives the animal. Then C pays ten dollars to D for his cow, but the animal is not handed over. C invokes the A/B case as a precedent; it is decided that the ruling is broader than stated, and this is rephrased to hold that all promises in the sale and purchase of cows are enforceable. Subsequent cases, dealing with pigs and fodder, yield the rule that all promises in trade are enforceable.

So far the judges have been successful in finding a more general statement of a ruling that remains unambiguous. But then a strange case occurs. X persuades Y that because horned animals resemble the devil, the tribal chief will soon decree that all cows be put to death. X thus acquires all of Y's cows for one dollar each and then pulls the deal on most of his neighbors. When the chief announces that cows, far from being diabolical, are the mainstay of a healthy economy, the market price for a cow rises to thirty dollars. Y sues X, who simply quotes the rule that all promises in trade are enforceable. If Y wins his case, how would you now reformulate the ruling?

This case offers scope for development by an imaginative mind (see H. R. Hartzler and H. T. Allan, *Introduction to Law*, Glenview, Ill.: Scott, Foresmen & Co., 1969, 92–96). Are we forced eventually to introduce some term such as *reasonable* and thus lose the clarity of rules that are applied in the same way to different cases?

6. Any student of history will supply examples of the many ways in which a question can be restated. Dispute about a tax on tea is turned into a question of colonialism. The alleged treason of a particular army officer becomes an international affair. The assassination of an archduke plunges the world into war. In such a chaos of questions, how does the historian himself find "historical facts"? Does he also exercise the choice that Oliphant described in terms of a stadium? Is it true, in history, that "conclusions and premises are two ways of stating the same thing"?

7. We expect some dispute about the question, Who started the war? But surely no problem is involved in a simple question like, Who discovered oxygen? Joseph Priestley obtained the gas from the red oxide of mercury in 1774. Unfortunately, he referred to the gas as "air without phlogiston," invoking a theory that is no longer popular. So the books tell us that it was Lavoisier who discovered oxygen. What he did was to repeat Priestley's experiment, but with interpretations that are more congenial today. Nevertheless, Lavoisier referred to oxygen as the "principle of acidity," which remains the etymology of our word for the gas. The theory that oxygen is the source of all acids is rejected today. So who discovered oxygen? Adam, because he breathed it, and facts are independent of theory? Or no one, because our theory of oxygen is still open to reinterpretation?

8. A Connecticut law of 1879 prohibited the sale of contraceptives. Three times a dispute over this statute reached the U.S. Supreme Court, in 1943, 1961, and 1965, ending in a declaration that the law was unconstitutional (Griswold v. Connecticut, 381 U.S. 479, 85 Sup.Ct. 1678). Would you say that this statute *became* unconstitutional in 1965 or was so even in 1879? Could it be part of the therapeutic task of a court to delay a precise answer for which conditions are not ready? Is there some analogy in the "non-directive counseling" conducted by a psychologist?

31. MANUFACTURERS' LIABILITY

[Legal reasoning] is not simply deductive. In the long run a circular motion can be seen. The first stage is the creation of the legal concept which is built up as cases are compared. The period is one in which the court fumbles for a phrase. Several phrases may be tried out; the misuse or misunderstanding of words itself may have an effect. The concept sounds like another, and the jump to the second is made. The second stage is the period when the concept is more or less fixed,

although reasoning by example continues to classify items inside and out of the concept. The third stage is the breakdown of the concept, as reasoning by example has moved so far ahead as to make it clear that the suggestive influence of the word is no longer desired.
(Edward H. Levi, *An Introduction to Legal Reasoning*)[24]

Generalities about the way lawyers and judges reason from case to case require an extended illustration. A classic example will be outlined below, showing a hundred years in the career of rules that try to define the liability of a manufacturer for negligence, when harm from his products results to someone other than the immediate purchaser.[25]

Search for a Concept

When X manufactures an article and sells it to Y, a contract is involved such that Y can claim for failure of the article to be what it should be or was represented as being. But suppose that Y sells, or otherwise transmits, the article to Z before the defect appears. Can Z claim against the producer, X? The question is most important where injury results.

There is an ancient rule in the common law that a manufacturer or supplier is not liable to a remote purchaser. Liability of the producer is limited by "privity of contract" to the only party with whom he entered into a contract, the initial purchaser. We shall see in a moment what happened to this rule where negligence could be proved. But we should be careful not to transplant our current views of consumer protection to the nineteenth century. Then it was held that no one could be responsible to the whole world. A line had to be drawn somewhere, and the logical place was the one established by the contract into which the producer knowingly entered. His "neighbor" was the person he actually met.

However, even in the nineteenth century some hesitations were felt. No one worried much about a carpenter making chairs for sale. If one collapses, you may hurt more than your dignity. But no serious danger is put loose in the world. Suppose, though, that I am a pharmacist and the product I set abroad consists of bottles labeled as aspirin but containing, through my negligence, drugs with serious consequences if consumed as aspirin? There is some difference between substandard chairs and mislabeled poison. Should the producer have wider, even unlimited, liability in the latter case? And if so, how to draw the distinction? What sort of goods?

---

24. Edward H. Levi, *An Introduction to Legal Reasoning* (Chicago: Univ. of Chicago Press, 1949), 8–9. This slim book of a hundred pages offers an excellent introduction to reasoning from cases and from statutes. The author, a professor and dean of the University of Chicago Law School, was U.S. attorney general from 1975–1976.

25. Levi gives a fifteen-page summary of the cases and refers in a lengthy footnote (pp. 9–10) to other discussions. For the judicial opinions in the cases from 1852–1916, see H. J. Berman and W. R. Greiner, *The Nature and Functions of Law* (Mineola, N.Y.: Foundation Press, 1972), 433–79.

The cases start in England, and four may illustrate the fumbling search for appropriate legal concepts.

DIXON v. BELL (1816)

Bell sent his thirteen-year-old servant girl to get his gun. It happened to be loaded. She played with it and shot Dixon's son in the eye. Bell, though he did not fire the gun, was found liable because "his want of care left the gun in a state of doing mischief." Negligence was the ground for claim, and the article was classified as "mischievous."

LANGRIDGE v. LEVY (1837)

Langridge's father bought a gun from Levy, and it blew up in Langridge's hand. Here we seem to have a problem with privity of contract because the gun was not sold directly to the plaintiff. But the court ruled in his favor, avoiding the difficulty by claiming (1) that the father was an unconscious agent in a contract with the plaintiff and (2) that the sale involved fraud because Levy knew the gun was defective. That is, the court tried to maintain privity of contract and saw the defect as a matter of fraud rather than of negligence.

WINTERBOTTOM v. WRIGHT (1842)

Wright provided and repaired coaches under contract to the postmaster general. Winterbottom was a coachman employed by further contractors to drive for the post office; he was lamed for life when thrown from the seat as a result of a "latent defect" in one such coach. The court held that neither of the provisions of *Langridge* could be applied and that to extend Wright's liability beyond the claims of the immediate party in the contract (the post office) would lead to "absurd and outrageous consequences." Winterbottom got nothing from Wright. If we feel that this is inconsistent with the two previous cases, we may suspect that the problem lay in the absence of any concept that would cover the similarity without resort to the apparent subterfuges of *Langridge*.

LONGMEID v. HOLLIDAY (1851)

Holliday manufactured a naphtha lamp and sold it to Mr. Longmeid. When Longmeid's wife, the plaintiff in this case, lighted the lamp, it exploded and burned her. The court refused to use the dodges in *Langridge*, of seeing the husband as "unconscious agent" for the wife or of finding fraud in the contract. The holding in *Winterbottom* was followed closely. So the decision went against Mrs. Longmeid. But the court accepted a concept that was later, when expanded, to question the decision in this case and in *Winterbottom*. In referring to *Dixon v. Bell*, the court classified a loaded gun as "an instrument *in its nature dangerous*" and hence as an exception to the rule on manufacturers' liability. When articles are so classified, negligence on the part of the producer may extend his liability beyond the original contract. However, it was claimed, a carriage or a lamp is dangerous only through "defects discoverable by the exercise of ordinary care." An obscure concept had been proposed, and more than half a century would be taken to explore it through a wide range of applications.

Classification under the Concept

If the concept of being "naturally dangerous" were unambiguous, reasoning would take the form of a simple deduction, where the minor premise states that X (e.g., a loaded gun) is naturally dangerous, Y (e.g., a lamp) is not. Yet the way in which courts classified articles on one side or the other of the conceptual fence leads us to suspect that the boundary moved in the process. We now turn to a series of seven cases, the first six before the New York Court of Appeals.

THOMAS v. WINCHESTER (1852): 6 N.Y. 397

Winchester prepared and bottled vegetable extracts for sale. By mistake, an "extract of belladonna" was put in a bottle labeled "extract of dandelion" and sold to a druggist, who sold it to another, who sold it to Mrs. Thomas. She became duly sick, almost died, and then sued Winchester, who based his defense on "lack of privity with the plaintiff." The court decided for Mrs. Thomas by employing, with some critical ambiguities, the concept announced in *Longmeid* and reviewing the precedents in this light. Mislabeled poison, like a loaded gun, is in its nature dangerous to all. Negligence in preparation "puts human life in imminent danger.... Death or great bodily harm would be the natural consequence of sale." But neither a carriage nor a lamp is "imminently dangerous," and liability for negligence can be restricted by the contract of sale. Winterbottom might still wonder why he fell on the wrong side of the fence, but at least the courts had some rule to apply and some notable examples to discuss.

LOOP v. LITCHFIELD (1870): 42 N.Y. 351

Litchfield manufactured and sold a circular saw, mentioning some defects in the balance wheel to the purchaser. Five years later, the machine was used by Loop, a neighbor. The balance wheel broke and Loop was killed. The court denied recovery to his estate, indicating its strict application of the *Thomas* ruling by the following account of the defendant's case:

> Poison is a dangerous subject. Gunpowder is the same. A torpedo is a dangerous instrument, as is a spring gun, a loaded rifle or the like. They are instruments and articles in their nature calculated to do injury to mankind, and generally intended to accomplish that purpose. They are essentially, and in their elements, instruments of danger. Not so, however, an iron wheel, a few feet in diameter and a few inches in thickness although one

part may be weaker than another. If the article is abused by too long use, or by applying too much weight or speed, an injury may occur, as it may from an ordinary carriage wheel, a wagon axle, or the common chair in which we sit. There is scarcely an object in art or nature, from which injury may not occur under such circumstances. Yet they are not in their nature sources of danger, nor can they, with any regard to the accurate use of language, be called dangerous instruments.

LOSEE v. CLUTE (1873): 51 N.Y. 494

Clute manufactured a steam boiler from poor iron for a paper company. The boiler exploded after only three months and damaged Losee's buildings nearby. Recovery was denied, and *Loop* was quoted. The purchaser had tested the boiler and accepted it as sound.

DEVLIN v. SMITH et al. (1882): 89 N.Y. 470

Smith agreed to paint a courthouse dome and Stevenson contracted with him to build the scaffold. Devlin, a painter in the employ of Smith, fell ninety feet to his death when part of the scaffolding collapsed because improperly secured. The lower court found for both defendants. The appeals court affirmed as to Smith but ordered a new trial as to Stevenson. The previous cases were distinguished in this way. Where injury comes from a defective carriage, "misfortune to third persons, not parties to the contract, would not be a natural and necessary consequence of the builder's negligence, and such negligence is not an act imminently dangerous to human life." But where the injury comes from mislabeled drugs, the situation is different: "Liability to third parties has been held to exist when the defect is such as to render the article in itself imminently dangerous, and serious injury to any person using it is a natural and probable consequence of its use." As to the scaffold in the present dispute, "a stronger case where misfortune to third persons not parties to the contract would be a natural and necessary consequence of the builder's negligence can hardly be supposed, nor is it easy to imagine a more apt illustration of a case where such negligence would be an act imminently dangerous to human life." As Winterbottom hobbled through life, he might well have given thought to the metaphysical discussion of what is dangerous "in its nature," or "imminently," or "essentially," or is "in its nature calculated to do injury," or has injury as its "natural and necessary (or probable?) consequence."

TORGESEN v. SCHULTZ (1908): 192 N.Y. 156, 84 N.E. 956

Schultz manufactured siphon bottles of aerated water. Two were purchased from a druggist and delivered to a house where Torgesen, the domestic servant, received them on a hot day. She put them in a pan of ice and one exploded, with the result that she lost an eye. An instructor in physics at Columbia University reproduced the conditions in an experiment and found that five out of seventy-one bottles exploded. The court allowed recovery "under the doctrine of *Thomas v. Winchester* and similar cases based upon the duty of the vendor of an article dangerous in its nature, or likely to become so in the course of the ordinary usage to be contemplated by the vendor...."

STATLER v. RAY (1909): 195 N.Y. 478, 88 N.E. 1063

Ray manufactured a battery of steam-heated coffee urns for a restaurant. An explosion followed and Statler was killed. The court again allowed recovery, putting coffee urns in the class of guns and mislabeled poisons rather than in that of carriages and lamps. "In the case of an article of an inherently dangerous nature, a manufacturer may become liable for a negligent construction which, when added to the inherent character of the appliance, makes it immediately dangerous...." The term *inherent* has been added to the list of criteria, and *imminently* is translated as "immediately."

CADILLAC v. JOHNSON (1915): 221 F. 801

The problem enters the automobile age with an attempt by a federal court to halt the slide of such criteria in a direction favorable to the plaintiff. A car manufactured by the Cadillac Motor Company was sold by a dealer to Johnson, who was injured when a wheel broke and the car turned over. Wheels in those days had wooden spokes, and these were held in this case to have been made of "dozy" wood. The court denied recovery by Johnson from Cadillac and offered a summary, with a few hypotheticals added, of the items that previous opinions in England and the United States had put on one or the other side of the boundary. There is an obvious analogy between cars and carriages, but the reader is likely to entertain a few questions.

> One who manufactures articles inherently dangerous, e.g., poisons, dynamite, gunpowder, torpedoes, bottles of water under gas pressure, is liable in tort to third parties which they injure, unless he has exercised reasonable care with reference to the articles manufactured.... On the other hand, one who manufactures articles dangerous only if defectively made, or installed, e.g., tables, chairs, pictures or mirrors hung on the walls, carriages, automobiles, and so on is not liable to third parties for injuries caused by them, except in cases of willful injury or fraud.[26]

A Landmark Case

A century has passed since Dixon's son was shot in the eye. If Professor Levi is correct in his analysis of legal reasoning, we are ready for the third stage, in

---

26. This decision was reversed in a new trial four years later: Johnson v. Cadillac (1919, 261 F. 878).

which a seemingly clear concept has become so ambiguous that it must break down and invite a reformulation of the question. Ordinary language will support some sense in which dynamite is dangerous and chairs are not. But the injury (say, partial paralysis) from a defective chair may be more serious than a surface wound that comes from dynamiting. Even a ball of string or a length of rope, if negligently made, can result in death: suppose Devlin's fate had rested on the more customary use of "lashing" rather than on nails in the scaffold? There may well be some basis for setting up a valid distinction, but more is required than the loose employment of undefined metaphysical terms.

Within a year, the *Cadillac* decision had been challenged in a state court. The similarities in the incident could scarcely have been closer. A car made by Buick was sold by a dealer to MacPherson, who was injured when a wheel broke. The trial court found for MacPherson, and Buick appealed. The Court of Appeals of New York affirmed the judgment, and it was Judge Cardozo who composed the majority opinion. He took occasion not only to review the line of precedents, but to suggest important questions about how the precedent doctrine is itself to be interpreted. Extracts follow from his opinion and from the dissenting opinion. Then some comments will be added.

MacPHERSON v. BUICK MOTOR CO.
Court of Appeals of New York, 1916

217 N.Y. 382, 111 N.E. 1050.

CARDOZO, J. . . . The question to be determined is whether the defendant owed a duty of care and vigilance to any one but the immediate purchaser. The foundations of this branch of the law, at least in this state, were laid in *Thomas v. Winchester*. A poison was falsely labeled. The sale was made to a druggist, who in turn sold to a customer. The customer recovered damages from the seller who affixed the label. "The defendant's negligence," it was said, "put human life in imminent danger." . . .

Thomas v. Winchester became quickly a landmark of the law. In the application of its principle there may at times have been uncertainty or even error. There has never in this state been doubt or disavowal of the principle itself. The chief cases are well known, yet to recall some of them will be helpful. *Loop v. Litchfield* is the earliest. It was the case of a defect in a small balance wheel used on a circular saw. The manufacturer pointed out the defect to the buyer, who wished a cheap article and was ready to assume the risk. The risk can hardly have been an imminent one, for the wheel lasted five years before it broke. In the meanwhile the buyer had made a lease of the machinery. It was held that the manufacturer was not answerable to the lessee. *Loop v. Litchfield* was followed in *Losee v. Clute*, the case of the explosion of a steam boiler. That decision has been criticized, but it must be confined to its special facts. It was put upon the ground that the risk of injury was too remote. The buyer in that case had not only accepted the boiler, but had tested it. The manufacturer knew that his own test was not the final one. The finality of the test has a bearing on the measure of diligence owing to persons other than the purchaser.

These early cases suggest a narrow construction of the rule. Later cases, however, evince a more liberal spirit. First in importance is *Devlin v. Smith*. The defendant, a contractor, built a scaffold for a painter. The painter's servants were injured. The contractor was held liable. He knew that the scaffold, if improperly constructed, was a most dangerous trap. He knew that it was to be used by the workmen. He was building it for that very purpose. Building it for their use, he owed them a duty, irrespective of his contract with their master, to build it with care. . . .

It may be that *Devlin v. Smith* and *Statler v. Ray* have extended the rule of *Thomas v. Winchester*. If so, this court is committed to the extension. The defendant argues that things imminently dangerous to life are poisons, explosives, deadly weapons—things whose normal function is to injure or destroy. But whatever the rule in *Thomas v. Winchester* may once have been, it has no longer that restricted meaning. A scaffold is not inherently a destructive instrument. It becomes destructive only if imperfectly constructed. A large coffee urn may have within itself, if negligently made, the potency of danger, yet no one thinks of it as an implement whose normal function is destruction. What is true of the coffee urn is equally true of bottles of aerated water (*Torgesen v. Schultz*). . . .

We hold, then, that the principle of *Thomas v. Winchester* is not limited to poisons, explosives, and things of like nature, to things which in their normal operation are implements of destruction. If the nature of a thing is such that it is reasonably certain to place life and limb in peril when negligently made, it is then a thing of danger. Its nature gives warning of the consequences to be expected. If to the element of danger there is added knowledge that the thing will be used by persons other than the purchaser, and used without new tests, then, irrespective of contract, the manufacturer of this thing of danger is under a duty to make it carefully. That is as far as we are required to go for the decision of this case. There must be knowledge of a danger, not merely possible, but probable. It is *possible* to use almost anything in a way that will make it dangerous if defective. . . .

It is possible that even knowledge of the danger and of the use will not always be enough. The proximity or remoteness of the relation is a factor to be considered. We are dealing now with the liability of the manufacturer of the finished product, who puts it on the market to be used without inspection by his customers. If he is negligent, where danger is to be foreseen, a liability will follow. We are not required at this time to say that it is legitimate to go back of the manufacturer of the finished product and hold the manufacturers of the component parts. To make their negligence a cause of imminent danger, an independent cause must often intervene; the manufacturer of the finished product must also fail in *his* duty of inspection. It may be that in those circumstances the negligence of the earlier members of the series is too remote to constitute, as to the ultimate user, an actionable wrong. We leave that question open. . . .

From this survey of the decisions, there thus emerges a definition of the duty of a manufacturer which enables us to measure this defendant's liability. Beyond all question, the nature of an automobile gives warning of probable danger if its construction is defective. This automobile was designed to go fifty miles an hour. Unless its wheels were sound and strong, injury was almost certain. It was as much a thing of danger as a defective engine for a railroad. The defendant knew the danger. It knew also that the car would be used by persons other than the buyer. This was apparent from its size; there were seats for three persons. It was apparent also from the fact that the buyer was a dealer in cars, who bought to resell. . . . Precedents drawn from the days of travel by stage coach do not fit the conditions of travel today. The principle that the danger must be imminent does not change, but the things subject to the principle do change. They are whatever the needs of life in a developing civilization require them to be. . . .

In this view of the defendant's liability there is nothing inconsistent with the theory of liability on which the case was tried. It is true that the court told the jury that "an automobile is not an inherently dangerous vehicle." The meaning, however, is made plain by the context. The meaning is that danger is not to be expected when the vehicle is well constructed. The court left it to the jury to say whether the defendant ought to have foreseen that the car, if negligently constructed, would become "imminently dangerous."

Subtle distinctions are drawn by the defendant between things inherently dangerous and things imminently dangerous, but the case does not turn upon these verbal niceties. If danger was to be expected as reasonably certain, there was a duty of vigilance, and this whether you call the danger inherent or imminent....

The judgment should be affirmed with costs.

WILLARD BARTLETT, CH. J. (dissenting)... It has heretofore been held in this state that the liability of the vendor of a manufactured article for negligence arising out of the existence of defects therein does not extend to strangers injured in consequence of such defects but is confined to the immediate vendee. The exceptions to this general rule which have thus far been recognized in New York are cases in which the article sold was of such character that danger to life or limb was involved in the ordinary use thereof; in other words, where the article sold was inherently dangerous. As has already been pointed out, the learned trial judge instructed the jury that an automobile is not an inherently dangerous vehicle....

The leading English authority in support of this rule, to which all the later cases on the same subject refer, is *Winterbottom v. Wright*, which was an action by the driver of a stage coach against a contractor who had agreed with the postmaster-general to provide and keep the vehicle in repair for the purpose of conveying the royal mail over a prescribed route. The coach broke down and upset, injuring the driver, who sought to recover against the contractor on account of its defective construction. The Court of Exchequer denied him any right of recovery on the ground that there was no privity of contract between the parties, the agreement having been made with the postmaster-general alone. "If the plaintiff can sue," said Lord Abinger, the Chief Baron, "every passenger or even any person passing along the road, who was injured by the upsetting of the coach, might bring a similar action. Unless we confine the operation of such contracts as this to the parties who enter into them, the most absurd and ourtrageous consequences, to which I can see no limit, would ensue."

... The case of *Devlin v. Smith* is cited as an authority in conflict with the view that the liability of the manufacturer and vendor extends to third parties only when the article manufactured and sold is inherently dangerous.... It seems to me clear from the language of Judge Rapallo, who wrote the opinion of the court, that the scaffold was deemed to be an inherently dangerous structure....

In the case at bar the defective wheel on an automobile moving only eight miles an hour was not any more dangerous to the occupants of the car than a similarly defective wheel would be to the occupants of a carriage drawn by a horse at the same speed; and yet unless the courts have been all wrong on this question up to the present time there would be no liability to strangers to the original sale in the case of the horse-drawn carriage.

... That the Federal courts still adhere to the general rule, as I have stated it, appears by the decision of the Circuit Court of Appeals in the Second Circuit, in March, 1915, in the case of *Cadillac Motor Car Co. v. Johnson*. That case, like this, was an action by a subvendee against a manufacturer of automobiles for negligence in failing to discover that one of its wheels was defective, the court holding that such an action could not be maintained. It is true there was a dissenting opinion in that case, but it was based chiefly on the proposition that rules applicable to stage coaches are archaic when applied to automobiles and that if the law did not afford a remedy to strangers to the contract the law should be changed. If this be true, the change should be effected by the legislature and not by the courts....

The language used by Cardozo does not announce the breakdown of an ancient rule. Claims based on defective products still require proof of negligence by the manufacturer, and privity of contract is not denied. Yet exceptions had been allowed from the beginning, and Cardozo's handling of the criteria so increased the scope for exceptions that the rigidity of the rule was greatly diminished. A sociologist or historian would probably say that the law had now developed from an age in which people buy from a producer they know personally to one in which few have ever met Henry Ford or even an official of his company; what goes on in courts does eventually reflect changes in the way we live and deal with others. However, Cardozo was writing as a judge faithful to some logic within the law. He did not tell us to forget the old and usher in the new. What he may be seen to support is a view of analogical reasoning that challenges the pretense of judges or lawyers to be in complete possession of concepts from which legal conclusions can be deduced.

Bartlett, in dissenting, is by no means opposed to a change in the law that will recognize the advance from stage coaches to automobiles. But he insists that such a change should be effected by the legislature. When it comes to case law, decisions should be based on a rule that appears from the precedents, and he reviews the verdicts on manufacturers' liability with the assumption that such a rule can be found. His own preferred statement is that exceptions to privity of contract are to be allowed only when the article is "inherently" dangerous. He was therefore forced to conclude that the judge in *Devlin* must have regarded a scaffold as inherently dangerous, though the precise term nowhere appears in the opinion, and Bartlett attempts no account of why this undefined concept applies to containers of coffee and of soda water but not to steam boilers and balance wheels.

Cardozo, at the end of his opinion, mentions that the trial court told the jury that "an automobile is not an inherently dangerous vehicle." And he offers a possible interpretation of the term. If the court in *Cadillac* had confined its examples to poisons and torpedoes, there is a sense in which these are "calculated to do injury" (*Loop*), whereas wheels on carriages, cars, or circular saws are not. Wheels would not then be inherently dangerous but could *become* "imminently" dangerous in some circumstances of manufacture and employment. We should thus be talking, not about the nature of a thing in itself, but about human intentions, expectations, and uses.

However, this distinction, though important and suggestive, will not give us the one sharp concept for which we have been looking. The courts show no consistency in talking this way. And even if they had so tidied up their words, their verdicts would remain a mystery. Balance wheels and steam boilers would have joined scaffolds and coffee urns in the class of "imminently though not inherently" dangerous articles; yet it remains a fact that Loop and Losee were defeated in court, while Devlin and Statler won.

Though Cardozo dismisses the "inherent/imminent" distinction as a "verbal nicety," his general approach may be so interpreted that this becomes one way of replacing crudely metaphysical language with more functional talk. "Inherent" suggests "natures" and "things in themselves." "Imminent" may more readily be applied to a range of human purposes and tests. Morphine is not inherently dangerous (any more than a car is), but we can sensibly discuss whether it is imminently so to various classes of patients. Doctors make such judgments each day of their lives, and they do so as physicians rather than as metaphysicians.

Also, why not abandon the search for any *one* clear distinction and remain satisfied, instead, with a view of legal cases in terms of "family resemblances"? A judicial opinion would, then, be more like a decision what to include in a book of games (or to exclude as not a game) than like a decision whether an immigrant is a citizen and can vote. Clarity is an ideal always to be respected, but it does come through definitions we impose, and these in turn through purposes we follow. Cases, like the life they report, do not belong to the world of geometry; they may call for a somewhat different type of reasoning.

Cardozo does not say this in so many words. However, he does tell a judge not to look for any one criterion but rather to apply an open-ended series of tests. Does the product pose "reasonable certainty of placing life and limb in peril when negligently made?" Is this danger "not merely possible but probable?" Is it reasonably certain that the article "will be used by persons other than by the purchaser?" That this will occur "without new tests?" How long is the chain of persons involved, from "the earlier members of the series to the ultimate user?" It is not suggested that a manufacturer is liable if he scores 80 percent on some such tests, nor is it proposed that there is any sharp distinction between satisfying a test and not. Yet admission of the complexity of a rule is far removed from legal anarchy.

This must be enough to serve as an illustration of a lengthy series of cases. The story obviously did not stop in 1916. We saw, from *Henningsen* (section 19), one of the turns it took. The assumption that negligence or fraud must be proved in claiming manufacturers' liability is no longer in force; for the question in that case, though partly about negligence, was largely concerned with an "implied warranty" that was supposed to come on sale of a car. This is no innovation of the past twenty-five years but involves notions that go back to the thirteenth century: sellers of defective food were held liable, even if not negligent, through some implicit assurance they gave the community at large. Another notion that has shown expanded application is that of "strict liability." How can a person be liable for harm when he took all reasonable precautions? There are considerable problems here, yet the claim persists and has much to do with the model of society that we bring to our legal reasoning (section 34 will return to the use by judges of such models and policies in their arguments).

FURTHER READING

Berman, H. J., and W. R. Greiner. *The Nature and Functions of Law.* Mineola, N.Y.: Foundation Press, 1972, 413–81.

Hazard, Leland. *Law and the Changing Environment.* San Francisco: Holden-Day, 1971, 206–53.

Levi, Edward H. *An Introduction to Legal Reasoning.* Chicago: Univ. of Chicago Press, 1949, 1–27.

Pound, Roscoe. *Introduction to the Philosophy of Law.* 2d ed. New Haven: Yale Univ. Press, 1954, 72–106.

QUESTIONS FOR DISCUSSION

1. In *MacPherson*, Judge Bartlett quotes an English judge as justifying (in 1842) the limitation of manufacturers' liability through privity of contract: "Unless we confine the operation of such contracts as this to the parties who enter into them, the most absurd and outrageous consequences, to which I see no limit, would ensue." Give other examples of, and assess, arguments from "outrageous consequences." Can you justify privity of contract in terms of a pre-industrial society where the producer and purchaser stood in a "primary relationship"? If a post office official (or the postmaster general himself) had been riding in the ill-fated mail coach and had been injured, could he have sued and won where Winterbottom lost?

2. The earliest formulations of the desired rule employ the terms "nature" (*Longmeid*) and "imminent" (*Thomas*). What do these words mean in ordinary, rather than philosophical, language? What is the nature of a gun? Of a carriage? Of a person? Would the bottle of belladonna have still been an imminent danger if it remained unopened for five years (see *Loop*)? Is the meaning of imminence to be defined in terms of a measure of time? Or is time but one factor in a multitude of tests that decide how "close" we are to danger and how "probable" it is?

3. Is gunpowder "essentially an instrument of danger" (*Loop*)? Can you distinguish between consequences that are "natural and necessary" and those that are not (*Devlin*)? Think about firing a rifle, dynamiting a tree trunk, dumping chemical wastes in a river.

4. Comment on this example of another judge's effort to defuse metaphysical distinctions in the law.

> Take the illustration given in an unpublished manuscript by a distinguished and helpful writer on the law of torts. A chauffeur negligently collides with another car which is filled with dynamite, although he could not know it. An explosion follows. A, walking on the sidewalk nearby, is killed. B, sitting in a window of a building opposite, is cut by flying glass. C, likewise sitting in a window a block away, is similarly injured. And a further illustration: A nursemaid, ten blocks away, startled by the noise, involuntarily drops a baby from her arms to the walk. We are told that C may not recover while A may. As to B, it is a question for court or jury. We will all agree that the baby might not.... It is all a question of expediency. There are no fixed rules to govern our judgment. There is little to guide us other than common sense.
>
> (Dissenting opinion in Palsgraf v. Long Island R.R. Co., 1928, 248 N.Y. 339, 162 N.E. 99)

5. Would Torgesen have won if the bottle had exploded when she dropped it on the kitchen floor? How can a manufacturer foresee all that even reasonable purchasers will do with his products? Suppose the belladonna had been correctly labeled and Mrs. Thomas was not wearing her glasses?

6. In *MacPherson*, it was Bartlett, rather than Cardozo, who mentioned that MacPherson was driving at only eight miles per hour, probably more slowly than Winterbottom. Is this fact "material"?

7. Comment on the suggestion that, whereas a torpedo is inherently dangerous, a scaffold is not, though it can become imminently dangerous through faulty construction (or perhaps long exposure to the rain). To which of the examples listed in *Loop* might such a distinction apply?

8. Admission to law school is based largely on a candidate's score in the Law School Admission Test and on his or her college transcript (Q.P.A.). Sometimes an interview is taken into account. Imagine that candidates are submitted to a variety of other tests (performance at a cocktail party?), and suppose that decisions are made by a panel of officials. Should each test be given a precise weight, or should the decision be based loosely on "overall impression"? The analogy may be weak, but does it illustrate Cardozo's suggestion in *MacPherson*?

9. In section 2 above, Scott Turow was quoted as saying that, of the professors he had at Harvard Law School, one who eventually turned out to be among the most popular was at first dismissed as thoroughly confused and confusing. He was, interestingly, the instructor in torts. He refused ever to give a clear statement of a legal rule but repeatedly offered actual or hypothetical cases to question any formulation that was supplied. "Suddenly I realized his point: there are no answers." Does this indicate a sound approach to analogical reasoning in case law?

32. ENACTED LAW

> *What does it mean to say of a relationship or a side of life, "Let's have some rules around here"? . . . Since rules work so differently in different hands, you are also being asked what the art of making rules—and of using them to organize and manage social relationships—consists of and how it is to be exercised.*
>
> (J. B. White, *The Legal Imagination*, 504)

In section 10 it was suggested that law can be seen as a spectrum that runs from the highly informal to the very formal. At one extreme (we called it the "left") is the family, which proceeds by shared ideals and implicit understandings rather than by formal rules. Primitive societies, so far as they rely upon customary law, would tend to the left. At the far right we can place total institutions, such as prisons, where a comprehensive set of written rules prescribes for even the most trivial behavior. The modern state will presumably be right of center, though we find a broad range among and within legal traditions.

Thus far, in this chapter, we have been concerned with case law, and examples have been taken from the common law. If the judge, in his very fidelity to the law he finds, is obliged in some sense to make law, he does so only "interstitially." When we speak of a "lawmaker," we think of other officials. These are elected legislators in Congress or Parliament, where the political system is a democracy; or we should include a king, dictator, or oligarchy in other systems.

None of these officials is, except in a very general way, bound by precedents. A legislature can make a law by a show of hands and thus simply abolish previous laws or extend them dramatically to cover new situations. Though the judge carefully avoids giving the impression that he is acting in his own name, the legislature is proud to announce its initiative, its own doing. We speak of an *act* of Congress or Parliament. So we shall, in this section, turn from case law to a few questions about "enacted law."

Such questions can certainly be located in the common law. With the great complexity and rapid changes of modern life, the courts have shown themselves ill equipped to adapt the law, and we are relying to an increasing extent on the enacted law of statutes and ordinances (a notable feature is the growth of administrative agencies). Though the criminal law developed out of judicial decisions, it is now assumed—with a few minor exceptions—that criminal law should be "codified" in a comprehensive set of statutes. In this country, a Conference of Commissioners on Uniform State Laws was set up in 1890 to draft and submit to the state legislatures a series of proposals for common codes of non-criminal law. Some of these proposals, notably the Uniform Commercial Code, have been largely adopted.

Codification, the assembling of a wide variety of rules into a system, belongs to what we are calling enacted law. Sometimes the process is seen as a clean break with the past: lawmaking is at work on a grand scale, rather than being limited to particular statutes. At other times, codification is presented as a gathering together of rules that already exist, but no pretense is made to hide the changes imposed by the very needs of a system. It is in the civil law tradition that codification has become a dominant ideal, though many of the problems we are to discuss may lessen the difference between the two traditions in practice.

Perhaps the basic question of the layperson here is why all law has not been codified. Surely the enactment of law in a few volumes, with detailed indices at the back, shows clear advantages over the dissipation of rulings in a library of judicial opinions? Have we not yet fully recognized legislation as the final stage of law? Why have we been so slow to take the most obvious step toward making law a discipline? This section will be concerned largely with problems and disadvantages of codification, but some evident merits must be mentioned.

Firstly, enacted law is more adaptable to new situations. Legislators can take large steps and confront whole problem areas when they find a change in the law to be advisable. Judges, bound by *stare decisis*, can but tamper with small points in particular cases; the development of the law concerning manufacturers' liability was painfully slow, clumsy, and piecemeal.

Secondly, the need for law to be public seems more easily met in statutes and codes than in case law. Judicial opinions, at least at the appellate level, are written and published, yet in such a way that they remain hidden from all but a professional class of lawyers. Also, case law is "unwritten" in the vital sense that the rule has to be extracted from cases and has no official statement; even lawyers disagree on precisely how to find the *ratio decidendi*. However, the very text of a statute is the rule.

Thirdly, enacted law can be cleanly prospective, whereas each change made by a judge seems to have retroactive force in the case he is deciding; both Elmer Palmer and the Buick Company found they had offended against a rule that they apparently did not know at the time.

Finally, it is claimed that enacted law is more appropriate in a democracy, where authority rests with the people. It is our elected representatives who make and unmake the statutes. Yet even where judges are elected, they are to a

Problems of Codification

> As in many Utopias, one of the objectives of the French Revolution was to make lawyers unnecessary. There was a desire for a legal system that was simple and nontechnical.... Thus the French Civil Code of 1804 was envisioned as a kind of popular book that could be put on the shelf next to the family Bible. It would be a handbook for the citizen, clearly organized and stated in straightforward language, that would allow citizens to determine their legal rights and obligations by themselves.
>
> (J. H. Merryman, *The Civil Law Tradition*, 29–30)

For examples of codification we can go back to Justinian in the sixth century (or perhaps to Hammurabi of Babylon in the eighteenth century B.C.), but it is in the last two hundred years that the great codes of the civil law tradition appeared. The rise of modern nations was largely responsible; to meet the needs of a centralized state, a unity had to be achieved out of the broad diversity of legal materials that came from the past. And this meant breaking the power of judges to formulate the law (the different course of events in England, with its early growth of royal power and royal courts, has already been discussed: see section 13).

However, a further important element in codification was the spirit of rationalism that ruled the thought of intellectuals in the Continental countries that had produced Descartes, Spinoza, and Leibniz. History was less rational than geometry. Law was a product of reason and should proceed deductively from general principles to particular rules that apply readily to individual cases.

Nowhere is this seen more clearly than in the Prussian Code of 1794, enacted under Frederick the Great. It contained over 16,000 articles (whereas the French Civil Code had 2,281). The claim was to provide a system of such detail that any specific case could be solved without ambiguity. The judge's function was largely a mechanical one: it was simply to apply the rules designed by the legislator. All contingencies were thought to be anticipated, and judges were not allowed to interpret the code. If any question did arise, it was to be put to a royal commission. This "Statutes Commission" published its solution to the many doubts that developed, and volumes of supplementary rules began appearing. The system soon proved unworkable, the commission was dissolved, and the judges were given back their right to interpret the law in applying it.

The French codes of 1804 and subsequent years owe their greater influence and durability to the experienced jurists who carried out the task. One of these, Portalis, described the smaller number of articles as "principles or maxims" that were to show their fruit only when cases came to trial and the articles were applied. That is, he left the detail to interpretations that would be made by his successors. This professionalism, however, was largely concealed by the rhetoric of the Revolution, which portrayed the code as a comprehensive system that contained the whole law in a form both understandable to the people and free from change at the hands of judges.

One example may be enough to suggest the subsequent history of the French codes, with judicial interpretation making a covert entry under the facade of a system of purely enacted law. As in the Prussia of Frederick the Great, many questions of interpretation began to appear. The legislature created a governmental department to oversee the courts and simply to quash any interpretations of the code that were deemed incorrect. This branch of the legislature, though it acted as a court, was maintained not to be one and was called the *Tribunal de Cassation (casser*: to break). However, by gradual and perhaps inevitable steps, this body became the *Cour de Cassation*, very much like a supreme court in the common law lands. It was staffed by judges and, in addition to telling lower courts that they had made the wrong decision, it gave the proper one and applied it to produce a new verdict.

Germany, which became one nation much later, and in an age when history commanded greater respect, took more time over drafting a code. The one that appeared in 1896 (to be effective in 1900), had none of the revolutionary fervor of the French codes. It was presented, not as a break with the past, but more as a system that was faithful to the full development of the German spirit and law. Also, its language was addressed to lawyers rather than to laypersons. Though the claim to serve as a comprehensive basis for all particular decisions was still made, it is in Germany that the need for judicial departures from the articles of a code became most evident. The economic disruption of the country after the First World War was such that drastic legal revisions were needed if life was to go on. With the currency falling to one trillionth of its prewar value, contracts could not be met and creditors were being paid in worthless money. The Supreme Court intervened with creative decisions that set aside any pretense to rely on particular statutes. Such moves by the judiciary provoked much theoretical discussion and have become known, from one study, as "the flight into general clauses."

This brief historical survey may suggest that the traditional account of the distinction between a legal system like ours, grounded in case law, and one such as the French or German, based on enacted law, needs many qualifications. There is certainly a difference of style. An American or English judge, even in a realm of law that is codified, will look for the meaning of a rule in the decisions of courts. He sees his task as being faithful to a historical process rather than as maintaining a system of propositions. A French or German judge will certainly study courtroom precedents, but for the rule of law he will refer back to the code. The enacted system is not openly to be extended. Nevertheless, the difference is by no means so sharp as it is made to appear. The distinction between merely "considering" precedents and actively "following" them may prove rather slight in practice.

Napoleon was no legal expert, but he took a genuine interest in the formation of the code that bears his name, and he rightly suspected that its effects would range further and last much longer than his military conquests. He at first thought "it would be possible to reduce laws to simple geometrical demonstrations, so that whoever could read and tie two ideas together would be able to pronounce on them." Later, however, he admitted the absurdity of this idea and put his finger on the basic dilemma of any codifier: "I saw that oversimplicity was the enemy of precision." This is a choice that faces not only codifiers, but any drafter of a statute for a legislature.

At the extreme of simplicity, a coherent system of law can be formed from general statements that carefully avoid descent into detail. But an experienced lawyer, reading such a code, will repeatedly demand, Give me some cases! At the other extreme, the codifier will try to state the law in a way that covers everything in detail. The gain in precision results in loss of simplicity and of systematic harmony. If articles of a code provide exactly for damage on the roads, in an age of horses, then extensive revision will be needed as damage begins to come from the density and speed of automobile traffic.

Drafting a Statute

When we turn from the vast enterprise of codification to the more limited one of writing a statute, similar problems occur. Should we leave the statute general and imprecise or should we aim to cover all eventualities? Precision is among the virtues, yet there is often greater merit in "open texture." To resume the trivial example of headwear in church, it is possible that an exact statement of the rules could be formulated for men; a qualification would be written for bishops and for babies, and toupees would remain inviolate. But what about the rule, deriving from St. Paul, that women should wear hats in church? Here it may be less easy for a statute to tell us all. One woman covers her head with a veil, another with a scarf, a third with a handkerchief, and the fourth puts a flower in her hair. If one flower does not satisfy, what about three or a floral headpiece? What about the woman who simply covers her head with her hand, or the pious one who employs the parish magazine? The ecclesiastical legislator will almost certainly seek no greater precision than requiring that the head be "decently" covered.

The example is facetious, yet students of constitutional law can certainly supply more serious ones. A constitution will be very precise when it tells how a president is to be elected, much less so when it stipulates that the state may not "deprive any person of life, liberty, or property, without due process of law." And statutes that seem to be precise are often advisedly interpreted in ways that open them to subsequent interpretation in the courts. The Sherman Antitrust Act of 1890 put its key provision in the sentence that "every contract, combination in the form of trust or otherwise, or conspiracy, in restraint of trade or commerce among the several states or with foreign nations, is hereby declared to be illegal." We are still asking what precisely does or does not constitute "restraint of trade or commerce" and what sort of "combinations" can be guilty of it. The courts have, in effect, inserted the word "unreasonable" before "restraint of trade."[27]

Another classic example of uncertainties left to the courts by a statute is the Mann Act of 1910:

> Any person who shall knowingly transport or cause to be transported, or aid or assist in obtaining transportation for, or in transporting, in interstate or foreign commerce or in any territory or in the District of Columbia, any woman or girl for the purpose of prostitution or debauchery, or for any other immoral purpose, or with the intent and purpose to induce, entice or compel such woman or girl to become a prostitute, or to give herself up to debauchery, or to give herself up to any other immoral practice ... shall be deemed guilty of a felony.

This lengthy sentence seems to aim at covering all the possibilities. But the critical points are left for the future, and the courts, to decide. Though this was known as the "White Slave Traffic Act," how narrow or broad is its scope? Does it extend to cases where a prostitute gladly allows herself to be so transported? Even if there is a plain meaning to "prostitution and debauchery," what is or is not intended to be included by adding the wide class of "any other immoral purpose or practice"? A study of the legislative history of this act suggests that there was little agreement among the legislators on such questions, no serious projection of cases to arise, and even a strange ignorance of the facts constituting an evil to be remedied. The law that was enacted was thrown to the courts for pertinent decisions about its meaning.[28]

This example may well suggest the problems of codification because it comes from the field of criminal law, where the importance of enactment is generally accepted. Since criminal penalties are more severe than civil ones, and the stigma of being a convict is so grave, it seems that the law here should be as public and as precise as we can make it. You may have to consult a lawyer to find exactly how your contract binds you, but you should not need professional help to learn what is a legitimate or a criminal entry into someone else's home.

The principle has been enunciated, since the time of the French Revolution, in the phrase "*nullum crimen sine lege*": no crime has been committed unless there has been a violation of a definite (enacted) law. Exceptions today are in the area of "victimless crimes."[29] What the principle opposes most strongly is any catchall clause in the criminal law, of a sort that would enable courts to

---

27. This example was mentioned above, in section 19, as illustrating Dworkin's distinction between rules and principles.

28. See Levi, *Introduction to Legal Reasoning*, 33–54.

29. See section 15 above. An interesting example of a modern "common law crime" is offered by State v. Bradbury (1939, 136 Me. 347, 9 A.2d 657). Though no statute covered the case, Bradbury was convicted of indecently burning the body of his sister after she died in old age. The appeals court upheld the verdict that

convict us on serious matters where the legislature has made no specific provision. Two clear examples follow. The first has been officially repealed, and the second died with the legislator.

> If a socially dangerous act is not directly provided for by the present code, the foundations and limits of responsibility for it shall be determined according to those articles of the code which provide for those crimes most similar to it in kind.
>
> (Article 16, Soviet Criminal Code of 1926)

> Whoever commits an action which is deserving of punishment according to the sound principles of the people shall be punished. If no determinate penal law is applicable to the action, it shall be punished according to whatever law fits it best.
>
> (Nazi law of 1935)

There is a parallel, though distinct, principle that all criminal statutes are to be construed strictly by the courts. The leeway of interpretation for convicting a person of a crime should be less than for deciding between plaintiff and defendant in a civil court. It is, however, when we turn from criminal to civil cases that we find the most acute problems of whether any relevant statutes should be written precisely or should allow initiative for the courts. Following is an example that may indicate the question.[30]

Clara Smith was employed by Mr. and Mrs. Hiatt to care for their baby. One morning in 1946, Smith went into the kitchen to prepare milk for the child and slipped on some ice that had dropped to the floor while her employer was defrosting the refrigerator. There was evidence of negligence on the part of Hiatt, none on the part of Smith. So when the latter sued to recover for the resulting injuries, there was every indication that she would win.

However, the Hiatts had a sharp lawyer. He scrutinized the Massachusetts statutes on the liability of towns for injuries "sustained upon a public way by reason of snow or ice thereon." All claims for such injuries had to be made in writing within ten days. This would seem not to apply to ice on a kitchen floor. Nevertheless, there followed a clause that extended these provisions to injuries from snow or ice on private premises, though thirty days were allowed for notice of claims. So the lawyer astutely based his defense on the fact that no such notice of claim had been submitted by the plaintiff within the thirty days required by enacted law.

The jury followed their common sense and found for Smith. The Hiatts took their lawyer's advice and appealed. The Supreme Judicial Court of Massachusetts proceeded to reverse the decision and deny the plaintiff all recovery as

---

this was a crime under the common law, since the act of cremating a body by forcing it into a basement furnace "would outrage the feelings and natural sentiments of the public."

30. Smith v. Hiatt (1952): 329 Mass. 488, 109 N.E.2d 133.

"she was not relieved from giving the written notice required by the statute." A previous case was cited where the court had ruled that the statute applied when snow had been tracked into a house from outside.

If you agree with the jury in thinking this verdict unjust, then who is to blame? Smith's lawyer, for failing to know the law and advise his client? The Hiatt's lawyer, for knowing the law all too well? The upper court judges, for refusing to go beyond the letter of the statute to its spirit? Or the legislators, for bad draftsmanship of the statute? If this, would you say they should have been more precise or less precise?

The Massachusetts legislators made amends three years after the decision, and too late to help Miss Smith. They chose the course of greater precision by inserting in the statute, after "snow and ice," the words "resulting from rain or snow or weather conditions." Was such precision the right course? Suppose Smith had slipped on icy condensation from an air conditioner, a result of the "weather conditions" of excessive humidity? No legislator can see all possible gaps in what he writes and anticipate all possible cases. Might it not have been better if the original statute, after talking about public ways, had simply said that "appropriate extensions of this statute apply to injuries on private premises, though thirty days are allowed for notice of claims"?

Two questions appear from such discussions. How precisely or how loosely should codes and statutes be drafted? And does enacted law hand the courts a ready-made document, a major premise from which conclusions can be derived by deduction, or does any formulation of the law rely upon an indefinite series of court decisions that seek its meaning in many cases not foreseen by the legislators?

These questions cannot altogether be separated. However, though an answer to the first must be left open, it seems that both the common law and civil law traditions depend on continuing judicial decisions in reply to the second question. Codes and statutes, the work of the legislator, are thrown to the courts for an understanding of whatever norm is at work. This becomes all the more obvious when we realize that both legislature and judiciary are staffed by legal professionals. The ideology of a code that dispenses with lawyers may still impress us. But the difficulties are great. And a reading of the statutes governing our life leaves us with the conclusion that they were written by lawyers for further lawyers to apply and interpret. Nevertheless, the question of intepreting rules and other statements takes us beyond the practices of any one profession, so a number of remarks on traditional theories of interpretation will be added in the following section.

FURTHER READING

Berman, Harold J., and W. R. Greiner. *The Nature and Functions of Law.* Mineola, N.Y.: Foundation Press, 1972, 116–33.

Bishin, William R., and C. D. Stone. *Law, Language, and Ethics.* Mineola, N.Y.: Foundation Press, 1972, 413–44.

Frank, Jerome. *Law and the Modern Mind.* 1930. Reprint. Gloucester, Mass.: Peter Smith, 1970, 200–209, 336–37.

Houghteling, James L. *The Dynamics of Law.* New York: Harcourt Brace & World, 1963, 99–114.

Liebesny, Herbert J. *Foreign Legal Systems.* Washington, D.C.: George Washington Univ. Press, 1981, 26–100.

Merryman, John H. *The Civil Law Tradition.* 1969. Revised ed., Stanford, Calif.: Stanford Univ. Press, 1985, chapter 5.

Stoljar, Samuel J., ed. *Problems of Codification.* Canberra: The Australian National University, 1977.

White, James B. *The Legal Imagination.* Boston: Little, Brown & Co., 1973, chapter 4.

QUESTIONS FOR DISCUSSION

1. It is understandable that the royal commission, set up by Frederick the Great to answer all questions on the interpretation of a code, should have failed. However, Judge Cardozo suggested that each state should establish a commission to review the whole law repeatedly, both enacted and judicial, and submit needed changes or clarifications to the legislature. New York adopted the idea. How do the two proposals differ, and what greater success do you see for the latter?

2. Suppose that manufacturers' liability had come under enacted law rather than case law. Try drafting an appropriate statute as it might have been written in 1850; in 1860; in 1915.

3. In the light of examples in sections 26 and 27, try drafting a statement to define how far a lawyer may go in maintaining the confidentiality of his relationship with a client and in advocating the client's cause in court. Notice the dangers of being too vague or too specific.

4. If you prefer examples from outside the law, turn your hand to formulating some rules that will cover situations with which you are familiar. How might a parent legislate for damage resulting from negligence by family members? How might the rules of soccer tell a referee when to wave play on after a penalty occurs? Contrast the wording of rules about a delay in meeting the repayment of a debt and in taking a test at school. Notice any use you make of such words as "reasonable," "appropriate," or "discretion."

5. Write a statute (or other rule) that you regard to be overexact. Think of cases that would show it to be so. For instance, a doctor prescribing a cure for his patient will be very precise on how many pills to swallow per day, much less so on how much exercise to take per day. Suppose, however, he tries to be as detailed in legislating for the latter as for the former?

6. The rules for contempt of court in the United States are left vague. Is it enough to forbid "conduct not befitting an American courtroom"? See, for example, Mayberry v. Pennsylvania (1971), 400 U.S. 455, 91 S.Ct. 499. What about the military phrase, "conduct unbecoming an officer and a gentleman"?

7. Oliver Wendell Holmes's statement has been quoted, that those who want to know what the law is should see it from the viewpoint of the "bad man." There are, however, degrees of "badness." Should a legislator, in drafting statutes of criminal law, adopt the viewpoint of a prison warden drawing up rules for inmates who have already been carefully selected from the population at large? Or should a legislator for the state or nation presuppose some "goodness" as limiting the precision he needs to incorporate in enacted rules? Again, where do you situate the question of "legalism"?

8. From what you know of business practices, suggest the lack of clarity in deciding which procedures are or are not "in restraint of trade." Could this ambiguity be overcome in a more detailed formulation?

9. Mr. Hays, a cattleman from Wichita, attended a convention in Oklahoma and met a prostitute there. He later paid her bus fare to come to Kansas for a weekend that was pleasurable for one and profitable for the other. Hays was sentenced to eighteen months in the penitentiary for violating the Mann Act. Rightly so?

10. Mr. and Mrs. Mortensen operated a house of prostitution in Nebraska. In 1940 they drove to Yellowstone Park and took two of their employees along for a needed holiday. They returned, across state lines, and brought the girls back into Nebraska where these resumed their work as prostitutes. The Mortensens were charged under the Mann Act. They were convicted, but the decision was reversed by the Supreme Court (Mortensen v. U.S., 1944, 322 U.S. 369, 64 S.Ct. 1037). Rightly so?

33. THEORIES OF INTERPRETATION

> *The interpretation of the meaning of statutes, as applied to justiciable controversies, is exclusively a judicial function. This duty requires one body of public servants, the judges, to construe the meaning of what another body, the legislators, has said. Obviously there is danger that the courts' conclusion as to legislative purpose will be unconsciously influenced by the judges' own views or by factors not considered by the enacting body.*
>
> (Justice Stanley F. Reed)[31]

> *Whoever hath an absolute authority to interpret any written or spoken laws, it is he who is truly the lawgiver to all intents and purposes, and not the person who first wrote or spoke them.*
>
> (Bishop Benjamin Hoadly, 1717)

Much of our life is spent interpreting the spoken or written words of others. Most statements carry a sufficiently obvious meaning that there is little burden of understanding. If, as summer wanes, I remark that the days are growing shorter, you will get my point. Even this innocent comment is theory-laden, and perhaps the tone of voice and the context must be estimated if my full meaning is to come across. But we do not have to look far to find statements that call for a more subtle form (and hence theory) of interpretation. Journalists devote columns to telling us what the party platform or the aside of an official "really" means. Literary critics write books to explain other books. Marriages founder on problems of interpretation.

No reader who has come this far will deny that law offers prime examples. Few fields place so acute a strain on our ability to disclose the "true sense" of writings that tradition hands us. Perhaps, if this has been our topic throughout, little can be added. Illustrations, from *Riggs* and the Speluncean Explorers to *MacPherson* and *Smith v. Hiatt*, have all tested our way of finding what a legislator or a line of precedents has to offer.

---

31. U.S. v. American Trucking Associations (1940): 310 U.S. 534, 544, 60 S.Ct. 1059, 1064.

This is a chapter on legal reasoning. The theme covers the manner in which we move validly from premises to conclusions. However, we could scarcely respect reasoning if we did not see this as a way to discover what is true. Since a valid argument from false premises can produce a false conclusion, we must now turn somewhat more explicitly to the question how we know which premises are true. Problems about the factual (or "minor") premise belong to chapter 4. It is the major premise that concerns us here. Judges cite, or imply, grounds for deciding on the facts. These reasons may come from a statute of criminal law, from an article in a code, from what we take to be the *ratio decidendi* in a line of precedents, from a current social policy, from some conception of the family or of the state (as in cases pertaining to battered wives or involving "strict liability"), from a view of natural rights, or from a concept of law as a whole.

Judges do not help us by clearly listing all such sources, any more than they tell us to which of the "basic theories of law" (chapter 3) they subscribe. So this section will start with what appears to be the most simple question: how a judge finds the meaning of an article of enacted law. The discussion will widen to include case law. Some of the more evidently normative questions, about the place of justice in the premises of legal reasoning, will be left to the following section.

All professions supply guidelines to their members. To what can judges turn? They can find, in the written law, a variety of canons of construction (interpretation). These, however, are of little more value than the proverbs of daily life. From the latter we learn that "many hands make light work." But we are also told that "too many cooks spoil the broth." Karl Llewellyn has listed more than twenty canons of strict construction, each one matched by a contrary canon for broad interpretation.[32] Thus we are informed that "exceptions not made [explicitly by the legislator] cannot be read," and then we get the liberal advice that "whatever is within the reason of the law is within the law itself."

Should we be surprised by such "antinomies" in the help that is given us with legal interpretation? There is something rather odd in trying to find how we should construe rules by thus multiplying the number of rules we have to interpret. The Anglo-American tradition of law has little to say on this question. More comment comes from the civil law tradition; codification focuses attention on the problem how enactments are to be understood.[33] So we may turn, for a start, to a remark on French law: "The notion of 'interpretation' of texts permits four distinct approaches, characterized in French legal doctrine as grammatical, logical, historical, and teleological".[34]

---

32. See Karl Llewellyn, "Remarks on the Theory of Appellate Decision and the Rules or Canons About How Statutes are to be Construed," *Vanderbilt Law Review* 3 (1950): 401–6.

33. "The task of lawyers in these countries is conceived as essentially one of *interpreting* legislative provisions and is thus unlike that of common law countries where the legal technique is characterized by the process of *distinguishing* judicial decisions" (David, *Major Legal Systems*, 90).

34. René David and Henry P. de Vries, *The French Legal System* (New York: Oceana Publications, 1958), 87.

We need spend little time on the first two. Indeed, the layperson might say that they refer to the obvious process of reading a law without any need to interpret it. Traffic rules offer evident examples. If the sign says No Right Turn On Red, a basic knowledge of English words and grammar suffices. Some context is always involved, but problems are unlikely. Do not expect a sympathetic hearing from police officer or judge if you say you thought that "red" referred to the road surface rather than the traffic light.

All legal systems require that we begin with the "plain meaning" of words. The sign in the auditorium said No Smoking. I was caught with a lighted cigarette from which I was inhaling. I have offended. The janitor who allowed steam to escape from the radiators did not break this rule. The question might, however, take us beyond grammar if the sign were only in the body of the auditorium and I were smoking in the lobby. Had the statute pertinent to *Temple v. Petersburg* (section 6) stated that no cemetery should be "established or extended," then there is unlikely to have been such a case for us to study.

Problems arise when, as in *Temple*, the denotation of words may or may not cover the case at bar. Does "establishing" include "extending"? Or, to go back to Roman law, the Twelve Tables allowed an offended person to bring an action when a tree he owned was chopped down without his permission. Could he do so if the plant was a vine and it was cut with a knife? The answer was, yes. The word *tree* was held to include vines, and cutting is a form of chopping.

If this example were from a contemporary statute, the defendant might appeal beyond the dictionary to other considerations. Did the legislators have in mind serious problems of deforestation rather than the protection of small fruit trees around the family home? Some historical inquiry could be demanded. But there is another, relatively simple, stage of interpretation before we plunge into the murky depths of legislative history. It is that of logic. How does a particular article fit with the other articles of a code?

Law, whether expressed in a comprehensive code or not, can exist only if it is systematic. One of King Rex's failures to make law, in Fuller's story (section 12), came with the imposition of duties in one section that would mean violating obligations in another. The law of an Indian tribe would fail if it prescribed that disputes be settled in court with a pipe of peace and also prohibited smoking in court. The judge might, following logic, exclude the litigants from the scope of the latter rule at time of settlement; or perhaps he would distinguish between ritual and casual smoking.

The example is contrived but the point is serious. The meaning of any sentence depends at least upon the full literary context. For this we must look to the entire statute and to other statutes with which there is to be coherence. Suppose a federal law states that a child can be brought into the country for adoption only with prior approval of the state in which he or she is to reside. But the state in question will not give such approval unless social workers have first visited the child in the adoptive parents' home. The case is an actual one, and it was resolved by sympathetic officials whose interpretation of the law might be put under the rubric of logical consistency. For our purposes, we may say that search for the plain meaning of legal statements involves logic as well as grammar.

Legislative Intention

> There was a law, that those who in a storm forsook the ship would forfeit all property therein; and that the ship and lading should belong entirely to those who staid in it. In a dangerous tempest all the mariners forsook the ship, except only one sick passenger, who, by reason of his disease, was unable to get out and escape. By chance the ship came safe to port. The sick man kept possession, and claimed the benefit of the law. Now here all the learned agree, that the sick man is not within the reason of the law; for the reason of making it was, to give encouragement to such as should venture their lives to save the vessel but this is a merit which he could never pretend to, who neither staid in the ship upon that account, nor contributed anything to its preservation.
>
> (Sir William Blackstone, *Commentaries*, book I, 61)

We need not appeal to the authority of the most famous jurist of the eighteenth century to say that plain meaning (grammar plus logic) does not settle all our problems of legal interpretation. Blackstone draws also upon what he calls "the reason of the law." The phrase covers many possibilities, but he evidently uses it here to mean the particular intention of those responsible for making a law. They could not have included in their project the granting of a whole ship and cargo to one whose sickness prevented him both from escaping and from contributing courageously to salvage operations.

We thus come to the form of interpretation that many of us would regard as offering a clear solution to any such problems. We encounter an odd piece of sculpture. What is it? What does it mean? Surely our first question is, Who made it? Ask him or her. There is the one who should know. So, for the meaning of a law, we turn to the intention of the legislator.

This makes sense, yet our problems may only be beginning. It will help to have an example in mind. A prominent illustration in such discussion has been a statute that prohibits certain uses of "vehicles" or of "motor vehicles." If we wish an actual case, it can be that of McBoyle v. United States (1931, 283 U.S. 25, 51 S.Ct. 340). Few judges have been less bound by literalism, by inflexible attention to the words and logic of the law, than Justice Holmes; so it is surprising to read his majority opinion in this case. McBoyle had flown, from Illinois to Oklahoma, an airplane that he knew to have been stolen. He was charged with violation of a 1919 federal law, that "whoever shall transport or cause to be transported in interstate or foreign commerce a motor vehicle, knowing the same to have been stolen, shall be punished...." The term *motor vehicle* was defined by the act to "include an automobile, automobile truck, automobile wagon, motor cycle or any other self-propelled vehicle not designed for running on rails." Holmes allowed that it is possible to set an airplane under that definition: it is self-propelled and does not run on rails. But he cited the list of examples and said that these "call up the popular picture ... of a vehicle running on land." So he reversed the lower court decision, concluding that McBoyle had not violated this particular statute.

The ruling may be justifiable in terms of the obvious meaning of words. Though the aircraft traveled a short distance on land in Illinois, before taking off, and in Oklahoma, after landing, few would call a plane a motor vehicle. In addition, policy questions were involved. Criminal statutes are to be given a strict interpretation. Also, it might be wise to limit federal encroachment on the responsibility of states to prosecute under their own law. However, most of us would want to know more about the federal law in question. Airplanes were scarce but not unknown in 1919. Did Congress really intend to exclude their theft from the "ill" that it sought to remedy with this law? Though Holmes makes passing reference to the fact that airplanes were not discussed in the debates before enactment, is this enough to exclude them from the scope of the legislation? The list of four examples was not exhaustive, else why add mention of "any other self-propelled vehicle not designed for running on rails"? The law was in fact amended in 1945 to add airplanes explicitly.

Wittgenstein offers a similar example: "Someone says to me, 'Shew the children a game.' I teach them gaming with dice, and the other says 'I didn't mean that sort of game.' Must the exclusion of the game with dice have come before his mind when he gave me the order?"[35] An experienced baby sitter would probably reply that it all depends on understandings between employer and employee. From what you know of some parents, gambling is obviously out. Others might be amused at the initiation of their children into what is so much a part of life.

Suppose a city ordinance bans "vehicles" from the park on Sundays. "Plain meaning" suffices for us to turn away a Buick or Cadillac, a truck or bus, and probably a motorcycle or combine harvester. Then we come to some more dubious examples: a horse-drawn carriage, a go-kart, a moped, a bicycle, a wheelbarrow, a skateboard, a toy car, a baby carriage.[36] Those familiar with the full range of the common law will know that an English court placed go-karts in the category of vehicles (Burns v. Currell, 1963, 2 Q.B. 433). And if a later page of the city ordinances specifies that a tax on vehicles applies to motorcycles and mopeds but not to bicycles, logical consistency may give further guidance. Yet sooner or later we shall probably ask *why* the city legislators restricted traffic in this way. Was it to eliminate noise? Was it to give safe use of the park roads to pedestrians? Was it to offer a purely rustic scene once a week in the city? Depending on the lawmakers' purpose, we decide on our classification.

---

35. Wittgenstein, *Philosophical Investigations*, section 70, note.

36. In 1977, a California appeals court found, in a case involving intoxication, that to pedal a moped with the engine off is "to drive a motor vehicle" (People v. Jordan: 1977, 75 Cal.App.3d Supp. 1, 142 Cal. Rptr. 401). Yet three years later, another appellate court in the same state decided that to ride a bicycle when intoxicated does not make one liable under the Vehicle Code (Clingenpeel v. Municipal Court: 1980, 108 Cal. App.3d 394, 166 Cal.Rptr. 573).

Horse carriages supply more noise than an electric car. No walker likes to be hit by a bicycle or even a skateboard. And a commercial barrow may be an unpleasant reminder of the weekday concerns of a busy town.

If we suppose, at present, that a knowledge of legislative intention would decide the meaning of a law, what practical problems do we face? In most cases the obvious difficulty is that those who made the law are no longer before us to be consulted. The king may still be alive, though with failing memory, but the Congress or Parliament now in session is unlikely to be the same as the one that made the law. A page of history can be worth a volume of logic, yet there is an interesting reluctance of courts to invite studies of legislative history.[37] This is often meager, contradictory, and difficult to appraise. Most of the work is done in the privacy of committees. And where records exist of public debates, their very publicity means that the legislators were conscious of a variety of audiences. Even if an individual had a coherent "mind" on the question, he is unlikely to expose it fully for the record; his language is calculated to please discordant groups. For the average judge, a study of legislative history is time consuming and of little value.

Let us, then, take the situation most favorable to an inquiry into legislative intention, where the relevant legislature is still in session. Here we face the many difficulties connected with the word *intention*. If I am asked whether I intended to push someone or to avoid paying my income tax, I may find a simple answer. But the search for intentions, even in an individual, gets more complex as the situation presents more sides. Why are you at college? Why, if you are seeking a divorce, did you ever marry the person? Why, if you are so critical of the firm, do you still work for it? And these problems are compounded when we ask for a common intention in a legislature of more than a hundred. It is unlikely that we could find a consistent intention in the many people who drafted a law, discussed it in committee, debated it in public, and said aye when the time for a decision finally came. The account of the Mann Act suggests that few had a firm grasp of the facts that were supposed to create a need for legislation.

More serious than the problem of multiple and confused intentions is the realization that an interpreting judge must look for a hypothetical intention.

> The fact is that the difficulties of so-called interpretation arise when the Legislature has had no meaning at all; when the question which is raised on the statute never occurred to it; when what the judges have to do is, not to determine what the Legislature did mean on a point which was present to its mind, but to guess what it would have intended on a point not present to its mind, if the point had been present.
> (John Chipman Gray, *The Nature and Sources of the Law*, 2d ed., 1921 [reprint, Buffalo, N.Y.: W. S. Hein & Co., 1983], 173)

---

37. For example, see Justice Jackson's opinion in Schwegmann Brothers v. Calvert Distillers Corporation (1951): 341 U.S. 384, 71 S.Ct. 745.

An odd circularity seems to be involved. No legislator can foresee all, or even many, of the cases that will fall under his law, so he leaves it to the judges to supply as cases arise. Then the judges turn back to him and ask what he intended, when he did not even think of the case at bar. We can escape from a futile circle by distinguishing between explicit intentions and underlying purposes. If the legislators in 1919 were deeply concerned to attack the social ills that came with theft of cars and trucks and similar vehicles, this purpose would presumably have covered airplanes, though imagination would have been required to anticipate so unusual a form of stealing and to form an explicit intention of excluding it. A judge, in trying to locate the underlying purposes in any body of legislation, is acting reasonably. Yet he seems already to have passed from a "historical" to a "teleological" approach.

Perhaps the notion of basic purposes is best seen if we think of an example where we have lost sight of these. There are, for instance, many provisions of Roman law that we simply cannot understand today, because we do not know the purposes behind them. Or suppose the day arrives when we no longer bury our dead, and we forget the deep associations that this practice carries. Legal historians will then read *Temple v. Petersburg* with little feeling for the issues that made it a serious dispute. Grammar, logic, and legislative intention are empty without a grasp of the more fundamental aims at work.

Beyond such practical problems in finding legislative intention is a theoretical question: Even if we know exactly what a legislator intended, do we thereby know what the law is? Justice Felix Frankfurter offers a striking comment:[38]

> The problems were different when judges were lawmakers and lawmakers were judges, before adjudication was separated from legislation. With easy confidence the great Hengham could stop counsel's argument as to the meaning of an Act of Parliament, when Hengham contemporaneously sat in Parliament, with "Do not gloss the statute; we understand it better than you do, for we made it." This was in 1305.
>
> Innocent as the Victorians were supposed to have been, Lord Halsbury was far less cocksure than Chief Justice Hengham that the author of a statute is its most dependable interpreter. With characteristic dogmatism he thought the opposite:
>
>> I have more than once had occasion to say that in construing a statute I believe the worst person to construe it is the person who is responsible for its drafting. He is very much disposed to confuse what he intended to do with the effect of the language which in fact has been employed....

If we see no distinction between a law and a command, then the person who makes a law is privileged to tell us what it means. The gunman who orders me

---

38. See Felix Frankfurter, Foreword to "A Symposium on Statutory Construction," *Vanderbilt Law Review* 3 (1950): 366.

to hand over my money stands supreme in deciding on all the details. No more is involved than his private will and the power he has to impose it. Yet the legislator is not just forcing his way on those too weak to resist. He offers a work of reason, subject to whatever is contained in our agreement to live by rational rules. He is not, alone or finally, the one to say what this is as a law. In the project of living according to rules, certain basic purposes are contained that bind those who make as well as those who receive. The purpose of law goes beyond the particular intentions of a legislator, but how far beyond is an open question.

Teleological Interpretation

> If the case still remains doubtful, it must be decided according to natural principles of law....
>
> (Austrian Civil Code, Article 7)

> If the case still remains doubtful, it must be decided according to the general principles of legal order of the state....
>
> (Italian Civil Code, Article 12)

> If no legal provision can be deduced from the written law, then the judge shall decide according to customary law or, in the absence of customary law, according to the rule which he would establish if he were the legislator.
>
> (Swiss Civil Code, Article 1)

These quotations cover an interesting range of possibilities. It is assumed in each that the grammatical, logical, and historical approaches have proved insufficient. Neither obvious wording, nor coherence, nor legislative intention tells us what a law means. We are instructed then to seek the purpose behind a law. But the range of "purpose" remains considerable. This may be the purpose of all law (natural principles). Or it may be the purpose embodied in maintaining the order appropriate to a particular state at a particular time. Or it may be the purpose of the judge himself, acting as a supplementary legislator. The comments below will investigate teleological interpretations that run from the universal principles of which natural law theorists speak to the particular policies that positivists allow an interpreting judge to follow.

At the beginning of this book, an indication was given of the meaning of *nature* in Greek philosophy, and of the connection between this term and *universal purposes*. The teachers of advocacy, the Sophists, tended to diminish the scope of such terms. When we find what people do and believe, especially beyond our own region and time, we realize that they live by an immense variety of conventions; it is difficult to discover any common nature for man or society or law. This means that each person or state lives according to whatever intentions happen to be imposed at the time; there are no universal principles that serve as a norm to judge particular goals.

Both Plato and Aristotle had a healthy sense for the relativity of things and the variety of customs. But each attacked the conclusions toward which the Sophists led. It is not so easy to reduce truth to opinion, or justice to the conventions that prevail. More than opinion is involved in the claim that "all is merely opinion." And those who preach tolerance for any doctrines of morality, or who claim the right to live as they choose, are affirming some universal values and obligations.

It was Aristotle especially who supplied a philosophical basis for the assorted approaches that became known as "natural law" theories. In his *Politics*, for example, he argues that the basic human groupings involve more than mere conventions. Though families and villages may assume many forms, they show a structure that comes from the nature of man. "And therefore, if the earlier forms of society are natural, so is the state, for it is the end (*telos*: purpose) of them, and the nature of a thing is its end" (Aristotle *Politics* 1252b).

The influence of Aristotle on Western law came from his adoption as the main philosophical source in the medieval universities. It was not religion that led to the revival of legal studies. The early Christians extolled charity rather than law; conflicts should be resolved through the ideals of brotherly love, not by resort to the tribunals of the pagans. Hence there was something revolutionary in the rise of the law faculties at Bologna and Paris and elsewhere. Society was to be based on the elaboration of a comprehensive system of law. None was then in existence, so two sources were employed. One was the long defunct but remarkable model of Roman law. The other was reason, the ability to work out what the laws should be in order to satisfy the nature of man and the universal norms of morality. The rediscovery of Aristotle, and his "baptism" by Aquinas and other medieval theologians, met an urgent need. From such enterprises we see how Continental law took on its academic and rationalist character, by contrast with the English law that was grounded in the practical concerns of an advocate to get his case heard and to win it in court.

With the Renaissance, the clerical hold upon law was broken. But natural law theories survived in a secularized form. Individuals were not at the mercy of whatever a legislator willed; they were endowed with natural rights, and these were to be ascertained by reason rather than by quoting authorities.[39] The doctrine of the basic equality of all human beings, so influential in the political revolutions of the eighteenth and nineteenth centuries, was drawn from reasoning about human nature and not from observing similarities among the many different things we do.

Natural law theories have found fewer proponents among legal writers in England and America than in the civil law tradition, and the rise of a more empirical and historical approach to law on the Continent reduced such theories

---

39. Blackstone makes a misleading statement when he writes that "this will of his Maker is called the law of nature" (Blackstone, *Commentaries*, book I, 39). Aquinas drew law from the reason of God, not from the divine will: God is no less bound by reason than we are. And secularized versions of natural law were designed to free us from the will of a legislator by subjecting him to the universal norms of reason.

to a minor role. There is, however, an interesting connection between natural law thinking and the development of the Continental codes. The ideal of a comprehensive and rational system of law was still at work: "Why not make the model law of the medieval universities, completed and refined by the Natural Law School, the living, real, and applied law of different countries?"[40]

If we go back to our question about the purposes a judge should employ when plain meaning and legislative intention are inadequate for interpreting a law, the reply from the natural law extreme is clear. The judge will look beyond the purposes of legislators, beyond any goals he may happen himself to favor, and even beyond the policies of his time and of the dominant social and political movements. All of these, as worthy as they may seem, can be wrong. Enacted law, it is held, must always be regulated and interpreted to satisfy controlling purposes that stem from the nature of man and of society and of the enterprise of living morally according to rules. There is no need to repeat here the way in which Lon Fuller has drawn upon such teleological notions (see section 22). A rule that denies the basic principles of living legally is no law at all.

It is not surprising that such a position has provoked bitter opposition. We may remember Justice Keen's criticism of similar arguments from Foster in the story of the speluncean explorers. It is all too easy to find holes in a statute and fill them with a "purpose" that one divines either in that statute or in law as such. Language of this sort, it is claimed, has been discredited along with the metaphysical pretension to identify the "natures" and "essences" of things.

Nevertheless, legal positivists and legal realists do allow for a more empirical discussion of purposes at work in law. A judge, they hold, carries some responsibility for changes in the law, and he is clearly not without guiding purposes in this task. He does go beyond the plain meaning of words and the intention of past legislators. To what?

If we return to *McBoyle v. United States*, we suspect that more was involved in Holmes's verdict than a search through the dictionary or an inquiry into whether Congress in 1919 thought of airplanes and excluded them. Holmes (as suggested) may have had certain purposes in mind, such as limiting the scope of federal responsibility and leaving the states to convict in a case of this sort. These purposes can be described as policies that vary from time to time.

Or suppose that Holmes, a realist with a firm sense of social change, had ruled against McBoyle? He might well have remarked quite simply that the airplane, which occupied only a small part of our life in 1919, was assuming a major role in the 1930s and would likely take over a dominant one in the future. He might even have foreseen the form of theft that we call hijacking. Society changes, and so do its ills and the policies to meet them. Such a decision would have involved teleological interpretation of an imaginative sort. But, again, these purposes are not the timeless ones of natural law. They are the fluctuating goals of a mobile society. Is not such interpretation what a layperson

---

40. David, *Major Legal Systems*, 60.

expects of a judge? Perhaps some "ought" is involved, yet this is not an application of moral principles that reason deduces as always valid. It is the technical and changeable "ought" of a parent who varies rules as the children get older, or of a politician who adapts his campaign to new problems and to shifts in public opinion.

The last hundred years have shown the rise, in the civil law countries, of what is called a "free" or "sociological" interpretation of codes. The Swiss code, quoted above and adopted in 1907, reflects this. The judge should, in the end, act according to the rule he would establish if he were the legislator. He is to be guided by a sound awareness of social developments and needs. If we are to speak of purposes, they are changing policies rather than eternal reasons.

Legal positivism and realism have so far been put together in their joint rejection of metaphysical purposes in the law. The differences between these two theories were discussed in chapter 3 (notably on pp. 210–11). The purpose embodied in current policies is set by the realist in his determination of what the current law really says, whereas the positivist distinguishes between the law that *is* (plain meaning and legislative intention) and the law that *ought to be* (where the judge uses his strong discretion to act as quasilegislator). The realist extends the scope of policy in judicial action to the full range of law. The positivist, however, is worried by this broad dependence of interpretation on teleology; he wants to limit talk of purposes to the "penumbra" of hard cases where grammar, logic, and legislative intention prove inadequate.

A lengthy example is needed of the dispute about purposes in the law, so we may look again at the classic exchange between Hart and Fuller, from which extracts were given in section 16. What follows includes relevant excerpts from Hart's account of how a judge is to interpret the law. Hart, it will be seen, attacks both legal realism and natural law on the extent of law that is open to teleological interpretation. Fuller replies in the name of a modified natural law theory; but much of what he argues can be adapted to support the parallel claim of legal realism that considerations of purpose apply to any determination of what the law means.

POSITIVISM AND THE SEPARATION OF LAW AND MORALS
by H. L. A. Hart

Harvard Law Review 71 (1958): 607–615.
Copyright © 1958 by the Harvard Law Review Association.
Printed with permission.

A legal rule forbids you to take a vehicle into the public park. Plainly this forbids an automobile, but what about bicycles, roller skates, toy automobiles? What about airplanes? Are these, as we say, to be called "vehicles" for the purpose of the rule or not? If we are to communicate with each other at all, and if, as in the most elementary form of law, we are to express our intentions that a certain type of behavior be regulated by rules, then the general words we use—like "vehicle" in the case I consider—must have some standard instance in which no doubts are felt about its application. There must be a core of settled meaning, but there will be, as well, a penumbra of debatable cases in which words are neither obviously applicable nor obviously ruled out.... The toy automobile cannot speak up and say, "I am a vehicle for the purpose of this legal rule," nor can the roller skates chorus, "We are not a vehicle." Fact situations do not await us neatly labeled, creased, and folded, nor is their legal classification written on them to be simply read off by the judge. Instead, in applying legal rules, someone must take the responsibility of deciding that words do or do not cover some case in hand with all the practical consequences involved in this decision.

We may call the problems which arise outside the hard core of standard instances or settled meaning "problems of the penumbra"; they are always with us whether in relation to such trivial things as the regulation of the use of the public park or in relation to the multi-dimensional generalities of a constitution. If a penumbra of uncertainty must surround all legal rules, then their application to specific cases in the penumbral area cannot be a matter of logical deduction, and so deductive reasoning, which for generations has been cherished as the very perfection of human reasoning, cannot serve as a model for what judges, or indeed anyone, should do in bringing particular cases under general rules. In this area men cannot live by deduction alone. And it follows that if legal arguments and legal decisions of penumbral questions are to be rational, their rationality must lie in something other than a logical relation to premises. So if it is rational or "sound" to argue and to decide that for the purposes of this rule an airplane is not a vehicle, this argument must be sound or rational without being logically conclusive. What is it then that makes such decisions correct or at least better than alternative decisions? Again, it seems true to say that the criterion which makes a decision sound in such cases is some concept of what the law ought to be; it is easy to slide from that into saying that it must be a moral judgment about what law ought to be. So here we touch upon a point of necessary "intersection between law and morals" which demonstrates the falsity or, at any rate, the misleading character of the Utilitarians' emphatic insistence on the separation of law as it is and ought to be. Surely, Bentham and Austin could only have written as they did because they misunderstood or neglected this aspect of the judicial process, because they ignored the problems of the penumbra.

The misconception of the judicial process which ignores the problems of the penumbra and which views the process as consisting pre-eminently in deductive reasoning is often stigmatized as the error of "formalism" or "literalism." My question now is, how and to what extent does the demonstration of this error show the utilitarian distinction to be wrong or misleading? ...

How does the wrongness of deciding cases in an automatic and mechanical way and the rightness of deciding cases by reference to social purposes show that the utilitarian insistence on the distinction between what the law is and what it ought to be is wrong? I take it that no one who wished to use these vices of formalism as proof that the distinction between what is and what ought to be is mistaken would deny that the decisions stigmatized as automatic are law; nor would he deny that the system in which such automatic decisions are made is a legal system. Surely he would say that they are law, but they are bad law, they ought not to be law. But this would be to use the distinction, not to refute it; and of course both Bentham and Austin used it to attack judges for failing to decide penumbral cases in accordance with the growing needs of society.

... I wish at this time to point out something obvious, but likely, if not stated, to tangle the issues. It does not follow that, because the opposite of a decision reached blindly in the formalist or literalist manner is a decision intelligently reached by reference to some conception of what ought to be, we have a junction of law and morals. We must, I think, beware of thinking in a too simple-minded fashion about the word "ought." This is not because there is no distinction to be made between law as it is and ought to be. Far from it. It is because the distinction should be between what is and what from many different points of view ought to be. The word "ought" merely reflects the presence of some standard of criticism; one of these standards is a moral standard but not all standards are moral. We say to our neighbour, "You ought not to lie," and that may certainly be a moral judgment, but we should remember that the baffled poisoner may say, "I ought to have given her a second dose." The point here is that intelligent decisions which we oppose to mechanical or formal decisions are not necessarily identical with decisions defensible on moral grounds. We may say of many a decision: "Yes, that is right; that is as it ought to be," and we may mean only that some accepted purpose or policy has been thereby advanced; we may not mean to endorse the moral propriety of the policy or the decision. So the contrast between the mechanical decision and the intelligent one can be reproduced inside a system dedicated to the pursuit of the most evil aims. It does not exist as a contrast to be found only in legal systems which, like our own, widely recognize principles of justice and moral claims of individuals.

An example may make this point plainer.... Under the Nazi regime men were sentenced by courts for criticism of the regime. Here the choice of sentence might be guided exclusively by consideration of what was needed to maintain the state's tyranny effectively. What sentence would both terrorize the public at large and keep the friends and family of the prisoner in suspense so that both hope and fear would cooperate as factors making for subservience? The prisoner of such a system would be regarded simply as an object to be used in pursuit of these aims. Yet, in contrast with a mechanical decision, decision on these grounds would be intelligent and purposive, and from one point of view the decision would be as it ought to be. Of course, I am not unaware that a whole philosophical tradition has sought to demonstrate the fact that we cannot correctly call decisions or behavior truly rational unless they are in conformity with moral aims and principles. But the example I have used seems to me to serve at least as a warning that we cannot use the errors of formalism as something which per se demonstrates the falsity of the utilitarian insistence on the distinction between law as it is and law as *morally* it ought to be.

We can now return to the main point. If it is true that the intelligent decision of penumbral questions is one made not mechanically but in the light of aims, purposes, and policies, though not necessarily in the light of anything we would call moral principles, is it wise to express this important fact by saying that the firm utilitarian distinction between what the law is and what it ought to be should be dropped? Perhaps the claim that it is wise cannot be theoretically refuted for it is, in effect, an *invitation* to revise our conception of what a legal rule is. We are invited to include in the "rule" the various aims and policies in the light of which its penumbral cases are decided on the ground that these aims have, because of their importance, as much right to be called law as the core of legal rules whose meaning is settled. But though an invitation cannot be refuted, it may be refused and I would proffer two reasons for refusing this invitation. First, everything we have learned about the judicial process can be expressed in other less mysterious ways. We can say laws are incurably incomplete and we must decide the penumbral cases rationally by reference to social aims. I think Holmes, who had such a vivid appreciation of the fact that "general propositions do not decide concrete cases," would have put it that way. Second, to insist on the utilitarian distinction is to emphasize that the hard core of settled meaning is law in some centrally important sense and that even if there are borderlines, there must first be lines. If this were not so the notion of rules controlling courts' decisions would be senseless as some of the "Realists"—in their most extreme moods, and, I think, on bad grounds—claimed.

By contrast, to soften the distinction, to assert mysteriously that there is some fused identity between law as it is and as it ought to be, is to suggest that all legal questions are fundamentally like those of the penumbra. It is to assert that there is no central element of actual law to be seen in the core of central meaning which rules have, that there is nothing in the nature of a legal rule inconsistent with *all* questions being open to reconsideration in the light of social policy. Of course, it is good to be occupied with the penumbra. Its problems are rightly the daily diet of the law schools. But to be occupied with the penumbra is one thing, to be preoccupied with it another. And preoccupation with the penumbra is, if I may say so, as rich a source of confusion in the American legal tradition as formalism in the English. Of course we might abandon the notion that rules have authority; we might cease to attach force or even meaning to an argument that a case falls clearly within a rule and the scope of a precedent. We might call all such reasoning "automatic" or "mechanical," which is already the routine invective of the courts. But until we decide that this *is* what we want, we should not encourage it by obliterating the Utilitarian distinction.[41]

POSITIVISM AND FIDELITY TO LAW
by Lon L. Fuller

Harvard Law Review 71 (1958): 661–69.
Copyright © 1958 by the Harvard Law Review Association.
Printed with permission.

It is essential that we be just as clear as we can be about the meaning of Professor Hart's doctrine of "the core and the penumbra," because I believe the casual reader is likely to misinterpret what he has to say. Such a reader is apt to suppose that Professor Hart is merely describing something that is a matter of everyday experience for the lawyer, namely, that in the interpretation of legal rules it is typically the case (though not universally so) that there are some situations which will seem to fall rather clearly within the rule, while others will be more doubtful. Professor Hart's thesis takes no such jejune form. His extended discussion of the core and the penumbra is not just a complicated way of recognizing that some cases are hard, while others are easy. Instead, on the basis of a theory about language meaning generally, he is proposing a theory of judicial interpretation which is, I believe, wholly novel. Certainly it has never been put forward in so uncompromising a form before.

As I understand Professor Hart's thesis (if we add some tacit assumptions implied by it, as well as some qualifications he would no doubt wish his readers to supply) a full statement would run something as follows: The task of interpretation is commonly that of determining the meaning of the individual words of a legal rule, like "vehicle" in a rule excluding vehicles from a park. More particularly, the task of interpretation is to determine the range of reference of such a word, or the aggregate of things to which it points. Communication is possible only because words have a "standard instance," or a "core of meaning" that remains relatively constant, whatever the context in which the word may

41. Suppose that Professor Hart had been the leader of the speluncean explorers. He was asked by his companions (while awaiting rescue) how he thought himself to have acted legally in giving morphine tablets to one of his colleagues despite an ordinance that "the practice of medicine by anyone not licensed by the Newgarth Medical Association is forbidden." The reader is invited to make his or her comments on the basis of this extract. My suggestion is that Hart would have limited this ordinance to the "core." Such rules about the practice of medicine evidently depend on standard instances in hospital or consulting room; they do not include, in their scope, the use of a layperson's first-aid kit on an expedition without licensed doctors (some appeal to legislative intention may buttress plain meaning here). What would Hart have said about the more critical question of Article 12–A? Would the application of this to the predicament of the cave belong to the penumbra of law? Would Hart have advised his colleagues that, if their case ever got to the Supreme Court, the justices would have to act as quasilegislators, outside the law that *is*? Can homicide, in such circumstances, be sufficiently remote from the standard instances of murder? The case is hypothetical but may suggest a rereading of Hart's article with such eminently practical questions in mind.

appear. Except in unusual circumstances, it will always be proper to regard a word like "vehicle" as embracing its "standard instance," that is, that aggregate of things it would include in all ordinary contexts, within or without the law. This meaning the word will have in any legal rule, whatever its purpose. In applying the word to its "standard instance," no creative role is assumed by the judge. He is simply applying the law "as it is."

In addition to a constant core, however, words also have a penumbra of meaning which, unlike the core, will vary from context to context. When the object in question (say, a tricycle) falls within this penumbral area, the judge is forced to assume a more creative role. He must now undertake, for the first time, an interpretation of the rule in the light of its purpose or aim. Having in mind what was sought by the regulation concerning parks, ought it to be considered as barring tricycles? When questions of this sort are decided there is at least an "intersection" of "is" and "ought," since the judge, in deciding what the rule "is," does so in the light of his notions of what "it ought to be" in order to carry out its purpose.

If I have properly interpreted Professor Hart's theory as it affects the "hard core," then I think it is quite untenable. The most obvious defect of his theory lies in its assumption that problems of interpretation typically turn on the meaning of individual words. Surely no judge applying a rule of the common law ever followed any such procedure as that described (and, I take it, prescribed) by Professor Hart; indeed, we do not normally even think of his problem as being one of "interpretation." Even in the case of statutes, we commonly have to assign meaning, not to a single word, but to a sentence, a paragraph, or a whole page or more of text. Surely a paragraph does not have a "standard instance" that remains constant whatever the context in which it appears. If a statute seems to have a kind of "core meaning" that we can apply without a too precise inquiry into its exact purpose, this is because we can see that, however one might formulate the precise objective of the statute, *this* case would still come within it.

Even in situations where our interpretive difficulties seem to head up in a single word, Professor Hart's analysis seems to me to give no real account of what does or should happen. In his illustration of the "vehicle," although he tells us this word has a core of meaning that in all contexts defines unequivocally a range of objects embraced by it, he never tells us what these objects might be. If the rule excluding vehicles from parks seems easy to apply in some cases, I submit this is because we can see clearly enough what the rule "is aiming at in general" so that we know there is no need to worry about the difference between Fords and Cadillacs. If in some cases we seem to be able to apply the rule without asking what its purpose is, this is not because we can treat a directive arrangement as if it had no purpose. It is rather because, for example, whether the rule be intended to preserve quiet in the park, or to save carefree strollers from injury, we know, "without thinking," that a noisy automobile must be excluded.

What would Professor Hart say if some local patriots wanted to mount on a pedestal in the park a truck used in World War II, while other citizens, regarding the proposed memorial as an eyesore, support their stand by the "no vehicle" rule? Does this truck, in perfect working order, fall within the core or the penumbra? . . .

Turning now to the phenomenon Professor Hart calls "preoccupation with the penumbra," we have to ask ourselves what is actually contributed to the process of interpretation by the common practice of supposing various "borderline" situations. Professor Hart seems to say, "Why, nothing at all, unless we are working with problems of the penumbra." If this is what he means, I find his view a puzzling one, for it still leaves unexplained why, under his theory, if one is dealing with a penumbral problem, it could be useful to think about other penumbral problems.

Throughout his whole discussion of interpretation, Professor Hart seems to assume that it is a kind of cataloguing procedure. A judge faced with a novel situation is like a library clerk who has to decide where to shelve a new book. There are easy cases: the *Bible* belongs under Religion, *The Wealth of Nations* under Economics, etc. Then there are hard cases, when the librarian has to exercise a kind of creative choice, as in deciding whether *Das Kapital* belongs under Politics or Economics, *Gulliver's Travels* under Fantasy or Philosophy. But whether the decision where to shelve is easy or hard, once it is made all the librarian has to do is to put the book away. And so it is with judges, Professor Hart seems to say, in all essential particulars. Surely the judicial process is something more than a cataloguing procedure. The judge does not discharge his responsibility when he pins an apt diagnostic label on the case. He has to do something about it, to treat it, if you will. It is this larger responsibility which explains why interpretative problems almost never turn on a single word, and also why lawyers for generations have found the putting of imaginary borderline cases useful, not only "on the penumbra," but in order to know where the penumbra begins....

When we look beyond individual words to the statute as a whole, it becomes apparent how the putting of hypothetical cases assists the interpretative process generally. By pulling our minds first in one direction, then in another, these cases help us to understand the fabric of thought before us. This fabric is something that we inevitably help to create as we strive (in accordance with our obligation of fidelity to law) to make the statute a coherent, workable whole.

I should have considered all these remarks much too trite to put down here if they did not seem to be demanded in an answer to the theory of interpretation proposed by Professor Hart, a theory by which he puts such store that he implies we cannot have fidelity to law in any meaningful sense unless we are prepared to accept it. Can it be possible that the positivistic philosophy demands that we abandon a view of interpretation which sees as its central concern, not words, but purpose and structure? If so, then the stakes in this battle of schools are indeed high....

I have stressed here the deficiencies of Professor Hart's theory as that theory affects judicial interpretation. I believe, however, that its defects go deeper and result ultimately from a mistaken theory about the meaning of language generally. Professor Hart seems to subscribe to what may be called "the pointer theory of meaning," a theory which ignores or minimizes the effect on the meaning of words of the speaker's purpose and the structure of language. Characteristically, this school of thought embraces the notion of "common usage." The reason is, of course, that it is only with the aid of this notion that it can seem to attain the inert datum of meaning it seeks, a meaning isolated from the effects of purpose and structure.[42]

Dworkin on Interpretation

When Charles left Sarah on her cliff edge, I ordered him to walk back to Lyme Regis. But he did not; he gratuitously turned and went down to the Dairy. Oh, but you say, come on—what I really mean is that the idea crossed my mind as I wrote that it might be more clever to have him stop and drink milk ... and meet Sarah again. That is certainly one explanation of what happened; but I can only report—and I am the most reliable

---

42. Suppose now that Fuller had been the leader of the speluncean explorers. Would he have seen any decisive difference between giving morphine to an injured colleague (in the absence of a doctor's license) and the killing of Whetmore (in the absence of a public executioner's status)? As author of the story, he clearly asks us to reflect on Hart's distinction between core and penumbra in a situation that returns us to basic questions about why we accept law at all. It does not follow that Fuller would have agreed with the perhaps specious arguments of his creature, Justice Foster. But would Fuller have been open to the possibility that an examination of the basic purposes of all law might justify homicide-by-lot in the dire conditions of the cave? He evidently has more in mind than trite questions about how to classify vehicles in a park.

witness—that the idea seemed to me to come clearly from Charles, not myself. It is not only that he has begun to gain an autonomy; I must respect it, and disrespect all my quasi-divine plans for him, if I wish him to be real.
(John Fowles, *The French Lieutenant's Woman*)

Hart's theory of interpretation can be read as an effort to avoid two extremes: the judge is neither entirely constrained nor entirely free in his decisions. The theory arranges for this by distinguishing between a core and a penumbra of law. In the core, the judge is held by the plain meaning of statutes or of a line of precedents. In the penumbra, the judge—though perhaps morally bound by some such principle as that of utility—is free of strictly legal norms and has strong discretion to turn the law in one direction or another through his or her legislative "creativity."

Neither legal realists nor natural law theorists are happy with this "geographical" solution. The former extend creativity to all cases: the law for any particular case can be said to exist only when the judge gives whatever decision he happens to think appropriate. The latter, by finding universal constraints in the very project of law, also (though differently) attack the distinction between core and penumbra.

Chapter 3 included an account of Ronald Dworkin's legal philosophy, one that is not easy to classify in traditional terms. Recent articles by Professor Dworkin have tried to indicate the general theory of interpretation that is involved.[43] He described himself, in his main work, as arguing against "classical theories of adjudication ... which suppose that a judge follows statutes or precedent until the clear direction of these runs out, after which he is free to strike out on his own."[44] In such terms the primary target is legal positivism, and Dworkin sees a more complex relationship between the freedom a judge enjoys and the "following" to which he is obliged. Firstly, the initiative allowed by interpretation is not confined to a relatively small number of perplexing cases. Secondly, the guidelines that the law offers exclude both strong discretion

---

43. Ronald Dworkin's articles appeared in a debate with Prof. Stanley Fish, of Johns Hopkins University. The initial articles were published in the *Texas Law Review* 60 (March 1982) and in *Critical Inquiry* 9 (Sept. 1982). The exchange was reprinted in *The Politics of Interpretation*, W. J. T. Mitchell, ed. (Chicago: Univ. of Chicago Press, 1982), 249–86. Dworkin's reply to Fish comes in the same book, pp. 287–313. Fish's further reply is to be found in an article entitled "Wrong Again," *Texas Law Review* 62 (1983): 299–316. In *A Matter of Principle* (Cambridge: Harvard Univ. Press, 1985), Dworkin reproduced his initial article, as chapter 6, and followed this with a brief new essay that drew on material in his reply to Fish.

Dworkin has come increasingly to set general questions of interpretation at the heart of his account of law. In *Law's Empire* (Cambridge: Harvard Univ. Press, 1986), he puts legal positivism, legal realism, and natural law together as "semantic theories," to which he opposes his own theory as "interpretive." In chapter 2 he discusses at length how we interpret a work of art, and he begins his vital chapter 7 with a further description of the enterprise (discussed below) in which several authors combine to write a chain novel. Chapter 9, on statutory interpretation, is of particular interest in offering a detailed account of how a judge who conscientiously looks for the underlying convictions in a legislator's "intention" is gradually led to adopt the full interpretive position held by Dworkin himself.

44. Ronald Dworkin, *Taking Rights Seriously* (Cambridge: Harvard Univ. Press, 1977), 118.

in penumbral cases and the extreme libertarianism that is implied by the provocative comments of some realists.

Dworkin, rather than turning directly to the law, raises basic questions about what we propose to do in interpreting a text rather than changing it into a new one. He declines to talk about "objectivity" and consigns such language to a naive "copy theory," which would suppose that the true meaning is somehow "just there" apart from our beliefs and convictions (Mitchell, *Politics of Interpretation*, 289-92). Instead, he starts with the fact that we do distinguish between *interpreting* and *inventing* a text, and that we do claim that our interpretation is right whereas someone else's is wrong. What is supposed by such a distinction and such a claim?

Examples are taken from literature. What do I mean when I offer my interpretation of a novel or play or poem? Appeal to the "plain meaning" of a work of literature is scarcely enough if there are serious rival interpretations. A common expedient is to argue that I have captured the *author's intention*, whereas you have strayed from it. There is a parallel to the legal positivist's view that propositions of law describe decisions taken by legislators in the past. However, Dworkin asks why the intention of the author (say at the moment the final galley proofs are sent to the printer) should fix for all time the meaning of a work of art. Indeed, he claims, part of an author's intention is to create something whose nature or meaning is not so circumscribed. As a striking illustration, Dworkin mentions the interplay of author and characters that John Fowles records in *The French Lieutenant's Woman*. The characters in a novel acquire, as writing proceeds, a mind of their own. In fact, Fowles is said to have altered his own interpretation on seeing the film made from his book (that is, the interpretation offered by Harold Pinter in his screenplay and by Meryl Streep in her acting). There is no privileged moment of meaning but a continuing process.

What limits are there to the creativity of interpretation? When is a work of art simply *changed*? Obviously, I cannot play around with the words of the text (though the telling of a joke, in various words, might suggest a remote qualification here). More serious are the requirements of coherence or integrity. An interpretation fails if it makes a large part of the text irrelevant. Dworkin's example is of an Agatha Christie novel taken as a philosophical treatise on death, though he admits that such an approach to Raymond Chandler's mysteries might be more plausible (Mitchell, 254; see pp. 279-81 for Fish's rebuttal in regard to Christie). The question, as in a chain of legal precedents, is whether we are dealing with "the same" or have passed on to what is different; Dworkin concedes that "any useful theory of identity will be controversial" (Mitchell, 253), but he insists there are boundaries we can cross only at risk of turning the literary work into "a shambles."

What, then, is required if we are to distinguish between interpreting a literary text and inventing a new one, and how can such a distinction allow us to say that one interpretation is better than another? Dworkin states his thesis as follows: "An interpretation of a piece of literature attempts to show which way of reading (or speaking or directing or acting) the text reveals it as the best work of art" (Mitchell, 253). Evidently there is wide disagreement on the normative questions about what makes for a good or bad work of art, and Dworkin allows that his thesis here is "banal." But the point he is concerned to establish is that, as interpreters, we are neither limited by the author's intention nor freed from all constraints.

Literature is offered as an analogy for law, and Dworkin makes the transition through an interesting proposal. Imagine that a group of authors come together to compose a novel. The casting of lots decides the order of play. One author is to write the first chapter, then send it to another for the second, and so on. What can we say about freedom and constraint as the work proceeds?

The first author may seem to have unlimited freedom, yet Dworkin notices an important qualification: "Even the first novelist has the responsibility of interpreting to the extent any writer must, which includes not only interpreting as he writes but interpreting the genre in which he sets out to write" (Mitchell, 262 n. 4). What is a novel (and, we may add, what is a chapter in a novel)? Views differ, yet the project is to write one. So the general structure of some enterprise will control all that is done, from the opening words. "The artist can create nothing without interpreting as he creates; since he intends to produce art, he must have at least a tacit theory of why what he produces is art and why it is a better work of art through this stroke of the pen or the brush or the chisel rather than that" (Mitchell, 261). The parallel to law, even safely within what Hart would call the "core," is evident.

The status of first author has particular bearing on enacted law. Dworkin expresses doubt that the positivist's analysis works even where it seems most obvious, in the example of a statute defining how a will is to be made if it is to be valid (reference to *Riggs*?). Though we appear well covered by appeal to plain meaning and legislative intent, there is a network of definitions, modes of inference, and assumptions about what we are doing in making a law.

When we turn to subsequent authors in the imaginary chain (which now looks suspiciously like a line of precedents in case law), what do we find? These writers are likewise bound by whatever is contained in the enterprise of producing a novel. There is, for instance, a clear distinction from the old parlor game of drawing a head, folding the paper, passing it to a second player for the torso, and similarly to a third for some legs. The formal structures of a novel exclude any such arbitrary shifts in design. But more than this. There are, according to Dworkin (though see Fish's denial: Mitchell, 274–75), material factors that increasingly limit the freedom of the writer to "strike out on his own." If Dickens's *Christmas Carol* had been so composed, the second author could possibly still have seen Scrooge as inherently evil. But the final writer could do so only at risk of destroying the point of this particular novel. (Suppose Scrooge's conversion were only sham, and Tiny Tim emerged as a calculating villain? Though any theory of identity may be controversial, would we still have the same story?)

There is no need to describe, at length, the analogy that Dworkin sees in the law. Judges interpreting precedents are in the position of the subsequent authors. On the one hand, there is no core of plain meaning, and no single author's intention is canonized. On the other hand, a judge is constrained by the requirements of "a complex chain enterprise of which these innumerable decisions, structures, conventions, and practices are the history" (Mitchell, 263). There are, again, the formal structures of the legal project itself—a judge is a law official, not a novelist. And this involves his commitment to basic moral principles. But material factors supervene. The history of a particular legal system will further limit a judge's interpretation in the light of "substantive claims about social goals and principles of justice" (266). Much as normative theories about good or bad art influence aesthetic judgment in diverse cultures, so political values rightly affect judicial interpretation in different legal systems. No two such systems agree entirely on the way that social and individual effort are best coordinated or disputes should be resolved. "A judge's duty is to interpret the legal history he finds, not to invent a better history" (264–65). Where judges in any jurisdiction tend to agree on this complex task, we have "easy cases"; where they evidently disagree, we have "hard cases." But the subtleties of finding and making cannot be resolved by assigning one to the core and one to the penumbra.

Since Dworkin declines to be classified with any of the traditional schools, the task of assessment is far from easy. His immediate critic, in this dispute, was Prof. Stanley Fish, who sees him as attacking both realism and positivism by invoking each as a reply to the other:

> Dworkin embraces both of the positions he criticizes. He posits for the first novelist a freedom that is equivalent to the freedom assumed by those who believe that judges (and other interpreters) are bound only by their personal preferences and desires; and he thinks of later novelists as bound by a previous history in a way that would be possible only if the shape and significance of that history were self-evident. Rather than avoiding the Scylla of legal realism ("making it up wholesale") and the Charybdis of strict constructionism ("finding the law just 'there' "), he commits himself to both.
>
> (in Mitchell, *Politics of Interpretation*, 275)

It is to Dworkin's argument for constraint in interpretation that Professor Fish devotes most space. In regard to the chain gang example from literature, he stresses the ability of any subsequent author to redirect the whole novel by seeing it as a social satire or a comedy of manners or a straightforward piece of realism. In law, he claims that a judge who "strikes out on a course of his own" may be open to criticism in terms of a particular judicial direction but not for violating judicial direction as such (Mitchell, *Politics of Interpretation*, 276; cf.

Fish, "Wrong Again," 306). The similarity of cases, and hence the path of legal history, is itself the result of, rather than the basis for, interpretation.

What is Fish's own view of the constraints on an interpreter? "My efforts [at interpretation] might very well fail in that no one else would be persuaded to my reading. But neither success nor failure would prove anything about what the text does or does not allow; rather it would attest to the degree to which I had mastered or failed to master the rules of argument and evidence as they are understood (tacitly, to be sure) by members of the professional community" (Mitchell, 281).

Those sympathetic to Dworkin's project are unlikely to accept this, and Dworkin puts his reply succinctly: "No one who has a new interpretation to offer believes his interpretation better because it will convince others, though he may believe that it will convince others because it is better" (Mitchell, 297). How this applies in literary criticism is not our concern. There is, though, a rather basic difference in the enterprise of law. We do not have to comment on novels, but we are obliged to live according to law. Dworkin does not say so explicitly, yet some (as we have seen) hold that the very effort to escape from the structures of law is made within those structures.

This remark may turn our attention to critics who have taken little place in the controversy. Dworkin, at the beginning of his initial article, tried briefly to distance himself from natural law theories. He insisted that he is not proposing a legal theory "which exists in virtue of objective moral truth rather than historical decision" (250), that he is concerned with an actual rather than an ideal political morality.

It would be interesting if Lon Fuller had lived a few more years and had been able to offer his comments on a theorist much closer to him than Hart was. Fuller would certainly have supported Dworkin against Fish in regard to structural constraints on legal interpretation. However, Fuller's "ideal" involved only the rather abstract principles that he identified as basic to all law, and that he saw as present "to a greater or lesser degree" in any actual legal system. He merely mentioned the possibility that these structures may take us further toward substantive conclusions about which interpretations are right or wrong. Yet Dworkin clearly expects the judge to have more definite guidelines, drawn from "institutional history." The character of Scrooge is constrained by the substance of the story and not merely by the formal requirements of writing a novel. As the chain of authors proceed down the road, they are led by more than the bare form of a common enterprise.

FURTHER READING

Bishin, William R., and C. D. Stone. *Law, Language, and Ethics.* Mineola, N.Y.: Foundation Press, 1972, 476–509.

David, René. *Major Legal Systems in the World Today.* New York: Free Press, 1978, 36–45, 107–18.

Houghteling, James. *The Dynamics of Law.* New York: Harcourt Brace & World, 1968, 115–45.

Liebesny, Herbert J. *Foreign Legal Systems.* Washington, D.C.: George Washington Univ. Press, 101–22.

Shuchman, Philip, ed. *Cohen and Cohen's Readings in Jurisprudence and Legal Philosophy.* Boston: Little, Brown & Co., 1979, 339–96.

White, James B. *The Legal Imagination.* Boston: Little, Brown & Co., 1973, 623–756.

QUESTIONS FOR DISCUSSION

1. The problem of interpreting laws is but one part of the basic topic of interpreting human expressions, such as novels and poems, sculpture and paintings, historical records, religious books. Is there a "plain meaning" to Melville's *Moby Dick*, or Leonardo's *Last Supper*, or the creation account in Genesis? For what do you look that goes beyond the evident story or scene? The intention of the author or artist? More than that?

2. The Sermon on the Mount (Matthew 5–7) is certainly more than a set of laws, but it does contain a fair number of rules and principles, and these show an interesting variety. Comment on problems of interpretation in some of them. For example: "Every one who divorces his wife, except on the ground of unchastity, makes her an adulteress; and whoever marries a divorced woman commits adultery." "Do not resist one who is evil. But if any one strikes you on the right cheek, turn to him the other also." "You must be perfect as your heavenly Father is perfect."

3. Suppose the parent in Wittgenstein's example wanted to give the baby sitter instructions that left no room for interpretation. How could this be done? By denoting all approved games? By some general statement without a list? A city ordinance requires "commercial vehicles" to drive in one lane of a highway and "pleasure vehicles" in another. What about hearses?

4. Because of your logical mind and way with words, you are asked to draft the rules of a club that you and five others have formed. The rules are adopted without dissent and you are congratulated. However, your foresight was not complete. Within a year the club has twenty members, and problems of interpretation begin to arise. Who is best placed to solve them? You? The original six? The twenty?

5. Is concern for purposes absent when a policeman stops a Buick from entering the park but present when he turns back a bicycle? Or should we distinguish between those purposes that are standardized and those that are disputable? Consider some apparently unambiguous orders: Finish the job in a week. Give an objective account.

6. Do you agree with Hart that if there are borderlines (beyond which a judge may decide on the basis of purposes) there must first be lines defining an area where words "have some standard instance in which no doubts are felt about their application"? What about murder, or treason, or violence? Does Hart say that meaning belongs to individual words?

7. It is true that not all uses of the word *ought* involve an appeal to moral principles. You ought to walk five miles a day (if you value health more than time and convenience). But is Hart right in suggesting that all judicial decisions in the penumbra can be so analyzed as a choice of means to effect social policies? What about the situation of German judges in Hitler's times (discussed in section 16)? Was judicial concern simply with means or also with ends? If the latter, could a judge keep all moral considerations out of his work in giving legal judgment? In less dramatic circumstances, would you expect a judge never to reflect on the ends of law?

8. If a rule is to be "rational," must it not in some sense be "moral"? Think again of the club for which you legislated (question 4). One of the new members protests that rule 12-A is unreasonable (suppose the six founding members thereby get more votes than the newcomers). Does the objector not mean that the rule offends against some "natural" (and moral) right?

9. Think of examples, from any literature course, of how time has produced variant interpretations of a classic text (e.g., *Hamlet* or *Paradise Lost*). Would the correct interpretation be the one

that Shakespeare or Milton held at the time of writing? If not, what basis do we have for adjudicating between rival claims? Suppose, for example, you are teaching such a course; how could you show a student that he or she has missed the point of a text?

10. Apply such literary examples to statutory law. Judge Shauck, in *Deem v. Millikan* (see p. 28 above) faced a very similar appeal to that of *Riggs v. Palmer* three years earlier, but in a different state. Both cases called for a decision whether a murderer had forfeited his inheritance by murdering the testator, though the will satisfied the precise provisions of statutory law. Did Shauck and Earl simply come to different understandings of "author's intention"? Each happened to claim in his opinion that if he could summon up the past legislators, these would agree with him! Or did the judges differ by inclining toward Hart's and Dworkin's theories of interpretation, respectively? Shauck wrote, with sarcasm, that Earl's decision was "the manifest assertion of a wisdom believed to be superior to that of the legislature on a matter of policy." Did Earl's theory of interpretation claim that such judicial wisdom involves reference to more than the plain meaning of a text, and what an author happens to intend, and what current policies dictate or allow?

11. Apply Dworkin's example of a chain novel to some line of precedents in law. Was Judge Cardozo, in *MacPherson*, in a situation analogous to that of an author who appears toward the end of the chain? List some similarities and differences. Does Cardozo make gallant (if vain) efforts to discover coherence in the precedents "where the devil himself couldn't find any"? Or is Cardozo really "striking out on his own" and covering such creativity by a lengthy rationalization? If your answer is "somewhere in between," how would you define the problem of freedom and constraint so as to preserve the distinction between making and interpreting?

34. JUST DECISIONS

> *The law does not perfectly comprehend what is noblest and most just for all and therefore cannot enforce what is best. The differences of men and actions, and the endless irregular movements of human beings, do not admit of any universal and simple rule.... Then if the law is not the perfection of right, why are we compelled to make laws at all? The reason of this has next to be investigated.*
>
> (Plato *The Statesman* 294)

> *An ethics, like a metaphysics, is no more certain and no less dangerous because it is unconsciously held. There are few judges, psychoanalysts, or economists today who do not begin a consideration of their typical problems with some formula designed to cause all moral ideals to disappear and to produce an issue purified for the procedure of positive empirical science. But the ideals have generally retired to hats from which later wonders will magically arise.... The objection, then, is not that jurists have renounced ethical judgment but that they have renounced ethical science....*
>
> *Every decision is a choice between different rules which logically fit all past decisions but logically dictate conflicting results in the instant case. Logic provides the springboard but it does not guarantee the success of any particular dive.*
>
> (Felix Cohen, *Ethical Systems and Legal Ideals*, 1933 [reprint, Westport, Conn.: Greenwood Press, 1976], 3–5, 35)

Plato likens the true statesman to a ship's captain who "lays down no written enactments but supplies a law in action by practical application of his knowledge of seamanship to the needs of the voyage" (Plato *The Statesman* 297). Since most political leaders (and perhaps most captains) fall short of this ideal, we discover an obvious justification for a legal system. We likewise find a need for constant interpretation of legal rules in order to approach the requirements of a superior "law in action." It is, in our own society, the vocation of a judge to meet this need.

Few judges would take seriously the metaphysics of "eternal Forms," which Plato offered as a guide for statesmen. Yet these Forms are probably to be understood as moral principles, and all judges (Cohen points out) have at least a tacit ethics behind their interpretation of legal rules. The courts do not live by logic alone. Nor, if they are to be courts rather than casinos, is the "extra" to be set in the realm of arbitrary choices or of merely personal preferences. Even what may be called a hunch is taken by the judge as an intuition of what is right, not simply of what he or she wants.

The previous section, on theories of interpretation, produced a short list of the many factors involved when we take the viewpoint of the agent and ask how judgment is to be given. The constraints offered by the plain meaning of a text, by the intention of legislators, and by the integrity of a body of law, all come from some conception of fidelity to the judicial role and of justice toward people who should have equality before the law. The freedom (rather than license) to assign greater weight to some of the competing social or economic policies refers us to an implicit political and moral philosophy. And the identification of guiding principles, along with their classification as legal or extralegal, draws upon some basic theory of law, some idea of what the legal enterprise is about.

This final section will not retrace the course of chapter 3, where the fundamental legal philosophies were examined, largely in terms of the way that moral considerations enter into the law. Our viewpoint in this section is mainly that of the layperson who evaluates the decision of a judge.[45] Knowing little of the details of law, what do we expect from a court of justice? The reply that we want to win is plainly superficial—we are not merely hoping for our number to be drawn in the state lottery. We count upon an adequate hearing, a regard for our individuality and for all relevant factors in our case. We expect such consideration that we win or lose fairly.

Notice that we are asking for something more than what we describe as logic or as mechanical procedure ("slot machine jurisprudence"). The court, if it is seen to be offering guidelines for the way we plan a good life, must not appear as an impersonal bureaucracy. Taking two examples from this chapter, we

---

45. There are obvious simplifications in this question. Firstly, we neglect the distribution of decision-making responsibility between judges and other legal officials, such as police, prosecutors, and juries. Secondly, we gloss over many of the distinctions between trial and upper courts, enacted and case law, statutory and constitutional law, etc. It is significant, but perhaps unfortunate, that most current discussion of judicial decision making in this country has come from studies of the U.S. Supreme Court.

should lose our respect for law if we encountered only the unimaginative treatment accorded to the plaintiff in *Smith v. Hiatt*. We look, not for disregard of the rules, but for the more "creative" treatment of problems that was illustrated in *Tuttle v. Buck*. The Hiatts, though happy to win, may have admitted privately that they owed their victory to the crafty research and pleading of a lawyer rather than to the rounded justice of the law; they would have protested if they had lost a further case because of a more wily advocate in opposition and a court that considered only the plain meaning in a rule. Even Buck may have recognized some justice in his defeat, as he turned to other plans at his bank, trusting that he would find a less subtle court if challenged.

As lay critics of judicial decisions, however, we should be wary of hasty generalization. Is justice always on the side of creative interpretation and opposed to rule-bound decisions? Could we not suffer grave injustice at the hands of a judge who thought himself free to strike a course of his own? We must try to be somewhat more precise about the relation between following and making, and about the bearing of this on what we expect in the name of a just decision.

Morality and Equity

The question what is or is not a "moral consideration" is itself dependent on moral theory. But the ordinary person is unlikely to be interested. Without being able to offer precise definitions, he distinguishes between the *technical* question whether he ought to commit his savings to a bank that offers strangely high interest rates and the *moral* question whether he ought to claim a further exemption on his income tax returns by listing the name of his parrot as a dependent. He may lose more from a wrong decision in the former than in the latter. But the former touches what he *has*, the latter what he *is* as a person.

For instance, contrast your assessment of the treatment you receive at the hands of a stockbroker and of a judge. You could suffer a greater financial loss from miscalculations about the stock of a new company. But poor judgment about your innocence or rights in a court of law does far more than lower your capital. In this sense there is little difference between a legal and a moral verdict: both go to the heart of your being (though you may, of course, appeal from legal guilt to moral innocence).

It is also helpful to see legal reasoning as one form of moral reasoning. "Secondary rules" are more evidently involved in the former, but there is a similar move from strict rules to underlying principles. If the rule (legal or moral) prohibits telling lies, I ask whether I am justified in so doing to save someone's life or reputation. The theory of justification may be the same in both court and confessional. There is some important difference from the way I explain why I made a poor investment.

There is also a significant difference between legal/moral rules and those of a game. Though we have suggested some qualifications, the rules of a game are usually sufficient to determine the decision of a referee. He is seldom asked to adapt them to meet a particular situation. A touchdown is a touchdown. But the enterprise of law is less specific than the project for a gain in territory. Judges repeatedly face the claim that settled rules fail to fit particular cases in our unsettled life. To return to Plato's analogy, the experienced captain will not sacrifice his ship and crew by a narrow following of the rules for navigation; higher ideals or principles allow him to "bend" particular rules in order to meet exceptional circumstances.

This introduces once more the topic of "equity." The term goes back at least as far as Aristotle and was discussed in section 8 above. Included in all uses of the notion is the claim that justice somehow defies rule-like statements and calls for "individualization." In the development of the common law, equity was granted through an appeal from the rules employed by ordinary courts to the conscience of the king and his chancellor. But it was never made clear what higher norms of law were thus invoked. The assumption of many authors seems to be not only that formal rules miss the particularity of a case, but that the difference calls for an intuitive judgment that cannot be reduced to further rules.

It is not in question whether judges may *find* their decision by some intuitive process. The claim seems to be that *justification* of the decision as correct can itself be no more than intuitive. There is a serious problem here, since the need for a judicial verdict arises only because the parties have disagreed; hence the intuition cannot be universal. A resolution of the dispute that denies all means of public persuasion (argument) cannot make the legal system worthy of respect—certainly not from the loser and perhaps not from the winner. Judicial reasoning, however obscure its course, is grounded in our basic requirement, as rational beings, to understand and to accept. There is no need to dwell again on the problems of kadi justice and on the structure of generality that is basic to a legal system. I may like to speak of my case as unique. But then it would be ineffable, and I should not take it to a court of law.[46]

Judges themselves often, in the name of justice, express dissatisfaction with the way in which a case is presented to them, and with the rules that are cited on either side. Remember, for instance, Cardozo's biting comments on a "jurisprudence of conceptions" that extends definitions "to a dryly logical extreme" (*Hynes v. N.Y.C. R. Co.*, section 10 above). Yet Cardozo wrote a lengthy opinion to explain why the law allowed the mother of Harvey Hynes to recover from the railroad, and these pages offered, for subsequent judges (and swimmers), a more detailed formulation of the rules of trespass.

If [one who appeals to equity] is saying merely that *for any given set of rules*, it will probably happen that some unjust results will occur when these

---

46. It is an interesting question, though far beyond the scope of this book, whether religious belief puts us in a different situation. Did Job finally accept his sufferings because he recognized that there was no reason for them? Or did he accept them by recognizing the inadequacy of his terrestrial reasons?

rules are applied in all relevant instances, then the thesis is unobjectionable. But if something more is meant, if it is insisted that the continual revision of the rules would still not alleviate the problem, then the theory is less intelligible.... To make an exception to a rule is simply to introduce two more restrictive rules in place of the original.[47]

The contrast mentioned above, between *Smith v. Hiatt* and *Tuttle v. Buck*, was described as a distinction between rule-bound decisions and those that display "creativity." This term is often used in evaluating what judges do, but it is ambiguous. Only God can create out of nothing (and some myths deny even this). To speak of a judicial verdict as creative is certainly to say that it went somehow beyond the rules at hand. But we may mean only that the judge, respecting his obligation to take all into account, made some important distinction in those rules. Or it may mean that he put them in some broader context allowing further rules to be considered. Or it may mean that he went beyond all written rules to unwritten principles. Yet he is still engaged in a form of "finding." The quality of inventiveness remains within the discipline of discovery. Once again, to interpret a text is not to make a new one.

Utility and Principles

Creative decisions have been set in opposition to those that seem to be dictated by the rules; there we have the "easy cases," where every judge within a jurisdiction would come to the same verdict. The majority of cases in a traffic court may fall into this category. However, the mechanical nature of the process need not make the notion of a just decision inappropriate. Though material principles of relevance are not required, the formal principle of justice is clearly pertinent, that like cases be treated in a like manner. Injustice would come if some odd version of individualizing the law allowed one motorist to be fined, and another not, when both were caught pleasure-driving on the same road at the same time at 20 m.p.h. over the limit.

Creative decisions are called for in "hard cases." This term is much used in current discussion, though precise definitions are not always given.[48] For our limited purposes it is enough to think of cases where judges, faithful to their

---

47. Richard A. Wasserstrom, *The Judicial Decision* (Stanford, Calif.: Stanford Univ. Press, 1961), 108–9. Chapter 5 of that book offers an account and criticism of various notions of equity.

48. Here is an interesting definition, from a utilitarian. "It is a case in which existing law and statutes, the existing system of judicial precedents, and of other immediately relevant rules of decision tend to generate or fit a result that offends the judge's intuitions about benefit and harm" (Thomas Morawetz, *The Philosophy of Law* [New York: Macmillan, 1980], 117).

Though much discussion of Ronald Dworkin's theory of law has concentrated on an article he entitled "Hard Cases" (reprinted as chapter 4 of *Taking Rights Seriously*), he denies that a judge needs one method for hard cases and another for easy ones. The same method is at work, but its application is either hard or easy. In chess, "good players and I draw the distinction between hard and easy cases differently, not because we use different theories about what makes a move a good one, but because we have different skill in applying the single theory we share" (*Law's Empire*, 449 n. 14).

task, could disagree. In trial courts, they come to different verdicts where similar rules and similar facts appear to be involved. At the appellate level we have cases that produce a divided court (though it is certainly not to be assumed that a "unanimous court" has avoided serious disagreement).

How broad is the region covered by hard cases? The phrase we used, "fidelity to the judicial task," is a loose one and allows for many ways of mapping the terrain. Legal realists seem to suggest a maximum territory; at least, Hart accuses them of "preoccupation with the penumbra." Hart's own theory of law tends to restrict the range of genuine legal disagreement: the core is the home of "standard instances," and the penumbra is a region where judges turn outside the law to make their decisions. Yet our question is about what the judge, to be just, is expected to do in hard cases rather than about how many of these he or she encounters per year.

If we claim that Judge A's decision was just and Judge B's decision unjust, this may be because A took into account the full complexity of what was submitted for judgment, whereas B went strictly "according to the book." However, more subtle problems arise when both A and B go beyond a strict reading of the rules. Where this happens, a common way of imputing injustice is to claim that one of the decisions was biased. For instance, the judge may be said to favor the plaintiff over the defendant in negligence cases, or generally some class of persons in some type of case. He may be seen as a lobbyist for special interests or particular points of view. For example, he serves big business or brings strict religious conceptions to divorce and custody cases.

Though all of us are quick to make accusations of bias, we have difficulty defining its boundaries. Was Cardozo biased toward widowed mothers and against large corporations? Perhaps a biased decision is contrasted with one that is disinterested. A disinterested judgment is not one that is lacking in conviction; indeed, a judge may be said to have a passion for fairness. But good judgment is altruistic—its concern is for the rights and good of people in general, so that one's own profit and the advancement of one's particular interests will come (if at all) as a by-product.

These general and imprecise remarks could be relevant to our evaluation of judicial decisions that seem to depend on the support offered for *policies*. A trial court judge may, in his or her decisions, show the influence of current social policies that demand strict measures against violent crime, or drunken driving, or the collapse of family life. Appellate judges are notably exposed to political and economic policies that favor or oppose deregulation in business, or the power of labor unions, or the privilege of journalists to conceal their sources. How are we to view the decisions that are given? As an exercise of bias, or as a proper form of judgment that draws on values as well as on logic?

Perhaps the most common reply today is one that converts the judge's moral task into a matter of *calculation*. The greatest attraction of utilitarianism may lie in its claim to reduce moral reasoning to an objective and uniform procedure. There is but one principle, of utility: we should make the decision that maximizes benefits to people and minimizes harm. Hence, even if I personally suffer from the judge's decision, I can recognize it as a just one because it supports policies that will, overall, contribute to the good of the society affected by this verdict. During the first half of this century in Western nations, such calculations set on the side of justice those decisions that favored the growth of union power. Now (some claim, or calculate) the pendulum of social benefit may be swinging the other way.

Our concern is with utilitarianism as a basis for evaluating judicial decisions in hard cases and not as a way to assess decision making in general. There are important distinctions. Suppose I am a wealthy landlord and you are renting one of my many houses. I receive an attractive offer for purchase, so I notify you that the lease will not be renewed when it expires next month. You reply that your mother, who is living with you, is seriously ill and that any move at this time would cause grave hardship. What should I do if I am to decide morally by using the principle of utility? As with all hypothetical illustrations, more details may be required than are supplied. However, it is plausible that the maximizing of benefits would direct me to renew the lease. Other purchasers will come along, and my gain from an immediate sale is more than balanced by the harm inflicted on your family. Are there also "indirect" consequences to be weighed? Possibly, but they are remote and trivial. The example of my altruism is unlikely to send shock waves through the community of landlords or to undermine a capitalist economy.

Suppose, however, I adopt a harsh line and the dispute goes to court. How is the judge to give a just verdict if he is a utilitarian? Is he likewise to balance only my small gain against your great loss? No, because what I have called the indirect consequences now loom much larger. Chief of these is the effect that any court decision has upon the law itself. What I do as a landlord does not bind others. But court decisions (at the appellate level and, remotely, at lower levels) serve as precedents for later ones. The consistency of treatment between parties to old and new cases is a benefit that comes from our very system of case law. As landlords or renters we base all we do on some estimate of laws that are general and constant. Though the judge decides each case on its merits, and views with sympathy both sides in their complexity, he speaks for all within that system of law and must include the stability and coherence of the system in his calculations. Think, for instance, of the way in which the opinion of the appellate judge in *Haslem v. Lockwood* differed from that of the court president in the "case of the spoiled chiles" (section 23).

The problem of conflict between individualized verdicts and legal constancy is an ancient one, and the cases and discussions of chapter 1 can be read as illustrations of it. Indeed, one of the most important recent books on judicial decision making takes this as the basis for its study. In *The Judicial Decision*, Richard Wasserstrom defends a utilitarian approach but expounds a theory that tries to take into account everything a judge should regard when calculating how benefits outweigh harm. So far we have considered only the good or bad consequences for the parties to a dispute and for the system of law. Wasserstrom, however, introduces a third consideration that must come before a judge in any hard case. It is the benefit and harm to all those affected by the decision in more specific ways than those which protect or undermine a system of rules. He gives the following illustration.[49]

Widow Jones, living with her six children on a farm, cannot meet the mortgage payment that falls due in a snowy winter. The mortgage is held by Bachelor Smith, already the richest man in town. He goes to court in order to foreclose and evict. What decision would a court be justified in giving?

The sympathies of the reader are easy to predict, and (1) we may agree that "it would be a heartless and inhuman judge who would fail to see that consideration of her interests" leads to a decision for Jones in the name of utility. However (2) the judge's benevolence toward Jones is opposed by clear rules about mortgages. Can he emulate Cardozo by finding a creative solution that allows the widow and six children to remain on the farm and yet avoids damage to the laws of property? Perhaps, and utility would be sustained. Yet (3) Wasserstrom advises the judge to look further into the more detailed results. "One of the significant consequences of deciding mortgage cases in this way would be that persons who were most in financial need and who were most likely to remain in financial need would be unable to borrow money from prospective creditors.... Potential creditors might quite understandably be reluctant to lend money to those persons who would be hurt most by forfeiture of the mortgaged property in case of default." In simple terms, a decision in favor of Widow Jones might—for all the attention to her particular distress—produce great harm to the class of widows (and of people in need to borrow money). The judge may be preventing them from getting a mortgage at all. The example can be generalized to indicate the full complexity of any judicial decision based on utility.

In conformity with such discussions is the view that the law is goal oriented, and that policies (e.g., support of the poor or of democracy or of safety and public health) specify goals relevant to a particular judicial decision. The judge reasons that X is a goal the law ought to maintain and that Y is a necessary means to X; hence his conclusion is an application of Y to the case before him. The "careful" utilitarian (as Wasserstrom calls him) will see the intricacy at all stages of the argument. There are many conflicting goals that the law is said to support, and there are competing means to each. Yet the utilitarian presents his theory as the best way to tackle the network of problems: we attend only to the objective calculation of consequences.

Let us turn, however, to another way in which judges seem to derive their premises for reasoning. The case of Pavesich v. New England Life Insurance Co. (1904, 122 Ga. 190, 50 S.E. 68) is of interest, both because it illustrates another style of legal argument and because it seems flatly to contradict a

---

49. Wasserstrom, *Judicial Decision*, 140–44.

decision of only two years before in another state.[50] The insurance firm was sued by the plaintiff for using his photograph in an advertisement without his consent and in spite of the fact that he had no policy with the defendant company. The Supreme Court of Georgia ruled for Pavesich on the grounds that his right of privacy had been violated. This brief extract may indicate the tenor of the argument.

> The right of privacy has its foundation in the instincts of nature. It is recognized intuitively, consciousness being the witness that can be called to establish its existence. Any person whose intellect is in a normal condition recognizes [this right] at once.... We are utterly at variance with [the earlier New York opinion] that the existence of this right can not be legitimately inferred from what has been said by commentators upon the legal rights of individuals.... The conclusion reached by us seems to be thoroughly in accord with natural justice, with the principles of the law of every civilized nation, and especially with the elastic principles of the common law....

Comments have been made before on the often unfortunate language of those who appeal to natural law. "Intuitive recognition" makes a less stringent demand for acceptance than calculation. We wonder what the "instincts of nature" tell us and why we should respect them (unless the term *nature*, and the viewpoint involved, is much clarified). The New York judges may have had intellects no less "normal" than those of their brethren in Georgia. But let us recognize an important move from a goal-oriented to a rights-oriented style of reasoning. Utilitarians can support some talk of rights. However, these remain instrumental, statements of the means that calculation shows to be generally required for maximizing utility. The notion that individuals have rights serving as a "trump" over any possible concurrence of policies comes from another stable.

The contemporary theorist who has most systematically defended an appeal to the rights of individuals as a premise in legal reasoning is Ronald Dworkin. His position was discussed at length in section 19, and no summary will be attempted here. He refuses to be aligned with traditional natural law theories, but he argues for the conclusion that judicial reasoning is (should be?) based on *principles* embedded in the law rather than on the *policies* appropriate to a legislator (or to Hart's judge, who serves as a quasilegislator in the penumbra).

The question is far from academic, even if we adopt the limited perspective of a layperson who evaluates judicial decisions. There is a ring to the claim that "my rights have been violated"; we find a weak echo in the remark that "on balance, the judge made a poor assessment of current policies and of the benefits they confer." The term *principle* is vague, yet most of us have used it.

---

50. Roberson v. Rochester Folding Box Co. (1902): 171 N.Y. 538, 64 N.E.2d 442. Both cases are discussed in Golding, *Legal Reasoning*, 60–74.

On matters of freedom, for example, there is a difference between saying that current resources or policies dictate what you can print and saying that you have a right to make such statements, from your basic dignity as a person. If someone censored even this innocuous comment, I should find it difficult to erase the word principle from my reply.

Critics of Dworkin have understandably asked for the cash value of his theory in contemporary discussions. It is in hard cases, where the question is most pertinent, that we find it most difficult to see exactly where the turn from policies to principles is leading us. For example, is universal education a principle or a policy? At what age does it pass from one to the other? Which of these terms applies to the provision of "minimal subsistence"? At what income level do basic rights change into variable policies? Principles, no less than policies, will clash; how are we to decide between principles, "on principle"?[51]

Traditional natural law theories have tended to offer the judge an armory of principles or rights that would reduce the task of giving good judgment to a procedure scarcely less mechanical than that of "slot machine jurisprudence." We turn to celestial principles much as to terrestrial rules. Aquinas (as indicated in chapter 3) may have been more cautious. Lon Fuller certainly is, limiting the principles of natural law to the rather abstract guidelines that offer an "internal morality." Dworkin looks for more than Fuller in seeing legal interpretation as a herculean inquiry into institutional history. Yet there is one principle that seems to be independent of this: it is our basic right to "equal concern and respect." As suggested before (at the end of section 19), this may have to do with the basic question why we submit to the enterprise of living legally. It is here that teleological interpretation is involved in its most general form.

The opening page of this book quoted Auden's derisive view of the judge as proclaiming that the law is the law. The rest of the book has intimated that the law is the law only because we accept it as such, on moral grounds rooted in our recognition of others as persons rather than things.

A contemporary writer, after discussing the legal philosophies of Hart, Dworkin, and Fuller, presents his own approach as one he calls "functional natural law."[52] A functional concept is one where, if we are to say what something means, we must show what it is *for* (e.g., a wrench, but not a sunset). Hart is criticized, in this account, for neglecting the functional aspects of the concept of law. The function of law is difficult to specify, and the reluctance of a positivist to consider such broad purposes is understandable. However, a theory of law that simply neglects them offers no access to the basic question why a legal system is accepted, and thus exists, *as such* (rather than as, say, a mere means of forcing compliance).

---

51. See Morawetz, *Philosophy of Law*, 116. It may be noticed that Dworkin does allow and expect a judge to base the interpretation of a *statute* on justifications from policy as well as from principle, though he admits it may "be problematic which form of justification would be more appropriate" (*Law's Empire*, 339).

52. Theodore M. Benditt, *Law as Rule and Principle* (Stanford, Calif.: Stanford Univ. Press, 1978), chapter 5.

I suggest that doing a better job of resolving or regulating conflicts that arise among people is in part a matter of doing it with less friction and resistance on the part of those individuals.... This amounts to saying, I think, that the law achieves this end well only if its rules are such that the addressees of the rules (or as many of them as possible) can accept the rules—i.e. take an internal point of view toward them. We can accordingly ascribe the following function to a legal system, viz. to regulate the conduct of the individuals to whom the rules of the system apply in such a way that most of the rules of the system, and indeed the system itself, can be accepted by those individuals.[53]

Perhaps the final section of this book has been biased toward such an account because we have adopted the viewpoint of the "addressees" in evaluating judicial decisions. However, it is safe to remark that, if the law is *for* anyone, it is for us rather than for judges or other legal professionals. Hart bases a system of law on a rule of recognition whose existence depends only on the empirical fact that legal officials follow it as the norm of validity for rules; the external point of view takes over when we come to the end (or ground) of our inquiry. Nevertheless: "We might say, aphoristically, that the possibility of a legal system is just the possibility of the internal point of view being taken by the ordinary individuals."[54]

Most of us show a surprising indifference toward the particular rules of law. Yet we are committed, personally and morally, to accepting a system of law. We realize that the existence of such an enterprise affects what we are, as persons in community.

The conclusion from such general comments would be that we recognize a judge's decision, not simply because it helps us win, or because it shows some private preferences, or because we share in an undefinable intuition, or even because we see ourselves in agreement with the policies on which the judge seems to draw. We respect his or her decision basically because we regard it as helping to make the law more worthy of our respect. We can still, in spite of any immediate loss, share with the judge in the moral enterprise of living legally.[55]

The Fusion of Approaches

For the final pages we may return to the conflicts of a particular case. Appeals courts show disagreement among their members, not only on a decision, but also on ways of coming to a decision. The following extract reprints the account

53. Ibid., 103–4.
54. Ibid., 106.
55. This is far from saying that a judge is expected to solicit applause. Respect, though difficult to define, is not the same as popularity. I may ask why you count popularity as so important, but I am unlikely to ask why you hope to be worthy of respect. A contemporary novelist suggests that we subordinate even rationality and justice to this: "Judge's decisions must appear to be rational, fair as well as practical, if the courts are to retain the respect of the people" (Henry Denker, *Outrage*, 266).

given by one law professor of how judges diverge and "fuse" in arriving at a decision that the court offers as rational and just.

ON LAW AND JUSTICE
by Paul A. Freund

Cambridge: The Belknap Press of Harvard University Press, pp. 78–81.
Copyright © 1968 by the President and Fellows of Harvard College.
Excerpted by permission of the publishers.

Sinclair Refining Co. v. Atkinson (370 U.S. 195, 82 Sup.Ct. 1328), decided by the Supreme Court of the United States in 1962, is an interesting and not atypical case presenting problems of rationality in decision-making that may illuminate the meaning and relation of creativity, the application of rules, and calculation.

The facts were not in dispute for purposes of the case. The company and a union of its employees entered into a collective bargaining agreement which provided for arbitration of grievances and renounced strikes or slowdowns over any causes that were arbitrable. In violation of the agreement the union repeatedly engaged in work stoppages on account of arbitrable grievances and did not resort to the arbitration procedure. The company brought suit in a federal court to enjoin such work stoppages. For its defense the union relied on the Norris-LaGuardia Act of 1932, section 7 of which prohibits the federal courts from issuing injunctions against concerted non-violent activity by a union growing out of a labor dispute.

If this were all, it might appear that the course of decision is plain; that the rule of the Norris-LaGuardia Act compels the Court to refuse an injunction. The "rule" is clear; it need not be extracted from decisions, it is actually codified; and it is not of convenient vagueness like standards ("due process" or "prudent investment") or principles ("no one may profit by his own wrong at the expense of another"). And yet this result might well cause disquiet. Does the Act really fetter the courts in enforcing the obligations of a collective agreement? The background of the Act was a history of federal courts' intervention to restrain strikes and picketing in an era before rights of union organization and bargaining were secured; injunctions served to intensify the inferior position of workers and caused widespread hostility and disrespect on the part of labor toward law and courts. So viewed, would not an application of the Act in the circumstances of the present case be perverse? Already the neatness of "applying a rule" is becoming blurred. The calculation of consequences and the investigation of purposes suggest the possibility, at least, that the rule is more complex than it seems. Any reformulation must not do violence to the potentialities of language used; but the term "labor dispute" may be sufficiently protean to exclude cases where there is a breach of an arbitration agreement and of a no-strike clause. Whether this would involve too much creativity on the part of judges is the resulting question. If this were the whole case, the Justices might well have concluded unanimously that on balance this degree of creativity should be left to Congress.

But that was not the whole case. Other data were at hand that bore some relevance to the process of decision. In 1934, without amending the Norris-LaGuardia Act, Congress provided in the Railway Labor Act for compulsory arbitration of certain disputes, and the Court thereafter held that despite Norris-LaGuardia an injunction could be issued against a strike called in violation of the later statutory plan. At this point in the analysis, the present Court might rationally have (a) overruled the railway labor decision as an excess of judicial law making; (b) followed it as a precedent where, as here, a plan of arbitration (though here voluntarily adopted) was in force; or (c) distinguished it as apposite only to a legislative scheme of arbitration. The "rule" of the precedent might have been either (b) or (c), depending on the emphasis placed on the factor of legislative intervention.

But there was in fact additional legislative intervention in the background. In 1947, the Taft-Hartley Act conferred authority on the federal courts to entertain suits for the violation of contracts between employers and employees. This provision, the Court had held, authorized mandatory orders compelling a union or an employer to submit a dispute to arbitration. But did it authorize the kind of negative injunction forbidden generally by the Norris-LaGuardia Act? Now, obviously, the decision could not even in form be rested on "application of a rule." There was at least another coordinate rule to be taken into account, that of the 1947 Act.

In the actual decision, the Court divided. The majority opinion was written by Justice Black, who had been a member of the Senate when the Norris-LaGuardia Act was passed in 1932. The dissent, joined in by Justices Douglas and Harlan, was written by Justice Brennan, who had extensive experience in labor law before going on the bench.

The difference in approach of the two groups loses its significance if it is looked at simply as a difference in the application of a rule. Justice Black took the Norris-LaGuardia Act as the primary datum; held the railway cases inapposite; and stressed what would be the legislative character of a repeal of section 7, which Congress had declined to do. The calculation of consequences was for Congress; in any event they were not too serious, since an action for damages and a mandatory order to arbitrate were still available. Justice Brennan took as his primary datum a pattern of legislation, and asked not whether the earlier provision had been repealed but whether it could be "accommodated" with the later legislation. This he did because the consequences of the Norris-LaGuardia Act on the beneficent practices of arbitration agreements he regarded as deeply upsetting. And so he essayed a more creative role, seeking to find connections and reconciliation between otherwise discrete legislative provisions, converting inharmonious rules, if you will, into a more refined and comprehensive principle whose touchstone would be the promotion and safeguarding of collective bargaining. This he attempted to achieve by regarding the Norris-LaGuardia Act as a non-rigid direction, to be followed generally but not in the special circumstances of a case falling within the fostering policy of the later Act.

It is not important here to appraise the two opinions in their outcomes. What is of interest, I believe, is the fusion in actual practice of the types of rationality classically described as rule-application, creativity, and calculation. In that fusion each element, while not losing its distinctiveness, takes on some of the qualities of the others. That this is psychologically true, it may be argued, does not establish that it is logically valid or philosophically useful; perhaps the psychological impurities ought to be burned away in the interest of clear and distinct ideas. It is really, I suggest, a matter of pragmatic emphasis: which aspect, the distinctiveness of the types of rationality or their interaction, is it more useful to stress. I can only say that I believe the interaction to be not merely a valid description but a process the receptive awareness of which can enrich the resourcefulness and fruitfulness of the judicial process.

FURTHER READING

A list of books on justice and the law is supplied in section 8. Richard Wasserstrom's *The Judicial Decision* (1961) is the most accessible account of decision making in the law, from a utilitarian standpoint. Ronald Dworkin's *Taking Rights Seriously* (1977) can be read as an extended reply to this approach. Felix Cohen's *Ethical Systems and Legal Ideals* (1933; reprint 1976) has much to say of interest, from the position of a legal realist. For an application of such questions to constitutional law, see John Hart Ely, *Democracy and Distrust* (1980).

Two recent introductory textbooks give good accounts of the bearing of moral theory on judicial decisions:
Morawetz, Thomas. *The Philosophy of Law.* New York: Macmillan, 1980, chapter 2.

Murphy, Jeffrie, and Jules L. Coleman. *The Philosophy of Law.* Totowa, N.J.: Rowman & Allanheld, 1984, chapter 2.

QUESTIONS FOR DISCUSSION

1. The term *creativity* has run an ambiguous course through this section. How do you use the word in speaking of your acquaintances, of books, of your own decisions? If the creative person goes beyond established rules or procedures, is he or she engaged in "making" or in "finding"? Are original ideas merely novel ways of assembling old material (as the politician may rearrange groupings of legislators)? Or does originality involve a new way of seeing the old, a reformulation of questions? Apply your conclusions to a judge's creativity (or lack of it) in any case you have studied (e.g., the Georgetown Unversity Hospital case or *People v. Sherwood*).

2. Why does the rule book cover particular cases in a game but not always in law? Chapter 2 considered many instances where inadequate rules led a judge to find an answer in custom. Yet the solution then became, in some form or other, a written rule. Justice was individualized by a more detailed statement, though the process might well have to be repeated later. Is this what you expect when you hope for special consideration? If not, what do you want?

3. Any line of precedents in our developing law is likely to offer illustrations of judicial disagreement and to raise questions about the source of judicial reasons (premises). Reference was made, in the bibliography for section 29, to a series of six North Carolina cases that trace this state's case law on wife-beating from 1837 to 1874. A complete reversal seems to have occurred. In the second case (Joyner v. Joyner (1862, 59 N.C. 322), Chief Justice Pearson writes: "The wife must be subject to her husband.... Unto the woman it is said: 'Thy desire shall be to thy husband, and he shall rule over thee'; Genesis 3:16. It follows that the law gives the husband power to use such a degree of force as necessary to make the wife behave herself and know her place." Was Pearson biased, or did he make a legitimate appeal to policies in force at the time? Would you allow your own conception of the family or of individual dignity to enter into your reasoning? If so, would this be bias, or a matter of policy, of one of principle? If you rely on social policies, does it follow that the *law* thereby gives certain powers?

4. Reread Cardozo's verdict in *MacPherson* (section 31). It is often cited as an example of judicial creativity, yet he pays scrupulous attention to the precedents and he claims that "the principle ... does not change." What premises nevertheless crept in from outside the plain meaning of previous opinions? Notice, for instance, the difference in the way Cardozo and Bartlett read the *Devlin* decision. Does the appearance of "a more liberal spirit" serve as a legitimate basis for "extending rules"? Does Bartlett put too much weight on the benefits supplied by constancy in the law? Why should Cardozo not simply have said that the move from carriages to automobiles calls for a revision (or re-balancing) of the social policies that negligence law serves?

5. If you are a utilitarian, how would you justify the rule that promises should be kept? Suggest other rules about promises that would be *more* justifiable on utilitarian grounds. What difference would it make if these were legal rules rather than purely moral ones?

6. Reread the extract from Justice Blackmun's dissenting opinion in *Furman v. Georgia* (p. 210 above). Could his "excruciating agony of spirit" have been avoided if he had been more open to a utilitarian theory of judicial decision making? Would his opponents on the court have said they were allowing personal preferences to guide their judgment? What is wrong with crossing the policy line?

7. In addition to mentioning the solidly utilitarian question whether capital punishment serves any useful purpose, Blackmun remarks that the death penalty is opposed to his philosophical convictions and to our reverence for life. Here he presumably refers to moral principles independent of that of utility. How might he have justified a court decision against capital punishment on such grounds? Is not respect for persons (and certainly for their life and continuing ability to work

out their own moral destiny) part of the very structure of law, hence a legal as well as a moral principle?

8. In Griswold v. Connecticut (1965, 381 U.S. 479, 85 S.Ct. 1678), Justice Douglas, delivering the opinion of the court, argued in favor of a constitutional right of privacy on the ground that "specific guarantees in the Bill of Rights have penumbras, formed by emanations from those guarantees that help give them life and substance." Was he acting as a legislator in such a penumbra and deciding what does or does not belong according to current social policies? Could he have agreed that people might not have had such a right (relevant to the specific question of contraception) when the original Connecticut statute was passed in 1879, but that they had acquired it through subsequent changes in the social scene?

9. In a concurring opinion, Justice Goldberg wrote that "the right of privacy is a fundamental personal right, emanating from the totality of the constitutional scheme under which we live." Judge Learned Hand had remarked that the addition of such adjectives as "fundamental" and "essential" merely disguises personal preferences (Learned Hand, *The Bill of Rights* [Cambridge: Harvard Univ. Press, 1958], 70). But is Goldberg suggesting, along with Dworkin, that a judge's duty is to discover the basic principles embedded in the pertinent law, and that these—rather than preferences or policies—justify rights that are not specifically mentioned in the law?

10. List and classify the reasons produced on both sides of the *Sinclair* case. What inquiry was made into legislative intention for the three acts involved? Which side placed more weight on constancy in the law? Were principles at stake as well as policies? Does the commentator view "creativity" simply as the initiative that we associate with legislators, rather than with judges, or as the discovery of a more basic coherence in the law ("converting inharmonious rules into a comprehensive principle....")? Remember that Justice Black, writing for the majority here as for the minority in *Griswold*, delegates the "calculation of consequences" to Congress. The commentator is certainly right in saying that no judge shows any one form of legal reasoning in its purity. Would you, however, support Freund's comment that we are left with a question of "pragmatic emphasis"? Can we remain with a fusion of psychology and logic as our final word on legal reasoning? Notice that Freund himself interprets the meaning of the Norris-LaGuardia Act in terms of the need to avoid "disrespect toward law and courts." Is he referring to basic principles that go beyond current policies?

INDEX OF CASES

Baker v. Libbie, 333
Baltimore & Ohio Railroad v. Goodman, 91
Baxter v. Baxter, 231
Betts v. Brady, 305n
Brown v. Board of Education, 208
Burns v. Currell, 367

Cadillac Motor Co. v. Johnson, 347, 350
Clingenpeel v. Municipal Court, 367n

Deem v. Millikan, 28, 385
De Flaundres v. Rycheman, 153
Depue v. Flatau, 141
Devlin v. Smith, 346, 348–49, 350, 398
Dixon v. Bell, 344
Donoghue v. Stevenson, 328

Egerton v. Brownlow, 208

Furman v. Georgia, 210, 217–18, 398

Georgetown College, Application of, 47–48, 51, 59
Gideon v. Wainwright, 305n
Griswold v. Connecticut, 342, 399

Haslem v. Lockwood, 250–51, 391
Henningsen v. Bloomfield Motors, 190–91, 338, 352
Hynes v. New York Central Railroad, 92, 209, 256, 388

Johnson v. Cadillac Motor Co., 347n
Joyner v. Joyner, 398

Langridge v. Levy, 344
Longmeid v. Holliday, 344
Loop v. Litchfield, 345, 348
Losee v. Clute, 346, 348

McBoyle v. United States, 366–67, 372
MacPherson v. Buick Motor Co., 348–53, 385, 398
Mayberry v. Pennsylvania, 362
Miller v. Miller, 93
Miranda v. Arizona, 133
Mortensen v. United States, 363

Neiman v. Hurff, 27
New York Times Co. v. United States, 302n
North Carolina v. Alford, 128

Oleff v. Hodapp, 27

Palsgraf v. Long Island Railroad, 353
Pavesich v. New England Life Insurance, 392–93
People v. Conley, 44n
People v. Jordan, 367n
People v. Sherwood, 49–51, 256
Poe v. Ullman, 89
Pokora v. Wabash Railroad, 91

Queen v. Courvoisier, 287–91
Queen v. Dudley and Stephens, 29–30
Quinlan, In the Matter of Karen, 44–45

Repouille v. United States, 214–15
Riggs v. Palmer, 22–29, 38–39, 124, 190, 385
Robertson v. Rochester Folding Box Co., 393n
Rochin v. California, 219n

Savannah, F. & W. Railroad v. Daniels, 258
Schwegmann Bros. v. Calvert Distilleries, 368n
Sinclair Refining Co. v. Atkinson, 396–97, 399
Smith v. Bocklitz, 252
Smith v. Hiatt, 360–61, 387
Sodero v. Sodero, 230
State v. Bradbury, 359n
Statler v. Ray, 347, 349

Tedla v. Ellman, 91
Temple v. City of Petersburg, 42–43, 189–90, 365, 369
Terry v. Ohio, 138
Thomas v. Winchester, 345, 348
Torgesen v. Schultz, 346–47, 349
Tuttle v. Buck, 322–24, 329, 387

Union Pacific Railroad v. Cappier, 141
United States v. American Trucking Associations, 363
United States v. Holmes, 29, 38, 220–21, 281

Vegelahn v. Guntner, 209
Villers v. Monsley, 329

Webb v. McGowin, 151
Winterbottom v. Wright, 344, 350

INDEX OF NAMES

Abelard, Peter, 62
Abinger, Lord (James Scarlett), 350
Adams, Henry, 62, 70
Adolphus, John, 288–89
Allan, Harry T., 217, 342
Allen, Sir Carleton Kemp, 97, 328
Aquinas, Saint Thomas:
    content of natural law, 231–34
    freedom and necessity, 226
    grades of being, 226
    and Hart, 233-34
    influence on Western law, 225, 371
    intellectualism, 226–27, 371n
    legal advocacy, 287
    legal obligation, 227, 232–33
    mutability of law, 232
    types of law, 227–29
    validity of positive law, 229, 232–33
Aristotle:
    analogical reasoning, 329, 334–35
    deduction and induction, 333
    distributive justice, 64
    equality, 65–66, 318
    equity, 61, 66–70, 388
    friendship, 142
    grades of being, 224–25
    influence on Western law, 371
    the just mean, 241
    natural law, 222, 225n, 371
    negative proof, 113, 117, 223–24
    principles of justice, 65–66
    proportions in justice, 61, 63–67, 70
    rationality, 224–25, 330n
Arnold, Thurman, 11n
Auden, W.H., 1, 394
Auerbach, Jerold S., 6
Augustine (of Hippo), Saint, 219, 229
Austin, John:
    and Aquinas, 227, 235
    criticism by Hart, 176–78
    custom and law, 172–73
    general jurisprudence, 172, 175
    independence of law and morality, 157, 171–72, 243
    judicial legislation, 210, 315, 374
    laws as commands, 165, 170–71
    sanctions in law, 76, 165, 170
    the sovereign, 139, 165, 170, 173, 175, 227
    writings, 173
Austin, John Langshaw, 50

Bacon, Matthew, 24, 28
Bakunin, Michael, 103
Bard, Morton, 138
Barrett, William, 330n
Bartlett, Joseph W., 6
Bartlett, Willard (Justice), 350, 351, 398

Barton, John H., 84
Bedau, Hugo A., 69
Bedford, Sybille, 247, 268–72
Belford (Ulanov), Ann, 70
Bender, Edward J., 5
Benditt, Theodore M., 173, 201, 394–95
Bentham, Jeremy, 157, 167–68, 173, 226, 374
Bergson, Henri, 324
Berman, Harold J., 127n
Best, Sir William (Justice), 208–9
Bird, Otto A., 69
Bishin, William R., 257
Black, Hugo (Justice), 305, 397, 399
Blackmun, Harry A. (Justice), 209–10, 217, 398
Blackstone, Sir William, 171–72, 366, 371n
Bloomstein, Morris J., 265
Boas, George, 63
Bodde, Derk, 97
Bohannan, Paul, 80n, 84, 124–25, 217
Bolt, Robert, 229
Bonsignore, John J., 10n
Boswell, James, 285, 286
de Bracton, Henry, 319n, 322
Brand, Norman, 50
Brandeis, Louis (Justice), 207–8
Brecht, Bertolt, 256
Brennan, William J. (Justice), 397
Brett, George, 21
Brodie, Benjamin, 310
Brody, Burton F., 38
Brougham, Lord Henry, 3, 295
Brown, Brendan F., 231, 234

Cahn, Edmond, 69
Calabresi, Guido, 257
Caligula, 27
Cardozo, Benjamin (Justice):
    interpretation of precedents, 348–52, 398
    judicial decisions, 92, 209, 256, 310–11
    jurisprudence of conceptions, 92
    law and custom, 91, 201, 209
    law and literature, 50
    law and morality, 211, 214
    legal review commissions, 362
Carlin, Jerome E., 6
Carroll, Lewis, 105, 322
Cassirer, Ernst, 341
Chandler, Raymond, 380
Chapman, John W., 94n, 150
Cheatham, Eliott E., 15
Chen, Philip M., 97
Christie, Agatha, 380
Christie, George C., 217
Churchill, Sir Winston, 54
Clark, David S., 120, 127
Cohen, Felix S., 84, 277–81, 286, 385
Cohen, Jerome A., 97

403

Index of Names

Cohen, Marshall, 189n
Cohen, Morris R., 84
Coke, Sir Edward, 55, 247
Coleman, Jules L., 398
Collingwood, Robin George, 116
Confucius, 4, 96–97
Cook, Walter Wheeler, 204
Coons, John E., 56–60, 99, 329
Cooper, Frank E., 50
Copernicus, Nicolaus, 278, 279, 281, 308, 333
Countryman, Vern, 14
Cozzens, James G., 314
Croce, Benedetto, 107–8
Crouch, Leonard C. (Judge), 49–51, 256
Curtis, Charles P., 283–87

Danelski, David, 302
D'Arcy, Eric, 253n
Darwin, Charles, 100, 221
Daumier, Honoré, 277, 285
David, René, 97, 127, 225n, 364, 372
Davis, Karl, 138, 139
Davis, Kenneth Culp, 138
Davis, Michael, 295
Davis, Philip E., 27
Dean, John, 5
Dean, Karen, 301n
Denker, Henry, 395n
Descartes, René, 11, 45
Devlin, Sir Patrick:
    enforcement of morals, 143–47
    his critics, 147–50
Dewey, John, 337–38
Diamond, Arthur S., 84
Dickens, Charles, 289, 298, 381
DiPerna, Paula, 265
Dobbyn, John F., 15
Dorgelès, Roland, 315
Douglas, William O. (Justice), 397, 399
Dreyfus, Alfred, 174
Dworkin, Ronald:
    autonomous institutions, 21
    borderline and pivotal cases, 193n
    commands and rules, 183n
    consent to an enterprise, 20
    criticism of Hart on custom, 89n
    discretion, strong and weak, 134–37, 189–90, 193, 201
    enforcement of morals, 149–50, 152
    hard cases and skill, 389n
    integrity, 197n
    interpretation, theory of, 196–97, 379–83
    liberty, 226n
    natural law, rejection of, 198–99, 383
    philosophy, importance of, 196, 198
    precedents, 196–97, 321n, 381–82
    preferences, personal and external, 150n
    principles and policies, 194–95, 201–2, 323n, 382, 393–94
    principles and rights, 194–95, 199–200, 399
    principles and rules, 189–93, 201, 323n
    right to equal concern and respect, 199–200, 223, 245, 394
    writings, 188–89, 201, 379n

Earl, Robert (Judge), 22–25, 28–29, 68, 385
Eddy, Mary Baker, 333
Edwards, Harry T., 128
Ehrlich, Eugen, 86, 89–90, 106, 128, 206–7, 217
Ehrlich, Thomas, 15
Ehrmann, Henry W., 127

Eichmann, Adolf, 187
Elliston, Frederick, 295
Ely, John Hart, 198, 208n
d'Entrèves, Alessandro Passerin, 235, 242n
Euclid, 155, 278, 280, 301, 332

Feibleman, James K., 69
Feifer, George, 268n, 275
Feinberg, Joel, 150
Finnis, John, 229n
Fish, Stanley, 379n, 380, 382–83
Fisher, Roger, 340
Ford, Stephen D., 97
Forsyth, William, 265
Fowler, Henry Watson, 19
Fowles, John, 378–80
Frank, Hans, 55
Frank, Jerome (Judge):
    adversary system, 260n, 265
    definition of law, 205
    fact skepticism, 251–52, 255–56
    justice, 60–63, 66, 97n
    legal realism, 203
    precedents, 320, 328
    primacy of conclusions, 312n
    psychology of judges, 298n, 303
    public opinion, 215
    writings, 60, 217
Frankel, Marvin E., 265
Frankfurter, Felix (Justice), 89, 191, 209, 219n, 275, 369
Franklin, Marc A., 257, 328
Frederick the Great, 356
Freedman, Monroe, 292n, 294
Freud, Sigmund, 236, 303, 306, 314
Freund, Paul A., 43n, 396–97
Friedland, Martin, 266
Friedman, Lawrence M., 217
Frost, Robert, 263
Fuller, Lon L.:
    on Austin, 76n, 171, 243
    duty and aspiration, 241–42
    enterprise of law, 29, 187, 236–39, 243–45
    internal morality of law, 159–64, 239, 242–45, 394
    interpretation and purpose, 51, 376–78
    on judicial behavioralism, 306
    on Kelsen, 182
    on legal education, 237
    structures of law, 114–16, 140, 159–64, 233, 238–41, 383
    writings, 29, 38, 94n, 106, 128, 245

Galileo, 74, 112, 166, 221n, 256, 306, 308, 338
Garlan, Edwin N., 217
de Gaulle, Charles, 332
Gibson, James L., 313
Glendon, Mary Ann, 127
Gluckman, Max, 84
Godwin, William, 103, 107
Goffman, Erving, 9–10
Goldberg, Arthur (Justice), 399
Golding, Martin P., 106, 183, 231n, 336n, 393n
Goldman, Sheldon, 313
Goodhart, Arthur L., 326
Gopen, George D., 50
Gordley, James R., 128
Goulden, Joseph C., 6
Gray, John C. (Judge), 26–27, 59
Gray, John Chipman, 368
Green, Mark, 6, 69

Greenawalt, Kent, 134n, 135–37
Greene, Graham, 236
Greiner, William R., 127n
Grey, Thomas, 150
Griffith, J.A.G., 54
Grossman, Joel C., 306n
Guthrie, W.K.C., 7n

Haines, Charles Grove, 298
Hall, Jerome, 97
Halsbury, Lord (H.S. Giffard), 369
Hammurabi, 356
Hampshire, Stuart, 306n
Hand, Learned (Judge), 1, 198n, 209, 215, 399
Harlan, John Marshall (Justice), 397
Harnett, Bertram, 15
Hart, H.L.A.:
    on Austin, 157, 176–78
    enforcement of morals, 140, 147–48
    government, philosophy of, 188
    independence of law and morality, 156–59, 181, 187, 374–76
    internal and external viewpoints, 175, 178–79, 182–83, 212n
    interpretation, theory of, 211, 373–76, 379, 390
    judges as deputy legislators, 190
    legal obligation, 178–79, 182–85, 234
    natural law, 157–59, 233–34
    positivism and facts, 158–59, 186
    precedents, 318, 328
    pre-legal societies, 88–89, 176, 179–80, 240
    primary and secondary rules, 88, 179–80
    rule of recognition, 88–89, 139, 180–84, 193, 244, 395
    succession in law, 139, 177
    writings, 150, 173, 186
Hartzler, H. Richard, 217, 342
Hazard, Geoffrey C., Jr., 15, 295
Hazard, Leland, 352
Hegel, G.W.F., 206, 228
de Hengham, Ralph (Justice), 369
Hensley, Thomas R., 301n
Heymann, Philip B., 257
Hitler, Adolf, 55, 59, 104–5, 107, 159–61, 164, 183n
Hoadly, Bishop Benjamin, 363
Hobbes, Thomas, 96n, 116, 167, 221n
Hoebel, E. Adamson, 75–84, 87, 109, 120, 139, 259–60
Hohfeld, Wesley, 172n
Holmes, Oliver Wendell, Jr. (Justice):
    law and experience, 202–3, 247
    law as prediction, 204, 297
    policy and judicial decisions, 209, 367, 372, 376
    rules and standards, 91, 201, 366–67
    viewpoint of the "bad man," 204, 362
Hooker, Richard, 5
Houghteling, James L., Jr., 362
Huizinga, Johan, 259–60
Hume, David, 166, 174, 188, 226, 237, 240, 333
Hutcheson, Joseph C., Jr. (Judge), 309–12, 314

Jackson, Robert H. (Justice), 302, 368n
Jahnige, Thomas P., 313
James, William, 311
Jenkins, Iredell, 116
von Jhering, Rudolf, 207n
Job, Book of, 388n
Johnson, Samuel, 285, 286
Jones, Harry W., 206, 216
Justinian, 121, 148, 169, 356

Kadish, M.R. and S.H., 138, 183–86
Kafka, Franz, 16
Kalven, Harry, 266
Kant, Immanuel:
    creativity of mind, 237, 240, 248–49, 255n
    freedom and prediction, 307n
    hypothetical imperatives, 185–86, 213
    laws and principles, 225
    persons as ends in themselves, 241, 243
    social contract, 116
Kearney, Hugh, 286
Kekulé, August, 313
Kelsen, Hans, 69, 176, 181–82, 240n
Kenety, William H., 257
Kim, Hyung I., 97
King, Martin Luther, Jr., 219, 230
Kinyon, Stanley, 15
Kipling, Rudyard, 99
Kort, Fred, 304n
Krader, Lawrence, 84
Kropotkin, Peter, 103
Kuhn, Thomas, 74n, 286

Landsman, Stephan, 266
Laski, Harold J., 54
Lasswell, Harold, 313
Lavoisier, Antoine-Laurent, 342
Lawlor, Reed C., 305n
Leonardo da Vinci, 314
Levi, Edward H., 342–43, 347, 359n
Lewis, Peter, 138
Li, Victor H., 97
Lieberman, Jethro K., 6
Liebesny, Herbert J., 122nn, 123n
Llewellyn, Karl:
    canons of construction, 364
    Cheyenne law, 80–84, 120
    legal realism, 204, 325n
    precedents, 324–28
    prediction, 305
Locke, John, 110, 117, 255
Loevinger, Lee, 296, 299–300
Loftus, Elizabeth F., 254n
London, Ephraim, 50
Louis IX, 99
Louis XII, 3
Luban, David, 291n
Luijpen, William A., 235
Luther, Martin, 109

Macaulay, Stewart, 217
MacCormick, Neil, 169n, 186, 199
McDonald, Lynn, 138
Mackie, John, 196n, 202
Maine, Sir Henry:
    on Austin, 106, 176, 206
    the common law, 123n
    Greek law, 61–62, 69
    individual and community, 100
    natural law, 219n
    stages of law, 100–102, 104
    status and contract, 111
    writings, 84, 100, 106
Malinowski, Bronislaw, 76n, 84
Marke, Julius J., 5
Martin, Billy, 21
Marx, Karl, 103, 192, 206, 228, 241, 306
Masters, Roger, 305n
Mead, Margaret, 236
von Mehren, Arthur T., 128
Mellinkoff, David, 15, 50, 287–91

406 Index of Names

Merriam, Charles, 300
Merryman, John H., 120, 127, 128, 356
Mersky, Roy M., 5
Mill, John Stuart, 139, 143, 170, 175
Miller, Wilbur K. (Judge), 47–48, 51, 59
Mitchell, W.J.T., 379n
de Montaigne, Michel, 298
Morawetz, Thomas, 18n, 150, 389n, 394n
Moore, Sir Thomas, 229, 230–31
Morgan, John Pierpont, 292
Morison, William L., 173
Morris, Clarence, 69, 97, 341
Murphy, Jeffrie, 398
Murphy, Walter F., 58

Nader, Laura, 84, 249–50
Nader, Ralph, 6, 10
Nagel, Stuart S., 304, 313
Napoleon (Bonaparte), 358
Newman, Katherine S., 84
Newton, Sir Isaac, 253, 255n, 308, 310
Nietzsche, Friedrich, 58
Northrop, F.C.S., 153

O'Connor, Daniel John, 235
Oliphant, Herman, 340, 342
Osborn, John J., 15
Ovid, 102–4

Parke, Sir James, 208
Pascal, Blaise, 63, 70
Patterson, L. Ray, 15
Pearson, Richmond M. (Justice), 398
Pennock, J. Roland, 94n, 150
Perelman, Chaim, 341
Phillips, Charles, 288–91
Piaget, Jean:
    animism to conservation, 73–74, 85, 280n
    moral development of children, 20, 151
    sameness and transduction, 334
    structuralism, 240n
Pinter, Harold, 380
Plato:
    convention vs. nature, 7–8, 28–29, 112–13, 222–23, 371
    idealism, 7, 15
    influence on Western law, 95
    law and the statesman, 385–86, 388
    mathematical forms, 248, 336
    moral philosophy, 241
    opinion and truth, 280, 371
    Protagoras' self-contradiction, 222
    thought as dialogue, 222–23, 266
Pohlman, H.L., 217
Poincaré, Henri, 310
Polanyi, Michael, 74n
Portalis, Jean-Etienne-Marie, 356
Posner, Richard (Judge), 202
Pospisil, Leonard, 84, 126–27
Pound, Roscoe, 2n, 15, 69, 99n, 207
Priestley, Joseph, 342
Pritchett, C. Herman, 300, 313
Probert, Walter, 50
Protagoras, 222
Proudhon, Pierre-Joseph, 107
Ptolemy, 112, 278, 279, 281

Rabelais, François, 310
Radbruch, Gustav, 157–58, 160–62, 164, 239
Radin, Max, 311, 341

Rapallo, Charles A. (Judge), 350
Ratcliffe, James M., 151
Rawle, William, 243–44
Rawls, John, 116, 198, 200, 261–64
Raz, Joseph, 187, 201
Reed, Stanley F. (Justice), 363
Reich, Charles A., 130–34, 136
Rheinstein, Max, 58, 121
Rihani, Ameen, 99
Roberts, Simon, 84
Rodell, Fred, 6
Rohde, David, 313
Röhm, Ernst, 105, 159
Rommen, Heinrich, 235
Roosevelt, Theodore, 62
Ross, Sir David, 169n
Rossman, George, 50

Sarat, Austin, 313
Sartre, Jean-Paul, 58, 216, 225n, 307n
von Savigny, Karl Friedrich, 206, 209, 213n, 217
Schlesinger, Rudolf B., 128
Schroeder, Theodore, 298n
Schubert, Glendon, 298, 301, 302, 304–5, 313
Schur, Edwin M., 106
Schwartz, Murray, 15
Scott, Captain Robert Falcon, 71, 72
Seligman, Joel, 15
Selznick, Philip, 106, 237
Shakespeare, William, 3, 60, 285
Shapiro, Martin, 207n
Shauck, John A. (Judge), 28, 385
Shellow, Robert, 138
Shklar, Judith, 53–56, 58–59, 98, 329
Shuchman, Philip, 84
Simmel, Georg, 244
Simon, Yves, 235
Skinner, B.F., 113, 300
Smart, J.J.C., 173
Smith, John Cyril, 116
Snow, C.P., 21
Socrates, 10–12, 143, 222–23, 241, 332–33
Sophists, 7, 15, 28–29, 95, 112–13, 222–23, 370–71
Spaeth, Harold, 313
Spenser, Edmund, 106
Spinoza, Benedict de, 226n
Stern, Philip M., 4n
Stevens, Robert, 15
Stoljar, Samuel J., 362
Stone, Christopher D., 257
Stone, Julius, 69, 328n, 341
Stone, Roy L., 257, 331, 335
Stravinsky, Igor, 72
Streep, Meryl, 380
Strick, Anne, 69, 267
Stryker, Lloyd P., 50
Summers, Robert S., 156
Sumner, William G., 214

Tamm, Edward A. (Judge), 47, 51
Tate, C. Neal, 299n, 302n, 305, 313
Taylor, John F.A., 109–12
Ten, C.L., 201
Terrill, Ross, 98
de Tocqueville, Alexis, 40–41, 55, 207
Todd, Harry F., 84
Toffler, Alvin, 138
Tolstoy, Count Leo, 103
Train, Arthur, 249
Tulin, Leon A., 312n

Index of Names

Turow, Scott, 11–14, 266, 354
Tyndall, John, 310

Ulanov, Barry, 70
Ulman, Joseph N. (Judge), 1, 307–8, 314
Unger, Roberto Mangabeira, 94n, 98, 219n

Voltaire, 174
de Vries, Henry P., 364

Warren, Earl (Justice), 208
Wasserstein, Bruce, 69
Wasserstrom, Richard A., 67–68, 151, 320n, 388–89, 391–92
Watson, Alan, 127
Watson, J.B., 300
Weber, Max, 55–56, 59, 128, 184
Weinreb, Lloyd L., 180n, 201
Weisstub, David N., 116
Wellman, Francis L., 266

White, James B., xviii n., 50, 354
White, James J., 128
White, John O., 50
Whitehead, Alfred N., 128, 165
Wigmore, John Henry, 61, 84
Williams, Bernard, 173
Wilson, James Q., 138
Wilson, Woodrow, 3
Winston, Kenneth I., 238n
Wittgenstein, Ludwig, 43–44, 51, 68, 336, 341, 367, 384
Wolff, Robert P., 58
Wordsworth, William, 253
Wright, J. Skelly (Judge), 47, 51
Wright, Jack, 138

Zane, John M., 331–32
Zeisel, Hans, 266
Zelermyer, William, 341

SUBJECT INDEX

Acceptance of law (*see also* Fidelity to law, Respect for law):
   Dworkin, 183n, 200
   Fuller, 163–64, 187, 236–38, 243–45
   Hart, 182–85, 187
   Kadish, 183–84
   law vs. power, 102, 105, 109–12, 126–27, 200, 222–23, 234, 260, 324, 394–95
Adversary system:
   contrast with inquisitorial system, 269–70, 272–74, 294
   criticisms, 264, 267
   defense, 264–65
   in legal education, 8–14
   multiplicity of perspectives, 264–65, 272, 281, 338–39
   origins, 259–61
Advocates, legal (*see also* Lawyers):
   concern with victory, 8, 260, 284–85, 294
   defense of the guilty, 282–83, 289–91, 293–94
   ethical problems in counseling clients, 292–95
   harm to others, 276, 283–85, 289–91, 293, 295
   integrity of adjudication, 264–65, 281, 285
   as liars, 277–86, 296
   role morality, 291n
   vicarious conduct, 283–84
Analogy:
   in language (*see also* Legal language: open texture), 43–44, 51
   in reasoning, 123, 322, 331–37, 343–54
Analytical jurisprudence, 172, 196
Anarchism, 102–4, 107, 154
Animism, 73–74, 85, 221–22, 280n, 299
Arbitration, 55, 61, 124–27, 237–38, 274, 339–41, 396–97

Behavioralism, judicial:
   criticisms, 305–6
   history, 300, 304–5
   judicial attitudes and attributes, 303–5
   judicial decisions, 301–2
   and viewpoint, 306–7
Biology and viewpoint, 224
Biopolitics, 305n
Borderline and pivotal cases (Dworkin), 193n

Canons of construction, 24, 364
Cheyenne law:
   adjudication and negotiation, 81–84, 152
   heroic stories, 80–81, 142
   purification for murder, 120
Chinese law:
   absence of courts and lawyers, 3–4, 97
   customary law, 94–95, 105–6
   equity, 56, 97
   li and *fa*, 95–96, 98

Civil law tradition:
   codification, 122, 206, 356–57
   and common law, 22n, 40, 121–24, 316, 357–58
   criminal trials, 268–72
   interpretation, 364
   and natural law, 25, 371–72
   trials as conferences, 272–74
Codification (*see also* Statutes):
   advantages, 35, 355–56
   Aquinas, 229
   criminal law, 359–60
   history, 356–57
   Maine, 101
   tacit, 172n
Coherence of law, 40, 115, 124, 158–59, 162, 365–66, 380–82, 391
Commands and rules, 104–6, 165, 170–73, 176–78, 183n, 187, 318, 369–70
Commercial law, 86, 89–90
Common law:
   and civil law, 22n, 40, 121–24, 316, 357–58
   history, 122–23, 319–20, 388
Communist law, 41, 64, 121, 267–69, 275, 360
Community of ideas (Devlin), 144–45, 151–52
Constancy of law, 40, 53–56, 59, 61–62, 115, 125, 298, 321, 391–92
Core and penumbra of law, 210–11, 373–79, 382, 390
Creation myths, 41, 73, 111, 117, 165–66, 310
Criminal law:
   and civil law, 23n, 118–20
   codification, 359–60
   enforcement of morals (*see*)
Custom:
   Austin, 172–73
   in commercial law, 86, 89–90
   in families, 86, 93, 98
   Hart, 88–89, 176, 240
   in judicial practice, 92
   and legal realism, 206–7
   and legislation, 94–96, 98, 102, 104–6, 130, 133, 172–73, 209, 370
   as living law, 86, 89–95, 120, 206–9, 249–50
   Maine, 100–101, 176
   of the road, 91–92
   Savigny, 206, 209
   in the state, 94–97, 105–6

Decision making (*see* Judicial decisions)
Deduction, 123, 317, 331–34
Descriptive (vs. normative) laws, 59, 85, 96, 107–9, 111–12, 115, 178–79, 204, 207–8, 211–12, 221–22, 234, 296, 306–7, 314, 336
Development of law:
   in China, 94–97
   civil law and criminal law, 119–20
   common law and civil law, 121–23
   Maine's stages, 100–102

409

Discretion:
:   in applying rules of games, 18–20, 137–38, 202
    Dworkin's distinctions, 134–37, 189–90, 193, 201
    Greenawalt's criticisms, 135–36
    Kadish on discretion to disobey, 183–84
    in law enforcement, 129, 136
    unlimited and principled, 137–38, 161

Enforcement of morals:
:   common law crimes, 359n
    Devlin: public morality, 144–45
    Devlin: right to legal enforcement, 145–46
    Devlin: ways to find moral convictions, 146–47
    Dworkin: norms for public morality, 148–50
    Hart: criticism of Devlin, 147–48
    supererogation, 141–43
Enterprise of law (*see also* Acceptance, Fidelity, Structures, Respect):
:   Aquinas, 232–33
    Dworkin, 20, 193, 382, 394
    Fuller, 29, 114–16, 187, 236–39, 243–45
    J.F.A. Taylor, 109–12
Equity:
:   Aristotle, 61–62, 67–70
    in China, 56, 97
    equitable construction, 24, 388–89
    extralegal mercy, 31, 33, 63, 66–67
    and juries, 310, 314
    kadi justice, 56, 59, 99, 106, 114, 314, 321
Eskimo law, 75–80, 85, 259–60
Extracurial factors, 36–37, 39, 297, 300, 303–5

Facts (*see also* Descriptive laws, Perception):
:   in coherence theory of truth, 277–81
    and commands, 171
    dependence on questions, 252–56, 258, 294–95, 342
    Greeks on law and fact, 61, 69
    in judicial decisions (*see* Behavioralism, Legal realism)
    material and immaterial, 326–28, 335
    matters of fact and relations of ideas, 166, 174, 188, 333
    objectivity, 252–56, 296–98
    and reasons, 165–66, 171, 174, 228
Family law (*see* Marriage and family)
Family resemblances (Wittgenstein), 336, 352
Feeling:
:   Cardozo: the inadequacy of, 211
    Devlin: norm for moral consensus, 146–47
    Dworkin: criticism of Devlin, 149–50
    intuitive decisions, 297–98, 307–13
    and the legal mind, 12–13, 47–51
Fictions, legal, 62, 101
Fideism, 330
Fidelity to law, 33, 159–64, 186, 233–34
Forbearance (*see also* Respect for persons), 86, 109–12, 200, 223, 260
Freedom:
:   degrees of, 59, 226, 235
    J.S. Mill, 139, 143
    and prediction, 307, 314
    and rules, 58, 59
    de Tocqueville, 40, 55
Friendship, 142

Games:
:   discretion of referees, 18–20, 137–38, 197, 202
    family resemblances, 336, 341
    primary and secondary rules, 88n
    pure procedural justice, 262–63

Generality of law (*see also* Publicity), 3n, 56–59, 65–66, 99, 105, 114, 117, 124, 177, 318, 321, 388–89, 391
Good samaritan, 141–43
Greek law, 61–62, 69

Identity (*see* Same and different)
Imperatives, hypothetical, 109, 185, 213, 234, 236, 242
Induction, 317, 333–34
Inquisitorial system, 269–70, 272–74
Integrity (Dworkin), 197n, 380–82
Intention (*see also* Viewpoints):
:   and facts, 103, 252–56, 258
    hypothetical, 28, 368–69
    legislative, 24–25, 34–35, 39, 366–70, 380–81, 385, 396–97
    and prediction, 116, 212, 306–7
    and sameness, 256, 318–19, 334–36
Interpretation:
:   of codes, 356–58, 364, 370
    in core and penumbra, 373–78
    Dworkin, 196–97, 379–83
    Fuller, 51, 376–78
    Hart, 211, 373–76, 379, 390
    and history, 255, 258, 342
    and judicial legislation, 155, 167–68, 190–92, 207–11, 370, 372–76, 390–92, 396–97
    and legislative intention, 24–25, 34–35, 39, 366–70, 380–81, 385, 396–97
    and natural law, 25, 31–32, 370–72
    in Nazi law, 160–61, 360
    plain meaning, 26, 34, 39, 42, 211, 365–67, 373–78
Intuition (*see also* Equity), 297–98, 307–13
Is/ought distinction (*see* Descriptive laws, Imperatives, Morality, Naturalistic fallacy)

Judicial behavioralism (*see* Behavioralism)
Judicial decisions (*see also* Discretion, Interpretation, Precedents):
:   and decisions in general, 391–92
    dependence on advocacy, 264–65
    discovery vs. justification, 307–13, 317, 330–31, 337–39, 388
    in games, 17–21, 135, 137–38, 197
    as hunches, 297–98, 307–13
    measurement and prediction (*see* Behavioralism)
    moral considerations (Aquinas), 229, 232–33
    moral considerations (Dworkin), 194–200
    moral considerations (legal realism), 206–16
    moral considerations (utilitarianism), 390–92
    policy legislation, 155, 167–68, 190–92, 202, 207–11, 370, 372–76, 382, 390–92, 396–97
    as therapeutic, 76, 127, 260, 267–68, 274, 339–41
    unwritten principles, 24–25, 32–34, 57, 91–92, 137–38, 183–84, 190–93
Jural postulates, 75–77
Jurimetrics, 299–300
Jury:
:   and equity, 37, 310, 314
    in Germany, 268–69, 271–72
    in Greece, 61
    history (common law), 254–55, 260–61, 272
    legislation by, 256–57
    the reasonable man, 146
    special verdicts, 30
    triers of fact, 253

Subject Index 411

Justice (*see also* Equity):
    absence in primitive trials, 79, 259–60
    distributive and corrective, 64, 118
    formal and material principles, 65–66, 318–19, 321, 388–89
    in games, 17–21
    kadi, 55, 59, 99, 106, 114, 314, 321
    and legalism, 55
    and mercy, 31, 33, 60–63
    and other virtues, 63, 66–67, 141–43
    procedural, 46–48, 259, 261–65, 282, 285
    and truth, 284
    and validity of law, 219, 229

Lacrosse: primary and secondary rules, 88n
Language (*see* Legal language)
Language-games (Wittgenstein), 43–44, 51
Law enforcement (*see also* Enforcement of morals):
    agencies in primitive societies, 76, 87
    judgment exercised by police, 129
    maintenance of order, 130–32
    need for rules of procedure, 132
    presuppositions of such rules, 133–34, 138–39
Law schools (*see* Legal education)
Lawyers (*see also* Advocates):
    common criticisms, 1–6, 45, 97, 277, 283–85
    as counselors, 292–98
    as creators of social order, 73, 126–27, 237–38
    in France and Germany, 106, 268–74
    as generalists, 46
    legalistic mentality, 42–45, 53–59, 254
    de Tocqueville, 40, 55
Legal education (*see also* Legal language):
    in civil law countries, 122
    Fuller's criticism, 237
    Goffman's criticism, 9–10
    Socratic method, 10–12, 14
    training to think like a lawyer, 9–16, 54
Legalism (*see also* Advocates):
    and anarchism, 104
    in China, 4, 96
    J.E. Coons, 56–59, 329
    letter over spirit, 35, 42–48, 92, 94, 362
    and precedents, 321
    and professional or human relevance, 254
    in religion, 3, 5, 6, 59
    Judith Shklar, 53–56, 58–59, 329
Legal language (*see also* Interpretation):
    abstraction in, 9, 41, 80n
    formalism and inhumanity, 12–14, 35, 45–48, 92, 360–61, 374
    as an instrument, 45–46, 51
    open texture, 18, 68, 90–91, 136, 189–90, 241, 342, 358–59, 361, 362
    and perception, 43–44, 49–50, 252–56, 294
    how to read cases, 22–23
    de Tocqueville, 40
Legal obligation (*see also* Is/ought), 109–14, 161–64, 170, 172, 177–78, 181–88, 211–13, 227, 233–34, 238–39, 243
Legal positivism (*see also* Austin, Hart):
    in China (legalists), 95–96
    factual basis of law (*see also* Descriptive laws), 158–59, 166–67, 186, 199, 228
    five theses (Hart), 156
    history, 165–69
    independence of law and morality, 26, 34–35, 39, 154, 156–59, 167–68, 171–72, 181, 243, 373–76
    judicial legislation, 154–55, 167–68, 190, 373–76, 390–92
    opposition to legal realism, 155, 166–67, 173, 181–82, 203, 210–11, 212n, 375–76
    "pedigree" of law, 88–89, 125, 139, 179–84, 188, 195–96, 237, 395
    verification, 15, 223, 248
Legal realism (*see also* Frank, Holmes, Llewellyn):
    and behavioralism, 297, 305
    custom and mores, 206–7, 209, 214–16
    general position, 36–39, 155, 203–5
    history, 206–8
    judicial legislation, 155, 207–11, 372–73
    law as prediction, 39, 204–5, 297, 303–6
    opposition to natural law, 39, 155–56, 216, 221n
    opposition to positivism, 155, 166–67, 173, 181–82, 203, 210–11, 212n, 375–76
    pure procedural justice, 263
Legal systems:
    Aquinas, 232–33
    Benditt, 394–95
    Dworkin, 200
    Fuller, 243–45
    Hart, 179–80
    enforcement agencies, 76, 79, 87
    judicial agencies, 81–83, 87
    legislative agencies, 81–84, 88–89, 102
    Western assumptions, 125
Legislation (*see also* Legal positivism, Rules):
    agencies in primitive law, 81–84
    as basic source of law, 8, 26, 35, 154, 170–73
    and custom, 94–96, 98, 102, 104–6, 130, 133, 172–73, 209, 370
    enforcement of morals (*see*)
    intention of legislators, 24–25, 34–35, 39, 366–70, 380–81, 385, 396–97
    judicial (and policy), 155, 167–68, 190–92, 202, 207–11, 370, 372–76, 382, 390–92, 396–97
    limits, 24–25, 31–32, 105–6, 114–16, 219, 159–64, 171–72, 181, 221, 229–30, 232–33, 240–41
    Maine, 101–2, 176
Living law, 86, 89–95, 120, 206–9, 249–50

Malice, 44
Mann Act (1910), 359, 363
Marriage and family, 58, 76, 86, 93, 98, 142, 145, 217, 231, 398
Marxist views of law, 3–4, 103–4, 299, 306, 321
Matters of fact, 166, 174, 182, 188, 199, 333
Mediation:
    and adjudication, 126–27
    in China, 97
    creation of social order, 237–40
    police as mediators, 129–30
    therapeutic settlement, 339–40
    among the Tiv, 124–25
Metaphysics (*see also* Natural law):
    application to legal questions, 5–6, 103, 155–56, 219–20, 231–32, 333, 345–53
    Aquinas, 226
    Aristotle, 224–25
    Bentham's rejection, 167
    Cardozo's rejection, 349–50
    Dworkin's rejection, 198–99
    Fuller's rejection, 242
    Hart's rejection, 186
    Hume's rejection, 166
    Kelsen's rejection, 176, 181–182

Subject Index

Morality and law (*see also* Advocates, Enforcement of morals, Judicial decisions, Justice, Respect, Rights):
    Aquinas, 231–33
    Dworkin, 194–200
    Fuller, 159–64, 239, 242–45
    independence (positivism), 26, 34–35, 39, 154, 156–59, 167–68, 171–72, 181, 243, 373–76
    norms for legal validity, 24–25, 31–32, 105–6, 114–16, 219, 221, 229–30, 232–33, 240–41
Mores (and public opinion), 36–37, 39, 124–25, 155, 209, 211–16

Naturalistic fallacy, 212–13, 227, 231–32, 233
Natural law (*see also* Aquinas, Fuller, Structures of law):
    Aristotle, 222, 224–25, 371
    in China (*li*), 95–96
    convention vs. nature, 7, 28–29, 65, 95–96, 102–3, 112–13, 115–16, 222–24, 370–72
    Dworkin, 198–99, 383
    functional, 394
    "Golden Age," 102–3
    Hart, 233–34
    history, 219, 225–26, 371–72
    and interpretation, 24–25, 31–33, 371–72
    and obligation, 161–64, 185–86, 227, 233–34, 238–39, 243
    and privacy, 393
    purpose of all law, 31–32, 38, 227, 238, 244–45, 370, 395
    Radbruch, 157–58, 160–62, 164, 239
    state of nature, 29, 31–32, 38, 220–21, 246
    transcendent law, 101
    validity of positive law, 24–25, 31–32, 114–16, 159–64, 171–72, 219, 221, 229–30, 232–33, 240–41
Negative proof, 113, 117, 222–24, 234, 235, 240, 306, 307n, 314
Negotiation:
    and adjudication, 61, 81–84, 124–27
    and legalism, 55
    in plea bargaining, 128–29
    presuppositions, 109–10
    therapeutic settlement, 339–41
Normative laws (*see* Descriptive)
Norris-LaGuardia Act (1932), 396–97, 399

Objectivity and subjectivity:
    in facts, 252–56, 296–97, 299
    in interpretation (Dworkin), 380–83
    in intuitive decisions, 66, 297–98, 307–13
    in morality, 27, 39, 197, 202, 211–12
    quantification, 9, 14, 103, 256, 297, 300
    viewpoint, 178–79, 223, 297–98, 306–7
Obligation (*see* Legal obligation)

Paradigms, 74, 280n, 308, 338
Paraduction, 335
Pedigree of law (*see* Legal positivism)
Penumbra and core of law, 210–11, 377–79, 382, 390
Perception and rules, 9, 43–44, 74, 111, 256, 258, 278–80
Perjury, 292–94
Pivotal and borderline cases (Dworkin), 193n
Plain meaning, 26, 34, 39, 42, 211, 365–67, 373–78
Plea bargaining, 128–29
Police (*see* Law enforcement)
Policy, public (*see also* Principles), 36–37, 208–10, 336, 391–92, 396–99

Positivism (*see* Legal positivism)
Practices, closed and open, 18–21
Precedents:
    case of first impression, 81, 322–24
    history, 319–20
    induction and analogy, 334–37, 381–82
    justification and criticism, 196–97, 320–21
    manufacturers' liability, 343–53
    in primitive law, 126–27
    strict and loose application, 319–20, 324–29
    and therapeutic settlement, 339–41
    de Tocqueville, 40
Prediction, 39, 116, 204–5, 212, 296–307, 314
Preferences, personal and external (Dworkin), 150n
Principles:
    in common law, 25, 137, 192–93
    and equity, 68–69
    in games and grammar, 19–20, 137–38
    jural postulates, 75
    in justice, 65–66
    and policies, 194–95, 201–2, 323n, 394, 399
    premises of all law, 31–32, 38
    and rules, 90–94, 137–38, 150, 183–84, 189–93, 201, 307, 323–24, 329, 337, 388–89, 396
    as structures (Fuller), 114–16, 238–41
Privacy as a right, 393, 399
Privity of contract, 343
Procedural justice (law), 46–48, 259–65, 282, 285
Prosecutors, 37, 69, 128, 138–39, 270–72, 303
Publicity of law (*see also* Generality), 27–28, 105, 114–15, 160–61, 163, 321, 355, 388
Public opinion (*see* Mores)
Purpose:
    in Aristotle, 371
    in biology, 224
    Fuller on interpretation, 51, 376–78
    in games and grammar, 19–21, 116
    of all law, 31–32, 38, 227, 238, 244–45, 395
    of laws of inheritance, 24–25
    of laws against murder, 33, 34–35, 38
    legislative, 24–25, 34–35, 39, 366–70, 380–81, 385, 396–97
    of marriage, 231

Questions:
    and facts, 252–56, 258, 277–81, 294, 342
    foundational, 338–39
    reformulation of, 265, 337–42
    "why?," 306

Railway Labor Act (1934), 396
Ratio decidendi, 180, 319, 325–28, 335, 355
Realism (*see* Legal realism)
Reason:
    Aquinas, 225–27, 371n
    Aristotle, 224–25, 330n
    in common law and civil law, 123–24, 316
    deduction, induction, analogy, 123, 317, 331–37, 342–53
    and detachment, 330
    Devlin on the reasonable man, 146
    Dewey, 337–39
    Dworkin on moral positions, 149–50
    Dworkin's "rationalism," 199
    Fuller, 243–45
    Hume, 166, 174, 188, 333
    intellectualism and voluntarism, 165–66, 171, 227, 371n
    intuitive and discursive, 307–13, 330–31
    and the mores, 36–37, 81–82, 211–16

negative proof, 113, 117, 222–24, 234, 235, 240, 306, 307n, 314
and prediction, 296–307
in science, 165–67, 174, 296–97, 342
truth and validity, 317, 330, 364
Max Weber, 55–56
Respect (*see also* Acceptance, Forbearance):
for law, 183n, 200, 388, 395
for persons, 46, 86, 109–12, 116, 117, 131, 199–200, 218, 234, 236, 238–39, 243–45, 283, 398–99
Retroactivity:
in case law, 27, 124, 355
Fuller, 115, 159, 163, 242–43
Hart, 158
Rights:
Dworkin, 194–200, 223, 245, 393–94
and external preferences, 150n
and forbearance, 86, 109–12, 200, 223
and legalism, 53–54
of a litigant, 193–95, 199
of privacy, 393, 399
in a state of nature, 220
United Nations Declaration of, 218
and utilitarianism, 169, 194, 393
Role morality, 72, 291n
Roman law, 61, 101, 121–22, 225, 242, 365, 369, 371
Rules:
as basis for legalism, 53–59
and commands, 105–6, 165, 170–73, 177, 183n, 187, 318, 369–70
and custom, 86, 132–34, 173, 249–53
and freedom, 58, 59
in games and grammar, 17–21, 88n
in Greek law, 61–62
open texture, 18–19, 68, 90–91, 136, 189–90, 241, 342, 358–59, 361, 362
for perception, 9, 43–44, 74, 85, 111, 256, 258, 278–80
primary and secondary, 88–89, 179–80
and principles (*see* Principles and rules)
of recognition, 88–89, 139, 180–84, 193, 236, 244, 395
and roles, 71–72, 76, 79, 93
and supererogation, 80–81, 141–43, 151

Same and different, 256, 318–19, 334–37, 342–53, 380–83
Science (*see also* Behavioralism, Descriptive laws, Prediction):
abstraction and objectivity, 9, 255–56, 297–98
animism and conservation, 73–74, 85, 221–22, 280n, 299
evolutionary theories, 100, 308
and explanation, 174, 305–7
induction and analogy, 331, 333–37
intuitive elements, 310, 312–13
laws: found or made?, 106–7, 111–12, 255–56
observation vs. reason, 166–67, 174, 296–97
paradigms, 74, 280n, 308, 338
rules for perception, 74, 85, 256, 258, 278–80, 342
Self-defense, 33, 35, 38
Settlement of disputes, 127, 136, 339–41
Sherman Act (1890), 193, 358–59
Social contract theory of law, 32, 109–12, 116, 221n
Social engineering, 45, 207
Socratic method, 10–12, 14, 222–23
Stages of law (*see* Development)

State of nature, 29, 31–32, 38, 220–21, 246
Status and contract (Maine), 111
Statutes (*see also* Codification, Interpretation):
catchall provisions, 72, 107, 131, 360
in China (*fa*), 95–97
criminal, 119–20, 360
Nazi, 160–61, 360
open texture, 18–19, 68, 90–91, 136, 189–90, 358–59, 361, 362
as rules or principles, 193, 359–60
Structuralism, 240
Structures of law (*see also* Coherence, Constancy, Generality, Publicity, Retroactivity):
Fuller, 114–16, 140, 159–64, 233, 238–41, 325, 383
limits of law, 24–25, 31–32, 102–6, 112–13, 219, 229–30
Subjectivity (*see* Objectivity)
Supererogation, 141–43

Taft–Hartley Act (1947), 397
Tiv law, 124–25
Transduction, 334
Trials:
in China, 97
civil, in France and Germany, 273–74
criminal, in Germany, 268–72
by ordeal, 260
and play, 79, 259–60, 295
as therapeutic, 76, 127, 260, 267–68, 274, 339–41
among the Tiv, 124–25
types of procedural justice, 261–65
Truth (*see also* Advocates):
as adversarial, 264–65, 272, 337–38
and causality, 306, 307n
correspondence and coherence theories, 277–83
Greek vs. Hebraic notions, 330
in legal education, 12–14
in positivism, 15, 165–67, 223, 248
and the Sophists, 7, 15, 112–13, 222–23, 370–71
subordination to other values, 283–86
and validity, 317, 330, 364

United Nations Declaration of Rights, 218
Usury, 231
Utilitarianism:
basic position, 168–69, 174
criticism (Dworkin), 194–95
in judicial decisions, 156–57, 202, 208–9, 372–76, 390–92
relation to legal positivism, 154–55, 169

Validity:
of arguments, 317, 330, 364
of laws, 88, 114–16, 157, 159–64, 171–72, 181, 219, 229–30, 232–33, 240–41
"Vehicles" in law, 103, 211, 366–67, 373–74, 376–77
Victimless crimes (*see* Enforcement of morals)
Viewpoints, internal and external, 108–9, 175, 178–79, 182–87, 199, 200, 203, 211–12, 216, 220–25, 227, 297–98, 306–7, 395
Voluntarism, 166, 171, 227, 235–36, 371n

War crimes, 107
Weimar Constitution, 105
Wolfenden Report, 140, 143, 145–47